VRML 2.0 Sourcebook
Second Edition

ANDREA L. AMES
DAVID R. NADEAU
JOHN L. MORELAND

John Wiley & Sons, Inc.

New York • *Chichester* • *Weinheim* • *Toronto* • *Brisbane* • *Singapore*

Executive Publisher: Katherine Schowalter
Editor: Tim Ryan
Assistant Editor: Kathryn A. Malm
Managing Editor: Micheline Frederick
Electronic Products, Associate Editor: Mike Green
Text Design & Composition: North Market Street Graphics

Library of Congress Cataloging-in-Publication Data:
Ames, Andrea L.
    The VRML 2.0 sourcebook / Andrea L. Ames, David R. Nadeau, John L.
  Moreland. — 2nd ed.
      p.   cm.
    Rev. ed. of: VRML sourcebook. c1996.
    Includes index.
    ISBN 0-471-16507-7 (paper/CD-ROM : alk. paper)
    1. Hypertext systems.   2. VRML (Document markup language)
  3. Virtual reality. I. Nadeau, David R. II. Moreland, John L.
  III. Ames, Andrea L. VRML sourcebook. IV. Title.
QA76.76.H94A52 1997   96-42409
006—dc20   CIP

10 9 8 7 6 5

Contents

v

Chapter 8 Animating Position, Orientation, and Scale   109

Chapter 9 Sensing Viewer Actions   135

Chapter 10   Controlling Appearance with Materials   161

Chapter 13   Building Shapes with Points, Lines, and Faces   209

Chapter 14   Building Elevation Grids   241

Chapter 15 Building Extruded Shapes   251

Chapter 16 Binding Colors to Points, Lines, Faces, and Coordinates   275

Chapter 17   Mapping Textures   297

Chapter 18   Controlling Texture Mapping   335

Chapter 19   Controlling Shading   373

Chapter 20   Lighting Your Worlds   407

Chapter 31   Creating New Node Types   603

Appendix A   Radians and Degrees   623

Preface

Welcome to the second edition of *The VRML Sourcebook: The VRML 2.0 Sourcebook*! As in the first book, our goal is to introduce you to the Virtual Reality Modeling Language (VRML) in a friendly, practical, and nontechnical way. To do this, we've provided a book filled with useful and interesting examples, so you can start building your own VRML worlds right away.

The book is practical and task-oriented in style and structure. In other words, we answer your "What if I want to . . . ?" questions rather than explaining how to use the syntax first. This way, you can find the information you want even if you don't know, for example, what an **IndexedFaceSet** node does.

Using VRML requires that you understand a bit about computers and programming and a bit about computer graphics. We do not assume you understand these extensively, and we provide background concepts whenever necessary. The book is neither meant to be a computer graphics primer nor a basic programming text, however.

Intended Audience

The VRML 2.0 Sourcebook is written for a variety of people, and we structured the book to enable each of our audience segments to access the information it needs quickly and easily.

Computer Hobbyist or Enthusiast

You may be a computer hobbyist or enthusiast. If so, we wrote this book primarily for you! You may have a computer at home or at school and enjoy using it to fiddle with interesting technology. Maybe you've taken a computer class; written some programs in Basic, Pascal, Perl, C, or C++; or written some DOS batch files, HyperCard/HyperTalk scripts, or UNIX shell scripts. You probably have Internet access and enjoy surfing the Web, reading Internet news, and conversing with your friends using electronic mail. Maybe you've written your own HTML pages and have your own home page. Essentially, you are your own system administrator, maintaining your PC or Macintosh system software and enjoying the time you spend with your computer.

Technical or Nontechnical Artist; Multimedia Author

You may be a computer hobbyist or enthusiast *and* an artist, an artist looking for a new medium, or a multimedia author. As well as the knowledge of the hobbyist, you might also create two- and three-dimensional graphics on your PC or Mac with commercial software. You probably understand a bit about lighting models, morphing, and paint programs. Even if VRML is your first foray into computer-based art, this book is for you.

Virtual Reality Hobbyist or Enthusiast

As a virtual reality (VR) enthusiast, you may have no computer background other than playing games. You probably keep up with the latest developments in cool VR games and other environments. You probably own all the latest CD-ROM games and hold the high scores at your house. You can use this book with no prior technical knowledge to create your *own* VR worlds.

Technical Experts and Application Developers

Although we wrote this book primarily for a nontechnical audience, we tried to include something for everyone. If you're interested in more syntax explanation and clarification than that provided in the VRML specification, you'll find it here. Although we've kept the language nontechnical, the technical material is covered in detail.

How to Best Use This Book

As we've stated, *The VRML 2.0 Sourcebook* is written for a variety of people, and we structured the book to enable each portion of our audience to access the information it needs quickly and easily. For each of our potential audiences, we've provided a pathway through the book.

Computer Hobbyist or Enthusiast or Technical or Nontechnical Artist

Depending on your understanding of 3-D graphics concepts, you may want to read thoroughly or only skim the conceptual computer graphics and VRML discussions. These are found in each chapter's "Understanding . . ." section—the first section in each chapter. For example, positioning objects within your world (called "translation") is discussed in Chapter 5. The first section, "Understanding More About Coordinate Systems," builds on the discussion of coordinate systems in Chapter 2 and describes how coordinate systems and shape positioning relate.

To get the best understanding of VRML, read carefully the syntax sections. These are practical, syntax-oriented VRML discussions. For example, the **translation** field of the **Transform** node—with which you specify how a shape is positioned in your world—is discussed in the section entitled "The **Transform** Node Syntax" in Chapter 5. Each chapter contains one or more ". . . Syntax" sections like this.

The examples in the "Experimenting with . . ." section of each chapter illustrate using the VRML syntax, 3-D, computer graphics, and VRML concepts discussed in the conceptual sections of each chapter. Not only do they reinforce the ideas you've just read, they give you templates for building your own worlds.

Virtual Reality Hobbyist or Enthusiast

If you want to get a solid understanding of VRML, thoroughly read the "Understanding . . ." sections that discuss computer graphics and VRML concepts and the ". . . Syntax" sections describing the practical uses of the language.

The examples in the "Experimenting with . . ." section of each chapter illustrate how you can use VRML syntax to apply the 3-D, computer graphics, and VRML concepts discussed in the conceptual sections of each chapter. If you want to start building cool worlds right away, skim the conceptual information and start creating the example files in the "Experimenting with . . ." sections.

Technical Experts and Application Developers

Skim the table of contents for the ". . . Syntax" sections of each chapter. In those sections, you will find the meat of VRML. For further explanation about how the VRML specification has specified particular 3-D computer graphics concepts and techniques, see the conceptual "Understanding . . ." sections.

Conventions

This book relies on certain formatting and typographical conventions to convey information about VRML and to help you better access and understand that information.

Typographical Conventions

The following table shows the typographical conventions used throughout this book and describes what they mean.

Table P.1   Typographical Conventions

Typographical Convention	*Indicates*
Bold type in the body type style	Syntax: nodes, fields, eventIns, eventOuts, etc.
Italic in the body type style	New terms that are defined in the surrounding text.
`Regular type` in the monospaced type style	VRML text, file names, and field values, such as coordinates.
Bold page numbers in the index	The syntax box in which this node, field, and so on is described can be found on that page.
Italicized page numbers in the index	The term's definition can be found on that page.

Formatting Conventions

We've developed the following formatting conventions to help you easily find specific kinds of information throughout the book.

Figures

For every concept and example, we provide figures to illustrate the concepts or to provide the example VRML text and show the results of viewing that example text with your browser.

In some cases, figures provide example VRML text and images that illustrate what you will see when you view the VRML text with your browser. In these figures, the image is shown with a black background (the default VRML background color), indicating that you will see a scene just like that shown in the image. These figures are included in the "Experimenting with . . ." sections.

For example, the image shown in Figure P.1 illustrates how you can build a simple hut. (The image in this figure is identical to the image shown in Figure 5.8. The figure is not identical, however, as Figure 5.8 also provides the VRML text used to create the hut.)

Figure P.1   *A hut.*

Instead of images with black backgrounds, other figures provide example VRML text and a diagram, or a series of diagrams, with a white background so that you can see the axes, arrows, labels, and so on, necessary to understand the diagram. These diagrams illustrate not only what you will see when you view the VRML text with your browser but also what's happening behind the scenes as your browser reads the VRML file. Diagram series typically illustrate a breakdown of complex changes occurring as a result of your VRML text. In each diagram series:

- Grayed axes indicate the original or parent axes of the scene.
- Black axes indicate the new axes, typically resulting from a transformation. These axes provide a visual contrast to the gray axes, making it more apparent what changes have taken place from one diagram in the series to another.
- Arrows are provided to indicate changes in specific directions.

For example, the diagram series in Figure P.2 illustrates what happens when you position a cylinder with the **translation** field of a **Transform** node. (The diagram series in this figure is identical to Figure 5.3. The figure is not identical, however, as Figure 5.3 also provides the VRML text used to position the cylinder.)

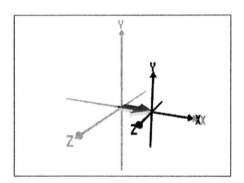 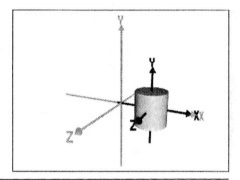

Figure P.2 *Translating +2.0 units along the X axis and building a cylinder.*

Sometimes these diagrams do not include VRML text when the images show texture images, for example, or when they are *not* included in the "Experimenting with . . ." sections. When figures are not included in the "Experimenting with . . ." section of a chapter, they are meant only to illustrate the concepts being discussed.

Syntax Boxes

The default syntax is always presented in a syntax box, which lists the VRML node and, in tabular form:

- The node's fields (for example, "**appearance**")
- The default values of each field (for example, "**NULL**")

- The type of each field (for example, "exposedField")
- A comment about the type of data of each field value (for example, "SFNode")

Syntax boxes accompany detailed syntax discussions that thoroughly explain all the components within the box. For example, the following syntax box from Chapter 3 shows the syntax of the **Shape** node.

SYNTAX	Shape node

```
Shape {
    appearance    NULL    # exposedField  SFNode
    geometry      NULL    # exposedField  SFNode
}
```

Sidebars

Sidebars are interesting and noteworthy topics that appear throughout the book. They are typically peripherally related to the discussion topic within which they are found. They are separated a bit from the main discussion, and they are prefaced by the word "Sidebar" in a small, gray box. They are also presented in the sans serif typeface, differing from the body text of the book. The following sidebar from Chapter 4 shows the sidebar style.

SIDEBAR: FONT USE BY DIFFERENT BROWSERS Different VRML browsers use different internal fonts to implement the serif, sans, and typewriter font families. For instance, while Times Roman is the typical font family used for serif, other possibilities include font families such as New York and Palatino. The font family actually displayed depends on your VRML browser.

Tips

Tips are special techniques that appear throughout the body of the book. They typically contain shortcuts, optimization ideas, usage warnings, and other techniques to help you more efficiently author your VRML worlds. They are separated a bit from the main discussion, and they are prefaced by the word "Tip" in a small, black box. They are also presented in the sans serif typeface, differing from the body text of the book. The following tip from Chapter 4 shows the tip style.

TIP For maximum portability of your VRML worlds, restrict your use of international language features to the English language. Many VRML browsers will not support the full range of languages, territories, and international characters theoretically available within VRML.

Colophon

Text drafts were written and edited using Microsoft Word on PCs.

VRML examples were created on PCs and SGI UNIX workstations using a text editor, SGI's Cosmo Player, and Netscape Navigator 3.0. Some VRML shapes were automatically generated using C and Perl programs running on SGI UNIX workstations. The mannequin in Chapter 26 was created using MetaTools Poser on a Macintosh, dumped to DXF format, converted to VRML 1.0 using an Abaco Systems geometry translator, then converted to VRML 2.0 using an SGI geometry translator.

Hand-painted texture images were created on PCs using Adobe PhotoShop and MetaTools Kai's Power Tools 3.0 plug-ins. Mountain background panorama texture images were created using MetaTools Bryce on Macintoshes. Texture images based on real-world objects were photographed using an Apple QuickTake digital camera, uploaded to a Macintosh, then copied to a PC for touch-up in Adobe PhotoShop. Movie textures were captured from video using Macintoshes and edited there using Adobe Premiere.

Synthesized sounds were created using a Yamaha SY99 synthesizer, then recorded and edited on PCs using Syntrillium's CoolEdit. Vocal sounds were created using a microphone and Syntrillium's CoolEdit on PCs.

Images were captured on SGI UNIX workstations using SGI's Cosmo Player and Cosmo Create 3D. Images were converted to their final TIFF format using SDSC's ImageTools. Final pages were produced using Macintoshes and QuarkXPress software.

CD-ROM and Web site HTML pages were created using a text editor and automatically generated using Perl programs running on SGI UNIX workstations. CD-ROM software, tools, VRML objects, textures, and so on, were assembled and tested on PCs. All CD-ROM contents were transferred to a Macintosh, and the CD-ROM golden master was burned using Astarte's Toast CD-ROM Pro.

Acknowledgments

Many, *many* people contributed to this book—in large and small ways. None are insignificant, and all are appreciated! First and foremost, I thank the San Diego Supercomputer Center (SDSC) for the unfailing support I've received as a Junior Fellow. This book would not be possible without the tireless dedication to knowledge and the unparalleled expertise and talent of the SDSC family. Special thanks to Ann Redelfs and Peter Taylor for making the Junior Fellows program a reality.

I thank my cohorts in crime, John and Dave, for another exhausting and exhilarating experience. And thanks for the support of Informix Software, Inc. Thanks to the great folks at Wiley—Tim, Micheline, et al.—for your professionalism, patience, help, and support on a *very* difficult, ever changing project. Thanks, also, to Silicon Graphics Inc. for their "Cosmic" support. And thanks to our readers—keep that e-mail coming! We love to hear your comments. This book is for you!

Thanks to Ma and Wendy for the last-minute production help and for your love, support, and encouragement. And to Nich, my funny monkey, for being a constant source of entertainment and joy. Thanks to Dad and Kit for your unfailing love and encouragement—it means *so* much to me. Thanks to Gram, Uncle Bud and Aunt Liz, and Uncle Chuck for your love and support. Special thanks to Valerie Young for your influence on this person and this book—it's priceless and immeasurable. Thanks to the roommates—you know who you are—for respecting the ribbon as much as you were able and to Robert Lincoln for helping us all to respect each other.

I thank Rob for his constant love, and I'm deeply grateful to my own, personal support system: Rob, John, Rich, Jen, and Larry—I'd be nowhere without you guys; I love you. Thanks for kicking me in the butt when I need it, for picking me up afterward, and for being there with "a dose" when I need it. Special thanks to Norma Clark for being the best damn tax accountant *anywhere*, for knowing more about law and personal finance—not to mention taxes—than anyone else I know, and for your incredible and enthusiastic support. And thanks to the wonderful and incredibly talented Spotted Peccary crew: Paul, JJ and Peggy, and Howard and Debra.

For their professional and personal encouragement and support, I thank Jennifer Atkinson, Mike Bailey, Tom Barnett, Gavin Bell, Steve Blair, Lisa Braz,

Patrick Brown, Gina Caputo, Dru Clark, Tom Comey, Laura Crowley, Cheryl Disch, Felicia Douglas, Jennifer Fell, Andrew Gross, George Hayhoe, Helen Hegelheimer, Noah Heldman, Eric and Margie Hunter, Paul Jasper, Helena Jerney, Anke Kamrath, Sid Karin, Todd Katz, Jayne Keller, Sean Kenefick, Kevin Landel, Kerri Lawnsby, Cheryl Lockett-Zubak, Brenda Long, Amy Longshore, Lauren Mund, Larry O'Toole, Nick and Andrea Pesut, Tom Perrine, Henry Ptasinski, Rama Ramachandran, Ann Redelfs, Sarah Richards-Gross, Lynn Rollins, Robert Russ, Ron and Saundra Russ, Tracey Sconyers, Mark Sheddon, Brett Shellhammer, Stephanie Sides, Charlotte Smart, Liz Smith, Allan "My Evil Twin" and Nancy Snavely, Rozeanne Steckler, Debbie Stine, Shawn Strande, Lee Taylor, Rich "the Bear" Toscano, Ed Wagner, Len Wanger, Tony Wolfram, Donna Woodka, Scott and Carla Whyte, Peg Zawryt and Dema Zlotin.

Andrea (andrea@sdsc.edu)

Thanks first to my coauthors, Andrea and John, for being part of a fascinating and productive team. Together we've learned a great deal about publishing, and gained a greater appreciation of the works of other intrepid book authors.

Thanks to everyone at the San Diego Supercomputer Center (SDSC) for their encouragement, advice, and technical support. Thanks to Charlotte Smart for keeping me organized and down to earth, to Mike Bailey for his confidence in me, and Reagan Moore for his everlasting patience and concern. Thanks to Charles Eubanks for his knowledge of VRML software and his help in maintaining the VRML Repository. Thanks to Henry Ptasinski and Max Okumoto for building an SGI system for home use, Jeff Makey for building SGI systems at SDSC, Kurt Mueller for constant technical assistance on PC systems, and Andrew Gross for a raised eyebrow at the chaos.

Very special thanks to Helga Thorvaldsdottir, Jackie Nyder, David Frerichs, and Kevin Hartz from Silicon Graphics for their incredible support in providing us with alpha and beta releases of Cosmo Player and Cosmo Worlds. We could not have done this book without their patience, their technical support, and of course their excellent software.

Thanks to Norma Clark for being as anal as we are (if not more so!) and for being such an enthusiastic fan of our work.

Thanks to the VRML community for producing an awesome VRML 2.0 specification, and to Rikk Carey for his work in orchestrating the process. Thanks to our readers for their feedback on our first book, *The VRML Sourcebook*, and on our work with the VRML Repository. Thanks as well to John Wiley & Sons, our publishers, and to Tim Ryan, our editor. We know this book has been a challenge for all of us!

Thanks to Gale Chan, Michael Schiesser, and Franz Friedrich for keeping me centered. Thanks to Mike Heck, of Template Graphics Software, for input on the book chapter order. And for their support, thanks to Allan Snavely, Sid Karin, and Anke Kamrath.

And finally, thanks to my brother, Steve, for his patience, helpful advice, kid stories, and wry humor, and to Matthew and Peter for being oblivious to it all.

Dave (nadeau@sdsc.edu)

Thanks to Rama Ramachandran for Teucher's chocolate fixes, Henry Ptasinski for building home-office SGI systems, the lunch crew—Andrew Gross and Sarah Richards-Gross, Henry Ptasinski, and Max Okumoto—for keeping me fed with good food, Thai House—Sert, Lek, Paul, and the rest of the crew—for continuing to create the tastiest Thai food on the planet.

Thanks to my family—Jules, Linda, Jay, Kim, and Jonah—for their continuing moral support and understanding of the complete loss of contact. . . . And to my Grandma—Oh, Grandma! Thanks to Pete and Effie for yacht/mountain de-kinking sessions, for marketing me and the book, and for stocking good tequila. Thanks to Ron, Tinka, Greg, Michelle, Veronica, John, Sandy, and Joe for providing an environment that feels "normal" during the holiday season (compared to the insane periods of bookwriting the rest of the year).

Thanks to Charlotte Smart for managing the sterling VRML 95 conference, to Charles Eubanks for maintaining the VRML Repository and keeping a look out for where the VRML wind was blowing, to Jeff Makey for building usable SGI systems for us, and to Henry Ptasinski for building SGI systems for the first book—sorry!

Thanks to my "old" friends—Matt, Dione, and Eric—for letting me "brag" without sounding like I'm bragging and to Kevin Landel for helping to indoctrinate other nuts into my pilgrimagelike, ski-trip getaways. Thanks to Norma Clark for all the great advice, for keeping me out of the poky, and for your support as one of our biggest fans.

Thanks to my SDSC management—Allan Snavely, Anke Kamrath, Mark Sheddon, and Sid Karin—for supporting, enabling, and encouraging VRML research; to my SDSC Vis colleague, Mike Bailey, for unfaltering guidance on the real tough graphics problems. Thanks to Andrea, the most professional, technically savvy, organized, and best technical writer I know. This book would simply not have ever happened without you. Thanks to Dave, one of the most technically and artistically gifted people I've ever worked with.

Thanks to our loyal readers (you know who you are!) for using our book and for all the great feedback and wonderful comments and to Wiley for continuing to print our books.

John (moreland@sdsc.edu)

## CHAPTER 1

Introduction to VRML

TIP If you are already familiar with VRML 1.0, you might want to skip to the section in this chapter entitled "Important Web Sites."

VRML is an acronym for the *Virtual Reality Modeling Language.* Using VRML you can craft your own three-dimensional virtual worlds on the Internet. You can build your own virtual rooms, buildings, cities, mountains, and planets. You can fill your virtual worlds with virtual furniture, cars, people, spacecraft, or anything else you can dream up. Your imagination is the only limit.

The most exciting feature of VRML is that it enables you to create dynamic worlds and sensory-rich virtual environments on the Internet, including the ability to:

- *Animate* objects in your worlds, making them move
- Play sounds and movies within your worlds
- Allow users to interact with your worlds
- Control and enhance worlds with *scripts,* small programs you create to act on your VRML worlds

This book discusses *VRML 2.0,* the second and most recent revision of the VRML specification.

The Internet and the World Wide Web

The *Internet* is an international network of computers connecting together universities, companies, research laboratories, homes, and government offices. You can think of the Internet as a giant, electronic highway system.

The *World Wide Web* (*WWW,* or the *Web*) is a complex spider's web of information available via the Internet. You can think of Web information as one kind of traffic on the electronic highway. Other kinds of Internet traffic include electronic mail (or *e-mail*), audio and video broadcasts, electronic news (or *net news*), and all the data traffic necessary to manage the Internet itself.

Browsing the Web

You can travel the Internet using a wide variety of applications, the most common of which are *Web browsers*, applications that enable you to display the incredible amount of information available on the Web.

Common Web browsers include Netscape Navigator, Microsoft Internet Explorer, and others. All of these Web browsers primarily display formatted text documents and any images embedded within them. The text formatting is controlled with a language called *HTML*, which is an acronym for *HyperText Markup Language*. HTML commands are embedded within the text to achieve various text and image formatting.

Using HTML, you can author your own text documents for the Web. For instance, many companies have Web documents describing their products and services, pricing, organizational structure, and company policies. Individuals may have Web documents for their clubs, scout troops, or school activities.

Within an HTML document you can embed *links* that connect your document to other documents on the Web. Each link is *anchored* to, or refers to, a word, phrase, or line of text in your document. Most Web browsers display these links by underlining the anchor text on the page.

Clicking on anchor text directs the Web browser to follow a link and retrieve the Web document to which the link connects. That retrieved Web document may also contain links, which lead you to more documents and their links, and so on. By following links in an HTML document, you can browse the vast spider's web of information on the Internet.

Figure 1.1 shows the Netscape Navigator Web browser displaying a text document which provides information about VRML. Each of the underlined words and phrases in the document are anchors for links to other documents.

MIME Content Types

MIME is an acronym for *Multipurpose Internet Mail Extensions* and is a software standard that defines a simple mechanism to describe the type of content in a file sent via the Internet. All Web browsers understand *MIME content types* and use them to automatically decide how to display information in the browser window. For example, if a MIME content type indicates that a file contains HTML text, then the browser formats the HTML text and displays it in the window. Similarly, if a MIME content type indicates a file contains audio data, then the browser plays the audio through the computer's speakers.

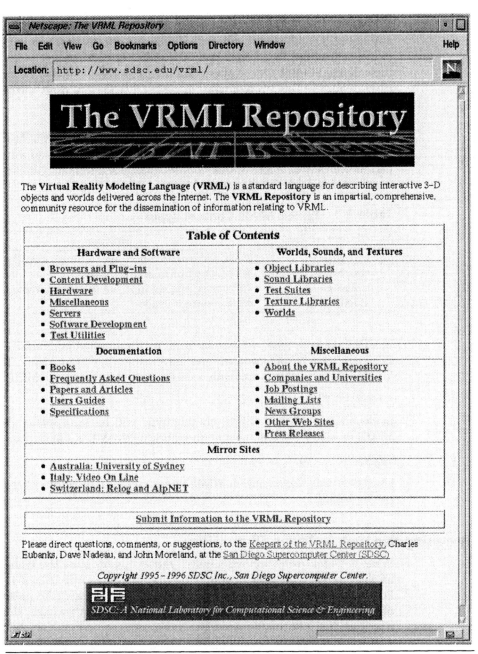

Figure 1.1   *A Web page displayed with the Netscape Navigator Web browser.*

SIDEBAR: THE MIME SPECIFICATION The exact format of MIME content types and how they are used by Internet software is the subject of an Internet community specification: RFC 1521. Web browsers support the full range of MIME features defined in this specification, but common use involves only a small subset of these features. This book covers the most commonly used MIME features. See Appendix B for references to the full MIME specification.

A MIME content type is specified in two parts separated by a slash. The first part indicates the *general type* of the content, such as text, audio, or video. The second part indicates the *subtype* of that content and is used to specify the exact format the content takes. Table 1.1 lists typical MIME content types.

Table 1.1   Typical MIME Content Types

MIME Content Type	Meaning
text/plain	Plain, unformatted text, such as in an e-mail message
text/html	HTML text, such as a Web page
image/gif	GIF image, such as a picture used on a Web page
video/mpeg	MPEG-encoded video

MIME content types are standardized by the Internet community. Temporary or extremely new MIME content types have names that start with x- (for extension). VRML is so new that it currently uses the following extension MIME content type:

```
x-world/x-vrml
```

In the future, VRML's MIME content type will be incorporated into the formal MIME standard and will become the following MIME content type:

```
model/vrml
```

Until that time, the extension MIME content type is the primary type in widespread use for VRML.

Browsing the Web in Three Dimensions

When a Web browser follows a link, it retrieves a file from the Web and checks the MIME content type that describes the information in the file. If it contains text, HTML, or images, the Web browser displays the document. To present other types of information, such as sounds, movies, and 3-D VRML worlds, the Web browser may pass that information to *helper applications*, programs that specifically understand the content and format of those other types of information, or to Web browser *plug-ins*, programs that enable you to view non-HTML information within the Web browser window.

To view VRML documents, you need a VRML helper application or plug-in called a *VRML browser.* The list of available VRML browsers is growing rapidly. Some of the more common VRML browsers available at the time of this writing are Silicon Graphics' CosmoPlayer, Sony's Community Place, Intervista's World View, VREAM's Wirl, and Dimension X's Liquid Reality.

Figure 1.2 shows Silicon Graphics' CosmoPlayer—a VRML browser/Netscape Navigator plug-in—displaying within the Netscape Navigator window the dungeon example from a later chapter in this book.

In VRML you can create links that are anchored to shapes in the VRML world. Typical anchor shapes include doors, windows, books, and maps. Clicking an anchor shape directs the VRML browser to follow the link and retrieve the VRML document to which the link connects. That document may also contain links for you to follow, and so on. By following links in a VRML document, you can browse the Web in 3D, stepping from virtual world to virtual world as you travel the Internet.

Configuring Your Web Browser

Because HTML and VRML Web browsers are typically acquired separately, you must configure your HTML Web browser so that it knows about your VRML Web browser and can automatically start the VRML browser when a file with VRML's MIME content type is found. Check both your HTML and VRML browser manuals to see how to configure them. Look for sections discussing helper applications and MIME content types.

Uniform Resource Locators

A link in an HTML or VRML document is the address of a document on the Web, similar to a street address for a house. Web document addresses are specified with *URLs*, which is an acronym for *Uniform Resource Locators*.

SIDEBAR: THE URL SPECIFICATION The exact format of URLs is the subject of two Internet community specifications: RFC 1736 and RFC 1808. Web browsers support the full range of features discussed in these specifications, but common use involves only a small subset of these features. This book covers only the commonly used URL features. See Appendix B for references to the full URL specifications.

A URL Web address is made up of three main parts:

- The name of the communications protocol necessary to retrieve a file
- The name of the computer, or *host*, on the Internet
- The directory path and file name for the file to be retrieved from the host

For example, the following URL is the Web address for an HTML document describing the San Diego Supercomputer Center's VRML Repository, the principal Internet site for information on VRML:

```
http://www.sdsc.edu/vrml
```

Figure 1.2 *A VRML page displayed within a Netscape Navigator window via the Silicon Graphics CosmoPlayer VRML browser, a Netscape plug-in.*

The string http: in this URL is the name of the *hypertext transfer protocol (http)* communications scheme used by most Web browsers. Most URL Web addresses use this protocol. Other communications protocols include ftp: for the *file transfer protocol (ftp)* used to copy and move files around the Internet and file: to refer to a file on your own hard disk.

The string www.sdsc.edu in the example URL is the name of a host on the Internet. This particular host is the World Wide Web host at SDSC (the San Diego Supercomputer Center) on the campus of the University of California in San Diego. The .edu at the end of the host name designates SDSC as an educational site on the Internet. Such a designation is reserved for universities, schools, and other educational organizations. Other common designations include .com for commercial companies, .org for nonprofit organizations, and .gov for government sites.

Finally, the string /vrml at the end of the example URL points to the name of a file to retrieve from SDSC. In this case, this is an HTML document describing the VRML Repository.

Using any Web browser, you can enter a URL, such as the one just cited, and the browser will retrieve the file from the Internet and display it on your screen.

A common, shortened URL drops the communications scheme (like http:) and host name from the URL and specifies only the file name. When this shortened URL is used, your Web browser automatically fills in the communication scheme and host name using defaults. Because the use of defaults makes the shortened URL relative to a default host, a shortened URL is known as a *relative URL*.

For example, if the relative URL appears in an HTML document retrieved from http://www.sdsc.edu/vrml, then the default scheme is http:, and the default host is www.sdsc.edu. If you use a relative URL by typing it into your Web browser directly, then the default scheme is file: (your hard disk), and the default host is your computer.

In this book, all URLs used in VRML examples are relative URLs. This ensures that all VRML examples will work on your computer, regardless of what name you've given it.

Important Web Sites

There are two important Web sites to know about for VRML and this book: the VRML Repository and John Wiley & Sons.

The VRML Repository is the principal Internet site for up-to-date information on VRML software, example worlds, documentation, and more. The repository also maintains a list of all of the VRML browsers currently available and how to get more information about them. The URL for the VRML Repository is:

http://www.sdsc.edu/vrml

The second important Web site to know is the John Wiley & Sons Web site. This site includes all of the VRML examples in this book and on the book's CD-ROM. Also included at the Wiley Web site are updates and errata for this book. The URL for Wiley's Web site is:

http://www.wiley.com/compbooks/

The VRML 2.0 Specification

VRML's features are defined by a public VRML 2.0 specification document. VRML is a rapidly evolving standard with a tremendous amount of support from the software community. As VRML evolves, so will the VRML specification document. You are encouraged to check the VRML Repository for the latest information on the VRML specification and the software that supports it.

SIDEBAR: THE VRML 2.0 SPECIFICATION   The exact features of VRML 2.0 are the subject of a standard managed by the International Standards Organization (ISO): ISO/IEC 14772. This specification contains in-depth discussion of all VRML 2.0 features, including those primarily of interest to developers of VRML browsers and other VRML applications. This book focuses on those VRML 2.0 features used to author, or create, VRML worlds. The full specification is available at the VRML Repository. See also Appendix B for references to the VRML 2.0 specification.

Creating Your Own Worlds with VRML

To create your own virtual world with VRML you'll need your VRML browser and any word processor. VRML files are text files that give your VRML browser instructions about how to draw 3-D shapes for your virtual worlds.

Starting in your word processor, you'll type VRML instructions, such as those shown in the examples throughout this book. Next, you'll save your file as a text file, then load it into your VRML browser to view it in 3-D. To add more to your world, return to the word processor, type in a few more VRML instructions, save the file, and read it back into your VRML browser. Repeating this sequence of operations enables you to gradually construct your own virtual worlds.

Three-dimensional drawing applications are also being developed to help you create VRML files. Using these applications, you can quickly create VRML files that you can then view using your VRML browser and edit further with your word processor.

Summary

The Internet is a vast electronic highway linking together educational, commercial, and government institutions throughout the world. The World Wide Web links together one type of information traffic on the Internet.

Web browsers enable you to travel the Web, browsing through archives of shareware, sounds, movies, and documents on any topic. Text documents are described using HTML (HyperText Markup Language). Three-dimensional virtual worlds are described using VRML (Virtual Reality Modeling Language).

To view VRML worlds, use a VRML browser, typically configured as a helper application or plug-in for your HTML Web browser. Once configured, VRML information received by your HTML Web browser is automatically displayed by your VRML browser.

A document on the Web is addressed using its URL (Uniform Resource Locator). A URL names the communications protocol to use when retrieving the document (typically `http:`), the Internet host from which to retrieve the document, and the name of the document.

CHAPTER 2

Key Concepts

In construction, houses and office buildings are built using blueprints that specify the building materials and layout of the building. Your VRML file serves as the blueprint for building the virtual world you create. It specifies and organizes the structure of your VRML world.

The VRML File

A *VRML file* is a textual description of your VRML world. It is a file containing text that you create with any text editor or word processor. You can also create it using applications that enable you to edit worlds in three dimensions or utilities that translate other graphics file formats to VRML. Your VRML file describes how to build shapes, where to put them, what color to make them, and so on.

VRML file names end with the .wrl (sometimes pronounced *dot world*) extension, which indicates that the file contains a VRML world. We often refer to your VRML files as *worlds* in this book. When your browser reads a VRML file, it builds the world described in the file. As you move around within the world, your browser *draws*, or displays, the world.

The Parts of a VRML File

VRML files can contain four main types of components:

- The VRML header
- Prototypes
- Shapes, interpolators, sensors, and scripts
- Routes

11

Chapters 3 through 29 discuss shapes, interpolators, and sensors. Chapter 30 covers scripts, and Chapter 31 discusses prototypes. Routes are covered later in this chapter.

Not all files have all of these. The only required item is the VRML header. Without at least one shape, however, your browser will display nothing when reading a file.

The VRML header is required in every VRML file. A VRML file can also contain these items:

- Comments
- Nodes
- Fields and field values
- Defined node names
- Used node names

Figure 2.1 shows a VRML world comprised of a header and a group, which contains nodes, fields, and comments. Type the text in this figure exactly as it's shown, view it with a VRML browser, and you've created your first VRML world.

```
#VRML V2.0 utf8
# A brown hut
Group {
    children [
    # Draw the hut walls
        Shape {
            appearance DEF Brown Appearance {
                material Material {
                    diffuseColor 0.6 0.4 0.0
                }
            }
            geometry Cylinder {
                height 2.0
                radius 2.0
            }
        },
    # Draw the hut roof
        Transform {
            translation 0.0 2.0 0.0
            children Shape {
                appearance USE Brown
                geometry Cone {
                    height 2.0
                    bottomRadius 2.5
                }
            }
        }
    ]
}
```

Figure 2.1 *Your first VRML world.*

For now, don't worry about the details of nodes like **Appearance, Cylinder, Group, Material, Shape,** and **Transform.** We'll discuss them in detail later in the book; see Chapters 3 (Cylinder, Group, and Shape), 10 (Appearance and Material), and 5–7 (Transform).

Browsers skip spaces, commas, tabs, and blank lines in VRML files. You can format your file in any way you like, including any number of spaces and blank lines within your file. Browsers do not ignore case, however, as they recognize the difference between uppercase and lowercase letters. Note the use of uppercase letters in examples and syntax boxes throughout the rest of the book.

The VRML Header

Notice that the VRML file shown in Figure 2.1 starts with this line:

```
#VRML V2.0 utf8
```

This is the *VRML header*, which is required in any VRML file. It must be the first line of the file, and it must contain the exact text shown in the VRML header syntax box.

SYNTAX	The VRML header

```
#VRML V2.0 utf8
```

The header describes to the browser that this file is:

- A VRML file
- Compliant with version 2.0 of the VRML specification
- A file using the international UTF-8 character set

The *UTF-8 character set* is a standard way of typing characters in many languages, including English. This enables VRML to support English characters, such as A to Z, as well as characters such as those in Korean, Japanese, and Arabic. The UTF-8 character set contains all the characters found on any computer keyboard, so you can enter standard ASCII text into a UTF-8 VRML document.

> **SIDEBAR: THE UTF-8 CHARACTER SET**   UTF-8 is an acronym for *UCS Transform Format*, and *UCS* is an acronym for *Universal Character Set*. UTF-8 is defined by the International Standards Organization (ISO) specification ISO 10646-1:1993. VRML's UTF-8 also uses the pDAM 1-5 specification in order to support recent changes in the Korean Jamo language. See Appendix B for references to information about the UTF-8 character set.
>
> The ASCII character set used by most computers is a subset of UTF-8. Thus any character you type from your keyboard is also a UTF-8 character. You need not do anything special to write or read VRML files using UTF-8.

Comments

VRML comments allow you to include extra information in your VRML file that doesn't affect the appearance of your world. This allows you to add notes to the file about what it contains and what different parts of the file draw. When you work on that file months or years later, you'll have your notes to help you remember your intentions.

Comments begin with a pound sign (#) and end at the end of the line. Anything you type on a line following a pound sign will be skipped by the VRML browser.

The file shown in Figure 2.1 contains several comments—for example, to describe a portion of the file:

```
# Draw the hut walls
```

Nodes

A VRML file contains *nodes* that describe shapes and their properties in your world. These are the building blocks of VRML. Individual nodes describe shapes, colors, lights, viewpoints, how to position and orient shapes, animation timers, sensors, interpolators, and so on. Nodes generally contain:

- The type of node (required)
- A set of curly braces (required)
- Some number of fields (optional) and their values that define attributes of the node within the curly braces (see the next section for details about fields and field values)

The **Cylinder** node shown in Figure 2.1 contains all of these items:

```
Cylinder {
    height 2.0
    radius 2.0
}
```

Curly braces group all of the field information within the node. The fields grouped between the curly braces belong to the node. The shape or property defined by the node and its related fields are then considered a single entity in your world. Curly braces are required in nodes, but they need not be on separate lines.

Fields and Field Values

The example shown in Figure 2.1 contains two fields within the **Cylinder** node:

```
height 2.0
radius 2.0
```

Fields define the attributes of a node. In the **Cylinder** node shown in Figure 2.1, the **height** field defines the height of the cylinder to be 2.0 units, and the **radius** field defines the radius to be 2.0 units. Other nodes have fields to set colors, orient shapes, and set the brightness of lights. The order of fields within a node is not important; you can specify fields within a node in any order you wish and the result is the same.

Fields are optional within nodes because each field has a *default value* that is used by your VRML browser if you don't specify a value. For example, a default VRML cylinder has a radius of 1.0 VRML unit, and a height of 2.0 units (VRML units are described in the sidebar entitled "VRML Units"). You can change these sizes in the **Cylinder** node's fields, but if you omit the fields completely from the text of your VRML file, the browser automatically builds a default, 1.0-unit-radius, 2.0-unit-tall cylinder. Throughout the book, default field values are specified where VRML node and field syntax is discussed.

Field values define attributes like color, size, or position, and every value is of a specific *field type*, which describes the kind of values allowed in the field. These field types have names like "SFColor" and "SFImage."

Most field types come in two varieties: single-value types and multiple-value types. *Single-value types* are a single value, like a single color or a single number, and have names that begin with "SF." *Multiple-value types* may be many values, like a list of colors or numbers, and have names that begin with "MF." When specifying multiple-value field types, enclose the list of values within brackets, and optionally separate the items in the list with commas. Table 2.1 provides a brief overview of each of the VRML field types.

Table 2.1 Field Value Type Summary

Field Value Type	*Description*
SFBool	Boolean or logical values. Value can be either **TRUE** or **FALSE**. Typically used to turn on or turn off a shape or property feature.
SFColor/ MFColor	A group of three floating-point values (see SFFloat/MFFloat). Describe the amount of red, green, and blue to be mixed together to form a desired color. Typically used to select the color for a shape or light.
SFFloat/ MFFloat	Floating-point values. Large or small, positive or negative values with decimal points. Examples: 88.5, 3.1415, and −489.398. Used, for example, to specify the height and radius of cylinders.
SFImage	A list of values describing the colors of a digital picture. Used to create surface textures to color shapes.
SFInt32/ MFInt32	32-bit integer values. Large or small, positive or negative values without a decimal point. Examples: 42, 182, and −37. Typically used to indicate a selection among several discrete possibilities.
SFNode/ MFNode	A VRML node. Example: **Cylinder.** Typically used to indicate a property node that controls how a shape node will draw a shape.
SFRotation/ MFRotation	A group of four floating-point values (see SFFloat/MFFloat). The first three values define a rotation axis. The last value is a rotation angle measured in radians. Typically used to specify how to orient a shape.
SFString/ MFString	A list of characters enclosed within quotation marks. Typically used to specify the name of a choice of several options.
SFTime	A floating-point value (see SFFloat/MFFloat). Gives a real-world, absolute time, measured in seconds since 12:00 midnight, GMT, January 1, 1970. Typically used to select when to start or stop an animation.
SFVec2f/ MFVec2f	2-D floating-point vector (see SFFloat/MFFloat). A group of two floating-point values. Typically used to specify a 2-D position.
SFVec3f/ MFVec3f	3-D floating-point vector (see SFFloat/MFFloat). A group of three floating-point values. Typically used to specify a 3-D position.

> **SIDEBAR: VRML UNITS**   VRML units are not bound to any real-world unit of measurement, such as inches, centimeters, or picas. They describe a size or a distance within the context of your VRML world. You can think of a VRML unit as an inch, a meter, an angstrom, or a light-year—whatever unit of distance is most convenient for you. Most VRML authors define distances in units of meters. This makes it easier to combine together shapes built by you and other world authors to create larger, more complex worlds.

Defining Node Names

You can define a name for any node in your world. Names can be most any sequence of letters and numbers. Once a node has a name, you can use that node again later in the file. For instance, you can specify the name `my_chair` for a node or group of nodes that build a chair. Then, to put four chairs around a table, you could reuse the same `my_chair` shape three more times, without having to retype the whole chair description each time.

The node with the defined name is called the *original* node, and each reuse of that node is called an *instance.* You can only set field values when defining the original node. Each of the instances uses the original's field values without change. This enables you to define the node that makes up a chair once, then later instance that chair multiple times around a table without repeating the nodes and fields for each chair. Additionally, if you make a change to the original chair, all of the instances are immediately changed as well. This makes it easy to rapidly make changes throughout your world, modifying the style of a chair, window, door, or any other shape you have named.

To define a node for use in instancing, precede the node with the word "DEF" and a node name of your choosing. A VRML file can contain any number of named nodes. You cannot, however, create two nodes with the same name in the same file.

| SYNTAX | DEF |

    DEF node-name node-type { ... }

Node names are any convenient sequence of characters, and they are case-sensitive. For example, the names "ABC" and "abc" are considered different by the VRML browser. Node names may include letters, numbers, and underscores. The following are examples of legal node names:

```
my_chair        space_shuttle   Kitchen_Design_12
Pianokey        GurgleSound     Indy500
Bright_Light    Dark_brown      red_brick
```

Names cannot start with a number; cannot include nonprinting, ASCII characters, such as spaces, tabs, line feeds, form feeds, and carriage returns; and cannot include double or single quotes, pound signs, plus signs, minus signs, commas, periods, square brackets, back slashes, or curly braces. The following names are also prohibited, since they are words used for other, specific purposes within VRML:

```
DEF        EXTERNPROTO    FALSE        IS      NULL
PROTO      ROUTE          TO           TRUE    USE
eventIn    eventOut       exposedField field
```

A *node type* is a particular kind of node, like the **Cylinder** node.

To define a name for a **Cylinder** node, for example, use the **DEF** syntax:

```
DEF my_cylinder Cylinder { . . . }
```

where my_cylinder is the name of the node and Cylinder is the type of node to be named.

Using Node Names

Once you have defined a name for a node, you can use that node again and again within the same file by preceding the node name with the word "USE."

SYNTAX	USE
	USE *node-name*

You can use a node anywhere in your file where that node can be specified. You can even use a node as the value of a field that normally requires a full node description.

The same original node can be instanced with **USE** any number of times within the same file. All of the instances share the same description of the node, so if you change the original node, all the instances change as well.

Building Shapes in a VRML File

As discussed at the beginning of this chapter, a construction blueprint specifies the building blocks—materials and layout—of a house or office building. In VRML, the basic building blocks are shapes described by nodes and their accompanying fields and field values.

Describing Shapes

A VRML shape has a form, or *geometry*, that defines its 3-D structure, and it has an appearance based on the *material*, a color like red or blue, from which it is made and its surface *texture*, like wood or brick. In VRML, these shape attributes—geometry and appearance—are specified by field values within a **Shape** node.

The example shown in Figure 2.1 creates two shapes, the first is a cylinder and the second is a cone. Both of these shape nodes define the geometry of the shape and share a common appearance.

VRML supports several types of *primitive shape geometries*, which are predefined in VRML, including boxes, cylinders, cones, and spheres, as well as several *advanced shape geometries*, like extruded shapes and elevation grids. Using these shapes you can build larger, more complex shapes. Those, in turn, can be used to build still larger shapes.

Grouping Shapes

Shapes can be grouped together to build larger, more complex shapes. The cylinder and cone shown in Figure 2.1 are grouped together by the **Group** node to create a hut shape. You could group together multiple hut shapes to build a village shape, and multiple village shapes to build a kingdom shape, and so on.

The node that groups together the group's shapes is called the *parent*. The shapes that make up the group are called the group's *children*. A group can have any number of children. Groups can even have other groups as children. When one group is contained within a larger group, that first group is considered *nested* within the larger group. In the example above, the village shape is nested within the kingdom shape, and the hut shape is nested within the village shape.

VRML Space

The nodes and fields in a VRML file provide building instructions for creating the features of a virtual world. Like real-world building instructions, VRML building instructions must include precise sizes and distances to control the size and placement of shapes built within VRML's three-dimensional space.

Building in Two Dimensions

You may recall learning about the X axis, Y axis, coordinates, and the origin in school. Imagine a set of X and Y axes on a piece of graph paper, like those shown in Figure 2.2.

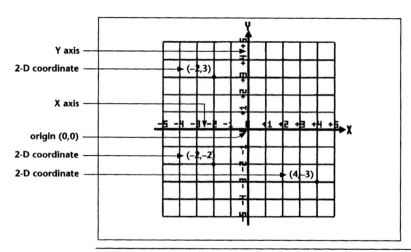

Figure 2.2   *X and Y axes, coordinates, and the origin on graph paper.*

These are the key things to understand about this *two-dimensional coordinate system:*

- The point at which the axes cross is called the *origin*, and is labeled (0.0,0.0).
- The *coordinates* shown in Figure 2.2 are made up of an X value and a Y value. *X values* correspond to the numbers along the X axis, and *Y values* correspond to the numbers along the Y axis. The shorthand used for describing these 2-D coordinates is (*x,y*), where *x* is the X value and *y* is the Y value.
- Numbers increase from left to right along the X axis and from bottom to top along the Y axis. Negative X values appear to the left of the origin and the Y axis, and negative Y values appear below the origin and the X axis.

Using this system, you can give precise building directions to a friend by specifying coordinates in terms of X and Y values. To draw a square on a piece of graph paper, you might give your friend these directions:

1. Put your pen down on the paper at (-2.0,-2.0) and drag it to (2.0,-2.0).
2. Without lifting the pen, drag it up the paper to (2.0,2.0).
3. Without lifting the pen, drag it to the left to (-2.0,2.0).
4. Still without lifting the pen, drag it down the paper to (-2.0,-2.0).
5. Stop drawing, and lift the pen off the paper.

Using these directions, your friend draws the square shown in Figure 2.3.

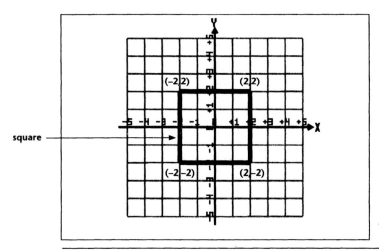

Figure 2.3 *The square your friend drew.*

Adding a Third Dimension

Using X and Y coordinates, you can give precise directions to draw any 2-D shape. VRML, however, builds shapes in *three* dimensions. You can extend your 2-D, graph-paper drawing space to create a 3-D *building* space by using a second piece of graph paper. Tape the first piece of graph paper to the wall, and place a second piece on the floor against the wall, as shown in Figure 2.4.

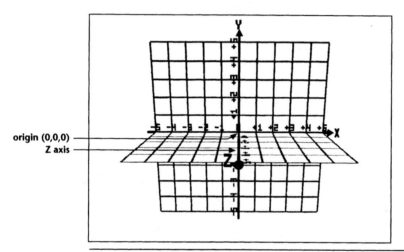

origin (0,0,0)
Z axis

Figure 2.4 *Graph paper in three dimensions.*

The second piece of graph paper contains a third axis, the *Z axis*, with numbers increasing as they proceed toward you and away from the wall. Three-dimensional shapes placed at higher values along the Z axis are closer to you. Shapes placed at lower values are farther away from you. Shapes placed at negative Z-axis values are on the other side of the wall from you. In the 3-D space, X is positive to the right, Y is positive upward, and Z is positive toward you in the space. (See the sidebar entitled "Right-Hand Rule for 3-D Axes" for a way to more easily remember how the Z axis is positioned in relation to the X and Y axes.)

The graph paper on the floor gives you a third building direction. Now, you can give precise directions to build 3-D shapes up and down and left and right on the wall graph paper, and toward you and away from you along the floor graph paper.

To find a position in your new 3-D space with an X value of 2, a Y value of 3, and a Z value of 5, find the point that is 2.0 units to the right of the origin, 3.0 units above the origin, and 5.0 units toward you from the origin—all at the same time! This point looks like that shown in Figure 2.5.

The midair point at the X value of 2.0, the Y value of 3.0, and the Z value of 5.0 can be written as (2.0,3.0,5.0), extending the 2-D coordinate shorthand used earlier. Such a trio of numbers is called a *3-D coordinate*. The special coordinate at (0.0,0.0,0.0) where the X, Y, and Z axes all cross is called the *3-D origin*, or more commonly, just the origin. The X, Y, and Z axes define a *3-D coordinate system*.

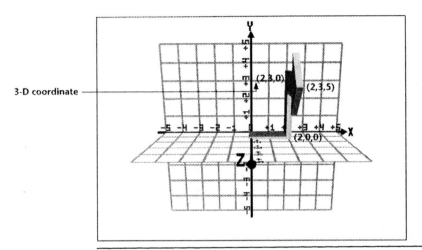

3-D coordinate

Figure 2.5 *The (2.0,3.0,5.0) coordinate in 3-D space.*

SIDEBAR: RIGHT-HAND RULE FOR 3-D AXES Position your right hand like the hand shown in Figure 2.6, with your thumb pointing in the positive X direction and your index finger pointing in the positive Y direction. Now, stick your middle finger straight out from your palm. Your middle finger now points in the positive Z direction, as shown in Figure 2.6.

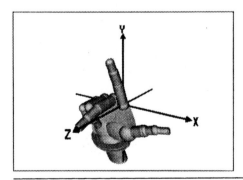

Figure 2.6 *The right-hand rule for three-dimensional axes.*

Events and Routes

Recall that a VRML file provides the building instructions for your world. To make your world dynamic those building instructions also may include "wiring" instructions. Such instructions describe how to wire nodes together so that, for example, clicking on a shape with your mouse can turn on a light, trigger a sound, or start up a machine.

VRML wiring involves:

- A pair of nodes to wire together
- A wiring *route*, or path, between the two nodes

Once a route is built between two nodes, the first node can send messages to the second node along that route. Such a message, called an *event*, contains a value, similar to field values within nodes. Typical event values include floating-point values, color values, or 3-D coordinate values. When a node receives an event, it reacts by turning on a light, playing a sound, starting an animation, or something else, depending on the features of that node. By wiring multiple nodes together you can create complex *circuits* through which you can route events to make your world dynamic.

Node Inputs and Outputs

Most types of VRML nodes can be wired into a circuit. Each node has input and output *jacks* to which you can optionally plug in wires. For instance, nodes that create lights in your world have an input jack for turning them on and off. If you wire to that jack, you can create a circuit that automatically turns the light on and off.

A node may have several input and output jacks available. A light, for instance, has input jacks to turn it on and off, change its brightness, change its color, and more. Some types of nodes have both input and output jacks, while others have only one or the other.

A node's input jack is called an eventIn. An *eventIn* receives events when it is connected to a route and when an event is sent to it. Similarly, an output jack is called an eventOut. An *eventOut* sends events out when it is connected to a route.

Consider the subset of **Collision** node syntax shown below. (For now, don't worry about what the **Collision** node does; it is discussed in Chapter 27.)

| SYNTAX | **Collision node** |

```
Collision {
    children        [ ]      # exposedField  MFNode
    proxy           NULL     # field         SFNode
    addChildren              # eventIn       MFNode
    removeChildren           # eventIn       MFNode
    collideTime              # eventOut      SFTime
}
```

The syntax box shows the following items of the selected **Collision** node syntax:

- The node (**Collision**)
- The node's fields (**children, proxy,** etc.)
- The fields' values (**[ ], NULL,** etc.)
- The type of each field (**exposedField, field,** etc.)
- The type of each field value (**MFNode, SFNode,** etc.)

Note that the node has two input jacks—**addChildren** and **removeChildren**—and one output jack, called **collideTime**. The node also has two fields: **children** and **proxy**.

Note that the **children** field in the syntax box above is an exposedField. An *exposedField* has two implicit jacks associated with it: one input jack to set its values and one output jack to send the field value each time the field changes. The implied input jack is always named **set_XXX,** where *XXX* is the name of the exposed field. Similarly, the implied output jack is always named **XXX_changed,** where *XXX* is the exposed field's name. For the **Collision** node's **children** exposed field, the implied jacks would be **set_children** and **children_changed**.

When building routes, you use the names of a node's eventOuts and eventIns to specify where to connect routes. For the **Collision** node above, you can create a route that connects to the node's eventIns (**addChildren** and **removeChildren**) and to its eventOut (**collideTime**). For an exposed field, you can wire a route to the implicit eventIn and eventOut (**set_children** and **children_changed**). You can also route to the exposed field itself (**children**), and your VRML browser will automatically use the implicit eventIn (if the route sends an event to the node) or eventOut (if the node is a receiver of events on the route).

Node Input and Output Types

Similar to a node's fields, each eventIn and eventOut for a node also has a type. An eventOut of type SFFloat, for example, outputs floating-point values when wired to a circuit. An eventOut of type SFColor sends colors. Similarly, an eventIn of type SFFloat can receive floating-point values, while one of type SFColor can receive colors.

When specifying routes, the output and the input jack types must match exactly. For example, you can send a floating-point event from an MFFloat eventOut to an MFFloat eventIn, but not to an SFFloat or MFColor eventIn.

Wiring Routes

A VRML circuit is built by describing a route from one node's eventOut to another node's eventIn. The circuit route remains dormant until an event is sent from the first node to the second node along the route. When the first node activates the route by sending an event, the event travels to the second node, and the node reacts. The type of reaction depends on:

- The type of node receiving the event
- The node input jack to which the route is wired
- The values contained in the event
- The current activities of the node

For example, when an event containing an SFBool **TRUE** value is sent to the **on** eventIn of a light node, the light turns on. Similarly, when an event containing a floating-point value is sent to the **intensity** eventIn of a light node, the light's brightness changes.

Summary

A VRML world is created by a browser reading and displaying a VRML file. The VRML file contains nodes. Files must also contain the VRML header, and they may contain comments. The nodes describe the shapes to be built and the properties of those shapes, like color and position. A node may contain fields and field values which describe attributes of that node, like height and radius.

The VRML building space is three-dimensional, described by an X axis from left to right, a Y axis from bottom to top, and a Z axis from the back of the space (away from you) forward (toward you). X is positive to the right, Y is positive upward, and Z is positive toward you in the space. You can specify where the browser begins building and where it moves around in this space using X, Y, and Z values to specify 3-D coordinates.

Circuits can be constructed by building routes between nodes. A route connects the eventOut of one node to the eventIn of another node. The first node can then send events to the second, causing the second node to react.

Building and Grouping Predefined Shapes

VRML provides several standard shapes with which you can begin building your worlds. These predefined, or *primitive*, shapes include the box, the cone, the cylinder, and the sphere.

Understanding Shapes and Grouping

Recall from Chapter 2 that a VRML shape has geometry and appearance, both defined by a **Shape** node. These characteristics define the shapes that your VRML browser builds and places within your world. A shape's exact geometry and appearance are controlled by your choice of nodes and by the values you choose for those nodes' fields.

The appearance of a shape is described by the **Appearance** and **Material** nodes. Using the default values of these nodes, you can create shaded white shapes. The shapes in this chapter use only these default values. Chapter 10 discusses shape appearances in depth.

VRML provides several primitive geometry nodes that you can use with the **Shape** node to build primitive shapes. These primitive geometries include the **Box, Cone, Cylinder,** and **Sphere** nodes. Each primitive geometry node has one or more fields that enable you to specify attributes like a box's dimensions, a sphere's radius, or the height of a cylinder or cone.

VRML's primitive shapes are always built centered at the origin. In later chapters you will learn how to move that origin to build shapes anywhere within your world.

Note that all primitive shapes are considered *solid;* you could fill one with water, and it wouldn't spill out no matter how you turn the shape. You cannot see the insides of solid shapes.

Recall from Chapter 2 that you can group together any number of nodes and then manipulate the group as a single entity. Recall, also, that a group can have any number of members, or children, which can be either shapes or other groups that contain shapes and groups. Finally, recall that the group node containing the child nodes is called a parent node.

Because groups can contain other groups, the parent of one group could be a child of a higher-level group. That higher-level group's parent could be the child of a still-higher-level group, and so on up to the highest- or top-level parent, called the *root.*

VRML provides several types of grouping nodes. This chapter introduces the **Group** node. The **Group** node among the other VRML grouping nodes is explained further in Chapters 5–7 and 11.

The **Shape** Node Syntax

All VRML shapes are built using the **Shape** node.

| SYNTAX | **Shape node** |

```
Shape {
    appearance    NULL    # exposedField  SFNode
    geometry      NULL    # exposedField  SFNode
}
```

The value of the **geometry** field specifies a node defining the 3-D form, or geometry, of the shape. Typical **geometry** field values include the primitive geometry **Box, Cone, Cylinder,** and **Sphere** nodes. The default **NULL** value for this field indicates the absence of geometry.

The value of the **geometry** exposed field can be changed by routing an event to the exposed field's implied **set_geometry** eventIn. When the event is received, the **geometry** field is set, and the new geometry is sent out the exposed field's implied **geometry_changed** eventOut.

The value of the **appearance** field specifies a node defining the appearance of the shape, including its color and surface texture. The **appearance** field values include the Appearance node and the default **NULL** value, which indicates a glowing white appearance.

The value of the **appearance** exposed field can be changed by routing an event to the exposed field's implied **set_appearance** eventIn. When the event is received, the **appearance** field is set, and the new appearance is sent out the exposed field's implied **appearance_changed** eventOut.

The **Appearance** Node Syntax

The **Appearance** node specifies appearance attributes and may be used as the value of the **appearance** field in a **Shape** node.

| SYNTAX | **Appearance node** |

```
Appearance {
    material          NULL   # exposedField    SFNode
    texture           NULL   # exposedField    SFNode
    textureTransform  NULL   # exposedField    SFNode
}
```

The value of the **material** field specifies a node defining the material attributes of the appearance. Typical **material** field values include the **Material** node. The default NULL value for this field indicates a default, glowing white material.

The remaining fields of the **Appearance** node—**texture** and **textureTransform**—are discussed in Chapters 17 and 18.

The **Material** Node Syntax

The **Material** node specifies material attributes and may be used as the value of the **material** field in an **Appearance** node.

| SYNTAX | **Material node** |

```
Material {
    ambientIntensity   0.2            # exposedField    SFFloat
    diffuseColor       0.8 0.8 0.8    # exposedField    SFColor
    emissiveColor      0.0 0.0 0.0    # exposedField    SFColor
    shininess          0.2            # exposedField    SFFloat
    specularColor      0.0 0.0 0.0    # exposedField    SFColor
    transparency       0.0            # exposedField    SFFloat
}
```

The default values for the **Material** node create shaded, white shapes. The **Material** node is discussed further in Chapter 10.

The **Box** Node Syntax

The **Box** node creates box-shaped primitive geometry and may be used as the value of the **geometry** field in a **Shape** node.

SYNTAX   **Box node**

```
Box {
     size    2.0 2.0 2.0    # field  SFVec3f
}
```

The value of the **size** field specifies the size of a 3-D rectangular box centered at the origin. The first value in the **size** field is the box's width in the X direction, the second value is the box's height in the Y direction, and the third value is the box's depth in the Z direction. All three size values must be greater than 0.0. The default **size** field values create a box 2.0 units wide, 2.0 units tall, and 2.0 units deep.

The **Cone** Node Syntax

The **Cone** node creates cone-shaped primitive geometry and may be used as the value of the **geometry** field in a **Shape** node.

SYNTAX   **Cone node**

```
Cone {
     bottomRadius    1.0      # field  SFFloat
     height          2.0      # field  SFFloat
     side            TRUE     # field  SFBool
     bottom          TRUE     # field  SFBool
}
```

The value of the **bottomRadius** field specifies the radius of the bottom of a 3-D cone centered at the origin with its axis lying along the Y axis. (A cone's *axis* is an imaginary line that runs through its center from bottom to top.) The **bottomRadius** field value must be greater than 0.0. The default **bottomRadius** field value creates a cone with a bottom radius of 1.0 unit.

The value of the **height** field specifies the cone's height in the Y direction. The **height** field value must be greater than 0.0. The default **height** field value creates a cone 2.0 units tall with the bottom of the cone 1.0 unit below the origin and the top 1.0 unit above the origin.

The value of the **side** field specifies whether or not the sloping sides of the cone are built. If the field value is **TRUE**, the sides are built; if the field value is **FALSE**, they are not. The default **side** field value creates a cone with sides.

The value of the **bottom** field specifies whether or not the circular bottom of the cone is built. If the field value is **TRUE**, the bottom is built; if the field value is **FALSE**, it is not. The default **bottom** field value creates a cone with a bottom.

While you can turn off both the sides and the bottom of the cone, when you do there is nothing left to build, and the cone is invisible. If you turn off the cone's bottom but not its sides, you can see inside of it. If you turn off the cone's sides but leave the bottom on, you'll see only the circular base of the cone.

The **Cylinder** Node Syntax

The **Cylinder** node creates cylinder-shaped primitive geometry and may be used as the value of the **geometry** field in a **Shape** node.

SYNTAX	Cylinder node

```
Cylinder {
    radius    1.0      # field  SFFloat
    height    2.0      # field  SFFloat
    side      TRUE     # field  SFBool
    top       TRUE     # field  SFBool
    bottom    TRUE     # field  SFBool
}
```

The value of the **radius** field specifies the radius of a 3-D cylinder centered at the origin with its axis lying along the Y axis. (A cylinder's *axis* is an imaginary line that runs through its center from bottom to top.) The **radius** field value must be greater than 0.0. The default **radius** field value creates a cylinder with a radius of 1.0 unit.

The value of the **height** field specifies the cylinder's height in the Y direction. The **height** field value must be greater than 0.0. The default **height** field value creates a cylinder 2.0 units tall with the bottom of the cylinder 1.0 unit below the origin and the top 1.0 unit above the origin.

The value of the **side** field specifies whether or not the curving sides of the cylinder are built. If the field value is **TRUE,** the sides are built; if the field value is **FALSE,** they are not. The default **side** field value creates a cylinder with sides.

The value of the **top** field specifies whether or not the circular top of the cylinder is built. If the field value is **TRUE,** the top is built; if the field value is **FALSE,** it is not. The default **top** field value creates a cylinder with a top.

The value of the **bottom** field specifies whether or not the circular bottom of the cylinder is built. If the field value is **TRUE,** the bottom is built; if the field value is **FALSE,** it is not. The default **bottom** field value creates a cylinder with a bottom.

While you can simultaneously turn off the sides, top, and bottom of the cylinder, when you do there is nothing left to build, and the cylinder is invisible. If you turn off the cylinder's top or bottom but not its sides, you can see inside of it. If you turn off the cylinder's sides but leave the top and/or bottom on, you'll see only the circular top and/or bottom of the cylinder.

The **Sphere** Node Syntax

The **Sphere** node creates sphere-shaped (a ball or globe) primitive geometry and may be used as the value of the **geometry** field in a **Shape** node.

SYNTAX   Sphere node

```
Sphere {
     radius    1.0     # field  SFFloat
}
```

The value of the **radius** field specifies the radius of a 3-D sphere centered at the origin. The **radius** field value must be greater than 0.0. The default **radius** field value creates a sphere with a radius of 1.0 unit.

The **Group** Node Syntax

VRML nodes can be grouped together using the **Group** node.

SYNTAX   Group node

```
Group {
     children        [ ]                # exposedField  MFNode
     bboxCenter      0.0 0.0 0.0        # field         SFVec3f
     bboxSize        -1.0 -1.0 -1.0     # field         SFVec3f
     addChildren                        # eventIn       MFNode
     removeChildren                     # eventOut      MFNode
}
```

The value of the **children** field specifies a list of child nodes to be included in the group. Typical **children** field values include **Shape** nodes and other **Group** nodes. When you display this file, your VRML browser builds the group by building each of the shapes and groups contained within the group. The default value for this field is an empty list of children.

The remaining fields of the **Group** node are discussed in Chapter 11.

Experimenting with Primitive Shapes and Grouping

The following examples provide a more detailed examination of the ways in which the **Shape, Group, Appearance, Material, Box, Cone, Cylinder,** and **Sphere** nodes can be used.

Experimenting with Boxes

You can build a box shape by using a **Box** node as the value of the **geometry** field in a **Shape** node, as shown in Figure 3.1.

```
#VRML V2.0 utf8
Shape {
    appearance Appearance {
        material Material { }
    }
    geometry Box { }
}
```

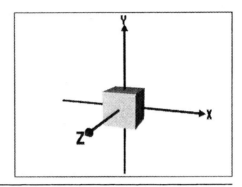

Figure 3.1   *Default box.*

This example creates a box shape without specifying the **Box** node's **size** field values. When you display this file, your VRML browser fills in the default values for the **size** field and creates a box with these characteristics:

- 2.0 units wide
- 2.0 units tall
- 2.0 units deep
- Centered at the origin

You can create a box with any dimensions by specifying values for the **size** field, as shown in Figure 3.2.

```
#VRML V2.0 utf8
Shape {
    appearance Appearance {
        material Material { }
    }
    geometry Box {
        size 1.0 3.0 5.0
    }
}
```

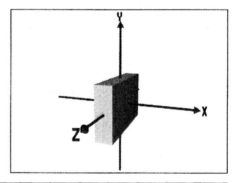

Figure 3.2   *A box with a small width, a medium height, and a large depth.*

Experimenting with Cones

You can build a cone shape by using a **Cone** node as the value of the **geometry** field in a **Shape** node, as shown in Figure 3.3.

```
#VRML V2.0 utf8
Shape {
    appearance Appearance {
        material Material { }
    }
    geometry Cone { }
}
```

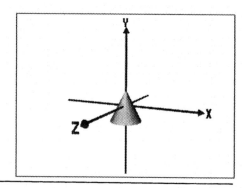

Figure 3.3 *Default cone.*

This example creates a cone shape without specifying the **Cone** node's **bottom-Radius** or **height** field values. When you display this file, your VRML browser fills in the default values and creates a cone with the following characteristics:

- 1.0-unit bottom radius (a 2.0-unit diameter)
- 2.0 units tall
- Centered at the origin

You can create a cone with any dimensions by specifying values for the **bottomRadius** and **height** fields, as shown in Figure 3.4.

```
#VRML V2.0 utf8
Shape {
    appearance Appearance {
        material Material { }
    }
    geometry Cone {
        bottomRadius 3.5
        height 1.5
    }
}
```

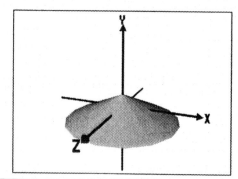

Figure 3.4 *A cone with a large bottom radius and a short height.*

Note that because you can't see the insides of solid shapes, when you turn off parts, the insides of the other parts seem to disappear.

Experimenting with Cylinders

You can build a cylinder shape by using a **Cylinder** node as the value of the **geometry** field in a **Shape** node, as shown in Figure 3.5.

```
#VRML V2.0 utf8
Shape {
    appearance Appearance {
        material Material { }
    }
    geometry Cylinder { }
}
```

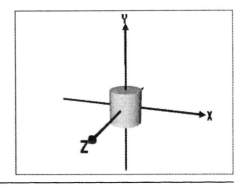

Figure 3.5   *Default cylinder.*

This example creates a cylinder shape without specifying the **Cylinder** node's **radius** or **height** field values. When you display this file, your VRML browser fills in the default values and creates a cylinder with the following characteristics:

- 1.0-unit radius (a 2.0-unit diameter)
- 2.0 units tall
- Centered at the origin

You can create a cylinder with any dimensions by specifying values for the **radius** and **height** fields, as shown in Figure 3.6.

```
#VRML V2.0 utf8
Shape {
    appearance Appearance {
        material Material { }
    }
    geometry Cylinder {
        radius 4.0
        height 1.0
    }
}
```

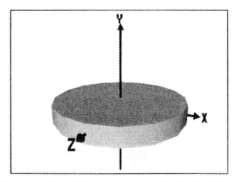

Figure 3.6   *A cylinder with a large radius and a short height.*

You can create a hollow ring by setting the **top** and **bottom** field values to **FALSE,** as shown in Figure 3.7.

```
#VRML V2.0 utf8
Shape {
    appearance Appearance {
        material Material { }
    }
```

Figure 3.7 continues

```
geometry Cylinder {
    radius 4.0
    height 1.0
    top     FALSE
    bottom FALSE
    }
}
```

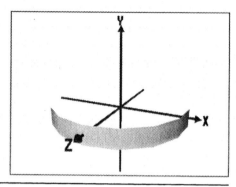

Figure 3.7 *A cylinder with a large radius, a short height, no top, and no bottom.*

Note that because you can't see the insides of solid shapes, when you turn off parts, the insides of the other parts seem to disappear.

Experimenting with Spheres

You can build a sphere shape by using a **Sphere** node as the value of the **geometry** field in a **Shape** node, as shown in Figure 3.8.

```
#VRML V2.0 utf8
Shape {
    appearance Appearance {
        material Material { }
    }
    geometry Sphere { }
}
```

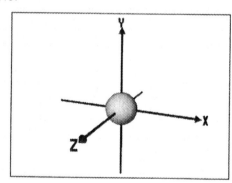

Figure 3.8 *Default sphere.*

This example creates a sphere shape without specifying the **Sphere** node's **radius** field value. When you display the file, your VRML browser fills in the default value and creates a sphere with the following characteristics:

- 1.0-unit radius (a 2.0-unit diameter)
- Centered at the origin

Experimenting with Groups

The examples thus far have shown a **Shape** node and its fields alone in each file. To include two or more **Shape** nodes in the same file, they can be grouped together within a **Group** node. Three, four, or more shapes can be added to the same group. You can combine together shapes of different sizes within the same group, and those shapes can overlap. This is important for creating complex shapes, like the 3-D plus sign shown in Figure 3.9.

```
#VRML V2.0 utf8
Group {
    children [
        Shape {
            appearance DEF White Appearance {
                material Material { }
            }
            geometry Box {
                size 25.0 2.0 2.0
            }
        },
        Shape {
            appearance USE White
            geometry Box {
                size 2.0 25.0 2.0
            }
        },
        Shape {
            appearance USE White
            geometry Box {
                size 2.0 2.0 25.0
            }
        }
    ]
}
```

Figure 3.9 *A 3-D plus sign.*

In Figure 3.9, the three **Shape** nodes using **Box** node primitive geometries create the three long poles of the plus sign. All three boxes cross in the middle, overlapping each other.

Each of the box shapes needs an appearance description. To save time, you can describe a standard shaded white appearance once using an **Appearance** node named "White" by the **DEF** syntax. You can then reuse the "White" **Appearance** node for the remaining two box shapes by using the USE syntax.

You can create more complicated shapes, for example, the space station shown in Figure 3.10, by combining different primitive geometries.

```
#VRML V2.0 utf8
Group {
    children [
        Shape {
            appearance DEF White Appearance {
                material Material { }
            }
        }
```

Figure 3.10 continues

```
            geometry Box {
                size 10.0 10.0 10.0
            }
    },
    Shape {
        appearance USE White
        geometry Sphere {
            radius 7.0
        }
    },
    Shape {
        appearance USE White
        geometry Cylinder {
            radius 12.5
            height 0.5
        }
    },
    Shape {
        appearance USE White
        geometry Cylinder {
            radius 4.0
            height 20.0
        }
    },
    Shape {
        appearance USE White
        geometry Cylinder {
            radius 3.0
            height 30.0
        }
    },
    Shape {
        appearance USE White
        geometry Cylinder {
            radius 1.0
            height 60.0
        }
    }
    }
  ]
}
```

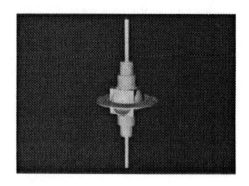

Figure 3.10 *A space station.*

Summary

Shapes are built using the **Shape** node with which you can specify a shape's geometry and appearance. Shapes are always built centered at the origin.

A shape's appearance is controlled by the **Appearance** and **Material** nodes. Without these, a shape is colored glowing white. Using the default values for the **Material** node, shapes are shaded white.

VRML's four primitive geometry nodes are the **Box** node, the **Cone** node, the **Cylinder** node, and the **Sphere** node. Each of these nodes contains fields which enable you to specify geometries of different sizes. Cylinders and cones have parts which can be turned on and off: the bottom and sides of a cone and the top, bottom, and sides of a cylinder. Cones and cylinders are built with their axes pointing upward along the Y axis.

Shapes can be grouped together in a **Group** node, and groups can contain shapes or other groups. A VRML file may contain any number of groups.

## CHAPTER 4

Building Text Shapes

Using VRML's text and font features, you can add 3-D text shapes to your world. To build text, you specify the VRML **Text** node as the value of the **Shape** node's **geometry** field. For each text geometry you can specify a list of text strings and the length of each string. Using the **FontStyle** node you can control the font family, style, and size of text geometry, as well as their spacing, justification, and more.

Understanding VRML Text

Recall from Chapter 3 that VRML geometry nodes, like **Box** and **Sphere,** are used to specify the geometry of shapes built by the **Shape** node. You can also use the VRML **Text** geometry node to create 3-D shapes for each character of one or more lines of text. Like the geometry nodes from Chapter 3, fields in the **Text** node enable you to specify the characters to build and the attributes controlling how each string of characters is built.

In addition to the shape and geometry nodes introduced so far, VRML supports a variety of nodes that help specify how shapes and geometry are created. These nodes, called *property* nodes, don't create shapes or geometry themselves, but rather encapsulate settings that you can use over and over again to control how shapes and geometry are built.

In the case of text shapes, it is often convenient to use the same font attributes for multiple text shapes. Rather than repeatedly specifying the font family, style, size, and so forth, for each text shape, you can encapsulate these settings within a **FontStyle** property node, then share that node among all of the text shapes intended to be the same font. Later, if you choose to make all of those text shapes a different font, you need only change the shared **FontStyle** node's fields in order to affect all of the text shapes at once.

Text Shapes

Text geometry is specified with the **Text** node. Fields in the **Text** node enable you to control:

- The text string, or series of characters, to be built
- The maximum permissible extent of the lines or columns of text
- The exact length of each line or column of text
- The font or typeface to use for the text, along with its style, justification, and other attributes

A *text string* is a series of characters that specifies the text geometry to be built. For instance, if you provide a text string like "ABC," you will get side-by-side, 3-D geometry for the letters "A," "B," and "C."

You can create a single line or multiple lines of text. All of the lines of text are built as 3-D geometry. Depending on the font style you choose, lines of text can be built from left to right (as, for example, English text is written) or right to left (as Arabic is written), and from top to bottom (as Chinese is written) or bottom to top. This enables you to accommodate the reading direction of any of the world's languages.

You can specify the maximum extent of lines or columns of text. Lines or columns longer than this maximum extent are compressed by reducing the size or spacing of the characters making up the lines or columns. This ensures that a block of text will fit within a prescribed part of your world, such as on a street sign.

You can also control the length of each line or column of text. Text geometry is compressed or expanded to match this length. This feature enables you to create special justification effects similar to those found in page-layout applications.

Font Styles

The shape and position of characters built by a **Text** node depends on the choice of properties in a **FontStyle** node. The fields of the **FontStyle** property node enable you to control:

- The font family defining the character shapes used for the text
- The font style of the text, such as bold, italic, or normal
- The font size of the text
- The spacing of the text lines or columns
- The justification of the lines or columns of text
- The orientation of the text: horizontal or vertical
- The flow direction of the text: from left to right, right to left, top to bottom, or bottom to top
- The specific language features to use

VRML provides three *font families* for text shapes: serif, sans, and typewriter. The *serif* font family is similar to the Times Roman font family found on most computers. Likewise, *sans* is similar to Helvetica, and *typewriter* is similar to Courier.

The serif and sans font families both use *variable-width characters* in which an "i," for example, takes up less space than a "W." Variable-width characters like these are used by word processors to give blocks of text a more uniform appearance.

The typewriter font family uses *fixed-width characters* in which an "i" takes the same amount of space as a "W." Fixed-width characters like these are typically used in computer command windows, such as those on DOS or UNIX computers.

All three VRML font families can be drawn at any font size. *Font size* specifies the character height in units, just like those used to set a cylinder's height or a sphere's radius.

You can specify plain, bold, italic, or bold and italic *font styles* for any of the three font families.

To support both line- and column-oriented text in different languages, VRML's **FontStyle** node enables you to select whether text should be built horizontally or vertically and to control whether text progresses from left to right or right to left and from top to bottom or bottom to top. You can also control the horizontal or vertical spacing between lines or columns of text, and indicate whether text should be justified at the beginning of lines or columns (in English, the left side, and called *left-justified*), at the end of lines or columns (in English, the right side, and called *right-justified*), or in the middle of lines or columns (called *centered*).

Character Sets

To enable VRML to display any character in any of the world's languages, VRML uses the UTF-8 character set encoding defined by the International Standards Organization (ISO) 10646-1:1993 standard and the pDAM 1-5 extension. These character set standards enable you to build shapes for any English alphabet character, as well as characters in Japanese, Arabic, Cyrillic, and other languages.

Character sets are not the same as fonts. A *character set* defines the alphabet available, while a *font* defines the aesthetic look of characters in that alphabet. For a single character set, you can have hundreds or thousands of different fonts, each providing a different look for those same characters. The popular Times Roman font, for instance, defines one look for a character set.

The UTF-8 character set encoding of the ISO standard includes all of the characters found on a typical computer keyboard. For example, to get an "A," type "A" into the text string of a **Text** node. International characters not found on the standard computer keyboard may be entered by typing in their UTF-8 codes. This requires special features in your text editor or in a VRML authoring application. Examples in this book use only the standard English-language characters (technically, the Latin character set) in text strings.

See Appendix B for references to more information about the UTF-8 character set, the ISO 10646-1:1993 standard, and the pDAM 1-5 extension.

TIP For maximum portability of your VRML worlds, restrict your use of UTF-8 characters to only those found on the computer keyboard. There are over 24,000 characters defined in the ISO 10646-1:1993 standard, but only 127 in the ASCII (American Standard Code for Information Interchange) character set used by most computers. Many VRML browsers will not support the full range of characters theoretically available within VRML. Additionally, because the UTF-8 encoding requires the use of 8-bit characters, instead of the more common 7-bit ASCII characters, many text editing applications will be unable to create UTF-8 characters or display them properly.

The **Text** Node Syntax

The **Text** node creates text geometry and may be used as the value for the **geometry** field in a **Shape** node.

SYNTAX	Text node

```
Text {
        string      [ ]      # exposedField  MFString
        length      [ ]      # exposedField  MFFloat
        maxExtent   0.0      # exposedField  SFFloat
        fontStyle   NULL     # exposedField  SFNode
```

The value of the **string** exposed field specifies one or more lines of text to build. Each line or column of text is enclosed within quotation marks. Carriage returns within quoted strings are ignored. To create more than one line or column of text, list the text strings enclosed by square brackets and optionally separated by commas. The default for this field is an empty list of strings, which creates no text geometry for the shape.

The value of the **string** exposed field can be changed by routing an event to the exposed field's implied **set_string** eventIn. When the event is received, the **string** field is set, and the new string is sent using the exposed field's implied **string_changed** eventOut.

The **Text** node builds flat text characters with a Z-axis depth of 0.0. By default, consecutive text string characters are placed side by side along the X axis from left to right. Consecutive text string lines are placed one below the other down the Y axis from top to bottom. You can change these defaults by setting fields of a **FontStyle** node that is specified as the value of the **fontStyle** field.

The value of the **length** exposed field specifies the desired length, in VRML units, of each line of text. To match the specified length, lines or columns of text are compressed or expanded by changing their character size or character spacing. A **length** field value of 0.0 specifies text strings that are built at their natural length without compressing or expanding.

Each line of text can have its own length by including multiple length values within square brackets and optionally separated by commas. In a list of **length** field values, the first value in the list controls the length of the first text string in the **string** field's value list. The second **length** field value controls the length of the second string, and so on. If there are fewer **length** field values than there are **string** field values, the remaining text strings are built at their natural lengths as if lengths of 0.0 had been specified. The default **length** field value is an empty list and is treated as if a list of 0.0 lengths had been specified.

The value of the **length** exposed field can be changed by routing an event to the exposed field's implied **set_length** eventIn. When the event is received, the **length** field is set, and the new length is sent using the exposed field's implied **length_ changed** eventOut.

The value of the **maxExtent** exposed field specifies the maximum permissible length, in VRML units, of any line or column of text. The **maxExtent** field value must be greater than or equal to 0.0. Lines or columns longer than the maximum extent are compressed by reducing their character size or character spacing. Lines or columns shorter than the maximum extent are not affected. The maximum extent is measured horizontally for horizontal text and vertically for vertical text. The default for this field is 0.0, which indicates that no extent limit be used.

The value of the **maxExtent** exposed field can be changed by routing an event to the exposed field's implied **set_maxExtent** eventIn. When the event is received, the **maxExtent** field is set, and the new maximum extent is sent using the exposed field's implied **maxExtent_changed** eventOut.

The first character of the first **string** field value in a **Text** node is typically positioned resting on the X axis with its lowest, left-most point at a Y coordinate of 0.0. Subsequent characters are placed to the right or left, above or below, based on features controlled using a **FontStyle** node. Similarly, spacing between and justification across lines or columns of text are controlled using the **FontStyle** node.

The value of the **fontStyle** exposed field specifies the characteristics defining the look of text created by the **Text** node. Typically the **fontStyle** field value is a **FontStyle** node. The default NULL value for this field indicates that the default font style should be used. The default font style instructs the **Text** node to build left-justified, serif text from left to right horizontally and from top to bottom vertically. The default font's size is 1.0 unit tall, and its spacing between text lines is 1.0 unit.

The value of the **fontStyle** exposed field can be changed by routing an event to the exposed field's implied **set_fontStyle** eventIn. When the event is received, the **fontStyle** field is set, and the new font style is sent using the exposed field's implied **fontStyle_changed** eventOut.

The **FontStyle** Node Syntax

The **FontStyle** node controls the characteristics defining the look of the text geometry created by a **Text** node. A **FontStyle** node may be used as the value of the **fontStyle** field in a **Text** node.

| SYNTAX | FontStyle node |

```
FontStyle {
     family          "SERIF"     # field  SFString
     style           "PLAIN"     # field  SFString
     size            1.0         # field  SFFloat
     spacing         1.0         # field  SFFloat
     justify         "BEGIN"     # field  SFString
     horizontal      TRUE        # field  SFBool
     leftToRight     TRUE        # field  SFBool
     topToBottom     TRUE        # field  SFBool
     language        ""          # field  SFString
}
```

The **family** field specifies which of the standard VRML font families to use. Valid **family** field values are described in Table 4.1. The default **family** field value is "SERIF". An empty string ("") also specifies the default font family.

Table 4.1   Valid **family** Field Values

family Field Value	*Description*
"SERIF"	A variable-width, serif font such as Times Roman (default)
"SANS"	A variable-width, sans serif font such as Helvetica
"TYPEWRITER"	A fixed-width font such as Courier

SIDEBAR: FONT USE BY DIFFERENT BROWSERS Different VRML browsers use different internal fonts to implement the serif, sans, and typewriter font families. For instance, while Times Roman is the typical font family used for serif, other possibilities include font families such as New York and Palatino. The font family actually displayed depends on your VRML browser.

The value of the **style** field specifies the text style to use. Valid **style** field values are described in Table 4.2. The default **style** field value is "PLAIN" (the empty string).

Table 4.2   Valid **style** Field Values

style Field Value	*Description*
"PLAIN"	Plain text (default)
"BOLD"	Bold text
"ITALIC"	Italic, or oblique, text
"BOLDITALIC"	Bold and italic text

The value of the **size** field specifies the height of the characters measured in VRML units. The default **size** field value is 1.0 unit.

The value of the **spacing** field specifies the vertical line spacing, in VRML units, of horizontal text or the horizontal column spacing of vertical text. In either case, consecutive lines or columns are built (size x spacing) units over, where *size* is the **size** field value, and *spacing* is the **spacing** field value. For typical horizontal, left-to-right, top-to-bottom text, the first line is built horizontally along the X axis, the second line is built (size x spacing) units *down* the Y axis, the third line is built 2 × (size x spacing) down the Y axis, and so on. The **default** value for the spacing field is 1.0.

The value of the **horizontal** field specifies whether text strings are built horizontally or vertically. When the field value is **TRUE,** each text string in the **Text** node's **string** field builds a horizontal line of text. When the field value is **FALSE,** each text string builds a vertical column of text. The default value for the horizontal field is **TRUE.**

All text shapes have a major direction and a minor direction, selected by the value choice for the **horizontal** field's value. For horizontal text, the *major direction* is horizontal along the X axis, and the *minor direction* is vertical along the Y axis. Similar for vertical text, the major direction is vertical along the Y axis, and the minor direction is horizontal along the X axis. In either case, a text shape is built by placing the characters of a text string side by side along the major direction (horizontal or vertical) and by placing consecutive text strings side by side along the minor direction (horizontal or vertical). Typically, the **horizontal** field value is **TRUE:** text string characters are placed horizontally side by side and consecutive text strings are placed vertically one below the other.

The values of the **horizontal, leftToRight,** and **topToBottom** fields are used in combination to control horizontal or vertical text placement. For horizontal text, the **leftToRight** field value specifies how consecutive characters in a text string are placed along the major direction (horizontal). When the **leftToRight** field value is **TRUE,** consecutive characters are placed side by side from left to right, progressing along the positive X axis. When the **leftToRight** field value is **FALSE,** consecutive characters are placed side by side from right to left, progressing along the negative X axis. In either case for horizontal text, the **topToBottom** field value specifies how consecutive text strings are placed along the minor direction (vertical). When the **topToBottom** field value is **TRUE,** consecutive strings are placed one below the other from top to bottom, progressing down the negative Y axis. When the **topTo-Bottom** field value is **FALSE,** consecutive strings are placed one above the other from bottom to top, progressing up the positive Y axis.

For vertical text, the effects of the **leftToRight** and **topToBottom** field values is similar. The **topToBottom** field value specifies how consecutive characters in a text string are placed along the major direction (vertical). When the **topToBottom** field value is **TRUE,** consecutive characters are placed one below the other from top to bottom, progressing down the negative Y axis. When the **topToBottom** field value is **FALSE,** consecutive characters are placed one above the other from bottom to top, progressing up the positive Y axis. In either case for vertical text, the **leftToRight** field value specifies how consecutive text strings are placed along the minor direction (horizontal). When the **leftToRight** field value is **TRUE,** consecutive strings are placed side by side from left to right, progressing along the positive X axis. When the **leftToRight** field value is **FALSE,** consecutive strings are placed side by side from right to left, progressing along the negative X axis.

The default values for the **leftToRight** and **topToBottom** fields are both **TRUE**. When the **horizontal** field value is **TRUE** as well, the result is typical, English-language text placement where characters in a string read from left to right and consecutive lines flow from top to bottom.

The value of the **justify** field specifies the way in which the text shape's block of text is positioned relative to the X and Y axes. The field value is a list of one or two justification selections. When two justification values are given, the values must be enclosed within square brackets and, optionally, separated by commas. The first justification value is called the *major justification* and controls justification along the major direction of the text (typically horizontal). The optional second justification value is called the *minor justification* and controls justification along the minor direction (typically vertical). Valid values for the major and minor justification values are "FIRST", "BEGIN", "MIDDLE", and "END". The default **justify** field value is "BEGIN", which specifies only the major justification value and leaves the minor justification value at the default value of "FIRST".

The meaning of the major and minor justification values depends on the values for the **horizontal, leftToRight,** and **bottomToTop** fields. Each variation is described in the following tables.

Table 4.3   justify Field Values for Major Justification of Horizontal Text

justify field *major value*	*leftToRight* *field value*	*Description*
"FIRST"	TRUE	Place the left edge of the text block at the Y axis.
	FALSE	Place the right edge of the text block at the Y axis.
"BEGIN"	TRUE	Place the left edge of the text block at the Y axis (default).
	FALSE	Place the right edge of the text block at the Y axis.
"MIDDLE"	TRUE	Place the middle of the text block at the Y axis.
	FALSE	Place the middle of the text block at the Y axis.
"END"	TRUE	Place the right edge of the text block at the Y axis.
	FALSE	Place the left edge of the text block at the Y axis.

Table 4.4   justify Field Values for Major Justification of Vertical Text

justify field *major value*	*topToBottom* *field value*	*Description*
"FIRST"	TRUE	Place the top edge of the text block at the X axis.
	FALSE	Place the bottom edge of the text block at the X axis.
"BEGIN"	TRUE	Place the top edge of the text block at the X axis.
	FALSE	Place the bottom edge of the text block at the X axis.
"MIDDLE"	TRUE	Place the middle of the text block at the X axis.
	FALSE	Place the middle of the text block at the X axis.
"END"	TRUE	Place the right edge of the text block at the X axis.
	FALSE	Place the left edge of the text block at the X axis.

Table 4.5 Justify Field Values for Minor Justification of Horizontal Text

justify field minor value	*topToBottom field value*	*Description*
"FIRST"	TRUE	Place the baseline of the first text line at the X axis.
	FALSE	Place the baseline of the first text line at the X axis.
"BEGIN"	TRUE	Place the top edge of the first text line at the X axis.
	FALSE	Place the bottom edge of the first text line at the X axis.
"MIDDLE"	TRUE	Place the middle of the text block at the X axis.
	FALSE	Place the middle of the text block at the X axis.
"END"	TRUE	Place the bottom edge of the last text line at the X axis.
	FALSE	Place the top edge of the last text line at the X axis.

Table 4.6 Justify Field Values for Minor Justification of Vertical Text

justify field minor value	*leftToRight field value*	*Description*
"FIRST"	TRUE	Place the left edge of the first text column at the Y axis.
	FALSE	Place the right edge of the first text column at the Y axis.
"BEGIN"	TRUE	Place the left edge of the first text column at the Y axis.
	FALSE	Place the right edge of the first text column at the Y axis.
"MIDDLE"	TRUE	Place the middle of the text block at the Y axis.
	FALSE	Place the middle of the text block at the Y axis.
"END"	TRUE	Place the right edge of the last text column at the Y axis.
	FALSE	Place the left edge of the last text column at the Y axis.

Table 4.7 summarizes the most common combined effects of the **justify, horizontal, leftToRight,** and **topToBottom** field values on the three-line **string** field value ["The", "VRML 2.0", "Sourcebook"]. In each image, the location of the origin relative to the text block is indicated by four symbols, one for each of the four possible minor justification values.

The value of the **language** field specifies the context of the language used in values of the **Text** node's **string** field. This field is typically not specified; its value is left as the default: "" (the empty string). When used, **language** field values help to clarify the choice of language used in **string** field values. This clarification makes it possible to more accurately build multilingual text strings based on the ISO 10646-1:1993 character standard and VRML's UTF-8 encoding.

Valid **language** field values are based on locale specifications outlined in several international standards, including that of POSIX and RFC 1766 (see Appendix B for references to these standards). Each **language** field value contains a required *language code* followed by an optional underscore and *territory code*. Language codes are specified in the ISO 639 standard, and territory codes are specified in the ISO 3166 standard. Table 4.5 describes examples of valid **language** field values. Full details on language and territory codes may be found in the ISO 639 and ISO 3166 standards (see Appendix B for references to these standards).

Table 4.7 Typical Combinations of Text Justification and Direction of Text Flow

horizontal		topToBottom		leftToRight		justify — Major Value			justify — Minor Value*			For This Effect
TRUE	FALSE	TRUE	FALSE	TRUE	FALSE	"FIRST" or "BEGIN"	"MIDDLE"	"END"	"FIRST" or "BEGIN"	"MIDDLE"	"END"	
✓		✓		✓		✓			✓			Qwerty 0123 Asdf
✓		✓		✓		✓			✓			Qwerty 0123 Asdf
✓		✓		✓		✓				✓		Qwerty 0123 Asdf

Use This Combination of Field Values

Table 4.7 (Continued)

For This Effect	horizontal TRUE	horizontal FALSE	topToBottom TRUE	topToBottom FALSE	leftToRight TRUE	leftToRight FALSE	Major Value "FIRST" or "BEGIN"	Major Value "MIDDLE"	Major Value "END"	Minor Value "FIRST" or "BEGIN"	Minor Value "MIDDLE"	Minor Value "END"
(Qwerty / 0123 / Asdf)	✓		✓		✓		✓					✓
(Qwerty / 0123 / Asdf)	✓		✓		✓			✓		✓		
(Qwerty / 0123 / Asdf)	✓		✓		✓				✓	✓		

Column groups: "Use This Combination of Field Values" spans horizontal, topToBottom, leftToRight, and justify (Major Value / Minor Value).

Table 4.7 (Continued)

For This Effect	Use This Combination of Field Values											
	horizontal		topToBottom		leftToRight		justify					
							Major Value			Minor Value*		
	TRUE	FALSE	TRUE	FALSE	TRUE	FALSE	"FIRST" or "BEGIN"	"MIDDLE"	"END"	"FIRST" or "BEGIN"	"MIDDLE"	"END"
Asdf / 0123 / Qwerty	✓		✓		✓		✓			✓		
ytrewQ / 3210 / fdsA	✓			✓		✓	✓			✓		
Q 0 A / w 1 s / e 2 d / r 3 f / t y		✓	✓		✓		✓			✓		

50

Table 4.7 (Continued)

For This Effect	Use This Combination of Field Values											
	horizontal		topToBottom		leftToRight		justify					
							Major Value			Minor Value*		
	TRUE	FALSE	TRUE	FALSE	TRUE	FALSE	"FIRST" or "BEGIN"	"MIDDLE"	"END"	"FIRST" or "BEGIN"	"MIDDLE"	"END"
(diagram 1)		✓	✓		✓		✓				✓	
(diagram 2)		✓	✓		✓		✓					✓
(diagram 3)		✓	✓		✓			✓		✓		

51

Table 4.7 (Continued)

For This Effect	Use This Combination of Field Values												
	horizontal		topToBottom		leftToRight			justify Major Value			justify Minor Value*		
	TRUE	FALSE	TRUE	FALSE	TRUE	FALSE	"FIRST" or "BEGIN"	"BEGIN" or "FIRST"	"MIDDLE"	"END"	"BEGIN" or "FIRST"	"MIDDLE"	"END"
Effect 1: Q w e0A r1s e2d v3f (↑y, →x)		✓	✓		✓					✓	✓		
Effect 2: y r3f e2d w1s Q0A (↑y, →x)		✓		✓	✓		✓				✓		
Effect 3: A0Q s1w d2e f3r t y (↓y, →x)		✓	✓			✓	✓				✓		

*justify field minor values are represented by four symbols. Sphere represents "FIRST"; Box represents "BEGIN"; Cone represents "MIDDLE"; and Cylinder represents "END".

✓ = Default; no need to specify fields with this value.

Table 4.8 Valid language Field Value Examples

	Description	
language Field Value	*Language*	*Territory*
ar	Arabic	
de	German	
de_DE	German	Germany
de_CH	German	Switzerland
en	English	
en_US	English	United States
en_GB	English	Great Britain
hi	Hindi	
jp	Japanese	
ru	Russian	
sa	Sanskrit	
sw	Swahili	
zh	Chinese	
zh_TW	Chinese	Taiwan
zh_CN	Chinese	China

TIP For maximum portability of your VRML worlds, restrict your use of international language features to the English language. Many VRML browsers will not support the full range of languages, territories, and international characters theoretically available within VRML.

Experimenting with Text Shapes

The following examples provide a more detailed examination of the ways in which the **Text** and **FontStyle** nodes can be used and how they interact with nodes discussed in previous chapters.

Building Text Shapes

You build a text shape by using a **Text** node as the geometry for a **Shape** node, as shown in Figure 4.1.

```
#VRML V2.0 utf8
Shape {
    appearance Appearance {
        material Material { }
    }
    geometry Text {
        string "Qwerty"
    }
}
```

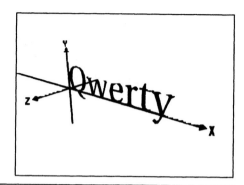

Figure 4.1 *A text shape.*

Figure 4.1 illustrates how you can create a text shape with a single string. You can create multistring text shapes by providing a list of strings as values for the **string** field, as shown in Figure 4.2.

```
#VRML V2.0 utf8
Shape {
    appearance Appearance {
        material Material { }
    }
    geometry Text {
        string [ "Qwerty", "0123" ]
    }
}
```

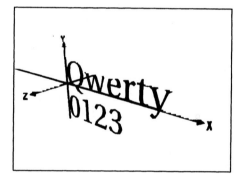

Figure 4.2 *A list of text strings.*

Controlling the Length of Text

Using the **Text** node's **length** field, you can vary the character spacing to compress or expand text lines or columns. Figure 4.3 shows how you can compress a text string by using a **length** field value, which is less than the natural length of the string.

```
#VRML V2.0 utf8
Shape {
    appearance Appearance {
        material Material { }
    }
    geometry Text {
        string "Qwerty"
        length 2.0
    }
}
```

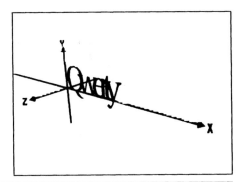

Figure 4.3 *Compressed text using a small **length** field value.*

When using multistring text shapes, you can specify a separate **length** field value for each string. For example, the VRML text in Figure 4.4 illustrates how you can compress the first string, but expand the second.

```
#VRML V2.0 utf8
Shape {
    appearance Appearance {
        material Material { }
    }
    geometry Text {
        string [ "Qwerty", "Qwerty" ]
        length  [ 3.0, 4.0 ]
    }
}
```

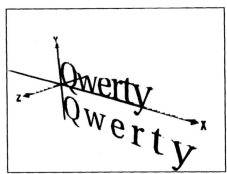

Figure 4.4 *A list of text strings with a list of lengths.*

Controlling the Maximum Extent of Text

Using the **Text** node's **maxExtent** field, you can limit the length of text lines to a maximum size. Lines or columns longer than this maximum are compressed to fit the maximum size. Figure 4.5 shows two lines of text, the first long and the second short. Using a medium-sized maximum extent, the long line is compressed down to the maximum, while the short line is left alone.

```
#VRML V2.0 utf8
Shape {
    appearance Appearance {
        material Material { }
    }
    geometry Text {
        string [ "Qwerty Uiop", "Asdf" ]
        maxExtent 4.0
    }
}
```

Figure 4.5   *Text limited by a maximum extent.*

Specifying Font Families and Styles

You can use a **FontStyle** node as the value of a **Text** node's **fontStyle** field. The **FontStyle** node controls font characteristics of text shapes. The **family** and **style** fields of a **FontStyle** node select the font family and style to use. Figure 4.6 shows plain (*a*) and bold (*b*) versions of the VRML serif font.

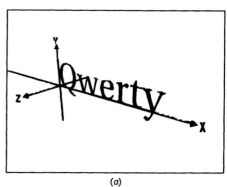

(*a*)

```
#VRML V2.0 utf8
Shape {
    appearance Appearance {
        material Material { }
    }
    geometry Text {
        string "Qwerty"
        fontStyle FontStyle {
            family "SERIF"
            style  "BOLD"
        }
    }
}
```

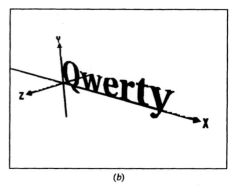

(*b*)

Figure 4.6   *(a) Text in a plain serif font, and (b) text in a bold serif font. (The VRML text in this figure builds the world shown in Figure 4.6b.)*

Controlling Font Size

Using the **FontStyle** node's **size** field, you can build large or small text shapes. Changing the size of the font changes the size of individual characters and the spacing between lines or columns of text. For instance, you can reduce the font size to one-half unit, as shown in Figure 4.7.

```
#VRML V2.0 utf8
Shape {
    appearance Appearance {
        material Material { }
    }
    geometry Text {
        string "Qwerty"
        fontStyle FontStyle {
            size 0.5
        }
    }
}
```

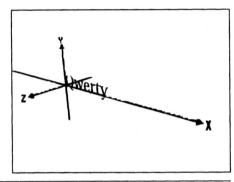

Figure 4.7 *Small text.*

Controlling Font Spacing

Using the **spacing** field of the **FontStyle** node, you can vary only the spacing between lines or columns of text, as shown in Figure 4.8.

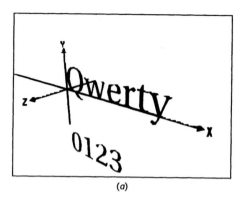

(a)

```
#VRML V2.0 utf8
Shape {
    appearance Appearance {
        material Material { }
    }
    geometry Text {
        string [ "Qwerty", "0123" ]
        fontStyle FontStyle {
            spacing 0.5
        }
    }
}
```

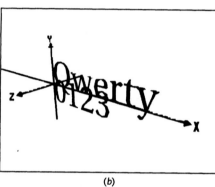

(b)

Figure 4.8 *(a) Text with more-than-default spacing between lines and (b) less-than-default spacing between lines causing the lines of text to overlap. (The VRML text in this figure builds the world shown in Figure 4.8b.)*

Building More than One Text Shape

Like the primitive shapes in Chapter 3, you can create more than one text shape by including them within a **Group** node's list of children. Figure 4.9 shows two text shapes: the first is right-justified, and the second is left-justified.

```
#VRML V2.0 utf8
Group {
    children [
        Shape {
            appearance DEF White Appearance {
                material Material { }
            }
            geometry Text {
                string "First"
                fontStyle FontStyle {
                    family  "SERIF"
                    style   "ITALIC"
                    justify "END"
                    size    1.0
                }
            }
        },
        Shape {
            appearance USE White
            geometry Text {
                string "Second"
                fontStyle FontStyle {
                    family  "SANS"
                    style   "BOLD"
                    justify "BEGIN"
                    size    1.0
                }
            }
        }
    ]
}
```

Figure 4.9 *Two text shapes with different types of justification.*

Combining Text and Primitive Shapes

You can also combine text shapes with the primitive shapes. The VRML text in Figure 4.10 builds two lines of text with a flattened box between them.

```
#VRML V2.0 utf8
Group {
    children [
        Shape {
            appearance DEF White Appearance {
                material Material { }
            }
            geometry Text {
                string [ "Above", "Below" ]
                fontStyle FontStyle {
                    justify "MIDDLE"
                }
            }
        },
        Shape {
            appearance USE White
            geometry Box {
                size 5.0 0.01 2.0
            }
        }
    ]
}
```

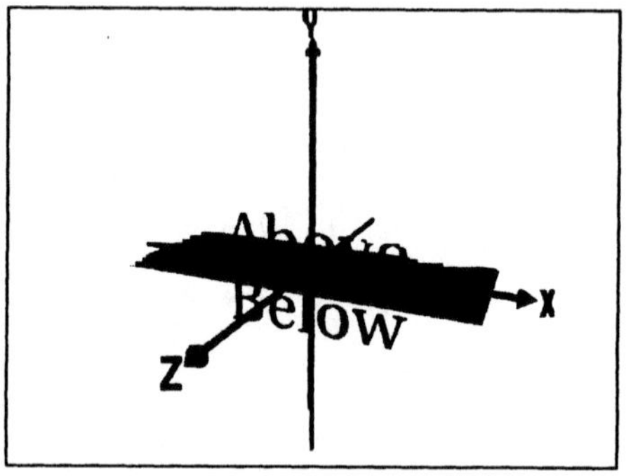

Figure 4.10 *Two lines of text with a flat box between them.*

Using **DEF** and **USE** to Share Font Styles

Recall from Chapter 2 that you can define a name for any node by preceding the node with the word DEF and a name of your choosing. Later, in the same VRML file, you can create another instance of that same node by preceding the name you chose with the word "USE." Using DEF and USE, you can repeatedly use the same node without having to type its full description over and over again. Using DEF and USE saves typing and shortens the length of your VRML files. Additionally, shapes named by DEF and instanced by USE all share the same node specification. If you change that node specification, all instances of that shape change as well.

Figure 4.11 illustrates how you can use DEF and USE to share font styles. The two Text nodes in the VRML text share the same FontStyle node.

```
#VRML V2.0 utf8
Group {
    children [
        Shape {
            appearance DEF White Appearance {
                material Material { }
            }
            geometry Text {
                string [ "Over", "Strike" ]
                fontStyle DEF myFontStyle FontStyle {
                    size    6.0
                    family  "TYPEWRITER"
                    justify "MIDDLE"
                }
            }
        },
        Shape {
            appearance USE White
            geometry Text {
                string [ "----", "------" ]
                fontStyle USE myFontStyle
            }
        }
    ]
}
```

Figure 4.11   *Using **DEF** and **USE** to share font properties.*

Summary

VRML's **Text** node enables you to build text shapes from single- or multiline text strings. You can specify text strings to be built, control the maximum extent of the text, and control the length of individual text lines or columns.

Using a **FontStyle** node as the value of the **fontStyle** field in a **Text** node, you can specify font characteristics for the characters specified with the **Text** node's **string** field value. You can choose a font family from the three families supported by VRML: serif, sans, and typewriter. For each family you can select whether the text should be created with plain, bold, italic, or bold and italic characters. You can control the font size, spacing, and justification, as well as whether the text is horizontal or vertical and whether it flows from left to right, right to left, top to bottom, or bottom to top.

## CHAPTER 5

Positioning Shapes

You can position shapes anywhere in your world. You can stack them on top of each other, inside each other, or hang them in midair. You can arrange multiple boxes as buildings along a city street, or make a row of Greek columns with cylinders. You can also position text shapes anywhere within your worlds to create signs on buildings, label items, and include notes in your worlds. Using the **Transform** grouping node and its **translation** field, you can position shapes and groups of shapes anywhere in your world.

Understanding More About Coordinate Systems

Recall the discussion of VRML space and the X, Y, and Z axes in Chapter 2. Recall also the 3-D axes shown in the diagrams of Chapters 3 and 4. These axes define a coordinate system for the shape shown in each diagram. The position of shapes in that coordinate system are specified as 3-D coordinates relative to that coordinate system's origin (the point where the X, Y, and Z axes meet). A coordinate like (3.0,2.0,5.0), for example, is 3.0 units along X, 2.0 units along Y, and 5.0 units along Z measured from the origin.

Recall from Chapter 3 that all of the primitive shapes (box, cone, cylinder, and sphere) created by the **Shape** node are built centered around the origin. Similarly, text shapes described in Chapter 4 are built relative to the origin and flow outward from that origin from left to right, right to left, top to bottom, or bottom to top. In all cases, shapes are built relative to the origin of a coordinate system.

In VRML you can create any number of coordinate systems. Each new coordinate system is positioned, or *translated*, relative to the origin of another coordinate system. When a new coordinate system is relative to another, we say that the new coordinate system is a *child coordinate system* that is *nested* within the *parent coordinate system.* That parent coordinate system can, in turn, be nested within another parent coordinate system, and so on. This parent-child relationship of coordinate systems creates a family tree of coordinate systems.

The top-most parent in the coordinate system tree is the VRML file's *root coordinate system.* Every VRML file has a root coordinate system. All of the examples in Chapters 3 and 4, for instance, built shapes centered at the origin of the automatically created root coordinate system. The **Transform** node creates new coordinate systems relative to the root coordinate system or to any other coordinate system.

Since all additional coordinate systems are descendants of the root coordinate system—directly or indirectly, depending on their position in the coordinate-system family tree—the VRML file's root coordinate system encompasses everything you build in a VRML file's world. The root coordinate system is, therefore, often called the *world coordinate system.*

The entire family tree of coordinate systems, including any shapes you build within those coordinate systems, is often called a *scene graph.*

Building Shapes in Coordinate Systems

Figure 5.1a shows a world coordinate system represented as a set of X, Y, and Z axes similar to those in the diagrams of Chapters 3 and 4. Figure 5.1b shows a child coordinate system translated −3.0 units along the X axis, 2.0 units along the Y axis, and 2.0 units along the Z axis relative to the world coordinate system shown in Figure 5.1a. The child coordinate system is also shown with its own X, Y, and Z axes.

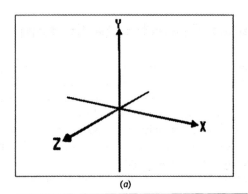 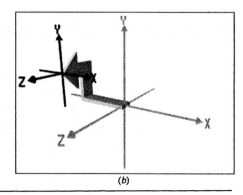

(a)   (b)

Figure 5.1 *(a) A world coordinate system, and (b) a child coordinate system translated relative to the world coordinate system by −3.0 units along the X axis, 2.0 units along the Y axis, and 2.0 units along the Z axis.*

Shapes are always built within a coordinate system. In Chapters 3 and 4, each of the shapes built by the **Shape** node were automatically positioned at the origin within the world coordinate system. If you create an additional coordinate system using the **Transform** node, any shape built within it is positioned at the origin of the new coordinate system. If a **Transform** node's coordinate-system origin is translated relative to its parent, any shapes in the **Transform** node's coordinate system translate along with the coordinate system and appear translated relative to the parent coordinate system.

To illustrate, Figure 5.2 shows the world and child coordinate systems of Figure 5.1. A new box shape has been built centered around the origin of the child coordinate system. Notice that since that child coordinate system is 3.0 units along the X axis and 2.0 units along the Y axis away from the world's origin, the *box* is 3.0 units in X and 2.0 units in Y away from the world's origin as well.

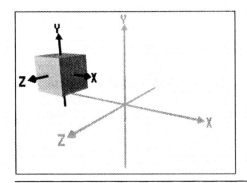

Figure 5.2   *A box shape in a child coordinate system.*

The ability to create coordinate systems is a very powerful feature of VRML. Consider, for instance, the steps you might use to build a lamp, place the lamp on a table, and place the table in a room.

1. Create a lamp, building each of its components relative to a *lamp coordinate system.*
2. Create a table, building each of its components relative to a *table coordinate system.*
3. Place the lamp on the table by positioning the *lamp coordinate system* relative to the *table coordinate system*. The *lamp coordinate system* is now a child of the *table coordinate system.*
4. Create a room, building each of its components relative to a *room coordinate system.*
5. Place the table (and its lamp) by positioning the *table coordinate system* relative to the *room coordinate system*. The *table coordinate system* is now a child of the *room coordinate system.*

The power of this approach is that you can create each piece of your world independently. The structure of the lamp is independent of where the lamp is put on the table. The structure of the table is independent of where the table is put in the room, and so on. If you want to move the table, translate the table's coordinate system. Since the lamp's coordinate system is a child of the table's coordinate system, when you move the table's coordinate system, the lamp's coordinate system moves as well.

This style of construction permeates VRML. Every shape you create is built within its own coordinate system. Those shape coordinate systems can then be grouped together within a parent's coordinate system. The parent can be grouped with more shapes and placed within a larger parent coordinate system, and so on.

Translating Coordinate Systems

Each time you create a new coordinate system with a **Transform** node, you specify its position, or *translation*, relative to a parent coordinate system. The *translation distance* is the number of VRML units in the X, Y, and Z directions between the parent's origin and the new coordinate system's origin. The translation distance for a new coordinate system determines the location of any shapes created within that new coordinate system, since those shapes are built around the new coordinate system's origin.

Grouping and Coordinate Systems

A **Transform** node is a group node similar to the **Group** node discussed in Chapter 3. Like the **Group** node, the **Transform** node contains a list of child nodes. Those children may be **Shape** nodes or other **Group** or **Transform** nodes. All of the child nodes of the **Transform** node are built at the origin within the **Transform** node's coordinate system. If the position of that coordinate system changes, then the positions of all the children of the **Transform** node change along with the changed coordinate system.

Like **Shape** and **Group** nodes, the **Transform** node may be the child of a parent **Group** or **Transform** node. The coordinate system of that parent node is the parent coordinate system of the **Transform** node's coordinate system.

If the **Transform** node is the top-level group for the VRML file, then the parent coordinate system is the world coordinate system of the VRML file.

The **Transform** Node Syntax

The **Transform** node creates a new coordinate system relative to its parent coordinate system. Shapes created as children of the **Transform** node are built relative to that new coordinate system's origin.

| SYNTAX | Transform node |

```
Transform {
    children          [ ]                      # exposedField   MFNode
    translation       0.0   0.0   0.0          # exposedField   SFVec3f
    rotation          0.0   0.0   1.0   0.0    # exposedField   SFRotation
    scale             1.0   1.0   1.0          # exposedField   SFVec3f
    scaleOrientation  0.0   0.0   1.0   0.0    # exposedField   SFRotation
    bboxCenter        0.0   0.0   0.0          # field          SFVec3f
    bboxSize         -1.0  -1.0  -1.0          # field          SFVec3f
    center            0.0   0.0   0.0          # exposedField   SFVec3f
    addChildren                                # eventIn        MFNode
    removeChildren                             # eventIn        MFNode
}
```

The value of the **children** exposed field specifies a list of child nodes to be included in the group. Typical **children** field values include **Shape** nodes and other **Group** and **Transform** nodes. The VRML browser builds the group by building each of the shapes and groups contained within the group. The default value for this field is an empty list of children.

The values of the **translation** exposed field specify the distances in the X, Y, and Z directions between the parent coordinate system origin and the origin of the new coordinate system. The first value in the **translation** field specifies the distance in the X direction, the second the distance in the Y direction, and the third the distance in the Z direction. Any of these distances may be positive or negative values. The default zero values for this field cause no translation in X, Y, or Z. This places the new coordinate system in exactly the same place as the parent coordinate system.

The value of the **translation** exposed field can be changed by routing an event to the exposed field's implied **set_translation** eventIn. When the event is received, the **translation** field is set, and the new translation is sent using the exposed field's implied **translation_changed** eventOut.

The remaining fields of the **Transform** node are discussed in Chapters 6 (**rotation** and **center**), 7 (**scale** and **scaleOrientation**), and 9 (bboxCenter, bboxSize, addChildren, and removeChildren).

Experimenting with Translation

The following examples provide a more detailed examination of the ways in which the **Transform** node's **children** and **translation** fields can be used and how they interact with nodes and fields discussed in previous chapters.

Translating in Different Directions

You can use the **Transform** node to create a new coordinate system that is translated in any direction away from the world coordinate system's origin. Figures 5.3 through 5.6 show the new coordinate system origin moved along the X, Y, or Z axes in both positive and negative directions.

```
#VRML V2.0 utf8
Transform {
    translation 2.0 0.0 0.0
    children [
        Shape {
            appearance Appearance {
                material Material { }
            }
            geometry Cylinder { }
        }
    ]
}
```

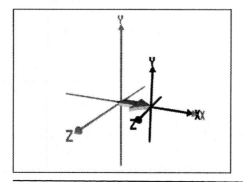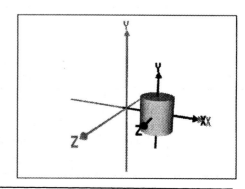

Figure 5.3   *Translating 2.0 units along the X axis, and building a cylinder.*

```
#VRML V2.0 utf8
Transform {
    translation -2.0 0.0 0.0
    children [
        Shape {
            appearance Appearance {
                material Material { }
            }
            geometry Cylinder { }
        }
    ]
}
```

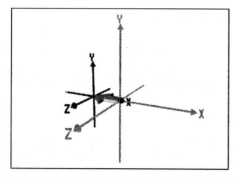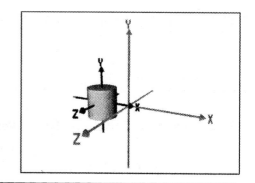

Figure 5.4   *Translating –2.0 units along the X axis, and building a cylinder.*

```
#VRML V2.0 utf8
Transform {
    translation 0.0 2.0 0.0
    children [
        Shape {
            appearance Appearance {
                material Material { }
            }
            geometry Cylinder { }
        }
    ]
}
```

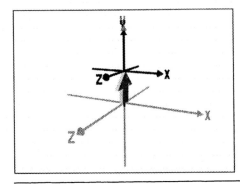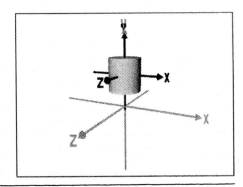

Figure 5.5 *Translating 2.0 units along the Y axis, and building a cylinder.*

```
#VRML V2.0 utf8
Transform {
    translation 0.0 0.0 2.0
    children [
        Shape {
            appearance Appearance {
                material Material { }
            }
            geometry Cylinder { }
        }
    ]
}
```

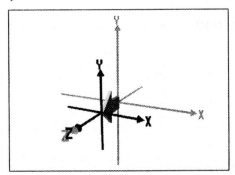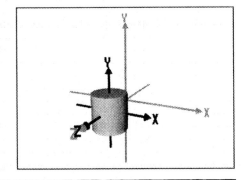

Figure 5.6 *Translating –2.0 units along the Z axis, and building a cylinder.*

Figures 5.3 through 5.6 show the translation of the new coordinate system in only one direction at a time. The **translation** field values in Figure 5.3, for example, specify an X-direction translation of 2.0 units, and no translation in the Y and Z directions. You can also specify two or all three of the **translation** field values to translate the new coordinate system's origin in any direction.

The example in Figure 5.7 illustrates how the new coordinate system can be translated in three directions at once: 2.0 units in the X direction, 1.0 unit in the Y direction, and −2.0 units in the Z direction.

```
#VRML V2.0 utf8
Transform {
    translation 2.0 1.0 -2.0
    children [
        Shape {
            appearance Appearance {
                material Material { }
            }
            geometry Cylinder { }
        }
    ]
}
```

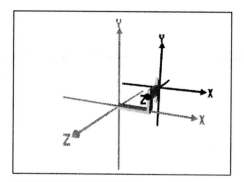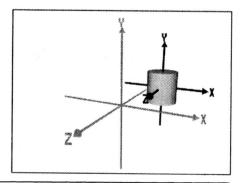

Figure 5.7 *Translating 2.0 units along the X axis, 1.0 unit along the Y axis, −2.0 units along the Z axis, and building a cylinder.*

Building Shapes in Multiple Coordinate Systems

Each of the previous examples created a new coordinate system relative to the automatically created world coordinate system. Each of the shapes grouped with the **Transform** grouping node were placed within the new coordinate system. You can also build shapes in the world coordinate system.

For example, you can build a hut similar to the one built in Chapter 2. A cylinder shape is used for the walls of the hut. A **Transform** node is used to translate up to the top of the walls and create a new coordinate system there. A cone shape is built within the new coordinate system to create the roof of the hut. The VRML text for the hut is shown in Figure 5.8.

```
#VRML V2.0 utf8
# A gray hut
Group {
    children [
    # Draw the hut walls
        Shape {
            appearance DEF White Appearance {
                material Material { }
            }
            geometry Cylinder {
                height 2.0
                radius 2.0
            }
        },
    # Draw the hut roof
        Transform {
            translation 0.0 2.0 0.0
            children [
                Shape {
                    appearance USE White
                    geometry Cone {
                        height 2.0
                        bottomRadius 2.5
                    }
                }
            ]
        }
    ]
}
```

Figure 5.8   *A hut.*

The VRML browser reads your file and builds the hut in stages, as shown in Figure 5.9.

1. Create a group of shapes, all to be built within the automatically created world coordinate system.

   a. Build a cylinder shape at the origin.

   b. Create a new group of shapes with its own coordinate system translated 2.0 units in the Y direction away from the world coordinate system.

      i. Build a cone shape at the origin.

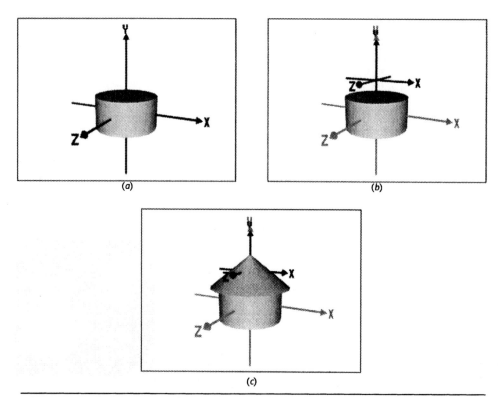

Figure 5.9 *(a) Step 1a: Building a cylinder shape for the walls of the hut, (b) step 1b: translating 2.0 units along the Y axis, and (c) step 1bi: building a cone shape for the hut's roof.*

Constructing Multiple Coordinate Systems

A VRML file may contain any number of **Transform** nodes, each defining their own new coordinate system. Figure 5.10 illustrates how you can build a temple archway by translating coordinate systems to build cylinders to the left and right of the archway and to build a box on top of the cylinders spanning the archway. To position the cylinders and box, each shape's coordinate system is translated.

```
#VRML V2.0 utf8
Group {
    children [
    # Ground
        Shape {
            appearance DEF White Appearance {
                material Material { }
            }
            geometry Box {
                size 25.0 0.1 25.0
            }
        },
```

Figure 5.10 continues

```
# Left Column
    Transform {
        translation -2.0 3.0 0.0
        children Shape {
            appearance USE White
            geometry Cylinder {
                radius 0.3
                height 6.0
            }
        }
    },
# Right Column
    Transform {
        translation 2.0 3.0 0.0
        children Shape {
            appearance USE White
            geometry Cylinder {
                radius 0.3
                height 6.0
            }
        }
    },
# Archway span
    Transform {
        translation 0.0 6.05 0.0
        children Shape {
            appearance USE White
            geometry Box {
                size 4.6 0.4 0.6
            }
        }
    }
    ]
}
```

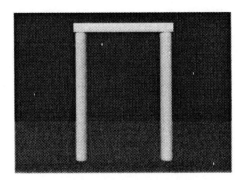

Figure 5.10 *Building an archway using multiple, translated coordinate systems.*

Nesting Coordinate Systems

The previous temple archway example built each piece of the archway in its own coordinate system, each relative to the world coordinate system. You can also create coordinate systems within coordinate systems, nesting them as deeply as you like.

Figure 5.11 shows a second archway built for the temple. The second archway is identical to the first archway (two cylinders and a box) but is contained within its own coordinate system. That coordinate system is translated in the Z direction relative to the world coordinate system.

```
#VRML V2.0 utf8
Group {
    children [
    # Ground
        Shape {
            appearance DEF White Appearance {
                material Material { }
            }
            geometry Box {
                size 25.0 0.1 25.0
            }
        },
    # First archway
    # Left Column
        DEF LeftColumn Transform {
            translation -2.0 3.0 0.0
            children DEF Column Shape {
                appearance USE White
                geometry Cylinder {
                    radius 0.3
                    height 6.0
                }
            }
        },
    # Right Column
        DEF RightColumn Transform {
            translation 2.0 3.0 0.0
            children USE Column
        },
    # Archway span
        DEF ArchwaySpan Transform {
            translation 0.0 6.05 0.0
            children Shape {
                appearance USE White
                geometry Box {
                    size 4.6 0.4 0.6
                }
            }
        },
    # Second archway
        Transform {
            translation 0.0 0.0 -2.0
            children [
                USE LeftColumn,
                USE RightColumn,
                USE ArchwaySpan
            ]
        }
    ]
}
```

Figure 5.11 *Nesting coordinate systems.*

Notice how **DEF** and **USE** are used in Figure 5.11 to enable shape specifications to be shared. The left and right columns of an archway are identical. Rather than specify both left and right columns, you build the left column and define the name "Column" for it. Then build the right column by using, or instancing, the left column shape over again.

Each archway contains identical archway parts, including their relative positioning. Rather than specify each archway's parts and positions, define a name for each positioned shape within the **Transform** node: "LeftColumn," "RightColumn," and "ArchwaySpan". Build the second archway by using these same positioned shapes over again.

Using **DEF** and **USE** saves typing and shortens the length of your VRML files. Additionally, shapes named by **DEF** and instanced by **USE** all share the same node specifications. If you change those node specifications, all instances of that shape change as well. For example, if you change the **radius** field value for the "Column" **Cylinder** node, the radii of all of the columns in the temple are affected.

You can extend the temple in Figure 5.11 to include additional archways by adding more **Transform** nodes like the last one in the VRML file. Each new **Transform** node creates and translates a new coordinate system and builds a new archway, reusing the same left and right columns and archway span.

Summary

The **Transform** node creates a new coordinate system relative to its parent's coordinate system. The new coordinate system has an origin translated in the X, Y, and Z directions away from the parent's coordinate system origin.

Similar to the **Group** node, the **Transform** node collects together a group of child nodes. Shapes built by those child nodes are built at the origin within the **Transform** node's coordinate system. If that coordinate system is repositioned, all of the **Transform** node's children are repositioned along with the coordinate system.

The world coordinate system in a VRML file is the top-level, parent coordinate system in a family tree of coordinate systems called a scene graph. The world coordinate system is constructed automatically by the VRML browser. A VRML file can include any number of nested child coordinate systems, each one positioned relative to its parent's coordinate system.

Rotating Shapes

Rotation enables you to make a car wheel from a cylinder, make a funnel from a cone, or balance a box on one corner. Using the **Transform** grouping node and its **rotation** and **center** fields, you can rotate shapes and groups of shapes about the origin of a coordinate system or about a center point you specify.

Understanding Rotated Coordinate Systems

Recall that a coordinate system is defined by a set of X, Y, and Z axes that cross at an origin. Positions within the coordinate system are specified by X, Y, and Z distances measured along each of the axes. Imagine, for instance, that you are building an airplane and the coordinate system origin for the airplane is placed in the middle of the passenger cabin with the X axis aimed along the right wing, the Y axis aimed up, and the Z axis aimed out toward the back of the plane. In this airplane coordinate system, the position of the pilot cabin is measured backward along the Z axis, the engines are positioned left and right along the X axis, and the tail is positioned forward along the Z axis and up along the Y axis. Figure 6.1 shows the origin and axes of the airplane's coordinate system.

Using this airplane coordinate system, you can position each shape on the airplane, including the doors, windows, seats, landing gear, suitcases, people, and so on. Such an airplane coordinate system can be created using the **Transform** node. By using the **translation** field of that node, you can position the entire coordinate system anywhere you like. If you animated the values of the **translation** field, the airplane would fly around your world, moving left and right, up and down, and forward and back relative to the origin of the parent coordinate system. (For details about translation animation, see Chapter 8.)

To make the airplane's flight more realistic, you must also control the airplane's orientation, or *rotation*, using the **rotation** field of the **Transform** node.

Figure 6.1   *An airplane and its coordinate system.*

You may wish to tilt the airplane upward during takeoff, turn it to face the direction in which it is flying, or bank it in a turn. Each of these operations is accomplished by rotating the airplane's coordinate system. Figures 6.2 *a*, *b*, and *c* show the airplane tilted up, turned, and banked, respectively. The dark X, Y, and Z axes show the orientation of the airplane's coordinate system, while the gray X, Y, and Z axes show the unchanged orientation of the parent coordinate system.

Notice that rotating the airplane's coordinate system does not affect how that airplane is itself built. The pilot's cabin is still positioned toward the front of the plane, the wings to the left and right, and the tail to the back. The placement of shapes within the airplane's coordinate system is independent of the position and orientation of that coordinate system relative to the parent coordinate system. This is a very powerful feature of VRML. You can build the airplane, or any other shape, then later position and orient its coordinate system in your world.

Specifying Rotation Axes

A *rotation axis* is an imaginary line about which a coordinate system is rotated. When you spin a toy top, for example, the top spins around an imaginary line running vertically through its center. That imaginary line is a rotation axis. Similarly, the Earth rotates about an imaginary line running through the North and South Poles. That line is a rotation axis.

A rotation axis can point in any direction. The rotation axis used to turn a car wheel, for example, points horizontally out of the center of the wheel. When rotating a coordinate system in VRML, you will specify a rotation axis *and* the direction for that rotation axis.

To specify a direction for a rotation axis, imagine drawing a line between two coordinates in space. One coordinate is always the origin (0.0,0.0,0.0). The second coordinate's location is specified by you. The imaginary line drawn between these two coordinates creates the rotation axis.

For example, to define a rotation axis for a toy top spinning about a vertical rotation axis, use an imaginary line that points straight up from the origin. The second

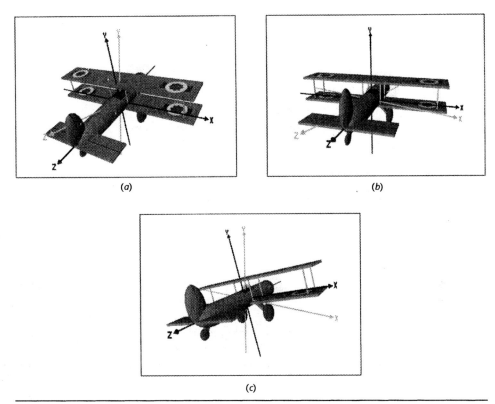

Figure 6.2 *An airplane's coordinate system (a) tilted up, (b) turned to the side, and (c) banked on its side.*

coordinate defining the line must be directly above the origin for the top to spin straight up, such as (0.0,1.0,0.0).

The distance between coordinates in a rotation axis doesn't matter. Any point on the imaginary line is valid. To define a rotation axis that points straight up along the Y axis, (0.0,2.0,0.0), (0.0,0.357,0.0), and (0.0,1.0,0.0) are all equivalent, because they all point straight up.

While you can specify a rotation axis in any direction, most rotation axes aim to the right along the X axis, up along the Y axis, or out along the Z axis. The rotation axis values used to create these axes are shown in Table 6.1.

Table 6.1   Values for Common Rotation Axes

Direction	*Rotation Axis Values*
To the right along the X axis	1.0 0.0 0.0
Up along the Y axis	0.0 1.0 0.0
Out along the Z axis	0.0 0.0 1.0

In the airplane example in Figure 6.2, a rotation around the X axis tilts the airplane up or down, a rotation around the Y axis turns it side to side, and a rotation around the Z axis banks it for a turn.

Specifying Rotation Angles

In addition to specifying a rotation axis, you must also indicate by how much you want the new coordinate system to rotate about that axis. The rotation amount is specified as a *rotation angle*, measured in *radians*. See the sidebar entitled "Radians" for more information.

SIDEBAR: RADIANS Most people are more familiar with measuring angles in degrees. In this book, we will discuss angles in terms of degrees but convert degrees to radians in VRML examples. Appendix A provides a conversion table and an explanation of degrees-to-radians conversion.

For example, to tilt an airplane's coordinate system up by 30.0 degrees during takeoff, use a rotation axis aimed along the X axis, and a rotation angle of 30.0 degrees (0.524 radians). To turn the airplane's coordinate system 20.0 degrees to the right, use a rotation axis aimed upward along the Y axis, and a rotation angle of 20.0 degrees (0.349 radians). To turn the airplane's coordinate system 10.0 degrees to bank for a left-hand turn, use a rotation axis aimed outward along the Z axis, and a rotation angle of 10.0 degrees (0.175 radians).

Rotation angles can be positive or negative. For example, to bank the airplane 10.0 degrees for a right-hand turn instead of a left-hand turn, use the same Z rotation axis and a rotation angle of –10.0 degrees (–0.175 radians).

It is easy to get confused about rotations and become unsure whether a positive or negative rotation amount turns shapes left or right, forward or back, up or down. See the sidebar entitled "The Right-Hand Rule for Rotation" for an easy way to determine which is which.

SIDEBAR: THE RIGHT-HAND RULE FOR ROTATION Imagine grabbing the rotation axis with your right hand, wrapping your fingers around the axis, and pointing your thumb in the positive direction of the axis as if you were hitchhiking. A *positive* rotation angle rotates a coordinate system around the axis in the same direction as the one in which your fingers are wrapped. A *negative* rotation angle rotates a coordinate system in the opposite direction. The diagrams in Figure 6.3 illustrate the right-hand rule around the X, Y, and Z axes, respectively.

For example, if you define a rotation axis of 0.0 0.0 1.0 that points out the positive Z axis, and you want to know which way a positive rotation turns a coordinate system, grab the axis and point your thumb straight out in the positive Z direction as shown in Figure 6.3c. A positive rotation angle rotates around the axis in the same direction as you wrap the fingers of your right hand, and the coordinate system's axes tilt to the left. A negative rotation angle turns in the opposite direction and tilts the coordinate system's axes to the right.

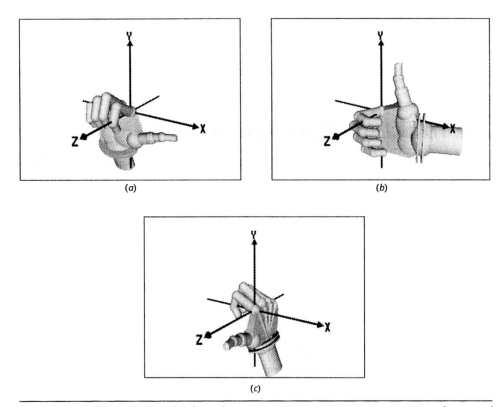

(a)

(b)

(c)

Figure 6.3 *The right-hand rule to determine a positive/negative rotation angle around (a) the X axis, (b) the Y axis, and (c) the Z axis.*

Translating *and* Rotating

Coordinate system translation and rotation can be used in combination within the same **Transform** node. To fly an airplane, for instance, use rotation to aim the aircraft's coordinate system along its flight path, and translation to position the aircraft's coordinate system. Similarly, to build a car wheel, use rotation to tilt a cylinder on its side, then translation to move the tilted coordinate system into place in the front or back of the car.

Specifying a Rotation Center

By default, the center of rotation, or *rotation center,* for a rotated coordinate system is the origin of that coordinate system. You can also specify a rotation center elsewhere in the coordinate system. This is often necessary when building articulated shapes, like the arm of an adjustable desk lamp or of a robot. In such cases, the rotation center is the joint at one end or the other of the arm. That joint may not be at the origin of the coordinate system.

Using the **Transform** node's **center** field, you can specify the 3-D coordinate for the rotation center within a new coordinate system. The rotation axis and angle used in the **rotation** field cause a rotation around the center point specified by the **center** field value instead of around the natural origin of the coordinate system.

The **Transform** Node Syntax

The **Transform** group node creates a new coordinate system relative to its parent coordinate system. Shapes created as children of the **Transform** group node are built relative to the new coordinate system's origin.

| SYNTAX | Transform node |

```
Transform {
    children          [ ]                    # exposedField  MFNode
    translation       0.0   0.0   0.0        # exposedField  SFVec3f
    rotation          0.0   0.0   1.0  0.0   # exposedField  SFRotation
    scale             1.0   1.0   1.0        # exposedField  SFVec3f
    scaleOrientation  0.0   0.0   1.0  0.0   # exposedField  SFRotation
    bboxCenter        0.0   0.0   0.0        # field         SFVec3f
    bboxSize         -1.0  -1.0  -1.0        # field         SFVec3f
    center            0.0   0.0   0.0        # exposedField  SFVec3f
    addChildren                              # eventIn       MFNode
    removeChildren                           # eventIn       MFNode
}
```

The values of the **children** and **translation** fields are discussed in Chapter 5.

The values of the **rotation** exposed field specify a rotation axis about which to rotate the new coordinate system and a rotation angle specifying the amount by which to rotate around that axis. The first three values in the field specify the X, Y, and Z components of a 3-D coordinate in the new, translated coordinate system. The imaginary line between that coordinate and the translated origin specifies the rotation axis. The fourth value in the **rotation** field specifies the positive or negative rotation angle measured in radians. The default values for the **rotation** field specify that no rotation is to occur.

The **rotation** exposed field value can be changed by routing an event to the exposed field's implied **set_rotation** eventIn. When the event is received, the **rotation** field is set, and the new rotation is sent using the exposed field's implied **rotation_changed** eventOut.

The values of the **center** field specify the 3-D coordinate in the new, translated coordinate system about which rotations are to occur. The default rotation center is the origin.

The **center** exposed field value can be changed by routing an event to the exposed field's implied **set_center** eventIn. When the event is received, the **center** field is set, and the new center is sent using the exposed field's implied **center_changed** eventOut.

The remaining fields of the **Transform** node are discussed in Chapters 7 (**scale** and **scaleOrientation**) and 9 (**bboxCenter, bboxSize, addChildren,** and **removeChildren**).

When **translation, center,** and **rotation** field values are used in combination, your browser follows a specific order. The new coordinate system is:

1. Rotated about the center point.
2. Translated relative to the parent coordinate system.

The **translation, center,** and **rotation** fields may be specified in any order in the **Transform** node, however, these fields are always applied in the order stated above.

Experimenting with Rotation

The following examples provide a more detailed examination of the ways in which the **Transform** node's **rotation** and **center** fields can be used and how they interact with nodes and fields discussed in previous chapters.

Rotating in Different Directions

You can use the **Transform** node to rotate a new coordinate system in any direction. Figures 6.4 through 6.7 show rotation by positive and negative angles around the X, Y, and Z axes.

```
#VRML V2.0 utf8
Transform {
    rotation 1.0 0.0 0.0  0.785
    children [
        Shape {
            appearance Appearance {
                material Material { }
            }
            geometry Box { }
        }
    ]
}
```

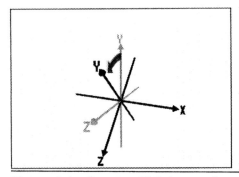 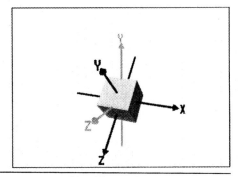

Figure 6.4 *Rotating 45.0 degrees about the X axis, and building a box.*

```
#VRML V2.0 utf8
Transform {
    rotation 1.0 0.0 0.0  -0.785
    children [
        Shape {
            appearance Appearance {
                material Material { }
            }
            geometry Box { }
        }
    ]
}
```

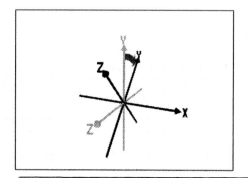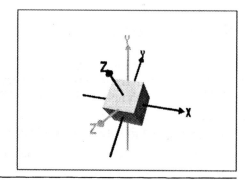

Figure 6.5   *Rotating −45.0 degrees about the X axis, and building a box.*

```
#VRML V2.0 utf8
Transform {
    rotation 0.0 1.0 0.0  0.785
    children [
        Shape {
            appearance Appearance {
                material Material { }
            }
            geometry Box { }
        }
    ]
}
```

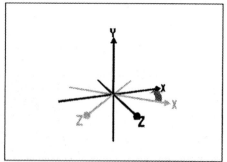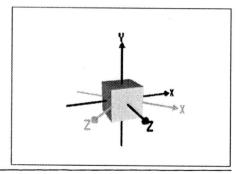

Figure 6.6   *Rotating 45.0 degrees about the Y axis, and building a box.*

```
#VRML V2.0 utf8
Transform {
    rotation 0.0 0.0 1.0   -0.785
    children [
        Shape {
            appearance Appearance {
                material Material { }
            }
            geometry Box { }
        }
    ]
}
```

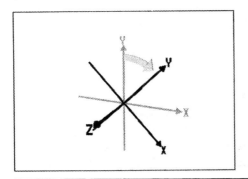 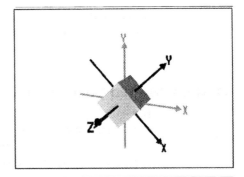

Figure 6.7   *Rotating −45.0 degrees about the Z axis, and building a box.*

Constructing Multiple Rotated Coordinate Systems

A VRML file may contain any number of **Transform** nodes, each defining its own new coordinate system. Figure 6.8 shows a 3-D asterisk created from one cylinder built within a vertical coordinate system and two cylinders built within rotated coordinate systems. To rotate the two nonvertical cylinders, each is built within its own rotated coordinate system. Note the use of **DEF** to name the cylinder shape and the use of **USE** to instance that shape for each of the nonvertical cylinders.

```
#VRML V2.0 utf8
Group {
    children [
    # Arm 1
        DEF Arm1 Shape {
            appearance Appearance {
                material Material { }
            }
            geometry Cylinder {
                height 1.0
                radius 0.1
            }
        },
```

Figure 6.8 continues

```
# Arm 2
   Transform {
        rotation 1.0 0.0 0.0  1.047
        children USE Arm1
   },
# Arm 3
   Transform {
        rotation 1.0 0.0 0.0  2.094
        children USE Arm1
   }
 ]
}
```

Figure 6.8 *A 3-D asterisk created with cylinders built within one vertical and two rotated coordinate systems.*

Nesting Rotated Coordinate Systems

In Figure 6.8, the tilted arms of the asterisk were built in their own coordinate systems, each rotated relative to the world coordinate system. You can also create coordinate systems within coordinate systems, nesting them as deeply as you like.

Figure 6.9 adds a second pair of cylinders built within rotated coordinate systems to create a more complex 3-D asterisk. The second pair of tilted cylinders are identical to the first pair, but the last two cylinders are each built within their own new coordinate system, and each of those new coordinate systems is rotated about the Y axis by 90.0 degrees relative to the world coordinate system.

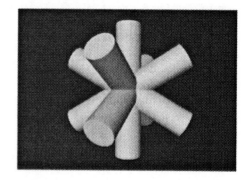

```
#VRML V2.0 utf8
Group {
    children [
    # Arm 1
        DEF Arm1 Shape {
            appearance Appearance {
                material Material { }
            }
            geometry Cylinder {
                height 1.0
                radius 0.1
            }
        },
    # Arm 2
        DEF Arm2 Transform {
            rotation 1.0 0.0 0.0  1.047
            children USE Arm1
        },
    # Arm 3
        DEF Arm3 Transform {
            rotation 1.0 0.0 0.0  2.094
            children USE Arm1
        },
```

Figure 6.9 continues

```
# Arms 4 and 5
    Transform {
        rotation 0.0 1.0 0.0  1.785
        children [
            USE Arm2,
            USE Arm3
        ]
    }
  ]
}
```

Figure 6.9 *A 3-D asterisk ball built with cylinders in rotated coordinate systems.*

Translating and Rotating Coordinate Systems

Recall the archway you built in Chapter 5. To give the arch a more Greek-architecture look, you can add a roof using two tilted, flattened boxes. Each box is created in its own coordinate system built by a **Transform** node. To place the new coordinate systems at roof level, the **Transform** node has a **translation** field value to move the coordinate system up and off the ground. To create a tilted roof, the **Transform** node has a **rotation** field value to tilt the coordinate system. Once translated and rotated, a box is built within that coordinate system. Figure 6.10 shows the temple archway with the tilted roof boxes added.

```
#VRML V2.0 utf8
Group {
    children [
    # Ground
        Shape {
            appearance DEF White Appearance {
                material Material { }
            }
            geometry Box {
                size 25.0 0.1 25.0
            }
        },
    # First archway
    # Left Column
        DEF LeftColumn Transform {
            translation -2.0 3.0 0.0
            children DEF Column Shape {
                appearance USE White
                geometry Cylinder {
                    radius 0.3
                    height 6.0
                }
            }
        },
```

Figure 6.10 continues

```
# Right Column
    DEF RightColumn Transform {
        translation 2.0 3.0 0.0
        children USE Column
    },
# Archway span
    DEF ArchwaySpan Transform {
        translation 0.0 6.05 0.0
        children Shape {
            appearance USE White
            geometry Box{
                size 4.6 0.4 0.6
            }
        }
    },
# Left Roof
    DEF LeftRoof Transform {
        translation -1.15 7.12 0.0
        rotation 0.0 0.0 1.0  0.524
        children DEF Roof Shape {
            appearance USE White
            geometry Box {
                size 2.86 0.4 0.6
            }
        }
    },
# Right Roof
    DEF LeftRoof Transform {
        translation 1.15 7.12 0.0
        rotation 0.0 0.0 1.0  -0.524
        children USE Roof
    }
]
}
```

Figure 6.10 *An archway with pieces of the roof built within translated, rotated coordinate systems.*

Rotating About a Center Point

Recall that shapes are always built centered at the origin of their parent's coordinate system. Rotations about the coordinate system origin rotate the shape about its center. The asterisk cylinder's coordinate systems in Figures 6.8 through 6.9 are all rotated about their centers in this way.

When building articulated shapes, like the arm of an adjustable desk lamp or of a robot, it is more natural to use a center of rotation placed at one end of the arm instead of at its center. Using the **Transform** node's **center** field, you can specify the location of the rotation center to be a more natural center for these types of shapes.

Figure 6.11 shows the base and lower arm of an adjustable desk lamp. The lower arm is rotated about a center point at the lower end of the arm. This simulates the existence of a pivot joint in the middle of the lamp base to which the lower end of the arm is attached. Varying the **rotation** field value tilts the arm.

```
#VRML V2.0 utf8
Group{
    children [
    # Lamp base
        Shape {
            appearance DEF White Appearance {
                material Material { }
            }
            geometry Cylinder {
                radius 0.1
                height 0.01
            }
        },
    # Base joint
        Transform {
            translation 0.0 0.15 0.0
            rotation    1.0 0.0 0.0   -0.7
            center      0.0 -0.15 0.0
            children [
                # Lower arm
                Shape {
                    appearance USE White
                    geometry Cylinder {
                        radius 0.01
                        height 0.3
                    }
                }
            ]
        }
    ]
}
```

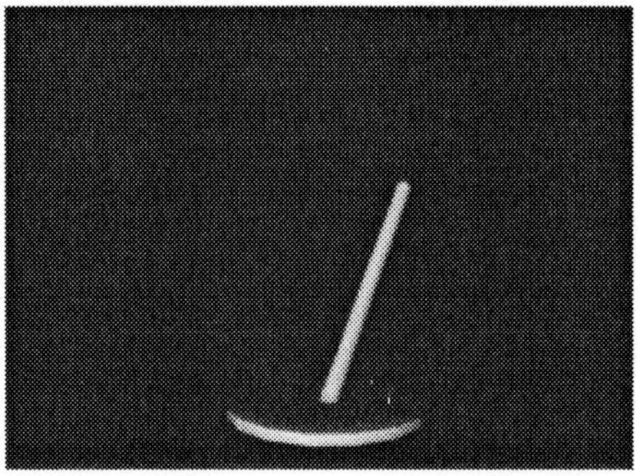

Figure 6.11 *The lower arm of a desk lamp, rotated using a center of rotation at the lower end of the arm.*

Figure 6.11 can be extended to add a second arm attached to the end of the first one. Like the first arm, the second arm, shown in Figure 6.12, uses a **Transform** node to create a new coordinate system, a **center** field to specify rotation about a joint at the lower end of the arm, and a **rotation** field to rotate the arm. Notice that the second arm is built within the coordinate system of the first arm. If the first arm is tilted by varying its **rotation** field values, the second arm moves in relation to the movement of the first arm.

```
#VRML V2.0 utf8
Group{
    children [
    # Lamp base
        Shape {
            appearance DEF White Appearance {
                material Material { }
            }
            geometry Cylinder {
                radius 0.1
                height 0.01
            }
        },
    # Base joint
        Transform {
            translation 0.0 0.15 0.0
            rotation    1.0 0.0 0.0  -0.7
            center      0.0 -0.15 0.0
            children [
            # Lower arm
                DEF LampArm Shape {
                    appearance USE White
                    geometry Cylinder {
                        radius 0.01
                        height 0.3
                    }
                },
            # Lower arm - second arm joint
                Transform {
                    translation 0.0 0.3 0.0
                    rotation    1.0 0.0 0.0  1.9
                    center      0.0 -0.15 0.0
                    children [
                    # Second arm
                        USE LampArm
                    ]
                }
            ]
        }
    ]
}
```

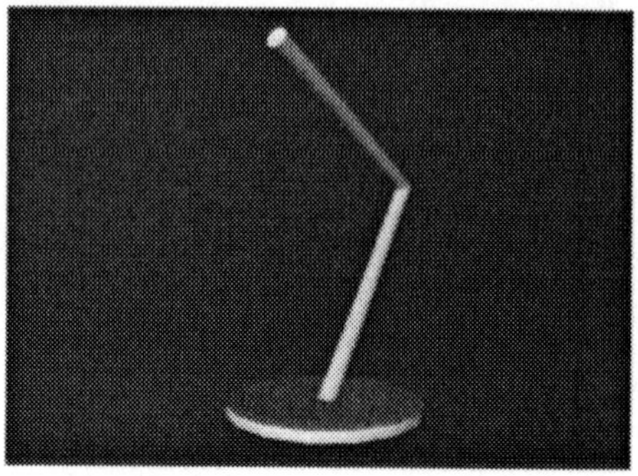

Figure 6.12 *The first and second arms of the desk lamp, each rotated using a center of rotation at the lower end of each arm.*

Summary

The **Transform** node creates a new coordinate system relative to its parent's coordinate system. The new coordinate system can be rotated relative to the parent's coordinate system by using the **rotation** field of the **Transform** node.

Similar to the **Group** node, the **Transform** node collects together a group of child nodes. Shapes built by those child nodes are positioned within the **Transform** node's coordinate system. If that coordinate system is rotated, all of the **Transform** node's children are rotated along with the coordinate system.

The **rotation** field value specifies a rotation axis and a rotation angle by which the new coordinate system is to be rotated. The rotation axis is an imaginary line drawn between the origin and a 3-D coordinate. The rotation angle, measured in radians, is the angle by which the coordinate system is rotated around the rotation axis. Commonly, rotation occurs around either the X, the Y, or the Z axis, but arbitrary diagonal rotation axes can be specified as well.

You can specify both the **translation** and **rotation** field values of the **Transform** node to orient *and* position the new coordinate system in your world. Using the **center** field, you can specify the center of rotation for orienting the coordinate system.

## CHAPTER 7

Scaling Shapes

Shapes can be any size in VRML. You can create shapes as large as planets in a solar system or as small as atoms in a molecule. You can create your own library of cities, cars, trees, and furniture, all in different sizes. Then you can combine shapes to create new worlds, enlarging some shapes and shrinking others to make their sizes compatible. Using the **Transform** grouping node and its **scale** and **scaleOrientation** fields, you can scale shapes and groups of shapes to any size you wish.

Understanding Scaled Coordinate Systems

Recall that a coordinate system is defined by a set of X, Y, and Z axes that cross at an origin. Using the **translation** field of a **Transform** node, you can create new coordinate systems and translate them relative to their parent coordinate systems. As the coordinate system is positioned, so are the shapes built within that coordinate system. Using the **rotation** field of a **Transform** node, you can rotate new coordinate systems relative to their parent coordinate system. Shapes built within the rotated coordinate system are rotated along with it.

VRML also enables you to **scale** a coordinate system, increasing or decreasing its size relative to a parent coordinate system. Shapes created within the scaled coordinate system are built at the new scale of the coordinate system. For example, Figure 7.1 shows a world coordinate system (bottom), and a scaled down coordinate system (top). In each coordinate system, an identical pair of shapes is built (a sphere and a cone) and separated by a 4-unit-long ruler. Notice that when the bottom coordinate system is scaled down, *everything* in the coordinate system shrinks, including the shapes (the sphere and cone) *and* the distance between those shapes (as indicated by the ruler).

By scaling coordinate systems, you can enlarge and shrink shapes or groups of shapes. This enables you to take a shape that is, perhaps, built too large for your desired application and shrink it down to fit. You could, for example, take a full-

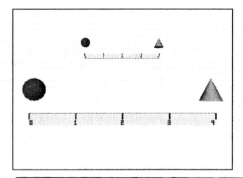

Figure 7.1   *A scaled (top) versus unscaled (bottom) coordinate system.*

size airplane shape and shrink it down to the size of a plastic model to put it on a shelf in a child's room. Figure 7.2 shows this airplane shape at its original size (bottom), and then scaled down to half its original size (top).

Notice that scaling the airplane's coordinate system does not affect how the airplane is built. The pilot's cockpit is still forward, the wings left and right, and the tail behind. The placement of shapes within the airplane's coordinate system is independent of the position, orientation, and scale of that coordinate system relative to the parent coordinate system. This is a very powerful feature of VRML. You can build the airplane, or any other shape, then later position, orient, and scale it to fit into your world. If you decide to scale the airplane differently, change the scaling of that airplane's coordinate system. The airplane will change in size, but its shape will remain unchanged.

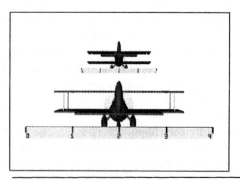

Figure 7.2   *An airplane at its original size (bottom) and scaled down to half size (top).*

Specifying Scale Factors

When something large, like an airplane, is scaled down to something small, like a model airplane, the size difference is called a *scale factor*. Similarly, when something small, like an ant, is scaled up to something large, like a monster, that size difference is also called a scale factor.

A scale factor is a multiplication factor. For example, to build a shape like a car at half its original size, use a scale factor of 0.5, and to build it at one-tenth its original size, use a scale factor of 0.1. Similarly, to build a shape at twice its original size, use a scale factor of 2.0. To create it at ten times its original size, use a scale factor of 10.0.

The **Transform** node's **scale** field uses three scale factors, one value for scaling in the X direction, one for scaling in the Y direction, and one for scaling in the Z direction. Using these independent scale factors you can grow or shrink a coordinate system by different amounts horizontally, vertically, and front to back. This warps the shapes built within the coordinate system, changing their shape as if they were made out of rubber. Figure 7.3 shows an airplane model (*a*), scaled down in X only (*b*), scaled down in Y only (*c*), and scaled down in Z only (*d*).

To increase or decrease the scale of a coordinate system without warping its shapes, specify the same scale factor for each of the X, Y, and Z directions. The air-

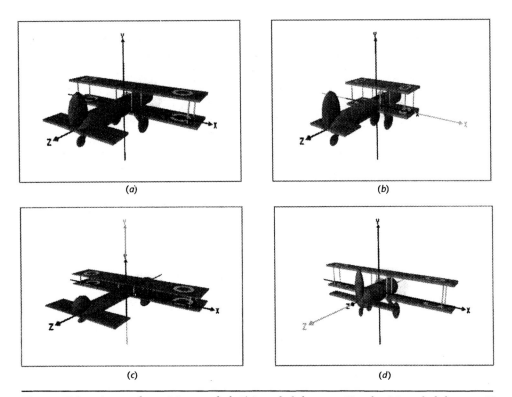

(a)   (b)

(c)   (d)

Figure 7.3 *An airplane (a) unscaled, (b) scaled down in X only, (c) scaled down in Y only, and (d) scaled down in Z only.*

plane in Figure 7.2, for instance, was reduced to half its size by scaling by a factor of 0.5 in X, Y, and Z simultaneously.

Translating, Rotating, and Scaling

Coordinate system translation, rotation, and scaling can be used in combination within the same **Transform** node. To fly a model plane, for instance, use scale to shrink the plane down to model size, rotation to orient it, and translation to position the plane. Similarly, to attack a city with a giant ant, scale the ant up to monstrous proportions, turn it to face the city, and then translate it to the city in preparation for battle.

Recall that when a coordinate system is scaled up or down, the shapes within it and the distances between those shapes change size as well. Knowing that distances, as well as shapes, are scaled when you scale a coordinate system, you can build shapes, like the airplane, without regard to how they are going to be used. You can choose any shape size and translation distance within your shape's coordinate system, and build an airplane that is 4.0 units, or 400.0 units, wingtip to wingtip. Later, when you want to use the airplane in a broader context, you can enlarge it or shrink it as necessary.

Using a Scale Orientation

The X, Y, and Z scale factors of the **Transform** node enable you to enlarge or shrink a coordinate system differently in the X, Y, and Z directions. There are times, however, when you may wish to stretch a coordinate system's shapes along an arbitrary diagonal axis. Such a stretch effect can be achieved in VRML by orienting the scale. In other words, only the direction of the scale is changed, the entire coordinate system is not reoriented.

To orient a scale, use the **Transform** node's **scaleOrientation** field and provide a rotation axis and angle, as in the **rotation** field. The rotation of the *scale orientation* is applied to the new coordinate system before the coordinate system is scaled, then undone afterward. This enables you to stretch the coordinate system in any direction, but doesn't leave the coordinate system rotated afterward. If you wish the coordinate system to remain rotated, you can use the **rotation** field as well to orient the coordinate system after scaling it.

Using a Scale Center

By default, the center of scaling, or *scale center,* for a scaled coordinate system is the origin of that coordinate system. You can also specify a scale center elsewhere in the coordinate system. This is sometimes necessary when building shapes where one end of the shape must remain where it is while the shape increases or decreases in size. A tree, for instance, increases in size as it grows, but the bottom of the trunk remains stationary during its growth. In the case of the tree, the center of scaling is the base of the trunk, even if that tree-trunk base is at the origin of the coordinate system.

Using the **Transform** node's **center** field, you can specify the 3-D coordinate for the scale center within the new coordinate system. The scale factor used in the **scale** field causes scaling relative to that center point instead of the origin.

The **center** field values are also used as the center of rotation. This enables you to both rotate and scale about the same center point at the same time.

The **Transform** Node Syntax

The **Transform** grouping node creates a new coordinate system relative to its parent coordinate system. Shapes created as children of the **Transform** group node are built relative to the new coordinate system's origin.

SYNTAX Transform node

```
Transform {
    children          [ ]                      # exposedField  MFNode
    translation       0.0  0.0  0.0            # exposedField  SFVec3f
    rotation          0.0  0.0  1.0   0.0      # exposedField  SFRotation
    scale             1.0  1.0  1.0            # exposedField  SFVec3f
    scaleOrientation  0.0  0.0  1.0   0.0      # exposedField  SFRotation
    bboxCenter        0.0  0.0  0.0            # field         SFVec3f
    bboxSize         -1.0 -1.0 -1.0            # field         SFVec3f
    center            0.0  0.0  0.0            # exposedField  SFVec3f
    addChildren                                # eventIn       MFNode
    removeChildren                             # eventIn       MFNode
}
```

The **children** and **translation** fields are discussed in Chapter 5, and the **rotation** field is discussed in Chapter 6.

The values of the **scale** exposed field specify scale factors in the X, Y, and Z directions for the new coordinate system. The first value in the **scale** field specifies the scale factor in the X direction, the second the scale factor in the Y direction, and the third the scale factor in the Z direction. The default 1.0 values for all three scale factors cause no change in scale in X, Y, or Z. This scales the new coordinate system the same as the parent coordinate system.

Scale factors must be positive values. Values between 0.0 and 1.0 reduce the size of the new coordinate system, while values larger than 1.0 increase its size. A scale factor of 0.0 shrinks the coordinate system to nothing.

The **scale** exposed field value can be changed by routing an event to the exposed field's implied **set_scale** eventIn. When the event is received, the **scale** field is set, and the new scale is sent using the exposed field's implied **scale_changed** eventOut.

The values of the **scaleOrientation** field specify a rotation axis and angle with which to rotate the new coordinate system prior to scaling, and then unrotate it after scaling. Like the **rotation** field, the first three values in the **scaleOrientation** field specify the X, Y, and Z components of a 3-D coordinate in the new, translated coordinate system. The imaginary line between that coordinate and the translated origin specifies the rotation axis for orienting the scale. The fourth value in the **scaleOrientation** field specifies the positive or negative rotation angle, measured in radians. The default values for the **scaleOrientation** field specify that no rotation for scaling is to occur.

The **scaleOrientation** exposed field value can be changed by routing an event to the exposed field's implied **set_scaleOrientation** eventIn. When the event is received, the **scaleOrientation** field is set, and the new orientation is sent using the exposed field's implied **scaleOrientation_changed** eventOut.

The **center** field values specify the 3-D coordinate in the new, translated coordinate system about which rotations and scales are to occur. The default rotation and scale center is the origin.

The **center** exposed field value can be changed by routing an event to the exposed field's implied **set_center** eventIn. When the event is received, the **center** field is set, and the new center is sent using the exposed field's implied **center_changed** eventOut.

The remaining fields of the **Transform** node—**bboxCenter, bboxSize, addChildren,** and **removeChildren**—are discussed in Chapter 9.

When **translation, center, rotation, scale,** and **scaleOrientation** field values are used in combination, the new coordinate system is:

1. Scaled about the center point, oriented first by the scale orientation.
2. Rotated about the center point.
3. Translated relative to the parent coordinate system.

The **translation, center, rotation, scale,** and **scaleOrientation** fields may be specified in any order within the **Transform** node, however, these fields are always applied in the order stated above.

Experimenting with Scaling

The following examples provide a more detailed examination of the ways in which the **Transform** node's **scale, scaleOrientation,** and **center** fields can be used and how they interact with nodes and fields discussed in previous chapters.

Scaling in Different Directions

You can use the **Transform** node to scale a new coordinate system in any direction. Figures 7.4 through 7.7 show a coordinate system, and a sphere built within it, scaled up and scaled down in first the X, then the Y, and finally the Z directions.

```
#VRML V2.0 utf8
Transform {
    scale 2.0 1.0 1.0
    children [
        Shape {
            appearance Appearance {
                material Material { }
            }
            geometry Sphere { }
        }
    ]
}
```

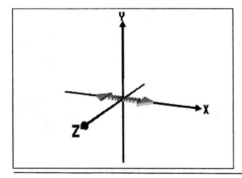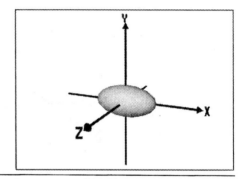

Figure 7.4 *Scaling up by 2.0 in the X-axis direction, and building a sphere.*

```
#VRML V2.0 utf8
Transform {
    scale 0.5 1.0 1.0
    children [
        Shape {
            appearance Appearance {
                material Material { }
            }
            geometry Sphere { }
        }
    ]
}
```

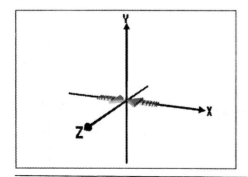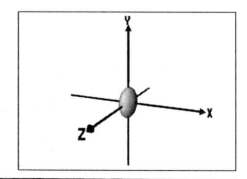

Figure 7.5 *Scaling down by 0.5 in the X-axis direction, and building a sphere.*

```
#VRML V2.0 utf8
Transform {
    scale 1.0 2.0 1.0
    children [
        Shape {
            appearance Appearance {
                material Material { }
            }
            geometry Sphere { }
        }
    ]
}
```

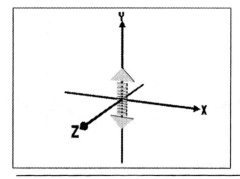 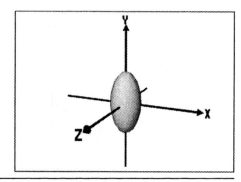

Figure 7.6   *Scaling up by 2.0 in the Y-axis direction, and building a sphere.*

```
#VRML V2.0 utf8
Transform {
    scale 1.0 1.0 0.5
    children [
        Shape {
            appearance Appearance {
                material Material { }
            }
            geometry Sphere { }
        }
    ]
}
```

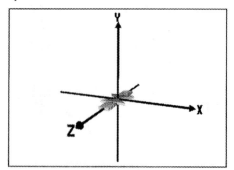 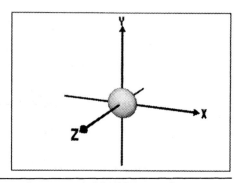

Figure 7.7   *Scaling down by 0.5 in the Z-axis direction, and building a sphere.*

Figures 7.4 through 7.7 show scaling in only one direction. You can also scale in two or all three directions at once. When you scale in more than one direction, the three scale field values may be the same or different. In Figure 7.8, the sphere's coordinate system is scaled up by 2.0 in the X direction, down by 0.5 in the Y direction, and up by 4.0 in the Z direction. Finally, the sphere is built.

```
#VRML V2.0 utf8
Transform {
    scale 2.0 0.5 4.0
    children [
        Shape {
            appearance Appearance {
                material Material { }
            }
            geometry Sphere { }
        }
    ]
}
```

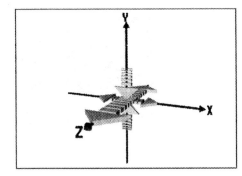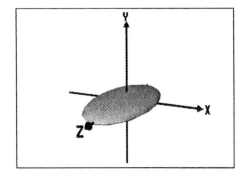

Figure 7.8 *Scaling up by 2.0 in the X direction, scaling down by 0.5 in the Y direction, scaling up by 4.0 in the Z direction, and building a sphere.*

Constructing Multiple Scaled Coordinate Systems

A VRML file may contain any number of **Transform** nodes, each defining its own new coordinate system. Figure 7.9 shows a simple spaceship built using a cylinder as a wing and a sphere as the fuselage. To create the wing, the cylinder is scaled up along the Z axis and down along the X axis. To create the fuselage, the sphere is scaled up along the X axis and down along the Y and Z axes.

```
#VRML V2.0 utf8
Group {
    children [
    # Wing
        Transform {
            scale 0.5 1.0 1.5
            children Shape {
                appearance DEF White Appearance {
                    material Material { }
                }
                geometry Cylinder {
                    radius 1.0
                    height 0.025
                }
            }
        },
    # Fuselage
        Transform {
            scale 2.0 0.2 0.5
            children Shape {
                appearance USE White
                geometry Sphere { }
            }
        }
    ]
}
```

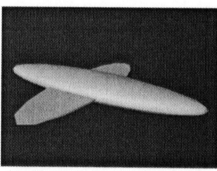

Figure 7.9   *A simple spaceship built with a cylinder and a sphere, each scaled within its own coordinate system.*

Nesting Scaled Coordinate Systems

The previous spaceship example built the wing and fuselage in their own coordinate systems, which are each scaled relative to the world coordinate system. You can also create coordinate systems within coordinate systems, nesting them as deeply as you like.

Figure 7.10 adds a second wing and fuselage shape pair to create a more detailed spaceship. The second wing and fuselage pair is identical to the first pair but is contained within its own new coordinate system. That coordinate system is scaled down along the X and Z axes, and up along the Y axis, relative to the world coordinate system. Notice the use of **DEF** and **USE** to reuse the wing and fuselage pair for the second, scaled pair.

```
#VRML V2.0 utf8
Group {
    children [
    # Wing
        DEF Wing Transform {
            scale 0.5 1.0 1.5
            children Shape {
                appearance DEF White Appearance {
                    material Material { }
                }
                geometry Cylinder {
                    radius 1.0
                    height 0.025
                }
            }
        },
    # Fuselage
        DEF Fuselage Transform {
            scale 2.0 0.2 0.5
            children Shape {
                appearance USE White
                geometry Sphere { }
            }
        },
    # Wing detail and fuselage dome
        Transform {
            scale 0.3 2.0 0.75
            children [
                USE Wing,
                USE Fuselage
            ]
        }
    ]
}
```

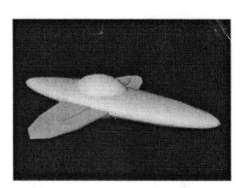

Figure 7.10 *A simple spaceship built with shapes in scaled coordinate systems.*

Translating and Scaling Coordinate Systems

Recall the archway you built in Chapter 5. To expand that architecture further, you can place smaller copies of the archway to the left and right of the original. Each smaller archway is created in its own coordinate system built by a **Transform** node. To place the smaller archways to the left and right of the central archway, the **Transform** node uses a **translation** field value to move the coordinate system to the left or right. To create the smaller version of the archway, its coordinate system is scaled down using the **Transform** node's **scale** field. Figure 7.11 shows the original temple archway and its new smaller side archways.

```
#VRML V2.0 utf8
Group {
    children [
    # Ground
        Shape {
            appearance DEF White Appearance {
                material Material { }
            }
            geometry Box {
                size 25.0 0.1 25.0
            }
        },
    # First archway
        DEF Archway Group {
            children [
            # Left Column
                DEF LeftColumn Transform {
                    translation -2.0 3.0 0.0
                    children DEF Column Shape {
                        appearance USE White
                        geometry Cylinder {
                            radius 0.3
                            height 6.0
                        }
                    }
                },
            # Right Column
                DEF RightColumn Transform {
                    translation 2.0 3.0 0.0
                    children USE Column
                },
            # Archway span
                DEF ArchwaySpan Transform {
                    translation 0.0 6.05 0.0
                    children Shape {
                        appearance USE White
                        geometry Box {
                            size 4.6 0.4 0.6
                        }
                    }
                },
            # Left Roof
                DEF LeftRoof Transform {
                    translation -1.15 7.12 0.0
                    rotation 0.0 0.0 1.0  0.524
                    children DEF Roof Shape {
                        appearance USE White
                        geometry Box {
                            size 2.86 0.4 0.6
                        }
                    }
                },
```

Figure 7.11 continues

```
# Right Roof
    DEF RightRoof Transform {
        translation 1.15 7.12 0.0
        rotation 0.0 0.0 1.0  -0.524
        children USE Roof
    }
]
},
# Left small archway
    Transform {
        translation -4.0 0.0 0.0
        scale 0.5 0.5 0.5
        children USE Archway
    },
# Right small archway
    Transform {
        translation 4.0 0.0 0.0
        scale 0.5 0.5 0.5
        children USE Archway
    }
]
}
```

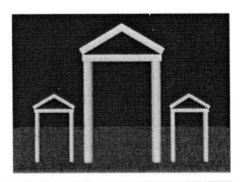

Figure 7.11 *An archway with smaller archways on each side created in translated, scaled coordinate systems.*

Scaling About a Center Point

Recall that shapes are always built centered at the origin of their parent's coordinate system. By default, scaling increases or decreases a coordinate system's size by expanding or shrinking everything outward from the coordinate system origin. The shapes in the simple spaceship in Figures 7.9 and 7.10 are scaled about their centers in this way.

When building shapes that should grow or shrink relative to a particular point on the shape, it is more natural to specify a center of scaling. A tree, for example, increases in size relative to the base of the trunk. The tip of the tree grows upward away from the trunk base, and the roots grow downward. The base of the trunk stays where it is. This is a natural center of scaling for the tree. Using the **Transform** node's **center** field, you can specify the location of the center of scaling for scale operations specified by the **scale** field values.

Figure 7.12 shows a very simple tree built using a cylinder for the trunk and a cone for the branches. The base of the trunk just touches a flattened box used as the ground. The origin of the tree's coordinate system is halfway up the tree trunk. A **Transform** node's **scale** field is used to scale the tree up. The **center** field sets the center of scaling to be at the base of the tree trunk, down along the Y axis by 1.0 unit from the tree's origin. When the tree is scaled up in this way, the base of the trunk stays touching the ground as the tree grows upward.

```
#VRML V2.0 utf8
Group {
    children [
    # Ground
        Shape {
            appearance DEF White Appearance {
                material Material { }
            }
            geometry Box {
                size 12.0 0.1 12.0
            }
        },
    # Tree
        Transform {
            translation 0.0 1.0 0.0
            scale       1.0 2.0 1.0
            center      0.0 -1.0 0.0
            children [
            # Trunk
                Shape {
                    appearance USE White
                    geometry Cylinder {
                        radius 0.5
                        height 2.0
                    }
                },
            # Branches
                Transform {
                    translation 0.0 3.0 0.0
                    children Shape {
                        appearance USE White
                        geometry Cone {
                            bottomRadius 2.0
                            height 4.0
                        }
                    }
                }
            ]
        }
    ]
}
```

Figure 7.12 *A tree (a) at its original size and (b) scaled up about a center point set at the base of the tree trunk. (This VRML text creates the image shown in Figure 7.12b.)*

Using a Scale Orientation

You can warp coordinate systems and their shapes by scaling up or down differently in the X, Y, and Z directions. This effect was used in the earlier simple spaceship examples to stretch cylinders and spheres into the spaceship's wing and fuselage. For additional warping control, you can use scale orientation to scale up and down along rotated X, Y, and Z axes. This enables you to scale shapes diagonally instead of just horizontally, vertically, and front to back.

Figure 7.13 shows the tree from Figure 7.12, but this tree is scaled diagonally to show the result of a long life in a windy area. A *scale orientation* is used that rotates the scaling direction 45.0 degrees around the Z axis. Once rotated, the tree's coordinate system is scaled up by 2.0 in the rotated Y direction, and 1.0 in the rotated X and Z directions. Note that these are the *rotated* X, Y, and Z directions. This use of scale orientation stretches the tree diagonally up and to the right.

Notice that even though the tree's coordinate system is scaled diagonally, the final tree isn't rotated. The base of the tree trunk is still flat on the ground. The rotation axis and angle used in the **scaleOrientation** field only affect the orientation of scaling. They do not leave the shape rotated. To rotate the shape use the **rotation** field.

```
#VRML V2.0 utf8
Group {
    children [
    # Ground
        Shape {
            appearance DEF White Appearance {
                material Material { }
            }
            geometry Box {
                size 12.0 0.1 12.0
            }
        },
    # Tree
        Transform {
            translation 0.0 1.0 0.0
            scale       1.0 2.0 1.0
            scaleOrientation 0.0 0.0 1.0 -0.785
            center      0.0 -1.0 0.0
            children [
            # Trunk
                Shape {
                    appearance USE White
                    geometry Cylinder {
                        radius 0.5
                        height 2.0
                    }
                },
```

Figure 7.13 continues

```
# Branches
   Transform {
       translation 0.0 3.0 0.0
       children Shape {
           appearance USE White
           geometry Cone {
               bottomRadius 2.0
               height 4.0
           }
       }
   }
   ]
   }
   ]
}
```

Figure 7.13   *A tree scaled along a diagonal axis using scale orientation.*

Summary

The **Transform** node creates a new coordinate system relative to its parent's coordinate system. The new coordinate system can be scaled relative to the parent's coordinate system by using the **scale** field of the **Transform** node.

Similar to the **Group** node, the **Transform** node collects together a group of child nodes. Shapes built by those child nodes are positioned within the **Transform** node's coordinate system. If that coordinate system is scaled, all of the **Transform** node's children are scaled along with the coordinate system.

The **scale** field value specifies three scale factors to increase or decrease the size of the coordinate system in the X, Y, and Z directions. To create a shrunken or grown shape without warping it, use the same scale factor for all three directions. To create a warped shape, use different scale factors for X, Y, and Z.

To scale in diagonal directions, you can rotate the scaling direction by using the **scaleOrientation** field. The **scaleOrientation** field value specifies a rotation axis and a rotation angle by which the new coordinate system is to be rotated for scaling. The rotation axis is an imaginary line drawn between the origin and a 3-D coordinate. The rotation angle, measured in radians, is the angle by which the coordinate system is rotated around the rotation axis. The scale orientation affects the orientation of scale operations, but leaves the coordinate system unrotated. To rotate the coordinate system, use the **rotation** field.

You can use the **translation, rotation,** and **scale** field values of the **Transform** node to position, orient, and scale the new coordinate system in your world. Using the **center** field, you can specify the center of rotation and scaling for the coordinate system.

## CHAPTER 8

Animating Position, Orientation, and Scale

To add movement to your world, you can animate the position, orientation, and scale of any coordinate system. As the coordinate system moves, any shapes built within the coordinate system move with it. By animating the coordinate system for a group of shapes, you can cause those shapes to fly about your world, translating, rotating, and scaling as you desire.

To start, stop, and otherwise control animation, the **TimeSensor** node acts as a clock. As time passes, this sensor generates events indicating changes in time. By routing these events from the **TimeSensor** node's eventOuts to other nodes, you can cause those nodes to change as the TimeSensor node's clock ticks.

To cause coordinate systems to translate, rotate, and scale, you can route **TimeSensor** node events to **PositionInterpolator** and **OrientationInterpolator** nodes. Each of these nodes generates new position and rotation values sent via its eventOuts. Routing these, in turn, to a **Transform** node causes the node's coordinate system to translate, rotate, or scale as the animation progresses.

Understanding Animation and Time

Animation is the change of something as time progresses. For instance, the change may be to a coordinate system's position, thereby causing the coordinate system and a group of shapes built within it to translate from place to place as time progresses. The change caused by an animation can be to a coordinate system's orientation and scale, as well.

Any animation requires two elements:

- A clock to control the playback of the animation
- A description of how something changes during the course of the animation

You can create a clock using the **TimeSensor** node. This node provides features for starting and stopping the animation, and controlling how quickly the animation plays.

To describe the changes to occur during an animation, you can use VRML's **PositionInterpolator** and **OrientationInterpolator** nodes. Both of these nodes use information from the clock to select an appropriate position or orientation from a list you provide. As the animation progresses, new positions and orientations are selected and output.

To create an animation circuit using these nodes, you can use VRML's **ROUTE** syntax to wire an output from a **TimeSensor** node to the input of a **PositionInter-polator** or **OrientationInterpolator** node. Then you can use another route to connect an output from an interpolator node to an input of a **Transform** node. Once wired, the **TimeSensor** node's clock can be started. Events will flow from the **TimeSensor** node to the interpolator, and from there to the **Transform** node, causing the node's coordinate system to translate, rotate, and scale as the animation plays back.

Absolute Time

A **TimeSensor** node acts like a real-world clock. When turned on, the sensor starts ticking until it is turned off. If the sensor is never turned off, it continues ticking until you load a new VRML file into your VRML browser, or until you quit your browser.

While a time sensor is ticking, it outputs events via its **time** eventOut that indicate the current time. You can route these events to other nodes to cause them to animate as the sensor ticks away.

To enable a time sensor to act like a real-world clock, the time output by a time sensor is an *absolute time*, measured in seconds since 12:00 midnight, GMT (Greenwich mean time), January 1, 1970. In absolute time, second 0 occurred at this date, second 1 at one second after this date, and so forth on up to the current date and time. Using these absolute times, nodes to which you wire the time sensor's outputs can cause animation changes to happen at specific dates and times.

> **SIDEBAR: ABSOLUTE TIME**   The use of 12:00 midnight, GMT, January 1, 1970, as a starting point for measuring absolute time is an obscure artifact of computer history. This date is rumored to be the birth date of the UNIX operating system, developed by AT&T Bell Labs in the early 1970s. The later, widespread use of UNIX on laboratory and departmental computers perpetuated the use of this same date as the starting point for time measurement. Most of today's computers now use this date as the starting time for time measurement on their internal clocks. VRML's use of this same starting time is an artifact of this widespread operating system convention.

A **TimeSensor** node can be started or stopped at a specific date and time by providing absolute times for the node's **startTime** and **stopTime** fields. Using these fields, you can turn the time sensor on and off, thereby starting and stopping any animation to which the sensor is wired.

Because figuring out a starting and stopping date and time measured in seconds from 12:00 midnight, GMT, January 1, 1970 is a daunting task, few people type values directly into the **startTime** and **stopTime** fields. Instead, these fields are typically wired into a circuit and set automatically using the output of other VRML nodes.

When a time sensor is started, it outputs a **TRUE** via its **isActive** eventOut. By wiring to this output, you can cause other animations in your world to start as well. Similarly, when the sensor is stopped, it outputs a **FALSE** via the **isActive** eventOut.

Fractional Time

You can use a time sensor's absolute-time event output to drive animation activities. However, it is often more convenient to design your animation to be independent of the exact date and time at which it is played back. Such an animation is typically described using fractional time. In *fractional time*, an animation is imagined as starting at fractional time 0.0, and running to fractional time 1.0. The exact, absolute times at which fractional times 0.0 and 1.0 occur are intentionally omitted from the animation description.

Using fractional time, an animation can be described independently of when or how often the animation is played back. For instance, an animation description might say to cause an airplane to take off at fractional time 0.0, fly about for awhile, then land and come to a halt at fractional time 1.0. Later, this animation description can be used to fly the airplane by starting it up at any absolute time just by saying, "Go now." Once started, the airplane goes through its moves from fractional time 0.0 to 1.0 as absolute time ticks away. The same animation can be played again later by saying, "Go now," again. The animation description is completely independent of when or how often it is played back.

The **TimeSensor** node outputs fractional times on its **fraction_changed** eventOut. You can use a time sensor's absolute or fractional time outputs, or both, to drive your animations. Fractional time 0.0 always occurs when the time sensor is started.

The length of time between fractional time 0.0 and 1.0 is also independent of absolute time. For instance, you can direct a time sensor to go from 0.0 to 1.0 in five seconds, thirty minutes, or any other time interval you like. The time it takes to cycle from 0.0 to 1.0 in fractional time is called the *cycle interval* and is specified using the **TimeSensor** node's **cycleInterval** field.

You can use short or long cycle intervals to control the speed with which an animation is played back. For instance, if the airplane animation above has a ten-minute cycle interval, then the airplane takes off and lands within the span of ten minutes. If, instead, the animation cycle interval is only two minutes, then the entire flight takes only two minutes.

Looping Fractional Time

A time sensor can create a time loop that cycles from fractional time 0.0 to 1.0, then starts over again after each interval. Using this feature, you can cause animations to repeat over and over until the time sensor is stopped. This feature is useful for creating endless animations, such as to make a shape spin continuously, or make a paper airplane fly in an endless loop around a room.

Looping is turned on within a time sensor when you specify a **TRUE** value for the node's **loop** field. When using loops, the **TimeSensor** node outputs the absolute time via its **cycleTime** eventOut each time the cycle starts over. You can use this absolute time to start and stop further animations or synchronize multiple animations in the same world.

Understanding Keyframe Animation

VRML provides several ways of describing animations. Two of the most common are through use of the **PositionInterpolator** and **OrientationInterpolator** nodes. Both of these nodes can use fractional time to compute and output a translation value or a rotation value. You can route these outputs to a **Transform** node to cause the node's coordinate system to translate or rotate.

Key Fractional Times and Values

An animation description must provide a position or orientation for each new time as the animation's fractional time progresses from 0.0 to 1.0. The most straightforward approach is for an animation description to use a table of orientations or rotations, one for each possible fractional time between 0.0 and 1.0. Unfortunately, there are an infinite number of possible fractional times between 0.0 and 1.0, which makes a table like this impractical.

Instead, animation descriptions use a technique called *keyframe animation*, where a position or rotation is specified for only a few, key fractional times. The position or rotation values at these times are called *key values*. The VRML interpolator nodes use these key fractional times and values as a rough sketch of the animation and fill in the values between those specified as needed. Using keyframe animation, an animation description specifies only a few positions and rotations, instead of an infinite number of them.

For example, to cause a car to drive from left to right as fractional time proceeds from 0.0 to 1.0, a keyframe animation could use just two key fractional times, 0.0 and 1.0, and two key values, the left position and the right position. The interpolator node automatically computes positions between these two key positions for fractional times between 0.0 and 1.0. At fractional time 0.5, for instance, the car's position is computed at exactly halfway between the first key position, at fractional time 0.0, and second key position, at fractional time 1.0.

The **PositionInterpolator** and **OrientationInterpolator** nodes both use a list of key fractional times and key values to describe an animation. Key fractional times are listed as values in an interpolator node's **key** field, while key values are listed in the node's **keyValue** field. Both of these fields can be provided with any number of key fractional times and values.

To wire an interpolator node into an animation circuit, the **fraction_changed** eventOut of a time sensor is routed to the **set_fraction** eventIn of the interpolator. Each time the time sensor outputs a new fractional time, the interpolator uses the input fractional time, computes a new position or rotation, then outputs it via its **value_changed** eventOut. That output is, in turn, wired to a **Transform** node to cause the node's coordinate system to translate and rotate as the time sensor ticks away.

Linear Interpolation

The **PositionInterpolator** and **OrientationInterpolator** nodes both use linear interpolation to compute intermediate values between the key values you provide. *Linear interpolation* can be visualized by first imagining two key-value positions plotted as dots on a piece of graph paper. Next, using an imaginary ruler, draw a *linear*, or straight, line between the two dots. All points along that drawn line, as shown in Figure 8.1, are intermediate positions between the first key-value position and the second.

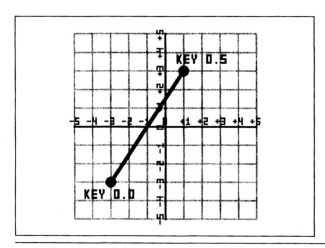

Figure 8.1   *Graph paper with two positions marked and a straight line drawn between them.*

A linear interpolator computes an intermediate position each time an output is needed. For example, if the first position is at key fractional time 0.0, and the second is at 0.5, then at fractional time 0.25, a position on the line halfway between the first and second positions is output.

Using linear interpolation, interpolator nodes can compute any number of intermediate values between your key positions or rotations. For example, if you provide two key positions to move a car from left to right as fractional time goes from 0.0 to 1.0, linear interpolation can compute the car's position for 3, 10, or even a 1,000 different fractional times between 0.0 to 1.0.

The use of interpolation is especially important when playing animation at different speeds. For a quick animation, your VRML browser may only have time to draw the world a few times between the time the animation starts and the time it stops. In this case, your browser may only need to linearly interpolate values at a few fractional times between the key fractional times you provide.

For a slow animation, your VRML browser may have the time to draw the world many times and may need a large number of interpolated positions and rotations. In this case, your browser may interpolate values at many fractional times between your key fractional times.

Using keyframe animation and linear interpolation, you can describe an animation independent of the playback speed of the animation. During playback, an appropriate number of intermediate values are computed automatically.

Linearly Interpolating Positions and Rotations

Linear interpolation can be used to interpolate between any two values. For a pair of key positions specified by 3-D coordinates, linear interpolation simultaneously interpolates between the key position's X, Y, and Z values. During an animation, this has the desired effect of simultaneously changing the X, Y, and Z components of the computed position, thereby smoothly sliding a shape from one computed position to another along a straight line.

When interpolating rotations, linear interpolation simultaneously interpolates between a pair of key rotation's X, Y, and Z rotation axis values and rotation angles. This has the desired effect of smoothly changing the axis of rotation and rotation angle as the animation progresses. Using this form of rotation interpolation, you can cause a shape to rotate from a first key angle to a second, letting the interpolator compute intermediate angles.

Interpolating with Multiple Key Values

Linear interpolation also can be used when an animation includes more than just two key positions or rotations. For example, Figure 8.2 extends the graph paper example in Figure 8.1 by adding a third key position. The first, second, and third key positions are key animation positions for key fractional times 0.0, 0.5, and 1.0. Straight lines between these key positions illustrate the path a shape should take as it animates from the first key position to the second, and then from the second to the third.

Using linear interpolation, at fractional time 0.25, the computed position is halfway between the first and second key positions. At fractional time 0.5, the com-

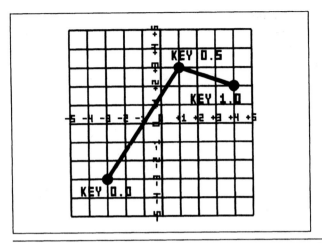

Figure 8.2 *Graph paper with three positions marked and straight lines drawn between them.*

puted position is exactly at the second key position. At fractional time 0.75, the computed position is halfway between the second and third positions.

Linear interpolation can be used in this manner to compute intermediate positions or rotations for any number of key positions and rotations.

Animating Scale

The computed output value of the **PositionInterpolator** node is of type SFVec3f, and is designed to be used as an input to nodes that use translation values or 3-D coordinates. The **Transform** node, for example, uses an SFVec3f value as the value of the **translation** field. The **PositionInterpolator** node is appropriate for animating this field to cause a coordinate system to translate.

In a similar fashion, the output of an **OrientationInterpolator** node is of type SFRotation, and is designed to be suitable as an input to nodes that use rotations. The **Transform** node's **rotation** field, for example, uses an SFRotation value to specify the rotation axis and angle by which the node's coordinate system is to be rotated. The **OrientationInterpolator** node is appropriate for animating this field to cause a coordinate system to rotate.

Any node that uses an SFVec3f value for a field can be animated using the **PositionInterpolator** node. The field animated need not be one that describes a position. For example, the **Transform** node's **scale** field uses an SFVec3f to describe the X, Y, and Z scaling factors by which to scale the node's coordinate system. You can use a **PositionInterpolator** node to animate these scale factors by routing the interpolator's outputs to the **Transform** node's **scale** field. This causes the **Transform** node's coordinate system to grow and shrink under the control of the animation key values in the **PositionInterpolator** node.

The **TimeSensor** Node Syntax

The **TimeSensor** node creates a clock that generates events to control animations.

SYNTAX	TimeSensor node

```
TimeSensor {
    enabled           TRUE    # exposedField  SFBool
    startTime         0.0     # exposedField  SFTime
    stopTime          0.0     # exposedField  SFTime
    cycleInterval     1.0     # exposedField  SFTime
    loop              FALSE   # exposedField  SFBool
    isActive                  # eventOut      SFBool
    time                      # eventOut      SFTime
    cycleTime                 # eventOut      SFTime
    fraction_changed          # eventOut      SFFloat
}
```

The value of the **enabled** exposed field specifies whether the time sensor is turned on or off. If the field value is TRUE, the time sensor is on, and the rest of the node's fields are used to control the output of the sensor. If the field is FALSE, the time sensor is off and no outputs are generated except those in response to changing an exposed field (for example, **enabled_changed**). The default value for the field is TRUE.

The value of the **startTime** exposed field specifies the time at which, if the sensor is enabled, it begins outputting events via its eventOuts. The **startTime** field value is an absolute time measured in seconds since 12:00 midnight, GMT, January 1, 1970. The default value is 0.0 seconds.

The value of the **stopTime** exposed field specifies the time at which the time sensor stops outputting events. The **stopTime** field value is an absolute time and has a default value of 0.0 seconds.

The value of the **cycleInterval** exposed field specifies the length of time the time sensor takes to vary its fractional time output from fractional time 0.0 to 1.0. The cycle interval value is a time interval, measured in seconds, and must be greater than 0.0. The default cycle interval is 1.0 second.

The value of the **loop** exposed field specifies whether the time sensor loops or not. If the field value is TRUE, the time sensor outputs floating-point fractional time values from 0.0 to 1.0 during the cycle interval. At the end of the interval, the fractional output returns to 0.0, and the sensor begins the cycle again. If the loop field value is FALSE, the time sensor does not loop. Instead, fractional time values are output from 0.0 to 1.0 for only one cycle, after which output ceases. The default value for the **loop** field is FALSE.

The **startTime, stopTime, cycleInterval,** and **loop** field values work together to control the time sensor's outputs. Once enabled, a time sensor remains dormant until the start time is reached. At that time, the sensor becomes active and begins generating events. If the **loop** field value is FALSE, then the time sensor generates events until either the stop time is reached, or one cycle has been completed at (startTime + cycleInterval), whichever comes first. If the **loop** field value is **TRUE**, then the time sensor generates events continually, through a potentially infinite number of cycles, until the stop time is reached. In the special case where the stop time is earlier than or equal to the start time, the stop time is ignored. This can be used to create time sensors that loop forever.

The **startTime, stopTime, cycleInterval,** and **loop** field values can be used together to create several standard effects, such as those listed in Table 8.1.

Table 8.1   Standard Effects Based on startTime, stopTime, cycleInterval, and loop Field Values

loop Field Value	*startTime, stopTime,* and *cycleInterval* Field Value Relationships	*Effect*
TRUE	stopTime ≤ startTime	Run forever
TRUE	startTime < stopTime	Run until **stopTime**
FALSE	stopTime ≤ startTime	Run for one cycle, then stop at (start Time + cycleInterval)
FALSE	startTime < (startTime + cycleInterval) ≤ stopTime	Run for one cycle, then stop at (start Time + cycleInterval)
FALSE	startTime < stopTime < (startTime + cycleInterval)	Run for less than one cycle, then stop at **stopTime**

The **isActive** eventOut outputs a single **TRUE** event value when the time sensor becomes active and starts outputting events. A single **FALSE** event value is sent when the time sensor stops outputting events and becomes inactive.

The **time** eventOut outputs an absolute time event value continuously as long as the time sensor is generating events.

The **cycleTime** eventOut outputs an absolute time event value each time the cycle starts over again. If the **loop** field value is **FALSE**, then a time is output from the **cycleTime** eventOut only at the start of the first, and only, cycle.

The **fraction_changed** eventOut outputs a fractional, floating-point time value between 0.0 and 1.0 as the time sensor progresses through a cycle. A fractional time value of 0.0 is output at the start of the cycle, a 1.0 at the end of the cycle, and intermediate fractional time values at times in between. If the **loop** field value is **FALSE**, fractional time values are output only during a single cycle. If the **loop** field value is **TRUE**, fractional time values are output repeatedly through each cycle, always starting over at 0.0 at the beginning of each cycle.

The value of the **enabled** exposed field can be changed by routing an event to the exposed field's implied **set_enabled** eventIn. If a **TRUE** event value is received, and the sensor is currently disabled, then the sensor becomes enabled. If a **FALSE** event value is received, and the sensor is currently enabled, then the sensor disables after outputting a final set of events via its eventOuts. If a **TRUE** event value is received, but the sensor is already enabled, or if a **FALSE** value is received, but the sensor is already disabled, then the event is ignored and the sensor is unchanged. In any case, each time the sensor changes from **TRUE** to **FALSE** or **FALSE** to **TRUE,** the new sensor enable value is output via the exposed field's implied **enabled_changed** eventOut.

The value of the **loop** exposed field can be changed by routing a **TRUE** or **FALSE** event to the exposed field's implied **set_loop** eventIn. If the **loop** field value is changed from **TRUE** to **FALSE,** and the sensor is currently active and generating events during a cycle, then the sensor continues to the end of the cycle, or to the stop time, before stopping. If the **loop** field value is changed from **FALSE** to **TRUE,** and the sensor is currently active, then the sensor loops until the stop time. In any case, when the **loop** field value is changed, the new value is output via the exposed field's implied **loop_changed** eventOut.

The values for the **startTime** and **cycleInterval** exposed fields can be changed by routing an event to the exposed field's implied **set_startTime** and **set_cycleInterval** eventIns, respectively. If the time sensor is active when a new value is received, the new value is ignored. Otherwise, the new value sets the exposed field and is output via the exposed field's implied **startTime_changed** and **cycleInterval_changed** eventOuts, respectively.

If the time sensor is not active when a new start time is received, the sensor's start time is changed. This may cause the sensor to become active if the new start time is the current time, or is soon enough in the past that the current time is less than (startTime + cycleInterval).

The value of the **stopTime** exposed field can be changed by routing an event to the exposed field's implied **set_stopTime** eventIn. If a new stop time is earlier than the start time, the new stop time value is ignored. Otherwise, the new stop time changes the **stopTime** field value and is output via the exposed field's implied **stopTime_changed** eventOut. The new stop time is also used to evaluate whether it is time to stop the time sensor based on the current time, the cycle interval, and the new stop time.

The **TimeSensor** node creates no shapes and has no visible effect on a world. A **TimeSensor** node may be included as the child of any grouping node, but is independent of the coordinate system in use. Typically, time sensors are placed at the end of the outermost group of a VRML file.

TIP The exact frequency with which a time sensor outputs events depends on the speed of your computer, the activities in progress on your computer, and the activities in progress within your VRML browser. On a slow or busy computer, your VRML browser may not get the opportunity to update the time sensor as frequently as on a fast or unloaded computer. Your VRML browser only guarantees to output events when the time sensor starts outputting events (the start time), and when it stops outputting events (the stop time or startTime + cycleInterval).

TIP Looping time sensors should be used with care since they can loop indefinitely and generate a large number of events. This large number of events can slow down your VRML browser, giving it less time to allocate to other timer sensors and build your world on the screen.

The **PositionInterpolator** Node Syntax

The **PositionInterpolator** node describes a series of key positions available for use in an animation.

SYNTAX | **PositionInterpolator node**

```
PositionInterpolator {
    key                [ ]    # exposedField  MFFloat
    keyValue           [ ]    # exposedField  MFVec3f
    set_fraction              # eventIn       SFFloat
    value_changed             # eventOut      SFVec3f
}
```

The value of the **key** exposed field specifies a list of key, fractional, floating-point times. Typically, fractional times are between 0.0 and 1.0, such as those output by a **TimeSensor** node's **fraction_changed** eventOut. Key fractional times, however, may be positive or negative floating-point values of any size. Key fractional times must be listed in nondecreasing order. The default value for the **key** field is an empty list.

The value of the **PositionInterpolator** node's **keyValue** exposed field specifies a list of key positions. Each key position is a group of three values containing an X, a Y, and a Z floating-point value making up a 3-D coordinate or translation distance. In some uses, key values also may be considered X, Y, and Z scaling factors or other groups of three of floating-point values. The default value for the **keyValue** field is an empty list.

The key fractional times and positions are used together so that the first key fractional time specifies the time for the first key position, the second key fractional time for the second key position, and so forth. The lists, together, may provide any number of fractional times and positions, but both lists must contain the same number of values.

When a **PositionInterpolator** node receives a fractional time, it computes a position based on the list of key positions and their corresponding key fractional times. The new computed position is output via the **value_changed** eventOut.

An output position for an input fractional time *t* is computed by the **PositionInterpolator** node by:

1. Scanning the key fractional times to find a pair of adjacent times *t1* and *t2*, where $t1 \le t \le t2$.

2. Retrieving the corresponding pair of key positions.

3. Computing an intermediate position by linearly interpolating between the key positions.

Two adjacent key fractional times *t1* and *t2* may have the same value in order to create a discontinuity, or jump, in the animation path. In this case, the key position corresponding to *t1* (the first of the two identical key fractional times) is used by the **PositionInterpolator** node when linearly interpolating for times less than *t1*, and the key position corresponding to *t2* (the second of the two times) is used when linearly interpolating for times greater than *t2*.

Typically, fractional times are sent to the **set_fraction** eventIn by wiring a route from the **fraction_changed** eventOut of a **TimeSensor** node. Fractional times also may be generated by alternate means, such as the output of nodes that generate generic, floating-point values.

The list of key fractional times or positions can be changed by sending values to the implied **set_key** and **set_keyValue** eventIns of the **key** and **keyValue** exposed fields. When values are received, the corresponding field values are changed, and the new values are output via the implied **key_changed** and **keyValue_changed** eventOuts of the exposed fields.

The **PositionInterpolator** node creates no shapes and has no visible effect on a world. A **PositionInterpolator** node may be included as the child of any grouping node but is independent of the coordinate system in use. Typically, interpolators are placed at the end of the outermost group of a VRML file.

The **OrientationInterpolator** Node Syntax

The **OrientationInterpolator** node describes a series of key rotations available for use in an animation.

| SYNTAX | OrientationInterpolator node |

```
OrientationInterpolator {
    key              [ ]    # exposedField   MFFloat
    keyValue         [ ]    # exposedField   MFRotation
    set_fraction            # eventIn        SFFloat
    value_changed           # eventOut       SFRotation
}
```

The value of the **key** exposed field is discussed in the section entitled "The **Position-Interpolator** Node Syntax."

The value of the **keyValue** exposed field specifies a list of key rotations. Each key rotation is a group of four values. The first three values specify the X, Y, and Z components of a rotation axis, while the fourth value specifies a rotation angle for rotating about that axis. (See Chapter 6 for discussion of rotation axes and angles.) The default value for the **keyValue** field is an empty list.

The key fractional times and rotations are used together so that the first key fractional time specifies the time for the first key rotation, the second key fractional time for the second key rotation, and so forth. The lists, together, may provide any number of fractional times and rotations, but both lists must contain the same number of values.

When a fractional time is received by the **OrientationInterpolator** node, it computes a rotation based on the list of key rotations and their corresponding key fractional times. The new computed rotation is output via the **value_changed** eventOut.

An output rotation for an input fractional time *t* is computed by the **Orientation-Interpolator** node by:

1. Scanning the key fractional times to find a pair of adjacent times *t1* and *t2*, where *t1* ≤ *t* ≤ *t2*.

2. Retrieving the corresponding pair of key rotations.

3. Computing an intermediate rotation by linearly interpolating between the key rotations.

Two adjacent key fractional times *t1* and *t2* may have the same value in order to create a discontinuity, or jump, in the animation path. In this case, the key rotation corresponding to *t1* (the first of the two identical key fractional times) is used by the **OrientationInterpolator** node when linearly interpolating for times less than *t1*, and the key rotation corresponding to *t2* (the second of the two times) is used when linearly interpolating for times greater than *t2*.

The **set_fraction** eventIn is discussed in the section entitled "The **PositionInterpolator** Node Syntax."

The list of key fractional times or rotations can be changed by sending values to the implied **set_key** and **set_keyValue** eventIns of the **key** and **keyValue** exposed fields. When values are received, the corresponding field values are changed and the new values are output via the implied **key_changed** and **keyValue_changed** eventOuts of the exposed fields.

The **OrientationInterpolator** node creates no shapes and has no visible effect on a world. An **OrientationInterpolator** node may be included as the child of any grouping node but is independent of the coordinate system in use. Typically, interpolators are placed at the end of the outermost group of a VRML file.

Experimenting with Shape Animation

The following examples provide a more detailed examination of the ways in which the **TimeSensor, PositionInterpolator,** and **OrientationInterpolator** nodes can be used and how they interact with nodes and fields discussed in previous chapters.

In reading the examples that follow, recall that the **Transform** node, discussed in Chapters 5–7, has exposed fields: **translation, rotation,** and **scale,** as well as several others. Since these fields are exposed, each field has an implied **set_translation, set_rotation,** and **set_scale** eventIn, respectively. These eventIns are used in the following examples as the destination for routes built using the **ROUTE** syntax discussed in Chapter 2.

All of the following examples use only the **fraction_changed** eventOut of the **TimeSensor** node. The remaining outputs are either rarely used or used only in combination with nodes discussed in later chapters.

All of the following examples use infinitely looping **TimeSensor** nodes. This is accomplished by setting the **startTime** and **stopTime** field values to the same value and setting the **loop** field value to **TRUE.** The examples that follow use the default **startTime** and **stopTime** of 0.0.

When using infinitely looping time sensors with these start and stop times, animation begins as soon as the VRML file is read by the browser, and continues until the next VRML file is read or until you exit from your VRML browser.

Nonlooping time sensors must be started or stopped through the use of other nodes, such as the **TouchSensor** node discussed in Chapter 10 or the **Proximity-Sensor** node discussed in Chapter 27. Examples using nonlooping time sensors are left to those later chapters.

Animating Position

The following example creates a simple animation that moves a cube back and forth in a bouncing path. To create this animation, the VRML text in this example first builds the following components:

- A **Transform** node, named "Cube," that creates the coordinate system to be moved. Within the coordinate system, a **Box** node builds a cube shape.
- A **TimeSensor** node, named "Clock," that creates the clock. The time sensor's fields specify that the clock has a cycle length of 4.0 seconds and that it loops forever.
- A **PositionInterpolator** node, named "CubePath," that describes a bouncing path using 13 key fractional times and positions.

These components are wired together using **ROUTE** instructions. The first **ROUTE** instruction wires a path from the **fraction_changed** eventOut of the **TimeSensor** node to the **set_fraction** eventIn of the **PositionInterpolator** node. The second **ROUTE** instruction wires a path from the **value_changed** eventOut of the **Posi-tionInterpolator** node to the implied **set_translation** eventIn of the **Transform** node.

As the time sensor ticks through each 4.0-second cycle, it outputs fractional time values varying from 0.0 to 1.0. These are received by the interpolator and used to compute a new position along the bouncing path. The new position is output and received by the **Transform** node, causing the node's coordinate system to be translated to the new position. Because the cube is built within the translated coordinate system, as the coordinate system moves, the cube moves along with it. The full effect is to cause a coordinate system and its cube shape to animate endlessly around a bouncing path.

Figure 8.3 shows the VRML text for this example. The lines and arrows drawn in the example text's margin show the wired routes from the **TimeSensor** node to the **PositionInterpolator** node and from the **PositionInterpolator** node to the **Transform** node.

```
#VRML V2.0 utf8
Group {
    children [
    # Moving box
       DEF Cube Transform {
            children Shape {
                appearance Appearance {
                    material Material { }
                }
                geometry Box { size 1.0 1.0 1.0 }
            }
        },
    # Animation clock
        DEF Clock TimeSensor {
            cycleInterval 4.0
            loop TRUE
        },
    # Animation path
        DEF CubePath PositionInterpolator {
            key [
                0.00, 0.11, 0.17, 0.22,
                0.33, 0.44, 0.50, 0.55,
                0.66, 0.77, 0.83, 0.88,
                0.99
            ]
            keyValue [
                0.0 0.0  0.0,  1.0 1.96 1.0,
                1.5 2.21 1.5,  2.0 1.96 2.0,
                3.0 0.0  3.0,  2.0 1.96 3.0,
                1.5 2.21 3.0,  1.0 1.96 3.0,
                0.0 0.0  3.0,  0.0 1.96 2.0,
                0.0 2.21 1.5,  0.0 1.96 1.0,
                0.0 0.0  0.0
            ]
        }
    ]
}
ROUTE Clock.fraction_changed TO CubePath.set_fraction
ROUTE CubePath.value_changed TO Cube.set_translation
```

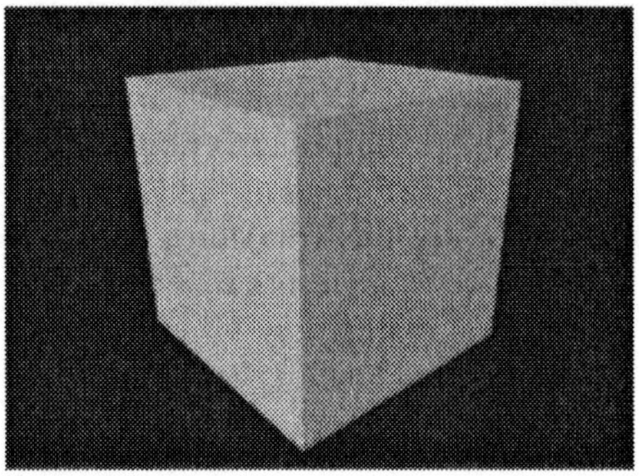

Figure 8.3 *An animation that moves a coordinate system and the cube built within it along a bouncing path.*

Animating Rotation

The following example creates an animation that endlessly spins a cylinder about the Z axis. The VRML text in this example first builds several components:

- A **Transform** node, named "Column," that creates the coordinate system to be rotated. Within the coordinate system, a **Cylinder** node builds a column shape.
- A **TimeSensor** node, named "Clock," that creates the clock. The time sensor's fields specify that the clock has a cycle length of 4.0 seconds and that it loops forever.
- An **OrientationInterpolator** node, named "ColumnPath," that describes a set of the key fractional times and rotations. All three key rotations rotate about the Z axis. The first rotation rotates by 0.0 degrees, the second by 180.0 degrees (3.14 radians), and the third by 360.0 degrees (6.28 radians).

These components are wired together using **ROUTE** instructions. The first **ROUTE** instruction wires a path from the **fraction_changed** eventOut of the **TimeSensor** node, to the **set_fraction** eventIn of the **OrientationInterpolator** node. The second **ROUTE** instruction wires a path from the **value_changed** eventOut of the **OrientationInterpolator** node to the implied **set_rotation** eventIn of the **Transform** node.

During the animation, the time sensor ticks through each 4.0-second cycle and outputs fractional time values from 0.0 to 1.0. These are received by the interpolator and used to compute a new rotation. The new rotation is output and received by the **Transform** node, causing the node's coordinate system to be rotated to a new angle. Because the column is built within the rotated coordinate system, as the coordinate system turns, the column turns along with it. The full effect is to cause a coordinate system and its column shape to animate endlessly in a 360.0-degree spin.

Figure 8.4 shows the VRML text for this example. The lines and arrows drawn in the example text's margin show the wired routes from the **TimeSensor** node to the **OrientationInterpolator** node and from the **OrientationInterpolator** node to the **Transform** node.

```
#VRML V2.0 utf8
Group {
    children [
    # Rotating cylinder
        DEF Column Transform {
            rotation 0.0 0.0 1.0 0.0
            children Shape {
                appearance Appearance {
                    material Material { }
                }
                geometry Cylinder {
                    height 1.0
                    radius 0.2
                }
            }
        },
    # Animation clock
        DEF Clock TimeSensor {
            cycleInterval 4.0
            loop TRUE
        },
    # Animation path
        DEF ColumnPath OrientationInterpolator {
            key [ 0.0, 0.50, 1.0 ]
            keyValue [
                0.0 0.0 1.0  0.0,
                0.0 0.0 1.0  3.14,
                0.0 0.0 1.0  6.28
            ]
        }
    ]
}
ROUTE Clock.fraction_changed    TO ColumnPath.set_fraction
ROUTE ColumnPath.value_changed TO Column.set_rotation
```

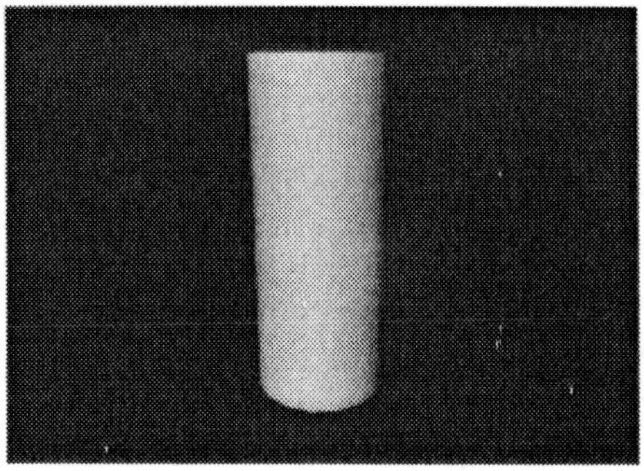

Figure 8.4 *An animation that rotates a coordinate system and the column built within it.*

Animating Scale

The following example creates an animation that repeatedly enlarges and reduces the size of a ball. The VRML text in this example first builds several components:

- A **Transform** node, named "Ball," that creates the coordinate system to be scaled. Within the coordinate system, a **Sphere** node builds a ball shape.
- A **TimeSensor** node, named "Clock," that creates the clock. The time sensor's fields specify that the clock has a cycle length of 2.0 seconds and that it loops forever.

- A **PositionInterpolator** node, named "BallPath," that describes the set of key fractional times and values. Rather than treat each key value as a position, this example uses each group of three of floating-point values as X, Y, and Z scale factors. The first key value scales by 1.0 in X, Y, and Z. The second scales up to 1.5 in X, Y, and Z, while the third scales down to 1.1, and the last scales back to 1.0.

These components are wired together using **ROUTE** instructions. The first **ROUTE** instruction wires a path from the **fraction_changed** eventOut of the **TimeSensor** node, to the **set_fraction** eventIn of the **PositionInterpolator** node. The second **ROUTE** instruction wires a path from the **value_changed** eventOut of the **PositionInterpolator** node to the implied set_scale eventIn of the **Transform** node.

During the animation, the time sensor ticks through each 2.0-second cycle and outputs fractional time values from 0.0 to 1.0. These are received by the interpolator and used to compute a new X, Y, and Z scale factor. The new scale factor is output and received by the **Transform** node, causing the node's coordinate system to be scaled up or down. Because the ball is built within the scaled coordinate system, as the coordinate system grows and shrinks, the ball scales along with it. The full effect is to cause a coordinate system and its ball shape to animate by growing larger, shrinking back to normal, and so on forever.

Figure 8.5 shows the VRML text for this example. The lines and arrows drawn in the example text's margin show the wired routes from the **TimeSensor** node to the **PositionInterpolator** node and from the **PositionInterpolator** node to the **Transform** node.

```
#VRML V2.0 utf8
Group {
    children [
    # Pulsing ball
        DEF Ball Transform {
            children Shape {
                appearance Appearance {
                    material Material { }
                }
                geometry Sphere { }
            }
        },
    # Animation clock
        DEF Clock TimeSensor {
            cycleInterval 2.0
            loop TRUE
        },
    # Animation path
        DEF BallPath PositionInterpolator {
            key [ 0.0, 0.20, 0.65, 1.0 ]
            keyValue [
                1.0 1.0 1.0,
                1.5 1.5 1.5,
                1.1 1.1 1.1,
                1.0 1.0 1.0,
            ]
```

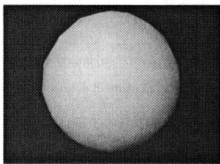

Figure 8.5 continues

```
        }
    ]
}
ROUTE Clock.fraction_changed TO BallPath.set_fraction
ROUTE BallPath.value_changed TO Ball.set_scale
```

Figure 8.5   *An animation that scales a coordinate system and the ball built within it.*

Animating Multiple Shapes Using One Interpolator

Each of the previous examples route the output of an interpolator to a single **Transform** node. Using additional routes, you can route the interpolator's output to multiple **Transform** nodes, causing multiple coordinate systems to translate, rotate, and scale at the same time. You can use this to create groups of synchronized animations, like dancers in a chorus line.

Figure 8.6 creates an animation that moves three side-by-side cubes in the bouncing path from Figure 8.3. The VRML text in this example first builds several components:

- Three **Transform** nodes named "Cube1," "Cube2," and "Cube3." Each **Transform** node contains a **Box** node.
- A **TimeSensor** node named "Clock." The time sensor specifies a 4.0-second cycle length.
- A single **PositionInterpolator** node named "CubePath." The key fractional times and values of the interpolator create a bouncing path.

The **TimeSensor** node's **fraction_changed** eventOut is routed to the **PositionInterpolator** node's **set_fraction** eventIn. The interpolator's **value_changed** eventOut is then routed to the three **Transform** node's implied **set_translation** eventIn.

As the animation plays through each 4.0-second cycle, the interpolator generates new positions. The same position output is used by each **Transform** node, causing all three side-by-side cubes to synchronously move along a bouncing path.

```
#VRML V2.0 utf8
Group {
    children [
    # Moving box
        DEF Cube1 Transform {
            children DEF ACube Shape {
                appearance Appearance {
                    material Material { }
                }
                geometry Box { size 1.0 1.0 1.0 }
            }
        },
        Transform {
            translation -2.0 0.0 0.0
            children DEF Cube2 Transform {
                children USE ACube
            }
```

Figure 8.6 continues

```
        },
        Transform {
            translation 2.0 0.0 0.0
            children DEF Cube3 Transform {
                children USE ACube
            }
        },
    # Animation clock
        DEF Clock TimeSensor {
            cycleInterval 4.0
            loop TRUE
        },
    # Animation path
        DEF CubePath PositionInterpolator {
            key [
                0.00, 0.11, 0.17, 0.22,
                0.33, 0.44, 0.50, 0.55,
                0.66, 0.77, 0.83, 0.88,
                0.99
            ]
            keyValue [
                0.0 0.0  0.0,   1.0 1.96 1.0,
                1.5 2.21 1.5,   2.0 1.96 2.0,
                3.0 0.0  3.0,   2.0 1.96 3.0,
                1.5 2.21 3.0,   1.0 1.96 3.0,
                0.0 0.0  3.0,   0.0 1.96 2.0,
                0.0 2.21 1.5,   0.0 1.96 1.0,
                0.0 0.0  0.0
            ]
        }
    ]
}
ROUTE Clock.fraction_changed TO CubePath.set_fraction
ROUTE CubePath.value_changed TO Cube1.set_translation
ROUTE CubePath.value_changed TO Cube2.set_translation
ROUTE CubePath.value_changed TO Cube3.set_translation
```

Figure 8.6   *One interpolator used to move three cubes.*

Using Multiple Interpolators

To create more complex animations, you can use multiple interpolators, each wired to the output of the same time sensor. Each time the time sensor outputs a new fractional time, all the interpolators wired to it receive a new time and compute a new key value. The key values output by the interpolators can be routed to one or more **Transform** nodes to cause multiple animation actions to occur simultaneously.

The VRML text in Figure 8.7 creates an animation that spins three bars, one each around the X, Y, and Z axes. Several components are built first:

- Three **Transform** nodes named "Bar1," "Bar2," and "Bar3." Each **Transform** node contains a **Box** node that builds a bar.

- A **TimeSensor** node, named "Clock," that creates the clock. The time sensor's fields specify that the animation clock has a cycle length of 4.0 seconds and that it loops forever.
- Three **OrientationInterpolator** nodes named "BarPath1," "BarPath2," and "BarPath3." The three nodes use key fractional times and values to create a 360.0-degree rotation path around the X, Y, or Z axis.

These nodes are wired together to connect the time sensor's **fraction_changed** eventOut to the **set_fraction** eventIn of each **OrientationInterpolator** node. Each interpolator node's **value_changed** eventOut is then routed to one of the three **Transform** node's implied **set_rotation** eventIn.

As the animation ticks through each 4.0-second cycle, the interpolators generate new X, Y, and Z rotations for the three bars. The effect is to create an interesting group of three rotating, intersecting bars that animate endlessly.

```
#VRML V2.0 utf8
Group {
    children [
    # Three rotating bars
        DEF Bar1 Transform {
            children Shape {
                appearance DEF White Appearance {
                    material Material { }
                }
                geometry Box { size 1.5 0.2 0.2 }
            }
        },
        DEF Bar2 Transform {
            children Shape {
                appearance USE White
                geometry Box { size 0.2 1.5 0.2 }
            }
        },
        DEF Bar3 Transform {
            children Shape {
                appearance USE White
                geometry Box { size 0.2 0.2 1.5 }
            }
        },
    # Animation clock
        DEF Clock TimeSensor {
            cycleInterval 4.0
            loop TRUE
        },
    # Animation paths, one for each bar
        DEF BarPath1 OrientationInterpolator {
            key [ 0.0, 0.50, 1.0 ]
            keyValue [
                0.0 0.0 1.0  0.0,
                0.0 0.0 1.0  3.14,
                0.0 0.0 1.0  6.28
            ]
        },
```

Figure 8.7 continues

```
DEF BarPath2 OrientationInterpolator {
    key [ 0.0, 0.50, 1.0 ]
    keyValue [
        1.0 0.0 0.0  0.0,
        1.0 0.0 0.0  3.14,
        1.0 0.0 0.0  6.28
    ]
},
DEF BarPath3 OrientationInterpolator
    key [ 0.0, 0.50, 1.0 ]
    keyValue [
        0.0 1.0 0.0  0.0,
        0.0 1.0 0.0  3.14,
        0.0 1.0 0.0  6.28
    ]
}
    ]
}
ROUTE Clock.fraction_changed TO BarPath1.set_fraction
ROUTE Clock.fraction_changed TO BarPath2.set_fraction
ROUTE Clock.fraction_changed TO BarPath3.set_fraction
ROUTE BarPath1.value_changed TO Bar1.set_rotation
ROUTE BarPath2.value_changed TO Bar2.set_rotation
ROUTE BarPath3.value_changed TO Bar3.set_rotation
```

Figure 8.7   *Three interpolators used to rotate three bars.*

The example in Figure 8.7 uses three **OrientationInterpolator** nodes. You can also mix in **PositionInterpolator** nodes to cause shapes to translate and scale, as well. For example, you can extend the preceding rotating bars example by adding two more interpolators: one interpolator to cause the entire group of shapes to translate around the bouncing path from Figure 8.3 and one interpolator to cause the entire group to grow and shrink using the scaling path from Figure 8.6.

Using Multiple Time Sensors

The prior examples each used a single **TimeSensor** node to clock all interpolators used in the animating world. Changing the cycle length on this time sensor changes the speed of all animating shapes. To individually control the speed of each animating shape, you can use multiple **TimeSensor** nodes, one per interpolator.

Figure 8.8 builds a simple solar system with a stationary sun sphere and three orbiting planet spheres. Each planet is built in its own coordinate system using its own **Transform** node. Three **OrientationInterpolator** nodes and three **TimeSensor** nodes are built as well, one of each for each planet. Routes are wired from each planet's clock to its interpolator and from there to its **Transform** node.

By using one **TimeSensor** node to control each planet's orbit time, this example can use a different cycle length for each planet. The first planet is given a quick orbit time of 2.0 seconds, the second a slower 3.5 seconds, and the third a slow 5.0 seconds.

```
#VRML V2.0 utf8
Group {
    children [
    # Stationary Sun
        Shape {
            appearance DEF White Appearance {
                material Material { }
            }
            geometry Sphere { }
        },
    # Several orbiting planets
        DEF Planet1 Transform {
            translation 2.0 0.0 0.0
            center -2.0 0.0 0.0
            children Shape {
                appearance USE White
                geometry Sphere { radius 0.2 }
            }
        },
        DEF Planet2 Transform {
            translation 3.0 0.0 0.0
            center -3.0 0.0 0.0
            children Shape {
                appearance USE White
                geometry Sphere { radius 0.3 }
            }
        },
        DEF Planet3 Transform {
            translation 4.0 0.0 0.0
            center -4.0 0.0 0.0
            children Shape {
                appearance USE White
                geometry Sphere { radius 0.5 }
            }
        },
    # Animation clocks, one per planet
        DEF Clock1 TimeSensor {
            cycleInterval 2.0
            loop TRUE
        },
        DEF Clock2 TimeSensor {
            cycleInterval 3.5
            loop TRUE
        },
        DEF Clock3 TimeSensor {
            cycleInterval 5.0
            loop TRUE
        },
```

Figure 8.8 continues

```
# Animation paths, one per planet
    DEF PlanetPath1 OrientationInterpolator {
        key [ 0.0, 0.50, 1.0 ]
        keyValue [
            0.0 0.0 1.0  0.0,
            0.0 0.0 1.0  3.14,
            0.0 0.0 1.0  6.28
        ]
    },
    DEF PlanetPath2 OrientationInterpolator {
        key [ 0.0, 0.50, 1.0 ]
        keyValue [
            0.0 0.0 1.0  0.0,
            0.0 0.0 1.0  3.14,
            0.0 0.0 1.0  6.28
        ]
    },
    DEF PlanetPath3 OrientationInterpolator {
        key [ 0.0, 0.50, 1.0 ]
        keyValue [
            0.0 0.0 1.0  0.0,
            0.0 0.0 1.0  3.14,
            0.0 0.0 1.0  6.28
        ]
    }
]
}
ROUTE Clock1.fraction_changed   TO PlanetPath1.set_fraction
ROUTE Clock2.fraction_changed   TO PlanetPath2.set_fraction
ROUTE Clock3.fraction_changed   TO PlanetPath3.set_fraction
ROUTE PlanetPath1.value_changed TO Planet1.set_rotation
ROUTE PlanetPath2.value_changed TO Planet2.set_rotation
ROUTE PlanetPath3.value_changed TO Planet3.set_rotation
```

Figure 8.8 *A group of three orbiting planets, each one using its own **TimeSensor** node to control its orbit time.*

Summary

The **TimeSensor** node creates a clock, which can be used to control animation. The times at which the time sensor starts and stops are set using the **startTime** and **stopTime** fields. Once started, the sensor loops through multiple cycles or a single cycle based on the value of the **loop** field. The length of a cycle, in seconds, is specified using the **cycleLength** field.

While running, the time sensor outputs a stream of events via multiple eventOuts. At each tick, the current absolute time is output via the **time** eventOut, while at the start of each cycle, the current absolute time is output via the **cycleTime** eventOut. During each cycle, the sensor outputs fractional times on its **fraction_changed** eventOut, varying the output from 0.0 at the start of the cycle, to 1.0 at the end.

TimeSensor node fractional times are typically wired to a **PositionInterpolator** node or an **OrientationInterpolator** node. Both nodes specify a list of key fractional times in the **key** field and a list of key values in the **keyValue** field. Each key fractional time specifies a time between 0.0 and 1.0 at which the corresponding key value (a position or a rotation) is to be output from the interpolator node. To create output values between key fractional times, the interpolator node linearly interpolates between adjacent key values in the list and outputs the computed position or rotation.

The **value_changed** eventOut of **PositionInterpolator** and **OrientationInterpolator** nodes is typically wired to a **Transform** node. By wiring a **PositionInterpolator** node to a **Transform** node's implied **set_translation** eventOut, the **Transform** node's coordinate system position can be animated. Similarly, an **OrientationInterpolator** node can be wired to a **Transform** node's implied **set_rotation** eventOut to cause the node's coordinate system orientation to be animated. Finally, a **PositionInterpolator** node's output can be interpreted as a group of three of X, Y, and Z scaling factors that, when routed to a **Transform** node's implied **set_scale** eventOut, can cause the coordinate system's size to be animated.

CHAPTER 9

Sensing Viewer Actions

To make your world interactive, you can attach to a shape a *sensor* that senses viewer actions with a pointing device, such as a mouse. When the viewer clicks on a shape with an attached sensor, the sensor outputs events that can be routed into other nodes to start animations.

The **TouchSensor** node detects a viewer's touch and outputs events describing when and where the viewer touched the sensed shape. The **CylinderSensor**, **PlaneSensor**, and **SphereSensor** nodes also detect when a viewer touches a sensed shape and provide outputs designed for use in changing the position and orientation of the shape.

Understanding How Viewer Actions Are Sensed

Most computers today provide a pointing device to move the cursor on the screen. (For more information, see the sidebars entitled "2-D Pointing Devices" and "3-D Pointing Devices.") A mouse with one, two, or three buttons is probably the most common pointing device, but joysticks, trackballs, touchpads, and other such devices are also available. To interact with an application, the viewer moves the cursor about to point at items of interest. When an interesting item is found, the viewer can perform one of three actions:

- *Move:* without pressing a mouse button, move the cursor over an item.
- *Click:* while the cursor is over an item, press a mouse button, then immediately release the button without moving the mouse.
- *Drag:* while the cursor is over an item, press a mouse button, move the mouse, then release the button.

In most applications, each of these actions causes something specific to happen. In Microsoft Windows, for instance, movement of the cursor so that it rests on a button causes a message to pop up telling viewers what will happen if they press the button. In a drawing application, clicking on a shape selects the shape so that its size or color can be changed. Similarly, in a drawing application, a drag action moves a shape across the screen.

In VRML, you can attach a sensor to a shape to detect move, click, and drag viewer actions. You can wire the outputs of a sensor into a circuit to cause shapes to move and animations to play when the viewer interacts with a *sensed shape*, a shape monitored by a sensor.

Sensing Touch

A **TouchSensor** node can be added to any group, such as those created by the **Group** and **Transform** nodes. When in such a group, the **TouchSensor** node senses when the viewer moves over, clicks, or drags on any shape built in that group. The ability of a **TouchSensor** node to sense all the shapes in a group enables you to create complex sensed shapes. You can, for instance, build an entire airplane within a group, then attach to the group a **TouchSensor** node. When the viewer clicks anywhere on the airplane, the sensor detects the touch and sends output. You can use the sensor output to trigger an animation that flys the airplane around the room.

A **TouchSensor** node can sense a viewer's move actions. When the viewer's cursor moves over a sensed group of shapes, the **TouchSensor** node outputs **TRUE** using its **isOver** eventOut. When the viewer moves the cursor off the shape, the node outputs **FALSE** using its **isOver** eventOut. Using these outputs, you can route the output of the **isOver** eventOut into the **set_enabled** eventIn of a **TimeSensor** node, causing the time sensor to start and stop an animation as the viewer's cursor moves over a shape and then off of it again.

A **TouchSensor** node also can sense click and drag actions. When the viewer moves the cursor over a sensed group of shapes and presses a mouse button, the **TouchSensor** node outputs **TRUE** using its **isActive** eventOut. When the viewer releases the mouse button, the **TouchSensor** node outputs **FALSE** using its **isActive** eventOut and sends the current absolute time using its **touchTime** eventOut. You can use these outputs to start and stop animations. For example, you can route the **touchTime** eventOut to the **set_startTime** eventIn of a **TimeSensor** node to cause an animation to start playing when a shape is touched.

During move, click, and drag actions, the **TouchSensor** node also outputs information about where on the shape the cursor is resting. These shape-location outputs can be used to control animation, as well.

Sensing Motion

In a standard drawing program, clicking and dragging a shape moves the shape around the screen. You can perform similar actions in a VRML world by using three special-purpose sensor nodes: **CylinderSensor, PlaneSensor,** and **SphereSensor.** All three nodes act similarly to the **TouchSensor** node, but they also provide outputs designed for use in moving and orienting shapes. Using these nodes, you can enable a viewer to pick up and move shapes in your world.

Similar to the **TouchSensor** node, the **CylinderSensor, PlaneSensor,** and **Sphere-Sensor** nodes all can be included within any group. When in a group, these nodes sense viewer actions on any shape in that group. When the viewer moves the cursor over a sensed group of shapes and presses a mouse button, the sensor outputs **TRUE** using its **isActive** eventOut. When the viewer releases the mouse button, the sensor outputs **FALSE** using its **isActive** eventOut. You can use this output to trigger an animation.

The **PlaneSensor** node senses viewer drag actions, computes translation distances, and outputs these using its **translation_changed** eventOut. By routing this output to the **set_translation** eventIn of a **Transform** node, the viewer can drag a shape around the world. To the viewer, it feels as if the shape is being dragged on a flat plane, like a floor or wall. For example, you can use a **PlaneSensor** node to enable a viewer to drag a chair across the floor of a room or position a painting on a wall.

The **SphereSensor** node senses viewer drag actions, computes rotation axes and angles, and outputs these using its **rotation_changed** eventOut. By routing this output to the **set_rotation** eventIn of a **Transform** node, the viewer can rotate a shape in your world. To the viewer, it feels as if the shape is a ball that can be rolled in any direction. For example, you can use a **SphereSensor** node to spin a globe or orient a spaceship.

The **CylinderSensor** node also senses viewer drag actions, computes rotation axes and angles, and outputs these using its **rotation_changed** eventOut. This output can be routed to the **set_rotation** eventIn of a **Transform** node to enable a viewer to turn a shape. To the viewer it feels as if the shape is a disk, like a record turntable, or as if the shape is a cylinder, like a rolling pin, that can be turned about an axis. For example, you can use a **CylinderSensor** node to turn a car wheel, swivel a chair, or turn a revolving door.

The **PlaneSensor** and **CylinderSensor** nodes have fields that enable you to limit the range of their motion. For a **CylinderSensor** node, for instance, you can limit the rotation angle to fall between a minimum and a maximum. Similarly, for a **Plane-Sensor** node, you can limit the translation to fall within a rectangular region with minimum and maximum limits.

Using Multiple Sensors

You can use multiple sensors, each sensing viewer actions on the same shapes. When you use multiple sensors, the sensors either override one another or work together depending on how the sensors are contained in groups.

Multiple Sensors in the Same Group

When multiple sensor nodes are siblings in the same group, they all simultaneously sense viewer actions on the same group of shapes.

For example, you can use a **TouchSensor** node to detect when the viewer's cursor has moved over a shape, and a **PlaneSensor** node to enable the viewer to drag the shape around. Both sensor nodes can be included in the same group to simultaneously detect viewer actions on the group's shapes.

Multiple Sensors in Nested Groups

When multiple sensors are in different groups, and those groups are nested within each other, then the sensor that is in the most nested group overrides those in outer groups.

For example, imagine building a lamp with an on/off switch. The on/off switch is contained in a group together with a **TouchSensor** node to turn the lamp on and off when the viewer touches the switch. The on/off switch group and its **TouchSensor** node are contained within a larger group that builds the lamp. The larger group includes a **PlaneSensor** node so that a viewer can move the lamp around on a table. The following abbreviated VRML text shows such a collection of nodes: a lamp with a nested group to build the lamp's on/off switch.

```
# Whole Lamp
Group {
    children [
        PlaneSensor { },
        ... shapes and groups to build the lamp body ...

        # On-off Switch
        Group {
            children [
                TouchSensor { },
                ... shapes and groups to build the lamp's on-off switch ...
            ]
        }
    ]
}
```

With this structure for building the lamp, there is a potential problem. The **Plane-Sensor** node senses the entire lamp shape. The **TouchSensor** node, however, senses only the on/off switch part of the shape. A potential problem occurs if the viewer touches the on/off switch that appears to be sensed by both sensor nodes.

In VRML, however, only the innermost sensor detects the touch. In this case, the **TouchSensor** node detects the touch to the on/off switch, and the **PlaneSensor** node ignores it. If, however, the viewer touches some other part of the lamp that isn't sensed by the **TouchSensor** node, then the **PlaneSensor** detects the touch and acts appropriately. So, nested sensors, like the **TouchSensor** node on the lamp, take priority over outer sensors, like the lamp's **PlaneSensor** node.

This behavior of sensors in nested groups enables you to build up complex shapes out of independent smaller shapes. You can, for instance, build a generic on/off switch shape with a **TouchSensor** node. You can test this generic switch shape and make sure it works independently of where you use it. That use might, for instance, be part of a lamp, a spaceship dashboard, or an elevator control panel. Each of those uses might add additional sensors to move the lamp, orient the dashboard, or open the elevator control panel. In each case, however, the additional sensors that manipulate the larger lamp, dashboard, or control panel shapes don't inhibit the on/off switch's functionality. Inner, nested sensors always take priority.

Sensor Offsets

Each time a viewer drags a shape sensed by a **CylinderSensor, PlaneSensor,** or **SphereSensor** node, the sensor outputs a series of values that are typically routed to a **Transform** node, causing the shape to move. When the viewer releases the mouse button and finishes the drag, the sensor stops outputting values, and the shape stops moving. When the viewer drags the shape again, the shape can either continue moving from the position where the viewer left it, or the shape can begin moving from initial values computed by the sensor. The choice between these two behaviors is controlled by the **autoOffset** field of the sensor nodes.

When the value of the **autoOffset** field is **TRUE,** the sensor remembers its prior translation or rotation value in the sensor's **offset** field. The next time the viewer drags the same shape, the offset is used so that the shape starts from its new position.

When the value of the **autoOffset** field is **FALSE,** the sensor does not remember its prior translation or rotation value. Each time the viewer drags the shape, translation or rotation starts from initial values computed by the sensor.

You can use these two offset behaviors to create different interaction styles for the shapes in your world. Typically, the **autoOffset** field value is **TRUE,** and sensors always remember where they last translated or rotated shapes.

Pointing Devices

When the viewer moves a 2- or 3-D pointing device, a cursor moves on the computer screen. As the cursor moves, an imaginary ray is repeatedly fired through the cursor and into the world. If the ray strikes a shape, then the cursor is said to be *over* that shape. As the cursor moves and fires the imaginary ray, the location at which the ray strikes the sensed shape is called the *hit point*. As the cursor moves over the shape, the hit-point location changes.

SIDEBAR: 2-D POINTING DEVICES Most computers today come equipped with a *2-D pointing device,* such as a mouse, trackball, trackpad, or joystick. Most VRML browsers will accept any of these as the pointing device for sensing viewer actions.

When using a 2-D pointing device with multiple buttons, such as a multibutton mouse, the leftmost button is typically considered the primary pointing-device button. It is this primary button that is sensed by the sensor nodes. The remaining buttons are ignored by the sensor nodes, but may be used by the VRML browser to access menus or control movement through the world.

SIDEBAR: 3-D POINTING DEVICES *Three-dimensional pointing devices,* such as a data glove or a CAVE wand, typically move a 3-D cursor in the virtual world. A *3-D cursor* can move horizontally and vertically, like a cursor controlled with a standard mouse, and it can also move forward and back within the world.

When using a 3-D cursor, the VRML sensor nodes only detect its presence over a shape if the 3-D cursor is on-screen. If the 3-D cursor is moved off the screen, the sensor nodes will not detect whether it is over a shape.

Since a 3-D cursor can move back away from the viewer in the world, there are times when the 3-D cursor may be obscured by shapes in the world. This can confuse what it means to be *over a shape.* In such situations, some VRML browsers may treat the cursor as being *over* the first shape struck by an imaginary straight line from the viewer through the 3-D cursor. That first shape may be behind, or even in front of, the 3-D cursor. Other VRML browsers will only consider a 3-D cursor to be over a shape if the shape is further away than the 3-D cursor.

When using a mouse, pressing the mouse's button is considered *touching* the sensed shape. When using a 3-D cursor, VRML browsers may instead register a touch when the 3-D cursor is moved close to, or touches, a sensed shape.

The **TouchSensor** Node Syntax

The TouchSensor node creates a sensor to detect viewer actions and convert them to outputs suitable for triggering animation. The TouchSensor node may be the child of any group, and it senses viewer actions for any shape built in that group or in any of that group's descendants. Pointer-device movement, such as that of a mouse, generates outputs when over a sensed shape. To the viewer, it feels as if the sensed shape is a button in a 3-D user interface. Touching the button shape generates outputs that are typically used to trigger animation in the world.

SYNTAX   TouchSensor node

```
TouchSensor {
    enabled              TRUE    # exposedField  SFBool
    isActive                     # eventOut      SFBool
    isOver                       # eventOut      SFBool
    touchTime                    # eventOut      SFTime
    hitPoint_changed             # eventOut      SFVec3f
    hitNormal_changed            # eventOut      SFVec3f
    hitTexCoord_changed          # eventOut      SFVec2f
}
```

The value of the **enabled** exposed field specifies whether the sensor is turned on or off. If the field value is **TRUE**, the sensor is on and can generate outputs. If the field is **FALSE**, the sensor is off and no outputs are generated, except those generated in response to a change in an exposed field (for example, **enabled_changed**). The default value for the field is **TRUE**.

When the viewer moves the cursor over a shape sensed by a **TouchSensor** node, the sensor node outputs **TRUE** using the **isOver** eventOut. When the viewer moves the cursor off the sensed shape, **FALSE** is output using the **isOver** eventOut.

As the viewer moves the cursor over a shape, the hit-point location's 3-D coordinate (in the sensor's parent group coordinate system) is output using the **hitPoint_changed** eventOut. Along with the changed hit point, the normal vector and texture coordinate at the sensed shape's hit point are output using the **hitTexCoord_changed** and **hitNormal_changed** eventOuts. Normal vectors and texture coordinates are discussed in Chapters 18 and 19, respectively.

When the viewer presses the pointing-device button while the cursor is over a sensed shape, the sensor node outputs **TRUE** using the **isActive** eventOut. When the viewer releases the pointing-device button, **FALSE** is output using the **isActive** eventOut. If the cursor is over the sensed shape when the viewer releases the pointing-device button, and **FALSE** is sent using the **isActive** eventOut, the current absolute time is also output using the **touchTime** eventOut.

While the pointing-device button is held down over a shape, and after **TRUE** has been output using the **isActive** eventOut, the sensor gains exclusive use of the pointing device until the viewer releases the pointing-device button and **FALSE** is output using the **isActive** eventOut. During this exclusive use, no other pointing-device sensors in the world can be activated.

You can change the value of the **enabled** exposed field by routing an event to the exposed field's implied **set_enabled** eventIn. If you change the field from **TRUE** to **FALSE,** and the sensor is currently active, then the sensor is deactivated, and **FALSE** is sent using the **isActive** eventOut. In any case, when you change the field value, the value is output using the exposed field's implied **enabled_changed** eventOut.

The sensor only updates its outputs as the viewer moves the cursor. If the cursor remains stationary, no outputs are generated. If the sensed shape moves out from under a stationary cursor, or another shape moves in the way, no changes are made to the sensor's outputs until the viewer moves the cursor.

If a sensor is instanced using **DEF** and **USE,** the sensor senses viewer actions over any shape in the parent group of any instance of the sensor.

The **PlaneSensor** Node Syntax

The **PlaneSensor** node creates a sensor to detect viewer actions and convert them to outputs suitable for manipulating shapes as if they were moving along a 2-D plane. The **PlaneSensor** node may be the child of any group, and it senses viewer actions for any shape built in that group or in any of that group's descendants. Sensor node outputs are typically routed to a **Transform** node to cause a shape to translate. Pointer-device movement, such as that of a mouse, while the pointer-device button is held down generates translation outputs that feels to the viewer as if the shape is sliding along the XY plane of the parent group's coordinate system.

SYNTAX	**PlaneSensor node**

```
PlaneSensor {
    enabled                 TRUE            # exposedField   SFBool
    autoOffset              TRUE            # exposedField   SFBool
    offset                  0.0  0.0 0.0    # exposedField   SFVec3f
    maxPosition            -1.0 -1.0        # exposedField   SFVec2f
    minPosition             0.0  0.0        # exposedField   SFVec2f
    isActive                                # eventOut       SFBool
    translation_changed                     # eventOut       SFVec3f
    trackPoint_changed                      # eventOut       SFVec3f
}
```

The value of the **enabled** exposed field is discussed in the section entitled "The **TouchSensor** Node Syntax."

When the viewer presses the pointing-device button while the cursor is over a sensed shape, the sensor node outputs **TRUE** using the **isActive** eventOut. When the viewer releases the pointing-device button, **FALSE** is output using the **isActive** eventOut.

Exclusive use of the pointing device while the button is pressed is discussed in the section entitled "The **TouchSensor** Node Syntax."

As the viewer moves the cursor over a sensed shape, the location of the hit point establishes the surface location of an imaginary, flat *track plane* that passes through the hit point and is oriented parallel to the XY plane in the sensor's parent group coordinate system. The hit point acts as the origin of the track plane. Each time the viewer moves the cursor while the pointing-device button is still pressed, a *track point* is slid along the track plane, starting from an initial position at the hit point. Horizontal cursor motion slides the track point horizontally, while vertical cursor motion slides the track point vertically on the plane. As the viewer changes the track point's location, the new track point's 3-D, track-plane coordinate is output using the **trackPoint_changed** eventOut.

The **autoOffset, offset, maxPosition,** and **minPosition** field values work together to convert the track point into a translation value output using the **translation_changed** eventOut each time the viewer changes the track point. This process includes:

- Computing the distance between the track point and the origin of the track plane to form a 3-D translation value
- Optionally offsetting the translation value by adding to it the value of the **offset** field
- Optionally limiting the translation to a range of X and Y values, as established by the values of the **minPosition** and **maxPosition** fields
- Outputting the offset, limited translation using the **translation_changed** eventOut

The output translation value is typically routed to a **Transform** node, causing a shape to translate within a plane as the viewer moves a pointing device. The track-point limits enable you to restrict the range of movement of the translated shape.

The limit and offset features controlled by these fields do not affect the track-point location output using the **trackPoint_changed** eventOut. These features only affect how the track point is used in computing the translation value output using the **translation_changed** eventOut.

Using the distance between the track point and the origin of the track plane, the browser computes a 3-D translation value. The value of the **autoOffset** field specifies whether or not the translation should be offset. When the **autoOffset** field value is **TRUE**, the 3-D translation value stored in the **offset** field is added to the translation. When the **autoOffset** field value is **FALSE**, the **offset** field value is not used, and the translation is not offset. The default value for the **autoOffset** field is **TRUE**, and the default **offset** field value is zero.

The values of the **minPosition** and **maxPosition** fields specify X and Y translation limits. The **minPosition** field value specifies the minimum allowed X and Y translation values, while the **maxPosition** field value specifies the maximum allowed X and Y values. Translation values that pass any limit are clamped back to that limit.

You can use the X component of the **minPosition** and **maxPosition** field values in three ways:

- If the minimum X value is less than the maximum X value, then the translation is limited to X-component values between the minimum and maximum.
- If the minimum X value is equal to the maximum X value, then the translation's X component is constrained to be that value.
- If the minimum X value is greater than the maximum X value, then the translation is unconstrained in the X direction.

You can use the Y component of the **minPosition** and **maxPosition** field values in ways analogous to the X component's use. By using these three behaviors, translation limits can be established in X, Y, or both directions. The default values for these fields establish no track-point limiting in the X or Y directions.

After offsetting and limiting the computed translation value, the value is output using the **translation_changed** eventOut.

When the viewer releases the pointing-device button, the sensor stops sending outputs. If the value of the **autoOffset** field is **TRUE**, the last output translation value is stored in the node's **offset** exposed field and is output using the implied **offset_changed** eventOut of the exposed field. Using VRML's offset feature ensures that each subsequent drag of a shape begins where the previous drag ended.

Changing the value of the **enabled** exposed field is discussed in the section entitled "The **TouchSensor** Node Syntax."

The values of the **autoOffset**, **offset**, **minPosition**, and **maxPosition** exposed fields can be changed by routing an event to the exposed fields' implied **set_autoOffset**, **set_offset**, **set_minPosition**, and **set_maxPosition** eventIns, respectively. When any of these fields are changed, the new value is output using the exposed field's implied **autoOffset_changed**, **offset_changed**, **minPosition_changed**, and **maxPosition_changed** eventOuts, respectively.

Discussion of sensor output is continued in the section entitled "The **TouchSensor** Node Syntax."

Using instances of sensors is discussed in the section entitled "The **TouchSensor** Node Syntax."

The **SphereSensor** Node Syntax

The **SphereSensor** node creates a sensor to detect viewer actions and convert them to outputs suitable for manipulating shapes in ways that feel to viewers as if they are turning a sphere. The **SphereSensor** node may be the child of any group, and it senses viewer actions for any shape built in that group or in any of that group's descendants. Sensor node outputs are typically routed to a **Transform** node to cause a shape to rotate. Pointer-device movement, such as that of a mouse, while the pointer-device button is held down generates rotation outputs that feel to viewers as if they are rolling a ball.

SYNTAX	SphereSensor node

```
SphereSensor {
    enabled             TRUE            # exposedField  SFBool
    autoOffset          TRUE            # exposedField  SFBool
    offset              0.0 1.0 0.0  0.0 # exposedField  SFRotation
    isActive                            # eventOut      SFBool
    rotation_changed                    # eventOut      SFRotation
    trackPoint_changed                  # eventOut      SFVec3f
}
```

The value of the **enabled** exposed field is discussed in the section entitled "The **TouchSensor** Node Syntax." The **isActive** eventOut is discussed in the section entitled "The **PlaneSensor** Node Syntax."

Exclusive use of the pointing device while the button is pressed is discussed in the section entitled "The **TouchSensor** Node Syntax."

As the viewer moves the cursor over a sensed shape, the location of the hit point establishes the surface location of an imaginary *track sphere* whose center is at the origin of the sensor's parent group coordinate system. The distance between the coordinate system origin and the hit point establishes the radius of the track sphere.

Each time the viewer moves the cursor while pressing the pointing-device button, a track point slides around the surface of the track sphere, starting from an initial position at the hit point. Side-to-side cursor motion slides the track point east and west, while vertical cursor motion slides the track point north and south on the sphere. As the viewer changes the track point's location, the new track point's 3-D, track-sphere coordinate is output using the **trackPoint_changed** eventOut.

The **autoOffset** and **offset** field values work together to convert the track point into a rotation value output using the **rotation_changed** eventOut each time the viewer changes the track point. This process includes:

- Computing a rotation axis and angle using the angular difference between the track point and hit point locations on the track sphere
- Optionally offsetting the rotation value by adding to it the value of the **offset** field
- Outputting the offset rotation using the **rotation_changed** eventOut

The offset features controlled by these fields do not affect the track-point location output on the **trackPoint_changed** eventOut. These features only affect how the track point is used in computing the rotation value output using the **rotation_changed** eventOut.

The value of the **autoOffset** field specifies whether the rotation should be offset. When the **autoOffset** field value is **TRUE,** the 3-D rotation value stored in the **offset** field is added to the rotation before the value is output using the **rotation_changed** eventOut. When the **autoOffset** field value is **FALSE,** the **offset** field value is not used, and the original rotation is output using the **rotation_changed** eventOut. The default value for the **autoOffset** field is **TRUE,** and the default **offset** field value is zero.

When the viewer releases the pointing-device button, the sensor stops sending outputs. If the value of the **autoOffset** field is **TRUE,** the last output rotation value is stored in the node's **offset** exposed field and is output using the implied **offset_changed** eventOut of the exposed field. Using VRML's offset feature ensures that each subsequent drag of a shape begins where the previous drag ended.

Changing the value of the **enabled** exposed field is discussed in the section entitled "The **TouchSensor** Node Syntax."

The values of the **autoOffset** and **offset** exposed fields can be changed by routing an event to the exposed fields' implied **set_autoOffset** and **set_offset** eventIns, respectively. When any of these fields are changed, the new value is output using the exposed field's implied **autoOffset_changed** and **offset_changed** eventOuts, respectively.

Discussion of sensor output is continued in the section entitled "The **TouchSensor** Node Syntax."

Using instances of sensors is discussed in the section entitled "The **TouchSensor** Node Syntax."

The **CylinderSensor** Node Syntax

The **CylinderSensor** node creates a sensor to detect viewer actions and convert them to output suitable for manipulating shapes in ways that feel to viewers as if they are turning a cylinder about an axis. The **CylinderSensor** node may be the child of any group, and it senses viewer actions for any shape built in that group or in any of that group's descendants. Sensor node outputs are typically routed to a **Transform** node to cause a shape to rotate. Pointer-device movement, such as that of a mouse, while the pointer-device button is held down generates rotation outputs that feel to the viewers as if they are turning the shape around the Y axis of the parent group's coordinate system.

SYNTAX   **CylinderSensor node**

```
CylinderSensor {
    enabled             TRUE      # exposedField  SFBool
    diskAngle           0.262     # exposedField  SFFloat
    autoOffset          TRUE      # exposedField  SFBool
    offset              0.0       # exposedField  SFFloat
    maxAngle            -1.0      # exposedField  SFFloat
    minAngle            0.0       # exposedField  SFFloat
    isActive                      # eventOut      SFBool
    rotation_changed              # eventOut      SFRotation
    trackPoint_changed            # eventOut      SFVec3f
}
```

The value of the **enabled** exposed field is discussed in the section entitled "The **TouchSensor** Node Syntax." The **isActive** eventOut is discussed in the section entitled "The **PlaneSensor** Node Syntax."

Exclusive use of the pointing device while the button is pressed is discussed in the section entitled "The **TouchSensor** Node Syntax."

As the viewer moves the cursor over a cylinder-sensed shape, an angle is formed between the imaginary straight line and the Y axis of the sensor's parent group coordinate system. This angle is compared to the value of the **diskAngle** field, and the **CylinderSensor** node adopts one of two related behaviors depending on this angle.

- When the viewer is above (or below) the sensed shape, looking down (or up) the Y axis, the angle between the imaginary straight line and the Y axis is small. If this is *less than* the value of the **diskAngle** field, the **CylinderSensor** node acts as if a disk is being rotated around the Y axis. Circular movement of the pointing device spins the disk, turning it counterclockwise as the pointing device moves in counterclockwise circles, and clockwise in response to clockwise movement.

  When the **CylinderSensor** node adopts this disklike behavior, the location of the hit point establishes the surface of a *track disk* in the XZ plane of the sensor's parent group coordinate system. The center of the track disk is at the origin of the coordinate system. The X axis of the coordinate system provides a zero line on the disk. When the viewer moves the cursor while pressing the pointing-device button, a track point slides around on the track disk beginning at the hit-point location. The cursor's counterclockwise, circular motion spins the track point around the track disk's Y axis in a counterclockwise direction. The cursor's clockwise motion spins the track point around the track disk's Y axis in a clockwise direction. As the viewer changes the track point's location, the new track point's 3-D, track-disk coordinate is output using the **trackPoint_changed** eventOut.

- When the viewer is beside or in front of the sensed shape, looking approximately perpendicular to the Y axis, the ray angle is large. If the angle between the imaginary straight line and the Y axis is *greater than* the value of the **diskAngle** field, the **CylinderSensor** node acts as if a vertical rolling pin is being rotated about the Y axis. Side-to-side movement of the pointing device rotates the rolling pin, turning it clockwise as the pointing device moves left and counterclockwise as the pointing device moves right.

When the **CylinderSensor** node adopts this rolling-pin-like behavior, the location of the hit point establishes the surface of a *track cylinder* aligned along the Y axis of the sensor's parent group coordinate system. The center of the track cylinder is at the origin of the coordinate system. The line from the nearest point on the Y axis to the hit point provides a zero-line radius for the cylinder. When the viewer moves the cursor while pressing the pointing-device button, a track point slides around on the surface of the track cylinder beginning at the hit-point location. The cursor's side-to-side motion slides the track point around the equator of the track cylinder. The cursor's vertical motion has no effect on the track point. As the viewer changes the track point's location, the new track point's 3-D, track-cylinder coordinate is output using the **trackPoint_changed** eventOut.

The default value for the **diskAngle** field is 15.0 degrees (0.262 radians). Typically, this disk angle provides an intuitive feel for the sensor. When the viewer is above a sensed shape, looking down, the **CylinderSensor** node provides a disk feel. When the viewer is beside the shape, the sensor provides a rolling pin feel.

The **autoOffset, offset, maxAngle,** and **minAngle** field values work together to convert the track point to a rotation value output using the **rotation_changed** eventOut each time the viewer changes the track point. This process includes:

- Computing a rotation axis and angle using the difference between the track point's location and the zero line on the track disk or track cylinder
- Optionally offsetting this rotation angle by adding to it the value of the **offset** field
- Optionally limiting the rotation angle to a range of angles, as established by the values of the **minAngle** and **maxAngle** fields
- Outputting the rotation value using the **rotation_changed** eventOut

The output rotation value is typically routed to a **Transform** node to cause a shape to rotate about the Y axis as the viewer moves the pointing device. The angle limits enable you to restrict the rotated shape's range of movement.

The offset and limit features controlled by these fields do not affect the track-point location output using the **trackPoint_changed** eventOut. These features only affect how the track point is used in computing the rotation value output using the **rotation_changed** eventOut.

The value of the **autoOffset** field specifies whether the rotation should be offset. When the **autoOffset** field value is **TRUE**, the rotation angle stored in the **offset** field is added to the computed rotation angle. When the **autoOffset** field value is **FALSE**, the **offset** field value is not used, and the rotation is not offset. The default value for the **autoOffset** field is **TRUE** and for the **offset** field is zero.

The values of the **minAngle** and **maxAngle** fields specify angular limits for the rotation, measured in radians. The **minAngle** field value specifies the minimum permitted angle while the **maxAngle** field value specifies the maximum permitted angle. Rotation angles less than or greater than these limits are clamped back to the limit. If the **minAngle** field value is greater than the **maxAngle** field value, then angles are unlimited. The default values for these fields indicate unlimited angles.

After offsetting and limiting the computed rotation value, the value is output on the **rotation_changed** eventOut.

The changing value of the **enabled** exposed field is discussed in the section entitled "The **TouchSensor** Node Syntax."

The values of the **autoOffset, offset, minAngle,** and **maxAngle** exposed fields can be changed by routing an event to the exposed fields' implied **set_autoOffset, set_offset, set_minAngle,** and **set_maxAngle** eventIns, respectively. When any of these fields are changed, the new value is output using the exposed field's implied **autoOffset_changed, offset_changed, minAngle_changed,** and **maxAngle_changed** eventOuts, respectively.

Discussion of sensor output is continued in the section entitled "The **TouchSensor** Node Syntax."

Using instances of sensors is discussed in the section entitled "The **TouchSensor** Node Syntax."

Experimenting with Sensors

The following examples provide a more detailed examination of the ways in which the **TouchSensor, PlaneSensor, SphereSensor,** and **CylinderSensor** nodes can be used and how they interact with nodes discussed in previous chapters.

In all of the following examples, the hit-point outputs from the **TouchSensor** node, and the track-point outputs from the **PlaneSensor, SphereSensor,** and **CylinderSensor** nodes are unused. Typically, the hit-point and track-point outputs are only used in conjunction with scripts and the **Script** node (discussed in Chapter 30).

Triggering Animation with Cursor Proximity

Recall that a **TimeSensor** node has an **enabled** exposed field. When this field's value is **FALSE,** the timer is dormant and outputs no values. If this field's value is **TRUE,** the timer starts running when the timer's start time is reached. If you wire the **Time-Sensor** node's **enabled** exposed field into a circuit, you can automatically enable and disable the timer, turning on and off any animation controlled by that timer.

The VRML text in Figure 9.1 builds a cube shape sensed by a **TouchSensor** node. The **TouchSensor** node's **isOver** eventOut is routed to a **TimeSensor** node. The **TimeSensor** node is routed to an **OrientationInterpolator** node which routes to the cube shape's **Transform** node. When the cursor moves over the cube, the **Touch-Sensor** node outputs TRUE using its **isOver** eventOut, which enables the **TimeSen-**

sor node, drives the **OrientationInterpolator** node, and spins the cube. When the cursor moves off the cube, **FALSE** is sent using the **TouchSensor** node's **isOver** eventOut, disabling the **TimeSensor** node and stopping the animation.

```
#VRML V2.0 utf8
Group {
    children [
    # Rotating Cube
        DEF Cube Transform {
            children Shape {
                appearance Appearance {
                    material Material { }
                }
                geometry Box { }
            }
        },
    # Sensor
        DEF Touch TouchSensor { },
    # Animation clock
        DEF Clock TimeSensor {
            enabled FALSE
            cycleInterval 4.0
            loop TRUE
        },
    # Animation path
        DEF CubePath OrientationInterpolator {
            key [ 0.0, 0.50, 1.0 ]
            keyValue [
                0.0 1.0 0.0  0.0,
                0.0 1.0 0.0  3.14,
                0.0 1.0 0.0  6.28
            ]
        }
    ]
}
ROUTE Touch.isOver          TO Clock.set_enabled
ROUTE Clock.fraction_changed TO CubePath.set_fraction
ROUTE CubePath.value_changed TO Cube.set_rotation
```

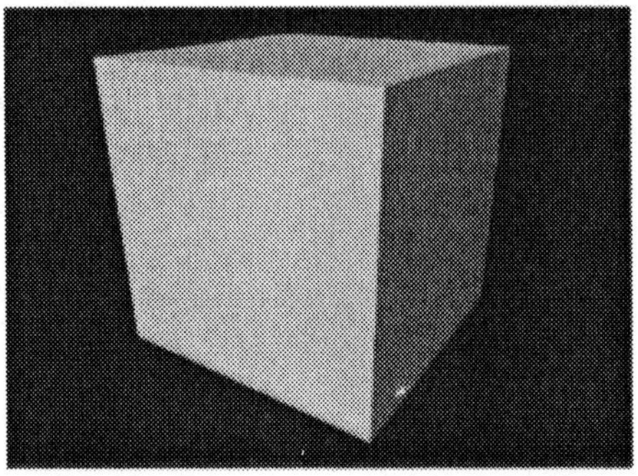

Figure 9.1   *A cube that spins when the viewer's cursor moves over it.*

Triggering Animations with Touch

Recall that a **TimeSensor** node has a start time and a stop time. If the start time is set to a time greater than or equal to the stop time, then the timer starts running at the start time and continues forever (if the **loop** field value is **TRUE**), or runs only for a single cycle (if the **loop** field value is **FALSE**). If you wire a circuit into a **Time-Sensor** node's **startTime** exposed field, you can set the time at which the sensor starts running, and thereby control the start time of any animation to which the **TimeSensor** node is wired.

In Figure 9.2, the **TouchSensor** node's **touchTime** eventOut is routed to a **Time-Sensor** node. The **TimeSensor** node output drives an **OrientationInterpolator** node, which routes to a cube shape's **Transform** node and spins the cube. When the viewer touches the sensed shape, the touch time sets the **TimeSensor** node's starting time, and the animation begins. By using **FALSE** value for the **TimeSensor** node's **loop** field, the timer runs for only a single cycle before stopping. When the viewer touches the sensed shape again, the **TimeSensor** node starts again, and the animation runs through another cycle.

```
#VRML V2.0 utf8
Group {
    children [
    # Rotating Cube
        DEF Cube Transform {
            children Shape {
                appearance Appearance {
                    material Material { }
                }
                geometry Box { }
            }
        },
    # Sensor
        DEF Touch TouchSensor { },
    # Animation clock
        DEF Clock TimeSensor { cycleInterval 4.0 },
    # Animation path
        DEF CubePath OrientationInterpolator {
            key [ 0.0, 0.50, 1.0 ]
            keyValue [
                0.0 1.0 0.0  0.0,
                0.0 1.0 0.0  3.14,
                0.0 1.0 0.0  6.28
            ]
        }
    ]
}
ROUTE Touch.touchTime        TO Clock.set_startTime
ROUTE Clock.fraction_changed TO CubePath.set_fraction
ROUTE CubePath.value_changed TO Cube.set_rotation
```

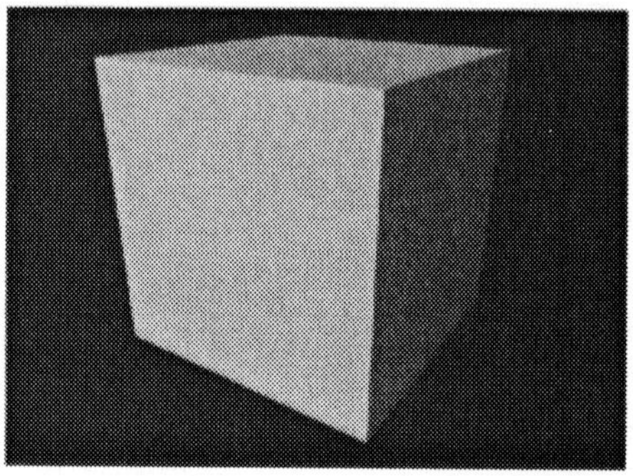

Figure 9.2 *A cube that spins when the viewer touches it.*

Translating Shapes on a Plane

The **translation changed** eventOut of a **PlaneSensor** node is designed to be routed to the **translation** exposed field of a **Transform** node. Once routed, the viewer can drag a sensed shape back and forth on the XY plane of the sensor's parent coordinate system.

Figure 9.3 builds a cube sensed by a **PlaneSensor** node. The sensor's **translation_changed** eventOut is routed to a **Transform** node surrounding the cube. When the viewer drags over the cube, the cube moves in the XY plane.

```
#VRML V2.0 utf8
Group {
    children [
        DEF Cube Transform {
            children Shape {
                appearance Appearance {
                    material Material { }
                }
                geometry Box { }
            }
        },
        DEF Sensor PlaneSensor { }
    ]
}
ROUTE Sensor.translation_changed TO Cube.set_translation
```

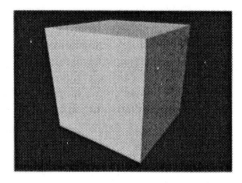

Figure 9.3 *A cube that translates in the XY plane when the viewer drags it.*

Using a **PlaneSensor** node, you can translate a shape in planes other than the XY plane by rotating the coordinate system of the translated shape. For example, Figure 9.4 uses the cube from Figure 9.3, but adds another **Transform** node around the cube and its **Transform** node. The outer **Transform** node rotates the coordinate system so that it lies flat along the world's horizontal XZ plane. Now, when the viewer drags the shape, the cube moves left and right, forward and back, along a horizontal plane. This technique enables the viewer to translate a shape in any direction.

```
#VRML V2.0 utf8
Group {
    children [
        Transform {
            rotation 1.0 0.0 0.0 -1.57
            children DEF Cube Transform {
                children Shape {
                    appearance Appearance {
                        material Material { }
                    }
                    geometry Box { }
                }
            }
        },
        DEF Sensor PlaneSensor {
            minPosition -2.0 -2.0
            maxPosition  2.0  2.0
        }
    ]
}
ROUTE Sensor.translation_changed TO Cube.set_translation
```

Figure 9.4 *A cube that translates within a limited range of the XZ plane when the viewer drags it.*

Figure 9.4 also uses the **minPosition** and **maxPosition** fields to limit the range of motion of the translating cube. Using these fields, you ensure that a shape moves within a constrained area, such as the floor space of a room.

Figure 9.5 uses multiple **PlaneSensor** nodes to build a world with four stacking blocks. Each block shape has its own **PlaneSensor** node. The viewer can drag each block around independently. Notice that the **PlaneSensor** node's **offset** field value is set to the initial, translated position of each block. This ensures that when the viewer starts dragging a block, the block moves relative to this initial position.

```
#VRML V2.0 utf8
Group {
    children [
        Group {
            children [
                DEF Block1 Transform {
                    children DEF BlockShape Shape {
                        appearance Appearance {
                            material Material { }
                        }
                        geometry Box { }
                    }
                },
                DEF Block1Sensor PlaneSensor {
                    offset 0.0 0.0 0.0
                }
            ]
        },
        Group {
            children [
                DEF Block2 Transform {
                    translation 2.5 0.0 0.0
                    children USE BlockShape
                },
                DEF Block2Sensor PlaneSensor {
                    offset 2.5 0.0 0.0
                }
            ]
        },
        Group {
            children [
                DEF Block3 Transform {
                    translation 1.5 2.0 0.0
                    children USE BlockShape
                },
                DEF Block3Sensor PlaneSensor {
                    offset 1.5 2.0 0.0
                }
            ]
        },
```

Figure 9.5 continues

```
        Group {
            children [
                DEF Block4 Transform {
                    translation 0.75 4.0 0.0
                    children USE BlockShape
                },
                DEF Block4Sensor PlaneSensor {
                    offset 0.75 4.0 0.0
                }
            ]
        }
    ]
}
ROUTE Block1Sensor.translation_changed TO Block1.set_translation
ROUTE Block2Sensor.translation_changed TO Block2.set_translation
ROUTE Block3Sensor.translation_changed TO Block3.set_translation
ROUTE Block4Sensor.translation_changed TO Block4.set_translation
```

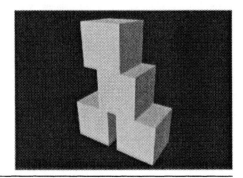

Figure 9.5   *Four stacking blocks.*

Rotating Shapes within a Sphere

You can rotate a shape in your world by using a **SphereSensor** node similar to the use of the **PlaneSensor** node in the previous examples. The viewer feels as if the shape is within a sphere that can be rolled.

Figure 9.6 builds two side-by-side shapes: a cube and a cone. Each shape is sensed by its own **SphereSensor** node. Dragging on a sensed shape causes the sensor to output a rotation using its **rotation_changed** eventOut. This is routed to a **Transform** node surrounding the shape, rotating it.

```
#VRML V2.0 utf8
Group {
    children [
        Group {
            children [
                DEF Shape1 Transform {
                    children Shape {
                        appearance DEF White Appearance {
                            material Material { }
                        }
                        geometry Box { }
                    }
                },
                DEF Shape1Sensor SphereSensor { }
            ]
        },
        Group {
            children [
                DEF Shape2 Transform {
                    translation 2.5 0.0 0.0
                    children Shape {
                        appearance USE White
                        geometry Cone { }
                    }
                },
                DEF Shape2Sensor SphereSensor { }
            ]
        }
    ]
}
ROUTE Shape1Sensor.rotation_changed TO Shape1.set_rotation
ROUTE Shape2Sensor.rotation_changed TO Shape2.set_rotation
```

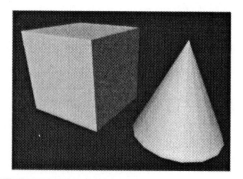

Figure 9.6 *Two shapes that rotate when the viewer drags them.*

Rotating Shapes within a Cylinder

A **CylinderSensor** node enables the viewer to rotate a shape around the Y axis, as if the shape were in a turning cylinder.

Figure 9.7 replaces the **SphereSensor** nodes of Figure 9.6 with **CylinderSensor** nodes. Dragging on a sensed shape causes the sensor to output a rotation and spin the shape.

```
#VRML V2.0 utf8
Group {
    children [
        Group {
            children [
                DEF Shape1 Transform {
                    children Shape {
                        appearance DEF White Appearance {
                            material Material { }
                        }
                        geometry Box { }
                    }
                },
                DEF Shape1Sensor CylinderSensor { }
            ]
        },
        Group {
            children [
                DEF Shape2 Transform {
                    translation 2.5 0.0 0.0
                    children Shape {
                        appearance USE White
                        geometry Cone { }
                    }
                },
                DEF Shape2Sensor CylinderSensor { }
            ]
        }
    ]
}
ROUTE Shape1Sensor.rotation_changed TO Shape1.set_rotation
ROUTE Shape2Sensor.rotation_changed TO Shape2.set_rotation
```

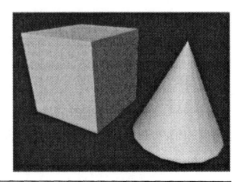

Figure 9.7   *Two shapes that rotate about the Y axis when the viewer drags them.*

Recall that a **CylinderSensor** node has two behaviors: a disklike spin or a rolling-pin-like roll. The viewer's orientation relative to the sensed shape and the value of the **diskAngle** field determine the behavior of the sensor.

Use your VRML browser's viewer-movement controls to position yourself in front of the sensed shape in Figure 9.7. To experience the rolling-pin-like motion, drag the shape with a side-to-side cursor movement. The shape rolls around the Y axis.

Use your VRML browser's viewer-movement controls to fly above the sensed shape in Figure 9.7 and look down at it. To experience the disklike spinning, drag the shape with a circular cursor movement. The shape spins around the Y axis.

Using Multiple Sensors in the Same Group

You can use multiple sensors to sense the same shape. Figure 9.8 uses a **TouchSensor** node and a **PlaneSensor** node on a cube shape. Both sensors are siblings in the same group. As in Figure 9.1, a **TouchSensor** node's **isOver** eventOut is routed to a **TimeSensor** node's **enabled** exposed field, and that sensor is routed to an **OrientationInterpolator** node and then to a **Transform** node. When the viewer's cursor moves over it, the cube spins. At the same time, a **PlaneSensor** node is routed to the same cube's **Transform** node. When the viewer drags the cube, it moves.

```
#VRML V2.0 utf8
Group {
    children [
    # Rotating Cube
        DEF Cube Transform {
            children Shape {
                appearance Appearance {
                    material Material { }
                }
                geometry Box { }
            }
        },
    # Sensors
        DEF Drag  PlaneSensor { },
        DEF Touch TouchSensor { },
    # Animation clock
        DEF Clock TimeSensor {
            enabled FALSE
            cycleInterval 4.0
            loop TRUE
        },
    # Animation path
        DEF CubePath OrientationInterpolator {
            key [ 0.0, 0.50, 1.0 ]
            keyValue [
                0.0 1.0 0.0  0.0,
                0.0 1.0 0.0  3.14,
                0.0 1.0 0.0  6.28
            ]
    }
```

Figure 9.8 continues

```
        ]
      }
      ROUTE Touch.isOver           TO Clock.set_enabled
      ROUTE Clock.fraction_changed TO CubePath.set_fraction
      ROUTE CubePath.value_changed TO Cube.set_rotation
      ROUTE Drag.translation_changed TO Cube.set_translation
```

Figure 9.8 *A cube that spins when the viewer's cursor moves over it and translates when the viewer drags it.*

Using Multiple Sensors in Nested Groups

Recall that when sensors are in nested groups, deeply nested sensors override those less deeply nested. For example, Figure 9.9 builds an adjustable desk lamp. The entire lamp shape is contained within a group that also contains a **PlaneSensor** node. When the viewer drags the lamp, it moves the lamp back and forth. Within the lamp group, a nested group contains the lamp's first arm, a **SphereSensor** node to rotate that arm, and a nested group to describe the second arm. The second arm group contains the lamp's second arm, a **SphereSensor** node to rotate the second arm, and another nested group to describe the lamp shade. Finally, the lamp shade group contains the lamp shade and a final **SphereSensor** node to rotate the lamp shade.

When the viewer clicks and drags on the lamp shade in the innermost nested group, then the **SphereSensor** node in that nested group is triggered, and the lamp shade rotates. The sensors in the outer groups of the lamp are overridden by the inner **SphereSensor** node for the lamp shade. If the viewer drags the second arm in the second-most nested group, the second arm's **SphereSensor** node triggers, and the second arm rotates. Again, the outer group's sensors are overridden by the inner sensor for the second arm. If the viewer drags the first arm, the first arm's **SphereSensor** node triggers, and the first arm rotates. Finally, if the viewer drags the lamp base in the outermost group, the **PlaneSensor** node in that group triggers, and the lamp slides.

```
#VRML V2.0 utf8
Group {
  children [
  # Lamp
    DEF MoveLamp PlaneSensor { },
    DEF Lamp Transform {
      children [
      # Lamp base
        Shape {
          appearance DEF White Appearance {
            material Material { }
          }
          geometry Cylinder {
            radius 0.1
            height 0.01
          }
        },
```

Figure 9.9 continues

```
# Base — First arm joint
Group {
  children [
    DEF MoveFirstArm SphereSensor {
      offset 1.0 0.0 0.0 -0.7
    },
    DEF FirstArm Transform {
      translation 0.0 0.15 0.0
      rotation    1.0 0.0 0.0  -0.7
      center      0.0 -0.15 0.0
      children [
      # Lower arm
        DEF LampArm Shape {
          appearance USE White
          geometry Cylinder {
            radius 0.01
            height 0.3
          }
        }
      },
      # First arm — second arm joint
      Group {
        children [
          DEF MoveSecondArm SphereSensor {
            offset 1.0 0.0 0.0 1.9
          },
          DEF SecondArm Transform {
            translation 0.0 0.3 0.0
            rotation  1.0 0.0 0.0  1.9
            center    0.0 -0.15 0.0
            children [
            # Second arm
              USE LampArm,
            # Second arm — shade joint
              Group {
                children [
                  DEF MoveLampShade SphereSensor {
                    offset 1.0 0.0 0.0 -1.25
                  },
                  DEF LampShade Transform {
                    translation 0.0 0.075 0.0
                    rotation  1.0 0.0 0.0  -1.25
                    center    0.0 0.075 0.0
                    children [
                    # Shade
                      Shape {
                        appearance USE White
                        geometry Cone {
                          height 0.15
                          bottomRadius 0.12
                          bottom FALSE
                        }
                      },
```

Figure 9.9 continues

```
                              # Light bulb
                               Transform {
                                  translation 0.0 -0.05 0.0
                                  children Shape {
                                     appearance USE White
                                     geometry Sphere {
                                        radius 0.05
                                     }
                                  }
                               }
                            ]
                          }
                        ]
                      }
                    ]
                  }
                ]
              }
            ]
          }
        ]
      }
    ]
  }
]
}
ROUTE MoveLamp.translation_changed    TO Lamp.set_translation
ROUTE MoveFirstArm.rotation_changed   TO FirstArm.set_rotation
ROUTE MoveSecondArm.rotation_changed  TO SecondArm.set_rotation
ROUTE MoveLampShade.rotation_changed  TO LampShade.set_rotation
```

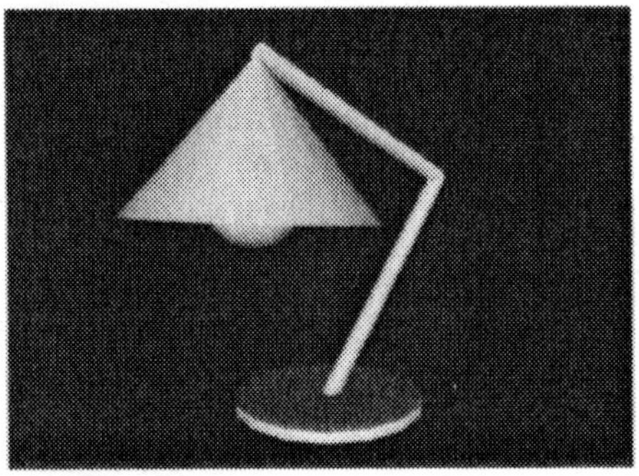

Figure 9.9 *A desk lamp that can be adjusted using nested sensors.*

Summary

The **TouchSensor, PlaneSensor, SphereSensor,** and **CylinderSensor** nodes sense viewer pointing-device move, click, and drag actions for shapes built within the same group as the sensor node. All four sensor nodes can be enabled and disabled using their **enable** fields. When disabled, these nodes ignore viewer actions. When enabled, viewer actions are converted to outputs that can be routed to other nodes to trigger animation or enable the viewer to manipulate shapes in the world.

The **TouchSensor** node is designed to sense a viewer's touch with the cursor. When the cursor is moved over a sensed shape, the **isOver** eventOut sends TRUE. When the cursor moves off of the sensed shape, FALSE is sent using the **isOver** eventOut. When the user presses the pointing-device button while over a sensed shape, the **TouchSensor** node sends TRUE using its **isActive** eventOut. Upon release of the pointing-device button, **FALSE** is sent using the **isActive** eventOut, and the current absolute time is sent using the **touchTime** eventOut.

For the **PlaneSensor**, **SphereSensor**, and **CylinderSensor** nodes, when the viewer presses the pointing-device button while over a sensed shape, the sensor sends **TRUE** using its **isActive** eventOut. Upon release of the pointing device button, **FALSE** is sent using the **isActive** eventOut.

During a drag, the **PlaneSensor** node converts side-to-side and vertical cursor motion over a sensed shape into a translation in the XY plane of the sensor's coordinate system. At each cursor movement, a translation value is output on the **translation_changed** eventOut and a track point location output on the **trackPoint_changed** eventOut. Typically, the translation value is routed to the **translation** exposed field of a **Transform** node.

The **SphereSensor** node converts side-to-side and vertical cursor motion over a sensed shape into an arbitrary rotation in the sensor's coordinate system. The behavior is that of rolling a ball. At each cursor movement, a rotation value is output on the **rotation_changed** eventOut and a track-point location output on the **trackPoint_changed** eventOut. Typically the rotation output is routed to the **rotation** exposed field of a **Transform** node.

The **CylinderSensor** node converts cursor motion over a sensed shape into rotation about the Y axis of the sensor's coordinate system. Two behaviors are provided by the sensor: a disklike spin and a rolling-pin-like roll. The selection between the disk or rolling pin is determined by comparing the node's **diskAngle** field value with an angle computed between the sensor's Y axis and the imaginary straight line that proceeds through the cursor and into the sensed shape. When this angle is less than the disk angle, the viewer must be oriented above or below the shape, and the sensor converts circular cursor motion into a rotation output. When the computed angle is greater than the disk angle, the viewer must be oriented beside or in front of the shape, and the sensor converts side-to-side cursor motion into a rotation output. In both cases, at each cursor movement, a rotation value is output using the **rotation_changed** eventOut and a track-point location output using the **trackPoint_changed** eventOut. Typically the rotation output is routed into a **Transform** node's **rotation** exposed field.

The range of motion possible with a **PlaneSensor** node can be controlled using the **minPosition** and **maxPosition** fields. Similarly, rotation outputs of the **CylinderSensor** node can be limited using the **minAngle** and **maxAngle** fields.

## CHAPTER 10

Controlling Appearance with Materials

You can control the appearance of any shape by specifying attributes of the material from which it is made. Material attributes include the shape's color, whether it glows, what color it glows, and whether it is semitransparent and by how much. Using the **Appearance** and **Material** nodes, you can control the shape color, glow color, and transparency amount. Using **ColorInterpolator** and **ScalarInterpolator** nodes, you can animate these shape attributes.

Understanding Appearance

Recall from Chapter 2 that VRML shapes are defined by their geometry and their appearance. In previous chapters you used primitive and text geometry nodes to specify the geometry of shapes built with a **Shape** node. The **Appearance** and **Material** nodes enable you to specify the appearance of shapes.

A shape's *appearance* is specified by two sets of attributes: those that indicate the shape's *material* color, like red or blue, and those that indicate the shape's surface color variation, or *texture*. Material attributes are specified by a **Material** node. Texture attributes are specified by one of several texturing nodes discussed in Chapters 17 and 18. The **Material** and texturing attribute nodes are each used as values in fields of an **Appearance** node. Finally, the **Appearance** node is used as a value in the **appearance** field of a **Shape** node.

By separating appearance attributes from those specifying a shape's geometry, you can create a set of standard appearances for repeated use in your VRML world. For example, you can create an **Appearance** node that specifies a red brick coloration and use **DEF** to give that node the name "Red Bricks." Later in your VRML file, you can instance this appearance for each shape you want to be colored like red bricks. If you change the values of the red brick **Appearance** node's field, all of the red brick shapes using that appearance also change.

Similarly, the material and texture attributes of an appearance are separated into the **Material** and texturing nodes, respectively. This enables you to create standard materials and textures for repeated use in the rest of your VRML file. You can, for instance, create a **Material** node that specifies a ruby red and use **DEF** to give that node the name "RubyRed." Later in your VRML file, you can instance this material in multiple **Appearance** nodes. If you change the ruby red specification, all of the **Appearance** nodes that use it will change as well.

RGB Colors

Imagine that you had to make a list of all the colors in the world: red, magenta, blue, mauve, purple, and so on. English color names like these are not very precise. They are too vague and too limited. VRML has a more accurate way of describing color so that you can be as precise about color as you are, for example, about shape positioning, rotating, and scaling.

If you've taken an art class, you may remember experimenting with paint colors. Starting with just a few colors of paint, you can create a huge variety of colors by mixing them together in different proportions. To make orange, mix a dab of yellow paint with a dab of red paint. To make purple, mix a dab of red with a dab of blue. To make a color lighter, add white, and to make it darker, add black.

You can carefully measure the amount of each basic color you use to create a new color, then give the measurements to a friend. By mixing the same paints in the same amounts, your friend can create exactly the same color you did. Color measurements like this are used to create all the shades of paint you find in a paint store.

Similar to mixing colors of paint, you can also mix colors of light. To make orange light, mix red light and yellow light. To make purple light, mix red light and blue light. To make a light brighter, turn up its intensity. To make a light darker, turn down its intensity.

VRML uses precise color measurements to specify the amount of red, green, and blue light to mix together to define virtual pen colors. These color measurements are called *RGB colors*, because they indicate how to combine amounts of red (R), green (G), and blue (B) light.

RGB colors contain three floating-point values, each one between 0.0 and 1.0. The first value in an RGB color specifies the amount of red to use, the second the amount of green, and the third the amount of blue. A value of 0.0 for a red, green, or blue amount means that color is turned off. A value of 1.0 for a red, green, or blue amount means that color is turned on completely. Values between 0.0 and 1.0 mean a color should be turned on partially.

Using RGB colors, you can precisely create an enormous number of colors. Table 10.1 lists a small sampling of RGB colors and their corresponding red, green, and blue values.

Table 10.1 Sample RGB Colors

Red	Green	Blue	Description
1.0	0.0	0.0	Pure red
0.0	1.0	0.0	Pure green
0.0	0.0	1.0	Pure blue
1.0	1.0	1.0	White
0.0	0.0	0.0	Black
1.0	1.0	0.0	Yellow
0.0	1.0	1.0	Cyan
1.0	0.0	1.0	Magenta
0.75	0.75	0.75	Light gray
0.5	0.5	0.5	Medium gray
0.25	0.25	0.25	Dark gray
0.5	0.0	0.0	Dark red
0.0	0.5	0.0	Dark green
0.0	0.0	0.5	Dark blue

Shading

When light shines on a shape, such as the sphere in Figure 10.1*a*, the sides facing the light are bright, and the sides facing away from the light are dark. Sides of the shape that partially face the light have an intermediate brightness that depends on how much they face the light. Artists call these variations in brightness *shading*.

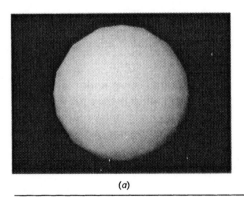
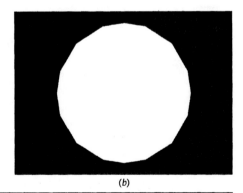

(a) (b)

Figure 10.1 *Comparing (a) a shaded sphere with (b) an unshaded one.*

Shading gives you the sense that a shape is three-dimensional. Compare, for instance, the shape in Figure 10.1*a* with the shape in Figure 10.1*b*. Both shapes have a circular outline, but one is clearly a sphere, while the other looks more like a flat circle. Actually, they are both drawn using a VRML **Sphere** node. The first sphere is shaded and looks three-dimensional. The second sphere is not shaded and looks flat.

Your VRML browser shades shapes by automatically computing the way a light brightens some sides of a shape while leaving other sides dark. To perform this shading, however, the browser must know where the light is in relation to the shape. For instance, if the light is to the right of the shape, then the right sides are built bright, and the left sides built dark. If the light is to the left of the shape, then the left sides are built bright, and the right sides built dark.

Your VRML browser automatically includes a light for the viewer in every world. This automatic light is positioned so that it shines on the world's shapes from the viewpoint viewers use to view your world. If the viewer moves to the right, so does the light. If the viewer moves to the left, so does the light. Because this light moves with viewers as their viewpoint changes, it is often called a *headlight*. You can imagine, in fact, that the headlight is attached to viewers' heads like the miner's light shown in Figure 10.2. As viewers look about your VRML world, the headlight always shines directly in front of them.

Figure 10.2   *Your headlight, like a miner's headlight.*

You can place additional lights in your world using the VRML lighting nodes: **PointLight, DirectionalLight,** and **SpotLight.** These nodes are discussed in Chapter 20. Many people find that the headlight is all that they need to properly light their world.

Whether you use the headlight or the lighting nodes, you can control how shapes are shaded using the **Material** node.

Glowing Effects

Glowing shapes include lightbulbs, computer screens, and neon signs. Shapes that glow emit their own light. A brightly glowing shape, like a lightbulb or the sun, appears simply as a mass of color. Shading effects on the shape are washed out by the shape's own glow. Using VRML's **Material** node, you can specify that a shape glows by specifying an *emissive color*—the color of its glow.

For example, Figure 10.3 shows a VRML-generated image of a hanging lightbulb. Figure 10.3*a* shows the lightbulb turned off, and Figure 10.3*b* shows the lightbulb turned on. The turned-off bulb is shaded by your browser and is clearly a sphere. The turned-on bulb glows so brightly that the shading is washed out. The bulb appears as a circular mass of light.

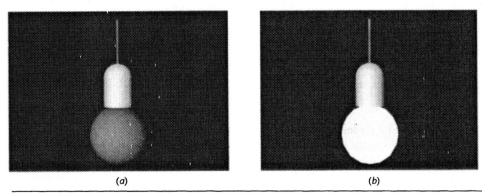

(a)   *(b)*

Figure 10.3   *Comparing shading of a lightbulb (a) when turned off versus (b) turned on.*

Transparency

Opaque shapes block light, while *transparent* shapes let light pass straight through them. *Semitransparent* shapes block a little of the light while letting the rest through. Windows, for instance, are almost completely transparent. Screen doors are semitransparent, and walls are opaque. Using VRML's **Material** node you can specify a shape's transparency when built by the VRML browser.

Understanding Material Animation

Recall that the **PositionInterpolator** and **OrientationInterpolator** nodes are used to smoothly animate the position or rotation of a shape as time ticks by. VRML provides two additional interpolator nodes that can be used to animate color and transparency values in a **Material** node: the **ColorInterpolator** and **ScalarInterpolator** nodes.

The **ColorInterpolator** node uses a list of key fractional times and key colors in its **key** and **keyValue** fields. When driven by the fractional time output of a **TimeSensor** node, the **ColorInterpolator** node uses linear interpolation to compute intermediate colors. Each new computed color is output using the node's **value_changed** eventOut. You can route this output to the color fields of a **Material** node to animate the shape color or glow color.

Similarly, the **ScalarInterpolator** node uses a list of key fractional times and key floating-point values in its **key** and **keyValue** fields. When driven by a **TimeSensor** node, the **ScalarInterpolator** node uses linear interpolation to compute intermediate floating-point values, which it outputs using its **value_changed** eventOut. You can route this output to the **transparency** field of a **Material** node to animate a shape's transparency.

You also can use a **ScalarInterpolator** node to send floating-point values to any node that uses a single floating-point value as the value of an exposed field. For instance, you can use a **ScalarInterpolator** node to generate fractional times that you can route to the **set_fraction** eventIn of other interpolators. You can use this technique to gain fine control over details of your animation.

HSV Colors

The **ColorInterpolator** node interpolates between colors to compute an intermediate color to output using its **value_changed** eventOut. The **ColorInterpolator** node could have been designed to compute intermediate RGB colors by independently interpolating between reds, greens, and blues in a manner analogous to interpolating between X, Y, and Z values in a **PositionInterpolator** node. Unfortunately, this produces odd intermediate colors that you would not want.

Instead, the **ColorInterpolator** node automatically converts your RGB colors into a second form of color specification, called *HSV colors*. Interpolation of these HSV colors produces a more natural result that is automatically converted back to an RGB color before it is output by the interpolator node. This automatic conversion to and from HSV colors means you never have to specify HSV colors yourself. Nevertheless, you get the benefit of using HSV colors for interpolation.

An HSV color is similar to an RGB color, but uses a different way of measuring color. Each HSV color specifies the hue (H), saturation (S), and value (V) of a color. The *hue* is a number between 0.0 and 1.0 that selects a color from a red-green-blue-red color wheel. Hue is often what people mean when they talk about a color. A red apple, for instance, has a red hue.

The *saturation* part of an HSV color is a number between 0.0 and 1.0 that selects how much white should be mixed with the color. For a saturation value of 0.0, a great deal of white is mixed with the hue, while a saturation value of 1.0 adds no white. The addition of white makes a color seem more pastel, so a saturation value of around 0.75 and a hue of red makes a pastel pink color.

The *value* part of an HSV color is a number between 0.0 and 1.0 that selects the brightness of the color. For a value of 0.0, the color is turned way down and produces black. For a value of 1.0, the color is at full brightness.

Animating Colors

HSV colors provide an important way to describe colors that is particularly useful when animating them. To illustrate, Tables 10.2 and 10.3 show two key RGB colors, bright red and bright blue, that are in an interpolator's key value list. Table 10.2 shows how intermediate colors would be computed if a **ColorInterpolator** node used RGB color interpolation. Table 10.3 shows how intermediate colors are actually computed by the **ColorInterpolator** node's use of HSV color interpolation.

Table 10.2   Color Interpolation Using RGB Colors

Fractional Time	Key RGB Color	Computed RGB Color	Output RGB Color	Description
0.00	1.00 0.00 0.00	1.00 0.00 0.00	1.00 0.00 0.00	Bright red
0.25		0.75 0.00 0.25	0.75 0.00 0.25	Dark red-blue
0.50		0.50 0.00 0.50	0.50 0.00 0.50	Medium gray
0.75		0.25 0.00 0.75	0.25 0.00 0.75	Dark blue-red
1.00	0.00 0.00 1.00	0.00 0.00 1.00	0.00 0.00 1.00	Bright blue

Table 10.3   Color Interpolation Using HSV Colors

Fractional Time	Key RGB Color	Computed HSV Color	Output RGB Color	Description
0.00	1.00 0.00 0.00	1.00 0.00 0.00	1.00 0.00 0.00	Bright red
0.25		0.92 0.00 0.00	1.00 0.00 0.50	Bright red-blue
0.50		0.83 0.00 0.00	1.00 0.00 1.00	Bright purple
0.75		0.75 0.00 0.00	0.50 0.00 1.00	Bright blue-red
1.00	0.00 0.00 1.00	0.67 0.00 0.00	0.00 0.00 1.00	Bright blue

In Table 10.2, notice that the intermediate RGB colors gradually reduce the red component of the computed RGB color while increasing the blue component. At halfway between the key red and blue colors, the computed RGB color is a medium gray. If you used these computed colors in an animation, the animation from red to blue would cause your shape to darken to gray halfway through the animation.

Table 10.3 shows interpolation using HSV colors instead. Notice that the intermediate HSV colors maintain full saturation and value for the colors, and that the resulting output RGB colors stay bright as the hue varies from red to blue during the animation. The intermediate colors do not darken and turn gray. The **ColorInterpolator** node's use of HSV color interpolation produces a more natural result and the interpolator handles the conversion to and from HSV colors automatically.

The **Shape** Node Syntax

All VRML shapes are built using the **Shape** node.

| SYNTAX | **Shape node** |

```
Shape {
    appearance    NULL    # exposedField   SFNode
    geometry      NULL    # exposedField   SFNode
}
```

The value of the **geometry** field is discussed in Chapter 3.

The value of the **appearance** field specifies a node that defines the appearance of the shape, including the shape's color and surface texture. Typical **appearance** field values include the **Appearance** node. The default **NULL** value for this field indicates a default, glowing white appearance.

The appearance and geometry of a shape can be changed by sending values to the implied **set_appearance** and **set_geometry** eventIns of the **appearance** and **geometry** exposed fields. When values are received by these inputs, the corresponding field values are changed, and the new values output by the implied **appearance_changed** and **geometry_changed** eventOuts of the exposed fields.

The **Appearance** Node Syntax

The **Appearance** node specifies appearance attributes and may be used as the value of the **appearance** field in a **Shape** node.

SYNTAX   **Appearance node**

```
Appearance {
    material            NULL    # exposedField  SFNode
    texture             NULL    # exposedField  SFNode
    textureTransform    NULL    # exposedField  SFNode
}
```

The value of the **material** field specifies a node defining the material attributes of the appearance. Typical **material** field values include the **Material** node. The default **NULL** value for this field indicates a default, glowing white material.

The appearance material can be changed by sending a value to the implied **set_material** eventIn of the **material** exposed field. When a value is received by this input, the corresponding field value is changed and the new value output by the implied **material_changed** eventOut of the exposed field.

The remaining fields of the **Appearance** node are discussed in Chapters 17 (texture) and 18 (textureTransform).

The **Material** Node Syntax

The **Material** node specifies material attributes and may be used as the value of the **material** field in an **Appearance** node.

SYNTAX **Material node**

```
Material {
    diffuseColor       0.8 0.8 0.8    # exposedField  SFColor
    emissiveColor      0.0 0.0 0.0    # exposedField  SFColor
    transparency       0.0            # exposedField  SFFloat
    ambientIntensity   0.2            # exposedField  SFFloat
    specularColor      0.0 0.0 0.0    # exposedField  SFColor
    shininess          0.2            # exposedField  SFFloat
}
```

The value of the **diffuseColor** exposed field specifies an RGB color for the material. The RGB color is specified as three floating-point values between 0.0 and 1.0 that indicate the amount of red (R), green (G), and blue (B) light to be mixed together to form the color. The VRML browser automatically computes darker colors as it shades the side of a shape, gradually darkening the shading color as it progresses from the lighted sides of the shape to the unlighted sides. The default value for this field is the medium-bright white used in the examples thus far in this book.

The value of the **emissiveColor** exposed field specifies the RGB glow color. The RGB color is specified as three floating-point values between 0.0 and 1.0 that indicate the amount of red (R), green (G), and blue (B) light to be mixed together to form the color. Brighter emissive colors make shapes appear to emit more light and thus glow more brightly. The default value for this field is black, which indicates no glow.

TIP Glowing shapes do not light up shapes around them. The glow caused by using the **emissiveColor** field only indicates that shapes be built brighter than usual, as if they emitted light. For example, if you turn off the default headlight of your VRML browser, shapes that are shaded with emissive colors are still visible. Other shapes are left shaded dark.

The value of the **transparency** exposed field specifies a transparency factor between 0.0 and 1.0. A transparency factor of 0.0 creates shapes that are opaque, while a factor of 1.0 makes them completely transparent. The default transparency factor is 0.0.

SIDEBAR: TRANSPARENCY Different VRML browsers use different techniques for drawing transparent shapes. Some browsers and graphics hardware use a *screen-door effect* that overlays on transparent shapes a kind of screen-door mesh known as a *dither* pattern. The **transparency** field controls the density of that screen so that a high transparency value creates a more see-through mesh, while a low transparency value makes the mesh more opaque.

Other browsers and graphics hardware use a *color-blending effect* that computes how colors blend when colored shapes show through semitransparent colored shapes. Using this color-blending method, no screen meshes are used. When available, this color blending method produces more realistic transparency results.

The color and transparency of a material can be changed by sending values to the implied **set_diffuseColor, set_emissiveColor,** and **set_transparency** eventIns of the **diffuseColor, emissiveColor,** and **transparency** exposed fields, respectively. When values are received by these inputs, the corresponding field values are changed, and the new values are output by the implied **diffuseColor_changed, emissiveColor_changed,** and **transparency_changed** eventOuts of the exposed fields.

The remaining fields of the Material node—**ambientIntensity, specularColor,** and **shininess**—are discussed in Chapter 21.

SIDEBAR: MATERIAL FEATURE SUPPORT Some VRML browsers may not support the full range of features specified by the **Material** node. Table 10.4 shows how VRML browsers may handle unsupported **Material** node features.

Table 10.4   How VRML Browsers May Handle Unsupported Material Node Features

Unsupported Feature	Action
Transparency	When a VRML browser doesn't support transparency, it treats **transparency** field values as if they select only between full opacity and full transparency. If the **transparency** field value is between 0.0 and 0.5, the shape is drawn fully opaque. Otherwise the shape is drawn fully transparent.
Emissive color and diffuse color specified together	When a VRML browser cannot support the simultaneous use of diffuse and emissive color, it ignores one or the other. When the **diffuseColor** field value is 0.0 0.0 0.0 (black), the **emissiveColor** field's value is used as the shape color, the and **diffuseColor** field value is ignored. Otherwise the **emissiveColor** field value is ignored and only the **diffuseColor** field value is used as the shape color.

The **ColorInterpolator** Node Syntax

The **ColorInterpolator** node describes a series of key colors available for use in an animation.

SYNTAX   ColorInterpolator node

```
ColorInterpolator {
    key             [ ]    # exposedField  MFFloat
    keyValue        [ ]    # exposedField  MFColor
    set_fraction           # eventIn       SFFloat
    value_changed          # eventOut      SFColor
}
```

The value of the **key** exposed field specifies a list of key, floating-point, fractional times. Typically, fractional times are between 0.0 and 1.0, such as those output by a **TimeSensor** node's **fraction_changed** eventOut. Key fractional times, however, may be positive or negative floating-point values of any size. Key fractional times must be listed in nondecreasing order. The default value for the **key** field is an empty list.

The value of the **keyValue** exposed field specifies a list of key RGB colors. Each RGB color is specified as three floating-point values between 0.0 and 1.0 that specify the amount of red (R), green (G), and blue (B) light to be mixed together to form the color. The default value for the **keyValue** field is an empty list.

The key fractional times and colors are used together so that the first key fractional time specifies the time for the first key color, the second key fractional time for the second key color, and so forth. The lists may provide any number of fractional times and colors, but both lists must contain the same number of values.

When a fractional time is received by the **set_fraction** eventIn, the **ColorInterpolator** node computes an RGB color based on the list of key colors and their corresponding key fractional times. The new, computed RGB color is output using the **value_changed** eventOut.

An output color for an input fractional time t is computed by the **ColorInterpolator** node by:

1. Scanning the key fractional times to find a pair of adjacent times $t1$ and $t2$, where $t1 \leq t \leq t2$.

2. Retrieving the corresponding pair of key colors.

3. Computing an intermediate color by linearly interpolating between the key colors.

Color interpolation is performed internally by the **ColorInterpolator** node using HSV colors that are automatically computed based on the RGB colors provided in the **keyValue** field.

Two adjacent key fractional times $t1$ and $t2$ may have the same value, creating a discontinuity, or jump, in the animation path. In this case, the key color corresponding to $t1$ (the first of the two identical key fractional times) is used by the **ColorInterpolator** node when linearly interpolating for times less than $t1$, and the key color corresponding to $t2$ (the second of the two times) is used when linearly interpolating for times greater than $t2$.

Typically, fractional times are sent to the **set_fraction** eventIn by wiring a route from the **fraction_changed** eventOut of a **TimeSensor** node. Fractional times also may be generated by other means, such as by nodes that generate generic, floating-point values, like the **ScalarInterpolator** node.

The list of key fractional times or colors can be changed by sending values to the implied **set_key** and **set_keyValue** eventIns of the **key** and **keyValue** exposed fields. When values are received by these inputs, the corresponding field values are changed, and the new values are output using the implied **key_changed** and **key-Value_changed** eventOuts of the exposed fields.

The **ColorInterpolator** node creates no shapes, and alone it has no visible effect on a world. A **ColorInterpolator** node may be included as the child of any grouping node but is independent of the coordinate system in use. Typically, interpolators are placed at the end of the outermost group of a VRML file.

The **ScalarInterpolator** Node Syntax

The ScalarInterpolator node describes a series of key colors available for use in an animation.

| SYNTAX | ScalarInterpolator node |

```
ScalarInterpolator {
      key            [ ]    # exposedField    MFFloat
      keyValue       [ ]    # exposedField    MFFloat
      set_fraction          # eventIn         SFFloat
      value_changed         # eventOut        SFFloat
}
```

The value of the **key** exposed field is discussed in the section entitled "The **ColorInterpolator** Node Syntax."

The value of the **keyValue** exposed field specifies a list of key floating-point values. The default value for the **keyValue** field is an empty list.

The key fractional times and values are used together so that the first key fractional time specifies the time for the first key value, the second key fractional time for the second key value, and so forth. The lists may provide any number of fractional times and floating-point values, but both lists must contain the same number of values.

When a fractional time is received by the **set_fraction** eventIn, the **ScalarInterpolator** node computes a floating-point value based on the list of key values and their corresponding key fractional times. The new, computed floating-point value is output using the **value_changed** eventOut.

An output floating-point value for an input fractional time t is computed by the **ScalarInterpolator** node by:

1. Scanning the key fractional times to find a pair of adjacent times $t1$ and $t2$, where $t1 \leq t \leq t2$.

2. Retrieving the corresponding pair of key values.

3. Computing an intermediate value by linearly interpolating between the key values.

Two adjacent key fractional times $t1$ and $t2$ may have the same value, creating a discontinuity, or jump, in the animation path. In this case, the key floating-point value corresponding to $t1$ (the first of the two identical key fractional times) is used by the **ScalarInterpolator** node when linearly interpolating for times less than $t1$, and the key floating-point value corresponding to $t2$ (the second of the two times) is used when linearly interpolating for times greater than $t2$.

Discussion of the **set_fraction** eventIn continues in the section entitled "The **ColorInterpolator** Node Syntax."

The list of key fractional times or floating-point values can be changed by sending values to the implied **set_key** and **set_keyValue** eventIns of the **key** and **keyValue** exposed fields. When values are received by these inputs, the corresponding field values are changed and the new values output using the implied **key_changed** and **keyValue_changed** eventOuts of the exposed fields.

The **ScalarInterpolator** node creates no shapes, and alone it has no visible effect on a world. A **ScalarInterpolator** node may be included as the child of any grouping node but is independent of the coordinate system in use. Typically, interpolators are placed at the end of the outermost group of a VRML file.

Experimenting with Appearances and Materials

The following examples provide a more detailed examination of the ways in which the **Appearance, Material, ColorInterpolator,** and **ScalarInterpolator** nodes can be used and how they interact with nodes discussed in previous chapters.

Using Appearance and Material

Using **Appearance** and **Material** nodes, you can specify the color of a shape built using a **Shape** node. Figure 10.4 shows a sphere shaded bright red. A **Sphere** node specifies the geometry of the shape, while an **Appearance** node and a **Material** node set the shape's color. The **diffuseColor** field value of the **Material** node selects a bright red color that mixes a red-light value of 1.0, a green-light value of 0.0, and a blue-light value of 0.0.

```
#VRML V2.0 utf8
Shape {
    appearance Appearance {
        material Material {
            diffuseColor 1.0 0.0 0.0
        }
    }
    geometry Sphere { }
}
```

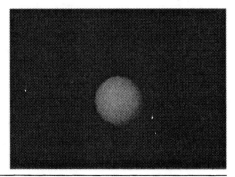

Figure 10.4 *A bright red sphere.*

Specifying the Appearance and Material of Multiple Shapes

Each **Shape** node in a VRML file may use its own **Appearance** node. Figure 10.5 shows a simple space station built using a sphere, a flat cylinder, and a tall cylinder. The sphere shape uses **Appearance** and **Material** nodes to make it bright red, the flat cylinder shape uses **Appearance** and **Material** nodes to make it blue, and the tall sphere shape uses **Appearance** and **Material** nodes to make it purple.

```
#VRML V2.0 utf8
Group {
    children [
    # Station Shapes
        Shape {
            appearance Appearance {
                material Material {
                    diffuseColor 1.0 0.0 0.0
                }
            }
            geometry Sphere { }
        },
        Shape {
            appearance Appearance {
                material Material {
                    diffuseColor 0.5 0.25 1.0
                }
            }
            geometry Cylinder {
                radius 2.0
                height 0.05
            }
        },
        Shape {
            appearance Appearance {
                material Material {
                    diffuseColor 0.75 0.0 1.0
                }
            }
            geometry Cylinder {
                radius 0.15
                height 5.0
            }
        }
    ]
}
```

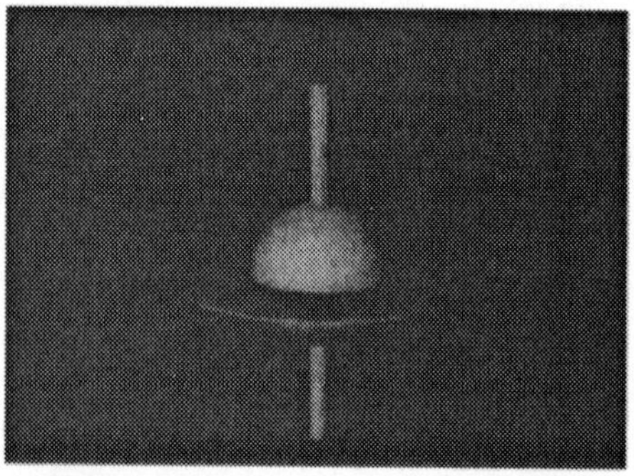

Figure 10.5 *A simple, multicolored space station.*

Animating Color

Using a **ColorInterpolator** node, you can animate the color of a shape. Figure 10.6 uses a **ColorInterpolator** node to animate the color of the central sphere on the simple space station. The interpolator uses a set of key colors to generate a color output that varies from red to green, to blue, and back to red. The **value_changed** eventOut of the **ColorInterpolator** node is routed to the implied **set_diffuseColor** eventIn of the sphere shape's **Material** node. A **TimeSensor** node acts as the clock for the animation.

```
#VRML V2.0 utf8
Group {
    children [
    # Station Shapes
        Shape {
            appearance Appearance {
                material DEF BallColor Material {
                    diffuseColor 1.0 0.0 0.0
                }
            }
            geometry Sphere { }
        },
        Shape {
            appearance Appearance {
                material Material {
                    diffuseColor 0.5 0.25 1.0
                }
            }
            geometry Cylinder {
                radius 2.0
                height 0.05
            }
        },
        Shape {
            appearance Appearance {
                material Material {
                    diffuseColor 0.75 0.0 1.0
                }
            }
            geometry Cylinder {
                radius 0.15
                height 5.0
            }
        },
    # Animation clock
        DEF Clock TimeSensor {
            cycleInterval 4.0
            loop TRUE
        },
```

Figure 10.6 continues

```
# Animation path
    DEF ColorPath ColorInterpolator {
        key [ 0.0, 0.33, 0.67, 1.0 ]
        keyValue [
            1.0 0.0 0.0,  0.0 1.0 0.0,
            0.0 0.0 1.0,  1.0 0.0 0.0,
        ]
    }
]
}
ROUTE Clock.fraction_changed  TO ColorPath.set_fraction
ROUTE ColorPath.value_changed TO BallColor.set_diffuseColor
```

Figure 10.6 *A multicolored space station where the central sphere animates from red, to green, to blue, and back to red.*

Making Shapes Glow

The VRML text in Figure 10.7 builds the hanging lightbulb shown in Figure 10.3*b*. The lightbulb wire is drawn in a dark gray, the lightbulb socket in brass, and the lightbulb itself glows a pure white. The **Material** node used for the lightbulb's sphere specifies an **emissiveColor** field value to cause the bulb to glow bright white. The **diffuseColor** field value of the same node sets the shading color to black, which *turns off* shading and gives the shape a more pure glow.

```
#VRML V2.0 utf8
Group {
    children [
    # Dark gray light bulb hanging wire
        Shape {
            appearance Appearance {
                material Material {
                    diffuseColor 0.4 0.4 0.4
                }
            }
            geometry Cylinder {
                radius 0.05
                height 2.0
            }
        },
    # Yellowish light bulb socket
        Transform {
            translation 0.0 -1.0 0.0
            children Shape {
                appearance Appearance {
                    material Material {
                        diffuseColor 1.0 1.0 0.4
                    }
                }
                geometry Sphere { radius 0.5 }
            }
        },
```

Figure 10.7 continues

```
        Transform {
            translation 0.0 -1.5 0.0
            children Shape {
                appearance Appearance {
                    material Material {
                        diffuseColor 1.0 1.0 0.4
                    }
                }
                geometry Cylinder {
                    radius 0.5
                    height 1.0
                }
            }
        },
# White light bulb
        Transform {
            translation 0.0 -2.95 0.0
            children Shape {
                appearance Appearance {
                    material Material {
                        diffuseColor  1.0 1.0 1.0
                        emissiveColor 1.0 1.0 1.0
                    }
                }
                geometry Sphere { }
            }
        }
    ]
}
```

Figure 10.7   *A lightbulb, turned on.*

Making Shapes Blink

A **ColorInterpolator** node's **value_changed** eventOut can be routed to a **Material** node's **emissiveColor** exposed field to cause the glow color of a shape to animate. You can create a blinking light effect by using alternating colors in the key value list for the interpolator node.

Recall that the key fractional times in an interpolator specify the times associated with the corresponding key colors. Typically, each new key time is greater than the previous one in the list. To create a blinking effect, however, you can place two identical key times side by side in the list. When you do this, the key color corresponding to the first of the two identical key fractional times is used when interpolating for times earlier than the first time, and the key color corresponding to the second of the two fractional times is used when interpolating for times greater than the second time. The effect is to create a discontinuity, or jump, in the animation output as time passes the time selected by the identical key times. This is exactly what you need in order to create an abrupt on-off blinking animation.

Figure 10.8 builds a sphere, a timer, and a color interpolator. The timer drives the interpolator, which in turn outputs colors to the **emissiveColor** exposed field of the sphere shape's **Material** node. The **ColorInterpolator** node uses key fractional times and colors creating a blinking effect that cycles from green to blue and back.

```
#VRML V2.0 utf8
Group {
    children [
    # Blinking ball
        Shape {
            appearance Appearance {
                material DEF BallColor Material {
                    diffuseColor 0.4 0.4 0.4
                }
            }
            geometry Sphere { }
        },
    # Animation clock
        DEF Clock TimeSensor {
            cycleInterval 1.0
            loop TRUE
        },
    # Animation path
        DEF ColorPath ColorInterpolator {
            key [ 0.0, 0.5, 0.5, 1.0 ]
            keyValue [
                0.0 1.0 0.0,   0.0 1.0 0.0,
                0.0 0.0 1.0,   0.0 0.0 1.0,
            ]
        }
    ]
}
ROUTE Clock.fraction_changed  TO ColorPath.set_fraction
ROUTE ColorPath.value_changed TO BallColor.set_emissiveColor
```

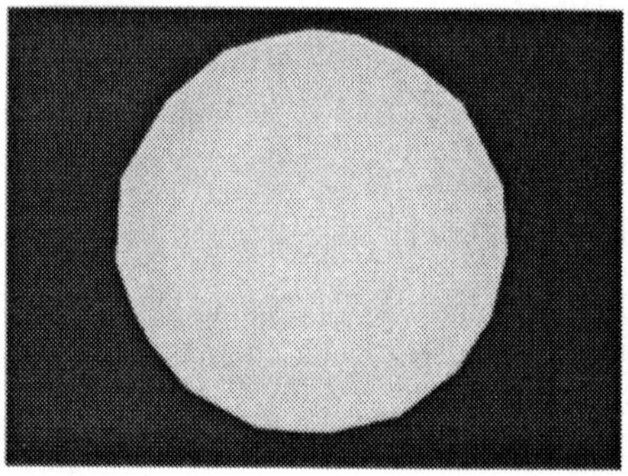

Figure 10.8 *A blinking sphere.*

Using Multiple Color Interpolators

You can use any number of **ColorInterpolator** nodes in the same world. Figure 10.9 extends the blinking sphere example to add two more blinking spheres. Each sphere shape has its own **TimeSensor** node and its own **ColorInterpolator** node to change the emissive color of the shape. Using different cycle intervals for the time sensors, the spheres blink with no obvious pattern, which creates the appearance of random blinking, like twinkling lights in a distant city.

```
#VRML V2.0 utf8
Group {
    children [
    # Blinking balls
        Transform {
            translation -2.0 0.0 0.0
            children Shape {
                appearance Appearance {
                    material DEF Ball1Color Material {
                        diffuseColor 0.4 0.4 0.4
                    }
                }
                geometry DEF ABall Sphere { }
            }
        },
        Shape {
            appearance Appearance {
                material DEF Ball2Color Material {
                    diffuseColor 0.4 0.4 0.4
                }
            }
            geometry USE ABall
        },
        Transform {
            translation  2.0 0.0 0.0
            children Shape {
                appearance Appearance {
                    material DEF Ball3Color Material {
                        diffuseColor 0.4 0.4 0.4
                    }
                }
                geometry USE ABall
            }
        },
    # Animation clocks
        DEF Clock1 TimeSensor {
            cycleInterval 1.0
            loop TRUE
        },
        DEF Clock2 TimeSensor {
            cycleInterval 1.3
            loop TRUE
        },
        DEF Clock3 TimeSensor {
            cycleInterval 0.7
            loop TRUE
        },
```

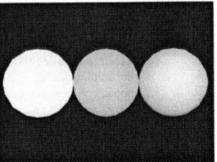

Figure 10.9 continues

```
# Animation paths
    DEF Color1Path ColorInterpolator {
        key [ 0.0, 0.5, 0.5, 1.0 ]
        keyValue [
            1.0 1.0 0.0,   1.0 1.0 0.0,
            0.0 1.0 0.0,   0.0 1.0 0.0,
        ]
    },
    DEF Color2Path ColorInterpolator {
        key [ 0.0, 0.5, 0.5, 1.0 ]
        keyValue [
            0.0 1.0 0.0,   0.0 1.0 0.0,
            0.0 0.0 1.0,   0.0 0.0 1.0,
        ]
    },
    DEF Color3Path ColorInterpolator {
        key [ 0.0, 0.5, 0.5, 1.0 ]
        keyValue [
            0.5 0.5 0.5,   0.5 0.5 0.5,
            1.0 1.0 1.0,   1.0 1.0 1.0,
        ]
    }
  ]
}
ROUTE Clock1.fraction_changed  TO Color1Path.set_fraction
ROUTE Clock2.fraction_changed  TO Color2Path.set_fraction
ROUTE Clock3.fraction_changed  TO Color3Path.set_fraction
ROUTE Color1Path.value_changed TO Ball1Color.set_emissiveColor
ROUTE Color2Path.value_changed TO Ball2Color.set_emissiveColor
ROUTE Color3Path.value_changed TO Ball3Color.set_emissiveColor
```

Figure 10.9   *Three blinking spheres.*

Making Shapes Transparent

The **transparency** field of the **Material** node enables you to control the transparency of a shape built by the browser. The default value is 0.0, which makes a shape opaque. As you increase the transparency value, a shape is built more and more transparent. A value of 1.0 directs the browser to build the shape entirely transparent, or invisible.

The VRML text in Figure 10.10 builds the simple space station but changes the transparency of the central, red sphere to be half-transparent. This creates the illusion that the central sphere is glass.

```
#VRML V2.0 utf8
Group {
    children [
    # Station Shapes
        Shape {
            appearance Appearance {
                material Material {
                    diffuseColor 1.0 0.0 0.0
                    transparency 0.5
                }
            }
            geometry Sphere { }
        },
        Shape {
            appearance Appearance {
                material Material {
                    diffuseColor 0.5 0.25 1.0
                }
            }
            geometry Cylinder {
                radius 2.0
                height 0.05
            }
        },
        Shape {
            appearance Appearance {
                material Material {
                    diffuseColor 0.75 0.0 1.0
                }
            }
            geometry Cylinder {
                radius 0.15
                height 5.0
            }
        }
    ]
}
```

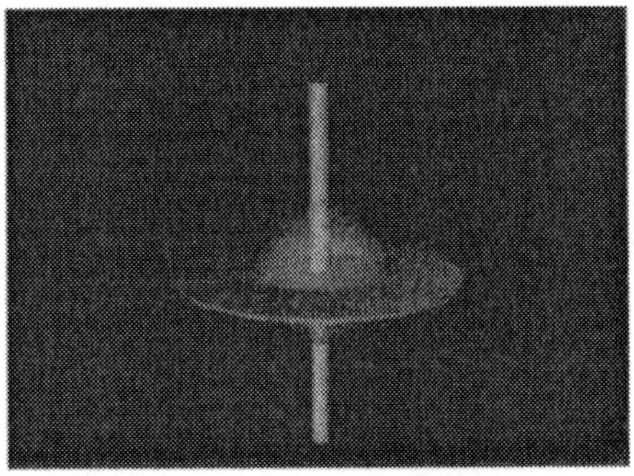

Figure 10.10 *A simple space station with a half-transparent central sphere.*

TIP You can use transparency to help you find and correct problems in complex VRML files. If you temporarily change the **transparency** field of **Material** nodes, you change some of your file's shapes to semitransparent. This reduces the clutter of a complex world and lets you see inside shapes. This may help you to see where shapes aren't lining up correctly. After you've corrected your file, turn the semitransparent shapes opaque again by changing **Material** node **transparency** fields back to 0.0.

Animating Transparency

You can use a **ScalarInterpolator** node's floating-point value output to animate the transparency indicated by a **Material** node. Figure 10.11 extends the simple space station example by adding **TimeSensor** and **ScalarInterpolator** nodes. The **TimeSensor** node drives the interpolator, which generates floating-point transparency values that vary from 0.0 (opaque) to 1.0 (transparent) and back again. The **value_changed** eventOut of the interpolator is routed to the **Material** node's **transparency** exposed field to cause the central sphere's transparency level to vary.

```
#VRML V2.0 utf8
Group {
    children [
    # Station Shapes
        Shape {
            appearance Appearance {
                material DEF BallColor Material {
                    diffuseColor 1.0 0.0 0.0
                }
            }
            geometry Sphere { }
        },
        Shape {
            appearance Appearance {
                material Material {
                    diffuseColor 0.5 0.25 1.0
                }
            }
            geometry Cylinder {
                radius 2.0
                height 0.05
            }
        },
        Shape {
            appearance Appearance {
                material Material {
                    diffuseColor 0.75 0.0 1.0
                }
            }
            geometry Cylinder {
                radius 0.15
                height 5.0
            }
        },
    # Animation clock
        DEF Clock TimeSensor {
            cycleInterval 4.0
            loop TRUE
        },
```

Figure 10.11 continues

```
# Animation path
    DEF TransparencyPath ScalarInterpolator {
        key [ 0.0, 0.5, 1.0 ]
        keyValue [ 0.0, 1.0, 0.0 ]
    }
   ]
}
ROUTE Clock.fraction_changed        TO TransparencyPath.set_fraction
ROUTE TransparencyPath.value_changed TO BallColor.set_transparency
```

Figure 10.11 *A simple space station with animating transparency for the central sphere.*

Controlling Animation Using Scalar Interpolation

The **ScalarInterpolator** node outputs a generic, floating-point value that you can use for any purpose, not just the animation of a **Material** node's transparency factor. For instance, you can route the output of a **ScalarInterpolator** node to the **set_fraction** eventIn of another interpolator node. This enables you to change an animation's notion of time. Instead of fractional times always smoothly progressing from 0.0 to 1.0, you can use a **ScalarInterpolator** node to convert an incoming fractional time into an outgoing one that varies in any way you please, including making time go backward.

Figure 10.12 uses a **ScalarInterpolator** node to map incoming 0.0 to 1.0 fractional times, into outgoing times that cycle from 0.0 to 1.0, then from 1.0 to 0.0. The interpolator outputs fractional times that go forward for a while, then reverse direction and come back. The **ScalarInterpolator** node's **value_changed** eventOut is routed to a **PositionInterpolator** node that routes to a **Transform** node to cause a box to bounce. Because of the reversed-time effect caused by the **ScalarInterpolator** node, the box appears to bounce forward for a while and then change direction and bounce back again when the scalar interpolator's output time changes and flows backward.

```
#VRML V2.0 utf8
Group {
    children [
    # Moving box
        DEF Cube Transform {
            children Shape {
                appearance Appearance {
                    material Material {
                        diffuseColor 1.0 1.0 0.0
                    }
                }
                geometry Box { size 1.0 1.0 1.0 }
            }
        },
```

Figure 10.12 continues

```
# Animation clock
    DEF Clock TimeSensor {
        cycleInterval 4.0
        loop TRUE
    },
# Animation controller
    DEF CubeController ScalarInterpolator {
        key     [ 0.0, 0.5, 1.0 ]
        keyValue [ 0.0, 1.0, 0.0 ]
    },
# Animation path
    DEF CubePath PositionInterpolator {
        key [
            0.00, 0.11, 0.17, 0.22,
            0.33, 0.44, 0.50, 0.55,
            0.66, 0.77, 0.83, 0.88,
            0.99
        ]
        keyValue [
            0.0 0.0  0.0,   1.0 1.96 1.0,
            1.5 2.21 1.5,   2.0 1.96 2.0,
            3.0 0.0  3.0,   2.0 1.96 3.0,
            1.5 2.21 3.0,   1.0 1.96 3.0,
            0.0 0.0  3.0,   0.0 1.96 2.0,
            0.0 2.21 1.5,   0.0 1.96 1.0,
            0.0 0.0  0.0
        ]
    }
    ]
}
]
}
ROUTE Clock.fraction_changed         TO CubeController.set_fraction
ROUTE CubeController.value_changed TO CubePath.set_fraction
ROUTE CubePath.value_changed        TO Cube.set_translation
```

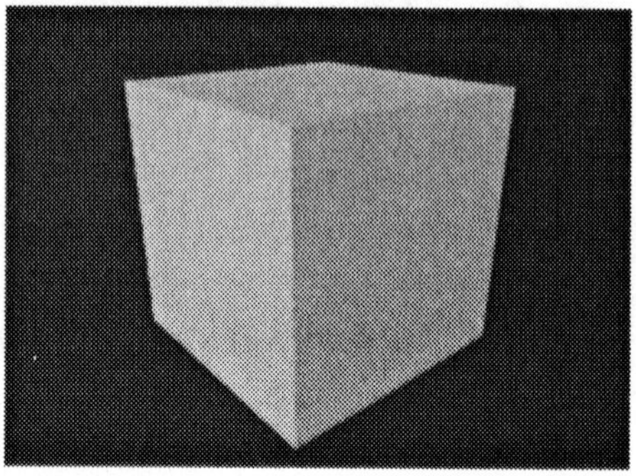

Figure 10.12 *A cube that bounces forward and back as an interpolator remaps time.*

Summary

The **appearance** field of a **Shape** node may be set to an **Appearance** node to control the appearance of the shape when shaded by the VRML browser.

The **material** field of the **Appearance** node may be set to a **Material** node to control material appearance attributes such as the shape's color, glow color, and transparency factor.

Using the **Material** node's **diffuseColor** field, you can control a shape's shading color. Colors are specified using RGB colors that specify the amount of red (R), green (G), and blue (B) light to mix together to achieve the desired color. The browser automatically shades shapes based on what sides face toward or away from lights in the world.

VRML browsers provide all worlds with a headlight. The headlight is automatically positioned so that it always points in the direction in which you are looking in your VRML world.

By setting the **emissiveColor** field of the **Material** node, you can build shapes that appear to glow. The glowing color is specified using an RGB color. A **Material** node can have both the **emissiveColor** and the **diffuseColor** fields set, each with a different color.

Using the **transparency** field of the **Material** node, you can build semitransparent shapes. Transparency values vary from 0.0 (opaque) to 1.0 (fully transparent).

A shape's color can be animated by using a **ColorInterpolator** node, and its transparency can be animated by using a **ScalarInterpolator** node. Both nodes use a list of key fractional times, in the **key** field, and key values, in the **keyValue** field. Each key fractional time typically specifies a time between 0.0 and 1.0 at which the corresponding key value (a color or a floating-point value) is to be output from the interpolator node. For input fractional times between key fractional times, the interpolator node linearly interpolates between adjacent key values in the list and outputs the computed color or floating-point value.

## CHAPTER 11

Grouping Nodes

You can group together any number of nodes and then manipulate the group as a whole. For instance, you can place shapes to build a building within a **Transform** grouping node, then translate, rotate, and scale the building as a whole to place it on a city block. The buildings making up the city block can, in turn, be a group that you translate, rotate, and scale to place within a city. Using VRML's grouping nodes and this kind of group hierarchy, you can manipulate large parts of a world at once.

Understanding Grouping

Recall from Chapters 2 and 3 that the VRML grouping nodes each collect together a list of nodes to be members of a group. Each of the VRML grouping nodes provide grouping abilities. To these abilities, each node adds its own additional features. For instance, the **Transform** node creates a new coordinate system for its group.

Basic Groups

The **Group** node provides basic node grouping features. Using the **children** field of the **Group** node, you can group together any number of nodes. The group as a whole can then be given a defined name using **DEF** and repeatedly instanced later in the VRML file using **USE**.

Switch Groups

The **Switch** grouping node extends the basic grouping abilities of the **Group** node. The **Switch** node uses the group of children as a list of choices and selects only one at a time to be built. Using the **whichChoice** field in the **Switch** node, you can select which child to build in the group.

Switch nodes can be used to group together different versions of a shape, such as different designs for a living room sofa. By changing the **whichChoice** field value, you can quickly switch between sofa designs without changing much in your VRML file.

Transform Groups

The **Transform** grouping node extends the basic grouping abilities of the **Group** node by creating a new coordinate system for the group. The new coordinate system can be translated, rotated, and scaled using the **translation, rotation, scale, center,** and **scaleOrientation** fields described in Chapters 5 through 7. This enables you to place the group anywhere within your world, orient it, and resize it depending on its use.

Billboard Groups

The **Billboard** group node extends the basic grouping abilities of the **Group** node by creating a special purpose billboard coordinate system. The *billboard* coordinate system is automatically rotated so that the shapes in the group, as a unit, always turn to face the viewer, even as the viewer moves around the group. The effect is called *billboarding*, because you can use it to make an advertisement billboard always turn to face the viewer. Billboarding can be used for a wide variety of effects, like signs, help messages, advertisements, annotations, control panels, and status displays.

You can specify the axis about which the billboard group rotates as it turns to face the viewer, and billboard group rotation is then restricted to that axis. Typically this is a vertical axis, but it can be any axis you choose. Consider, for example, using a vertical billboard axis. As the viewer moves around the group, the group pivots about the vertical axis to face the viewer. However, if the viewer rises up above the group, looking down at the group, no rotation about a vertical axis can orient the group to tilt upward facing the hovering viewer. Instead the group pivots about the vertical rotation axis to face viewers as if they weren't hovering.

You can also specify that the billboard group swivels arbitrarily to face the viewer, rotating around any axis as necessary.

Bounding Boxes

To build worlds as fast as possible, your VRML browser constantly examines the layout of your world in relation to the viewing position. Shapes in front of the viewer must be drawn, but shapes behind the viewer can be skipped to save drawing time. Sorting shapes into those that are visible and those that aren't is called *visibility culling*. The more quickly this is done, the more quickly your VRML browser can draw your world.

To speed visibility culling, the browser builds its own invisible boxes, called *bounding boxes*, around each group of shapes in **Group, Billboard,** and **Transform** groups. These boxes are just large enough to encompass, or *bound*, the shapes within the group.

Instead of checking the visibility of every shape within a group, the browser first checks the visibility of the bounding box. If the bounding box isn't visible, then none of the shapes within the box are visible, and the browser need not check each shape individually. If the bounding box is visible, then the browser checks each shape within the group to see if it is visible. On average, bounding-box checking dramatically speeds visibility culling and world building by your browser.

You can set the bounding box size and center for the **Group, Billboard,** and **Transform** nodes. This enables you to provide explicit hints to the browser to help it speed up visibility culling. You are also free to leave these fields unspecified, in which case your VRML browser computes their values itself.

The **Group** Node Syntax

VRML nodes can be grouped together using the **Group** node.

| SYNTAX | **Group node** |

```
Group {
    children          [ ]                 # exposedField   MFNode
    bboxSize          -1.0 -1.0 -1.0      # field          SFVec3f
    bboxCenter         0.0  0.0  0.0      # field          SFVec3f
    addChildren                           # eventIn        MFNode
    removeChildren                        # eventOut       MFNode
}
```

The value of the **children** exposed field specifies a list of children nodes to be included in the group. Typical **children** field values include **Shape** nodes and other grouping nodes. The VRML browser builds the group by building each of the shapes and groups contained within the group. The default value for this field is an empty list of children.

The value of the **bboxSize** field specifies the size of a bounding box sufficiently large to contain all of the shapes within the group. The first value gives the width of the box in the X direction, the second value the height of the box in the Y direction, and the third the depth of the box in the Z direction. The default for this field is a bounding box with a −1.0-unit width, height, and depth, which indicates that the VRML browser automatically computes the bounding box.

The value of the **bboxCenter** field specifies the center of the bounding box. The field value is a 3-D coordinate within the group's coordinate system. The default value is the origin. If the VRML browser automatically computes the bounding box size, it automatically computes the bounding box center, as well.

The list of children in the group can be set, added to, or removed from using the implied **set_children** eventIn of the **children** exposed field and the **addChildren** and removeChildren eventIns. When a list of node values is sent to the implied **set_children** eventIn, the list of nodes in the **children** field is replaced with the incoming node list. When a list of nodes is sent to the **addChildren** eventIn, each node in the incoming list is added to the list of nodes in the **children** field (if the node isn't already in that list of children). When a list of nodes is sent to the **removeChildren** eventIn, each node in the incoming list is compared to the list of children, and if found, the node is removed from the list. In all three cases, if the list of children is changed, the new list of children is sent using the implied **children_changed** eventOut of the **children** exposed field.

The **Switch** Node Syntax

VRML nodes can be grouped together using the **Switch** node.

SYNTAX	Switch node

```
Switch {
    choice        [ ]       # exposedField  MFNode
    whichChoice   -1        # exposedField  SFInt32
}
```

The value of the **choice** exposed field specifies a list of child nodes to be included in the group. Typical **choice** field values include **Shape** nodes and other grouping nodes. The VRML browser builds the group by building only one of the shapes and groups contained within the group. The default value for this field is an empty list of children.

The value of the **whichChoice** exposed field selects which chosen, single child in the group is to be built. Children are numbered starting with 0 for the first child in the **choice** field value list. If the **whichChoice** field value is less than 0, or greater than or equal to the number of nodes in the **choice** field's list of children, then none of the shapes in the group are built. The default value for this field is -1, which specifies that none of the group's shapes are to be built.

The current child choice can be changed by sending a value to the implied **set_whichChoice** eventIn of the **whichChoice** exposed field. When a value is received by this input, the corresponding field value is changed, and the new value is output using the implied **whichChoice_changed** eventOut of the exposed field.

The list of children in the group can be set using the implied **set_choice** eventIn of the **choice** exposed field. When a list of node values is sent to the implied **set_choice** eventIn, the children list value of the **choice** field is replaced with the incoming node list. When the list of children is changed, the new list of children is sent using the implied **choice_changed** eventOut of the **choice** exposed field.

All children of the **Switch** node continue to receive and send events regardless of the choice specified within the **whichChoice** field.

The **Transform** Node Syntax

The **Transform** grouping node creates a new coordinate system relative to its parent coordinate system. Shapes created as children of the **Transform** node are built relative to the new coordinate system's origin.

SYNTAX | **Transform node**

```
Transform {
    children         [ ]                        # exposedField  MFNode
    translation      0.0  0.0  0.0              # exposedField  SFVec3f
    rotation         0.0  0.0  1.0      0.0     # exposedField  SFRotation
    scale            1.0  1.0  1.0              # exposedField  SFVec3f
    scaleOrientation 0.0  0.0  1.0      0.0     # exposedField  SFRotation
    center           0.0  0.0  0.0              # exposedField  SFVec3f
    bboxSize        -1.0 -1.0 -1.0              # field         SFVec3f
    bboxCenter       0.0  0.0  0.0              # field         SFVec3f
    addChildren                                 # eventIn       MFNode
    removeChildren                              # eventIn       MFNode
}
```

The **children** and **translation** fields are discussed in Chapter 5, the **rotation** field is discussed in Chapter 6, and the **scale, scaleOrientation,** and **center** fields are discussed in Chapter 7.

The value of the **bboxSize** field is discussed in the section entitled "The **Group** Node Syntax." Remember that the **Transform** node's bounding-box size is relative to the new coordinate system created by the **Transform** node.

The value of the **bboxCenter** field is discussed in the section entitled "The **Group** Node Syntax." Remember that the **Transform** node's bounding-box center is relative to the new coordinate system created by the **Transform** node.

The **addChildren** and **removeChildren** eventIns are also discussed in the section entitled "The **Group** Node Syntax."

The **Billboard** Node Syntax

The **Billboard** group node creates a new coordinate system relative to its parent coordinate system. Shapes created as children of the **Billboard** group node are built relative to the new coordinate system's origin.

| SYNTAX | **Billboard node** |

```
Billboard {
        children          [ ]                     # exposedField  MFNode
        axisOfRotation    0.0  1.0  0.0            # exposedField  SFVec3f
        bboxCenter        0.0  0.0  0.0            # field         SFVec3f
        bboxSize         -1.0 -1.0 -1.0            # field         SFVec3f
        addChildren                               # eventIn       MFNode
        removeChildren                            # eventIn       MFNode
}
```

The **children** exposed field value is discussed in the section entitled "The **Group** Node Syntax."

The value of the **axisOfRotation** exposed field specifies an arbitrary axis about which to automatically rotate the group. As the viewer moves within the world, the rotation angle about this axis is continually updated so that the group's Z axis always points toward the viewer. The rotation axis can be any arbitrary axis. The default rotation axis is a vertical axis pointing straight up the Y axis of the group's coordinate system. A rotation axis of 0.0,0.0,0.0 indicates that the group should be rotated arbitrarily, without regard to a specific rotation axis.

The rotation axis can be changed by sending a value to the implied **set_axisOfRotation** eventIn of the **axisOfRotation** exposed field. When a value is received by this input, the corresponding field value is changed, and the new value output using the implied **axisOfRotation_changed** eventOut of the exposed field.

The **bboxSize** and the **bboxCenter** field values and the **addChildren** and **removeChildren** eventIns are discussed in the section entitled "The **Group** Node Syntax."

A **Billboard** node can be given a defined name using **DEF** and instanced multiple times using **USE**. Each instance acts independently of any other instance. In other words, each instance turns an appropriate angle about the rotation axis so that the billboard always faces the viewer.

Experimenting with Grouping

The following examples provide a more detailed examination of the ways in which the **Group, Switch, Transform,** and **Billboard** nodes can be used and how they interact with nodes discussed in previous chapters.

Switching Between Shapes

Using a **Switch** node, you can build multiple versions of a shape, include all of them in your VRML world, then select between them to quickly try out each one in context. The VRML text in Figure 11.1 creates three versions of a café sign and includes all three within a **Switch** node. Setting the **whichChoice** field of the node to 0 selects the first version of the sign, setting the field to 1 selects the second version, and setting it to 2 selects the third version.

```
#VRML V2.0 utf8
Switch {
    whichChoice 2
    choice [
    # Version 0:   simple round background
        Group {
            children [
                DEF Cafe Shape {
                    appearance DEF GlowWhite Appearance {
                        material Material {
                            emissiveColor 1.0 1.0 1.0
                            diffuseColor  0.0 0.0 0.0
                        }
                    }
                    geometry Text {
                        string "Cafe"
                        fontStyle FontStyle {
                            justify "MIDDLE"
                        }
                    }
                },
                DEF BlueDisk Transform {
                    translation 0.0 0.3 -0.10
                    rotation    1.0 0.0 0.0 -1.57
                    children Shape {
                        appearance Appearance {
                            material Material {
                                diffuseColor  0.0 0.3 0.8
                            }
                        }
                        geometry Cylinder {
                            radius 1.3
                            height 0.1
                        }
                    }
                }
            ]
        },
    # Version 1:   round background with white edge
        Group {
            children [
                USE Cafe,
                USE BlueDisk,
                DEF WhiteDisk Transform {
                    translation 0.0 0.3 -0.10
                    rotation    1.0 0.0 0.0 -1.57
                    children Shape {
                        appearance USE GlowWhite
                        geometry Cylinder {
                            radius 1.4
                            height 0.08
                        }
                    }
                }
            ]
        },
```

Figure 11.1 continues

```
# Version 2:  round background, white edge, red box
    Group {
        children [
            USE Cafe,
            USE BlueDisk,
            USE WhiteDisk,
            DEF RedAndWhiteBoxes Transform {
                translation 0.0 0.3 -0.10
                children [
                    Shape {
                        appearance Appearance {
                            material Material {
                                diffuseColor 0.8 0.0 0.0
                            }
                        }
                        geometry Box {
                            size 4.0 1.2 0.06
                        }
                    },
                    Shape {
                        appearance USE GlowWhite
                        geometry Box {
                            size 4.2 1.4 0.04
                        }
                    }
                ]
            }
        ]
    }
}
```

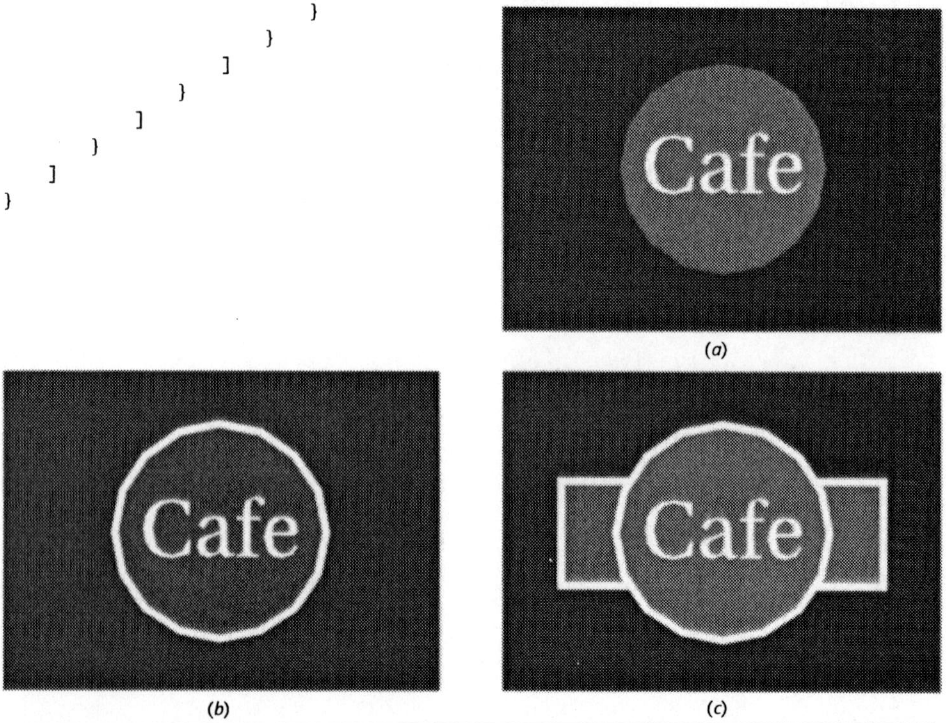

(a)

(b)

(c)

Figure 11.1 *Three versions of a café sign within a* **Switch** *node with the* **whichChoice** *field set to (a) 0, (b) 1, and (c) 2. (The VRML text shown in this figure creates the image shown in Figure 11.1c.)*

Creating Billboard Groups

Shapes built within a billboard group are automatically rotated to face the viewer as the viewer moves through your world. You can use this to ensure that signs are always readable. Figure 11.2 places the fanciest version of the café sign from Figure 11.1 in a **Billboard** group node with a vertical axis of rotation. Three **Box** nodes are added outside the **Billboard** group node, creating a base and ground for the sign.

```
#VRML V2.0 utf8
Group {
    children [
    # Cafe Sign in a Billboard group
        Billboard {
            axisOfRotation 0.0 1.0 0.0
            children [
                DEF Cafe Shape {
                    appearance DEF GlowWhite Appearance {
                        material Material {
                            emissiveColor 1.0 1.0 1.0
                            diffuseColor  0.0 0.0 0.0
                        }
                    }
                    geometry Text {
                        string "Cafe"
                        fontStyle FontStyle {
                            justify "MIDDLE"
                        }
                    }
                },
                DEF BlueDisk Transform {
                    translation 0.0 0.3 -0.10
                    rotation    1.0 0.0 0.0 -1.57
                    children Shape {
                        appearance Appearance {
                            material Material {
                                diffuseColor  0.0 0.3 0.8
                            }
                        }
                        geometry Cylinder {
                            radius 1.3
                            height 0.1
                        }
                    }
                },
```

Figure 11.2 continues

```
DEF WhiteDisk Transform {
    translation 0.0 0.3 -0.10
    rotation    1.0 0.0 0.0 -1.57
    children [
        Shape {
            appearance USE GlowWhite
            geometry Cylinder {
                radius 1.4
                height 0.08
            }
        }
    ]
},
DEF RedAndWhiteBoxes Transform {
    translation 0.0 0.3 -0.10
    children [
        Shape {
            appearance Appearance {
                material Material {
                    diffuseColor 0.8 0.0 0.0
                }
            }
            geometry Box {
                size 4.0 1.2 0.06
            }
        },
        Shape {
            appearance USE GlowWhite
            geometry Box {
                size 4.2 1.4 0.04
            }
        }
    ]
}
]
},
# Non-billboard sign pole and ground
DEF Pole Transform {
    translation 0.0 -3.1 -0.10
    children Shape {
        appearance DEF Gray Appearance {
            material Material {
                diffuseColor 0.6 0.6 0.6
            }
        }
        geometry Box {
            size 0.4 4.0 0.4
        }
    }
},
```

Figure 11.2 continues

```
DEF PoleBase Transform {
    translation 0.0 -5.2 -0.10
    children Shape {
        appearance USE Gray
        geometry Box {
            size 1.0 0.2 1.0
        }
    }
},
DEF Ground Transform {
    translation 0.0 -5.35 -0.10
    children Shape {
        appearance USE Gray
        geometry Box {
            size 10.0 0.1 10.0
        }
    }
}
        ]
    }
```

Figure 11.2 *A café sign within a billboard group.*

As the viewer moves around the sign, the pole and ground remain stationary, but the café sign automatically pivots about a vertical axis to follow the viewer. If the viewer moves upward and hovers looking down at the sign from an angle, the sign pivots on the vertical axis, but does not tilt upward to face the viewer. To make the sign tilt upward, change the **axisOfRotation** field value of the **Billboard** node to 0.0 0.0 0.0, like this:

```
Billboard {
    axisOfRotation 0.0 0.0 0.0
    children [
            .
    ]
}
```

Using Bounding Boxes

Recall the 3-D plus sign you built in Chapter 3 using three **Box** nodes as children of a **Group** node. To speed the browser's visibility culling, you can specify a bounding box for this group of boxes. To determine the bounding-box size for any group, examine the group's shapes and find those that extend farthest in the X, Y, and Z directions. Use these maximum extents to compute the size and center of a box large enough to hold all of the group's shapes.

The first box in the 3-D plus sign group is the widest at 25.0 units left to right. The second box in the group is the tallest at 25.0 units top to bottom. The third box in the group is the deepest at 25.0 units front to back. A bounding box big enough to encompass all three boxes is 25.0 units wide, 25.0 units tall, and 25.0 units deep, centered at the origin. The VRML text in Figure 11.3 shows a **Group** node with the bboxSize and bboxCenter field values set for this bounding box. The image in Figure 11.3 shows the 3-D plus sign and an outline showing the group's bounding box. The bounding box is actually invisible and is maintained by the VRML browser only to speed visibility culling.

```
#VRML V2.0 utf8
Group {
    bboxCenter 0.0 0.0 0.0
    bboxSize    25.0 25.0 25.0
    children [
        Shape {
            appearance Appearance {
                material Material {
                    diffuseColor 0.0 1.0 0.0
                }
            }
            geometry Box {
                size 25.0 2.0 2.0
            }
        },
        Shape {
            appearance Appearance {
                material Material {
                    diffuseColor 1.0 1.0 0.0
                }
            }
            geometry Box {
                size 2.0 25.0 2.0
            }
        },
        Shape {
            appearance Appearance {
                material Material {
                    diffuseColor 0.5 1.0 0.0
                }
            }
            geometry Box {
                size 2.0 2.0 25.0
            }
        }
    ]
}
```

Figure 11.3   *A group of shapes with a bounding box.*

You can also specify the bounding box for **Transform** and **Billboard** node groups. The bounding box size and center for these groups is specified relative to the group's coordinate system. Figure 11.4 builds two 3-D plus signs, each within a **Transform** group node. The first group is translated along the X axis, while the second is rotated around the Y axis. Since the geometry is the same in each **Transform** node group, so is the bounding box for the group.

```
#VRML V2.0 utf8
Group {
    children [
    # Translated Shape
        Transform {
            translation 20.0  0.0   0.0
            bboxCenter   0.0  0.0   0.0
            bboxSize    25.0 25.0 25.0
            children [
                DEF Widest Shape {
                    appearance Appearance {
                        material Material {
                            diffuseColor 0.0 1.0 0.0
                        }
                    }
                    geometry Box {
                        size 25.0 2.0 2.0
                    }
                },
                DEF Tallest Shape {
                    appearance Appearance {
                        material Material {
                            diffuseColor 1.0 1.0 0.0
                        }
                    }
                    geometry Box {
                        size 2.0 25.0 2.0
                    }
                },
                DEF Deepest Shape {
                    appearance Appearance {
                        material Material {
                            diffuseColor 0.5 1.0 0.0
                        }
                    }
                    geometry Box {
                        size 2.0 2.0 25.0
                    }
                }
            ]
        },
```

Figure 11.4 continues

```
# Rotated Shape
   Transform {
        rotation      0.0  1.0  0.0  0.785
        bboxCenter    0.0  0.0  0.0
        bboxSize     25.0 25.0 25.0
        children [
            USE Widest,
            USE Tallest,
            USE Deepest
        ]
    }
  ]
}
```

Figure 11.4 *Two transformed groups of shapes, each with its own bounding box.*

The **Group** node containing both shapes in Figure 11.4 was not given a specific bounding box. A bounding box can be computed for that **Group** node by examining the group's shapes, but computing your own bounding boxes can be quite time consuming, particularly when shapes are complicated or involve many nested **Transform** groups. Since VRML browsers can easily compute bounding boxes themselves, it is usually better to leave the **bboxSize** and **bboxCenter** fields unspecified, and let the browser fill in their values.

Summary

Nodes can be grouped together as children of VRML's grouping nodes: **Group, Switch, Transform,** and **Billboard.** Groups can contain shapes or more groups. A VRML file may contain any number of groups.

All shapes within a **Group, Transform,** or **Billboard** node are built by the VRML browser. In a **Switch** node, only the shape selected by the **whichChoice** field value is built. A negative value for this field indicates that none of the shapes within the switch group are to be built.

Transform and **Billboard** node groups create their own, new coordinate systems to contain the shapes within the group. The coordinate system of a **Transform** node can be translated, rotated, and scaled relative to the parent coordinate system. The coordinate system of a **Billboard** node is automatically rotated around a chosen axis of rotation so that the group's Z axis always points at the viewer. If the axis of rotation is 0.0 0.0 0.0, the group rotates freely to face the viewer, independent of a rotation axis. Billboard groups can be used to make signs and shapes always orient to face the viewer regardless of the viewer's position in your world.

Group, Billboard, and **Transform** node groups use bounding boxes that provide hints to the VRML browser to speed visibility culling for the shapes in the group. A bounding box is an invisible box positioned in the group's coordinate system and sized just large enough to encompass all shapes in the group.

## CHAPTER 12

Inlining Files

In each of the examples in previous chapters, you created a shape or shapes within a single VRML file. As you assemble these shapes together to create more complex shapes and worlds, your VRML files get larger and harder to manage. *Inlining* is a world-construction technique that enables you to keep each of the pieces of your VRML worlds in separate, smaller files. To construct a world using each of those pieces, you can create a VRML file containing **Inline** nodes. Each **Inline** node provides the file name of a piece to use in your new world. Your VRML browser reads each of the inlined files and assembles the world for you.

Typically, the file names you specify within **Inline** nodes are the names of files on your local hard disk. You can also use a full URL to specify the address of a file anywhere on the Web. Using URLs, you can inline shapes created by other VRML authors on the Web. This enables you to build very complex worlds without authoring each shape yourself.

Understanding Inlining

Inlining enables you to build each of the shapes for your world in a separate VRML file. You can independently test those shapes to make sure they look right on their own. Then you can inline one or more of those shape files to build a larger VRML file. That larger file can be inlined into a larger file, and so on. This inline assembly technique enables you to gradually build complex worlds from individual pieces, each stored in its own VRML file.

Like the VRML **Group** node, an **Inline** node groups shapes within your world. Unlike the **Group** node, an **Inline** node specifies the name of a VRML file from which the child nodes are read, instead of specifying the child nodes themselves. When the VRML browser reads any VRML file, it looks for **Inline** nodes and the files they list. Each inlined file is automatically read, as well, and the world constructed within the VRML browser.

A VRML file, such as one to create a table, can be inlined into as many other VRML files as you like. You can create a library of standard shapes that you inline as you need them in each world you create. If you change a library shape, like the table, all of the worlds in which that table is used change, as well.

Lists of URLs

The **url** field value of an **Inline** node specifies a URL, which is the location of a file to be inlined into your VRML world. The URL tells the VRML browser how to get the file, where to get the file, and the name of the file to get. URLs can indicate files on the Web or on your local hard disk. (See Chapter 1 for a discussion of URLs.)

Accessing your local disk is much faster than retrieving a file from the Web. Similarly, some sites on the Web are much faster than others. If your hard disk, a fast Web site, and a slow Web site all have the same VRML file available, you would naturally choose to get the file from your hard disk instead of from the Web sites. If your hard disk didn't have the file, but the fast and slow Web sites did, you would naturally choose to get the file from the fast Web site instead of the slow one. This is an example of prioritizing a list of locations where the VRML file you want may be found.

In VRML, anywhere you can specify a URL, you can also specify a list of URLs that provide a prioritized list of places where the browser can find the VRML file you want. Your VRML browser starts looking for the file by using the first URL in the list. If your browser finds the VRML file, it reads the file and skips the rest of the URLs in the list. If your browser can't find the file specified by the first URL in the list, then it tries the second one, and so on.

Inline Bounding Boxes

Like the **Group, Billboard,** and **Transform** grouping nodes, the **Inline** node includes fields in which you can specify the size and center of a bounding box for the inlined file's shapes. This bounding box is used by your VRML browser to speed visibility culling. (For more bounding box information, see Chapter 11.)

Your VRML browser can also use the bounding box to delay reading the inlined VRML file. If the bounding is outside the currently viewed part of the world, your VRML browser can postpone reading the inlined file's shapes until they would be visible.

DEF and USE within Inline Files

When using inlined files, the names you define with **DEF** may only be used again later within the *same* file. A defined name in an inlined file is not recognized if instanced by USE within the inlining file. Similarly, a defined name in the inlining file is not recognized within the inlined file. This limitation on the recognition of defined names enables you to define names in your files without regard to whether those same names are used in your other files.

The **Inline** Node Syntax

Any VRML file can be inlined using an **Inline** node. The **Inline** node can be used as the child of any grouping node.

| SYNTAX | **Inline node** |

```
Inline {
    url              [ ]                      # exposedField  MFString
    bboxCenter       -1.0 -1.0 -1.0           # field         SFVec3f
    bboxSize          0.0  0.0  0.0           # field         SFVec3f
}
```

The value of the **url** exposed field specifies a prioritized list of URLs, ordered from highest priority to lowest. The VRML browser typically starts by trying to open the file specified by the first URL in the list. If the file cannot be found, the browser tries the second URL in the list, and so on. When a URL is found that can be opened, the groups and shapes within that file are read and treated as children of the **Inline** node as if the **Inline** node were a **Group** node. If none of the URLs can be opened, then no inline shapes are built, and the **Inline** node is treated like a **Group** node without any children. The default value for the **url** field is an empty list of URLs, indicating that no file is opened and no inline shapes read in.

Some VRML browsers read shapes using a lower-priority URL while they wait to read shapes from a higher-priority URL over a slower connection. When the higher-priority URL shapes become available, the lower-priority shapes are automatically replaced with the higher-priority shapes.

The URL list can be changed by sending a value to the implied **set_url** eventIn of the **url** exposed field. When a value is received by this input, the corresponding field value is changed, and the new value is output using the implied **url_changed** eventOut of the exposed field.

Changing the **url** field value using the **set_url** eventIn causes the previously inlined nodes to be discarded and replaced with those in the newly selected inline file. If the previously inlined nodes include **Script** nodes, as discussed in Chapter 30, then each program script for each discarded **Script** node is shut down before it is replaced by the nodes from the newly selected inline file.

The **bboxSize** field value is discussed in Chapter 11.

The **bboxCenter** field value is discussed in Chapter 11.

Some VRML browsers display a line-drawn box the same size and location as the bounding box while they wait to read shapes from one of the URLs. When the URL's shapes become available, the line-drawn box is automatically replaced with the shapes.

Some VRML browsers delay reading shapes from any inline URL until the bounding box for the **Inline** node becomes visible to the viewer. This saves computation and communications effort in retrieving inlined shapes that the viewer may never turn toward and see.

Inlined files must be VRML files. The results are undefined if inlined files are not VRML files.

> **SIDEBAR: DELAYING INLINES** **Inline** nodes can be implemented by VRML browsers using several approaches. Two common approaches are: to read the inlined VRML file's contents immediately upon encountering the **Inline** node or to schedule reading the inlined file at some later time.
>
> Browsers that implement the first approach may not respond while they read each of the VRML files referenced by **Inline** nodes in the world. Only when all files contributing to the world have been retrieved and read is any part of the world displayed. This approach ensures that the world the viewer sees is always accurate and complete.
>
> The delay caused by waiting for all of the inlined files to be read in can leave users frustrated and wondering if their VRML browser has died. Therefore, many VRML browsers instead choose to display as much of the VRML world as possible, as soon as possible. This gives the user something to see, and possibly interact with, while the rest of the inlined files are being read in. Such browsers then schedule some or all of the inlined files to be retrieved when time permits.
>
> While the user is interacting with the partial world, the VRML browser periodically checks its list of scheduled inline files. Picking the top file off the list, the browser creates a new task to retrieve the file and read it into memory shared between the browser and the new task. When the task is finished, the browser is notified, and it adds the new inlined shapes to the portion of the world being displayed for the user. During this process it appears to users as if the world is being built before their eyes.
>
> Browsers that schedule tasks to read inline files usually have a menu item or a configuration file that enables the user to select the maximum number of inline reading tasks the browser can have running at any one time. With larger numbers there will be more tasks. If those tasks are all trying to access the same hard disk, or communicate over the same modem, then increasing the number of tasks won't necessarily speed up inline reading. A task limit of one or two is usually optimal.

Experimenting with Inlining

The following examples provide a more detailed examination of the ways in which the **Inline** node can be used and how it interacts with nodes discussed in previous chapters.

Using Inlining to Assemble a World

You can create a row of archways from the simple archway you built in Chapter 5 by inlining an archway and repeatedly instancing it.

Figure 12.1 shows the simple archway with two columns, a box spanning the columns, and two tilted boxes making up the archway roof. For use in the next two examples, save this archway in a file called *"arch.wrl"*.

```
#VRML V2.0 utf8
Group {
    children [
    # First archway
    # Left Column
        DEF LeftColumn Transform {
            translation -2.0 3.0 0.0
            children DEF Column Shape {
                appearance DEF White Appearance {
                    material Material { }
                }
                geometry Cylinder {
                    radius 0.3
                    height 6.0
                }
            }
        },
    # Right Column
        DEF RightColumn Transform {
            translation 2.0 3.0 0.0
            children USE Column
        },
    # Archway span
        DEF ArchwaySpan Transform {
            translation 0.0 6.05 0.0
            children Shape {
                appearance USE White
                geometry Box {
                    size 4.6 0.4 0.6
                }
            }
        },
    # Left Roof
        DEF LeftRoof Transform {
            translation -1.15 7.12 0.0
            rotation 0.0 0.0 1.0  0.524
            children DEF Roof Shape {
                appearance USE White
                geometry Box {
                    size 2.86 0.4 0.6
                }
            }
        },
```

Figure 12.1 continues

```
# Right Roof
    DEF LeftRoof Transform {
        translation 1.15 7.12 0.0
        rotation 0.0 0.0 1.0  -0.524
        children USE Roof
    }
]
}
```

Figure 12.1 *A simple arch.*

Figure 12.2 inlines the archway in "arch.wrl." The archway is then instanced multiple times to build a row of archways.

```
#VRML V2.0 utf8
Group {
    children [
        DEF Arch Inline {
            bboxSize    5.0 8.0 2.0
            bboxCenter 1.0 4.0 0.0
            url "arch.wrl"
        },
        Transform {
            translation 0.0 0.0 -2.0
            children USE Arch
        },
        Transform {
            translation 0.0 0.0 -4.0
            children USE Arch
        },
        Transform {
            translation 0.0 0.0 -6.0
            children USE Arch
        },
        Transform {
            translation 0.0 0.0 -8.0
            children USE Arch
        }
    ]
}
```

Figure 12.2 *A row of archways built by inlining one archway from "arch.wrl" and repeatedly instancing it.*

Nesting Inlined Files

A VRML file that uses **Inline** nodes can also be inlined. If you typed the archway row from Figure 12.2, name the file "archrow.wrl." The VRML text in Figure 12.3 shows how you can inline the archway row in "archrow.wrl" and instance it multiple times to create a simple temple.

```
#VRML V2.0 utf8
Group {
    children [
    # Ground
        Shape {
            appearance Appearance {
                material Material {
                    diffuseColor 0.0 1.0 0.0
                }
            }
            geometry Box {
                size 50.0 0.1 50.0
            }
        },
    # Back archway row
        Transform {
            translation 0.0 0.0 -4.0
            children DEF ArchRow Inline {
                bboxSize    5.0 8.0 10.0
                bboxCenter 1.0 4.0 -5.0
                url "archrow.wrl"
            }
        },
    # Front archway row
        Transform {
            translation 0.0 0.0 4.0
            rotation 0.0 1.0 0.0 3.14
            children USE ArchRow
        },
    # Left archway row
        Transform {
            translation -4.0 0.0 0.0
            rotation 0.0 1.0 0.0 1.57
            children USE ArchRow
        },
    # Right archway row
        Transform {
            translation 4.0 0.0 0.0
            rotation 0.0 1.0 0.0 -1.57
            children USE ArchRow
        }
    ]
}
```

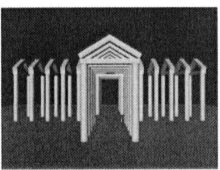

Figure 12.3 *A simple temple built by inlining one archway row from* "archrow.wrl" *and repeatedly instancing it.*

Summary

The **Inline** node specifies a prioritized list of URLs for a VRML file whose shapes are to be included in your world. The URL list includes full or relative URLs ordered from highest priority to lowest priority. Your VRML browser tries the highest-priority URL first. Only if it can't find that file does it try the second-highest-priority URL, and so on through the list. When it finds a file that it can open, it reads the nodes from that file and adds them as children of the **Inline** node, treating it like a **Group** node.

To speed the VRML browser's visibility culling, you can specify the center location and size of a bounding box large enough to encompass the contents of the inlined file. Your browser may also use the bounding box to delay reading in a VRML file until needed.

## CHAPTER 13

Building Shapes with Points, Lines, and Faces

The primitive geometry nodes can be used to create a variety of simple shapes, but they are insufficient when your goal is to create more complex shapes, particularly those with smooth, flowing curves. Fortunately, VRML provides a very flexible set of nodes for you to construct such geometries using points, lines, and faces.

A VRML *point* is a dot located within your 3-D world. Using sets of points in a **PointSet** node, you can draw star fields and scatter plots.

A VRML *line* is a straight line connecting two points in your 3-D world. Using sets of lines in a **IndexedLineSet** node, you can draw line plots, curves, and grids.

A VRML *face* is a flat shape, like a triangle, square, or octagon. The outline, or *perimeter*, of a face is made by connecting together a series of points, one for each corner of the face. The interior of the face is filled in by the VRML browser and shaded. By arranging many adjacent sets of faces in an **IndexedFaceSet** node, you can construct complex faceted surfaces. In fact, the VRML primitive geometries are actually constructed from faces. Using sets of faces, you can create your own faceted shapes. By using a large number of tiny facets, you can closely approximate any smooth surface. You can create the curved body of a sports car, the rolling hills of a landscape, the rounded shape of a computer mouse, or the smooth curves of a vase.

The **PointSet, IndexedLineSet,** and **IndexedFaceSet** nodes each use the **Coordinate** node to specify the 3-D locations for points in a point set, the end points for lines in a line set, and the corners for faces in a face set. You can animate these 3-D locations by using a **CoordinateInterpolator** node, and thereby create shapes that warp and change during an animation.

Understanding Point Sets

A VRML *point* is a dot located within your world. A *point set* is a collection of these dots, each with its own location.

Recall from Chapter 2 that you can specify a location in a 3-D world by using a coordinate made up of three values: an X, a Y, and a Z value. You can use lists of X, Y, and Z coordinates to specify the 3-D location of each point within a point set. For example, to build points at the four corners of a square, you'll need a coordinate list specifying the X, Y, and Z values for the four corners. Table 13.1 shows these four coordinates.

Table 13.1   Coordinates for the Four Corners of a Square

Coordinate Index	Coordinate (X, Y, Z)
0	-1.0 -1.0 0.0
1	1.0 -1.0 0.0
2	1.0 1.0 0.0
3	-1.0 1.0 0.0

Coordinates such as those in Table 13.1 are specified using a **Coordinate** node. The list of X, Y, Z values are specified as the value of the **point** field in the node. Figure 13.1 shows points built at each of the coordinates in Table 13.1.

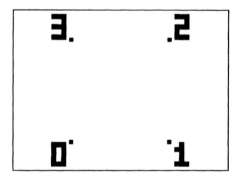

Figure 13.1   *A set of points at the corners of a square.*

Point-set geometries are built by providing a **Coordinate** node as the value of the coord field in a **PointSet** geometry node. Like other geometry nodes, the **PointSet** geometry node is used as the value of the **geometry** field in a **Shape** node to create a shape in your world. The shape you build with the **Shape** node can be given a color using an **Appearance** node and can be built within groups and new coordinate systems, just like other VRML shapes.

> **SIDEBAR: COORDINATES VERSUS VERTICES**   A coordinate is also called a *vertex,* and two or more coordinates are called *vertices.* A coordinate is a generic 3-D location, while a vertex is a coordinate used to build a shape. (We avoid this subtle distinction and primarily use the term coordinate in this book.)

Understanding Line Sets

A VRML *line* is a straight line connecting two end points, each one located within your world. A *line set* is a collection of these lines.

Like points in a point set, the end points of lines in a line set are specified using coordinates. To build a line, you specify the coordinate to start from and the coordinate to end with, and the VRML browser builds a straight line between the two.

You can connect multiple lines together into a *polyline.* A polyline has a starting coordinate, several intermediate coordinates, and an ending coordinate. The VRML browser builds a straight line from the starting coordinate to the first intermediate coordinate, from there to the second intermediate coordinate, and so on, finishing the polyline on the ending coordinate.

Using Coordinate Indexes to Build Polylines

VRML polylines are built just like drawing figures in a connect-the-dots game. The dots used to build a polyline are located by a list of coordinates. If you want the first coordinate in a coordinate list to be connected to the second coordinate, you specify that the VRML browser should build a line from *coordinate1* to *coordinate2.* If you want a line from the second coordinate to the third coordinate, you specify that a line should be built from *coordinate2* to *coordinate3.* The connect-the-dots numbers 1, 2, and 3 are *coordinate indexes.* Coordinate indexes indicate the coordinates you want to connect together, selecting them from a coordinate list. The coordinate list specifies the actual X, Y, and Z values for each coordinate.

For example, to build a Z-shaped polyline connecting four coordinates together, you need the coordinate list specifying the X, Y, Z values for the four coordinates, and the coordinate indexes specifying the order in which those coordinates are to be connected. Table 13.2 shows four coordinates for the Z-shaped polyline.

Table 13.2   Coordinates for the Four Corners of a Z-Shaped Polyline

Coordinate Index	*Coordinate (X, Y, Z)*
0	-1.0 -1.0 0.0
1	1.0 -1.0 0.0
2	1.0 1.0 0.0
3	-1.0 1.0 0.0

Coordinates like those in Table 13.2 are specified using a **Coordinate** node. The X, Y, Z values in the list are specified as the value of the **point** field in the node. The coordinates in the **point** field's list are implicitly numbered starting at 0. The first coordinate in the list has a coordinate index of 0, the second an index of 1, and so forth.

To build the Z-shaped polyline shown in Figure 13.2 using the coordinates above, you can specify a list of coordinate indexes such as these:

```
3, 2, 0, 1
```

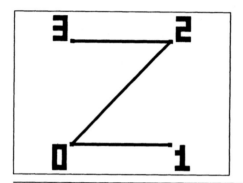

Figure 13.2   *A polyline connecting coordinates to make a "Z" shape.*

Using the same coordinates, you can build several different polylines by connecting the coordinates together differently. You can, for example, create an N-shaped polyline by using the following coordinate index list:

```
0, 3, 1, 2
```

If you use the same coordinate index more than once in the index list, you can create loops, triangles, squares, and circles. The following coordinate index list creates a square by using the same coordinate index (0) as both the starting and ending index in the list:

```
0, 1, 2, 3, 0
```

It is often convenient to build sets of polylines, each one using its own coordinate index list, but sharing the same coordinate list. VRML enables you to mark the end of one polyline and the beginning of the next by using the special coordinate index -1. For example the following coordinate index list creates three polylines:

```
0, 1, 2, 3, 0, -1,  0, 2, -1,  1, 3
```

The first coordinate index list above (0, 1, 2, 3, 0) builds a square polyline ending on index 0. The -1 marks the end of that polyline and the beginning of the next. The second list (0, 2) builds a straight diagonal line from index 0 at the lower-left corner of the square to index 2 at the upper-right corner. The next -1 marks the end of that polyline. The third list (1, 3) builds a straight diagonal line from index 1 at the lower-right to index 3 at the upper-left of the square. Figure 13.3 shows the results.

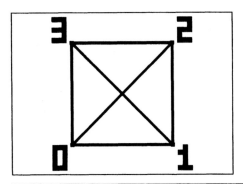

Figure 13.3   *Three polylines building a square and crossed diagonals.*

Building 3-D Shapes Using Polylines

Using 3-D coordinates, you can build polylines that depict 3-D shapes. Table 13.3 shows the 3-D coordinates for the eight corners of a box.

Table 13.3   Coordinates for the Corners of a 3-D Box

Coordinate Index	Coordinate (X, Y, Z)
0	-1.0 1.0 1.0
1	1.0 1.0 1.0
2	1.0 1.0 -1.0
3	-1.0 1.0 -1.0
4	-1.0 -1.0 1.0
5	1.0 -1.0 1.0
6	1.0 -1.0 -1.0
7	-1.0 -1.0 -1.0

To build the box using the coordinates from Table 13.1, you can build six poly-lines. The first polyline outlines the top of the box, and the second the bottom of the box. The remaining four polylines create the four vertical edges of the box. The following is the coordinate index list for these polylines:

```
0, 1, 2, 3, 0, -1,   4, 5, 6, 7, 4, -1,   0, 4, -1,   1, 5, -1,   2, 6, -1, 3, 7
```

Figure 13.4 shows the box polyline built using the above coordinate index list.

The **IndexedLineSet** geometry node enables you to create polylines like those above. The coordinate list for the polylines is specified by a **Coordinate** node used as the value of the **coord** field in an **IndexedLineSet** geometry node. To specify which coordinates are to be connected together by lines, you provide a list of coordinate indexes within the **IndexedLineSet** node's **coordIndex** field. Then use the **Indexed-LineSet** node as the value of the **geometry** field in a **Shape** node to create a shape in

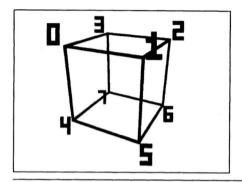

Figure 13.4 *A 3-D polyline box.*

your world. Like other shapes, you can give line-set shapes a color, group them, and build them within any coordinate system.

Understanding Face Sets

A VRML face is a flat shape like a triangle, square, or octagon. A *face set* is a collection of these faces.

To build a face, you specify the perimeter of the face using a chain of coordinates, similar to the way you specify a polyline. The area within the face's perimeter is filled in by the VRML browser and shaded to make it look solid.

The similarity of faces and polylines extends into terminology, as well: A face is also known as a *polygon*. Triangles, squares, octagons, and circles are all examples of polygons. (We use the term "face" throughout this book.)

Using Coordinate Indexes to Build Faces

Like the connect-the-dots strategy for building polylines, you build faces by specifying a starting coordinate index and a list of intermediate coordinate indexes for coordinates along the face perimeter. Your VRML browser automatically connects the coordinates together, then closes the perimeter by connecting the last intermediate coordinate back to the starting coordinate.

For example, to build a square face you need the coordinate list specifying the X, Y, and Z values of the square's four corners and the coordinate indexes to specify the

Table 13.4   Coordinates for the Four Corners of a Square

Coordinate Index	Coordinate (X, Y, Z)
0	-1.0 -1.0 0.0
1	1.0 -1.0 0.0
2	1.0 1.0 0.0
3	-1.0 1.0 0.0

order in which those coordinates are to be connected together for the face's perimeter. Table 13.4 shows four coordinates for the square.

To build the square using the coordinates in Table 13.4, you can specify a list of coordinate indexes, like this:

```
0, 1, 2, 3
```

Notice that the square's coordinate index list doesn't need to repeat the first index again as the last index. Unlike with polylines, your VRML browser automatically closes the square by connecting the last index back to the first when building faces, as shown in Figure 13.5

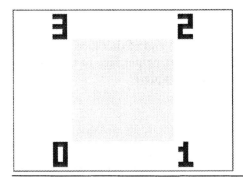

Figure 13.5   *A face built using four coordinates.*

Using the same coordinates, you can build several different faces by simply connecting them together differently. You can, for example, create a triangle by using the following coordinate index list:

```
1, 2, 3
```

A coordinate index list specifies the order of coordinates along a face's perimeter. The choice of starting index doesn't matter. For instance, the following three coordinate index lists all create the same triangular face:

```
1, 2, 3
2, 3, 1
3, 1, 2
```

Starting at index 1, you can create a triangle by tracing its perimeter in either the clockwise or the counterclockwise direction. Both of the coordinate index lists in Table 13.5 create the same triangle but trace its perimeter in opposite directions.

Table 13.5   Coordinate Index Lists for a Triangle

Coordinate Index List	Direction
1, 2, 3	Counterclockwise
3, 2, 1	Clockwise

Always build your VRML faces using coordinate indexes listed in counterclockwise order. This convention enables your VRML browser to decide which side of the face is the front and which is the back. The front of a face is the side of the face you see if you trace its perimeter in a counterclockwise fashion. By default, only the front sides of faces are drawn. If you look at a face from the back, it will be invisible.

Like line sets, it is often convenient to list the coordinate indexes for multiple faces within a set of faces. Each face in the set uses the same coordinate list, but with its own list of coordinate indexes. VRML enables you to mark the end of one face and the beginning of the next by using the special coordinate index -1. For example the following coordinate index list creates two triangular faces:

```
0, 1, 2, -1, 0, 2, 3
```

The first coordinate index list above (0, 1, 2) builds a triangular face in the lower-right corner of a square. The -1 marks the end of that face and the beginning of the next. The second list (0, 2, 3) builds a triangular face in the upper-left corner of a square. Together these two triangles fill a square.

Building 3-D Shapes Using Faces

Using 3-D coordinates, you can build face sets that create 3-D shapes, similar to VRML's text and primitives (see the sidebar entitled "Faces in Text and Primitive Geometries"). Table 13.6 shows the 3-D coordinates for the eight corners of a box.

Table 13.6   Coordinates for the Corners of a 3-D Box

Coordinate Index	Coordinate (X, Y, Z)
0	-1.0 1.0 1.0
1	1.0 1.0 1.0
2	1.0 1.0 -1.0
3	-1.0 1.0 -1.0
4	-1.0 -1.0 1.0
5	1.0 -1.0 1.0
6	1.0 -1.0 -1.0
7	-1.0 -1.0 -1.0

To build the box shown in Figure 13.6 using the coordinates in Table 13.6, you can build six faces, one for each side of the box. This is the coordinate index list for these faces:

```
0, 1, 2, 3, -1,  7, 6, 5, 4, -1,  0, 4, 5, 1, -1,
1, 5, 6, 2, -1,  2, 6, 7, 3, -1,  3, 7, 4, 0
```

The **IndexedFaceSet** geometry node enables you to create faces like these. The coordinate list for building faces is specified within a **Coordinate** node used as the value of the **coord** field in an **IndexedFaceSet** geometry node. To specify which coordinates are to be connected together to form face perimeters, you provide a list

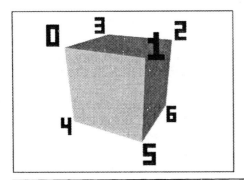

Figure 13.6 *A box built using six faces.*

of coordinate indexes within the **IndexedFaceSet** node's **coordIndex** field. The **IndexedFaceSet** node is then used as the value of the **geometry** field in a **Shape** node to create a shape in your world. Like other shapes, you can give face-set shapes a color, group them, and build them within any coordinate system.

SIDEBAR: FACES IN PRIMITIVE AND TEXT GEOMETRIES The primitive and text geometry nodes—**Box, Cone, Cylinder, Sphere,** and **Text**—build their geometries using face sets. The **Box** node, for instance, creates six faces, one each for the six sides of the box like that shown in Figure 13.6.

Determining the number of faces used to build the curved sides of cones, cylinders, and spheres is left to your VRML browser. Typically, the number of faces for a cylinder's sides may be 18 or more. Similarly, a sphere may use 60 or more. Some VRML browsers may vary the number of faces on a primitive shape, increasing the number as the viewer moves closer to the shape, and decreasing the number as the viewer moves away. This variation in the face count ensures that a cone, cylinder, or sphere always looks smooth. If you create your own cone, cylinder, or sphere out of faces in an **IndexedFaceSet** node, however, there will always be the same number of faces in the shape, regardless of the viewer's distance from it.

Like the primitive shapes, VRML text shapes are also built out of faces. The number of faces per character depends on the character's shape, the font style in use, and the implementation of your VRML browser. Typically, a single, Latin-alphabet character may have ten or more faces. Some VRML browsers may vary the number of faces in a character, increasing and decreasing the face count as the viewer moves closer or farther away from the character. If you build your own characters by using faces in an **IndexedFaceSet** node, however, the number of faces in the characters will not vary with viewer distance.

The VRML **LOD** node, which enables you to control the level of detail of your own shapes in a manner similar to the detail control often done automatically for cones, cylinders, spheres, and text characters, is discussed in Chapter 25.

Nonplanar Faces

Mathematically, a *planar* face is one in which all of its coordinates lie on a plane. More simply, a planar face is flat. If you toss a planar face on a table, it lies flat, and all of its perimeter coordinates simultaneously touch the tabletop. A triangle, for instance, is always planar.

A *nonplanar* face is one in which the coordinates *don't* all lie on a plane. If you toss a nonplanar face on a table, it does not lie flat, and at least one coordinate does not touch the tabletop. For example, while a perfectly flat piece of paper is planar, the same piece of paper is nonplanar when one corner of it is curled.

Similar to most computer graphics software, VRML can reliably draw only planar faces. To draw nonplanar faces, your VRML browser can automatically split nonplanar faces into multiple planar faces, typically triangles. This can be a problem, however, because there is always more than one way to split any nonplanar face into multiple planar faces.

For example, imagine a square with one corner lifted to make it nonplanar. Figure 13.7*a* and *b* show the square after the corner is lifted. Because the square with the corner lifted is no longer planar, your VRML browser must break the square into triangles before drawing it. Figure 13.7*a* and *b* show the two ways your browser may

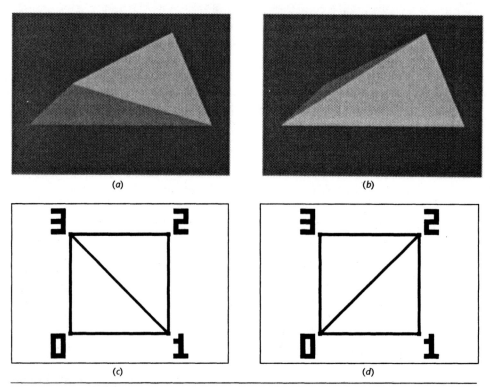

(a)   (b)

(c)   (d)

Figure 13.7   *Splitting a square with one corner lifted: (a) and (b) the square with one corner lifted but split differently; (c) and (d) top-view diagrams showing how the square is split.*

split the square, and *c* and *d* show top-view diagrams of the square illustrating the ways in which the square is split into triangles. Notice that the two ways of splitting the same nonplanar square create very different shaded results.

Both of the splits in Figure 13.7 are correct, but the results are very different. If you use nonplanar faces, the automatic splitting performed by the VRML browser may create either result. The browser may even split nonplanar faces differently depending on your viewpoint. This can make a shape look the way you intended from one angle, but look wrong from another angle.

In VRML you cannot control how the browser splits nonplanar faces. Instead, you should manually split nonplanar faces into triangles. This guarantees that you always get the effect you want.

Building Complex Faces

The previous examples use three and four coordinates to make triangles and squares. You can use longer lists of coordinates to create complex faces, such as the silhouette of a person's face or the outline of a guitar body. Complex faces have one of two forms:

- *Concave faces:* faces with inlets, or caves. The outline of a "C" is concave.
- *Convex faces:* faces without inlets, or caves. The outer perimeter of an "O" is convex.

Squares, triangles, pentagons, and octagons are all examples of convex faces. The silhouette of a person's face, however, is concave since it dips in and out as it passes over the brow ridge, under the nose, across the lips, and under the chin.

By default, your VRML browser assumes that all faces you build are convex. To enable you to build concave faces, you can set the **convex** field value in an **Indexed-FaceSet** node to **FALSE**. Your VRML browser will automatically convert the concave faces you build in that node to multiple, convex faces, typically triangles. Figure 13.8, for instance, shows how a concave face silhouette can be split into multiple triangles by your browser.

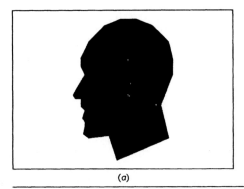
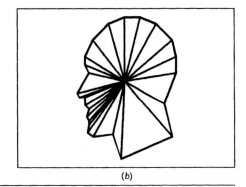

(a)   (b)

Figure 13.8   (a) *The concave shape of a person's face, and (b) the face split into multiple convex triangles.*

Building Solid Shapes

A *solid* shape is one that is built of faces that enclose a volume. Cubes, pyramids, and spheres are solid shapes. It doesn't matter what is contained inside the cube, pyramid, or sphere shape. The shape is solid if it can enclose a volume of something, whatever that is.

One way to check to see if a shape is a solid is to imagine that the shape is filled with water. If the water cannot pour out, then the shape is solid. For instance, a cube is solid, but a cube without the top face is not solid, since you could turn it upside down and pour water out of it.

An interesting property of solid shapes is that from any viewing position outside of the shape, the front side of one or more faces making up the shape, *always* blocks your view of the back side of any other face on the shape. Imagine, for instance, that the six sides of a solid cube are colored red on the outside, and blue on the inside. No matter how you turn the cube about, you will never see the blue inside. You have to tear open the cube to see the blue, but by so doing, you destroy its solidity.

By default, your VRML browser assumes that all faces in a face set combine to build one or more solid shapes. Because the shapes are all solid, the back sides of the shapes are never visible. Your browser can safely skip drawing the back side of a face, saving drawing time. Because the browser is skipping, or *culling*, back-facing faces, this shape-drawing optimization is called *backface culling*.

There are times, however, when you may wish to create shapes that are not solid. An open box, for instance, is not solid. If the viewer is looking inside the box, then the back sides of the faces making up the box's sides must be drawn and cannot be backface culled. You can enable or disable backface culling for shapes by setting the **solid** field value in the **IndexedFaceSet** node.

Smoothly Shading Shapes

Typically, the faces in a face set are used to build curvy shapes, such as car bodies, that are hard to build using the VRML primitive geometries alone. Each face in the face set creates a *facet*, or flat area, as if the curvy shape was chiseled out of stone. If you use a small number of large faces, you get a very rough approximation of the curvy shape. If you use a large number of small faces, you get a better approximation of the curvy shape. If you could use an infinite number of extremely tiny faces, you could create a perfect approximation of the curvy shape. (In practice, you can't use an infinite number of faces in a face set. The best you have is a good approximation that uses a moderate number of faces.)

When your VRML browser shades a face set, each of the faces are shaded to make the shape look three-dimensional. If you've used a low number of faces, your shape will look faceted and rough. If your intent was to approximate a smooth surface, like a car body, then this faceted shading is undesirable.

You have two choices to avoid faceted shading: (1) use many more faces to approximate the smooth shape, or (2) shade the faces differently so that it *looks* like you used lots of faces. Since the speed of your VRML browser decreases as you add more faces to a scene (see the sidebar entitled "Drawing Speed and World Complexity"), it is usually better to take advantage of shading tricks that make a small number of faces look like you used a large number. This technique of shading faces to make them look like they are part of a smooth shape is called *smooth shading.*

To accomplish smooth shading, your VRML browser gradually varies the brightness of a face as it shades it from edge to edge. This shading trick obscures the facets of a shape by making it harder to see where two faces butt up against each other. The actual faces haven't changed at all, only the way in which they are shaded.

Smooth shading makes any shape look smooth. However, sometimes there are parts of a shape that you don't want to be smoothed over. For this kind of shape, you need control over smooth shading so that sharp parts of the shape remain sharp, and smooth parts of the shape are shaded smoothly.

Sharpness and smoothness on a faceted shape can be indicated by the angle at which adjacent faces meet. If adjacent faces meet with a small angle between them, then the faces are probably facets on a smooth part of the shape. To make the shape appear smooth, faces with a small angle between them should be smooth shaded. If adjacent faces meet with a large angle between them, then the faces are probably part of a sharp feature on the shape. To make this part of the shape appear sharp, these faces should not be smooth shaded. The angle at which two adjacent faces meet is called the *crease angle.* As the term implies, a large angle indicates a crease, while a small angle indicates a smooth, nearly flat part of the shape.

Figure 13.9 shows an edge-on view of two pairs of faces. Figure 13.9*a* shows two faces that meet at a shallow crease angle. Figure 13.9*b* shows two faces that meet at a sharp crease angle.

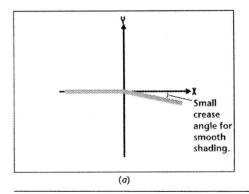 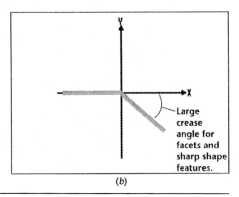

(a)   (b)

Figure 13.9 *An edge-on view of two pairs of adjacent faces: (a) two faces with a small crease angle, and (b) two faces with a large crease angle.*

To control smooth shading, you set a crease-angle threshold using the **creaseAngle** field value of the **IndexedFaceSet** node. Any pair of faces in the face set that meet with a crease angle less than the threshold are smoothly shaded so that the edge where they join is obscured. Any pair of faces that meet with a crease angle larger than the threshold, are not smoothly shaded.

SIDEBAR: DRAWING SPEED AND WORLD COMPLEXITY Whether shapes are built using the primitive and text geometry nodes or using the point-, line-, or face-set nodes, the number of coordinates and faces in your world has a dramatic effect on the drawing speed for the world. Increasing the number of coordinates and faces increases the amount of work necessary for your VRML browser to draw your world. Ideally, your VRML browser and your computer are fast enough to finish drawing your world in about $\frac{1}{30}$ of a second or less. At this speed, movement through the world will feel smooth and responsive. However, as the complexity of your world increases and your browser gains faces to draw at each movement, the drawing time can increase to more than $\frac{1}{30}$ of a second. As this happens, movement through the world begins to feel sluggish or jerky. It is to your advantage to keep your worlds as simple as practical and avoid using more faces than you absolutely need.

The tight correlation between the number of faces in your world and the speed with which the world can be drawn emphasizes the importance of giving your VRML browser every opportunity it can get to simplify its job. By setting the **solid** field value to **TRUE** in an **IndexedFaceSet** node, you enable your browser to skip drawing the back sides of faces in the face set. This can significantly reduce the amount of work your browser must do to draw your world. This, in turn, gives you the opportunity to add more detail to your world and still achieve smooth and responsive movement within it.

Understanding Coordinate Animation

You can use a **CoordinateInterpolator** node to animate coordinate positions in a **Coordinate** node. The **CoordinateInterpolator** node specifies a list of key fractional times and key coordinates in its **key** and **keyValue** fields. When driven by the fractional time output of a **TimeSensor** node, the **CoordinateInterpolator** node uses linear interpolation to compute intermediate lists of coordinates. Each new, computed coordinate list is output using the node's **value_changed** eventOut. You can route this output to a **Coordinate** node to animate a shape's coordinates.

A CoordinateInterpolator node outputs a whole list of values at each clock tick. You can use this coordinate-list output to completely change the list of coordinates in use by a shape. This type of coordinate animation can be used to warp a shape as the animation progresses.

For instance, if the interpolator's coordinate list at fractional time 0.0 describes a sphere, and the coordinate list at fractional time 1.0 describes a pillow sofa, then animating between the two coordinate lists evolves the shape from a sphere to a sofa. This form of shape animation is known as a *geometric morph*, or *morph*.

The **Coordinate** Node Syntax

The **Coordinate** node creates a list of coordinates and may be used as the value for the **coord** field of coordinate-based geometry nodes, such as the **PointSet, Indexed-LineSet,** and **IndexedFaceSet** nodes.

| SYNTAX | Coordinate node |

```
Coordinate {
    point    [ ]     # exposedField  MFVec3f
}
```

The value of the **point** exposed field specifies a list of 3-D coordinates used as geometry coordinates for a shape. Each 3-D coordinate is a three-part, floating-point value, one each for the X, Y, and Z distances from the origin. The default value for the **point** field is an empty list of coordinates.

When used by geometry nodes that use coordinate indexes, the first coordinate in the **Coordinate** node's list has index 0, the second index 1, and so forth.

The coordinate list can be changed by sending a value to the implied **set_point** eventIn of the **point** exposed field. When a value is received by this input, the coordinate list is changed, and the new coordinate list is output using the implied **point_changed** eventOut of the exposed field. The **CoordinateInterpolator** node is a typical source for coordinate-list values routed to the implied **set_point** eventIn.

The **CoordinateInterpolator** Node Syntax

The **CoordinateInterpolator** node describes a series of key colors available for use in an animation.

| SYNTAX | CoordinateInterpolator node |

```
CoordinateInterpolator {
    key             [ ]     # exposedField  MFFloat
    keyValue        [ ]     # exposedField  MFVec3f
    set_fraction            # eventIn       SFFloat
    value_changed           # eventOut      MFVec3f
}
```

The value of the **key** exposed field specifies a list of key, fractional, floating-point times. Typically, fractional times are between 0.0 and 1.0, such as those output by a **TimeSensor** node's **fraction_changed** eventOut. Key fractional times, however, may be positive or negative floating-point values of any size. Key fractional times must be listed in nondecreasing order. The default value for the **key** field is an empty list.

The value of the **keyValue** exposed field specifies a list of key 3-D coordinates. Each 3-D coordinate is specified as three floating-point values, one each for the X,

Y, and Z distances from the origin. The default value for the **keyValue** field is an empty list.

The key fractional times and key coordinates are used together to specify sublists of coordinates between which the node interpolates to generate an output coordinate list. In its simplest form, a sublist contains only one coordinate for each fractional time. For instance, if there are N fractional time values, then there are exactly N key coordinates in the **keyValue** field. The first key fractional time specifies the time for the first key coordinate, the second key fractional time the time for the second key coordinate, and so forth. In this simple form of the interpolator, each output coordinate list contains only one coordinate.

In a more complex form, the **keyValue** exposed field provides two or more key coordinates for each key fractional time. For instance, if there are N key fractional times, and M key coordinates for each time, then the **keyValue** field contains $N \times M$ coordinates, and the node's output contains M coordinates.

When a fractional time is received by the **set_fraction** eventIn, the **CoordinateInterpolator** node computes a sublist of coordinates based on the list of key fractional times and their corresponding key coordinate sublists. The new, computed coordinate list is output on the **value_changed** eventOut.

An output coordinate list for an input fractional time t is computed by the **CoordinateInterpolator** node by:

1. Scanning the key fractional times to find a pair of adjacent times $t1$ and $t2$, where $t1 \leq t \leq t2$.
2. Retrieving the corresponding pair of key coordinate sublists.
3. Computing an intermediate coordinate sublist computed by linearly interpolating between the key coordinate sublists.

Two adjacent key fractional times $t1$ and $t2$ may have the same value in order to create a discontinuity, or jump, in the animation path. In this case, the key coordinate sublist corresponding to $t1$ (the first of the two times) is used by the **CoordinateInterpolator** node when linearly interpolating for times less than $t1$, and the key coordinate sublist corresponding to $t2$ (the second of the two times) is used when linearly interpolating for times greater than $t2$.

Typically, fractional times are sent to the **set_fraction** eventIn by wiring a route from the **fraction_changed** eventOut of a **TimeSensor** node. Fractional times may also be generated by alternate means, such as the output of nodes that generate generic, floating-point values.

The list of key fractional times or coordinates can be changed by sending values to the implied **set_key** and **set_keyValue** eventIns of the **key** and **keyValue** exposed fields. When values are received by these inputs, the corresponding field values are changed, and the new values are output using the implied **key_changed** and **keyValue_changed** eventOuts of the exposed fields.

The **CoordinateInterpolator** node creates no shapes and has no visible effect on a world. A **CoordinateInterpolator** node may be a child of any grouping node but is independent of the coordinate system in use. Typically, interpolators are placed at the end of the outermost group of a VRML file.

The **PointSet** Node Syntax

The **PointSet** node creates point geometry and may be used as the value of the **geometry** field in a **Shape** node.

SYNTAX   **PointSet node**

```
PointSet {
      coord    NULL    # exposedField  SFNode
      color    NULL    # exposedField  SFNode
}
```

The value of the **coord** exposed field specifies a node listing the coordinates used to locate each point in the point set. Typical **coord** field values include the **Coordinate** node. The default **NULL** value for this field indicates an empty coordinate list and indicates that no points are to be built by the **PointSet** node.

Points are built one at a time, in order, starting with the first coordinate in the list and using all the coordinates from the coordinate list specified in the **coord** field.

The coordinate node value can be changed by sending a value to the implied **set_coord** eventIn of the **coord** exposed field. When a value is received by this input, the coordinate node is changed, and the new coordinate node is output using the implied **coord_changed** eventOut of the exposed field.

The **Appearance** node for the shape's **Shape** node specifies an overall color for the point set. Point-set shapes are always drawn using the **emissiveColor** field value of the **Appearance** node's **Material** node.

T I P   The default **emissiveColor** field value for a **Material** node is *black*. If you draw a point set using this default value, you will get black points. Since the default background color for a world is also black, you may not be able to see the black points. To avoid this, always set the **emissiveColor** field of the point-set shape's **Material** node to be something other than black.

You can color individual points using the **PointSet** node's **color** field, which is discussed in Chapter 16. The individually colored points are always drawn as if they are emissive.

Point set shapes cannot be textured using texture node values selected by an **Appearance** node. (See Chapters 17 and 18 for texture discussions.) Additionally, point set shapes are not subject to collision detection, as controlled by the **Collision** node, which is discussed in Chapter 27.

The **IndexedLineSet** Node Syntax

The **IndexedLineSet** node creates polyline geometry and may be used as the value for the **geometry** field of a **Shape** node.

SYNTAX   **IndexedLineSet node**

```
IndexedLineSet {
    coord            NULL    # exposedField  SFNode
    coordIndex       [ ]     # field         MFInt32
    color            NULL    # exposedField  SFNode
    colorIndex       [ ]     # field         MFInt32
    colorPerVertex   TRUE    # field         SFBool
    set_coordIndex           # eventIn       MFInt32
    set_colorIndex           # eventIn       MFInt32
}
```

The value of the **coord** exposed field specifies a node listing the coordinates available for building lines within the line set. Typical **coord** field values include the **Coordinate** node. The default **NULL** value for this field indicates an empty coordinate list and indicates that no lines are to be built by the **IndexedLineSet** node.

The value of the **coordIndex** field specifies a list of coordinate indexes describing the path of one or more polylines. Each value is an integer index specifying a coordinate from the coordinate list in the **coord** field. The default value for the **coordIndex** field is an empty coordinate index list and indicates that no lines are to be built.

A coordinate index list can specify one or many polylines. Each polyline connects together a string of coordinate indexes up to the end of the index list or up to an index of -1. The next coordinate index following a -1 starts a new polyline that ends at the next -1 index or at the end of the index list.

The coordinate node value can be changed by sending a value to the implied **set_coord** eventIn of the **coord** exposed field. When a value is received by this input, the coordinate node is changed, and the new coordinate node is output using the implied **coord_changed** eventOut of the exposed field.

The coordinate index list can be changed by sending a list of coordinate indexes to the **set_coordIndex** eventIn.

The **Appearance** node for the shape's **Shape** node specifies an overall color for the point set. Point-set shapes are always drawn using the **emissiveColor** field value of the **Appearance** node's **Material** node.

T I P   The default **emissiveColor** field value for a **Material** node is *black.* If you draw a line set using this default value, you will get black lines. Since the default background color for a world is also black, you may not be able to see the black lines. To avoid this, always set the **emissiveColor** field of the line-set shape's **Material** node to be something other than black.

You can color individual lines by using the **color, colorIndex, set_colorIndex,** and **colorPerVertex** fields discussed in Chapter 16. The individually colored lines are always drawn as if they are emissive.

Line set shapes cannot be textured using texture node values selected by an **Appearance** node. (See Chapters 17 and 18 for texture discussions.) Additionally, line set shapes are not subject to collision detection, as controlled by the **Collision** node, which is discussed in Chapter 27.

The **IndexedFaceSet** Node Syntax

The **IndexedFaceSet** node creates face geometry and may be used as the value for the **geometry** field of a **Shape** node.

SYNTAX | IndexedFaceSet node

```
IndexedFaceSet {
        coord               NULL       # exposedField   SFNode
        coordIndex          [ ]        # field          MFInt32
        texCoord            NULL       # exposedField   SFNode
        texCoordIndex       [ ]        # field          MFInt32
        color               NULL       # exposedField   SFNode
        colorindex          [ ]        # field          MFInt32
        colorPerVertex      TRUE       # field          SFBool
        normal              NULL       # exposedField   SFNode
        normalIndex         [ ]        # field          MFInt32
        normalPerVertex     TRUE       # field          SFBool
        ccw                 TRUE       # field          SFBool
        convex              TRUE       # field          SFBool
        solid               TRUE       # field          SFBool
        creaseAngle         0.0        # field          SFFloat
        set_coordIndex                 # eventIn        MFInt32
        set_texCoordIndex              # eventIn        MFInt32
        set_colorIndex                 # eventIn        MFInt32
        set_normalIndex                # eventIn        MFInt32
}
```

The value of the **coord** exposed field specifies a node listing the coordinates available for building faces within the face set. Typical **coord** field values include the **Coordinate** node. The default **NULL** value for this field indicates an empty coordinate list and indicates that no faces are to be built by the **IndexedFaceSet** node.

The value of the **coordIndex** field specifies a list of coordinate indexes describing the perimeter of one or more faces. Each value is an integer index selecting a coordinate from the coordinate list specified by the **coord** field. The default value for the **coordIndex** field is an empty coordinate index list and indicates that no faces are to be built.

A coordinate index list can specify the perimeter of one or many faces. Each face connects together a string of coordinate indexes up to the end of the index list or up to an index of -1. The face is automatically closed by connecting the last index before the -1 to the first index in the face's list. The next coordinate index following a -1 starts a new face that ends at the next -1 index or at the end of the index list and is closed by connecting the last index of the new face back to its first index.

The ccw field specifies a **TRUE** or **FALSE** value indicating whether the faces in the face set are indexed in counterclockwise order (**TRUE**) or in clockwise or an unknown order (**FALSE**). The front of a face is the side of the face you see if the coordinate indexes trace its perimeter in a counterclockwise (**TRUE**) or clockwise (**FALSE**) fashion. Depending on the value for the **solid** field, the back sides of faces may be skipped to save drawing time. The front sides of faces are always drawn. The default value for the ccw field is **TRUE**, which indicates that counterclockwise face perimeters are in use.

The **convex** field specifies a **TRUE** or **FALSE** value indicating whether all of the faces in the face set are convex. When **FALSE**, the VRML browser automatically splits concave faces into multiple convex faces. When **TRUE**, the VRML browser assumes that no such splitting is needed, saving processing time for the face set. The default value for the **convex** field is **TRUE**, indicating that all faces in the face set are convex and do not need splitting.

The **solid** field specifies a **TRUE** or **FALSE** value indicating whether the geometry specified by the faces in the face set is solid. The front sides of solid shapes' nearer faces always obscure the back sides of more distant faces on the same shape. When the VRML browser knows that a face set is solid, it can skip drawing the back sides of faces and speed drawing time. The default value for the **solid** field is **TRUE**, which indicates that the face builds a solid shape and that the backs of faces can be skipped.

The value of the **creaseAngle** field specifies a crease-angle threshold, measured in radians. Adjacent faces with an angle between them smaller than the crease-angle threshold are smoothly shaded to obscure the edge between them. Adjacent faces with an angle between them larger than the crease-angle threshold are shaded without a smoothing effect, leaving the edge between them clear. The crease angle must be a value greater than or equal to 0.0. The default value for the **creaseAngle** field is 0.0 degrees, which indicates that the shape should not be smoothly shaded.

The coordinate node value can be changed by sending a value to the implied **set_coord** eventIn of the **coord** exposed field. When a value is received by this input, the coordinate node is changed, and the new coordinate node is output using the implied **coord_changed** eventOut of the exposed field.

The coordinate index list can be changed by sending a list of coordinate indexes to the **set_coordIndex** eventIn.

The **Appearance** node for the shape's **Shape** node specifies an overall color for the face set. You can color individual faces by using the **color, colorIndex, set_colorIndex,** and **colorPerVertex** fields, which are discussed in Chapter 16.

The remaining fields and eventIns of the **IndexedFaceSet** node are discussed in Chapters 18 (**texCoord, texCoordIndex,** and **set_texCoordIndex**) and 19 (**normal, normalIndex, set_normalIndex,** and **normalPerVertex**).

Experimenting with Point, Line, and Face Sets

The following examples provide a more detailed examination of the ways in which the **Coordinate, CoordinateInterpolator, PointSet, IndexedLineSet,** and **Indexed-**

FaceSet nodes can be used and how they interact with nodes discussed in previous chapters.

Building a Shape Using Points, Lines, and Faces

The strong similarity of the **PointSet, IndexedLineSet,** and **IndexedFaceSet** nodes enables you to create shapes as points, lines, or faces with very few differences in the VRML text you type in. The next three examples build a 3-D box, first using points (Figure 13.10) at the box's corners, second using lines (Figure 13.11) along the box's edges, and third using faces (Figure 13.12) for the sides of the box. All three examples use the same coordinate list.

```
#VRML V2.0 utf8
Shape {
    appearance Appearance {
        material Material {
            emissiveColor 1.0 1.0 1.0
        }
    }
    geometry PointSet {
        coord Coordinate {
            point [
            # Coordinates around the top of the cube
                -1.0  1.0  1.0,
                 1.0  1.0  1.0,
                 1.0  1.0 -1.0,
                -1.0  1.0 -1.0,
            # Coordinates around the bottom of the cube
                -1.0 -1.0  1.0,
                 1.0 -1.0  1.0,
                 1.0 -1.0 -1.0,
                -1.0 -1.0 -1.0
            ]
        }
    }
}
```

Figure 13.10 *Points in a point set mark the eight corners of a box.*

```
#VRML V2.0 utf8
Shape {
    appearance Appearance {
        material Material {
            emissiveColor 1.0 1.0 1.0
        }
    }
```

Figure 13.11 continues

```
geometry IndexedLineSet {
    coord Coordinate {
        point [
        # Coordinates around the top of the cube
            -1.0  1.0  1.0,
             1.0  1.0  1.0,
             1.0  1.0 -1.0,
            -1.0  1.0 -1.0,
        # Coordinates around the bottom of the cube
            -1.0 -1.0  1.0,
             1.0 -1.0  1.0,
             1.0 -1.0 -1.0,
            -1.0 -1.0 -1.0
        ]
    }
    coordIndex [
    # top
        0, 1, 2, 3, 0, -1,
    # bottom
        4, 5, 6, 7, 4, -1,
    # vertical edges
        0, 4, -1,
        1, 5, -1,
        2, 6, -1,
        3, 7
    ]
}
}
```

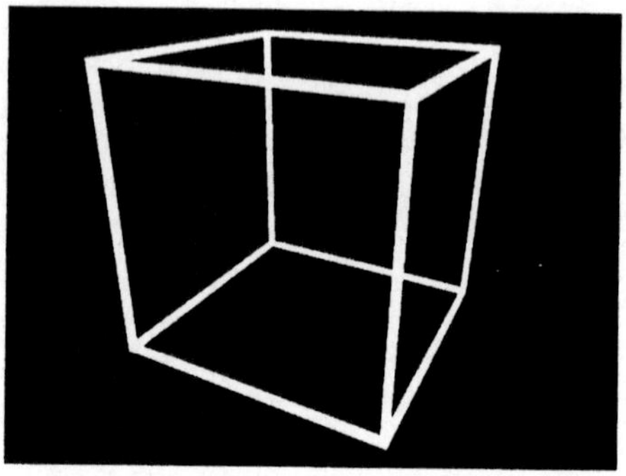

Figure 13.11   *Lines in a line set mark the 12 edges of a box.*

```
#VRML V2.0 utf8
Shape {
    appearance Appearance {
        material Material { }
    }
    geometry IndexedFaceSet {
        coord Coordinate {
            point [
            # Coordinates around the top of the cube
                -1.0  1.0  1.0,
                 1.0  1.0  1.0,
                 1.0  1.0 -1.0,
                -1.0  1.0 -1.0,
            # Coordinates around the bottom of the cube
                -1.0 -1.0  1.0,
                 1.0 -1.0  1.0,
                 1.0 -1.0 -1.0,
                -1.0 -1.0 -1.0
            ]
        }
        coordIndex [
        # top
            0, 1, 2, 3, -1,
        # bottom
            7, 6, 5, 4, -1,
        # front
            0, 4, 5, 1, -1,
        # right
            1, 5, 6, 2, -1,
        # back
            2, 6, 7, 3, -1,
        # left
            3, 7, 4, 0
        ]
    }
}
```

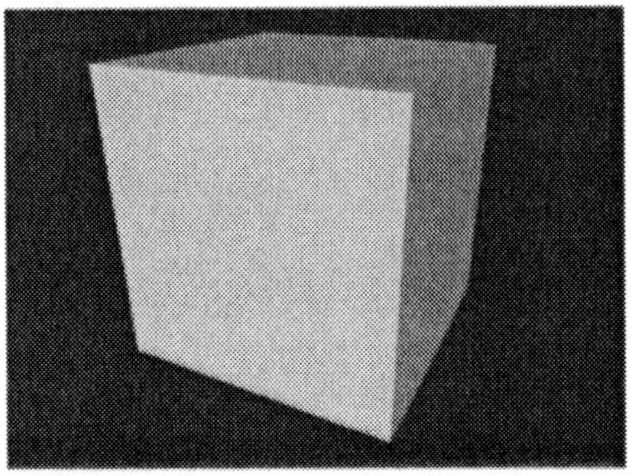

Figure 13.12 *Faces in a face set build the six faces of a cube.*

Building Concave Faces

Simple shapes, like the box in Figure 13.12, are most often built using convex faces, like triangles or rectangles. To build more complex shapes, you may find it convenient to use concave faces instead. When you use concave faces in a face set, you must set the **convex** field value to **FALSE**. This alerts the VRML browser that it may need to process the faces in the face set to automatically split them into convex faces before drawing them.

Figure 13.13 builds a 3-D lightning bolt. The front and back faces of the lightning bolt have crooked inlets to the left and right and are therefore concave faces. The sides of the lightning bolt are simple triangles and squares, and are therefore convex. The coordinate indexes to build the convex and concave faces are combined into a single **IndexedFaceSet** node and the **convex** field value set to **FALSE**.

```
#VRML V2.0 utf8
Shape {
    appearance Appearance {
        material Material {
            diffuseColor 1.0 1.0 0.0
        }
    }
    geometry IndexedFaceSet {
        coord Coordinate {
            point [
            # Lighting bolt tip
                0.0  0.0  0.0,
            # Front perimeter
                5.5  5.0  0.88,
                4.0  5.5  0.968,
                7.0  8.0  1.408,
                4.0  9.0  1.584,
                1.0  5.0  0.88,
                2.5  4.5  0.792,
            # Back perimeter
                5.5  5.0 -0.88,
                4.0  5.5 -0.968,
                7.0  8.0 -1.408,
                4.0  9.0 -1.584,
                1.0  5.0 -0.88,
                2.5  4.5 -0.792,
            ]
        }
        coordIndex [
        # Front
            0,  1,  2,  3,  4,  5,  6, -1,
        # Back
            0, 12, 11, 10,  9,  8,  7, -1,
        # Sides
            0,  7,  1, -1,
            1,  7,  8,  2, -1,
            2,  8,  9,  3, -1,
            3,  9, 10,  4, -1,
            4, 10, 11,  5, -1,
            5, 11, 12,  6, -1,
            6, 12,  0, -1,
        ]
        convex FALSE
    }
}
```

Figure 13.13 *A 3-D lightning bolt using concave faces.*

Building Nonsolid Shapes

Recall that a solid shape is one where the front sides of the faces on the shape always obscure the back sides of faces on that shape. Boxes and spheres, for instance, are solid. In VRML you can also build nonsolid shapes. Typically these include flat or curved sheets of faces, like those making up a room wall, a vaulted ceiling, or a curved car body. In these cases, the front and back of the faces on the shape should always be drawn. This enables you to see the wall or ceiling from either side.

To create nonsolid shapes, set the **solid** field value to **FALSE** within an Indexed-**FaceSet** node. Figure 13.14 uses this feature to build a curving part of a vaulted ceiling that you can use to build a vaulted ceiling in a building. Since the faces that make up the piece of vaulted ceiling do not enclose a volume, the ceiling is not solid. If you turn the shape, you can see both the front and back sides of the faces making up the shape.

```
#VRML V2.0 utf8
Shape {
    appearance Appearance {
        material Material { }
    }
    geometry IndexedFaceSet {
        coord Coordinate {
            point [
            # Circular arc
                -1.0  0.0    1.0,   -1.0  0.26  0.97,
                -1.0  0.5    0.87,  -1.0  0.71  0.71,
                -1.0  0.87   0.5,   -1.0  0.97  0.26,
                -1.0  1.0    0.0,   -1.0  0.97 -0.26,
                -1.0  0.87  -0.5,   -1.0  0.71 -0.71,
                -1.0  0.5   -0.87,  -1.0  0.26 -0.97,
                -1.0  0.0   -1.0,
            # Angled circular arc
                -1.0  0.0    1.0,   -0.97 0.26  0.97,
                -0.87 0.5    0.87,  -0.71 0.71  0.71,
                -0.5  0.87   0.5,   -0.26 0.96  0.26,
                 0.0  1.0    0.0,   -0.26 0.96 -0.26,
                -0.5  0.87  -0.5,   -0.71 0.71 -0.71,
                -0.87 0.5   -0.87,  -0.97 0.26 -0.97,
                -1.0  0.0   -1.0,
            ]
        }
    }
```

Figure 13.14 continues

```
coordIndex [
      0, 13, 14,   1, -1,
      1, 14, 15,   2, -1,
      2, 15, 16,   3, -1,
      3, 16, 17,   4, -1,
      4, 17, 18,   5, -1,
      5, 18, 19,   6, -1,
      6, 19, 20,   7, -1,
      7, 20, 21,   8, -1,
      8, 21, 22,   9, -1,
      9, 22, 23, 10, -1,
     10, 23, 24, 11, -1,
     11, 24, 25, 12, -1,
   ]
   solid FALSE
  }
}
```

Figure 13.14   *A nonsolid vaulted ceiling piece.*

Building Smooth Shapes

The vaulted ceiling in Figure 13.14 appears faceted. To make the shape appear smooth, you can either use a larger number of faces, or you can direct the VRML browser to smoothly shade each face on the shape. The latter approach is both easier to author and faster for the VRML browser to draw.

To smoothly shade the vaulted ceiling built in Figure 13.14, you can add the following **creaseAngle** field to the end of the **IndexedFaceSet** node:

```
creaseAngle 0.785
```

By using a crease-angle threshold larger than the largest angle between two adjacent faces, the VRML browser is directed to smoothly shade across the edges of every face on the ceiling, as shown in Figure 13.15.

Figure 13.15   *A smoothly shaded vaulted ceiling piece.*

Combining Face Shapes

Like all other shapes in VRML, you can build point-, line-, and face-set shapes within a **Shape** node, and include those shapes as the children of a **Transform** node. Similarly, point-, line-, and face-set shapes can be placed in separate files and inlined into larger worlds using the **Inline** node. This enables you to combine together primitive, text, and point-, line-, and face-set shapes in any way you like to build more complex worlds.

If you typed the VRML text for the vaulted ceiling piece in Figure 13.14 and added the **creaseAngle** field, name the file "vault.wrl." Figure 13.16 uses this file within an **Inline** node and builds the four quadrants of a vaulted ceiling. The vaulted ceiling is then instanced four more times, and columns are added to create part of a medieval building.

```
#VRML V2.0 utf8
Group {
    children [
    # Center vaulted ceiling
        DEF Ceiling Transform {
            translation 0.0 2.0 0.0
            children [
                DEF Vault Inline {
                    url "vault.wrl"
                },
                Transform { rotation 0.0 1.0 0.0 1.57
                    children USE Vault
                },
                Transform { rotation 0.0 1.0 0.0 3.14
                    children USE Vault
                },
                Transform { rotation 0.0 1.0 0.0 -1.57
                    children USE Vault
                }
            ]
        },
    # Left, right, front, and back vaulted ceilings
        Transform { translation -2.0 0.0  0.0  children USE Ceiling },
        Transform { translation  2.0 0.0  0.0  children USE Ceiling },
        Transform { translation  0.0 0.0 -2.0  children USE Ceiling },
        Transform { translation  0.0 0.0  2.0  children USE Ceiling },
    # Columns supporting the vaulted ceilings
        Transform {
            translation -3.0 1.0 -1.0
            children DEF Column Shape {
                appearance Appearance {
                    material Material { }
                }
                geometry Cylinder {
                    height 2.0
                    radius 0.05
                }
            }
        },
```

Figure 13.16 continues

```
Transform { translation -1.0 1.0 -1.0  children USE Column },
Transform { translation  1.0 1.0 -1.0  children USE Column },
Transform { translation  3.0 1.0 -1.0  children USE Column },
Transform { translation -3.0 1.0  1.0  children USE Column },
Transform { translation -1.0 1.0  1.0  children USE Column },
Transform { translation  1.0 1.0  1.0  children USE Column },
Transform { translation  3.0 1.0  1.0  children USE Column },
Transform { translation -1.0 1.0 -3.0  children USE Column },
Transform { translation -1.0 1.0  3.0  children USE Column },
Transform { translation  1.0 1.0 -3.0  children USE Column },
Transform { translation  1.0 1.0  3.0  children USE Column }
        ]
}
```

Figure 13.16 *A vaulted ceiling piece used repeatedly to build part of a medieval building.*

Animating Coordinates

Using a **CoordinateInterpolator** node, you can animate the locations of coordinates used to build a shape. Figure 13.17 shows a **CoordinateInterpolator** node used to animate the eight coordinates of a box. The interpolator specifies three sublists of eight coordinates each to morph the box from a normal box into one with an enlarged top and shrunk bottom, and then back again. The **value_changed** eventOut of the **CoordinateInterpolator** node is routed into the **set_point** eventIn of the box shape's **Coordinate** node. A **TimeSensor** node acts as the clock for the animation.

```
#VRML V2.0 utf8
Group {
    children [
    # Morphing shape
        Shape {
            appearance Appearance {
                material Material {
                    diffuseColor 0.0 1.0 1.0
                }
            }
            geometry IndexedFaceSet {
                coord DEF CubeCoordinates Coordinate {
                    point [
                    # Coordinates around top of cube
                        -1.0  1.0  1.0,
                         1.0  1.0  1.0,
                         1.0  1.0 -1.0,
                        -1.0  1.0 -1.0,
                    # Coordinates around bottom of cube
                        -1.0 -1.0  1.0,
                         1.0 -1.0  1.0,
                         1.0 -1.0 -1.0,
                        -1.0 -1.0 -1.0
                    ]
                }
```

Figure 13.17 continues

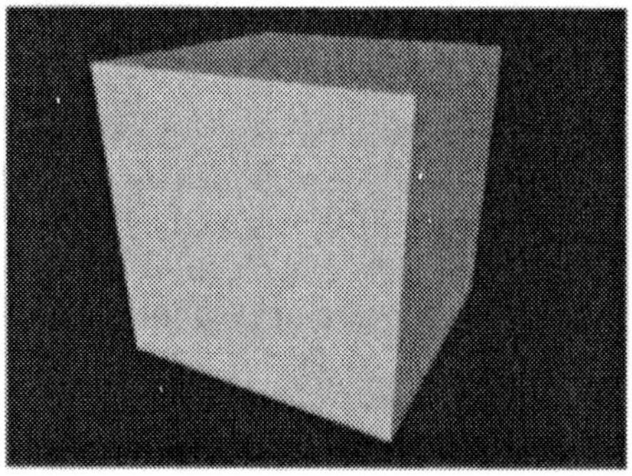

```
            coordIndex [
                # top
                0, 1, 2, 3, -1,
                # bottom
                7, 6, 5, 4, -1,
                # front
                0, 4, 5, 1, -1,
                # right
                1, 5, 6, 2, -1,
                # back
                2, 6, 7, 3, -1,
                # left
                3, 7, 4, 0
            ]
        }
    },
# Animation clock
    DEF Clock TimeSensor {
        cycleInterval 4.0
        loop TRUE
    },
# Animation morph
    DEF CubeMorph CoordinateInterpolator {
        key [ 0.0, 0.5, 1.0 ]
        keyValue [
        # time 0.0 coordinates (cube)
            -1.0  1.0  1.0,    1.0  1.0  1.0,
             1.0  1.0 -1.0,   -1.0  1.0 -1.0,
            -1.0 -1.0  1.0,    1.0 -1.0  1.0,
             1.0 -1.0 -1.0,   -1.0 -1.0 -1.0,
        # time 0.5 coordinates (warped cube)
            -1.5  1.0  1.5,    1.5  1.0  1.5,
             1.5  1.0 -1.5,   -1.5  1.0 -1.5,
            -0.5 -1.0  0.5,    0.5 -1.0  0.5,
             0.5 -1.0 -0.5,   -0.5 -1.0 -0.5,
        # time 1.0 coordinates (cube)
            -1.0  1.0  1.0,    1.0  1.0  1.0,
             1.0  1.0 -1.0,   -1.0  1.0 -1.0,
            -1.0 -1.0  1.0,    1.0 -1.0  1.0,
             1.0 -1.0 -1.0,   -1.0 -1.0 -1.0
        ]
    }
    ]
}
ROUTE Clock.fraction_changed  TO CubeMorph.set_fraction
ROUTE CubeMorph.value_changed TO CubeCoordinates.set_point
```

Figure 13.17   *A morphing box shape.*

Summary

A point is a dot located at a coordinate in your 3-D world. A point set is a group of these dots specified by a **PointSet** node.

A line is a straight line drawn between two coordinates in your 3-D world. A polyline is a chain of lines where the end of one is the start of the next. A line set is a group of polylines specified by an **IndexedLineSet** node.

A face is a flat shape whose perimeter traces a closed path through a series of coordinates in your 3-D world. A face set is a group of these faces specified by an **IndexedFaceSet** node.

The **PointSet, IndexedLineSet,** and **IndexedFaceSet** nodes each specify the geometry of a shape. All three can be used as the value of the **geometry** field in a **Shape** node.

The **coord** field of the **PointSet, IndexedLineSet,** and **IndexedFaceSet** nodes takes a **Coordinate** node as its value. The **Coordinate** node provides a list of 3-D coordinates. Each coordinate is made up of an X, a Y, and a Z distance measured from the origin of the coordinate system. Coordinates in the list are implicitly numbered, or indexed, starting with zero for the first coordinate.

A shape's coordinates can be animated using a **CoordinateInterpolator** node. The interpolator specifies a list of key fractional times in the **key** field and key coordinate sublists in the **keyValue** field. Each key fractional time specifies a time between 0.0 and 1.0 at which the corresponding key coordinate sublist is to be output from the interpolator node. For input fractional times between key fractional times, the interpolator node linearly interpolates between adjacent key coordinate sublists in the list and outputs the computed coordinate list.

The **coordIndex** field value of the **IndexedLineSet** and **IndexedFaceSet** nodes specifies a list of coordinate indexes. Each coordinate index selects a coordinate from the node's coordinate list. For lines, the coordinate indexes specify the path of a polyline. For faces, the coordinate indexes specify the perimeter of a face. The special coordinate index -1 may be used to mark the end of one polyline or face and the beginning of the next. In this way the **IndexedLineSet** and **IndexedFaceSet** nodes may specify any number of polylines or faces using coordinate indexes selecting coordinates from the same coordinate list.

To build closed polyline shapes, like a triangle or circle, the last coordinate index in a polyline's coordinate index list should be the same as the first coordinate index in that list.

When building faces, the VRML browser automatically closes the perimeter by connecting the last coordinate index in the face's list back to the first in the list.

Faces in a face set should be planar. When planar faces are set flat on a table, all of their coordinates simultaneously touch the tabletop. When confronted with nonplanar faces, your VRML browser splits them into triangles. The exact splitting algorithm is not under your control and can create unexpected results. To avoid these problems, it is better to split nonplanar faces yourself.

The **ccw** field value of an **IndexedFaceSet** node specifies whether the coordinate indexes describing the perimeters of the faces in the face set are to be used in counterclockwise (**TRUE**) or clockwise (**FALSE**) order. Counterclockwise is the default.

The **convex** field value specifies whether the faces in a face set are convex (**TRUE**) or concave (**FALSE**). Convex faces have no inlets, or caves, while concave faces have inlets. Convex faces are the default. When faces are specified as being concave, your VRML browser will automatically split them into convex faces for you.

The **solid** field value specifies whether the collection of faces in a face set describe a closed solid (**TRUE**), like a box or sphere, or a nonsolid (**FALSE**), like a flat or curving sheet. Solid shapes are the default. The front side of a solid shape's faces always block the viewer's view of the back side of other faces on that shape. Knowing that a shape is solid enables your VRML browser to skip building the back sides of faces, speeding drawing.

The **creaseAngle** field value specifies a crease-angle threshold. Within a face set, adjacent faces that meet at an angle less than this threshold are smoothly shaded to obscure the edge between the faces. Faces that meet at an angle larger than the crease-angle threshold are not smoothly shaded.

Like all VRML shapes, point-, line-, and face-set shapes can be built within groups, placed in coordinate systems by the **Transform** node, and colored using **Appearance** and **Material** nodes.

CHAPTER 14

Building Elevation Grids

Using the **IndexedFaceSet** node discussed in Chapter 13, you can build arbitrarily complex 3-D shapes. One common 3-D shape is a bumpy terrain, like a mountain range. You can build terrain like this by using a grid of adjacent square faces in an **IndexedFaceSet** node. For each face in the grid, the X and Z coordinate values indicate the corners of a face within the terrain, and the Y coordinate values specify the height, or *elevation*, of the face's corners. By using a large number of faces in the grid, you can create very complex terrain.

This type of grid is so commonly needed by VRML authors that VRML provides the **ElevationGrid** node designed specifically to build terrain grids. Using this node you specify the dimensions of a terrain grid and the elevation at each grid point. Faces are automatically built for each grid square to create your bumpy terrain.

Understanding Elevation Grids

The **ElevationGrid** node builds faces for a terrain using a grid of elevation values that you provide. The number of rows and columns for the grid, and the spacing between those rows and columns, are under your control.

One way to build an elevation grid is to begin first with a flat grid, such as the one in Figure 14.1a. Next, select one of the grid points and change its height, raising it to create a mountain peak, or lowering it to create an ocean or a crater. Figure 14.1b shows the center grid point raised to create a mountain peak. Continuing this process, you can create an arbitrarily bumpy terrain, like that shown in Figure 14.1c.

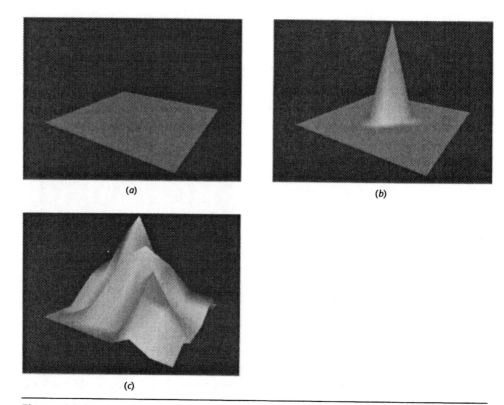

Figure 14.1   *Creating an elevation grid by (a) starting with a flat grid, (b) raising up the center point to make a mountain peak, and (c) setting elevations for all the grid points.*

The **ElevationGrid** Node Syntax

The ElevationGrid node creates face geometry and may be used as the value of the **geometry** field in a **Shape** node.

The values of the **xDimension** and **zDimension** fields specify the number of grid points in the X and Z directions, respectively. To build a grid, both of these field's values must be greater than one. The total number of grid points in the elevation grid is (**xDimension** × **zDimension**). The default zero value for these fields indicates no grid is to be built.

SYNTAX	ElevationGrid node			

```
ElevationGrid {
    xDimension      0         # field         SFInt32
    xSpacing        0.0       # field         SFFloat
    zDimension      0         # field         SFInt32
    zSpacing        0.0       # field         SFFloat
    height          [ ]       # field         MFFloat
    color           NULL      # exposedField  SFNode
    colorPerVertex  TRUE      # field         SFBool
    normal          NULL      # exposedField  SFNode
    normalPerVertex TRUE      # field         SFBool
    texCoord        NULL      # exposedField  SFNode
    ccw             TRUE      # field         SFBool
    solid           TRUE      # field         SFBool
    creaseAngle     0.0       # field         SFFloat
    set_height                # eventIn       MFFloat
}
```

The values of the **xSpacing** and **ySpacing** fields specify the distance between rows and columns in the grid. The **xSpacing** field value specifies the distance between columns, measured in the X direction.

Similarly, the **ySpacing** field value specifies the distance between rows, measured in the Z direction. Both values must be greater than or equal to zero. The default grid spacing is 0.0 units in both the X and Z directions.

The value of the **height** field specifies a list of elevations, one for each grid point, measured in the Y direction. Elevation values are listed by row for **zDimension** rows, each with **xDimension**-height values. Height values can be positive or negative. The default value for the **height** field is an empty height list, which indicates that no elevation grid is to be built.

When the elevation grid is built, the first grid point of the first row is placed at the origin in the coordinate system. The second grid point in the first row is placed to the right along the X axis by the positive distance specified by the value of the **xSpacing** field. The third grid point in the first row is placed the same distance farther along the X axis, and so on for all **xDimension** grid points on the row.

The second row of the elevation grid is placed in front of the first row, positioned forward along the Z axis by the positive distance specified by the value of the **zSpacing** field. The third row is placed in front of the second row by the same distance along the Z axis, and so on for all **zDimension** rows in the grid.

Faces are automatically built between rows and columns of the grid. The **ccw** field specifies a **TRUE** or **FALSE** value indicating whether the faces built for the elevation grid should be created with a counterclockwise (**TRUE**) or clockwise (**FALSE**) perimeter. When the **ccw** field value is **TRUE**, the front sides of faces face upward along the Y axis. Depending on the value of the **solid** field, the back sides of faces may be skipped to save drawing time. The front sides of faces are always drawn. The default value for the **ccw** field is **TRUE**.

The **solid** field contains a **TRUE** or **FALSE** value that indicates whether the geometry specified by the elevation grid is to be treated as a solid shape. The front sides of nearer faces of a solid shape always obscure the back sides of more distant faces on that shape. When the VRML browser knows that the shape is solid, it can skip drawing the back sides of faces and speed drawing time. The default value of the **solid** field is **TRUE**, which indicates that the elevation grid is solid and that the backs of faces can be skipped.

In practice, there is no way to construct a solid elevation grid that encloses a volume. The name for the **solid** field is chosen to be consistent with that in the **IndexedFaceSet** node. In the elevation grid context, the **solid** field can be thought of as indicating whether an elevation grid will only be viewed from the top. If so, the back sides of grid faces are never seen, just as in a solid shape built with the **IndexedFaceSet** node. Since terrain is, typically, only viewed from the top, the **solid** field value is typically **TRUE.**

The **creaseAngle** field value specifies a crease-angle threshold, measured in radians. Adjacent faces in the grid with an angle between them smaller than the crease-angle threshold are smoothly shaded to obscure the edge between them. Adjacent faces with an angle between them larger than the crease-angle threshold will be shaded without a smoothing effect, leaving the edge between them clear as if for a sharp crease in the shape. The crease angle must be a value greater than or equal to 0.0. The default value for the **creaseAngle** field is 0.0 degrees, which indicates that no smooth shading should be used.

The height list can be changed by sending a list of heights to the **set_height** eventIn.

The **Appearance** node for the shape's **Shape** node specifies an overall color for the elevation grid. You can color individual faces in the grid using the **color** and **colorPerVertex** fields discussed in Chapter 16.

The remaining fields of the **ElevationGrid** node are discussed in Chapters 18 (**texCoord**) and 19 (**normal** and **normalPerVertex**).

Experimenting with Elevation Grids

The following examples provide a more detailed examination of the ways in which the **ElevationGrid** node can be used and how they interact with nodes discussed in previous chapters.

Building a Mountain

Figure 14.2 builds a mountain using an elevation grid with nine rows and nine columns per row. The height values are chosen to create a peak in the center, and ridges running downward away from the peak.

```
#VRML V2.0 utf8
Shape {
    appearance Appearance {
        material Material { }
    }
    geometry ElevationGrid {
        xDimension  9
        zDimension  9
        xSpacing    1.0
        zSpacing    1.0
        solid       FALSE
        creaseAngle 0.785
        height [
            0.0, 0.0, 0.5, 1.0, 0.5, 0.0, 0.0, 0.0, 0.0,
            0.0, 0.0, 0.0, 0.0, 2.5, 0.5, 0.0, 0.0, 0.0,
            0.0, 0.0, 0.5, 0.5, 3.0, 1.0, 0.5, 0.0, 1.0,
            0.0, 0.0, 0.5, 2.0, 4.5, 2.5, 1.0, 1.5, 0.5,
            1.0, 2.5, 3.0, 4.5, 5.5, 3.5, 3.0, 1.0, 0.0,
            0.5, 2.0, 2.0, 2.5, 3.5, 4.0, 2.0, 0.5, 0.0,
            0.0, 0.0, 0.5, 1.5, 1.0, 2.0, 3.0, 1.5, 0.0,
            0.0, 0.0, 0.0, 0.0, 0.0, 0.0, 2.0, 1.5, 0.5,
            0.0, 0.0, 0.0, 0.0, 0.0, 0.0, 0.5, 0.0, 0.0,
        ]
    }
}
```

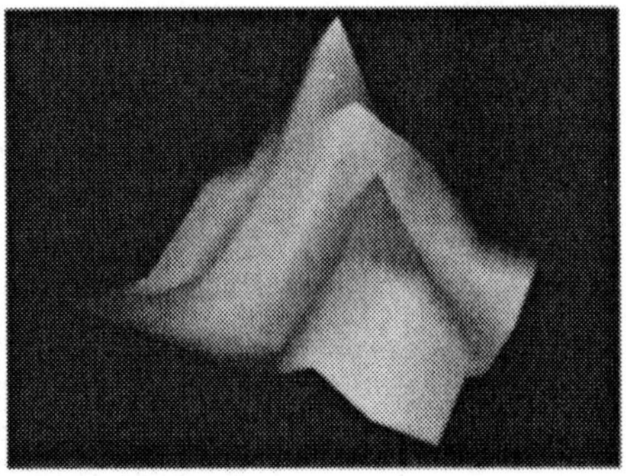

Figure 14.2 *A mountain using a 9 × 9 elevation grid.*

Building Smooth Surfaces

The mountain in Figure 14.2 appears coarse and spiked. To create smoother mountains, you can use a larger size grid and smaller grid spacing. It is typical to find elevation grids with 100 or more grid points per side, creating a grid with 10,000 or more height values.

TIP Large elevating grids are best authored using VRML world-building applications or custom programs designed to automatically output large grids.

Figure 14.3 shows a smooth ribbon in the shape of a sine wave. This shape was automatically computed using a simple program. The ribbon uses two duplicate rows, each with 20 columns. The large number of columns helps to make the surface of the ribbon appear smoother.

Notice that the **xSpacing** and **zSpacing** field values for the **ElevationGrid** node use an X spacing of 1.0 unit and a Z spacing of 4.0 units. The larger Z step increases the distance between the first and second rows in order to create a wide ribbon.

```
#VRML V2.0 utf8
Shape {
    appearance Appearance {
        material Material {
            diffuseColor 1.0 1.0 0.0
        }
    }
    geometry ElevationGrid {
        xDimension  2
        zDimension  20
        xSpacing    1.0
        zSpacing    4.0
        solid       FALSE
        creaseAngle 0.785
        height [
            0.00,  0.59,  0.95,  0.95,  0.59,
            0.00, -0.59, -0.95, -0.95, -0.59,
            0.00,  0.59,  0.95,  0.95,  0.59,
            0.00, -0.59, -0.95, -0.95, -0.59,
            0.00,  0.59,  0.95,  0.95,  0.59,
            0.00, -0.59, -0.95, -0.95, -0.59,
            0.00,  0.59,  0.95,  0.95,  0.59,
            0.00, -0.59, -0.95, -0.95, -0.59,
        ]
    }
}
```

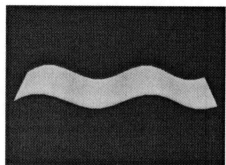

Figure 14.3   *A ribbon using a 20 × 2 elevation grid.*

Surface computation programs can easily generate very large and detailed surfaces. Figure 14.4 shows two versions of an elevation grid generated by computing the height using a sine function on the distance a grid point is from the center of the grid. This creates a puddle-splash terrain.

Figure 14.4*a* has only ten rows and ten columns, which is clearly too little to bring out the structure of the puddle splash. Figure 14.4*b* uses 40 rows and 40 columns. The higher-detail elevation grid creates a smoother, puddle-splash terrain with 1,600 height values.

```
#VRML V2.0 utf8
Shape {
    appearance Appearance {
        material Material {
            diffuseColor 0.0 0.6 1.0
        }
    }
```

Figure 14.4 continues

```
geometry ElevationGrid {
    xDimension  10
    zDimension  10
    xSpacing    0.100000
    zSpacing    0.100000
    solid       FALSE
    creaseAngle 3.14
    height [
          0.08,  0.03, -0.05, -0.08, -0.07,
         -0.07, -0.07, -0.08, -0.05,  0.03,
          0.03, -0.06, -0.07, -0.01,  0.04,
          0.05,  0.04, -0.01, -0.07, -0.06,
         -0.05, -0.07,  0.02,  0.08,  0.06,
          0.05,  0.06,  0.08,  0.02, -0.07,
         -0.08, -0.01,  0.08,  0.02, -0.05,
         -0.07, -0.05,  0.02,  0.08, -0.01,
         -0.07,  0.04,  0.06, -0.05, -0.06,
         -0.02, -0.06, -0.05,  0.06,  0.04,
         -0.07,  0.05,  0.05, -0.07, -0.02,
          0.08, -0.02, -0.07,  0.05,  0.05,
         -0.07,  0.04,  0.06, -0.05, -0.06,
         -0.02, -0.06, -0.05,  0.06,  0.04,
         -0.08, -0.01,  0.08,  0.02, -0.05,
         -0.07, -0.05,  0.02,  0.08, -0.01,
         -0.05, -0.07,  0.02,  0.08,  0.06,
          0.05,  0.06,  0.08,  0.02, -0.07,
          0.03, -0.06, -0.07, -0.01,  0.04,
          0.05,  0.04, -0.01, -0.07, -0.06,
    ]
  }
}
```

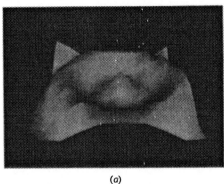 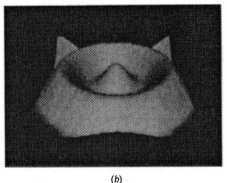

(a)   *(b)*

Figure 14.4 *A puddle splash having (a) a 10 × 10 elevation grid and (b) a 40 × 40 elevation grid. (The VRML text in this figure builds the world shown in Figure 14.4a.)*

Automatic elevation grid generators also can be used to convert to VRML elevation data available from government agencies and to generate terrain based on fractal- and image-processing techniques. Figure 14.5 shows a valley terrain built using an automatic terrain-generator application.

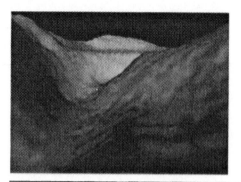

Figure 14.5 *An elevation grid built using an automatic terrain-generator application.*

Combining Elevation Grids

As with all VRML shapes, you can combine multiple elevation grids together to create more complex shapes. You can also use elevation grids to create shapes that are not terrain shapes.

If you've typed the ribbon in Figure 14.3, name the file "ribbon.wrl." The VRML text in Figure 14.6 specifies this file within an **Inline** node and repeatedly instances the ribbon to create a medallion.

```
#VRML V2.0 utf8
Group {
    children [
        DEF ThreeRibbon Group {
            children [
                DEF OneRibbon Transform {
                    translation 0.0 0.0 -2.0
                    children Inline {
                        url "ribbon.wrl"
                    }
                },
                Transform {
                    rotation 0.0 1.0 0.0  0.52
                    children USE OneRibbon
                },
                Transform {
                    rotation 0.0 1.0 0.0  1.05
                    children USE OneRibbon
                }
            ]
        },
```

Figure 14.6 continues

```
Transform {
    rotation 0.0 1.0 0.0  1.57
    children USE ThreeRibbon
},
Transform {
    rotation 0.0 1.0 0.0  3.14
    children USE ThreeRibbon
},
Transform {
    rotation 0.0 1.0 0.0  4.71
    children USE ThreeRibbon
}
]
}
```

Figure 14.6 *A medallion built from 12 elevation-grid ribbons.*

Summary

The VRML **ElevationGrid** node is designed to easily and efficiently build terrain shapes. The node enables you to define the X and Z dimensions of a terrain grid, and set the height in the Y direction for each grid point in the grid. Faces are automatically generated and shaded for the grid.

The number of grid points in the X and Z directions are set using the **xDimension** and **zDimension** fields, respectively. The **xSpacing** and **zSpacing** field values specify the spacing between grid rows and columns. The **height** field value specifies a list of elevations, one per grid point.

Faces are automatically built for each square of the grid. These faces can be built with counterclockwise or clockwise perimeters, specified by the value of the **ccw** field.

The entire elevation grid may be treated as a solid by setting the value of the **solid** field. When considered a solid, your VRML browser skips building the back side of any elevation grid face, saving drawing time.

The **creaseAngle** field value specifies a crease-angle threshold. Adjacent grid faces that meet at an angle less than this threshold are smoothly shaded to obscure the edge between the faces. Faces that meet at an angle larger than the crease-angle threshold are not smoothly shaded.

## CHAPTER 15

Building Extruded Shapes

Extrusion is a real-world manufacturing process that forces a stream of raw material, like hot metal, through a hole in a plate. Through the hole comes a long strand of material whose cross section is the shape of the plate hole. Wire, aluminum moldings, and steel I beams are typical products of extrusion. A similar extrusion process is used when sausage and noodles are made.

The VRML **Extrusion** geometry node mimics the real-world extrusion process. The node enables you to specify a 2-D outline, or *cross section*, for an extruded shape. The cross section is then swept along a 3-D curve, or *spine*, to create extrusion geometry for a **Shape** node. The extrusion process is a little like using a bubble wand to make long bubbles. The bubble wand's circular shape is the cross section, and the spine is the path of the wand as you wave it through the air. The extruded bubble is the resulting geometry of the extrusion.

Understanding Extrusion

The **Extrusion** node is an intuitive way of building face geometries for a wide range of common shapes. There are four key features of any extrusion:

- The cross section to extrude
- The spine specifying the path of the extrusion
- The scale of the cross section at points along the spine
- The orientation of the cross section at points along the spine

Cross Sections

A cross section is a 2-D outline, such as a square or circle. You specify the perimeter of the cross section using a chain of 2-D coordinates, similar to the way you specify coordinates for the perimeter of a face in a face set. These 2-D coordinates are listed in the **crossSection** field of the **Extrusion** node.

Extrusion cross sections can be closed or open. A *closed* cross section, such as a circle, starts and ends on the same 2-D coordinate. An *open* cross section, such as an arc, starts and ends on different coordinates.

Figure 15.1 shows three possible cross sections, including a square, a circle, and a half circle. The square and the circle are closed cross sections, while the half circle is an open cross section. All cross sections are specified using 2-D coordinates in the horizontal, XZ plane.

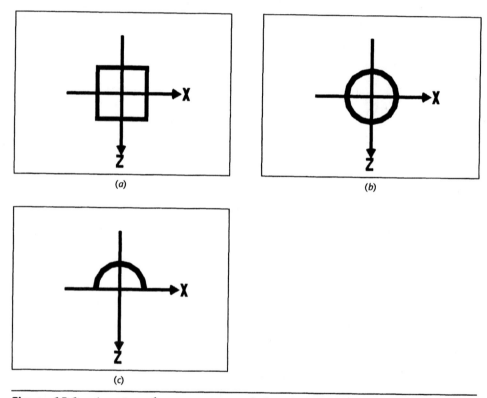

(a)

(b)

(c)

Figure 15.1   *A variety of cross sections, including (a) a square, (b) a circle, and (c) a half circle.*

Spines

A spine is a 3-D path for the extrusion, like a straight line or a curve. Similar to a polyline in an **IndexedLineSet** node, you specify an extrusion spine using a chain of 3-D coordinates. These 3-D coordinates are listed in the **spine** field of the **Extrusion** node.

The extrusion spine can be closed or open. A *closed* spine, such as a circle or a figure eight, starts and ends on the same 3-D coordinate. An *open* spine, such as a spiral, starts and ends on different coordinates.

Figure 15.2 shows three possible spines, including a straight spine, a circle, and a spring helix. The circle in Figure 15.1*b* is a closed spine, while the other two spines are open spines.

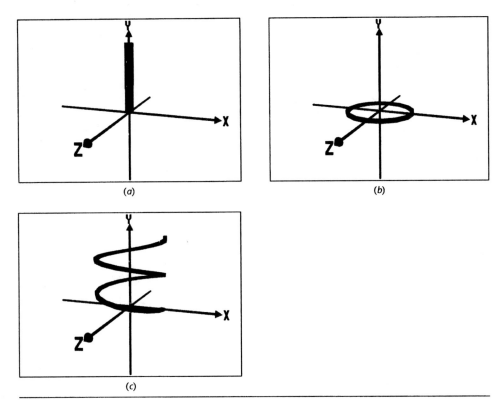

(a)   (b)

(c)

Figure 15.2   *A variety of spines, including (a) a straight spine, (b) a circle, and (c) a spring helix.*

Extruding a Cross Section along a Spine

You can create an extrusion shape by sweeping the 2-D cross section along the path of the 3-D spine. As the cross section sweeps along the spine, it leaves behind it a group of faces that create the skin of the extruded shape. As noted earlier, you can think of extrusion as similar to using a bubble wand. In the terminology of the VRML **Extrusion** node, the tubular bubble is an extruded geometry made up of faces, such as those in an **IndexedFaceSet** node.

Figure 15.3 shows three extruded shapes created by sweeping the cross sections in Figure 15.1 along the spines in Figure 15.2. Figure 15.3*a* shows a square cross section swept along a straight spine to create a simple bar. Figure 15.3*b* shows a circle swept along a circular spine to create a donut, or *torus*. Figure 15.3*c* shows a half-circle cross section swept along a helical spine to create a playground slide.

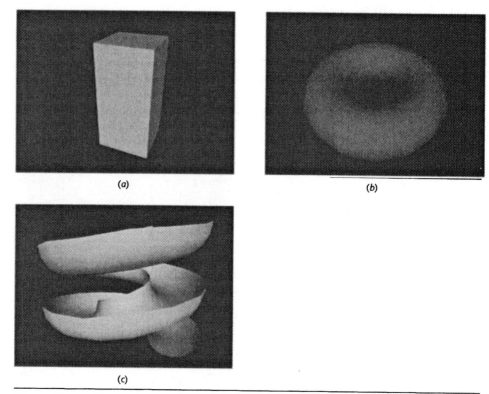

(a)

Figure 15.3 *Cross sections swept along spines to create (a) a bar, (b) a torus, and (c) a helical playground slide.*

Beginning and Ending Caps

By default, VRML builds faces, or *caps*, at the beginning and end of an extruded shape. For the bar in Figure 15.3*a*, the caps are the top and bottom of the bar. You can enable or disable the building of beginning and ending caps using the **beginCap** and **endCap** fields. This enables you to create tubes and other hollow extruded shapes. Figure 15.4 shows the bar from Figure 15.3*a* without caps.

Figure 15.4 *A square tube created by extruding a square without building the beginning and ending caps.*

Cross-Section Scaling

The extrusion process proceeds in stages:

1. Your cross section is placed at the first coordinate on the spine.
2. A copy of your cross section is placed at the next coordinate along the spine.
3. Faces are built that connect the first cross section to the second, creating the extrusion skin.
4. Steps 2 and 3 are repeated again for the next segment in the spine, and so forth, until the end of the spine is built.

Each time the cross section is placed at a spine coordinate (steps 1 and 2 above), you can scale the cross section up or down by specifying a scale factor in the **scale** field of the **Extrusion** node. You can even specify different scaling factors for the width and depth of the 2-D cross section. Using scaling you can widen and narrow the shape at each coordinate along the spine.

For example, you can put a bulge in the middle of an extrusion with a three-coordinate spine by scaling up the cross section at the middle coordinate in the spine and no scaling at the first and last spine coordinates. Similarly, you could create the flaring bell of a trumpet by scaling up the cross section at the end of a spine.

Figure 15.5 shows two extruded shapes that scale the cross section up or down at each coordinate along the spine. Figure 15.5*a* shows a bulging bar created by scaling a square cross section up at the middle coordinate of a three-coordinate straight spine. Figure 15.5*b* shows a beaded helix with a circular cross section that repeatedly scales up and down along the helical spine.

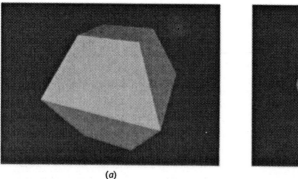
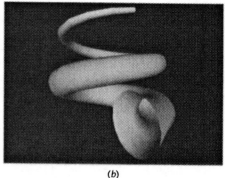

(a)   (b)

Figure 15.5 *Scaling the cross section at each coordinate along a spine to create (a) a bulging bar and (b) a beaded helix.*

Automatic Cross-Section Orientation

During extrusion, the cross-section copies placed at each coordinate along the spine are automatically oriented so that they face forward along the path of the spine. For example, first imagine that a cross section is laid flat on a table. Then imagine a candle in the middle of the cross section. The upward-pointing candle indicates the direction the cross section is facing. When extruding, the cross section is automatically rotated so that its upward-pointing face is aimed forward along the spine. This automatic cross-section rotation ensures that the cross section is swept uniformly along the spine so that you don't get any strange kinks in a smoothly curving spine.

The forward direction at a particular coordinate along the spine is determined using the spine's tangent at that coordinate. For example, imagine tying a ball to the end of a string and swinging that ball in a circular path around your head while you hold on to the string end. Now imagine letting go of the string so that the ball flies away from you in a straight line and continues forward in the direction it was traveling at the instant you let go. That forward direction is the *tangent* to the circular path at that location on the path. For the **Extrusion** node your VRML browser automatically computes the tangents for each spine coordinate and uses the forward directions defined by these tangents to orient the cross section as it sweeps along the path.

SIDEBAR: SPINE TANGENTS Alignment of the cross section with the spine requires that the VRML browser compute a forward direction for the spine at each spine coordinate. This forward direction is the tangent to the spine at a particular coordinate. Using this computed tangent, the browser computes the rotations necessary to automatically orient the extrusion cross section so that it faces forward along the tangent.

For a spine coordinate i, in a list of n spine coordinates, the VRML browser computes the tangent as follows:

- If i is not 0 (i.e., not the first spine coordinate) and i is not $(n-1)$ (i.e., not the last spine coordinate), then the X, Y, and Z components of the tangent are computed as:

```
tangent.x = spine.x[i + 1] - spine.x[i - 1]
tangent.y = spine.y[i + 1] - spine.y[i - 1]
tangent.z = spine.z[i + 1] - spine.z[i - 1]
```

where `tangent.x` refers to the X component of the tangent, `spine.x[i + 1]` refers to the X component of the $i + 1$th coordinate of the spine, and so on.

- If i is either the first or last coordinate in the spine, and if the first and last coordinates are the same (in other words the spine is a closed curve), then only one tangent is computed for both coordinates. This ensures that there is no discontinuity at the junction of the spine end with the spine beginning. For a closed spine, the tangent at the first (0) and last ($n - 1$) coordinates is computed as:

```
tangent.x = spine.x[1] - spine.x[n - 2]
tangent.y = spine.y[1] - spine.y[n - 2]
tangent.z = spine.z[1] - spine.z[n - 2]
```

- If i is either the first or last coordinate in the spine, and if the first and last coordinates are different (in other words the spine is an open curve), separate tangents are computed for each coordinate. For an open spine, the tangent at the first (0) coordinate is computed as:

```
tangent.x = spine.x[1] - spine.x[0]
tangent.y = spine.y[1] - spine.y[0]
tangent.z = spine.z[1] - spine.z[0]
```

and the tangent at the last ($n - 1$) coordinate is computed as:

```
tangent.x = spine.x[n - 1] - spine.x[n - 2]
tangent.y = spine.y[n - 1] - spine.y[n - 2]
tangent.z = spine.z[n - 1] - spine.z[n - 2]
```

Cross-Section Orientation

Along with automatic cross-section rotation, you can specify your own cross-section rotation for each coordinate on the spine. Using cross-section rotation, you can cause a cross section to twist and turn as it is swept along the spine. To create a twisting ribbon, for instance, you can sweep a thin, linelike cross section along the ribbon's spine and make the ribbon twist and curl by rotating the cross section as the spine turns.

You can specify cross-section rotations that rotate about any axis by any angle. If you rotate about the Y axis, you can create a twist in the extrusion. If you rotate about the X or Z axes, you can create kinks and flattened spots in the extrusion.

Figure 15.6 shows extruded shapes with rotated cross sections. Figure 15.6a shows a twisted bar created by rotating a square cross section about the Y axis as it is swept along a straight spine. In Figure 15.6b a lipstick shape is created by rotating a circular cross section about the X axis as it is swept along a straight spine pointing upward along the Y axis.

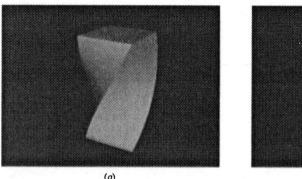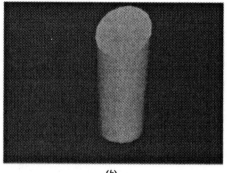

(a)   (b)

Figure 15.6   *Rotating the cross section at each coordinate along a spine to create (a) a twisted bar and (b) a lipstick shape.*

The **Extrusion** Node Syntax

The **Extrusion** node creates face geometry and may be used as the value of the geometry field in a **Shape** node.

SYNTAX

Extrusion node

```
Extrusion {
   crossSection   [
                              1.0  1.0,      ˙
                              1.0 -1.0,
                             -1.0 -1.0,
                             -1.0  1.0,
                              1.0  1.0 ]          # field    MFVec2f
   spine                 [ 0.0  0.0  0.0,
                           0.0  1.0  0.0 ]        # field    MFVec3f
   scale                 1.0  1.0                 # field    MFVec2f
   orientation           0.0  0.0  1.0    0.0     # field    MFRotation
   beginCap              TRUE                     # field    SFBool
   endCap                TRUE                     # field    SFBool
   ccw                   TRUE                     # field    SFBool
   solid                 TRUE                     # field    SFBool
   convex                TRUE                     # field    SFBool
   creaseAngle           0.0                      # field    SFFloat
   set_spine                                      # eventIn  MFVec3f
   set_crossSection                              # eventIn  MFVec2f
   set_scale                                      # eventIn  MFVec2f
   set_orientation                               # eventIn  MFRotation
}
```

The value of the **crossSection** field specifies a list of 2-D coordinates that define an open or closed outline to be extruded along the spine of the extrusion. The cross section is best envisioned as a flat outline built on the XZ plane so that the first value of each 2-D coordinate is a distance along the X axis and the second value a distance along the Z axis. In this position, the cross section faces upward along the positive Y axis. The default value for the **crossSection** field is a square.

The value of the **spine** field specifies a list of 3-D coordinates that define an open or closed path along which the cross section is swept to create the extrusion. The default value for the **spine** field is a straight path pointing upward along the Y axis.

The value of the **scale** field specifies a list of cross-section, scale-factor pairs to use at each coordinate along the spine. The first value in each scale-factor pair specifies an X scaling factor and the second a Z scaling factor for the cross section. Scaling factors between 0.0 and 1.0 reduce the size of the cross section, while those larger than 1.0 increase the cross-section size. A scaling factor of 1.0 leaves the cross-section size unchanged. Negative scaling factors are not valid. The **scale** field must include either one scale-factor pair or one pair for each coordinate in the spine. When only one scale-factor pair is specified, that pair is used for all coordinates along the spine. The default value of the **scale** field is a single scale-factor pair that scales by 1.0 in X and Z.

The value of the **orientation** field specifies a list of cross-section rotations to use at each coordinate along the spine. Each rotation value specifies a rotation axis and angle, exactly like that in the **rotation** field of the **Transform** node. The **orientation** field must include either one rotation value or one rotation value for each coordinate in the spine. When only one rotation value is provided, that value is used for all coordinates along the spine. The default value of the **orientation** field is a single rotation of 0.0 radians.

The VRML browser builds extruded shapes using the cross-section, spine, scaling, and rotation values with the following steps at each spine coordinate in this way:

1. Lay the cross section from the **crossSection** field flat on the XZ plane. In this configuration, the cross section's Y axis points upward.

2. Scale the cross section about its origin using the current spine coordinate's X and Z scale factors from the **scale** field value list.

3. Automatically orient the cross section to aim its Y axis along the tangent to the spine at the current spine coordinate.

4. Further rotate the cross section using the current spine coordinate's rotation axis and angle found in the **orientation** field value list.

5. Automatically translate the cross section to the current spine coordinate using the 3-D coordinate found in the **spine** field value list.

6. If the current spine coordinate in step 5 is not the first coordinate of the spine, build faces connecting the current spine coordinate's cross section to the cross section at the previous spine coordinate.

The **beginCap** and **endCap** fields each specify a TRUE or FALSE value indicating whether beginning and ending cap faces should be built for the ends of the extrusion. When **TRUE,** a flat cap face is built using the 2-D coordinates of the **crossSec-**

tion field. If the cross section is not a closed outline, the cap face closes the outline by connecting the last cross-section coordinate back to the first. When a **beginCap** or **endCap** field value is FALSE, a cap face is not built for the end of the extrusion. The default value for these fields is TRUE.

The **ccw** field specifies a TRUE or FALSE value indicating whether the cross section (and the faces automatically generated for the extrusion) are specified with coordinate indexes ordered in a counterclockwise order (TRUE) or in a clockwise order (FALSE). The front of a face is the side of the face you see if the coordinate indexes trace its perimeter in a counterclockwise (TRUE) or clockwise (FALSE) direction. Depending upon the value of the **solid** field, the back sides of faces may be skipped to save drawing time. The front sides of faces are always drawn. The default value of the **ccw** field is TRUE, which indicates that counterclockwise face perimeters are to be used.

The **convex** field specifies a TRUE or FALSE value indicating whether the cross section is convex (it has no inlets, or caves). When FALSE, the VRML browser automatically splits concave cross sections into multiple convex faces when building beginning or ending cap faces. When TRUE, the VRML browser assumes no splitting is needed, saving processing time. The default value for the **convex** field is TRUE.

The **convex** field value only affects how beginning and ending cap faces are built. If you turn off both beginning and ending caps using the **beginCap** and **endCap** fields, then no cap faces are built and the **convex** field is ignored.

The value of the **solid** field specifies a TRUE or FALSE value that indicates whether the geometry specified by the faces in the extrusion is that of a solid shape. When solid shapes are built, the front sides of nearer faces of the shape always obscure the back sides of more distant faces on that shape. When you specify that an extrusion is solid the browser can skip drawing the back sides of faces, speeding drawing. The default value for the **solid** field is TRUE, which indicates that the face builds a solid shape and the backs of faces can be skipped.

TIP Extrusions that use closed cross sections and build both end caps are always solid. The VRML browser is able to better optimize drawing these extrusions if you set the **solid** field value to **TRUE**. Extrusions with open cross sections or no end cap on one or both ends are not considered solid. If the viewer can see both the inside and the outside of your extrusion, you should set the **solid** field value to **FALSE** so that the back sides of faces are drawn when the viewer looks inside the extrusion. If the viewer will never look inside the extrusion, set the **solid** field value to **TRUE**. This enables the VRML browser to skip back faces and speed drawing.

The value of the **creaseAngle** field specifies a crease-angle threshold measured in radians. Adjacent extrusion faces that have an angle between them that is smaller than the crease-angle threshold are smoothly shaded to obscure the edge between them. Adjacent faces that have an angle between them that is larger than the crease-angle threshold are shaded without a smoothing effect, leaving the edge between them sharp. The crease angle must be a value greater than or equal to 0.0. The default value for the **creaseAngle** field is 0.0 degrees, which indicates that the shape should not be smoothly shaded.

The cross section, spine, list of scale factors, and list of rotations can be changed by sending a list of values to the **set_crossSection**, **set_spine**, **set_scale**, and **set_orientation** eventIns, respectively.

The **Appearance** node for the shape's **Shape** node specifies an overall color for the extrusion's faces.

Experimenting with Extrusions

The following examples provide a more detailed examination of the ways in which the **Extrusion** node can be used and how they interact with nodes discussed in previous chapters.

Building a Shape Using Extrusion

Figure 15.7 shows an **Extrusion** geometry node used to build a simple cylinder. The extrusion's cross section is a circle, and the spine is a straight line going up the Y axis.

```
#VRML V2.0 utf8
Shape {
    appearance Appearance {
        material Material {
            diffuseColor 0.0 0.7 1.0
        }
    }
    geometry Extrusion {
        creaseAngle 0.785
        crossSection [
            1.00  0.00,    0.92 -0.38,
            0.71 -0.71,    0.38 -0.92,
            0.00 -1.00,   -0.38 -0.92,
           -0.71 -0.71,   -0.92 -0.38,
           -1.00 -0.00,   -0.92  0.38,
           -0.71  0.71,   -0.38  0.92,
            0.00  1.00,    0.38  0.92,
            0.71  0.71,    0.92  0.38,
            1.00  0.00
        ]
        spine [ 0.0 -1.0 0.0,  0.0 1.0 0.0 ]
    }
}
```

Figure 15.7 *An extruded cylinder built using a circular cross section swept along a straight spine.*

The cylinder created in Figure 15.7 looks like the default cylinder created using the **Cylinder** geometry node. In fact, using the **Extrusion** node, you can create all four of the primitive geometry nodes: **Box**, **Cone**, **Cylinder**, and **Sphere**. The **Box** node, for instance, is simply a square cross section extruded along a straight spine.

The **Cone** and **Sphere** nodes can be mimicked with the **Extrusion** node by using the node's **scale** field to gradually scale a circular cross section as it is swept upward along a straight spine.

Using Open Cross Sections

The cylinder created in Figure 15.8 uses a closed, circular cross section. You can also specify open cross sections with differing first and last coordinates.

The VRML text in Figure 15.8 creates a half cylinder by using only half of the circular cross section used in Figure 15.7 with a straight-line spine. Slicing the cylinder in this way reveals the interior of the extrusion. The interior surface of the cylinder is made up of the back sides of faces that simultaneously make up the outside of the cylinder. As with faces in an **IndexedFaceSet**, to instruct the VRML browser to draw the back sides of faces as well as their front sides, set the **solid** field value to **FALSE**.

```
#VRML V2.0 utf8
Shape {
    appearance Appearance {
        material Material {
            diffuseColor 0.0 0.7 1.0
        }
    }
    geometry Extrusion {
        solid FALSE
        creaseAngle 0.785
        crossSection [
            1.00   0.00,    0.92 -0.38,
            0.71 -0.71,    0.38 -0.92,
            0.00 -1.00,   -0.38 -0.92,
           -0.71 -0.71,   -0.92 -0.38,
           -1.00 -0.00,
        ]
        spine [ 0.0 -1.0 0.0,  0.0 1.0 0.0 ]
    }
}
```

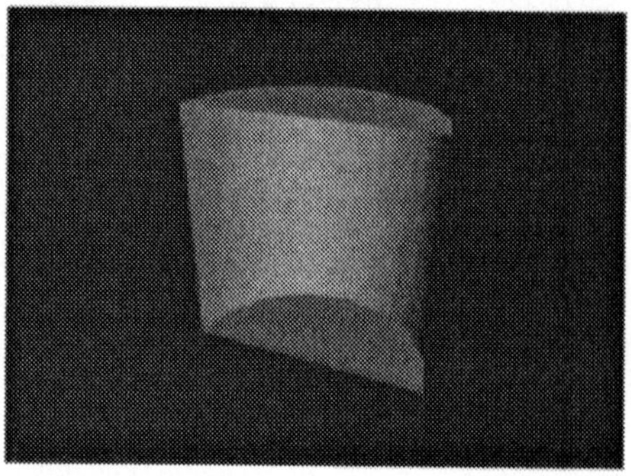

Figure 15.8 *An extruded half cylinder built using half of a circular cross section swept along a straight spine.*

Turning Off Extrusion Caps

The half cylinder in Figure 15.8 has beginning and ending caps at its bottom and top. The VRML text in Figure 15.9 builds the same half cylinder but turns off the beginning and ending caps by setting the **beginCap** and **endCap** field values to **FALSE**.

```
#VRML V2.0 utf8
Shape {
    appearance Appearance {
        material Material {
            diffuseColor 0.0 0.7 1.0
        }
    }
    geometry Extrusion {
        solid    FALSE
        beginCap FALSE
        endCap   FALSE
        creaseAngle 0.785
        crossSection [
              1.00  0.00,   0.92 -0.38,
              0.71 -0.71,   0.38 -0.92,
              0.00 -1.00,  -0.38 -0.92,
             -0.71 -0.71,  -0.92 -0.38,
             -1.00 -0.00,
        ]
        spine [ 0.0 -1.0 0.0,  0.0 1.0 0.0 ]
    }
}
```

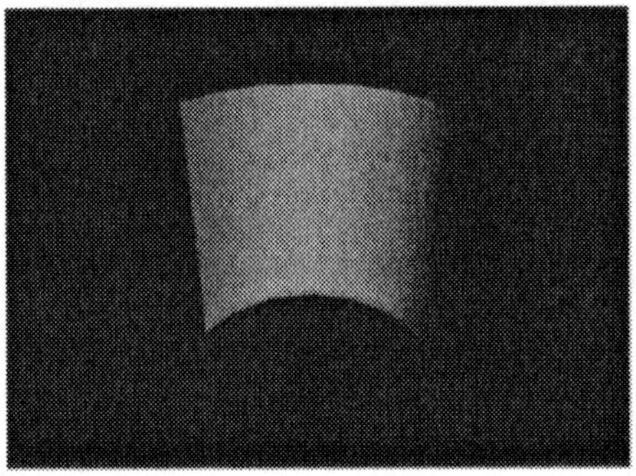

Figure 15.9 *An extruded half cylinder with its beginning and ending caps turned off.*

Using Concave Cross Sections

You can extrude cross sections of arbitrary complexity, including concave cross sections. One creative use of extrusion is to build the walls of a room. Start by creating a concave cross section that outlines the inner and outer perimeter of a room. To build the room, the VRML text directs the cross section to loop through the interior of the room, exit the room at a doorway, loop around the outside of the room, and connect back to the interior perimeter at the same doorway. The cross section is then extruded upward along a straight spine the height of the room.

Figure 15.10 builds this extruded room. Note that the **Extrusion** node's **convex** field value is **FALSE,** since the cross section is concave.

```
#VRML V2.0 utf8
Group {
    children [
        Shape {
            appearance Appearance {
                material Material {
                    diffuseColor 1.0 0.9 0.7
                }
            }
            geometry Extrusion {
                convex FALSE
                crossSection [
                # Room outline
                    -0.5  1.0,   -0.5  0.8,
                    -1.8  0.8,   -1.8 -0.8,
                     1.8 -0.8,    1.8  0.8,
                     0.5  0.8,    0.5  1.0,
                     2.0  1.0,    2.0 -1.0,
                    -2.0 -1.0,   -2.0  1.0,
                    -0.5  1.0
                ]
                spine [
                # Straight-line
                    0.0 0.0 0.0,
                    0.0 2.0 0.0
                ]
            }
        }
    ]
}
```

Figure 15.10 *An extruded room using a floor plan as the cross section.*

Using Curved Spines

Each of the previous examples have extruded along straight cross sections. You can extrude along any chain of 3-D coordinates you choose. The VRML text in Figure 15.11 builds a playground slide by extruding a half-circle cross section along a helical spine. The **creaseAngle** field value is set to 90.0 degrees (1.57 radians) to smoothly shade the shape.

```
#VRML V2.0 utf8
Shape {
    appearance Appearance {
        material Material {
            diffuseColor 0.0 1.0 0.7
        }
    }
    geometry Extrusion {
        creaseAngle 1.57
        endCap    FALSE
        beginCap FALSE
        solid     FALSE
        crossSection [
        # Half-circle
            -1.00  0.00,  -0.92 -0.38,
            -0.71 -0.71,  -0.38 -0.92,
             0.00 -1.00,   0.38 -0.92,
             0.71 -0.71,   0.92 -0.38,
             1.00  0.00,
        ]
        spine [
        # Helix
             2.00 0.00 -0.00,   1.85 0.12 -0.77,
             1.41 0.24 -1.41,   0.77 0.36 -1.85,
             0.00 0.48 -2.00,  -0.77 0.61 -1.85,
            -1.41 0.73 -1.41,  -1.85 0.85 -0.77,
            -2.00 0.97  0.00,  -1.85 1.09  0.77,
            -1.41 1.21  1.41,  -0.77 1.33  1.85,
             0.00 1.45  2.00,   0.77 1.58  1.85,
             1.41 1.70  1.41,   1.85 1.82  0.77,
             2.00 1.94  0.00,   1.85 2.06 -0.77,
             1.41 2.18 -1.41,   0.77 2.30 -1.85,
             0.00 2.42 -2.00,  -0.77 2.55 -1.85,
            -1.41 2.67 -1.41,  -1.85 2.79 -0.77,
            -2.00 2.91  0.00,  -1.85 3.03  0.77,
            -1.41 3.15  1.41,  -0.77 3.27  1.85,
             0.00 3.39  2.00,   0.77 3.52  1.85,
             1.41 3.64  1.41,   1.85 3.76  0.77,
             2.00 3.88  0.00,
        ]
    }
}
```

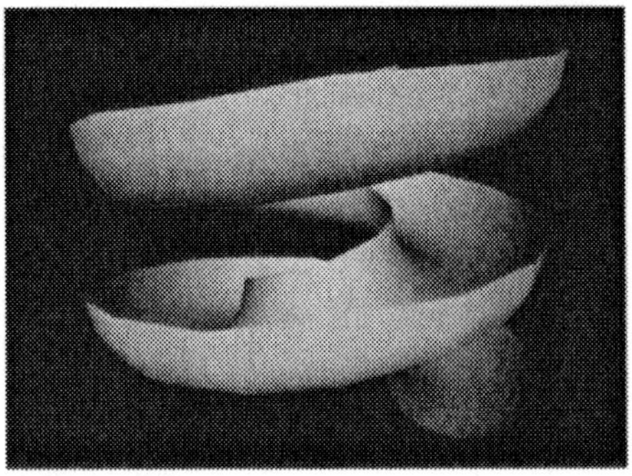

Figure 15.11 *A playground slide built by extruding a half-circle cross section along a helical spine.*

Using Closed Spines

The helical spine in Figure 15.11 is an open spine. You can also specify closed spines that have the same first and last spine coordinates. The VRML text in Figure 15.12 specifies a circular cross section and extrudes it along a closed circular spine. This creates a donut, or torus, shape.

Whenever you use a closed spine, such as that in Figure 15.11, the extrusion's beginning and ending coordinates lie on top of each other. In this situation, the beginning and ending caps, when generated, also lie atop each other. Since you rarely need both caps on closed spine shapes, you should turn one or both off by setting the **beginCap** or **endCap** field value to **FALSE**. For shapes that use closed cross sections swept along closed spines, such as the torus below, both caps are hidden within the interior of the extruded shape. Since neither cap can be seen, both caps should be turned off.

```
#VRML V2.0 utf8
Shape {
    appearance Appearance {
        material Material {
            diffuseColor 1.0 0.0 1.0
        }
    }
    geometry Extrusion {
        creaseAngle 1.57
        beginCap FALSE
        endCap   FALSE
        crossSection [
        # Circle
            1.00  0.00,    0.92 -0.38,
            0.71 -0.71,    0.38 -0.92,
            0.00 -1.00,   -0.38 -0.92,
           -0.71 -0.71,   -0.92 -0.38,
           -1.00 -0.00,   -0.92  0.38,
           -0.71  0.71,   -0.38  0.92,
            0.00  1.00,    0.38  0.92,
            0.71  0.71,    0.92  0.38,
            1.00  0.00
        ]
        spine [
        # Circle
            2.00 0.0  0.00,    1.85 0.0  0.77,
            1.41 0.0  1.41,    0.77 0.0  1.85,
            0.00 0.0  2.00,   -0.77 0.0  1.85,
           -1.41 0.0  1.41,   -1.85 0.0  0.77,
           -2.00 0.0  0.00,   -1.85 0.0 -0.77,
           -1.41 0.0 -1.41,   -0.77 0.0 -1.85,
            0.00 0.0 -2.00,    0.77 0.0 -1.85,
            1.41 0.0 -1.41,    1.85 0.0 -0.77,
            2.00 0.0  0.00,
        ]
    }
}
```

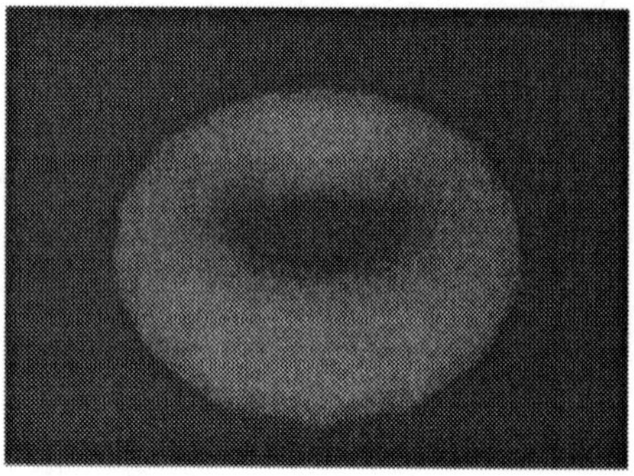

Figure 15.12 A *torus built using a circular cross section swept along a circular spine.*

Scaling Cross Sections

Using the **scale** field, you can provide a cross-section, scale-factor pair for each coordinate on the spine. You can use cross-section scaling to taper shapes. The VRML text in Figure 15.13 builds a pyramid using an extruded square that is scaled by a factor of 0.01 at the apex.

```
#VRML V2.0 utf8
Shape {
    appearance Appearance {
        material Material {
            diffuseColor 1.0 0.5 0.0
        }
    }
    geometry Extrusion {
        crossSection [
        # Square
            -1.0   1.0,    1.0  1.0,
             1.0  -1.0,   -1.0 -1.0,
            -1.0   1.0
        ]
        spine [ 0.0 0.0 0.0,   0.0 1.0 0.0 ]
        scale [ 1.0 1.0,       0.01 0.01 ]
    }
}
```

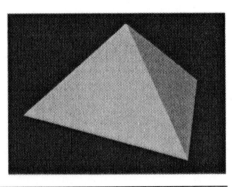

Figure 15.13 *A pyramid built by scaling a square cross section to 0.01 at the pyramid apex.*

When using curved spines, you can scale the cross section at each coordinate along the spine. The VRML text in Figure 15.14 builds a vase by scaling a circular cross section at each coordinate along a straight spine.

```
#VRML V2.0 utf8
Shape {
    appearance Appearance {
        material Material {
            diffuseColor 1.0 0.8 0.0
        }
    }
    geometry Extrusion {
        creaseAngle 1.57
        endCap FALSE
        solid  FALSE
        crossSection [
        # Circle
            1.00  0.00,    0.92 -0.38,
            0.71 -0.71,    0.38 -0.92,
            0.00 -1.00,   -0.38 -0.92,
           -0.71 -0.71,   -0.92 -0.38,
           -1.00 -0.00,   -0.92  0.38,
           -0.71  0.71,   -0.38  0.92,
            0.00  1.00,    0.38  0.92,
            0.71  0.71,    0.92  0.38,
            1.00  0.00
        ]
        spine [
        # Straight-line
            0.0 0.0 0.0,   0.0 0.4 0.0,
            0.0 0.8 0.0,   0.0 1.2 0.0,
            0.0 1.6 0.0,   0.0 2.0 0.0,
            0.0 2.4 0.0,   0.0 2.8 0.0,
            0.0 3.2 0.0,   0.0 3.6 0.0,
            0.0 4.0 0.0
        ]
        scale [
            1.8  1.8,    1.95 1.95,
            2.0  2.0,    1.95 1.95
            1.8  1.8,    1.5  1.5
            1.2  1.2,    1.05 1.05,
            1.0  1.0,    1.05 1.05,
            1.15 1.15,
        ]
    }
}
```

Figure 15.14 *A vase built by scaling a circular cross section at each coordinate along a straight spine.*

Rotating Cross Sections

Using the **orientation** field of the **Extrusion** node, you can rotate the cross section at each coordinate on the spine. If you rotate around the cross section's Y axis, you can create a twist in the extruded shape. Figure 15.15 shows Y-axis, cross-section rotation used to build a twisted bar from a square cross section and a straight spine.

```
#VRML V2.0 utf8
Shape {
    appearance Appearance {
        material Material {
            diffuseColor 1.0 0.5 0.0
        }
    }
    geometry Extrusion {
        creaseAngle 0.785
        crossSection [
        # Square
            -1.0  1.0,    1.0  1.0,
             1.0 -1.0,   -1.0 -1.0,
            -1.0  1.0
        ]
        spine [
        # Straight-line
            0.0 0.0 0.0,
            0.0 0.5 0.0,
            0.0 1.0 0.0,
            0.0 1.5 0.0,
            0.0 2.0 0.0,
            0.0 2.5 0.0,
            0.0 3.0 0.0,
            0.0 3.5 0.0,
            0.0 4.0 0.0
        ]
        orientation [
            0.0 1.0 0.0 0.0,
            0.0 1.0 0.0 0.175,
            0.0 1.0 0.0 0.349,
            0.0 1.0 0.0 0.524,
            0.0 1.0 0.0 0.698,
            0.0 1.0 0.0 0.873,
            0.0 1.0 0.0 1.047,
            0.0 1.0 0.0 1.222,
            0.0 1.0 0.0 1.396,
        ]
    }
}
```

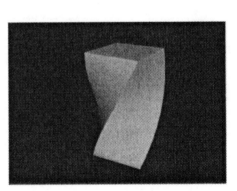

Figure 15.15 *A bar twisted using Y-axis, cross-section rotation at each spine coordinate.*

You can rotate cross sections about arbitrary rotation axes. For example, if you rotate the cross section about its X axis at each spine coordinate, you can create kinks in the extrusion or bevels at the extrusion ends. Figure 15.16 shows X-axis, cross-section rotation used to bevel the end of an extruded cylinder, creating a lipstick shape.

```
#VRML V2.0 utf8
Shape {
    appearance Appearance {
        material Material {
            diffuseColor 1.0 0.3 0.3
        }
    }
    geometry Extrusion {
        creaseAngle 1.57
        crossSection [
        # Circle
            1.00   0.00,    0.92 -0.38,
            0.71 -0.71,    0.38 -0.92,
            0.00 -1.00,   -0.38 -0.92,
           -0.71 -0.71,   -0.92 -0.38,
           -1.00 -0.0,    -0.92  0.38,
           -0.71  0.71,   -0.38  0.92,
            0.00  1.00,    0.38  0.92,
            0.71  0.71,    0.92  0.38,
            1.00  0.00
        ]
        spine [
        # Straight-line
            0.0 0.0 0.0,   0.0 4.0 0.0,
        ]
        orientation [
            0.0 1.0 0.0 0.0,   1.0 0.0 0.0 0.785
        ]
    }
}
```

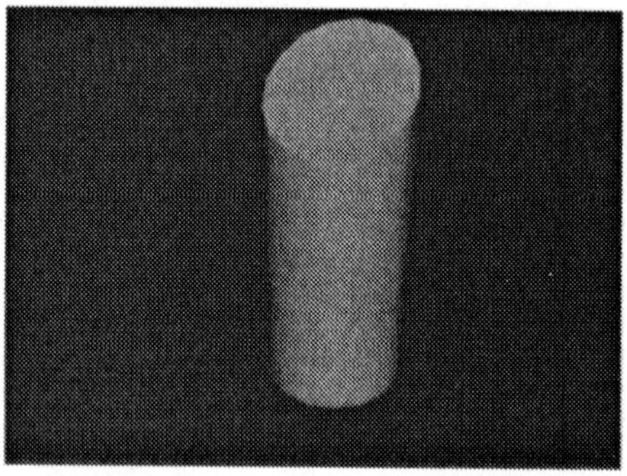

Figure 15.16 *A lipstick shape created by rotating a circular cross section about the X axis as it is extruded.*

Animating Spines

You can use a **CoordinateInterpolator** node to generate new, 3-D spine coordinates and route them into the **set_spine** eventIn of the **Extrusion** node. Each time the spine changes, the extrusion shape is rebuilt. This animates the extrusion shape and enables you to warp and wiggle it.

The VRML text in Figure 15.17 builds an animated snake that wiggles back and forth on the ground. The snake's cross section is a circle that is flattened at the head and tapers at the tail due to scale factors in the **scale** field. The snake's body is built using a sine-wave-shaped spine. A **CoordinateInterpolator** node repeatedly changes the spine, evolving from one sine wave to the next. A **TimeSensor** node clocks the animation.

```
#VRML V2.0 utf8
Group {
    children [

    # Ground
        Shape {
            appearance Appearance {
                material Material {
                    diffuseColor 0.6 0.6 0.0
                }
            }
            geometry Box { size 20.0 0.01 20.0 }
        },
    # Snake shape
        Transform {
            translation 0.0 0.3 0.0
            children Shape {
                appearance Appearance {
                    material Material {
                        diffuseColor 0.0 1.0 0.2
                    }
                }
                geometry DEF Snake Extrusion {
                    creaseAngle 1.57
                    crossSection [
                    # Circle
                        1.00  0.00,   0.92 -0.38,
                        0.71 -0.71,   0.38 -0.92,
                        0.00 -1.00,  -0.38 -0.92,
                       -0.71 -0.71,  -0.92 -0.38,
                       -1.00 -0.00,  -0.92  0.38,
                       -0.71  0.71,  -0.38  0.92,
                        0.00  1.00,   0.38  0.92,
                        0.71  0.71,   0.92  0.38,
                        1.00  0.00
                    ]
                    spine [
                    # Sine wave
                       -4.100 0.0  0.000,  -4.000 0.0  0.000,
                       -3.529 0.0  0.674,  -3.059 0.0  0.996,
                       -2.588 0.0  0.798,  -2.118 0.0  0.184,
                       -1.647 0.0 -0.526,  -1.176 0.0 -0.962,
                       -0.706 0.0 -0.895,  -0.235 0.0 -0.361,
                        0.235 0.0  0.361,   0.706 0.0  0.895,
                        1.176 0.0  0.962,   1.647 0.0  0.526,
                        2.118 0.0 -0.184,   2.588 0.0 -0.798,
                        3.059 0.0 -0.996,   3.529 0.0 -0.674,
                        4.000 0.0  0.000,
                    ]
```

Figure 15.17 continues

```
                    scale [
                        0.050 0.020,   0.200 0.100,
                        0.400 0.150,   0.300 0.300,
                        0.300 0.300,   0.300 0.300,
                        0.300 0.300,   0.300 0.300,
                        0.300 0.300,   0.300 0.300,
                        0.290 0.290,   0.290 0.290,
                        0.290 0.290,   0.280 0.280,
                        0.280 0.280,   0.250 0.250,
                        0.200 0.200,   0.100 0.100,
                        0.050 0.050,
                    ]
                }
            }
        },
# Animation clock
    DEF Clock TimeSensor {
        cycleInterval 4.0
        loop TRUE
    },
# Animation morph
    DEF SnakeWiggle CoordinateInterpolator {
        key [ 0.0, 0.25, 0.50, 0.75, 1.0 ]
        keyValue [
        # time 0.0 position
            -4.100 0.0  0.000,   -4.000 0.0  0.000,
            -3.529 0.0  0.674,   -3.059 0.0  0.996,
            -2.588 0.0  0.798,   -2.118 0.0  0.184,
            -1.647 0.0 -0.526,   -1.176 0.0 -0.962,
            -0.706 0.0 -0.895,   -0.235 0.0 -0.361,
             0.235 0.0  0.361,    0.706 0.0  0.895,
             1.176 0.0  0.962,    1.647 0.0  0.526,
             2.118 0.0 -0.184,    2.588 0.0 -0.798,
             3.059 0.0 -0.996,    3.529 0.0 -0.674,
             4.000 0.0  0.000,
        # time 0.25 position
            -4.100 0.0 -1.000,   -4.000 0.0 -1.000,
            -3.529 0.0 -0.739,   -3.059 0.0 -0.092,
            -2.588 0.0  0.603,   -2.118 0.0  0.983,
            -1.647 0.0  0.850,   -1.176 0.0  0.274,
            -0.706 0.0 -0.446,   -0.235 0.0 -0.932,
             0.235 0.0 -0.932,    0.706 0.0 -0.446,
             1.176 0.0  0.274,    1.647 0.0  0.850,
             2.118 0.0  0.983,    2.588 0.0  0.603,
             3.059 0.0 -0.092,    3.529 0.0 -0.739,
             4.000 0.0 -1.000,
```

Figure 15.17 continues

```
# time 0.50 position
    -4.100 0.0   0.000,   -4.000 0.0   0.000,
    -3.529 0.0  -0.674,   -3.059 0.0  -0.996,
    -2.588 0.0  -0.798,   -2.118 0.0  -0.184,
    -1.647 0.0   0.526,   -1.176 0.0   0.962,
    -0.706 0.0   0.895,   -0.235 0.0   0.361,
     0.235 0.0  -0.361,    0.706 0.0  -0.895,
     1.176 0.0  -0.962,    1.647 0.0  -0.526,
     2.118 0.0   0.184,    2.588 0.0   0.798,
     3.059 0.0   0.996,    3.529 0.0   0.674,
     4.000 0.0   0.000,
# time 0.75 position
    -4.100 0.0   1.000,   -4.000 0.0   1.000,
    -3.529 0.0   0.739,   -3.059 0.0   0.092,
    -2.588 0.0  -0.603,   -2.118 0.0  -0.983,
    -1.647 0.0  -0.850,   -1.176 0.0  -0.274,
    -0.706 0.0   0.446,   -0.235 0.0   0.932,
     0.235 0.0   0.932,    0.706 0.0   0.446,
     1.176 0.0  -0.274,    1.647 0.0  -0.850,
     2.118 0.0  -0.983,    2.588 0.0  -0.603,
     3.059 0.0   0.092,    3.529 0.0   0.739,
     4.000 0.0   1.000,
# time 1.0 position
    -4.100 0.0   0.000,   -4.000 0.0   0.000,
    -3.529 0.0   0.674,   -3.059 0.0   0.996,
    -2.588 0.0   0.798,   -2.118 0.0   0.184,
    -1.647 0.0  -0.526,   -1.176 0.0  -0.962,
    -0.706 0.0  -0.895,   -0.235 0.0  -0.361,
     0.235 0.0   0.361,    0.706 0.0   0.895,
     1.176 0.0   0.962,    1.647 0.0   0.526,
     2.118 0.0  -0.184,    2.588 0.0  -0.798,
     3.059 0.0  -0.996,    3.529 0.0  -0.674,
     4.000 0.0   0.000,
  ]
 }
 ]
}
ROUTE Clock.fraction_changed      TO SnakeWiggle.set_fraction
ROUTE SnakeWiggle.value_changed TO Snake.set_spine
```

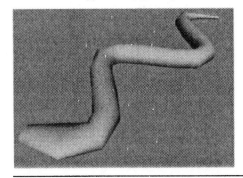

Figure 15.17 *A wiggling snake whose spine is animated using a* **CoordinateInterpolator** *node.*

Summary

The **Extrusion** geometry node builds geometry for a **Shape** node by sweeping a 2-D cross section along a 3-D path.

The **crossSection** field value specifies a list of 2-D coordinates that describe the perimeter of the cross section. The cross section can have an open or closed perimeter.

The **spine** field value specifies a list of 3-D coordinates that describe the path along which the cross section is swept. The spine can be an open or closed curve.

The cross section can be scaled and rotated at each coordinate of the spine by specifying a list of scaling factors in the **scale** field and a list of rotation axes and angles in the **orientation** field. Both lists should have just one value or the same number of values as there are coordinates in the spine.

The beginning and ending caps of the spine can be turned on and off using the **beginCap** and **endCap** fields, respectively. When turned on, cap faces are built by closing the cross section to create a face for one or both ends of the extrusion.

The **ccw** field value specifies whether the coordinates describing the perimeters for faces in the extrusion are to be traced in counterclockwise (**TRUE**) or clockwise (**FALSE**) order. Counterclockwise is the default.

The **convex** field value specifies whether the cross section is convex (**TRUE**) or concave (**FALSE**). Convex cross sections have no inlets, or caves, while concave cross sections have inlets. Convex cross sections are the default.

The **solid** field value selects whether the collection of faces in an extrusion describe a closed solid (**TRUE**), such as a bar, or a nonsolid (**FALSE**), such as a tube. Solid shapes are the default.

The **creaseAngle** field value specifies a crease-angle threshold. Adjacent faces that meet at an angle less than this threshold are smoothly shaded to obscure the edge between the faces. Faces that meet at an angle larger than the crease-angle threshold are not smoothly shaded to obscure the edge between them.

Binding Colors to Points, Lines, Faces, and Coordinates

Using the **Appearance** and **Material** nodes, you can specify a color to shade an entire shape, such as a set of faces or an elevation grid. Using the **Color** node, you can bind specific colors to the individual points, lines, faces, and coordinates of a shape.

With point, line, and face coloring, you can specify a different color for each point, line, and face in a **PointSet, IndexedLineSet, IndexedFaceSet,** or **ElevationGrid** node. Using coordinate coloring, you can specify a different color for each coordinate of each line or face. When the VRML browser builds shapes with colored coordinates, it smoothly varies the color from coordinate to coordinate across each line or face.

Understanding Color Binding

Appearance and **Material** nodes enable you to specify the overall color and transparency attributes of a shape. Using these general-purpose nodes, you can describe an appearance that is independent of what shape is being shaded. For instance, you can create an **Appearance** node that makes shapes red, then use that same node to make red boxes, red spheres, red face sets, or red elevation grids.

To control the color of individual points, lines, faces, and coordinates, your color specification must be tuned to the actual shape being colored. The general-purpose features of the **Appearance** and **Material** nodes are not appropriate. Instead, VRML provides shape-specific color control using several coloring fields within the **PointSet**, **IndexedLineSet**, **IndexedFaceSet**, and **ElevationGrid** nodes.

Color Lists

The shape-specific coloring features of the **PointSet**, **IndexedLineSet**, **IndexedFace-Set**, and **ElevationGrid** nodes require a list of colors to use when coloring the shape. You can then direct how colors in that list are bound to the individual points, lines, faces, or coordinates of a shape.

Colors are listed in a **Color** node similar to the way coordinates are listed in a **Coordinate** node. Each color in the color list is an RGB (red, green, blue) color value, exactly like those used for the **diffuseColor** and **emissiveColor** fields of the **Material** node. Like the coordinates in a **Coordinate** node's value list, the colors in a **Color** node are implicitly numbered, or *indexed*, starting with a *color index* of 0 for the first color, 1 for the second, and so on.

Coloring Point Sets

Recall that the locations of points built with a **PointSet** node are specified using a **Coordinate** node as the value of the **coord** field. The first point in the set is located at the first 3-D coordinate in the **Coordinate** node's coordinate list, the second point is located at the second coordinate, and so on.

Similarly, you can color the individual points in a point set by providing a **Color** node as the **color** field value of a **PointSet** node. The first point in the set is colored using the first color in the **Color** node's color list, the second point is colored using the second color in the list, and so on.

Coloring Line Sets

Like point sets, polylines in an **IndexedLineSet** node are built using a coordinate list provided by a **Coordinate** node. Coordinate indexes specify coordinates from the list to be built and chained together to create one or more polylines.

You can color portions of a line set by providing a **Color** node as the **color** field of an **IndexedLineSet** node. By providing a list of color indexes in a **colorIndex** field, you can specify a different color for each polyline in the line set. Alternately, you can provide a color index for each coordinate of each polyline in the line set. Using coordinate colors, you can cause colors to smoothly vary from one part of a polyline to the next.

Coloring Face Sets

Similar to point and line sets, face sets in an **IndexedFaceSet** node are built using a coordinate list provided by a **Coordinate** node. Coordinate indexes specify coordinates from the list to be built and chained together to form the perimeter of one or more faces.

You can color portions of a face set by providing a **Color** node for the **color** field of an **IndexedFaceSet** node. By providing a list of color indexes in a **colorIndex** field, you can specify a different color for each face in the face set. You also can provide a color index for each coordinate of each face in the face set. Face-coordinate coloring enables you to create rainbowlike effects by varying the color from corner to corner across the interior of a face.

Coloring Elevation Grids

Recall that an elevation grid built by an **ElevationGrid** node uses a list of heights, one for each grid point in a 2-D grid. The node automatically builds faces for each grid square.

You can color portions of an elevation grid by providing a **Color** node for the **color** field of an **ElevationGrid** node. Colors in the color list are automatically assigned to portions of the elevation grid. You can control this automatic assignment and specify whether colors should apply to an entire grid square or to individual grid points.

When colors are applied square by square, the first color in the list colors the first grid square, the second color the second square, and so on. You can use this feature to create a checkerboard pattern across an elevation grid.

When colors are applied to individual grid points, the first color in the list colors the first grid point, the second color the second grid point, and so on. The faces automatically built by the **ElevationGrid** node use these grid-point colors as colors for face coordinates. This enables you to smoothly vary colors across the faces of an elevation grid. For example, you can use white for the peaks of a mountain, smoothly shade downward through green at the middle elevations, and into blues for low-lying lakes and streams.

Colors and Materials

You can specify a **Color** node to control coloring parts of a shape, and you can specify **Appearance** and **Material** nodes to control the overall appearance of a shape. When a **Material** node and a **Color** node are used to color the same shape, the **Color** node's color specification takes priority, overriding the **diffuseColor** field value of the **Material** node. The other fields of the **Material** node remain in effect. This enables you to use a **Material** node to set the transparency factor for a shape, and a **Color** node to vary color across the shape.

The **Color** Node Syntax

The **Color** node creates a list of colors and may be used as the value of the **color** field in coordinate-based geometry nodes, such as the **PointSet**, **IndexedLineSet**, **IndexedFaceSet**, and **ElevationGrid** nodes.

| SYNTAX | Color node |

```
Color {
    color    [ ]     # exposedField MFColor
}
```

The value of the **color** exposed field specifies a list of colors used as geometry colors for a shape. Each color is specified as three floating-point values, one each for the red, green, and blue components of a color. The default value for the **color** field is an empty list of colors.

When specified within geometry nodes that use color indexes, the first color in the **Color** node's list has an index of 0, the second an index of 1, and so on.

The color list can be changed by sending values to the implied **set_color** eventIn of the **color** exposed field. When a list of values is received by this input, the **color** field values are changed, and the new color list is output using the implied **color_changed** eventOut of the exposed field.

The **PointSet** Node Syntax

The **PointSet** node creates point geometry and may be used as the value of the **geometry** field in a **Shape** node.

| SYNTAX | PointSet node |

```
PointSet {
    coord    NULL    # exposedField  SFNode
    color    NULL    # exposedField  SFNode
}
```

The **coord** field is discussed in Chapter 13.

The value of the **color** exposed field specifies a node that provides the colors used to color each point in the point set. Typical **color** field values include the **Color** node. The first point is colored with the first color in the color list, the second point with the second color, and so forth. There must be at least as many colors in the color list as there are coordinates in the coordinates list. The default **NULL** value for this field indicates an empty color list.

The color node value can be changed by sending a value to the implied **set_color** eventIn of the **color** exposed field. When a value is received by this input, the color node is changed, and the new color node is output using the implied **color_changed** eventOut of the exposed field.

Point colors can be set by a **Color** node, by a **Material** node, or by both, using the following rules:

- If no **Color** node and no **Material** node are specified, then all points in the point set are shaded black.

- If no **Color** node is specified, but a **Material** node is provided, then all points in the point set are shaded using the colors in the **Material** node.

- If a **Color** node is specified, but no **Material** node is provided, then all points in the point set are shaded using the colors in the **Color** node.

- If both a **Color** node and a **Material** node are specified, then all points in the point set are shaded using the overall attributes from the **Material** node, such as transparency, but the **Material** node's **diffuseColor** and **emissiveColor** fields are ignored. Instead, colors from the **Color** node control coloration across the surface of the shape.

In all cases, point sets are shaded by treating the color choice as emissive, creating glowing point shapes.

The **IndexedLineSet** Node Syntax

The **IndexedLineSet** node creates polyline geometry and may be used as the value for the **geometry** field of a **Shape** node.

SYNTAX	IndexedLineSet node

```
IndexedLineSet {
    coord            NULL    # exposedField  SFNode
    coordIndex       [ ]     # field         MFInt32
    color            NULL    # exposedField  SFNode
    colorIndex       [ ]     # field         MFInt32
    colorPerVertex   TRUE    # field         SFBool
    set_coordIndex           # eventIn       MFInt32
    set_colorIndex           # eventIn       MFInt32
}
```

The **coord, coordIndex,** and **set_coordIndex** fields are discussed in Chapter 13.

The value of the **color** exposed field specifies a node that provides the colors used to color the lines in the line set. Typical **color** field values include the **Color** node. The default **NULL** value for this field indicates an empty color list.

The value of the **colorIndex** field provides a list of color indexes that specify the colors to use when coloring polylines in the line set. Each value is an integer index specifying a color from the color list in the **color** field. The default value for the **colorIndex** field is an empty color index list.

The **colorPerVertex** field specifies a **TRUE** or **FALSE** value that indicates whether colors from the **Color** node's color list are used for each polyline (**FALSE**) or for each coordinate index of each polyline (**TRUE**). The default value for the **colorPer-Vertex** field is **TRUE**.

When the **colorIndex** field value is not empty:

- A **colorPerVertex** field value of **FALSE** indicates that one color index from the color index list is specified for each polyline in the line set. The first color index specifies the color for the first polyline, the second color index for the second polyline, and so on. There must be one color index for each polyline in the line set.

- A **colorPerVertex** field value of **TRUE** indicates that one color index from the color index list is used for each coordinate index in the line set. The first color index specifies the color for the first coordinate index, the second color index for the second coordinate index, and so on. There must be one color index for each coordinate index, including the -1 coordinate indexes used as polyline separators.

TIP Some VRML browsers do not support line coordinate coloring (**colorPerVertex** field value of **TRUE**). These browsers will average together the coordinate colors of a polyline, then color the entire polyline using the average color.

When the **colorIndex** field value is empty:

- A **colorPerVertex** field value of **FALSE** indicates that colors are used from the color list, in order, one per polyline. The first color in the list is used for the first polyline, the second color for the second polyline, and so on. There must be one color in the color list for each polyline in the line set.

- A **colorPerVertex** field value of **TRUE** indicates that the coordinate indexes in the **coordIndex** field are used as color indexes. The first coordinate index specifies both the coordinate and the color for the first coordinate, the second coordinate index for the second coordinate, and so on.

The **Color** node value can be changed by sending a value to the implied **set_color** eventIn of the **color** exposed field. When a value is received by this input, the color node is changed, and the new color node is output using the implied **color_changed** eventOut of the exposed field.

The color index list can be changed by sending a list of color indexes to the **set_colorIndex** eventIn.

Line colors can be set by a **Color** node, by a **Material** node, or by both, using the following rules:

- If no **Color** node and no **Material** node are specified, then all lines in the line set are shaded white.

- If no **Color** node is specified, but a **Material** node is provided, then all lines in the line set are shaded using the colors in the **Material** node.

- If a **Color** node is specified, but no **Material** node is provided, then all lines in the line set are shaded using the colors in the **Color** node.

- If both a **Color** node and a **Material** node are specified, then all lines in the line set are shaded using the overall attributes from the **Material**

node, such as transparency, but the **Material** node's **diffuseColor** and
emissiveColor fields are ignored. Instead, colors selected from the **Color**
node control coloring across the surface of the shape.

In all cases, line sets are shaded by treating the color choice as emissive, thereby creating glowing line shapes.

The **IndexedFaceSet** Node Syntax

The **IndexedFaceSet** node creates face geometry and may be used as the value of the
geometry field in a **Shape** node.

| SYNTAX | IndexedFaceSet node |

```
IndexedFaceSet {
        coord               NULL      # exposedField  SFNode
        coordIndex          [ ]       # field         MFInt32
        texCoord            NULL      # exposedField  SFNode
        texCoordIndex       [ ]       # field         MFInt32
        color               NULL      # exposedField  SFNode
        colorindex          [ ]       # field         MFInt32
        colorPerVertex      TRUE      # field         SFBool
        normal              NULL      # exposedField  SFNode
        normalIndex         [ ]       # field         MFInt32
        normalPerVertex     TRUE      # field         SFBool
        ccw                 TRUE      # field         SFBool
        convex              TRUE      # field         SFBool
        solid               TRUE      # field         SFBool
        creaseAngle         0.0       # field         SFFloat
        set_coordIndex                # eventIn       MFInt32
        set_texCoordIndex             # eventIn       MFInt32
        set_colorIndex                # eventIn       MFInt32
        set_normalIndex               # eventIn       MFInt32
}
```

The **coord, coordIndex, set_coordIndex, ccw, convex, solid,** and **creaseAngle** fields
are discussed in Chapter 13.

The value of the **color** exposed field specifies a node that provides the colors used
to color the faces in the face set. Typical **color** field values include the **Color** node.
The default **NULL** value for this field indicates an empty color list.

The value of the **colorIndex** provides a list of color indexes that specify the colors
to use when coloring faces in the face set. Each value is an integer index specifying
a color from the color list in the **color** field. The default value for the **colorIndex**
field is an empty color index list.

The **colorPerVertex** field specifies a **TRUE** or **FALSE** value indicating whether
colors from the **Color** node's color list are used for each face (**FALSE**) or for each
coordinate index of each face (**TRUE**). The default value for the **colorPerVertex**
field is **TRUE**.

When the **colorIndex** field value is not empty:

- A **colorPerVertex** field value of **FALSE** indicates one color index from the color index list is used for each face in the face set. The first color index specifies the color for the first face, the second color index for the second face, and so on. There must be one color index for each face in the face set.
- A **colorPerVertex** field value of **TRUE** indicates that one color index from the color index list is used for each coordinate index in the face set. The first color index specifies the color for the first coordinate index, the second color index for the second coordinate index, and so on. There must be one color index for each coordinate index, including the -1 coordinate indexes used as face separators.

T I P   Some VRML browsers do not support face-coordinate coloring (**color-PerVertex** field value of **TRUE**). These browsers will average together the coordinate colors of a face, then color the entire face using the average color.

A **colorIndex** field value is empty:

- When the **colorPerVertex** field value of **FALSE** indicates that colors are used from the color list, in order, one per face. The first color in the list is used for the first face, the second color for the second face, and so on. There must be one color in the color list for each face in the face set.
- A **colorPerVertex** field value of **TRUE** indicates that the coordinate indexes in the **coordIndex** field are used as color indexes. The first coordinate index specifies both the coordinate and the color for the first coordinate, the second coordinate index for the second coordinate, and so on.

The **Color** node value can be changed by sending a value to the implied **set_color** eventIn of the **color** exposed field. When a value is received by this input, the color node is changed, and the new color node is output using the implied **color_changed** eventOut of the exposed field.

The color index list can be changed by sending a list of color indexes to the **set_colorIndex** eventIn.

Face colors can be set by a **Color** node, by a **Material** node, or by both, using the following rules:

- If no **Color** node and no **Material** node are given, then all faces in the face set are shaded black.
- If no **Color** node is specified, but a **Material** node is provided, then all faces in the face set are shaded using the colors in the **Material** node. Faces are drawn as shaded or emissive surfaces depending on the use of the **diffuseColor** and **emissiveColor** fields of the **Material** node.
- If a **Color** node is specified, but no **Material** node is provided, then all faces in the face set are shaded using the colors in the **Color** node. These colors are treated as if they are emissive colors, creating glowing shapes.

- If both a **Color** node and a **Material** node are specified, then all faces in the face set are shaded using the overall attributes from the **Material** node, such as transparency, but the **Material** node's **diffuseColor** field is ignored; instead, colors selected from the **Color** node control coloring across the surface of the shape.

The remaining fields of the **IndexedFaceSet** node are discussed in Chapters 18 (**texCoord, texCoordIndex,** and **set_texCoordIndex**) and 19 (**normal, normalIndex, set_normalIndex,** and **normalPerVertex**).

The **ElevationGrid** Node Syntax

The **ElevationGrid** node creates face geometry that may be used as the value for the **geometry** field of a **Shape** node.

| SYNTAX | ElevationGrid node |

```
ElevationGrid {
        xDimension        0          # field         SFInt32
        xSpacing          0.0        # field         SFFloat
        zDimension        0          # field         SFInt32
        zSpacing          0.0        # field         SFFloat
        height            [ ]        # field         MFFloat
        color             NULL       # exposedField  SFNode
        colorPerVertex    TRUE       # field         SFBool
        normal            NULL       # exposedField  SFNode
        normalPerVertex   TRUE       # field         SFBool
        texCoord          NULL       # exposedField  SFNode
        ccw               TRUE       # field         SFBool
        solid             TRUE       # field         SFBool
        creaseAngle       0.0        # field         SFFloat
        set_height                   # eventIn       MFFloat
}
```

The **xDimension, zDimension, xSpacing, zSpacing, height, set_height, ccw, crease-Angle,** and **solid** fields are discussed in Chapter 14.

The value of the **color** exposed field specifies a node that provides the colors used to color the faces built for the elevation grid. Typical **color** field values include the **Color** node. The default NULL value for this field indicates an empty color list.

The **colorPerVertex** field specifies a TRUE or FALSE value indicating whether colors from the **Color** node's color list are used for each grid square (**FALSE**) or each grid point (**TRUE**) of the elevation grid. The default value for the **colorPerVertex** field is **TRUE**.

TIP Some VRML browsers do not support elevation-grid-point coloring (**colorPerVertex** field value of **TRUE**). These browsers will average together the colors for each corner of a grid square, then color the entire square using the average color.

When the **colorPerVertex** field value is **FALSE**, one color from the **color** field's color list is used for each square in the elevation grid. The first color is used for the first square of the first row of the grid, the second color for the second square of the first row, and so on. There must be one color for each square in the elevation grid. The number of grid squares in the elevation grid is computed as:

```
(xDimension-1) x (zDimension-1)
```

When the **colorPerVertex** field value is **TRUE**, one color from the **color** field's color list is used for each grid point in the elevation grid. The first color is used for the first grid point of the first row of the grid, the second color for the second grid point of the first row, and so on. There must be one color for each grid point in the elevation grid. The number of grid points in the elevation grid is computed as:

```
xDimension x zDimension
```

The **Color** node value can be changed by sending a value to the implied **set_color** eventIn of the **color** exposed field. When a value is received by this input, the color node is changed, and the new color node is output using the implied **color_changed** eventOut of the exposed field.

Elevation grid colors can be set by a **Color** node, by a **Material** node, or by both, using the following rules:

- If no **Color** node and no **Material** node are specified, then all faces built for the elevation grid are shaded white.
- If no **Color** node is specified, but a **Material** node is provided, then all faces built for the elevation grid are shaded using the colors in the **Material** node. Elevation grid faces are drawn as shaded or emissive surfaces depending on the use of the **diffuseColor** and **emissiveColor** fields of the **Material** node.
- If a **Color** node is specified, but no **Material** node is provided, then all faces built for the elevation grid are shaded using the colors in the **Color** node. These colors are treated as if they are emissive colors, creating glowing shapes.
- If both a **Color** node and a **Material** node are specified, then all faces built for the elevation grid are shaded using the overall attributes from the **Material** node, such as transparency, but the **Material** node's **diffuseColor** field is ignored; instead, colors selected from the **Color** node control coloring across the surface of the shape.

The remaining fields of the **ElevationGrid** node are discussed in Chapters 18 (**tex-Coord**) and 19 (**normal** and **normalPerVertex**).

Experimenting with Color Binding

The following examples provide a more detailed examination of the ways in which the **Color** node can be used with the **PointSet, IndexedLineSet, IndexedFaceSet,** and **ElevationGrid** nodes and how they interact with nodes discussed in previous chapters.

Coloring Points in a Point Set

You can use a point set to create a scatter plot, like that in Figure 16.1. An **Indexed-LineSet** node is used to create the X and Y axes of the plot, giving them an overall white color using a **Material** node. A **PointSet** node is used to locate the points on the plot, and a **Color** node is used to give each plotted point a color.

```
#VRML V2.0 utf8
Group {
    children [
    # Axes
        Shape {
            appearance Appearance {
                material Material {
                    emissiveColor 1.0 1.0 1.0
                    diffuseColor  1.0 1.0 1.0
                }
            }
            geometry IndexedLineSet {
                coord Coordinate {
                    point [
                        0.0 0.0 0.0, 10.0 0.0 0.0, 0.0 8.0 0.0
                    ]
                }
                coordIndex [ 0, 1, -1,  0, 2, -1 ]
            }
        },
    # Scatter plot with different color points
        Shape {
            # no appearance, use emissive coloring
            geometry PointSet {
                coord Coordinate {
                    point [
                    # Green points
                        1.0 1.0 0.0,   2.0 4.0 0.0,
                        3.0 5.0 0.0,   4.0 4.0 0.0,
                        5.0 6.0 0.0,   6.0 7.0 0.0,
                        7.0 5.0 0.0,   8.0 6.0 0.0,
                        9.0 4.0 0.0,  10.0 3.0 0.0,
                    # Yellow points
                        1.0 3.0 0.0,   2.0 2.0 0.0,
                        3.0 2.0 0.0,   4.0 1.0 0.0,
                        5.0 2.0 0.0,   6.0 4.0 0.0,
                        7.0 3.0 0.0,   8.0 5.0 0.0,
                        9.0 5.0 0.0,  10.0 6.0 0.0,
                    ]
                }
            }
```

Figure 16.1 continues

```
color Color {
    color [
    # Green points
        0.0 1.0 0.0,    0.0 1.0 0.0,
        0.0 1.0 0.0,    0.0 1.0 0.0,
        0.0 1.0 0.0,    0.0 1.0 0.0,
        0.0 1.0 0.0,    0.0 1.0 0.0,
        0.0 1.0 0.0,    0.0 1.0 0.0,
    # Yellow points
        1.0 1.0 0.0,    1.0 1.0 0.0,
        1.0 1.0 0.0,    1.0 1.0 0.0,
        1.0 1.0 0.0,    1.0 1.0 0.0,
        1.0 1.0 0.0,    1.0 1.0 0.0,
        1.0 1.0 0.0,    1.0 1.0 0.0,
    ]
}
        }
    }
    ]
}
```

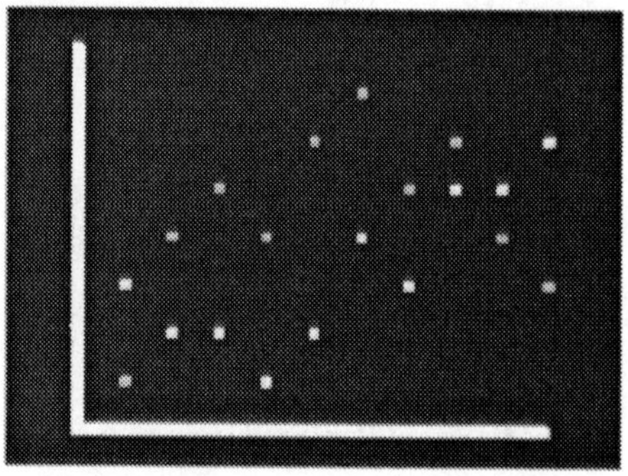

Figure 16.1 *A scatter plot with the points colored using colors from a **Color** node.*

Coloring Polylines in a Line Set

Figure 16.2 creates a line plot with two zig-zagging polylines built by an **Indexed-LineSet** node. The **colorPerVertex** field value is set to **FALSE**, and a **Color** node and color indexes are used to specify a color for each polyline in the line set. A second **IndexedLineSet** node is used to create the white X and Y axes of the plot.

```
#VRML V2.0 utf8
Group {
    children [
    # Axes
        Shape {
            appearance Appearance {
                material Material {
                    emissiveColor 1.0 1.0 1.0
                    diffuseColor  1.0 1.0 1.0
                }
            }
        }
```

Figure 16.2 continues

```
        geometry IndexedLineSet {
            coord Coordinate {
                point [
                    0.0 0.0 0.0, 10.0 0.0 0.0, 0.0 8.0 0.0
                ]
            }
            coordIndex [ 0, 1, -1,  0, 2, -1 ]
        }
    },
# Line plot with different color lines
    Shape {
        # no appearance, use emissive coloring
        geometry IndexedLineSet {
            coord Coordinate {
                point [
                # Green line
                    1.0 1.0 0.0,    2.0 4.0 0.0,
                    3.0 5.0 0.0,    4.0 4.0 0.0,
                    5.0 6.0 0.0,    6.0 7.0 0.0,
                    7.0 5.0 0.0,    8.0 6.0 0.0,
                    9.0 4.0 0.0,   10.0 3.0 0.0,
                # Yellow line
                    1.0 3.0 0.0,    2.0 2.0 0.0,
                    3.0 2.0 0.0,    4.0 1.0 0.0,
                    5.0 2.0 0.0,    6.0 4.0 0.0,
                    7.0 3.0 0.0,    8.0 5.0 0.0,
                    9.0 5.0 0.0,   10.0 6.0 0.0,
                ]
            }
            coordIndex [
            # Green line
                0, 1, 2, 3, 4, 5, 6, 7, 8, 9, -1,
            # Yellow line
                10, 11, 12, 13, 14, 15, 16, 17, 18, 19, -1
            ]
            colorPerVertex FALSE
            color Color {
                color [ 0.0 1.0 0.0,    1.0 1.0 0.0 ]
            }
            colorIndex [ 0, 1 ]
        }
    }
  ]
}
```

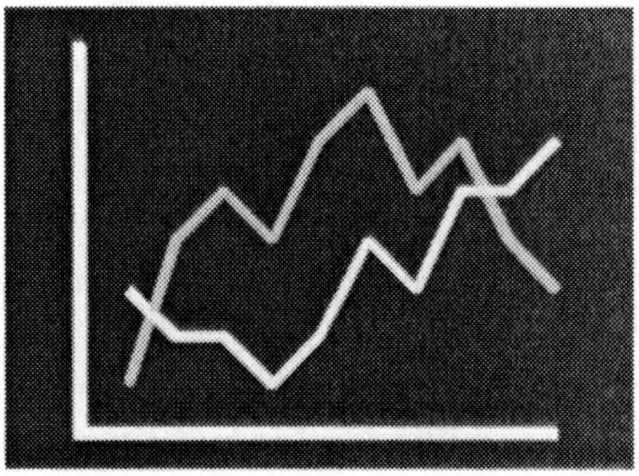

Figure 16.2 *A line plot with the polylines colored using colors from a **Color** node.*

Coloring Coordinates in a Line Set

The polylines in Figure 16.2 are each colored uniformly from beginning to end. You can also control the color of each coordinate along each polyline by setting the colorPerVertex field value to TRUE.

Figure 16.3 builds a thistlelike star burst using a series of lines radiating from a central coordinate. For each line, the center coordinate's color is set to yellow, and the outer coordinate's color is set to red. When drawn, each line's color smoothly varies from yellow to red.

```
#VRML V2.0 utf8
Group {
    children [
        DEF Burst Shape {
            # no appearance, use emissive coloring
            geometry IndexedLineSet {
                coord Coordinate {
                    point [
                         0.00  0.00 0.00,   1.00  0.00 0.00,
                         0.92  0.38 0.00,   0.71  0.71 0.00,
                         0.38  0.92 0.00,   0.00  1.00 0.00,
                        -0.38  0.92 0.00,  -0.71  0.71 0.00,
                        -0.92  0.38 0.00,  -1.00  0.00 0.00,
                        -0.92 -0.38 0.00,  -0.71 -0.71 0.00,
                        -0.38 -0.92 0.00,   0.00 -1.00 0.00,
                         0.38 -0.92 0.00,   0.71 -0.71 0.00,
                         0.92 -0.38 0.00,
                    ]
                }
                coordIndex [
                     0,  1, -1,   0,  2, -1,
                     0,  3, -1,   0,  4, -1,
                     0,  5, -1,   0,  6, -1,
                     0,  7, -1,   0,  8, -1,
                     0,  9, -1,   0, 10, -1,
                     0, 11, -1,   0, 12, -1,
                     0, 13, -1,   0, 14, -1,
                     0, 15, -1,   0, 16, -1
                ]
                colorPerVertex TRUE
                color Color {
                    color [
                        1.0 1.0 0.0,   # burst center color
                        1.0 0.3 0.3    # burst ends color
                    ]
                }
```

Figure 16.3 continues

```
            colorIndex [
                 0,  1,  0,   0,  1,  0,
                 0,  1,  0,   0,  1,  0,
                 0,  1,  0,   0,  1,  0,
                 0,  1,  0,   0,  1,  0,
                 0,  1,  0,   0,  1,  0,
                 0,  1,  0,   0,  1,  0,
                 0,  1,  0,   0,  1,  0,
                 0,  1,  0,   0,  1,  0,
            ]
        }
    },
    Transform { rotation 0.0 1.0 0.0  0.785 children USE Burst },
    Transform { rotation 0.0 1.0 0.0  1.57  children USE Burst },
    Transform { rotation 0.0 1.0 0.0  2.355 children USE Burst }
    ]
}
```

Figure 16.3 *A star burst of lines colored using colors from a* **Color** *node for each line coordinate.*

Coloring Faces in a Face Set

Figure 16.4 builds a book out of faces in a face set. The book face set uses two colors, brown and white, both specified in a **Color** node. The three faces making up the cover (front, back, and spine) are colored with the first color, and the three faces making up the book's paper edges are colored with the second.

```
#VRML V2.0 utf8
Shape {
    appearance Appearance {
        material Material { }
    }
    geometry IndexedFaceSet {
        coord Coordinate {
            point [
            # Around the front of the book
                -0.095 -0.115 0.04,   0.095 -0.115 0.04,
                 0.095  0.115 0.04,  -0.095  0.115 0.04,
```

Figure 16.4 continues

```
        # Around the back of the book
            -0.095 -0.115 0.00,    0.095 -0.115 0.00,
             0.095  0.115 0.00,   -0.095  0.115 0.00
        ]
    }
    coordIndex [
    # Cover front, back, and spine cover (brown)
        0, 1, 2, 3, -1,   7, 6, 5, 4, -1,   0, 3, 7, 4, -1,
    # Paper bottom, right, and top edges (white)
        0, 4, 5, 1, -1,   1, 5, 6, 2, -1,   2, 6, 7, 3
    ]
    colorPerVertex FALSE
    color Color {
        color [
            0.7 0.5 0.2, # cover
            0.8 0.8 0.8  # paper edges
        ]
    }
    colorIndex [
        0, 0, 0, # cover
        1, 1, 1  # paper edges
    ]
    }
}
```

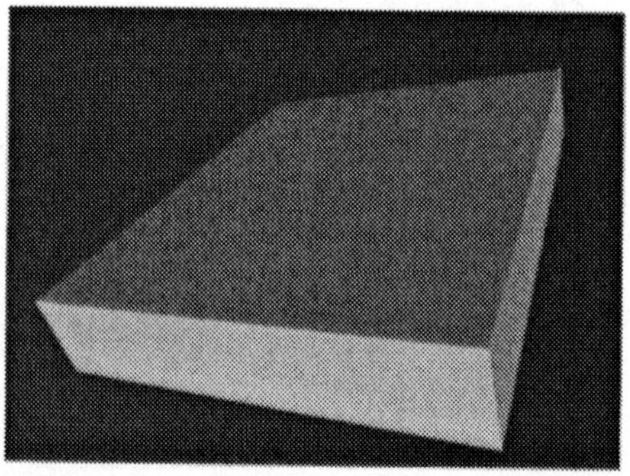

Figure 16.4 *A book with its faces individually colored using colors from a* **Color** *node.*

Coloring Coordinates in a Face Set

You can specify a color for each coordinate of each face in a face set by setting the **colorPerVertex** field value to **TRUE** and providing one color index for each coordinate index. Figure 16.5 creates flames on a log by repeatedly using a face set of four triangles. By binding orange, yellow, and red to the three coordinates of each triangle, a smooth color gradation across the triangle is created. Notice also that no **Material** node is used. This ensures that the coordinate colors are interpreted as emissive, creating a glowing-fire effect.

```
#VRML V2.0 utf8
Group {
    children [
    # A log
        Transform {
            translation 0.0 -0.4 0.0
            rotation    0.0 0.0 1.0 -1.57
            children Shape {
                appearance Appearance {
                    material Material {
                        diffuseColor 0.5 0.3 0.0
                    }
                }
            }
```

Figure 16.5 continues

```
                    geometry Cylinder {
                        height 2.9
                        radius 0.4
                    }
                }
            },
    # A set of flames
        DEF Flames Shape {
            # No appearance, use emissive coloring
            geometry IndexedFaceSet {
                coord Coordinate {
                    point [
                        -0.7 0.0 0.0,  -0.8 1.5 0.0,  -1.0 0.0 0.0,
                        -0.5 0.0 0.01, -0.7 1.2 0.01, -0.9 0.0 0.01,
                        -0.1 0.0 0.0,  -0.2 1.6 0.0,  -0.4 0.0 0.0,
                         0.3 0.0 0.01,  0.2 1.0 0.01,  0.0 0.0 0.0,
                    ]
                }
                coordIndex [
                    0, 1, 2, -1,  3,  4,  5, -1,
                    6, 7, 8, -1,  9, 10, 11, -1
                ]
                solid FALSE
                colorPerVertex TRUE
                color Color {
                    color [
                        1.0 0.0 0.0,  1.0 0.5 0.0,  1.0 0.1 0.0,
                        0.8 0.0 0.0,  1.0 0.9 0.0,  1.0 0.0 0.0,
                    ]
                }
                colorIndex [
                    3, 4, 5, 0,   0, 1, 2, 0,
                    3, 4, 5, 0,   0, 1, 2, 0
                ]
            }
        },
    # Repeat the flames to make a roaring fire
        Transform {
            translation 0.8 0.0 0.02
            scale 1.0 1.3 1.0
            children USE Flames
        },
        Transform {
            translation 1.1 0.0 0.04
            scale 1.0 0.5 1.0
            children USE Flames
        },
        Transform {
            translation -0.3 0.0 0.06
            scale 1.0 1.1 1.0
            children USE Flames
        },
```

Figure 16.5 continues

```
Transform {
    translation -0.1 0.0 0.08
    scale 1.0 0.4 1.0
    children USE Flames
},
Transform {
    translation 0.8 0.0 0.10
    scale 1.0 1.1 1.0
    children USE Flames
}
]
}
```

Figure 16.5   *A log and fire using faces colored with colors from a **Color** node.*

Coloring Grid Squares in an Elevation Grid

Figure 16.6 builds a red and black checkerboard using an **ElevationGrid** node and a height list containing only heights of 0.0. By setting the **colorPerVertex** field value to **FALSE**, one color from the **Color** node is assigned to each grid square, row by row, throughout the grid.

```
#VRML V2.0 utf8
Shape {
    appearance Appearance {
        material Material { }
    }
    geometry ElevationGrid {
        xDimension 8
        zDimension 8
        xSpacing    1.0
        zSpacing    1.0
        solid       FALSE
        height [
            0.0, 0.0, 0.0, 0.0, 0.0, 0.0, 0.0, 0.0,
            0.0, 0.0, 0.0, 0.0, 0.0, 0.0, 0.0, 0.0,
            0.0, 0.0, 0.0, 0.0, 0.0, 0.0, 0.0, 0.0,
            0.0, 0.0, 0.0, 0.0, 0.0, 0.0, 0.0, 0.0,
            0.0, 0.0, 0.0, 0.0, 0.0, 0.0, 0.0, 0.0,
            0.0, 0.0, 0.0, 0.0, 0.0, 0.0, 0.0, 0.0,
            0.0, 0.0, 0.0, 0.0, 0.0, 0.0, 0.0, 0.0,
            0.0, 0.0, 0.0, 0.0, 0.0, 0.0, 0.0, 0.0,
        ]
        colorPerVertex FALSE
```

Figure 16.6 continues

```
color DEF check Color {
    color [
        1.0 0.3 0.3,  0.2 0.2 0.2,  1.0 0.3 0.3,  0.2 0.2 0.2,
        1.0 0.3 0.3,  0.2 0.2 0.2,  1.0 0.3 0.3,  0.2 0.2 0.2,
        1.0 0.3 0.3,  0.2 0.2 0.2,  1.0 0.3 0.3,  0.2 0.2 0.2,
        1.0 0.3 0.3,  0.2 0.2 0.2,  1.0 0.3 0.3,  0.2 0.2 0.2,
        1.0 0.3 0.3,  0.2 0.2 0.2,  1.0 0.3 0.3,  0.2 0.2 0.2,
        1.0 0.3 0.3,  0.2 0.2 0.2,  1.0 0.3 0.3,  0.2 0.2 0.2,
        1.0 0.3 0.3,  0.2 0.2 0.2,  1.0 0.3 0.3,  0.2 0.2 0.2,
        1.0 0.3 0.3,  0.2 0.2 0.2,  1.0 0.3 0.3,  0.2 0.2 0.2,
        1.0 0.3 0.3,  0.2 0.2 0.2,  1.0 0.3 0.3,  0.2 0.2 0.2,
        1.0 0.3 0.3,  0.2 0.2 0.2,  1.0 0.3 0.3,  0.2 0.2 0.2,
        1.0 0.3 0.3,  0.2 0.2 0.2,  1.0 0.3 0.3,  0.2 0.2 0.2,
        1.0 0.3 0.3,  0.2 0.2 0.2,  1.0 0.3 0.3,  0.2 0.2 0.2,
        1.0 0.3 0.3,  0.2 0.2 0.2,
    ]
    }
  }
}
```

Figure 16.6 *A checkerboard built using elevation-grid squares and colored using colors from a Color node.*

Coloring Grid Points in an Elevation Grid

By setting the **colorPerVertex** field value to **TRUE** in an **ElevationGrid** node, you can cause colors to be assigned, one by one, to each grid point. Square faces built between the grid points show a smooth variation of colors from corner to corner.

Figure 16.7 colors the mountain you built in Chapter 14. The **Color** node contains one color for each grid point. Blue colors are used for low elevations, white for high elevations, and greens and browns for the middle elevations.

```
#VRML V2.0 utf8
Shape {
    appearance Appearance {
        material Material { }
    }
    geometry ElevationGrid {
        xDimension  9
        zDimension  9
        xSpacing    1.0
        zSpacing    1.0
        solid       FALSE
        creaseAngle 0.785
```

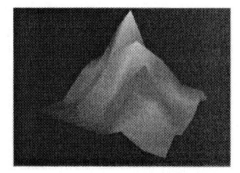

Figure 16.7 continues

```
height [
    0.0, 0.0, 0.5, 1.0, 0.5, 0.0, 0.0, 0.0, 0.0,
    0.0, 0.0, 0.0, 0.0, 2.5, 0.5, 0.0, 0.0, 0.0,
    0.0, 0.0, 0.5, 0.5, 3.0, 1.0, 0.5, 0.0, 1.0,
    0.0, 0.0, 0.5, 2.0, 4.5, 2.5, 1.0, 1.5, 0.5,
    1.0, 2.5, 3.0, 4.5, 5.5, 3.5, 3.0, 1.0, 0.0,
    0.5, 2.0, 2.0, 2.5, 3.5, 4.0, 2.0, 0.5, 0.0,
    0.0, 0.0, 0.5, 1.5, 1.0, 2.0, 3.0, 1.5, 0.0,
    0.0, 0.0, 0.0, 0.0, 0.0, 0.0, 2.0, 1.5, 0.5,
    0.0, 0.0, 0.0, 0.0, 0.0, 0.0, 0.5, 0.0, 0.0,
]
colorPerVertex TRUE
color Color {
    color [
        0.0 0.3 1.0,   0.0 0.3 1.0,   0.0 0.5 0.1,
        0.2 0.6 0.0,   0.0 0.5 0.1,   0.0 0.3 1.0,
        0.0 0.3 1.0,   0.0 0.3 1.0,   0.0 0.3 1.0,

        0.0 0.3 1.0,   0.0 0.3 1.0,   0.0 0.3 1.0,
        0.0 0.3 1.0,   0.5 0.4 0.0,   0.0 0.5 0.1,
        0.0 0.3 1.0,   0.0 0.3 1.0,   0.0 0.3 1.0,

        0.0 0.3 1.0,   0.0 0.3 1.0,   0.0 0.5 0.1,
        0.0 0.5 0.1,   0.5 0.4 0.0,   0.2 0.6 0.0,
        0.0 0.5 0.1,   0.0 0.3 1.0,   0.2 0.6 0.0,

        0.0 0.3 1.0,   0.0 0.3 1.0,   0.0 0.5 0.1,
        0.4 0.3 0.1,   0.7 0.7 0.7,   0.5 0.4 0.0,
        0.2 0.6 0.1,   0.3 0.6 0.6,   0.0 0.5 0.1,

        0.2 0.6 0.0,   0.5 0.4 0.0,   0.5 0.4 0.0,
        0.7 0.7 0.7,   0.8 0.8 0.8,   0.5 0.5 0.7,
        0.5 0.5 0.7,   0.2 0.6 0.0,   0.0 0.3 1.0,

        0.0 0.5 0.1,   0.2 0.6 0.1,   0.2 0.6 0.1,
        0.2 0.6 0.1,   0.5 0.5 0.7,   0.7 0.7 0.7,
        0.5 0.4 0.0,   0.0 0.5 0.1,   0.0 0.3 1.0,

        0.0 0.5 0.1,   0.0 0.3 1.0,   0.0 0.5 0.1,
        0.2 0.6 0.1,   0.2 0.6 0.0,   0.5 0.4 0.0,
        0.5 0.5 0.7,   0.2 0.6 0.0,   0.0 0.3 1.0,

        0.0 0.3 1.0,   0.0 0.3 1.0,   0.0 0.3 1.0,
        0.0 0.3 1.0,   0.0 0.3 1.0,   0.0 0.5 0.1,
        0.5 0.4 0.0,   0.2 0.6 0.0,   0.0 0.5 0.1,

        0.0 0.3 1.0,   0.0 0.3 1.0,   0.0 0.3 1.0,
        0.0 0.3 1.0,   0.0 0.3 1.0,   0.0 0.3 1.0,
        0.0 0.5 0.1,   0.0 0.3 1.0,   0.0 0.3 1.0,
    ]
  }
 }
}
```

Figure 16.7 *A mountain built using elevation-grid points and colored using colors from a **Color** node.*

Summary

You can specify colors for individual points, lines, faces, or coordinates in point sets, line sets, face sets, and elevation grids. The colors are specified in a **Color** node used as the value of the **color** field in these geometry nodes. The **Color** node's **color** field provides a list of RGB (red, green, blue) color values, like those used for the **diffuse-Color** or **emissiveColor** fields of the **Material** node. Colors in the list are implicitly numbered, or indexed starting with zero.

PointSet node colors are assigned, one by one, to the points in the point set in the same order as the coordinates in the point set's coordinate list.

You can assign colors to specific polylines, faces, or coordinates, within **Indexed-LineSet** and **IndexedFaceSet** nodes by providing a list of color indexes in the **color-Index** field. When the **colorPerVertex** field value is **FALSE**, each color index specifies a color for an entire polyline or face. When the **colorPerVertex** field value is **TRUE**, each color index specifies a color for a coordinate on a polyline or face. When a different color for each coordinate of a polyline is specified, colors are smoothly varied along the length of the line. When a different color for each coordinate of a face is specified, colors are smoothly varied across the interior of the face.

ElevationGrid node colors are assigned, one by one, to the grid squares or grid points of the elevation grid. When the **colorPerVertex** field value is **FALSE**, colors are assigned to grid squares, with the first color bound to the first square of the first row, the second color bound to the second square of the first row, and so on. When the **colorPerVertex** field value is **TRUE**, colors are assigned to grid points in the same manner. When each grid point is specified to be a different color, colors are smoothly varied across the square.

CHAPTER 17

Mapping Textures

The real world is filled with an extraordinary amount of visual detail. Consider a tree, for instance. From a distance, a tree appears to be a large greenish blob. As you near it, it resolves into a trunk and leafy canopy. Come closer still, and branches and clumps of leaves are visible, then individual leaves, the veins on the leaves, and so on. With all this detail, how closely must you simulate the real world to make your VRML world look believable?

In computer graphics, this visual detail is known as *texture*. Creating extraordinarily detailed shapes for every branch, leaf, or vein, of a tree is impractical. Instead, VRML enables you to take a picture of anything in the real world and paint, or *map*, it on any shape in your VRML world—a technique known as *texture mapping*.

Texture mapping saves a lot of time, since you no longer need to create shapes for every leaf on a tree, every brick in a building, every blade of grass in a lawn, and so on. Instead, take a picture of a tree, a brick wall, a grassy lawn, or anything else, scan it into your computer, and map it to a simple shape, like a square. When seen from a distance, such a texture mapped shape fools the viewer into believing they are seeing a tree, a brick wall, or grassy lawn. Only when viewed from close up does the illusion break down and the shape reveal itself to be a simple square painted with a picture of a real-world tree, brick wall, lawn, or something else.

You can use the **texture** field of the **Appearance** node, together with the **ImageTexture**, **PixelTexture**, and **MovieTexture** nodes, to specify textures to map to your shapes.

Understanding Texture Mapping

Texture mapping is a technique used to add detail to a world without creating shapes for every brick, leaf, cloud, or bit of wood grain. You can use any kind of

297

image as a texture image, including real-world photographs and *bitmapped art*, like that created with a paint application. Figure 17.1 shows a bookcase lined with books. Figure 17.1*a* shows the shapes without texture mapping. In Figure 17.1*b*, a wood-grain texture image of oak is mapped to the bookcase, and an image of book spines is mapped to a face for each book shelf. The addition of these texture images increases the realism of the shapes without adding any additional shapes to the world. Figure 17.1*c, d, e, f,* and *g,* show the five texture images used to texture map the bookcase and shelves.

You can texture map any VRML shape, except those created using **PointSet** or **IndexedLineSet** nodes. The bookcase in Figure 17.1 is built using several **Indexed-FaceSet** nodes. You can also apply textures to **Box, Cone, Cylinder, Sphere, Text, ElevationGrid,** and **Extrusion** node shapes.

TIP A painting and photo touchup application, like Adobe's PhotoShop, is an essential tool for creating and manipulating texture mapping images. Image processing tools, such as Kai's Power Tools for PhotoShop, also can be used to warp and modify texture images in creative ways. If you don't have the tools or the time to create your own texture images, you can purchase libraries of texture images on CD-ROM or browse the Internet for texture images created by other VRML authors.

Texture Images

You can think of a texture image as a 2-D grid, like a piece of graph paper, with each grid square colored a different color. The grid squares of the image are called *pixels,* which is an abbreviation for *picture element.* The *size* of an image is specified as the width and height of the image, measured in numbers of pixels. While texture images can be any size in VRML, they are typically quite small. Common texture-image sizes are 128 by 128 pixels, 64 by 64 pixels, or smaller. In comparison, your computer screen is 640 by 480 pixels or larger.

The pixel values for a texture image are typically stored in an image file. You can select an image file to use as a texture map with a URL. Using a URL to specify a texture-image file enables you to select texture images from anywhere on the Internet or from your local hard disk.

VRML texture-image files can store a single texture image or a movie containing a series of texture images, like the frames in a film. When you map a movie texture to a shape, the movie plays back on the shape as if the shape were a TV screen. You can also use movie textures to create moving clouds, flickering torches, or swirling whirlpools.

Typically, JPEG and GIF file formats are used for nonmovie texture images, and the MPEG format is used for movie textures. In this book, most nonmovie texture images are stored in the JPEG file format in the files with the `.jpg` file name extension. Movie textures are stored in the MPEG file format in files with the `.mpg` file name extension.

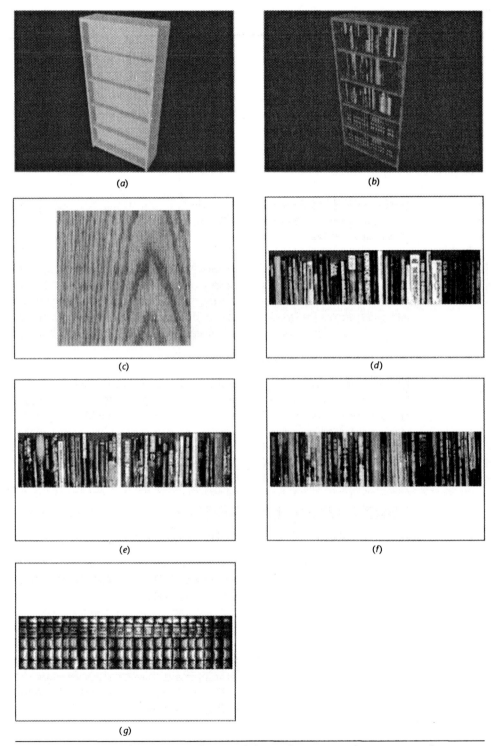

Figure 17.1 *A bookcase (a) without and (b) with textures. The images used to texture map the bookcase: (c) oak wood grain and (d–g) rows of books.*

TIP Some VRML browsers support additional image file formats, such as TIFF, BMP, PCX, and PICT. However, if you use any of these nonstandard formats for VRML, users of browsers that don't support these formats will be unable to view your worlds properly.

Image-File Formats

Over the years, hundreds of different methods have been developed for storing image pixels in files. Some methods are more efficient than others or offer additional features needed by a particular vendor's applications. VRML supports four of the most common of these *image-file formats* for storing texture images: JPEG, GIF, PNG, and MPEG.

TIP Painting, drawing, photo touchup, and digital video editing applications typically support a wide range of file formats to which to save your work. There are also a variety of file-format conversion tools available commercially (such as Equilibrium's DeBabelizer) and as shareware that can help you convert between file formats so that you can easily create JPEG, GIF, PNG, and MPEG files.

SIDEBAR: JPEG IMAGE-FILE FORMAT *JPEG* stands for "Joint Photographic Experts Group," the name of the committee that invented the file format. The JPEG image-file format is designed for storing high-quality images using a very clever storage compression algorithm. This format is the best of VRML's supported formats for storing nonmovie texture images.

On a PC, JPEG files are typically named with a .jpg file name extension. On a UNIX system, JPEG files often have .jpeg or .jfif file name extensions. On a Macintosh, the JPEG format is indicated by a "JPEG" file type.

SIDEBAR: GIF IMAGE-FILE FORMAT *GIF* stands for "Graphical Interchange Format." The GIF format was developed by CompuServe as a standard format for the distribution of images that is now ubiquitous on the Web and supported by all Web browsers. The GIF format is designed to store relatively low-quality images using a common compression scheme. This is the second-best format of VRML's supported, nonmovie, texture-image formats.

On a PC or UNIX system, GIF files are typically named with a .gif file name extension. On a Macintosh, the GIF format is indicated by a "GIFf" file type.

SIDEBAR: PNG IMAGE-FILE FORMAT *PNG* stands for "Portable Network Graphics." The PNG format is in development by Web application developers as a replacement for GIF. While the PNG format has a number of desirable features, it is not yet widely supported. For this reason, this is the third-best format for storing nonmovie texture images.

On a PC or UNIX system, PNG files are typically named with a .png file name extension. On a Macintosh, the PNG format is indicated by a "PNGf" file type.

MPEG stands for "Moving Picture Experts Group," the name of the inventors of the file format. Unlike JPEG, GIF, and PNG, the MPEG format is designed to store high-quality movie images using several clever storage compression schemes. In addition to movie images, the MPEG format can also store sound to go along with the movies. The MPEG format is the only file format supported by VRML for storing movie textures.

On a PC or UNIX system, MPEG files may have a variety of file name extensions, including .mpg, .mps, .mlv, and .mpv. On a Macintosh, the MPEG format is indicated by an "MPEG" file type.

Image Types

Texture images can be stored as color or grayscale images. A *color image* stores a color for each pixel in the image, while a *grayscale image* only stores a gray level for each pixel. You can use either color or grayscale images as textures for VRML shapes.

When you use a color texture image, the colors in the texture image are mapped to parts of your VRML shapes as if those shapes were being painted. If specified, the **diffuseColor** field of the shape **Material** node is ignored when using a color texture, but the remaining fields of the **Material** node still apply. This enables you to create semitransparent or glowing textured shapes.

When you use a grayscale texture image, the gray values in the image are multiplied with the **diffuseColor** field value of the shape **Material** node. This brightens and darkens the shape's color from point to point across the shape. You can use this effect to create light and dark patterns on colored shapes. The remaining fields of the **Material** node still apply, enabling you to create semitransparent or glowing textured shapes.

The JPEG, GIF, and PNG file formats support color and grayscale images. The MPEG format only supports color images.

SIDEBAR: IMAGE COLOR VALUES AND VRML COLOR VALUES Most color image file formats store each RGB color as three, 8-bit integers, one each for the red, green, and blue components of the RGB color. Each 8-bit integer holds a value between 0 and 255. VRML browsers automatically convert these three integers into a floating-point RGB color, such as that used in the **diffuseColor** field of a **Material** node. During the conversion, each red, green, and blue value between 0 and 255 is mapped to a value between 0.0 and 1.0 by dividing the file color value by 255.0.

Grayscale images are typically stored in an analogous fashion, with each gray value stored as a single 8-bit integer that varies between 0 (black) and 255 (white). VRML browsers automatically map each gray integer value to a value between 0.0 and 1.0 by dividing the file gray value by 255.0.

Transparency Images

In addition to storing a color or grayscale level at each pixel, some texture-image file formats can optionally store a transparency level for each pixel. A pixel's *transparency level* indicates whether the pixel should be transparent, opaque, or somewhere in between. Using pixel transparency you can create texture images with transparent holes in them.

When an image with pixel transparencies is texture mapped to a shape, the pixel transparencies control transparency from point to point across the shape. Where there is a transparent hole in the texture image, a corresponding transparent hole also occurs in the textured shape.

Figure 17.2*a* shows a texture image of a tree, and *b* shows the pixel transparencies for the tree image. The white parts of the transparency image correspond to the opaque parts of the texture, while the black parts are transparent holes in the image. In this example, the transparency image creates a white silhouette of the tree. Figure 17.2*c* shows an untextured row of flat faces in front of a brick wall, and *d* shows the same row of faces with the tree texture mapped to each. The textured faces have transparent holes anywhere tree-texture pixels are transparent.

(a)   (b)

(c)   (d)

Figure 17.2   *A texture image of a tree showing the (a) colored part of the image and (b) the transparent part of the image. A row of faces (c) without any texturing and (d) with the tree texture mapped to each.*

When you use a texture image with pixel transparencies, the transparency levels in the texture image override those in the **transparency** field value of the shape's **Material** node. The remaining fields of the **Material** node still apply.

The PNG file format supports pixel-transparency values. The JPEG and MPEG formats cannot store pixel transparencies, and neither can the most common form of the GIF format. The GIF format, however, can store a background color for the image that can be interpreted as transparency information. Most VRML browsers treat this background-color transparency as a simple form of pixel transparency.

> **SIDEBAR: IMAGE ALPHA VALUES AND VRML PIXEL TRANSPARENCIES** Most image-file formats that support pixel transparency, store each pixel's transparency information as an 8-bit integer alpha value. A pixel's *alpha value* indicates its level of opacity and varies between 0 and 255, where 0 is transparent and 255 is opaque. VRML browsers automatically convert each alpha integer into a floating-point pixel transparency. During the conversion, each alpha value between 0 and 255 is mapped to a value between 1.0 and 0.0 by dividing the file alpha value by 255.0 and subtracting the result from 1.0.

Texture Nodes

VRML provides three nodes for specifying a texture to be mapped to a shape: **ImageTexture**, **PixelTexture**, and **MovieTexture**. Any of these nodes can be used as the value of the **texture** field in a shape's **Appearance** node.

The **ImageTexture** node is the most common node used for texture mapping. Using this node, you provide the URL of a texture image file in JPEG, PNG, or GIF format. The VRML browser retrieves the texture image from the file and applies it to a shape.

The **PixelTexture** node provides an alternative way of specifying a texture image. Instead of providing the URL of a texture image file, you can specify the pixel values explicitly, one by one, from left to right and bottom to top for an image. This enables you to embed a texture image in the VRML file without storing the image in a separate image file.

The **MovieTexture** node is used to specify an MPEG movie-texture file for texture mapping. Using this node, you provide the URL of the MPEG file and field values to control when the movie is played back and how quickly it plays.

Understanding How Textures Are Mapped

When used as the value of the **texture** field in an **Appearance** node, the **ImageTexture**, **PixelTexture**, and **MovieTexture** nodes specify a texture image to map to a shape. The way the texture is mapped varies based on the geometry node used to build the shape.

Box Shapes

The **Box** node, builds a box with four sides, a top, and a bottom. When texture mapped, the texture image is applied to the box faces like this:

- The texture image appears right-side up on the front, back, left, and right sides of the box if you view each face with the box's top pointing upward along the positive Y axis.
- On the top of the box, the texture image appears right-side up if you tilt the top of the box down to face you while keeping the left face pointing to the left and the right face pointing to the right.
- On the bottom of the box, the texture image will appear right-side up if you tilt the bottom of the box up to face you while keeping the left face pointing to the left and the right face pointing to the right.

Cone Shapes

The **Cone** node builds a cone with sides and a bottom. When texture mapped, the texture image is applied to the cone like this:

- On the sides of the cone, the texture is wrapped around in a counter-clockwise direction (as viewed from above) starting at the back of the cone. The seam where the left and right edges of the texture image join runs vertically along the back of the cone. The top of the texture image is pinched together at the cone's tip.
- On the bottom of the cone, the texture image appears right-side up if you tilt the bottom of the cone up to face you without turning the cone about its axis.

Cylinder Shapes

The **Cylinder** node builds a cylinder with sides, a top, and a bottom. When texture mapped, the texture image is applied to the cylinder like this:

- On the sides of the cylinder, the texture is wrapped around in a counter-clockwise direction (as viewed from above) starting at the back of the cylinder. The seam where the left and right edges of the texture image join runs vertically along the back of the cylinder.
- On the top of the cylinder, the texture image appears right-side up if you tilt the top of the cylinder down to face you without turning the cylinder about its axis.
- On the bottom of the cylinder, the texture image appears right-side up if you tilt the bottom of the cylinder up to face you without turning the cylinder about its axis.

Sphere Shapes

The **Sphere** node builds a sphere. When texture mapped, the texture image is applied to the sphere like this:

> On the sides of the sphere, the texture is wrapped around in a counterclockwise direction (as viewed from above) starting at the back of the sphere. The seam where the left and right edges of the texture image join runs vertically along the back of the sphere. The top and bottom of the texture image are pinched together at the sphere's top and bottom poles.

Text Shapes

The **Text** node builds text shapes. When texture mapped, the texture image is applied to the text like this:

> The lower-left corner of the texture image is anchored at the origin of the text string (as determined by the text shape's justification). The image is stretched in a uniform manner horizontally and vertically so that the height of the texture image matches the height of the text font. Each character in the text string acts like a cookie cutter, stamping out side-by-side, character-shaped pieces of the texture image. At the left, right, bottom, and top edges of the texture image, additional duplicate copies of the texture image are added to create an infinite sheet of repeating texture images from which the text characters can stamp out pieces so that the sheet of repeating texture images spans the entire width and height of the text shape.

Point-Set Shapes

The **PointSet** node builds shapes out of points. Since points have no width or height, they cannot be texture mapped. Texture nodes are ignored when point sets are drawn.

Line-Set Shapes

The **IndexedLineSet** node builds shapes out of lines. Since lines have no thickness, they cannot be texture mapped. Texture nodes are ignored when line sets are drawn.

Face-Set Shapes

The **IndexedFaceSet** node builds shapes out of faces. When texture mapped, the texture image is applied to the entire shape like this:

> A bounding box for the shape is computed by the VRML browser, producing a width, height, and depth for the box. The texture image is projected onto the

face set shape as if from a slide projector. The projection is positioned and oriented so that the horizontal axis of the texture image extends side to side along the longest dimension of the bounding box, whether that be the box's width, height, or depth. The vertical axis of the texture-image projection is oriented to extend along the second-longest dimension of the bounding box. To avoid warping the texture image, the texture may be clipped off at the top if the second-longest dimension isn't equal to the longest dimension.

Texture images are rarely mapped to face sets using this automatic texture alignment. Instead, you can specify explicit mapping directions using the texture coordinate features of the **IndexedFaceSet** node discussed in Chapter 18.

Elevation-Grid Shapes

The **ElevationGrid** node builds shapes out of a grid of heights. When texture mapped, the texture image is applied to the entire grid like this:

> The texture image is aligned so that the left and right edges of the texture line up with the left and right edges of the grid, the bottom of the texture lines up along the first row of grid points, and the top of the texture lines up along the last row of grid points.

Recall that elevation grids are always built so that they extend to the right along the X axis and forward along the Z axis away from the origin. Using the default texture-mapping behavior preceding, texture images are mapped *upside down* when the elevation grid is viewed from above. You can compensate for this behavior by flipping your image upside down before mapping it to the elevation grid, which flips it back to a right side up orientation during texture mapping. You can also specify explicit mapping directions using texture-coordinate features of the **ElevationGrid** node discussed in Chapter 14.

Extrusion Shapes

The **Extrusion** node builds shapes out of a cross section swept along a spine. When texture mapped, the texture image is applied to the extruded shape like this:

- On the sides of the extrusion, the texture is wrapped around front to back. The left edge of the texture aligns with the first coordinate of the cross section, and the right edge of the texture aligns with the last coordinate of the cross section. If the cross section is a closed shape, such as a circle, then the seam where the left and right edges of the texture image join runs along the joint between the first and last cross-section coordinates. The bottom edge of the texture aligns with the first cross section of the extrusion placed at the first spine coordinate. The top edge of the texture aligns with the last cross section placed at the last spine coordinate.

- On the begin cap and end cap of the extrusion, the texture is aligned so that the horizontal direction on the texture lines up with the X axis direction of the cross section used to build the cap. Similarly, the vertical direction on the texture is aligned with the Z axis direction of the cross section. The texture image is stretched in a uniform manner so that it spans the begin or end cap edge to edge along the longest dimension of the cap.

The **Appearance** Node Syntax

The **Appearance** node specifies appearance attributes and may be used as the value of the **appearance** field in a **Shape** node.

SYNTAX	Appearance node

```
Appearance {
    material            NULL    # exposedField   SFNode
    texture             NULL    # exposedField   SFNode
    textureTransform    NULL    # exposedField   SFNode
}
```

The **material** exposed field is discussed in Chapter 10.

The value of the **texture** exposed field provides a node specifying a texture image to be applied to a shape. Typical **texture** field values include the **ImageTexture, PixelTexture,** and **MovieTexture** nodes. The default **NULL** value for this field indicates that no texture is to be applied.

The appearance texture can be changed by sending a value to the implied **set_texture** eventIn of the **texture** exposed field. When a value is received by this input, the corresponding field value is changed, and the new value is output using the implied **texture_changed** eventOut of the exposed field.

The remaining field of the **Appearance** node—**textureTransform**—is discussed in Chapter 18.

The **ImageTexture** Node Syntax

The **ImageTexture** node specifies texture-mapping attributes and may be used as the value of the **texture** field in an **Appearance** node.

SYNTAX	ImageTexture node

```
ImageTexture {
    url        [ ]      # exposedField   MFString
    repeatS    TRUE     # field          SFBool
    repeatT    TRUE     # field          SFBool
}
```

The value of the **url** exposed field specifies a prioritized list of URLs ordered from highest priority to lowest. The VRML browser typically tries to open the file specified by the first URL in the list. If the file cannot be found, the browser tries the second URL in the list, and so on. When a URL is found that can be opened, the file is read and used to texture map a shape. If none of the URLs can be opened, then no texturing takes place. The default value for the **url** field is an empty list of URLs.

The URL list can be changed by sending a value to the implied **set_url** eventIn of the **url** exposed field. When a value is received by this input, the field value is changed, and the new value is output using the implied **url_changed** eventOut of the exposed field.

Texture image files must be in the JPEG, GIF, or PNG image file formats. Images in these formats may provide color or grayscale values for each pixel and may include a pixel transparency value for each pixel.

Texture color and grayscale values control the color across the surface of a shape, combining with or overriding colors chosen in a shape's **Material** and **Color** nodes as follows:

- If the texture is a color image, the texture's colors override any color specified in a **Color** node or in the **diffuseColor** field of a **Material** node.
- If the texture is a grayscale image, the texture's grayscale values are multiplied with the color specified in a **Color** node or in the **diffuseColor** field of a **Material** node.

In either case, if the shape has no **Appearance** node, has no **Material** node, or the **Material** node's **diffuseColor** field value is zero, then the texture colors or grayscale values are treated as emissive colors and make the textured shape appear to glow. Otherwise, if the shape has an **Appearance** node and a **Material** node with a nonzero **diffuseColor** field value, then the shape is shaded using the texture color and grayscale values.

Texture transparency values control the transparency level across the surface of a shape, overriding any transparency value selected by a **Material** node, if present.

Textures are ignored for shapes built using **PointSet** and **IndexedLineSet** nodes.

The remaining fields of the **ImageTexture** node—**repeatS** and **repeatT**—are discussed in Chapter 18.

The **PixelTexture** Node Syntax

The **PixelTexture** node specifies texture-mapping attributes and may be used as the value of the **texture** field in an **Appearance** node.

PixelTexture node

```
PixelTexture {
    image      0 0 0    # exposedField  SFImage
    repeatS    TRUE     # field         SFBool
    repeatT    TRUE     # field         SFBool
}
```

The value of the **image** field specifies the image size and pixel values for a texture image used to texture map a shape. The first three integer values in the **image** field are, in order:

1. The width of the image, in pixels.
2. The height of the image, in pixels.
3. The number of 8-bit bytes for each pixel. Recognized values are shown in Table 17.1.

Table 17.1 Possible Values of the Third Image Field of the PixelTexture Node

Number of Bytes	Meaning
0	Disable texturing for the shape
1	Grayscale
2	Grayscale with alpha
3	RGB
4	RGB with alpha

Following the width, height, and number of bytes, the remaining values of the **image** field provide one integer value for each pixel in the image (if the number of bytes per pixel is not zero). The first pixel value provides the color for the left-most, bottom-most pixel in the texture image. Subsequent pixel values proceed left to right, then bottom to top, line by line, throughout the entire texture image. The last pixel value provides the color for the right-most, upper-most pixel in the texture image.

Integer pixel values are typically specified using hexadecimal notation (see the sidebar on "Hexadecimal Notation"). Pixel values are interpreted differently depending upon the number of bytes indicated for each pixel in the image, as shown in Table 17.2

Table 17.2 Pixel Value Interpretation Based on the Number of Bytes for Each Pixel

Number of Bytes	Pixel Value Interpretation
1	Each pixel value provides a 1-byte value, interpreted as a 1-byte, grayscale intensity varying from 0x00 (black) to 0xFF (white). Examples:

Pixel Integer	Meaning
0x00	Black
0x80	50% gray
0xFF	White

Number of Bytes	Pixel Value Interpretation
2	Each pixel value provides a 2-byte value, interpreted as a 1-byte, grayscale intensity, and a 1-byte, alpha opacity value varying from 0x00 (transparent) to 0xFF (opaque). The grayscale intensity is in the high byte and the alpha value in the low byte of the 2-byte integer. Examples:

Pixel Integer	Meaning
0x0000	Black, transparent
0x00FF	Black, opaque
0x80FF	Gray, opaque
0xFF80	White, half-transparent

Number of Bytes	Pixel Value Interpretation
3	Each pixel value provides a 3-byte value, interpreted as a 1-byte red level, a 1-byte green level, and a 1-byte blue level, each varying from 0x00 (none) to 0xFF (full). The red level is in the high byte, the green level in the middle byte, and the blue level in the low byte. Examples:

Pixel Integer	Meaning
0x000000	Black
0xFF0000	Red
0x00FF00	Green
0x0000FF	Blue
0xFFFF00	Yellow
0xFFFFFF	White

Number of Bytes	Pixel Value Interpretation
4	Each pixel value provides a 4-byte value, interpreted as 1-byte each of red, green, and blue levels and a 1-byte, alpha opacity value varying from 0x00 (transparent) to 0xFF (opaque). The red level is in the high byte, the green level in the middle-high byte, the blue level in the middle-low byte, and the alpha value in the low byte. Examples:

Pixel Integer	Meaning
0x00000000	Black, transparent
0xFF0000FF	Red, opaque
0x00FF0080	Green, half-transparent

TIP Most computer programming books teach counting hexadecimal and conversion by hand back and forth between hexadecimal, decimal, octal, and binary counting systems. In practice, however, most people just use a calculator that supports hexadecimal to decimal conversion, and back. Most software calculators for Macintoshes and PCs have a button on the user interface to do this kind of conversion.

Table 17.3 shows a few image pixel data examples.

Table 17.3   Image Pixel Data

Image Pixel Data	*Meaning*
0 0 0	Empty texture image
1 2 1 0×FF 0×00	1-pixel-wide, 2-pixel-high, grayscale image with a white bottom pixel (0×FF) and a black top pixel (0×00)
2 2 2 0×FF00 0×FF00 0×0080 0×0080	2-pixel-wide, 2-pixel-high, grayscale and alpha image with the bottom two pixels white and transparent (0×FF00) and the top two pixels black and half-transparent (0×0080)
2 1 3 0×FF0000 0×0000FF	2-pixel-wide, 1-pixel-high, RGB color image with the left pixel red (0×FF0000) and the right pixel blue (0×0000FF)
1 2 4 0×00FF0080 0×00FFFFFF	1-pixel-wide, 2-pixel-high, RGB color and alpha image with the bottom pixel green and half-transparent (0×00FF0080) and the top pixel cyan and opaque (0×00FFFFFF)

The default value of the **image** field is an image with a width of 0 pixels, a height of 0 pixels, and no bytes for each pixel. This default value creates an empty image and disables texture mapping.

The image values can be changed by sending a list of values to the implied **set_image** eventIn of the **image** exposed field. When a value is received by this input, the field value is changed, and the new value is output using the implied **image_changed** eventOut of the exposed field.

Color, grayscale, and alpha values modify the color and transparency levels across the surface of a shape, combining with and overriding fields in the shape's **Material** and **Color** nodes as discussed in the section entitled "The **Image Texture** Node Syntax."

Textures are ignored for shapes built using **PointSet** and **IndexedLineSet** nodes.

The remaining fields of the **PixelTexture** node—repeatS and repeatT—are discussed in Chapter 18.

SIDEBAR: HEXADECIMAL NOTATION *Hexadecimal notation* is a counting system based on a set of 16 digits including 10 numeric digits, 0 through 9, and 6 alphabetic digits, A through F. When using hexadecimal notation, counting goes 0, 1, 2, 3, 4, 5, 6, 7, 8, 9, A, B, C, D, E, F. After F, the next larger hexadecimal number is a 1 followed by a 0, written as 10. After 10 comes 11, 12, etc. up through 19,

1A, 1B, 1C, 1D, 1E, and 1F. After 1F, comes 20, 21, 22, etc. in a manner analogous to counting in standard decimal notation.

To more easily distinguish between 10 in decimal (with a value of ten) and 10 in hexadecimal (with a value of sixteen), hexadecimal notation adds *0x* to the beginning of each number. So, 0x10 is a hexadecimal number, while a plain 10 is a decimal number.

A convenient way of making sense out of a long hexadecimal-notation pixel value is to split it into groups of two hexadecimal digits, starting with the rightmost portion of the number. So, a pixel value like 0x813F9D is split into 0x81, 0x3F, and 0x9D. If this pixel value is an RGB color, then the right-most group (0x9D) is the amount of blue, the middle group (0x3F) is the amount of green, and the left-most group (0x81) is the amount of red. Using a hexadecimal to decimal conversion button on a calculator, these numbers become 129 (red), 63 (green), and 157 (blue) in decimal. These 1-byte, integer color values can be converted to VRML's floating-point RGB color values by dividing each one by 255.0. In this case the VRML RGB color is 0.506 0.247 0.616, which specifies a rich purple.

The **MovieTexture** Node Syntax

The **MovieTexture** node specifies texture-mapping attributes and may be used as the value for the **texture** field of an **Appearance** node. When a movie file containing audio is used, the **MovieTexture** node specifies sound that may be played back when the node is used as the value for the **source** field of the **Sound** node, discussed in Chapter 24.

| SYNTAX | MovieTexture node |

```
MovieTexture {
    url                  [ ]      # exposedField  MFString
    loop                 FALSE    # exposedField  SFBool
    speed                1.0      # exposedField  SFFloat
    startTime            0.0      # exposedField  SFTime
    stopTime             0.0      # exposedField  SFTime
    repeatS              TRUE     # field         SFBool
    repeatT              TRUE     # field         SFBool
    isActive                      # eventOut      SFBool
    duration_changed              # eventOut      SFFloat
}
```

The value of the **url** field and the implied **url_changed** eventOut are discussed in the section entitled "The **ImageTexture** Node Syntax."

Texture movie files must be in the MPEG image file format. The MPEG-1 Systems (audio and video) and MPEG-1 Video (video only) variants of the MPEG file format are supported (see the sidebar entitled "MPEG Variants").

SIDEBAR: MPEG VARIANTS The MPEG format is an evolving group of international standards for the compressed storage and transmission of video and audio. MPEG-1, the first version of MPEG, is designed to handle efficient video and audio playback from a hard disk or CD-ROM. The second version of MPEG, called MPEG-2, extends MPEG to handle playback over a slow network connection, like a computer modem. MPEG-3 is designed to handle high-definition television (HDTV) encoding and has now been renamed and rolled into MPEG-2. Finally, MPEG-4 is in development and will address extremely slow network connections, such as for a video telephone.

MPEG-1 and MPEG-2 each support three variants: Systems, Audio, and Video. MPEG-1 Systems encodes video and synchronized audio into the same file, MPEG-1 Audio encodes only audio, and MPEG-1 Video encodes only video. VRML's **Movie-Texture** node supports MPEG-1 Systems and MPEG-1 Video for the playback of video frames as textures on a shape. MPEG-1 Audio-only and MPEG-2 are not supported by VRML at this time.

Each MPEG movie has stored within it a series of movie frames, each one an image suitable for texture mapping to a shape. The number of frames in the movie determines the movie's *duration*. As soon as the movie is read in by the VRML browser, the movie's duration, measured in seconds, is determined and output on the **duration_changed** eventOut. The output duration is independent of the playback speed selected by the **speed** field. If there is a problem with the MPEG file, or the duration cannot be determined for some reason, a -1 is output using the **duration_changed** eventOut instead of the movie's duration in seconds.

The value of the **startTime** exposed field specifies the time at which the movie texture starts playing. The **startTime** field value is an absolute time measured in seconds since 12:00 midnight, GMT, January 1, 1970. The default value is 0.0 seconds.

The value of the **stopTime** exposed field specifies the time at which the movie texture stops playing. The **stopTime** field value is an absolute time and has a default value of 0.0 seconds.

The value of the **speed** exposed field specifies a multiplication factor for speeding or slowing playback of the movie texture. A value of 1.0 plays the movie at its normal speed. A value of 0.0 disables movie playback, freezing the movie on the first frame. A value between 0.0 and 1.0 slows the movie, while a value greater than 1.0 increases the movie playback speed. Negative speed values play the movie backward. The default value of 1.0 plays the movie forward at normal speed.

The value of the **loop** exposed field specifies whether the move playback loops or not. If the field value is **TRUE**, the movie plays repeatedly. If the loop field value is **FALSE**, the movie plays once, and then stops. The default value for the **loop** field is **FALSE**.

The **startTime, stopTime, speed,** and **loop** field values work together to control the **MovieTexture** node's texturing. A **MovieTexture** node remains dormant until the start time is reached. During this time, the first frame (or the last frame, if the speed is negative) in the movie is used as the shape texture. At the start time the

MovieTexture node becomes active, outputs **TRUE** using the **isActive** eventOut, and begins playing forward through movie frames (or backward, if the **speed** field value is negative). At each new movie frame, the shape texture is changed to the new movie frame. If the **loop** field value is **FALSE**, then the **MovieTexture** node generates textures until either the stop time is reached, or one cycle through the movie has been completed at (startTime + duration/speed), whichever comes first. If the **loop** field value is **TRUE**, then the **MovieTexture** node generates textures continually, through a potentially infinite number of playback cycles, until the stop time is reached. In the special case where the stop time is earlier than or equal to the start time, the stop time is ignored. This can be used to create movies that loop forever. In any case, when the movie stops, **FALSE** is output using the **isActive** eventOut, and the last frame played from the movie remains as the shape texture.

The **startTime, stopTime, speed,** and **loop** field values can be used together to create several standard effects, as shown in Table 17.4.

Table 17.4   Standard Effects Based on startTime, stopTime, speed, and loop Field Values

loop *field value*	startTime, stopTime, and speed *field value relationships*	*Effect*
TRUE	stopTime ≤ startTime	Run forever
TRUE	startTime < stopTime	Run until **stopTime**
FALSE	stopTime ≤ startTime	Run for one cycle, then stop at (startTime + duration/speed)
FALSE	startTime < (startTime + duration/speed) ≤ stopTime	Run for one cycle, then stop at (startTime + duration/speed)
FALSE	startTime < stopTime < (startTime + duration/speed)	Run for less than one cycle, then stop at **stopTime**

The value of the **speed** exposed field can be changed by routing an event to the exposed field's implied **set_speed** eventIn. If the node is active when the new value is received, the new value is ignored. Otherwise, the new speed value sets the exposed field and is output using the exposed field's implied **speed_changed** eventOut.

The value of the **loop** exposed field can be changed by routing a **TRUE** or **FALSE** event to the exposed field's implied **set_loop** eventIn. If the **loop** field value is changed from **TRUE** to **FALSE**, and the **MovieTexture** node is currently active and playing a movie during a cycle, then playback continues until the end of the cycle, or until the stop time, before stopping. If the **loop** field value is changed from **FALSE** to **TRUE**, and the node is currently active, then the playback loops until the stop time. In any case, the **loop** field value is changed, and the new value is output using the exposed field's implied **loop_changed** eventOut.

The value of the **startTime** exposed field can be changed by routing an event to the exposed field's implied **set_startTime** eventIn. If the node is active when a new value is received, the new value is ignored. Otherwise, the new value sets the exposed field and is output using the exposed field's implied **startTime_changed** eventOuts.

If the **MovieTexture** node is not active when a new start time is received, the node's start time is changed. This may cause the node to become active if the new start time is the current time or is recent enough that the current time is less than (`startTime + duration/speed`).

The value of the **stopTime** exposed field can be changed by routing an event to the exposed field's implied **set_stopTime** eventIn. If a new stop time is earlier than the start time, the new stop time value is ignored. Otherwise, the new stop time changes the **stopTime** field value and is output using the exposed field's implied **stopTime_changed** eventOut. The new stop time is also used to reevaluate whether it is time to stop the movie based on the current time, the duration, the speed, and the new stop time.

Color, grayscale, and alpha values modify the color and transparency level across the surface of a shape, combining with and overriding fields in the shape's **Material** and **Color** nodes as discussed in the section entitled "The **ImageTexture** Node Syntax".

Textures are ignored for shapes built using **PointSet** and **IndexedLineSet** nodes.

The remaining fields of the **MovieTexture** node—**repeatS** and **repeatT**—are discussed in Chapter 18.

Experimenting with Texture Mapping

The following examples provide a more detailed examination of the ways in which the **ImageTexture**, **PixelTexture**, and **MovieTexture** nodes can be used and how they interact with nodes discussed in previous chapters.

Mapping Textures to Primitive Shapes

Figure 17.3 shows a simple texture image used in several of the following examples.

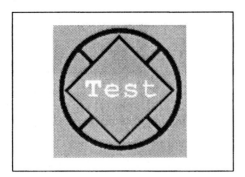

Figure 17.3 *A simple texture image.*

Figure 17.4*a* shows the simple texture image mapped to the sides of a box, *b* mapped to a cone, *c* mapped to a cylinder, and *d* mapped to a sphere. Notice how the texture image is stretched to fit around the circumference of a cone, cylinder, or sphere, and how it is oriented when mapped to the top and bottom of a box or cylinder, and the bottom of a cone. Notice also how the texture image is pinched at the top of a cone, and at the top and bottom of a sphere.

```
#VRML V2.0 utf8
Shape {
    appearance Appearance {
        material Material { }
        texture ImageTexture {
            url "testimg.jpg"
        }
    }
    geometry Box { }
}
```

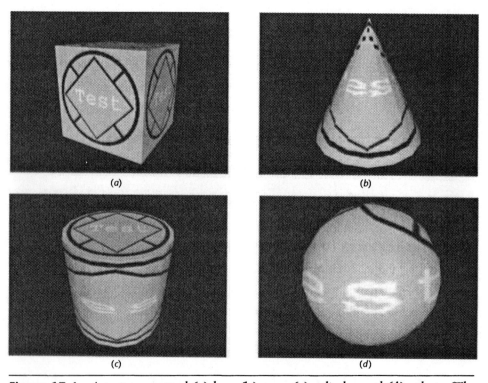

(a)   (b)

(c)   (d)

Figure 17.4 *A texture mapped (a) box, (b) cone, (c) cylinder, and (d) sphere. (The VRML text in this figure builds the texture-mapped box shown in Figure 17.4a.)*

Mapping Textures to Parts of Primitive Shapes

When a texture is mapped to a primitive shape, the same image is placed on all parts of the shape, including the top, bottom, and sides. To map a different image to each part of the shape, you can create three separate shapes, each with their own texture image.

The example in Figure 17.5 uses three texture images for the top (*a*), bottom (*b*), and sides (*c*) of a soft drink can and maps them to the top, bottom, and sides of a cylinder (*d*).

```
#VRML V2.0 utf8
Group {
    children [
    # Can top
        Shape {
            appearance Appearance {
                material Material { }
                texture ImageTexture {
                    url "cantop.jpg"
                }
            }
            geometry Cylinder {
                bottom FALSE
                side FALSE
                height 2.7
            }
        }
    # Can bottom
        Shape {
            appearance Appearance {
                material Material { }
                texture ImageTexture {
                    url "canbot.jpg"
                }
            }
            geometry Cylinder {
                top FALSE
                side FALSE
                height 2.7
            }
        }
    # Can side
        Shape {
            appearance Appearance {
                material Material { }
                texture ImageTexture {
                    url "canlabel.jpg"
                }
            }
```

Figure 17.5 continues

```
geometry Cylinder {
    top FALSE
    bottom FALSE
    height 2.7
}
            }
        ]
    }
```

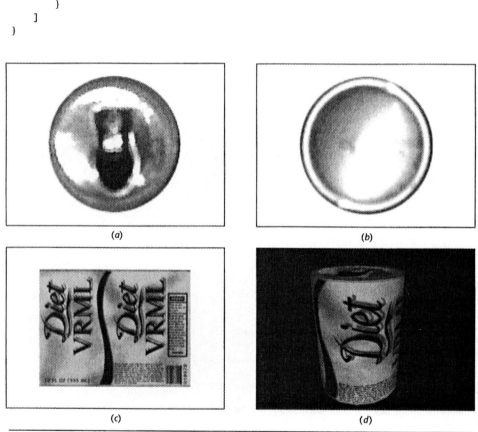

(a)   (b)

(c)   (d)

Figure 17.5 *Texture images for a soft drink can, including (a) the top, (b) the bottom, and (c) the sides. (d) A soft drink can built by texture mapping parts of a cylinder. (The VRML text in this figure builds the can shown in Figure 17.5d.)*

Mapping Textures to Text Shapes

The VRML text in Figure 17.6 maps a brick texture image, shown in Figure 17.6*a*, to text shapes built by a **Text** node, as shown in Figure 17.6*b*. Notice how the text characters act like cookie cutters stamping out pieces from an infinitely repeated texture image.

```
#VRML V2.0 utf8
Shape {
    appearance Appearance {
        material Material { }
        texture ImageTexture {
            url "brick.jpg"
        }
    }
    geometry Text {
        fontStyle FontStyle {
            style "BOLD"
        }
        string [ "Qwerty", "0123" ]
    }
}
```

 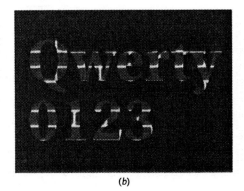

(a)   (b)

Figure 17.6 (a) *A brick texture image, and (b) the texture image mapped to a text shape. (The VRML text in this figure builds the texture-mapped text shown in Figure 17.6b.)*

Mapping Textures to Face-Set Shapes

Figure 17.7a shows a yellow and red flame texture, and *b* shows the texture mapped to a lightning bolt. When your VRML browser maps the image to the lightning bolt, it starts by computing a bounding box for the shape. The texture image is projected onto the lightning bolt, aligned so that the horizontal direction on the image maps to the longest dimension of the bounding box—in this case, the side-to-side dimension. The vertical direction of the texture image is aligned to fall along the second-longest dimension of the bounding box—in this case, the top-to-bottom dimension.

```
#VRML V2.0 utf8
Shape {
    appearance Appearance {
        material Material { }
        texture ImageTexture {
            url "bolt2.jpg"
        }
    }
}
```

Figure 17.7 continues

```
geometry IndexedFaceSet {
    coord Coordinate {
        point [
        # Lighting bolt tip
            0.0  0.0  0.0,
        # Front perimeter
            5.5  5.0  0.88,
            4.0  5.5  0.968,
            7.0  8.0  1.408,
            4.0  9.0  1.584,
            1.0  5.0  0.88,
            2.5  4.5  0.792,
        # Back perimeter
            5.5  5.0 -0.88,
            4.0  5.5 -0.968,
            7.0  8.0 -1.408,
            4.0  9.0 -1.584,
            1.0  5.0 -0.88,
            2.5  4.5 -0.792,
        ]
    }
    coordIndex [
    # Front
        0,  1,  2,  3,  4,  5,  6, -1,
    # Back
        0, 12, 11, 10,  9,  8,  7, -1,
    # Sides
        0,  7,  1, -1,
        1,  7,  8,  2, -1,
        2,  8,  9,  3, -1,
        3,  9, 10,  4, -1,
        4, 10, 11,  5, -1,
        5, 11, 12,  6, -1,
        6, 12,  0, -1,
    ]
    convex FALSE
    }
}
```

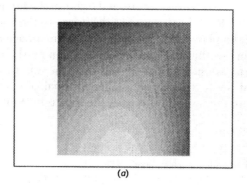
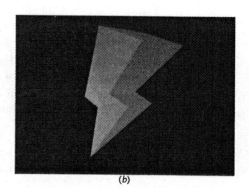

(a)   (b)

Figure 17.7   (a) *A flaming texture image, and* (b) *a lightning bolt with the flaming texture image. (The VRML text in this figure builds the lightning bolt shown in Figure 17.7b.)*

Mapping Textures to Elevation-Grid Shapes

Using texture mapping on **ElevationGrid** node shapes, you can map satellite photographs or terrain coloration images to terrain shapes. Figure 17.8*a* shows a handpainted terrain image, and *b* shows the terrain image texture mapped to the mountain elevation grid from Chapter 14. Note that the texture image is upside down to compensate for the upside-down texture mapping of the **ElevationGrid** node.

```
#VRML V2.0 utf8
Shape {
    appearance Appearance {
        material Material { }
        texture ImageTexture {
            url "mount.jpg"
        }
    }
    geometry ElevationGrid {
        xDimension 9
        zDimension 9
        xSpacing    1.0
        zSpacing    1.0
        solid       FALSE
        height [
            0.0, 0.0, 0.5, 1.0, 0.5, 0.0, 0.0, 0.0, 0.0,
            0.0, 0.0, 0.0, 0.0, 2.5, 0.5, 0.0, 0.0, 0.0,
            0.0, 0.0, 0.5, 0.5, 3.0, 1.0, 0.5, 0.0, 1.0,
            0.0, 0.0, 0.5, 2.0, 4.5, 2.5, 1.0, 1.5, 0.5,
            1.0, 2.5, 3.0, 4.5, 5.5, 3.5, 3.0, 1.0, 0.0,
            0.5, 2.0, 2.0, 2.5, 3.5, 4.0, 2.0, 0.5, 0.0,
            0.0, 0.0, 0.5, 1.5, 1.0, 2.0, 3.0, 1.5, 0.0,
            0.0, 0.0, 0.0, 0.0, 0.0, 0.0, 2.0, 1.5, 0.5,
            0.0, 0.0, 0.0, 0.0, 0.0, 0.0, 0.5, 0.0, 0.0,
        ]
    }
}
```

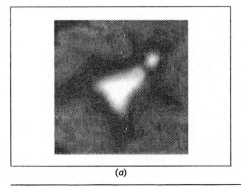
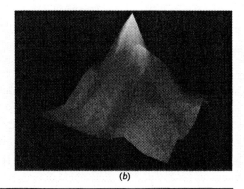

(*a*)   (*b*)

Figure 17.8 *(a) A terrain texture image, and (b) a mountain-shaped elevation grid texture mapped with the terrain image. (The VRML text in this figure builds the mountain shown in Figure 17.8 b.)*

Mapping Textures to Extrusion Shapes

You can map texture images to extruded shapes. A snake shape, for instance, can use a texture image to give the shape the appearance of scales. Similarly, an extrusion shape that creates a torus, or donut, can be texture mapped to add chocolate icing and sprinkles to the donut's top. Figure 17.9*a* shows a donut-icing texture image, and *b* shows the icing texture mapped to a donut-shaped extrusion.

```
#VRML V2.0 utf8
Shape {
    appearance Appearance {
        material Material { }
        texture ImageTexture {
            url "icing.jpg"
        }
    }
    geometry Extrusion {
        creaseAngle 1.57
        beginCap FALSE
        endCap  FALSE
        crossSection [
        # Circle
            1.00  0.00,   0.92 -0.38,
            0.71 -0.71,   0.38 -0.92,
            0.00 -1.00,  -0.38 -0.92,
           -0.71 -0.71,  -0.92 -0.38,
           -1.00 -0.00,  -0.92  0.38,
           -0.71  0.71,  -0.38  0.92,
            0.00  1.00,   0.38  0.92,
            0.71  0.71,   0.92  0.38,
            1.00  0.00
        ]
        spine [
        # Circle
            2.00 0.0  0.00,   1.85 0.0 -0.77,
            1.41 0.0 -1.41,   0.77 0.0 -1.85,
            0.00 0.0 -2.00,  -0.77 0.0 -1.85,
           -1.41 0.0 -1.41,  -1.85 0.0 -0.77,
           -2.00 0.0  0.00,  -1.85 0.0  0.77,
           -1.41 0.0  1.41,  -0.77 0.0  1.85,
            0.00 0.0  2.00,   0.77 0.0  1.85,
            1.41 0.0  1.41,   1.85 0.0  0.77,
            2.00 0.0  0.00,
        ]
    }
}
```

Figure 17.9 continues

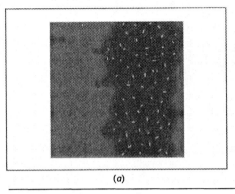

(a)   (b)

Figure 17.9 *(a) A donut-icing texture image, and (b) a chocolate donut texture mapped with the donut-icing image. (The VRML text in this figure builds the donut shown in Figure 17.9b.)*

Creating Holes Using Pixel Transparency

The color texture images in the previous examples control how color varies across a texture-mapped shape. You can also control how transparency varies across a shape by providing a pixel-transparency value for each pixel in the texture image. This enables you to create holes in the texture image that, when mapped to a shape, create transparent holes in the shape.

You can use texture transparency to create trees. Figure 17.10*a* shows a texture image of a tree. Figure 17.10*b* shows what the tree image's pixel transparencies look like if they are drawn as a grayscale image. On the pixel transparency image, black areas are transparent, and white areas are opaque. When this tree image is mapped to a shape, as shown in Figure 17.10*c*, portions of the shape covered by the tree are opaque and colored by the tree's leaf colors. Portions of the shape covered by the transparent background of the tree are transparent. Notice that the example does not include a **Material** node. This ensures that the tree texture's colors are used as emissive colors for the tree shape, and creates a more realistic appearance for the tree.

```
#VRML V2.0 utf8
Group {
    children [
    # Ground
        Shape {
            appearance Appearance {
                material Material { }
            }
```

Figure 17.10 continues

```
        geometry IndexedFaceSet {
            coord Coordinate {
                point [
                    -5.0 0.0  5.0,  5.0 0.0  5.0,
                     5.0 0.0 -5.0, -5.0 0.0 -5.0,
                ]
            }
            coordIndex [ 0, 1, 2, 3 ]
            solid FALSE
        }
    },
# Tree face
    Shape {
        appearance Appearance {
            # No material, use emissive texturing
            texture ImageTexture {
                url "tree1.png"
            }
        }
        geometry IndexedFaceSet {
            coord Coordinate {
                point [
                    -1.51 0.0 0.0,   1.51 0.0 0.0,
                     1.51 3.0 0.0,  -1.51 3.0 0.0,
                ]
            }
            coordIndex [ 0, 1, 2, 3 ]
            solid FALSE
        }
    }
]
}
```

Figure 17.10 continues

(a)

(b)   (c)

Figure 17.10 *A tree texture image showing (a) the image's colors and (b) the image's pixel transparencies viewed as a grayscale image. (c) A tree built by mapping a tree image, with pixel transparencies, on a rectangular face. (The VRML text in this figure builds the tree shown in Figure 17.10c.)*

When viewed face-on, the tree is fairly realistic. The illusion breaks down as you move around the tree's rectangular face and it becomes clear that the tree is just a flat image. You can avoid this by using a **Billboard** grouping node around the tree's rectangular face. Now, as you move around the world, the tree's face always turns to face you, and the flatness of the tree is less apparent.

Another way of sustaining the illusion that the tree is a 3-D tree and not just a textured rectangular is to texture map multiple tree faces and place them on top of each other, but rotated around the Y axis to create a plus-sign or asterisk pattern when viewed from above. This technique does not use a **Billboard** node for the tree, so as you move around the set of tree faces, your view of the tree changes. The use of additional tree faces, even when texture mapped with the same tree image, gives the tree a feeling of depth. The uneven edges of the tree image on each face obscure the fact that the tree is really just a collection of rectangular faces arranged in an asterisk pattern.

Using Grayscale Textures

Each of the previous examples have used color texture images. You can also use grayscale texture images. When mapped to a shape, the gray level of each texture image pixel is multiplied by the shape's color from the **diffuseColor** field value of the shape's **Material** node. This enables you to use a grayscale texture image to brighten and darken areas on a shape or to create patterns on colored shapes.

Figure 17.11a shows a grayscale texture image of stripes. Figure 17.11b maps this image on a green cylinder. Dark areas on the grayscale image create dark stripes on the green cylinder.

```
#VRML V2.0 utf8
Shape {
    appearance Appearance {
        material Material {
            diffuseColor 0.0 1.0 0.0
        }
        texture ImageTexture {
            url "lines_g.jpg"
        }
    }
    geometry Cylinder {
        height 2.0
        radius 1.0
    }
}
```

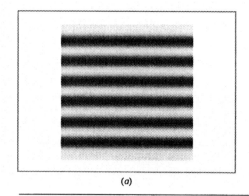

(a)   (b)

Figure 17.11 (a) A grayscale striped texture image, and (b) a green cylinder texture mapped with the grayscale striped image. (The VRML text in this figure builds the world shown in Figure 17.11b.)

Coloring Grayscale Textures

As shown in Figure 17.11*b*, a grayscale texture image affects the brightness of portions of a colored shape. In other words, the shape color is *coloring* the grayscale texture image. For instance, you can use a grayscale wood texture and color the texture to create different types of wood grains, like oak, pine, cherry wood, or other wood types. Figure 17.12*a* shows a grayscale wood texture. Figure 17.12*b* shows six different types of wood by mapping this texture to six colored squares.

```
#VRML V2.0 utf8
Group {
    children [
    # Top left
        Shape {
            appearance Appearance {
                material Material { diffuseColor 1.0 0.35 0.23 }
                texture DEF wood ImageTexture { url "wood_g.jpg" }
            }
            geometry DEF square IndexedFaceSet {
                coord Coordinate {
                    point [
                        0.0 1.0 0.0,  0.0 0.0 0.0,
                        1.1 0.0 0.0,  1.1 1.0 0.0
                    ]
                }
                coordIndex [ 0, 1, 2, 3 ]
            }
        },
    # Top center
        Transform {
            translation 1.25 0.0 0.0
            children Shape {
                appearance Appearance {
                    material Material { diffuseColor 1.0 0.45 0.23 }
                    texture USE wood
                }
                geometry USE square
            }
        },
    # Top right
        Transform {
            translation 2.50 0.0 0.0
            children Shape {
                appearance Appearance {
                    material Material { diffuseColor 1.0 0.55 0.23 }
                    texture USE wood
                }
                geometry USE square
            }
        },
```

Figure 17.12 continues

```
    # Bottom left
        Transform {
            translation 0.0 -1.25 0.0
            children Shape {
                appearance Appearance {
                    material Material { diffuseColor 1.0 0.65 0.53 }
                    texture USE wood
                }
                geometry USE square
            }
        },
    # Bottom center
        Transform {
            translation 1.25 -1.25 0.0
            children Shape {
                appearance Appearance {
                    material Material { diffuseColor 1.0 0.55 0.43 }
                    texture USE wood
                }
                geometry USE square
            }
        },
    # Bottom right
        Transform {
            translation 2.50 -1.25 0.0
            children Shape {
                appearance Appearance {
                    material Material { diffuseColor 1.0 0.55 0.53 }
                    texture USE wood
                }
                geometry USE square
            }
        }
    ]
}
```

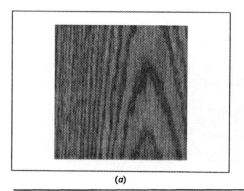

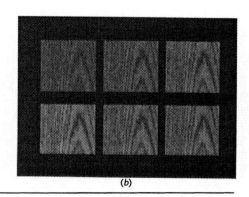

(a)   *(b)*

Figure 17.12   *(a) A grayscale wood texture image, and (b) six different wood types created by coloring a grayscale wood texture. (The VRML text in this figure builds the world shown in Figure 17.12b.)*

Embedding Texture Images in a VRML File

Texture images are typically stored in separate image files and mapped to world shapes using **ImageTexture** nodes. In some cases it is more convenient to include the texture image's pixel data in the VRML file itself. You can do this with the **Pixel-Texture** node instead of the **ImageTexture** node.

> **TIP** In most cases, inclusion of a texture image in the VRML file itself is only efficient if the texture image is very small, such as an image only a few pixels wide and high. This kind of texture image is commonly used to create color gradients and stripes.

Figure 17.13 uses a **PixelTexture** node to create a simple color gradient across a rectangular face. The **PixelTexture** node's image data creates a 1-pixel-wide, 2-pixel-high, 3-byte RGB color texture image. When mapped to the face, the first pixel value (yellow) is placed at the bottom of the face, and the second pixel value (red) is placed at the top of the face. Colors in the middle of the face vary from the bottom color to the top color. You can also create grayscale, grayscale-with-alpha, and color-with-alpha texture images using the **PixelTexture** node.

```
#VRML V2.0 utf8
Shape {
    appearance Appearance {
        material Material { }
        texture PixelTexture {
            image 1 2 3        # width, height, 3-byte RGB image
                0xFFFF00  # yellow at the bottom
                0xFF0000  # red at the top
        }
    }
    geometry IndexedFaceSet {
        coord Coordinate {
            point [
                -1.5 -1.0 0.0,   1.5 -1.0 0.0,
                 1.5  1.0 0.0,  -1.5  1.0 0.0,
            ]
        }
        coordIndex [ 0, 1, 2, 3 ]
        solid FALSE
    }
}
```

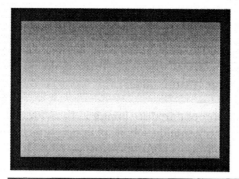

Figure 17.13 *A face with color varying from yellow to red.*

Using Movie Textures

Movie texture mapping using the **MovieTexture** node enables you to create moving texture images. You can use this feature of VRML for a wide variety of effects, for example, with a flickering flame, you can create animated torches in a dungeon.

Figure 17.14*a* shows the first frame from a movie depicting water swirling down a drain. Figure 17.14*b* uses this movie and a **MovieTexture** node to create a swirling whirlpool. To give the water an eerie glow, the movie texture is made emissive by not specifying a **Material** node.

```
#VRML V2.0 utf8
Group {
    children [
    # Ground
        Shape {
            appearance Appearance {
                material Material {
                    diffuseColor 0.0 0.7 0.0
                }
            }
            geometry Box { size 10.0 0.01 10.0 }
        },
    # Well wall
        Shape {
            appearance Appearance {
                material Material { }
                texture ImageTexture {
                    url "wellwall.jpg"
                }
            }
```

Figure 17.14 continues

```
geometry Extrusion {
    creaseAngle 1.57
    beginCap FALSE
    endCap   FALSE
    crossSection [
    # upside-down U-shape
        0.4  0.0,
        0.4 -0.7,
       -0.4 -0.7,
       -0.4  0.0,
    ]
    spine [
    # Circle
        2.00 0.0  0.00,   1.85 0.0  0.77,
        1.41 0.0  1.41,   0.77 0.0  1.85,
        0.00 0.0  2.00,  -0.77 0.0  1.85,
       -1.41 0.0  1.41,  -1.85 0.0  0.77,
       -2.00 0.0  0.00,  -1.85 0.0 -0.77,
       -1.41 0.0 -1.41,  -0.77 0.0 -1.85,
        0.00 0.0 -2.00,   0.77 0.0 -1.85,
        1.41 0.0 -1.41,   1.85 0.0 -0.77,
        2.00 0.0  0.00,
    ]
}
},
# Well water
    Shape {
        appearance Appearance {
            # No material, use emissive texturing
            texture MovieTexture {
                url "wrlpool.mpg"
                loop TRUE
            }
        }
        geometry IndexedFaceSet {
            solid FALSE
            coord Coordinate {
                point [
                # Circle
                    2.00 0.6  0.00,   1.85 0.6  0.67,
                    1.41 0.6  1.41,   0.67 0.6  1.85,
                    0.00 0.6  2.00,  -0.67 0.6  1.85,
                   -1.41 0.6  1.41,  -1.85 0.6  0.67,
                   -2.00 0.6  0.00,  -1.85 0.6 -0.67,
                   -1.41 0.6 -1.41,  -0.67 0.6 -1.85,
                    0.00 0.6 -2.00,   0.67 0.6 -1.85,
                    1.41 0.6 -1.41,   1.85 0.6 -0.67,
                    2.00 0.6  0.00,
                ]
            }
        }
```

Figure 17.14 continues

```
coordIndex [
    0, 1, 2, 3, 4, 5, 6, 7, 8, 9, 10,
    11, 12, 13, 14, 15, 16
]
            }
        }
    ]
}
```

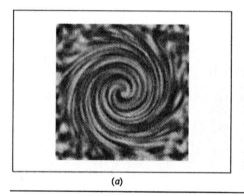
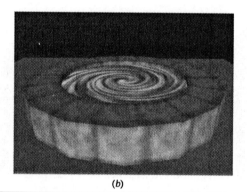

(a)   (b)

Figure 17.14 *(a) The first frame from a swirling water movie texture, and (b) a swirling whirlpool created using a movie texture. (The VRML text in this figure builds the whirlpool shown in Figure 17.14b.)*

T I P You can create movie textures by capturing frames from a real film or video, or you can create your own movies using animation and image processing applications. The swirling water movie in the previous example was created using Adobe Premiere, an application designed to edit movies on your computer. The individual frames of the movie were created by dabbing some dark blue pixels on a light blue background, then applying a twirl filter to the image to swirl the dark and light blues together as if going down a drain. The amount of swirling in the image was animated to create a series of frames for the movie. You can use similar techniques to create your own movie effects.

Summary

Texture mapping maps an image, such as brick or tree leaves, to the faces of a shape. This technique enables you to add realistic detail to a VRML world without creating individual shapes for every brick or tree leaf.

A texture for mapping is specified by setting the **texture** field value of a shape's **Appearance** node to be an **ImageTexture**, **PixelTexture**, or **MovieTexture** node.

An **ImageTexture** node specified a JPEG-, PNG-, or GIF-format image file using a URL as the value of the node's **url** field. The image file is read by your VRML browser, and its colors are used to color the faces of a textured shape.

Using a **PixelTexture** node, you can include an image within your VRML file by explicitly specifying the individual pixel colors in the node's **image** field. Similar to the **ImageTexture** node, the image in a **PixelTexture** node is used to color the faces of a textured shape.

A **MovieTexture** node specifies an MPEG-format movie file using a URL as the value of the node's **url** field. The movie file is read by your VRML browser and played back, frame by frame, as a texture on a shape. The colors of each movie frame color the faces of the textured shape.

For movie textures, the **speed** field value controls the playback speed, and the **loop** field value specifies whether the movie should be played back once or looped repeatedly. Movie playback begins at the start time set in the **startTime** field and ends at the stop time set in the **stopTime** field.

Texture images can be in color or grayscale. Color textures override the colors chosen by a **Color** node or by the **diffuseColor** field value in the shape's **Material** node. Grayscale textures multiply their gray level by the colors in a **Color** node or by the **diffuseColor** field in a **Material** node.

When pixel transparency values are present in a texture, the values vary the transparency level across the shape's faces. Using this feature, you can create holes in texture-mapped shapes.

Any shape can be texture mapped, except those built using **IndexedLineSet** or **PointSet** nodes.

## CHAPTER 18

Controlling Texture Mapping

Using texture-mapping control, you can position a texture on a shape, enlarge or shrink it, rotate it, and repeat the texture multiple times across the surface of a shape. For instance, you can take a texture image of a small number of bricks and repeat the texture over and over to cover an entire wall with bricks.

Texture-mapping controls also enable you to extract a piece of a texture image and use only that piece when texturing a shape. For instance, if you have a texture image of a computer keyboard, you can use VRML texture mapping controls to extract a piece of the image containing just the numeric keypad and map that piece of the shape.

Using texture coordinates in a **TextureCoordinate** node, you can specify a piece of a texture image and use the **TextureTransform** node to translate, rotate, and scale the texture coordinates.

Understanding Texture-Mapping Control

Texture mapping is a multistage process. The process always starts by reading or creating a texture image using the **ImageTexture, PixelTexture,** or **MovieTexture** nodes. Each of these nodes specifies a texture image that acts as the raw material for the remaining stages in the process.

You can imagine the texture image is a piece of rubber with an image painted on it. By default, the entire rubber image is stretched, wrapped around the shape to be textured, then stuck to the shape. You can override this default behavior, select a *piece* of the texture image and map only that piece to your shape. You can think of it as using a cookie cutter to stamp out pieces of a texture image, and then using glue to attach the pieces to a shape, stretching and pulling the pieces as necessary to make them fit. Using 2-D *texture coordinates,* you can describe the perimeter of a texture-image cookie cutter. For instance, if you describe a square using 2-D texture coordinates, you'll stamp out a square piece of the texture image. If you describe a triangle, you'll stamp out a triangular piece of the texture image.

The piece of texture image is mapped to a shape's face by aligning each corner of the image with a corner on the face. If a shape's face has four corners (four 3-D coordinates), then your piece of texture image must have four corners, as well.

The steps in the texture-mapping process are:

1. Select a texture image using an **ImageTexture, PixelTexture,** or **MovieTexture** node.

2. Use 2-D texture coordinates to describe the perimeter of a texture-map cookie cutter.

3. Stamp out a piece of the texture image.

4. Stretch the piece of texture image to fit a face on a shape, aligning each corner on the piece of texture image with a corresponding coordinate on the face.

The last three steps stamp out a single texture image piece and glue it to a single face on a shape. To texture map every face on the shape, these three steps are repeated for each face.

Texture Coordinates

Recall that to create an indexed-face-set face, you use a list of 3-D coordinates to trace out the perimeter of the face. Each 3-D coordinate specifies a location in space, measured in the X, Y, and Z directions relative to an origin in a 3-D coordinate system. Describing the shape of a 2-D, texture-image cookie cutter works in a similar fashion.

The shape of a 2-D texture cookie cutter is described using a list of 2-D texture coordinates that trace out the perimeter of the cookie cutter. Each 2-D coordinate specifies a location in a *texture coordinate system* where distances are measured in the S (horizontal) and T (vertical) directions spanning the texture image. The origin of the texture coordinate system is always at the lower-left corner of the texture image. Figure 18.1 shows the S and T directions of a texture coordinate system.

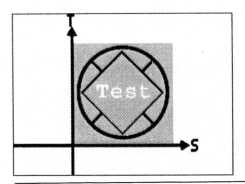

Figure 18.1   *The S and T directions of the texture coordinate system.*

S-texture-coordinate values can vary from 0.0 at the left edge of a texture image to 1.0 at the right edge. Similarly, T-texture-coordinate values can vary from 0.0 at the bottom edge to 1.0 at the top edge of a texture image. This range of S and T values is independent of the actual width and height in pixels of the texture image. Texture coordinate (1.0,1.0), for instance, is always the upper-right corner of the image, and coordinate (0.5,0.5), is always the center of the image. This use of generic texture coordinate values that always range from 0.0 to 1.0 enables you to specify a location on a texture image independent of the image's size.

To cut out a square piece of a texture image, you can define a square, cookie-cutter shape using a list of 2-D texture coordinates, such as those in Table 18.1. In this coordinate list, texture coordinate index 0 at coordinate (0.0,0.0) specifies the lower-left corner of the texture image, index 1 specifies the lower-right corner, index 2 the upper-right corner, and index 3 the upper-left corner. If you use this coordinate list to specify a texture cookie cutter, you will stamp out a piece of texture that contains the entire image.

Table 18.1   2-D Texture Coordinates Defining a Square Piece of Texture Image

Texture Coordinate Index	Coordinate (S, T)
0	0.0 0.0
1	1.0 0.0
2	1.0 1.0
3	0.0 1.0

To cut out a small square piece from the middle of the texture image, like that shown in Figure 18.2, you can use texture coordinates such as those in Table 18.2.

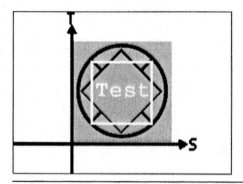

Figure 18.2 *A small, square texture piece selected from the middle of a texture image.*

Table 18.2 2-D Texture Coordinates Defining a Small, Square Piece from the Middle of a Texture Image

Texture Coordinate Index	Coordinate (S, T)
0	0.2 0.2
1	0.8 0.2
2	0.8 0.8
3	0.2 0.8

You can select texture image pieces of any size and shape using any number of 2-D texture coordinates. Figure 18.3 shows the texture image piece selected using the texture coordinates shown in Table 18.3.

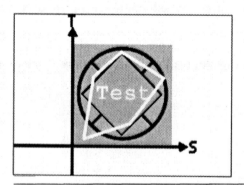

Figure 18.3 *A multisided texture piece selected from the middle of a texture image.*

Table 18.3   2-D Texture Coordinates Defining a Multisided Piece of Texture Image

Texture Coordinate Index	Coordinate (S, T)
0	0.1 0.1
1	0.6 0.2
2	0.9 0.7
3	0.5 0.9
4	0.2 0.7

Texture coordinates enable you to select a relevant piece of a texture image and map that to a shape. For example, Figure 18.4a shows a texture image of a circular pizza, and b shows a slice of the pizza selected and mapped to a face.

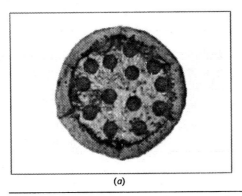
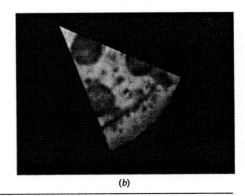

(a)   (b)

Figure 18.4 *Texture coordinates used with (a) a pizza texture image to (b) select a piece and map it to a face.*

All of the geometry types in VRML, including **Box, Cone, Cylinder, Sphere, Text, IndexedFaceSet, ElevationGrid,** and **Extrusion,** automatically create their own texture coordinates. This enables you to texture map cylinders, text, and other shapes without specifying texture coordinates.

When using the **IndexedFaceSet** and **ElevationGrid** nodes to specify shape geometry, you have the option of overriding the automatic creation of texture coordinates by providing your own texture coordinates in a **TextureCoordinate** node used as the value of the **texCoord** field in the **IndexedFaceSet** and **ElevationGrid** nodes.

Texture Binding

Using the texture coordinates of a texture cookie cutter, a piece of texture image is stamped out of a texture. To apply the piece to a face on a shape, each corner on the texture piece is bound to a 3-D coordinate on the face. If the texture piece and the 3-D face aren't quite the same size, then the texture image is stretched and pulled to fit the face.

In order for a piece of texture to fit a face on a shape, the texture piece and the face must each have the same number of coordinates. You can, for instance, map a square four-coordinate piece of texture to a rectangular, four-coordinate face, but you cannot map a triangular, three-coordinate piece of texture to the rectangular face.

Tables 18.4 and 18.5 provide the texture coordinates for a square region of a texture image and the 3-D coordinates for a square face in an indexed face set, respectively.

Table 18.4   2-D Texture Coordinates Defining a Square Piece of Texture Image

Texture Coordinate Index	*Coordinate (S, T)*
0	0.2 0.2
1	0.8 0.2
2	0.8 0.8
3	0.2 0.8

Table 18.5   3-D Coordinates Defining a Square Face in an Indexed Face Set

Face Coordinate Index	*Coordinate (X, Y, Z)*
0	-1.0 -1.0 0.0
1	1.0 -1.0 0.0
2	1.0 1.0 0.0
3	-1.0 1.0 0.0

To map the square texture image to the square face, each texture coordinate is aligned with a face coordinate, one by one, around the shape. You can, for example, align the first texture coordinate to the first face coordinate, the second texture coordinate to the second face coordinate, and so on, as shown in Table 18.6.

Table 18.6   Face and Texture Indexes Mapping Face Coordinates to Texture Coordinates

Face Coordinate Index	*Texture Coordinate Index*
0	0
1	1
2	2
3	3

Figure 18.5*a* shows the area of a texture image selected by the texture coordinates shown in Table 18.6. Figure 18.5*b* shows the piece of texture stamped out. Figure 18.5*c* shows the square face created by the face coordinates shown in Table 18.6, and *d* shows the face textured using the stamped-out piece of texture with the coordinates aligned based on the information in Table 18.6.

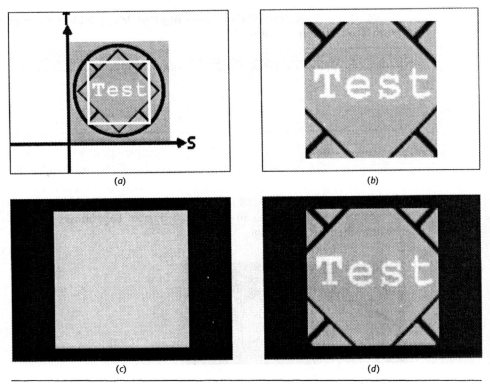

Figure 18.5 *The stages in mapping a texture to a face: (a) A texture image with an area selected, (b) the piece of texture stamped out of the texture image, (c) a face, and (d) the face textured with the stamped-out piece of texture.*

You can align any texture coordinate with any face coordinate. For instance, Figure 18.6 turns the stamped-out texture piece on its side by aligning it with the face's coordinates as they are mapped in Table 18.7.

Figure 18.6 *A texture image mapped sideways on a face.*

Table 18.7   Face and Texture Coordinates Mapped in an Order Different from That Shown in Table 18.6

Face Coordinate Index	Texture Coordinate Index
0	3
1	0
2	1
3	2

If the size of a face isn't the same as the size of a texture image, then the texture image is automatically stretched to fit the face. For example, you can stretch the square texture image from the previous examples so that it fits on a rectangular face defined by the coordinates in Table 18.8. Figure 18.7 shows the resulting face and the stretched texture image.

Figure 18.7   *A square piece of texture mapped on a rectangular face.*

Table 18.8   Face and Texture Coordinates Mapped to Stretch a Texture

Face Coordinate Index	Coordinate (X, Y, Z)
0	-2.0 -1.0 0.0
1	2.0 -1.0 0.0
2	2.0 1.0 0.0
3	-2.0 1.0 0.0

Stretching a texture to make it fit a face can be used to conform a texture to a desired shape. For instance, Figure 18.8a shows a texture image of a single square stone block. Figure 18.8b shows the stone-block texture image mapped to a series of block faces outlining the curved arch above a doorway. Notice that the square stone block texture image is stretched to fit the nonsquare block faces making up the curved arch.

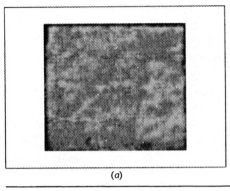
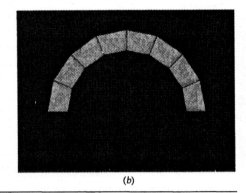

(a)   (b)

Figure 18.8 *(a) A square, stone-block texture image, and (b) the image stretched to fit each nonsquare face making up blocks above a curved doorway.*

When texture coordinates are automatically created by a VRML shape, those coordinates are also automatically aligned with faces on the shape. This gives you the option of texture mapping boxes, text, elevation grids, and so on without generating texture coordinates or specifying their alignment with shape faces.

For shapes created using the **IndexedFaceSet** node, you can specify a list of texture coordinates using a **TextureCoordinate** node and provide a list of texture coordinate indexes, one per face index, within the **texCoordIndex** field of the **IndexedFaceSet** node. The first texture coordinate index specifies a texture coordinate corresponding to the first face's first coordinate. The second texture coordinate index corresponds to the face's second coordinate, and so on. This process of assigning texture coordinates to face coordinates is similar to that of binding a different color to each face coordinate, as discussed in Chapter 16.

Wrapping Texture Coordinates

Recall that a texture image always extends from 0.0 to 1.0 in the S direction and from 0.0 to 1.0 in the T direction in the texture coordinate system. Each of the previous examples have used texture coordinates to select a region *within* the texture image. You can also use texture coordinates to select regions *outside* the texture image—beyond the left, right, bottom, or top edges of the image. When you do so, your texture coordinates are *wrapped* so that coordinates above the top of the image wrap to the bottom of the image, and coordinates below the bottom edge wrap back to the top. Likewise, texture coordinates to the left of the left edge wrap to the right edge, and coordinates to the right of the right edge wrap to the left edge.

You can think of the original texture image as repeating endlessly left-to-right and bottom-to-top in a giant sheet of texture images. When you select texture coordinates from the left edge of the original texture image, they fall on a copy of the image to the left of the original. Similarly, texture coordinates from the right, bottom, or top edges of the original image fall on copies to the right, below, or above the original image in the giant sheet of texture images.

Figure 18.9*a* shows a texture image. Figure 18.9*b* shows the same texture image and several of its duplicate neighbors surrounding it. Each of these neighbors have duplicate neighbors, and so on, repeating infinitely in all directions. The center image in this giant sheet of duplicate images is called the *original* texture image.

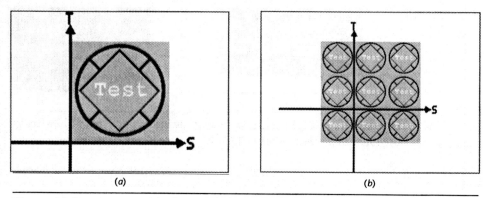

(a)   (b)

Figure 18.9 *A texture (a) alone and (b) with a few of its neighbors on all sides.*

A texture coordinate of (1.0,0.0) specifies a location on the right edge of the original texture image. A coordinate further to the right, such as (1.2,0.0), moves past the right edge of the original texture image and specifies a point on the left side of the duplicate neighbor texture to the right.

This infinite series of duplicate texture images creates a giant sheet of repeating texture images. Using your texture cookie cutter, you can stamp out a texture of any size anywhere on this sheet. For example, the texture coordinates in Table 18.9 select a large piece of this sheet so that the stamped-out piece contains several copies of the texture image.

Table 18.9   Face and Texture Coordinates Mapped to Copy the Texture within the Specified Piece of Texture

Texture Coordinate Index	Coordinate (S, T)
0	-0.5 -0.5
1	1.5 -0.5
2	1.5 1.5
3	-0.5 1.5

Figure 18.10*a* shows a portion of the texture sheet with the selected texture piece indicated, and *b* shows the piece of texture image stamped out by these texture coordinates.

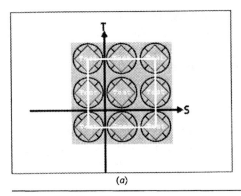
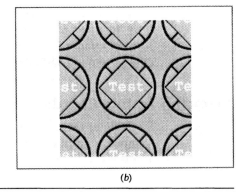

(a)   (b)

Figure 18.10 *Using texture coordinates spanning multiple texture copies: (a) a selected region of the texture sheet and (b) the stamped-out piece of texture.*

You can use texture-coordinate wrapping to create repeating patterns across shapes, such as for a brick wall or tiles on a floor. For each shape, select an appropriately large piece of the infinitely repeating, texture-image sheet, and map it to the shape. For example, Figure 18.11a shows a simple brick texture image, and b shows the texture image mapped to a wall. By selecting a large piece of the infinite brick texture sheet, the brick texture is repeated multiple times across the brick wall.

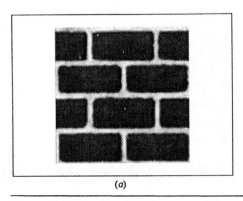
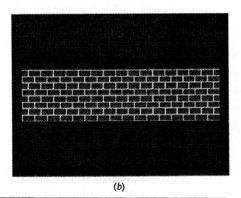

(a)   (b)

Figure 18.11 *(a) A brick texture (b) repeated across a wall shape using wrapped texture coordinates.*

Texture-coordinate wrapping enables you to repeat a texture many times across a shape. By default, texture-coordinate wrapping is turned on. You can turn wrapping off for the S, T, or both directions using the **repeatS** and **repeatT** fields in the **Image-Texture, PixelTexture,** and **MovieTexture** nodes.

TIP   Some texture images work well repeated, and others do not. The brick texture, for instance, repeats well. The brick texture image has been processed with a painting application so that each edge neatly butts up against its opposite edge without a visible seam. Many painting and image-processing applications have features to help you create repeatable texture images from scanned or painted images. You can also find repeatable texture images on the Web or purchase them in CD-ROM texture libraries.

Clamping Texture Coordinates

By *clamping* texture coordinates, you can prevent them from wrapping. You can use clamped texture coordinates to ensure that a texture image occurs just once on a shape, instead of repeating it over and over, like the brick wall example.

You can clamp in the S direction, in the T direction, or in both directions at once. When you clamp in the S direction, S-texture-coordinate values less than 0.0 (the left edge of the original texture image) or greater than 1.0 (the right edge of the image) are pulled and clamped to those edges. So, for instance, a texture coordinate like (2.5,0.0) beyond the right edge of the texture image is clamped to the right edge at (1.0,0.0). A texture coordinate like (-1.3,0.5) beyond the left edge is clamped to the left edge at (0.0,0.5).

Clamping in the T direction works in the same way. T-texture-coordinate values less than 0.0 (the bottom edge of the original texture image) or greater than 1.0 (the top edge of the image) are clamped back to those edges.

You can think of clamping as restricting the infinite sheet of texture images in the S, T, or both directions. Instead of repeating the texture image over and over in those directions, only the *edges* of the texture image are repeated infinitely. This creates a smearing effect that wipes the texture image's left edge infinitely to the left, the right edge infinitely to the right, bottom edge to the bottom, and top edge to the top.

For example, Figures 18.12*a* and *b* show the brick texture image placed in the middle of a square face. Figure 18.12*a* uses wrapping texture coordinates to repeat the brick texture edge to edge across the face. Figure 18.12*b* uses clamped texture coordinates, causing the left, right, bottom, and top edges of the texture image to smear outward to the edges of the face.

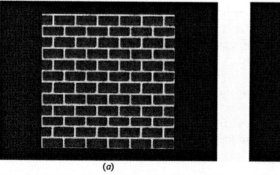 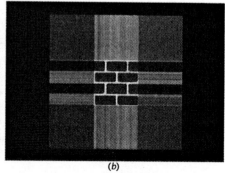

(a)   (b)

Figure 18.12   *A brick texture mapped to the center of a square* (a) *with wrapped texture coordinates and* (b) *with clamped texture coordinates.*

To control the smearing effect caused by texture-coordinate clamping, you can add a solid-color border to your texture image. Then, when the edges of the texture image are smeared across a face, it is the border pixels that are smeared. If you create a solid red border, for instance, the smear is a solid red. This prevents the striped smear effect shown in the brick example in Figure 18.12.

Texture-coordinate clamping is controlled using the **repeatS** and **repeatT** fields of the **ImageTexture, PixelTexture,** and **MovieTexture** nodes. When these fields have **TRUE** values, texture coordinates wrap, and no clamping occurs. When these fields have **FALSE** values, texture coordinates are clamped in either the S, T, or both directions.

Transforming Texture Coordinates

2-D texture coordinates describe a texture cookie-cutter shape within the texture coordinate system. Using a **TextureTransform** node, you can create a new texture coordinate system for your texture cookie cutter. By varying the **translation, rotation,** and **scale** field values of the **TextureTransform** node, you can position, orient, and resize the texture cookie cutter before using it to stamp out a piece of the texture and applying the piece of texture to a shape.

Texture-Coordinate Translation

Texture-coordinate translations are specified as distances measured in the S and T directions across a texture image. For example, translating texture coordinates to the right by 0.5 units slides the texture cookie cutter to the right by 0.5 units before stamping out a texture piece.

Figure 18.13*a* shows a texture image and the outline of a texture cookie cutter using texture coordinates that specify the entire image. Figure 18.13*b* shows the same cookie cutter translated to the right by 0.5 units. Figure 18.13*c* shows the stamped-out texture piece mapped to a square face. Notice that translating the texture cookie cutter to the *right* has the visual effect of shifting the texture to the *left* on the face.

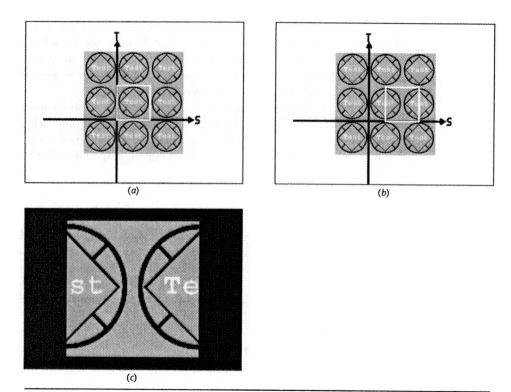

Figure 18.13 *(a) A portion of the infinite texture sheet with texture coordinates specifying a square the size and position of the original texture image, (b) the texture coordinates translated to the right by 0.5 units, and (c) the stamped-out piece of texture mapped to a square.*

Texture-Coordinate Rotation

Texture-coordinate rotation spins the texture cookie cutter around before it stamps out a piece of the texture image. Like shape rotations, texture rotations use an angle, measured in radians. Since the texture image is always on a 2-D plane, there is no need for a rotation axis such as that used in the **Transform** node. Rotation is always about an imaginary axis perpendicular to the plane of the texture-image sheet.

Figure 18.14*a* shows a texture cookie cutter rotated by 45.0 degrees counterclockwise around the origin of the texture coordinate system (remember that the origin is at the lower-left corner of the original texture image). Figure 18.14*b* shows the stamped out texture piece mapped to a square face. Notice that rotating the texture cookie cutter *counterclockwise* has the visual effect of rotating the texture *clockwise* on the face.

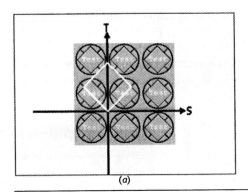
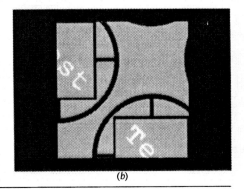

(a)   (b)

Figure 18.14 *(a) The texture coordinates of a square texture cookie cutter rotated counterclockwise by 45.0 degrees, and (b) the stamped-out piece of texture mapped to a square.*

You can also rotate texture coordinates around any location on the texture image. A typical center point is the center of the texture image at (0.5,0.5). Figure 18.15a shows a texture cookie cutter rotated by 45.0 degrees counterclockwise around (0.5,0.5). Figure 18.15b shows the stamped-out piece of texture mapped to a square face.

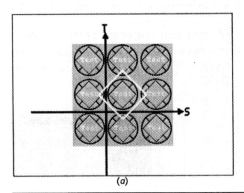
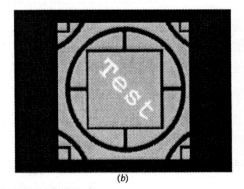

(a)   (b)

Figure 18.15 *(a) The texture coordinates of a square texture cookie cutter rotated counterclockwise by 45.0 degrees, and (b) the stamped-out piece of texture mapped to a square.*

Texture-Coordinate Scaling

Texture-coordinate scaling increases or decreases the size of the texture cookie cutter before it stamps out a piece of the texture. If you scale up the cookie cutter, it stamps out a larger piece of the texture image sheet. When using wrapping texture coordinates, that larger stamped-out piece includes a larger number of repeated texture images. In the same way, when you scale down the cookie cutter, it stamps out a smaller piece of the texture, which includes a smaller number of texture repeats from the texture sheet.

Figure 18.16*a* shows a texture cookie cutter scaled up by a factor of 2.0 relative to the texture-coordinate-system origin at the lower-left corner of the original texture image. Figure 18.16*b* shows the stamped-out piece of texture mapped to a square face. Notice that scaling the texture cookie cutter *up* has the visual effect of increasing the number of repeated textures on a shape, causing each texture to appear to *shrink* in size on the face.

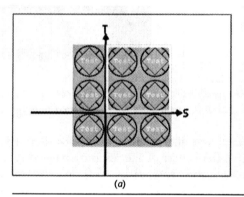 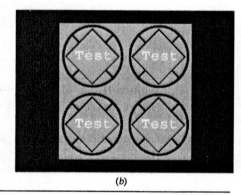

(a)   (b)

Figure 18.16 *(a) The texture coordinates of a square texture cookie cutter scaled up by a factor of 2.0, and (b) the stamped-out piece of texture mapped to a square.*

As with texture-coordinate rotation, you can select a center point for scaling texture coordinates. Figure 18.17*a* shows a texture cookie cutter scaled up by a factor of 2.0 using a center point at (0.5,0.5). Figure 18.17*b* shows the stamped-out piece of texture mapped to a square face.

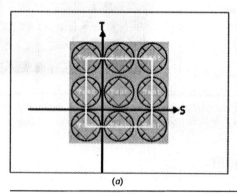 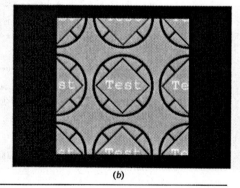

(a)   (b)

Figure 18.17 *(a) The texture coordinates of a square texture cookie cutter scaled up by a factor of 2.0 and using a center point (0.5,0.5), and (b) the stamped-out piece of texture mapped to a square.*

Texture Coordinate Translation, Rotation, and Scaling

You can use *texture transforms* to translate, rotate, and scale a texture cookie cutter so that the texture it stamps out fits the area in which you want to use the texture. For example, Figure 18.18*a* and *b* shows texture images of a fan and a small portion of a protective grill. Both images use pixel transparencies to indicate that the white background of the image should be transparent. Figure 18.18*c* shows the fan and grill images mapped to rectangular faces filling a window opening in a brick wall. The grill image mapping uses texture coordinate scaling to cause the grill image to repeat many times across the window opening. The fan-blade image uses texture rotation to turn the fan image to a desired orientation. You can also animate the fan-texture rotation angle so that the fan blades appear to rotate within the window.

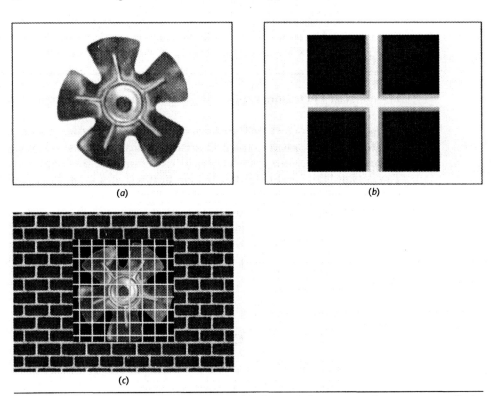

(a)

(b)

(c)

Figure 18.18 *Texture images of (a) fan blades and (b) a piece of a protective grill. (c) The texture images rotated and scaled to fit on faces filling a window.*

Texture-coordinate translation, rotation, and scaling are all controlled using a **TextureTransform** node as the value of the **textureTransform** field in a shape's **Appearance** node. Texture transforms affect texture coordinates if you provide them using the **TextureCoordinate** node for an **IndexedFaceSet** node, *and* if they are automatically created by shape geometry nodes. This enables you to translate, rotate, and scale textures even when texturing shapes that create their own texture coordinates, like the **Box, Cylinder, Cone, Sphere, Text, ElevationGrid,** and **Extrusion** nodes.

The **Appearance** Node Syntax

The **Appearance** node specifies appearance attributes and may be used as the value of the **appearance** field in a **Shape** node.

SYNTAX   Appearance node

```
Appearance {
    material          NULL    # exposedField   SFNode
    texture           NULL    # exposedField   SFNode
    textureTransform  NULL    # exposedField   SFNode
}
```

The **material** and **texture** exposed fields are discussed in Chapters 10 and 17, respectively.

The value of the **textureTransform** exposed field provides a node that specifies a transform to be applied to the 2-D texture coordinates used when texture mapping a shape. Typical **textureTransform** field values include the **TextureTransform** node. The default **NULL** value for this field indicates that no transform should be applied to texture coordinates.

The appearance texture transform can be changed by sending a value to the implied **set_textureTransform** eventIn of the **textureTransform** exposed field. When a value is received by this input, the corresponding field value is changed, and the new value is output using the implied **textureTransform_changed** eventOut of the exposed field.

The **ImageTexture** Node Syntax

The **ImageTexture** node specifies texture mapping attributes and may be used as the value of the **texture** field in an **Appearance** node.

SYNTAX   ImageTexture node

```
ImageTexture {
    url       [ ]    # exposedField   MFString
    repeatS   TRUE   # field          SFBool
    repeatT   TRUE   # field          SFBool
}
```

The **url** field is described in Chapter 17.

The **repeatS** and **repeatT** fields specify **TRUE** or **FALSE** values that indicate whether texture coordinates should wrap or be clamped. When **TRUE**, texture coordinates wrap and repeat within the texture coordinate system. When **FALSE**, texture coordinates are clamped and do not repeat. The **repeatS** and **repeatT** field values are independent, enabling wrapping and clamping to be independently controlled for the S and T directions in the texture coordinate system. The default value for these fields is **TRUE**, which enables texture-coordinate wrapping.

The **PixelTexture** Node Syntax

The **PixelTexture** node specifies texture-mapping attributes and may be used as the value of the **texture** field in an **Appearance** node.

| SYNTAX | **PixelTexture node** |

```
PixelTexture {
     image         0 0 0      # exposedField   SFImage
     repeatS       TRUE       # field          SFBool
     repeatT       TRUE       # field          SFBool
}
```

The **image** field is described in Chapter 17.

The **repeatS** and **repeatT** fields are described in the section entitled "The **Image-Texture** Node Syntax."

The **MovieTexture** Node Syntax

The **MovieTexture** node specifies texture-mapping attributes and may be used as the value of the **texture** field in an **Appearance** node. When a movie file containing audio is used, the **MovieTexture** node specifies sound that may be played back when the node is used as the value of the **source** field in the **Sound** node, which is discussed in Chapter 24.

| SYNTAX | **MovieTexture node** |

```
MovieTexture {
     url               [ ]        # exposedField   MFString
     loop              FALSE      # exposedField   SFBool
     speed             1.0        # exposedField   SFFloat
     startTime         0.0        # exposedField   SFTime
     stopTime          0.0        # exposedField   SFTime
     repeatS           TRUE       # field          SFBool
     repeatT           TRUE       # field          SFBool
     isActive                     # eventOut       SFBool
     duration_changed             # eventOut       SFFloat
}
```

The **url, loop, speed, startTime, stopTime, isActive,** and **duration_changed** fields are described in Chapter 17.

The **repeatS** and **repeatT** fields are described in the section entitled "The **Image-Texture** Node Syntax."

The **TextureCoordinate** Node Syntax

The **TextureCoordinate** node specifies a list of texture coordinates and may be used as the value of the **texCoord** field in the **IndexedFaceSet** and **ElevationGrid** nodes.

SYNTAX	TextureCoordinate node

```
TextureCoordinate {
    point    [ ]     # exposedField  MFVec2f
}
```

The value of the **point** exposed field provides a list of texture coordinates that specify locations in the texture coordinate system of a texture image. Each coordinate is specified as two floating-point values, one each for the S and T distances from the origin. The default value of the **point** field is an empty list of texture coordinates.

When specified within geometry nodes that use texture coordinate indexes, the first coordinate in the **TextureCoordinate** node's list corresponds to index 0, the second corresponds to index 1, and so on.

The coordinate list can be changed by sending a value to the implied **set_point** eventIn of the **point** exposed field. When a value is received by this input, the coordinate list is changed, and the new coordinate list is output using the implied **point_changed** eventOut of the exposed field.

The **TextureTransform** Node Syntax

The **TextureTransform** node builds a new texture coordinate system relative to the original texture coordinate system. The **TextureTransform** node may be used as the value of the **textureTransform** field in the **Appearance** node.

SYNTAX	TextureTransform node

```
TextureTransform {
    translation    0.0 0.0    # exposedField  SFVec2f
    rotation       0.0        # exposedField  SFFloat
    scale          1.0 1.0    # exposedField  SFVec2f
    center         0.0 0.0    # exposedField  SFVec2f
}
```

The value of the **translation** exposed field specifies the distances in the S and T directions between the origin of the original texture coordinate system and the origin of the new texture coordinate system. The first value in the **translation** field specifies the distance in the S direction and the second the distance in the T direction. Either of these distances may be positive or negative values. The default zero values for this field cause no translation in S or T. This places the new coordinate system directly on top of the original texture coordinate system.

The value of the **rotation** exposed field specifies a rotation angle, measured in radians, indicating how the new texture coordinate system is oriented relative to the original texture coordinate system. The default value for the **rotation** field specifies that no rotation occurs.

The value of the **scale** exposed field specifies scale factors in the S and T directions for the new texture coordinate system. The first value in the **scale** field specifies the scale factor in the S direction, and the second the scale factor in the T direction. The default 1.0 values for both scale factors cause no change in scale in S or T. This builds the new coordinate system at the same scale as the original texture coordinate system.

Scale factors must be greater than or equal to zero. Values between 0.0 and 1.0 reduce the size of the new coordinate system, while values larger than 1.0 increase its size. A scale factor of 0.0 shrinks the coordinate system down to nothing.

The value of the **center** exposed field specifies the 2-D texture coordinate in the new, translated coordinate system about which rotations and scales are to occur. The default rotation and scale center is the origin.

When **translation, rotation, scale,** and **center** field values are used in combination, the new coordinate system is scaled and rotated first about the center point, then translated relative to the parent coordinate system.

The translation, rotation, scale, and center values can be changed by sending values to the implied **set_translation, set_rotation, set_scale,** and **set_center** eventIns of the **translation, rotation, scale,** and **center** exposed fields, respectively. When values are received by these inputs, the corresponding field values are changed, and the new values are output using the implied **translation_changed, rotation_changed, scale_changed,** and **center_changed** eventOuts of the exposed fields.

The **IndexedFaceSet** Node Syntax

The **IndexedFaceSet** node creates face geometry and may be used as the value of the **geometry** field in a **Shape** node.

SYNTAX   **IndexedFaceSet node**

```
IndexedFaceSet {
    coord              NULL      # exposedField   SFNode
    coordIndex         [ ]       # field          MFInt32
    texCoord           NULL      # exposedField   SFNode
    texCoordIndex      [ ]       # field          MFInt32
    color              NULL      # exposedField   SFNode
    colorindex         [ ]       # field          MFInt32
    colorPerVertex     TRUE      # field          SFBool
    normal             NULL      # exposedField   SFNode
    normalIndex        [ ]       # field          MFInt32
    normalPerVertex    TRUE      # field          SFBool
    ccw                TRUE      # field          SFBool
    convex             TRUE      # field          SFBool
    solid              TRUE      # field          SFBool
    creaseAngle        0.0       # field          SFFloat
    set_coordIndex               # eventIn        MFInt32
    set_texCoordIndex            # eventIn        MFInt32
    set_colorIndex               # eventIn        MFInt32
    set_normalIndex              # eventIn        MFInt32
}
```

The **coord, coordIndex, set_coordIndex, ccw, convex, solid,** and **creaseAngle** fields are described in Chapter 13.

The **color, colorIndex, set_colorIndex,** and **colorPerVertex** fields are described in Chapter 16.

The value of the **texCoord** exposed field provides a node that specifies the texture coordinates available for texturing faces within the face set. Typical **texCoord** field values include the **TextureCoordinate** node. The default NULL value for this field indicates an empty texture coordinate list and enables automatic generation of texture coordinates as follows:

A bounding box for the shape is computed by the VRML browser producing a width, height, and depth for the box. The texture image is projected onto the face-set shape. The projection is positioned and oriented so that the horizontal axis of the texture image extends side to side along the longest dimension of the bounding box, whether that is the box's width, height, or depth. The vertical axis of the texture-image projection is oriented to extend along the second-longest dimension of the bounding box. To avoid warping the texture image, the texture may be clipped off at the top if the second-longest dimension isn't equal to the longest dimension.

The value of the **texCoordIndex** field specifies a list of texture-coordinate indexes describing the perimeter of one or more texture cookie cutters, one for each face in the face set. Each value in the list is an integer index corresponding to a texture coordinate from the texture coordinate list in the **texCoord** field. The default value for the **texCoordIndex** field is an empty texture-coordinate index list. When the tex-

CoordIndex field is empty, and a list of texture coordinates is specified in the **texCoord** field, the coordinate indexes listed in the **coordIndex** field are used as texture-coordinate indexes.

When texture-coordinate indexes are provided, there must be one index from the texture-coordinate index list for each coordinate index listed in the **coordIndex** field. The first texture-coordinate index corresponds to a texture coordinate to be aligned with the first coordinate index, the second texture-coordinate index corresponds to a texture coordinate to align with the second coordinate index, and so on. There must be one texture-coordinate index for each coordinate index, including -1 coordinate indexes used as face separators.

The texture-coordinate node value can be changed by sending a value to the implied **set_texCoord** eventIn of the **texCoord** exposed field. When a value is received by this input, the texture-coordinate node is changed, and the new texture-coordinate node is output using the implied **texCoord_changed** eventOut of the exposed field.

The texture-coordinate index list can be changed by sending a list of texture-coordinate indexes to the **set_texCoordIndex** eventIn.

The remaining fields of the **IndexedFaceSet** node—normal, normalIndex, set_normalIndex, and normalPerVertex—are discussed in Chapter 19.

The **ElevationGrid** Node Syntax

The **ElevationGrid** node creates face geometry and may be used as the value of the **geometry** field in a **Shape** node.

| SYNTAX | ElevationGrid node |

```
ElevationGrid {
    xDimension        0       # field         SFInt32
    xSpacing          0.0     # field         SFFloat
    zDimension        0       # field         SFInt32
    zSpacing          0.0     # field         SFFloat
    height            [ ]     # field         MFFloat
    color             NULL    # exposedField  SFNode
    colorPerVertex    TRUE    # field         SFBool
    normal            NULL    # exposedField  SFNode
    normalPerVertex   TRUE    # field         SFBool
    texCoord          NULL    # exposedField  SFNode
    ccw               TRUE    # field         SFBool
    solid             TRUE    # field         SFBool
    creaseAngle       0.0     # field         SFFloat
    set_height                # eventIn       MFFloat
}
```

The **xDimension, xSpacing, zDimension, zSpacing, height, set_height, ccw, solid,** and **creaseAngle** fields are as described in Chapter 14.

The **color** and **colorPerVertex** fields are as described in Chapter 16.

The value of the **texCoord** exposed field provides a node that specifies the texture coordinates available for texturing faces in the elevation grid. Typical **texCoord** field values include the **TextureCoordinate** node. The default **NULL** value for this field indicates an empty texture coordinate list, and enables automatic generation of texture coordinates as follows:

> Texture coordinates create a grid to lay over the top of the texture image. These coordinates align with the texture image so that the left and right edges of the texture line up with the left and right edges of the grid, the bottom of the texture lines up along the first row of grid points, and the top of the texture lines up along the last row of grid points.

When texture coordinates are provided, one texture coordinate from the **texCoord** field's texture-coordinate list is used for each grid point in the elevation grid. The first texture coordinate is used for the first grid point of the first row of the grid, the second texture coordinate for the second grid point of the first row, and so on. There must be one texture coordinate for each grid point in the elevation grid, computed as **xDimension × zDimension.**

The texture-coordinate node value can be changed by sending a value to the implied **set_texCoord** eventIn of the **texCoord** exposed field. When a value is received by this input, the texture-coordinate node is changed, and the new texture-coordinate node is output using the implied **texCoord_changed** eventOut of the exposed field.

The remaining fields of the **ElevationGrid** node—**normal** and **normalPerVertex**—are discussed in Chapter 19.

Experimenting with Texture-Mapping Control

The following examples provide a more detailed examination of the ways in which the **TextureCoordinate** and **TextureTransform** nodes can be used with the geometry nodes to control texture mapping.

Using Texture Coordinates

To control texture mapping of a face in a face set, you can provide your own texture coordinate list in a **TextureCoordinate** node and a texture-coordinate index for each coordinate index used to build the face. The texture coordinates specified by the texture-coordinate indexes define the perimeter of a texture cookie cutter that stamps out a texture image and glues it to the face.

Figure 18.19*a* shows a texture image, and *b* shows the texture image mapped to a square face. The VRML text in this figure is used to select this texture piece, stamp it out, and apply it to a square face in a face set.

```
#VRML V2.0 utf8
Shape {
    appearance Appearance {
        material Material { }
        texture ImageTexture {
            url "testimg.jpg"
        }
    }
    geometry IndexedFaceSet {
        coord Coordinate {
            point [
                -1.0 -1.0 0.0,
                 1.0 -1.0 0.0,
                 1.0  1.0 0.0,
                -1.0  1.0 0.0,
            ]
        }
        coordIndex [ 0, 1, 2, 3, ]
        texCoord TextureCoordinate {
            point [
                0.2 0.2,
                0.8 0.2,
                0.8 0.8,
                0.2 0.8,
            ]
        }
        texCoordIndex [ 0, 1, 2, 3, ]
        solid FALSE
    }
}
```

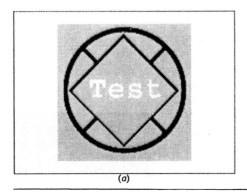 

(a) (b)

Figure 18.19 (a) *A texture image and* (b) *a square face texture mapped using texture coordinates to select the texture image. (The VRML text in this figure builds the world shown in Figure 18.19b.)*

The number of texture coordinates for a texture cookie cutter must match the number of coordinates used to build the face to be textured. The previous example uses four coordinates to select a square piece of texture. You can also select triangular, circular, or other shapes for texture pieces when mapping to triangular, circular, or other face shapes.

Figure 18.20*a* shows a texture image of a pizza. Figure 18.20*b* shows the VRML text to select a slice out of the pizza and map it to a face.

```
#VRML V2.0 utf8
Shape {
    appearance Appearance {
        material Material { }
        texture ImageTexture {
            url "pizza.jpg"
        }
    }
    geometry IndexedFaceSet {
        coord Coordinate {
            point [
            # Slice, pulled out of pizza
                0.50 0.0 0.50,   0.88 0.0 1.42,
                1.06 0.0 1.33,   1.21 0.0 1.21,
                1.33 0.0 1.06,   1.42 0.0 0.88
            ]
        }
        coordIndex [ 0, 1, 2, 3, 4, 5 ]
        texCoord TextureCoordinate {
            point [
            # Center point of pizza image
                0.50 0.50,
            # Slice perimeter
                0.68 0.07,   0.76 0.11,
                0.83 0.17,   0.89 0.24,
                0.93 0.32,
            ]
        }
        texCoordIndex [ 0, 1, 2, 3, 4, 5, ]
        solid FALSE
    }
}
```

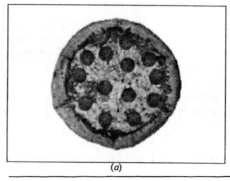

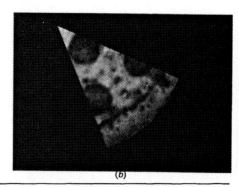

(a)   (b)

Figure 18.20 *(a) A pizza texture with a slice selected, and (b) a triangular face texture mapped with the pizza slice. (The VRML text in this figure builds the world shown in Figure 18.20b.)*

Using Texture Coordinates for Multiple Faces

You can provide texture coordinates for each face in a face set. Figure 18.21 uses the pizza texture from Figure 18.20 and builds both a pizza slice and the body of the pizza from which the slice is extracted. The pizza body and slice are both faces within the same face set.

```
#VRML V2.0 utf8
Shape {
    appearance Appearance {
        material Material { }
        texture ImageTexture {
            url "pizza.jpg"
        }
    }
    geometry IndexedFaceSet {
        coord Coordinate {
            point [
            # Slice, pulled out of pizza
                0.50 0.0  0.50,   0.88 0.0  1.42,
                1.06 0.0  1.33,   1.21 0.0  1.21,
                1.33 0.0  1.06,   1.42 0.0  0.88,
            # Rest of pizza
                0.00 0.0  0.00,   0.92 0.0  0.38,
                0.98 0.0  0.20,   1.00 0.0  0.00,
                0.98 0.0 -0.20,   0.92 0.0 -0.38,
                0.83 0.0 -0.56,   0.71 0.0 -0.71,
                0.56 0.0 -0.83,   0.38 0.0 -0.92,
                0.20 0.0 -0.98,   0.00 0.0 -1.00,
               -0.20 0.0 -0.98,  -0.38 0.0 -0.92,
               -0.56 0.0 -0.83,  -0.71 0.0 -0.71,
               -0.83 0.0 -0.56,  -0.92 0.0 -0.38,
               -0.98 0.0 -0.20,  -1.00 0.0  0.00,
               -0.98 0.0  0.20,  -0.92 0.0  0.38,
               -0.83 0.0  0.56,  -0.71 0.0  0.71,
               -0.56 0.0  0.83,  -0.38 0.0  0.92,
               -0.20 0.0  0.98,   0.00 0.0  1.00,
                0.20 0.0  0.98,   0.38 0.0  0.92
            ]
        }
        coordIndex [
        # Slice
            0,  1,  2,  3,  4,  5, -1,
        # Rest of pizza
            6,  7,  8,  9, 10, 11, 12, 13, 14, 15, 16,
           17, 18, 19, 20, 21, 22, 23, 24, 25, 26, 27,
           28, 29, 30, 31, 32, 33, 34, 35
        ]
```

Figure 18.21 continues

```
texCoord TextureCoordinate {
    point [
    # Center point of pizza image
        0.50 0.50,
    # Pizza perimeter
        0.96 0.41,   0.97 0.50,
        0.96 0.59,   0.93 0.68,
        0.89 0.76,   0.83 0.83,
        0.76 0.89,   0.68 0.93,
        0.59 0.96,   0.50 0.97,
        0.41 0.96,   0.32 0.93,
        0.24 0.89,   0.17 0.83,
        0.11 0.76,   0.07 0.68,
        0.04 0.59,   0.03 0.50,
        0.04 0.41,   0.07 0.32,
        0.11 0.24,   0.17 0.17,
        0.24 0.11,   0.32 0.07,
        0.41 0.04,   0.50 0.03,
        0.59 0.04,
    # Slice perimeter
        0.68 0.07,   0.76 0.11,
        0.83 0.17,   0.89 0.24,
        0.93 0.32
    ]
}
texCoordIndex [
# Slice
    0, 28, 29, 30, 31, 32, -1,
# Rest of pizza
    0,  32,  1,  2,  3,  4,  5,  6,  7,  8,  9, 10,
    11, 12, 13, 14, 15, 16, 17, 18, 19, 20, 21, 22,
    23, 24, 25, 26, 27, 28
]
solid FALSE
        }
    }
```

Figure 18.21 *A pizza and slice.*

Translating Texture Coordinates

The texture coordinates used in an **IndexedFaceSet** node specify the shape of a texture cookie cutter that stamps out a piece of texture and glues it to a face in the set. You can use a **TextureTransform** node in an **Appearance** node to translate the cookie cutter so that it stamps out a piece of texture from different regions of the texture image.

Figure 18.22 shows a virtual video wall made up of four virtual TV screens (simplified here to be four squares, but you could add the TV chassis, speakers, etc.). To build a single TV screen, one quarter of the video wall, the VRML text specifies an **IndexedFaceSet** node and texture coordinates that describe a texture cookie-cutter shape large enough to stamp out one-fourth of the video texture image.

```
#VRML V2.0 utf8
Group {
    children [
    # Lower-left video screen
        Shape {
            appearance Appearance {
                # no material, use emissive texturing
                texture DEF Video ImageTexture {
                    url "grand.jpg"
                }
            }
            geometry DEF Screen IndexedFaceSet {
                solid FALSE
                coord Coordinate {
                    point [
                        0.0 0.0 0.0,  1.0 0.0 0.0,
                        1.0 1.0 0.0,  0.0 1.0 0.0,
                    ]
                }
                coordIndex [ 0, 1, 2, 3 ]
                texCoord TextureCoordinate {
                    point [
                        0.0 0.0,  0.5 0.0,
                        0.5 0.5,  0.0 0.5,
                    ]
                }
                texCoordIndex [ 0, 1, 2, 3 ]
            }
        },
    # Lower-right video screen
        Transform {
            translation 1.1 0.0 0.0
            children Shape {
                appearance Appearance {
                # no material, use emissive texturing
                    texture USE Video
                    textureTransform TextureTransform {
                    # Slide to lower-right quadrant
                        translation 0.5 0.0
                    }
                }
                geometry USE Screen
            }
        },
```

Figure 18.22 continues

```
# Upper-left video screen
    Transform {
        translation 0.0 1.1 0.0
        children Shape {
            appearance Appearance {
            # no material, use emissive texturing
                texture USE Video
                textureTransform TextureTransform {
                # Slide to upper-left quadrant
                    translation 0.0 0.5
                }
            }
            geometry USE Screen
        }
    },
# Upper-right video screen
    Transform {
        translation 1.1 1.1 0.0
        children Shape {
            appearance Appearance {
            # no material, use emissive texturing
                texture USE Video
                textureTransform TextureTransform {
                # Slide to upper-right quadrant
                    translation 0.5 0.5
                }
            }
            geometry USE Screen
        }
    }
]
}
```

(a)   (b)

Figure 18.22   (a) *A mountain texture image and* (b) *a four-screen video wall; each screen is created by stamping out one-fourth of a mountain texture image and using a* **TextureTransform** *node to translate the texture cookie cutter. (The VRML text in this figure builds the world shown in Figure 18.22b.)*

To build the second TV screen, the first TV screen's geometry is used again, but a **TextureTransform** node translates the shape's texture cookie cutter to the right before stamping out another quarter of the video texture image. The third and fourth TV screens are built in the same way; each one uses the first TV screen's geometry, adding a **TextureTransform** node to translate the texture cookie cutter to a new video texture image quadrant before stamping out a texture piece.

The final video wall has four TV screens, each one showing one quadrant of the texture image. You can also use a **MovieTexture** node to create a moving texture image on your virtual video wall.

Scaling Texture Coordinates

You can use a **TextureTransform** node to control the number of times a texture image is repeated when mapped to a shape. Figure 18.23*a* shows a simple grillwork image, and *b* shows this grillwork repeated multiple times across a square face using texture coordinate scaling. Notice that scaling up texture coordinates looks as if the image is scaled down and repeats the texture image when applied to the face.

```
#VRML V2.0 utf8
Shape {
    appearance Appearance {
        material Material { }
        texture ImageTexture {
            url "grill.png"
        }
        textureTransform TextureTransform {
            scale 32.0 8.0
            center 0.5 0.5
        }
    }
    geometry IndexedFaceSet {
        solid FALSE
        coord Coordinate {
            point [
                -4.0 -1.0 0.1,   4.0 -1.0 0.1,
                 4.0  1.0 0.1,  -4.0  1.0 0.1,
            ]
        }
        coordIndex [ 0, 1, 2, 3 ]
        texCoord TextureCoordinate {
            point [
                0.0 0.0,  1.0 0.0,
                1.0 1.0,  0.0 1.0,
            ]
        }
        texCoordIndex [ 0, 1, 2, 3 ]
    }
}
```

Figure 18.23 continues

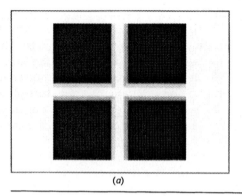 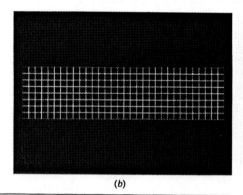

(a)   (b)

Figure 18.23 *(a) A small grillwork texture image and (b) the grillwork image repeated across a square face using texture-coordinate scaling. (The VRML text in this figure builds the world shown in Figure 18.23b.)*

Rotating Texture Coordinates

You can use a **TextureTransform** node to rotate texture coordinates. This rotates the texture image on the shape to which it is mapped.

To convert the grillwork rectangle in Figure 18.23 into a chain-link fence, Figure 18.24 rotates the grillwork image by 45.0 degrees (0.785 radians) and maps it to the rectangular face. To complete the fence, three fence posts are added.

```
#VRML V2.0 utf8
Group {
    children [
    # Chain-link fence
        Shape {
            appearance Appearance {
                material Material { }
                texture ImageTexture {
                    url "grill.png"
                }
                textureTransform TextureTransform {
                    rotation 0.785
                    scale 32.0 8.0
                    center 0.5 0.5
                }
            }
            geometry IndexedFaceSet {
                solid FALSE
                coord Coordinate {
                    point [
                        -4.0 -1.0 0.1,    4.0 -1.0 0.1,
                         4.0  1.0 0.1,   -4.0  1.0 0.1,
                    ]
                }
```

Figure 18.24 continues

```
            coordIndex [ 0, 1, 2, 3 ]
            texCoord TextureCoordinate {
                point [
                    0.0 0.0,  1.0 0.0,
                    1.0 1.0,  0.0 1.0,
                ]
            }
            texCoordIndex [ 0, 1, 2, 3 ]
        }
    },
# Fence posts
    DEF Post Shape {
        appearance Appearance {
            material Material { }
        }
        geometry Cylinder {
            height 2.0
            radius 0.1
        }
    },
    Transform { translation -4.0 0.0 0.0  children USE Post },
    Transform { translation  4.0 0.0 0.0  children USE Post }
    ]
}
```

Figure 18.24 *A rotated grillwork texture image mapped to a rectangular face to create a chain-link fence.*

Transforming Textures on Primitive Shapes

Each of the previous examples use explicit texture coordinates together with texture transforms to control the appearance of texture images mapped to a face-set shape. For primitive and text shapes, however, you cannot override the automatically created coordinates. Nevertheless, you can apply texture transforms to translate, rotate, and scale the automatically generated texture coordinates. This enables you to position, orient, and resize the appearance of textures mapped to primitive and text shapes.

Figure 18.25*a* shows a brick texture image, and *b* shows the brick texture mapped to a **Box** node's shape. A **TextureTransform** node scales up the **Box** node's automatic texture coordinates, causing the brick texture to repeat several times across each face of the box.

```
#VRML V2.0 utf8
Shape {
    appearance Appearance {
        material Material { }
        texture ImageTexture {
            url "brick.jpg"
        }
        textureTransform TextureTransform {
            scale 3.0 3.0
        }
    }
    geometry Box { }
}
```

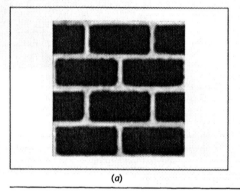
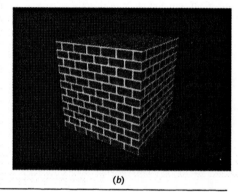

(a)   (b)

Figure 18.25   (a) A brick texture and (b) a brick texture repeatedly mapped to a **Box** node's shape using a **TextureTransform** node. (The VRML text in this figure builds the world shown in Figure 18.25b.)

Controlling Texture Mapping of an Elevation Grid

For most applications, the automatically computed texture coordinates for an ElevationGrid node are satisfactory. You can gain additional control by providing your own texture coordinates, one for each grid point. Using your own texture coordinates, you can stretch and warp the texture image as it is applied to the elevation grid. For terrain applications, this ability to stretch and warp the image enables you to adjust for curvature and warping present in the texture image. This can occur, for instance, when the texture image is a satellite photograph.

Figure 18.26a shows a satellite photograph of the San Diego bay area. The photograph is warped, as if taken from a sharp angle. Figure 18.26b shows this image mapped directly to a flat elevation grid using the automatic texture coordinates generated by the **ElevationGrid** node. The VRML text used to create Figure 18.26c maps the same image to the same elevation grid, but it uses custom texture coordinates to reverse the warping and invert the image so that it is right side up.

```
#VRML V2.0 utf8
Shape {
    appearance Appearance {
        material Material { }
        texture ImageTexture { url "sdbaywlr.jpg" }
    }
    geometry ElevationGrid {
        xDimension 5
        zDimension 5
        xSpacing    0.2
        zSpacing    0.2
        solid       FALSE
        height [
            0.0, 0.0, 0.0, 0.0, 0.0,
            0.0, 0.0, 0.0, 0.0, 0.0,
            0.0, 0.0, 0.0, 0.0, 0.0,
            0.0, 0.0, 0.0, 0.0, 0.0,
            0.0, 0.0, 0.0, 0.0, 0.0
        ]
        texCoord TextureCoordinate {
            point [
                0.250 1.000, 0.375 1.000, 0.500 1.000, 0.625 1.000, 0.750 1.000,
                0.188 0.750, 0.344 0.750, 0.500 0.750, 0.656 0.750, 0.812 0.750,
                0.125 0.500, 0.312 0.500, 0.500 0.500, 0.688 0.500, 0.875 0.500,
                0.062 0.250, 0.281 0.250, 0.500 0.250, 0.719 0.250, 0.938 0.250,
                0.000 0.000, 0.250 0.000, 0.500 0.000, 0.750 0.000, 1.000 0.000
            ]
        }
    }
}
```

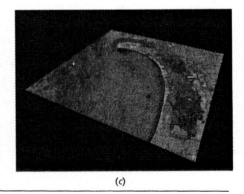

(a)

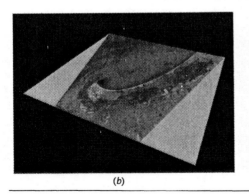

(b)   (c)

Figure 18.26   *(a) A warped, satellite-image texture of San Diego Bay, (b) a flat eleva-tion grid textured with the image of San Diego Bay, and (c) the same elevation grid using custom texture coordinates to reverse the warping and invert the San Diego Bay image as it is applied. (The VRML text in this figure builds the world shown in Figure 18.26c.)*

Animating Texture Transforms

You can animate a texture transform to translate, scale, or rotate a texture during an animation. The VRML text in Figure 18.27 creates a fan behind grillwork fencing. The grillwork texture can be seen in Figures 18.23 and 18.24. The fan image is mapped on a square face and rotated by animating the rotation angle of the face's **TextureTransform** node. A **TimeSensor** node provides the clock for the animation while a **ScalarInterpolator** node generates rotation angles.

```
#VRML V2.0 utf8
Group {
    children [
    # Rotating fan
        Shape {
            appearance Appearance {
                material Material { }
                texture ImageTexture {
                    url "fan.png"
                    repeatS FALSE
                    repeatT FALSE
                }
                textureTransform DEF FanRotation TextureTransform {
                    center 0.5 0.5
                }
            }
            geometry DEF Square IndexedFaceSet {
                coord Coordinate {
                    point [
                        -1.0 -1.0 -0.1,   1.0 -1.0 -0.1,
                         1.0  1.0 -0.1,  -1.0  1.0 -0.1,
                    ]
                }
                coordIndex [ 0, 1, 2, 3, ]
                texCoord TextureCoordinate {
                    point [
                        0.0 0.0,   1.0 0.0,
                        1.0 1.0,   0.0 1.0,
                    ]
                }
                texCoordIndex [ 0, 1, 2, 3, ]
                solid FALSE
            }
        },
    # Grill in front
        Transform {
            translation 0.0 0.0 0.1
            children Shape {
                appearance Appearance {
                    material Material { }
                    texture ImageTexture {
                        url "grill.png"
                    }
```

Figure 18.27 continues

```
                    textureTransform TextureTransform {
                        rotation 0.785
                        scale 8.0 8.0
                        center 0.5 0.5
                    }
                }
                geometry USE Square
            }
        },
    # Animation clock
        DEF Clock TimeSensor {
            cycleInterval 10.0
            loop TRUE
        },
    # Animation path
        DEF FanPath ScalarInterpolator {
            key      [ 0.0, 0.5,  1.0  ]
            keyValue [ 0.0, 3.14, 6.28 ]
        },
    ]
}
ROUTE Clock.fraction_changed TO FanPath.set_fraction
ROUTE FanPath.value_changed  TO FanRotation.set_rotation
```

Figure 18.27 *An animated, rotating fan texture.*

Summary

Texture mapping is a multistage process. The process starts by selecting a texture image using an **ImageTexture, PixelTexture,** or **MovieTexture** node as the value of the **texture** field of a shape's **Appearance** node.

In the second stage, texture coordinates are used to select a piece of the texture image. The texture coordinates can be thought of as describing the perimeter of a cookie cutter that is used to stamp out a piece of the texture image. Each texture coordinate selects a 2-D location in the texture coordinate system. The first value of the coordinate specifies the distance in the S direction (horizontal) and the second value the distance in the T direction (vertical), measured relative to the texture origin in the lower-left corner of the texture image. S and T values vary from 0.0 at the left and bottom edge of the image, to 1.0 at the right and top edge of the image.

Texture coordinates can extend beyond the edges of the texture image. When they do, they are clamped back to those edges or allowed to wrap around, depending upon the value of the **repeatS** and **repeatT** fields of the texture nodes. Then these fields have a **FALSE** value, texture coordinates outside of the range 0.0 to 1.0 are clamped back to this range. When these fields have a **TRUE** value, texture coordinates outside of this range wrap around, creating a repeating texture pattern on the textured shape.

All VRML geometry nodes automatically compute their own texture coordinates. For the **IndexedFaceSet** and **ElevationGrid** nodes, you can override these automatic texture coordinates and specify your own by using the **TextureCoordinate** node as the value of the **texCoord** field of these nodes. For the **ElevationGrid** node, your texture coordinates are automatically assigned to the grid, one point at a time as the grid is built. For the **IndexedFaceSet** node, you can assign texture coordinates to face coordinates by listing texture coordinate indexes in the **texCoordIndex** field of the node.

In the third stage of texture mapping, the texture coordinates are transformed by an optional texture transform set using the **TextureTransform** node as the value of the **textureTransform** field of the **Appearance** node. Similar to a 3-D coordinate system created using a **Transform** node, a texture transform creates a new texture coordinate system in which the texture coordinates select a texture piece. The new texture coordinate system can be translated, rotated, and scaled relative to the original texture coordinate system. If you think of the texture coordinates as describing a texture cookie cutter, then the texture transform translates, rotates, and scales that cookie cutter before it stamps out a piece of the texture image.

In the final stage of texture mapping, the stamped-out texture piece is applied to a face on the shape. Each corner of the stamped-out piece is aligned with a corner on the face, stretching the image as necessary to make it fit.

Controlling Shading

The brightness of a face on a VRML shape depends on how much it is lit by light in the virtual world. The more a face is oriented toward a light, the more brightly it is shaded by the VRML browser. A face that is oriented directly away from a light is shaded dark.

To decide whether a face is oriented toward or away from a light, the VRML browser automatically computes a *normal* for the face. You can think of a normal as an arrow that points straight out from the face, perpendicular to the face. If the face is oriented toward the right, then its normal arrow points to the right. If the face is oriented upward, then its normal arrow points upward.

If a face's normal points directly at a light, then the face must be oriented toward the light as well, and the VRML browser shades it bright. If a face's normal points away from a light, the face is shaded darker.

Computing face normals is usually the task of the VRML browser. You can override automatically computed normals and provide your own. This enables you to control exactly how faces on a shape are shaded.

You can provide your own normals for shapes built using the **IndexedFaceSet** and **ElevationGrid** geometry nodes. In both cases, you provide your own list of normals using the **Normal** node as the value of the **normal** field in these geometry nodes. You can even animate these normals using the **NormalInterpolator** node.

Understanding Normals

A normal is a way of indicating the orientation of a face. A face that is oriented to the right has a normal that points to the right. A face that is oriented upward has a normal that points upward, and so on. In this chapter's diagrams, normals are indicated with arrows that point outward from a face or coordinate. For instance, Figure 19.1 shows a cube and the normals for each of its six faces.

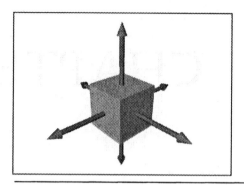

Figure 19.1   *A box with its normals indicated with arrows.*

Shading Based on Normal Directions

Recall that the VRML browser always creates a headlight to illuminate your VRML worlds. Imagine that headlight, as the name implies, positioned on your head in the world, as shown in Figure 19.2. As you move about the world, the light moves with you and always illuminates whatever you can see at the moment.

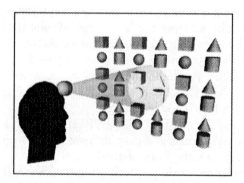

Figure 19.2   *Your headlight, like a miner's headlight.*

To shade a face, the VRML browser measures the angle between a face's normal and an imaginary line pointing away from the face directly toward a light. With the headlight, for instance, the imaginary line always points at you and your headlight.

When a face is facing you and your headlight, the angle between the face's normal and the light line is small, and the face is shaded brightly. As a face turns away from you, its normal points increasingly away from you and your headlight. Since your headlight illuminates the face less when it is turned edge-on, the VRML browser shades the face darker. Faces that are oriented directly away from you and your headlight are shaded darkest.

Notice that as the face points away from you more and more, the face is shaded darker and darker, and the angle between the normal and the light line increases. This link between shading darkness and the normal angle is what your VRML browser uses when it computes shading for your world. You can use this same link to compute your own normals to create specific shading effects.

Figure 19.3 shows a square face and how it is shaded as it is turned to face toward, and then away from, a light. In Figure 19.3*a*, the face is directly facing you and your headlight, so the face is shaded brightly. In Figure 19.3*b* the face is turned a bit to the right. Since it no longer directly faces you and your headlight, it is a bit darker. Figures 19.3*c* through *i* continue to turn the face away from you bit by bit. At each stage, the face is shaded more and more darkly. As you walk about within your virtual world, you see this effect, sometimes viewing brightly shaded faces from the front, and sometimes viewing darker shaded faces nearly edge-on.

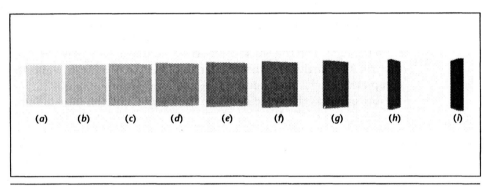

(a)　　*(b)*　　*(c)*　　*(d)*　　*(e)*　　*(f)*　　*(g)*　　*(h)*　　*(i)*

Figure 19.3　*A face shaded based on its orientation toward or away from the headlight.*

To further illustrate this shading effect, consider the top-view diagram in Figure 19.4 showing a single face viewed edge-on from above. Pointing out from the face is a normal arrow. The star burst indicates a light in the world, similar to your headlight. A light line is drawn from the face to the light. The most important part of this diagram is the angle between the normal arrow and the light line.

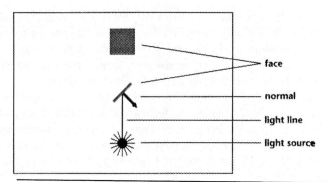

Figure 19.4 *A shaded face with its normal, a light source, and a light line.*

Figure 19.5 shows a series of diagrams like those in Figure 19.4. The first diagram shows the face directly facing the light. The next shows the face turned slightly away from the light, and so on, until the last shows the face oriented 90.0 degrees away from the light. The shaded squares above each diagram show the face's brightness at that rotation angle. The first shades the face the brightest, while the last shades it completely black since the face is aimed away from the light.

Notice that as the angle between the normal and the face-to-light line increases, the brightness of the face decreases.

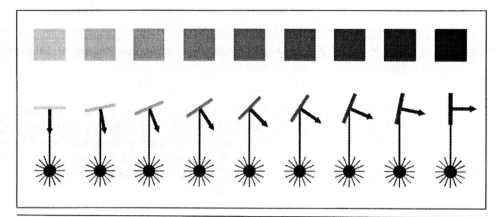

Figure 19.5 *Shading variations based on a face's orientation toward a light source.*

Figure 19.6 continues the diagram series begun in Figure 19.5 by swiveling the face entirely around from an initial position facing the light, to one facing directly away, and then back again. Notice that the face is shaded black for all positions where the face is edge-on or facing away from the light. The face is only shaded lighter when it faces the light at least a little bit.

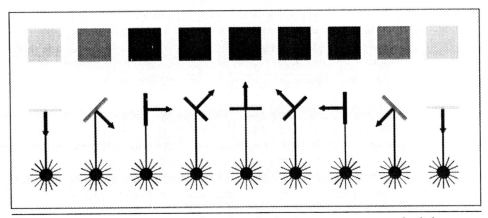

Figure 19.6 *Shading variations based on the face's orientation toward a light source.*

As these diagrams illustrate, the normal of a face is the key to understanding how the VRML browser shades faces. If the normal points toward a light, the face is shaded brightly. If it points away from a light, it is shaded dark.

Determining Normal Directions

The normal direction for a face is computed by looking at the order in which coordinates are specified to trace out the perimeter of a face. Consider the triangle in Figure 19.7. The coordinates for this triangle trace out a face perimeter starting at the top, continuing down and to the left, over to the right, and back again to the top of the triangle. This coordinate order creates a counterclockwise path about the triangle's perimeter. If you spin this triangle around to look at the opposite side, the coordinates will appear ordered clockwise.

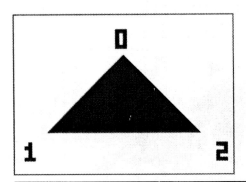

Figure 19.7 *A triangle described by an indexed face set.*

By default, VRML treats the side of a face where the coordinates appear ordered counterclockwise as the *front* of the face. The opposite side of the face is, of course, the *back* of the face. You can reverse this front and back distinction using the **ccw** field found in most coordinate-based geometry nodes. In any case, the normal for the face always points outward from the face's front, whichever side that is. (For an easy way to remember how the order of coordinates indicates the normal direction, see the sidebar entitled "Right-Hand Rule for Normals.")

SIDEBAR: RIGHT-HAND RULE FOR NORMALS Imagine that the fingers of your right hand are curling about the perimeter of a face, following the coordinates in the order specified in an **IndexedFaceSet** node. Stick your thumb out, as if hitch-hiking, and your thumb points in the direction of the face's normal. Figure 19.8*a* shows the right-hand rule applied to the triangle in Figure 19.7. You can view the same triangle from the back and again curl your fingers around the perimeter following the order in which the coordinates are specified in the **IndexedFaceSet** node. Figure 19.8*b* shows the result. Notice that no matter which side of the triangle you view, if you curl your fingers using the right-hand rule, your thumb always points out the front of the triangle. The same right-hand rule applies to any face with any number of coordinates. Figure 19.8*c* shows the rule applied to a more complicated face.

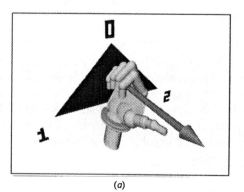

(a)

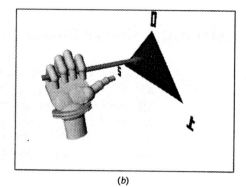

(b)

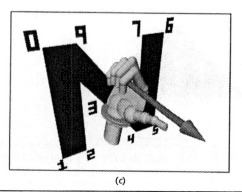

(c)

Figure 19.8 *(a) The right-hand rule for normals, (b) the right-hand rule from the back of the face, and (c) applying the right-hand rule to a more complex shape.*

Computing Normals

Normals can be computed by hand or using a computer program, like your VRML browser: To control shading, you or your browser will compute one normal for each face on a shape, or for more control, one normal for each coordinate of each face on a shape.

A normal for a face is computed using three consecutive coordinates around the perimeter of a face. For the triangle in Figure 19.7, the first three (and only three) coordinates are shown in Table 19.1.

Table 19.1   The Coordinates for the Triangle in Figure 19.6

Coordinate Index	Coordinate (X, Y, Z)
0	0.0 1.0 0.0
1	-1.0 0.0 0.0
2	1.0 0.0 0.0

To compute a normal, start by computing two vectors, one from coordinate 0 to coordinate 1 and the other from coordinate 1 to coordinate 2. A *vector* is an arrow pointing from a starting point to an ending point. It is represented as three X, Y, and Z values computed as the difference between the ending and starting X values of the arrow's points, the ending and starting Y values, and the ending and starting Z values. So, the vector from coordinate 0 to coordinate 1 of the triangle is this:

((-1.0 - 0.0), (0.0 - 1.0), (0.0 - 0.0)) - (-1.0, -1.0, 0.0)

The vector from coordinate 1 to coordinate 2 of the triangle is this:

((1.0 - -1.0), (0.0 - 0.0), (0.0 - 0.0)) - (2.0, 0.0, 0.0)

You can think of a vector as a translation distance in the X, Y, and Z directions that takes you from a starting point to an ending point. The vector from coordinate 0 to coordinate 1 indicates a translation in X by -1.0 unit, in Y by -1.0 unit, and in Z by 0.0 units. Figure 19.9 shows these two vectors computed.

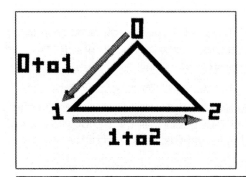

Figure 19.9   *Two vectors computed for the triangle.*

To be more generic when computing vectors from coordinate to coordinate, use a bit of algebra and label the X, Y, and Z components of each of the three coordinates with letters, as shown in Table 19.2.

Table 19.2   Coordinates Written Algebraically and Labeled with Letters

Coordinate Index	Coordinate (X, Y, Z)
0	X_0, Y_0, Z_0
1	X_1, Y_1, Z_1
2	X_2, Y_2, Z_2

Further labeling describes the two vectors of concern as *V* and *W*, where *V* is the vector from coordinate 0 to coordinate 1, and *W* is the vector from coordinate 1 to coordinate 2. Figure 19.10 shows the *V* and *W* vectors for the triangle. The calculation to compute these vectors, shown earlier, can now be written like this:

```
V - ( (X₁ - X₀), (Y₁ - Y₀), (Z₁ - Z₀) ) - (Xᵥ, Yᵥ, Zᵥ) - (-1.0, -1.0, 0.0)
W - ( (X₂ - X₁), (Y₂ - Y₁), (Z₂ - Z₁) ) - (Xᵥ, Yᵥ, Zᵥ) - (2.0, 0.0, 0.0)
```

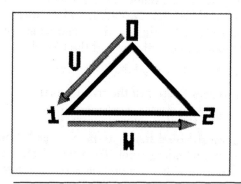

Figure 19.10   *The V and W vectors computed for the triangle.*

Using the *V* and *W* vectors, the face's normal vector *N* is computed by calculating the cross product of the two vectors. A *cross product* multiplies two vectors together to get a third vector and is computed like this:

```
N - ( (Yᵥ x Zᵥ - Zᵥ x Yᵥ), (Zᵥ x Xᵥ - Xᵥ x Zᵥ), (Xᵥ x Yᵥ - Yᵥ x Xᵥ) ) - (Xₙ, Yₙ, Zₙ)
```

This cross-product calculation produces a new vector that points directly outward from the face. This outward-pointing vector is the normal shown in Figure 19.11. The normal *N* for the preceding triangle is computed in this way:

```
N - ( (-1.0 x 0.0 - 0.0 x 0.0), (0.0 x 2.0 - -1.0 x 0.0), (-1.0 x 0.0 - -1.0 x 2.0) )
  - (0.0, 0.0, 2.0)
```

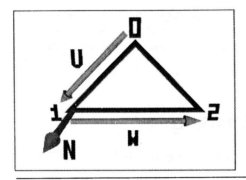

Figure 19.11 *The normal for the triangle.*

The normal **N** is a vector just like **V** and **W**. Recall that the triangle lies flat with a Z value of 0.0 for all three coordinates. The normal **N** points straight out from the front face of the triangle. This is the normal necessary to compute the brightness of the triangle.

Normal vectors used for shading are expected to be *unit vectors* such that the vector's magnitude is 1.0 (*vector magnitude* is computed as the square root of the sum of the squares of the X, Y, and Z components of a vector). The above normal, however, is not a unit vector and has a magnitude of

$$\sqrt{(0.0 \times 0.0 + 0.0 \times 0.0 + 2.0 \times 2.0)} = 2.0$$

You can make any vector into a unit vector by computing the magnitude and then dividing each X, Y, and Z value by that magnitude. Using algebra, the calculation to compute a vector magnitude **M** from a normal vector's X, Y, and Z components and compute a unit normal vector looks like this:

$$M = \sqrt{X^2 + Y^2 + Z^2}$$
$$N_{unit} = (X/M, Y/M, Z/M)$$

Shading always requires unit normal vectors. All normal vectors in the rest of this chapter have been converted to unit vectors.

The above calculations compute a single normal vector using the triangle coordinates 0, 1, and 2. This normal indicates the direction the entire triangle faces and enables the VRML browser to properly shade the face.

You can also compute a normal vector for each coordinate on a face. In fact, each time you compute a normal for a set of three coordinates, such as 0, 1, and 2 for the triangle, the vector you compute is the normal for the middle coordinate, such as coordinate 1 on the triangle. This is why the previous figures show the normal vector pointing outward from coordinate 1 when coordinates 0, 1, and 2 are used to compute the normal.

For a flat face, the normal at each coordinate around the face is the same. For a bent face, however, the normals at each of the bent face's coordinates may be different. Since a normal controls shading brightness, when a face has a different normal at each coordinate, your VRML browser computes a different shading brightness level at each coordinate. When the face is shaded, your VRML browser smoothly varies the shading brightness across the interior of the face which makes the face look bent.

Understanding Smooth Shading

Consider four rectangles arranged as facets in a half column. Figure 19.12*a* shows outlines of the four rectangles viewed from the front. Figure 19.12*b* shows the half column shaded, and *c* shows the half column's rectangles viewed from above.

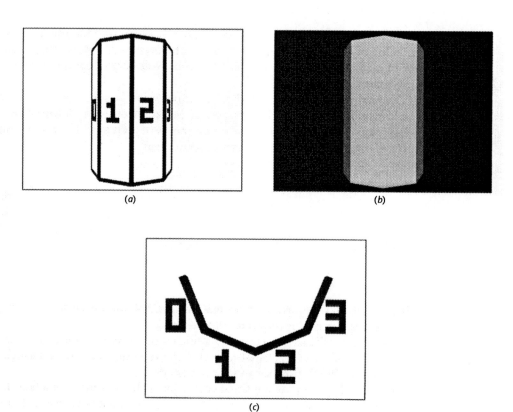

Figure 19.12 *Four rectangles composing a half column's facets (a) in outline form viewed from the front, (b) shaded and viewed from the front, and (c) in outline form viewed from above.*

Using automatically computed normals, the half column above clearly reveals its faceted structure. Imagine that you want to create the appearance of a smoothly rounded half column. The most direct approach is to use more rectangles to more closely approximate a rounded surface. The images in Figure 19.13 show the use of four (*a*), five (*b*), six (*c*), and seven (*d*) rectangular facets to approximate the curved surface of a rounded half column. As the number of facets increases, the shading of the half column makes it look more and more round.

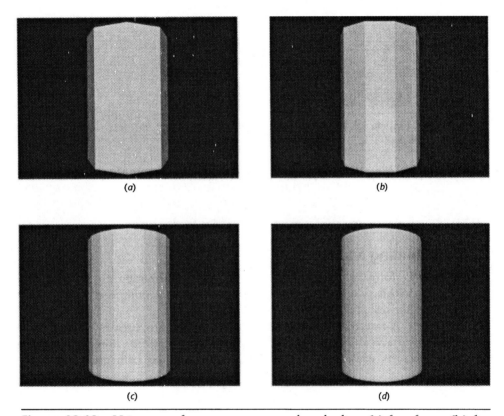

(a)   (b)   (c)   (d)

Figure 19.13 *Using more facets to create smoother shading: (a) four facets, (b) five facets, (c) six facets, and (d) seven facets.*

Unfortunately, using more rectangular faces means the VRML browser has more to draw, and it takes longer to draw your world. If you use large numbers of faces throughout your world to simulate smooth surfaces, you can end up with so many faces that your VRML browser takes many seconds, or even minutes, to build the world.

Using your own normals, however, you can create the smooth shading of a rounded half column, or other curved surface, using only a few faces and avoid slowing your VRML browser. To do this, you shade a flat face as if it were curved—a technique called *smooth shading.*

For example, in Figure 19.14, the faces of the half column use specially computed normals for each face coordinate. When shaded, the faces of this half column appear bent, as if curved to form a smoothly rounded surface.

Figure 19.14   *The shaded half column using normals that create a smooth-shading effect.*

Using the smooth-shading technique for computing normals, the half column's four faces are shaded so that they more closely approximate a smoothly rounded half column. Only by looking at the top and bottom edges of the half column is it obvious that the column is made of only four faces.

Smooth Shading and Normals

Performing smooth shading is the principal reason normal control is available in VRML. Using this technique, you can shade simple faceted shapes so that they look like smoothly curved surfaces.

A faceted shape, like the half column, approximates (rather poorly) the curved surface of a rounded half column. Figure 19.15*a* shows the top view of the four facets, while *b* shows the top view of a rounded half column.

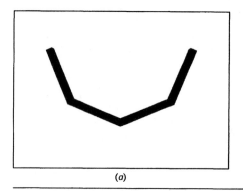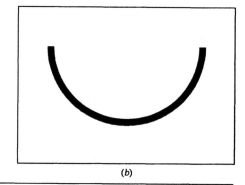

(a)   (b)

Figure 19.15   (a) *The top view of a half column built using four faces, and (b) the top view of a perfectly rounded half column.*

When the VRML browser automatically computes normals, it aims a normal straight out each face in the faceted column. Figure 19.16*a* shows the top view of the faceted column with normal arrows pointing out from each face. If you compute a perfectly smooth column, however, the normal at any point on the column points outward as if extending straight out from the center point of the column, similar to those in Figure 19.16*b*.

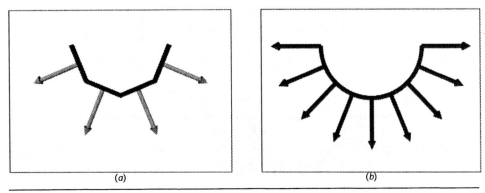

(a)   *(b)*

Figure 19.16   *The top view of a half column with normals (a) for each face in a faceted half column and (b) pointing outward from the center for a perfectly rounded half column.*

Figure 19.17*a* overlays the diagrams of the faceted column and the curved column. The normals at the centers of each face on the faceted column coincide perfectly with those of the curved column. The VRML browser's automatic normal computation usually creates a single normal for each face in a shape. All of the coordinates of a face share this normal. Figure 19.17*b* shows the faceted-column top view again, but this time each face's normal arrow is shown pointing out of each coordinate of each face.

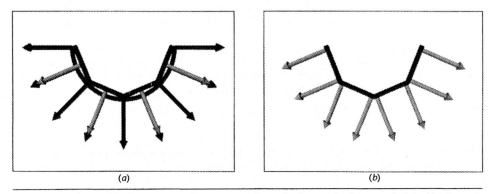

(a)   *(b)*

Figure 19.17   *(a) Comparing facet normals with the perfectly rounded half column's normals. (b) Top view of normals pointing out from each coordinate of a face.*

Figure 19.18 overlays the diagrams in Figures 19.16*b* and 19.17*b*. Notice that the normals used at the coordinates for the faceted column are wrong. The true, curved-column normals point straight out from the center of the column, but the faceted column's coordinate normals point off in one direction or another. Notice also that when a coordinate is shared between two adjacent faces, it is assigned a different normal for each face on the faceted column. The shared coordinate, however, represents a single point on the approximated curved column and should have only one normal. To smoothly shade the faceted half column, compute coordinate normals based on the true normals of the curved half column. Figure 19.18*b* shows the corrected normals pointing outward from each coordinate of the faceted half column.

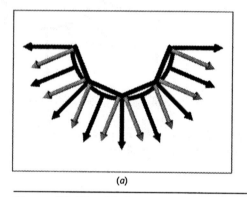
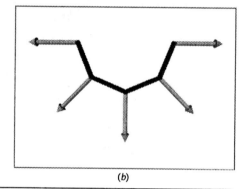

(a)   (b)

Figure 19.18   *(a) Comparing normals of facet coordinates and the perfectly rounded half column's normals, and (b) corrected normals pointing out from each face's coordinates.*

Using these new normals, the VRML browser can shade each face, gradually varying the face brightness from one edge to the other. Such shading closely approximates the shading that occurs on the smoothly rounded half column but uses only the four faces of the faceted half column. Figure 19.19*a* shows the original, faceted half column; *b* shows the smoothly shaded, faceted half column; and *c* shows the smoothly rounded half column. The shading of Figure 19.19*b* and *c* is quite close, and yet the half column has only four facets and is drawn considerably quicker than the smoothly rounded half column.

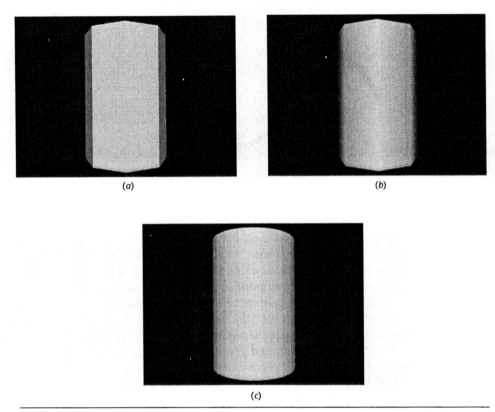

(a) (b)

(c)

Figure 19.19 *Comparing half-column shading: (a) faceted, (b) smoothly shaded and faceted, and (c) smoothly rounded.*

Computing Smooth-Shading Normals

Calculating normals for facets depends on the smooth surface you are trying to approximate. All of the previous examples have approximated a half column. The normals for such a surface always point straight out the half column's radius. Other curved shapes, however, may require more complicated normal computations. Figure 19.20, for instance, shows the normal arrows for a sideways S shape (a sine wave).

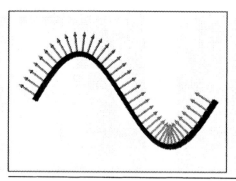

Figure 19.20   *The normals for a sine-wave shape.*

You can compute normals for curved shapes similar to these using several techniques. When a shape is known to be curved based on a mathematical equation, such as the outline of a circle or a sine wave, the easiest approach is to use that same curve equation to generate the normals. For each coordinate along the shape, compute a normal vector that is orthogonal (crosses the shape line at a 90.0-degree angle) at that vertex. For a circle, like the half column used in the previous examples, the normal always points straight out along a radius line from the circle's center point.

In other cases, the curved surface you are trying to approximate with facets isn't based on a mathematical equation. To compute curve normals for a surface like this, follow these steps:

1. Compute normals for each coordinate of each shape face using the vector, cross product, and magnitude calculations described in the section entitled "Computing Normals."

2. Look at adjacent faces on your shape. If there are two side-by-side faces with an edge in common, they must share at least two coordinates: one at each end of the common edge. At each shared coordinate, you calculated multiple normals in step 1: one normal for each face that shares that coordinate. Average those normals together to get a single normal for each coordinate.

3. Use the average coordinate normals calculated in step 2 as the smooth-shading coordinate normals for your shape.

Crease Angles

The **creaseAngle** field of the **IndexedFaceSet**, **Extrusion**, and **ElevationGrid** nodes controls how the VRML browser automatically computes normals if you do not specify your own. When adjacent faces have an angle between them that is less than the crease angle, the VRML browser computes normals to create a smooth-shading effect. The computation used by the browser to compute these normals is identical to the method outlined above.

When adjacent faces have an angle between them that is greater than the crease angle, the VRML browser computes one normal per face and does not average normals together at shared coordinates. This creates faceted shading.

Typically, it is more convenient to use the **creaseAngle** field than your own normals to create a smooth-shading effect. Providing your own normals is only necessary in relatively rare cases. Those cases include situations where some portions of a shape need faceted shading, while others need smooth shading. In such situations, no single crease angle will do. Instead, you can provide your own normals, computed such that smooth shading occurs only on those parts of a shape that you want to appear smooth.

Understanding Normal Binding

The normal-control features of the **IndexedFaceSet** and **ElevationGrid** nodes require a list of normals to use when shading the shape. You can then direct how normals in the list are bound to the individual faces or coordinates of a shape.

A normal list is analogous to the coordinate list some geometry nodes use to specify the coordinates of a shape. Normals are listed in a **Normal** node similar to the way coordinates are listed in a **Coordinate** node. Each normal in the normal list is a unit vector with X, Y, and Z values. Like the coordinates in a **Coordinate** node's value list, the normals in a **Normal** node are implicitly numbered, or indexed, starting with a *normal index* of 0 for the first normal, 1 for the second, and so on.

Face-Set Normals

You can provide normals for a face set by specifying a **Normal** node for the **normal** field of an **IndexedFaceSet** node. By specifying a list of normal indexes in a **normalIndex** field, you can specify a different normal for each face in the face set. This enables you to control shading on a face-by-face basis in the face set.

Alternately, you can provide a normal index for each coordinate of each face in the face set. This enables you to control shading effects that vary the brightness from corner to corner across the interior of a face.

Elevation-Grid Normals

You can provide normals for an elevation grid by specifying a **Normal** node for the **normal** field of an **ElevationGrid** node. Normals in the normal list are automatically assigned to portions of the elevation grid. You can control this automatic assignment and specify whether normals should apply to an entire grid square or to individual grid points.

When normals are applied to the grid squares, the first normal in the list controls the shading of the first grid square, the second normal the second square, and so on. You can use this to control shading on a face-by-face basis for each grid square in the elevation grid.

When normals are applied to individual grid points, the first normal in the list controls shading at the first grid point, the second normal at second grid point, and so forth. The faces automatically built by the **ElevationGrid** node use these grid-point normals as normals for face coordinates. This enables you to control shading effects that smoothly vary the brightness from corner to corner across the interior of each grid-square face.

Understanding Normal Animation

Recall that the **PositionInterpolator** and **OrientationInterpolator** nodes from Chapter 8 are used to smoothly animate the position or rotation of a shape as time ticks by. VRML also provides the **NormalInterpolator** node that can be used to animate normal vectors in a **Normal** node.

The **NormalInterpolator** node uses a list of key fractional times and key normal vectors in its **key** and **keyValue** fields. When driven by the fractional-time output of a **TimeSensor** node, the **NormalInterpolator** node uses linear interpolation to compute intermediate lists of normal vectors. Each new, computed, normal-vector list is output on the node's **value_changed** eventOut. You can route this output to a **Normal** node to cause a shape's normals to animate.

The **Normal** Node Syntax

The **Normal** node creates a list of normal vectors and may be used as the value of the **normal** field in coordinate-based geometry nodes, such as the **IndexedFaceSet** and **ElevationGrid** nodes.

SYNTAX	Normal node

```
Normal {
    vector    [ ]    # exposedField  MFVec3f
}
```

The value of the **vector** exposed field specifies a list of unit normal vectors that may be used as normals for a shape. Each normal is specified as three floating-point values, one each for the X, Y, and Z components of a vector. The default value of the **vector** field is an empty list of normals.

When used by geometry nodes that use normal indexes, the first normal in the **Normal** node's list has index 0, the second index 1, and so forth.

The normal vector list can be changed by sending a value to the implied **set_vector** eventIn of the **vector** exposed field. When a value is received by this input, the normal vector list is changed, and the new, normal vector list is output using the implied **vector_changed** eventOut of the exposed field. The **NormalInterpolator** node is a typical source for normal-vector-list values routed to the implied **set_vector** eventIn.

The **NormalInterpolator** Node Syntax

The **NormalInterpolator** node describes a series of key colors available for use in an animation.

| SYNTAX | NormalInterpolator node |

```
NormalInterpolator {
    key                 [ ]    # exposedField   MFFloat
    keyValue            [ ]    # exposedField   MFVec3f
    set_fraction               # eventIn        SFFloat
    value_changed              # eventOut       MFVec3f
}
```

The value of the **key** exposed field specifies a list of key floating-point fractional times. Typically, fractional times are between 0.0 and 1.0, such as those output by a **TimeSensor** node's **fraction_changed** eventOut. Key fractional times, however, may be positive or negative floating-point values of any size. Key fractional times must be listed in non-decreasing order. The default value of the **key** field is an empty list.

The value of the **keyValue** exposed field specifies a list of key normal vectors. Each normal vector is specified as three floating-point values, one each for the X, Y, and Z components of the vector. The default value of the **keyValue** field is an empty list.

The key fractional times and key normal vectors are used together to specify sublists of normal vectors between which the node interpolates to generate an output normal vector list. In the node's simplest form, a sublist contains only one normal vector for each fractional time. For instance, if there are N fractional time values, then there are exactly N key normal vectors in the **keyValue** field. The first key fractional time gives the time for the first key normal vector, the second key fractional time the time for the second key normal vector, and so forth. In this simple form of the interpolator, each output normal vector list contains only one normal vector.

In a more complex form of the interpolator node, the **keyValue** exposed field provides two or more key normal vectors for each key fractional time. For instance, if there are N key fractional times, and M key normal vectors for each time, then the **keyValue** field contains $N \times M$ normal vectors and the node's output contains M normal vectors.

When a fractional time is received by the **set_fraction** eventIn, the **NormalInterpolator** node computes a sublist of normal vectors based on the list of key fractional times and their corresponding key normal vector sublists. The new computed normal vector list is output on the **value_changed** eventOut. Output normal vectors are unit vectors.

Normal vectors output using the **value_changed** eventOut are interpolated from point to point as if on the surface of a sphere with a radius of 1.0. The pair of unit vectors *P* and *Q* are used as 3-D coordinates, indicating positions on the surface of the unit sphere. During interpolation, intermediate values between *P* and *Q* are computed along the shortest arcing path between *P* and *Q* on the sphere.

An output normal vector list for an input fractional time *t* is computed by the **NormalInterpolator** node by:

1. Scanning the key fractional times to find a pair of adjacent times *t1* and *t2*, where $t1 \leq t \leq t2$.

2. Retrieving the corresponding pair of key normal vector sublists.

3. Computing an intermediate normal vector sublist by linearly interpolating between the key normal vector sublists.

Two adjacent key fractional times *t1* and *t2* may have the same value in order to create a discontinuity, or jump, in the animation path. In this case, the key normal vector sublist corresponding to *t1* (the first of the two identical key fractional times) is used by the **NormalInterpolator** node when linearly interpolating for times less than *t1*, and the key normal vector sublist corresponding to *t2* (the second of the two times) is used when linearly interpolating for times greater than *t2*.

Fractional times are typically sent to the **set_fraction** eventIn by wiring a route from the **fraction_changed** eventOut of a **TimeSensor** node. Fractional times may also be generated by alternate means, such as by nodes that generate generic floating-point values, such as the **ScalarInterpolator** node.

The list of key fractional times or normal vectors can be changed by sending values to the implied **set_key** and **set_keyValue** eventIns of the **key** and **keyValue** exposed fields. When values are received by these inputs, the corresponding field values are changed, and the new values are output using the implied **key_changed** and **keyValue_changed** eventOuts of the exposed fields.

The **NormalInterpolator** node creates no shapes and has no visible effect on a world. A **NormalInterpolator** node may be included as the child of any grouping node but is independent of the coordinate system in use. Typically, interpolators are placed at the end of the outermost group of a VRML file.

The **IndexedFaceSet** Node Syntax

The **IndexedFaceSet** node creates face geometry and may be used as the value of the **geometry** field in a **Shape** node.

SYNTAX	IndexedFaceSet node

```
IndexedFaceSet {
    coord               NULL     # exposedField   SFNode
    coordIndex          [ ]      # field          MFInt32
    texCoord            NULL     # exposedField   SFNode
    texCoordIndex       [ ]      # field          MFInt32
    color               NULL     # exposedField   SFNode
    colorindex          [ ]      # field          MFInt32
    colorPerVertex      TRUE     # field          SFBool
    normal              NULL     # exposedfield   SFNode
    normalIndex         [ ]      # field          MFInt32
    normalPerVertex     TRUE     # field          SFBool
    ccw                 TRUE     # field          SFBool
    convex              TRUE     # field          SFBool
    solid               TRUE     # field          SFBool
    creaseAngle         0.0      # field          SFFloat
    set_coordIndex               # eventIn        MFInt32
    set_texCoordIndex            # eventIn        MFInt32
    set_colorIndex               # eventIn        MFInt32
    set_normalIndex              # eventIn        MFInt32
}
```

The **coord, coordIndex, set_coordIndex, ccw, convex, solid,** and **creaseAngle** fields are as described in Chapter 13.

The **color** and **colorIndex** fields and the **set_colorIndex** and **colorPerVertex** eventIns are as described in Chapter 16.

The **texCoord** and **texCoordIndex** fields and the **set_texCoordIndex** eventIn are as described in Chapter 17.

The value of the **normal** exposed field provides a node that specifies the unit normal vectors used to shade faces in the face set. Typical **normal** field values include the **Normal** node. The default NULL value for this field indicates an empty normal list. When this list is empty, normals are automatically computed for each face or coordinate in the face set, and the **normalIndex** and **normalPerVertex** field values are ignored.

The value of the **normalIndex** field specifies a list of normal indexes that specify normals to use when shading faces in the face set. Each value is an integer index specifying a normal from the normal list specified by the **normal** field. The default value for the **normalIndex** field is an empty normal index list.

The **normalPerVertex** field specifies a TRUE or FALSE value that indicates whether normals from the **Normal** node's normal list are used for each face **(FALSE)** or for each coordinate index of each face **(TRUE)**. The default value for the **normalPerVertex** field is TRUE.

When the **normalIndex** field value is not empty:

- A **normalPerVertex** field value of **FALSE** indicates that one normal index from the normal index list is used for each face in the face set. The first normal index specifies the normal for the first face, the second index for the second face, and so on. There must be one normal index for each face in the face set.

- A **normalPerVertex** field value of **TRUE** indicates that one normal index from the normal index list is used for each coordinate index used in the face set. The first normal index selects the normal for the first coordinate index, the second normal index for the second coordinate index, and so on. There must be one normal index for each coordinate index, including -1 coordinate indexes used as face separators.

When the **normalIndex** field value is empty:

- A **normalPerVertex** field value of **FALSE** indicates that normals are used from the normal list, in order, one per face. The first normal in the list is used for the first face, the second normal for the second face, and so forth. There must be one normal in the list for each face in the face set.
- A **normalPerVertex** field value of **TRUE** indicates that the coordinate indexes in the **coordIndex** field are used as normal indexes. The first coordinate index selects both the coordinate and the normal for the first coordinate, the second coordinate index for the second coordinate, and so on.

When the **normal** field is empty, normals are automatically computed for the faces in the face set. The **ccw** and **creaseAngle** field values can be used to control how these normals are computed.

When the **normal** field is not empty, normals are used from the specified **Normal** node and the **ccw** and **creaseAngle** field values are ignored.

The normal vector node value can be changed by sending a value to the implied **set_normal** eventIn of the **normal** exposed field. When a value is received by this input, the normal node is changed, and the new normal node is output using the implied **normal_changed** eventOut of the exposed field.

The normal index list can be changed by sending a list of normal indexes to the **set_normalIndex** eventIn.

The **ElevationGrid** Node Syntax

The **ElevationGrid** node creates face geometry and may be used as the value for the **geometry** field of a **Shape** node.

SYNTAX	**ElevationGrid node**			

```
ElevationGrid {
    xDimension      0        # field          SFInt32
    xSpacing        0.0      # field          SFFloat
    zDimension      0        # field          SFInt32
    zSpacing        0.0      # field          MFFloat
    height          [ ]      # field          MFFloat
    color           NULL     # exposedField   SFNode
    colorPerVertex  TRUE     # field          SFBool
    normal          NULL     # exposedField   SFNode
    normalPerVertex TRUE     # field          SFBool
    texCoord        NULL     # exposedField   SFNode
    ccw             TRUE     # field          SFBool
    solid           TRUE     # field          SFBool
    creaseAngle     0.0      # field          SFFloat
    set_height               # eventIn        MFFloat
}
```

The **xDimension, xSpacing, zDimension, zSpacing, height, set_height, ccw, solid,** and **creaseAngle** fields are as described in Chapter 14. The **color** and **colorPerVertex** fields are as described in Chapter 16. The **texCoord** field is discussed in Chapter 17.

The value of the **normal** exposed field provides a node that specifies the unit normal vectors used to shade faces built for the elevation grid. Typical **normal** field values include the **Normal** node. The default NULL value for this field indicates an empty normal list. When this list is empty, normals are automatically computed for each grid face in the elevation grid.

The **normalPerVertex** field specifies a **TRUE** or **FALSE** value that indicates whether normals are used for each grid square (**FALSE**) or each grid point (**TRUE**) in the elevation grid. The default value for the **normalPerVertex** field is TRUE.

When the **normalPerVertex** field value is **FALSE,** one normal from the **normal** field's normal list is used for each square in the elevation grid. The first normal is used for the first square of the first row of the grid, the second normal for the second square of the first row, and so forth. There must be one normal for each square in the elevation grid, computed as (xDimension–1)×(zDimension–1).

When the **normalPerVertex** field value is **TRUE,** one normal from the **normal** field's normal list is used for each grid point in the elevation grid. The first normal is used for the first grid point in the first row of the grid, the second normal for the second grid point in the first row, and so on. There must be one normal for each grid point in the elevation grid, computed as xDimension × zDimension.

When the **normal** field is empty, normals are automatically computed for the grid faces in the elevation grid. The **ccw** and **creaseAngle** field values can be used to control how these normals are computed.

When the **normal** field is not empty, normals are used from the specified **Normal** node and the **ccw** and **creaseAngle** field values are ignored.

The normal vector node value can be changed by sending a value to the implied **set_normal** eventIn of the **normal** exposed field. When a value is received by this input, the normal node is changed, and the new normal node is output using the implied **normal_changed** eventOut of the exposed field.

Experimenting with Normals

The following examples provide a more detailed examination of the ways in which the **Normal** and **NormalInterpolator** nodes can be used and how they interact with nodes discussed in previous chapters.

Using Normals

By default, your VRML browser automatically computes normals for you for all of your shapes. By overriding this automatic normal computation, you can apply your own normals and achieve nonstandard shading effects.

Figure 19.21 shows a square face whose front faces forward along the positive Z axis. If you used automatic normals, the face's normal would be the vector (0.0,0.0,1.0) aiming out the Z axis. The VRML text in Figure 19.21 overrides automatic normal computation by specifying a **Normal** node listing four normal vectors, one per coordinate on the face. The normals are all set to be (0.0,0.0,1.0), which is identical to what automatic normal computation would have created. Using these normals, the face is brightest when viewed from the front, and darkens as you look at the face from any edge.

```
#VRML V2.0 utf8
Shape {
    appearance Appearance {
        material Material { }
    }
    geometry IndexedFaceSet {
        coord Coordinate {
            point [
                -1.0 -1.0  0.0,   1.0 -1.0  0.0,
                 1.0  1.0  0.0,  -1.0  1.0  0.0,
            ]
        }
        coordIndex [ 0, 1, 2, 3 ]
        normalPerVertex TRUE
        normal Normal {
            vector [
                0.0  0.0  1.0,   0.0  0.0  1.0,
                0.0  0.0  1.0,   0.0  0.0  1.0,
            ]
        }
        normalIndex [ 0, 1, 2, 3 ]
    }
}
```

Figure 19.21 continues

Figure 19.21   *A square face and four normals.*

The VRML text in Figure 19.22 modifies the normals used in Figure 19.20. The normals bound to the upper and lower right-hand coordinates of the square are changed to the vector (1.0, 0.0, 0.0), which points straight to the right. Using these normals, the left side of the square appears brightest when viewed from the front (because the left-side normals point forward along positive Z), but from that angle the right side appears dark (because the right-side normals point to the right, not forward at the viewer's headlight). As you turn the square and look at it from the right edge, the right side brightens, and the left side darkens.

```
#VRML V2.0 utf8
Shape {
    appearance Appearance {
        material Material { }
    }
    geometry IndexedFaceSet {
        coord Coordinate {
            point [
                    -1.0 -1.0  0.0,   1.0 -1.0  0.0,
                     1.0  1.0  0.0,  -1.0  1.0  0.0,
            ]
        }
        coordIndex [ 0, 1, 2, 3 ]
        normalPerVertex TRUE
        normal Normal {
            vector [
                     0.0  0.0  1.0,   1.0  0.0  0.0,
                     1.0  0.0  0.0,   0.0  0.0  1.0,
            ]
        }
        normalIndex [ 0, 1, 2, 3 ]
    }
}
```

Figure 19.22 continues

Figure 19.22 *A square face with two normals pointing along the positive Z axis and two normals pointing along the positive X axis.*

Smoothly Shading a Half Column

The use of custom normals for the flat square face in Figure 19.22 above makes the face appear bent on the right side. You can use this shading illusion to cause any group of flat faces to appear to be bent, as if for a curved surface like a cylinder or sphere.

Figure 19.23 shows the faceted half column introduced earlier in this chapter. The **IndexedFaceSet** node used to build the half column includes no custom normals. Instead, automatic normals are computed that shade each face as if it were flat.

```
#VRML V2.0 utf8
Shape {
    appearance Appearance {
        material Material { }
    }
    geometry IndexedFaceSet {
        coord Coordinate {
            point [
                -2.00  3.00 0.00,
                -2.00 -3.00 0.00,
                -1.41  3.00 1.41,
                -1.41 -3.00 1.41,
                 0.00  3.00 2.00,
                 0.00 -3.00 2.00,
                 1.41  3.00 1.41,
                 1.41 -3.00 1.41,
                 2.00  3.00 0.00,
                 2.00 -3.00 0.00,
            ]
        }
    }
```

Figure 19.23 continues

```
        coordIndex [
            0, 1, 3, 2, -1,
            2, 3, 5, 4, -1,
            4, 5, 7, 6, -1,
            6, 7, 9, 8, -1,
        ]
    }
}
```

Figure 19.23   *A faceted half column.*

Figure 19.24 shows the same half column, but adds a **creaseAngle** field with a value of 90.0 degrees (1.57 radians). Since all angles between adjacent faces on the half column are less than 90.0 degrees, the VRML browser computes normals to create a smooth-shading effect that shades the faces as if they were curved surfaces. Notice that, at the left and right edges of the half column in Figure 19.24*a*, there are no normals to average together. Instead, these edges use normals that point outward from the face but don't quite match the radial normals needed to shade the half column correctly. For most uses, this is not a problem. This is shown more clearly in Figure 19.24*b*. Where two of these half columns are placed back-to-back so that the left edge of one butts up against the right edge of the other. If the normals at these edges were radial, there would be no visible seam.

```
#VRML V2.0 utf8
Shape {
    appearance Appearance {
        material Material { }
    }
    geometry IndexedFaceSet {
        creaseAngle 1.57
        coord Coordinate {
            point [
                -2.00   3.00 0.00,
                -2.00  -3.00 0.00,
                -1.41   3.00 1.41,
                -1.41  -3.00 1.41,
                 0.00   3.00 2.00,
                 0.00  -3.00 2.00,
                 1.41   3.00 1.41,
                 1.41  -3.00 1.41,
                 2.00   3.00 0.00,
                 2.00  -3.00 0.00,
            ]
        }
        coordIndex [
            0, 1, 3, 2,   -1,
            2, 3, 5, 4,   -1,
            4, 5, 7, 6,   -1,
            6, 7, 9, 8,   -1,
        ]
    }
}
```

Figure 19.24 continues

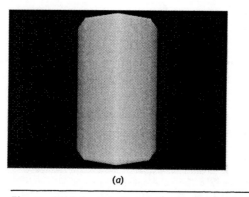 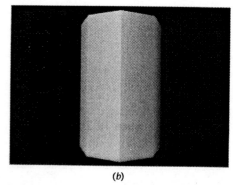

(a)   (b)

Figure 19.24   *(a) A smooth-shaded half column using a crease angle and (b) two half columns with a visible seam caused by inaccuracies in the crease-angle method of computing normals. (The VRML text in this figure builds the world shown in Figure 19.24a.)*

The crease angle approach to automatic normal computation lacks sufficient information to create these radial normals for all face coordinates. The best the browser can do is average together normals for coordinates shared by more than one face. You can compute correct normals because you know that the shape's faces approximate the curved surface of a column.

Figure 19.25*a* shows the half column with custom normals provided in a **Normal** node. These normals are all radial and are computed based on knowledge that the shape's faces approximate a curved surface. As shown in Figure 19.25*b*, the custom normals corrected the problem shown in Figure 19.24*b*.

```
#VRML V2.0 utf8
Group {
    children [
        Shape {
            appearance Appearance {
                material Material { }
            }
            geometry IndexedFaceSet {
                coord Coordinate {
                    point [
                        -2.00   3.00 0.00,
                        -2.00  -3.00 0.00,
                        -1.41   3.00 1.41,
                        -1.41  -3.00 1.41,
                         0.00   3.00 2.00,
                         0.00  -3.00 2.00,
                         1.41   3.00 1.41,
                         1.41  -3.00 1.41,
                         2.00   3.00 0.00,
                         2.00  -3.00 0.00,
                    ]
                }
}
```

Figure 19.25 continues

```
coordIndex [
    0, 1, 3, 2,    -1,
    2, 3, 5, 4,    -1,
    4, 5, 7, 6,    -1,
    6, 7, 9, 8,    -1,
]
normalPerVertex TRUE
normal Normal {
    vector [
        -1.00 0.00 0.00,
        -0.71 0.00 0.71,
         0.00 0.00 1.00,
         0.71 0.00 0.71,
         1.00 0.00 0.00,
    ]
}
normalIndex [
    0, 0, 1, 1,    -1,
    1, 1, 2, 2,    -1,
    2, 2, 3, 3,    -1,
    3, 3, 4, 4,    -1,
]
                    }
                }
            ]
        }
```

(a)   (b)

Figure 19.25 *(a) A smooth-shaded half column using custom normals, and (b) two half columns without a visible seam. (The VRML text in this figure builds the world shown in Figure 19.25a.)*

Smoothly Shading an Elevation Grid

You can provide your own normals for grid points in an elevation grid. This enables you to provide correct normals when the elevation grid represents an approximation of a smooth surface. You can also use elevation grid normals to create special shading effects.

Figure 19.26 shows a small, flat elevation grid. Grid-point normals are provided using a **Normal** node. To create an unusual shading effect, the normals for the center of the elevation grid are aimed outward, while those at the edges are aimed up. When viewed from directly above, this creates a darkened center to the grid. As you move down to ground level and view the center of the grid from a sharper angle, the center of the grid brightens.

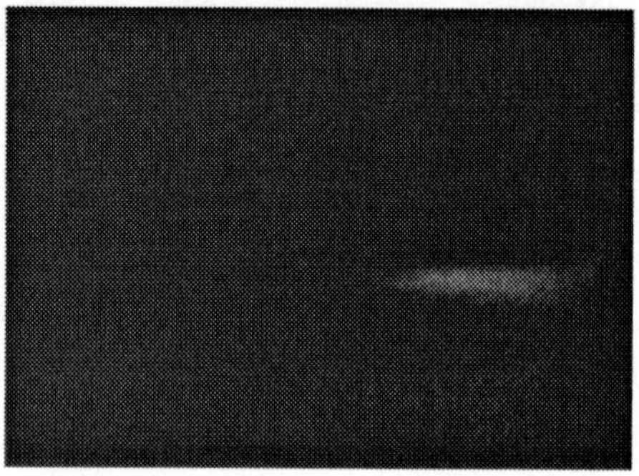

```
#VRML V2.0 utf8
Shape {
    appearance Appearance {
        material Material { }
    }
    geometry ElevationGrid {
        xDimension 5
        zDimension 5
        xSpacing    1.0
        zSpacing    1.0
        solid       FALSE
        height [
            0.0, 0.0, 0.0, 0.0, 0.0,
            0.0, 0.0, 0.0, 0.0, 0.0,
            0.0, 0.0, 0.0, 0.0, 0.0,
            0.0, 0.0, 0.0, 0.0, 0.0,
            0.0, 0.0, 0.0, 0.0, 0.0,
        ]
        normalPerVertex TRUE
        normal Normal {
            vector [
            # First row
                0.0 1.0  0.0,   0.0 1.0  0.0,
                0.0 1.0  0.0,   0.0 1.0  0.0,
                0.0 1.0  0.0,
            # Second row
                0.0 1.0  0.0,  -0.3 0.3 -0.3,
                0.0 0.5 -0.5,   0.3 0.3 -0.3,
                0.0 1.0  0.0,
            # Third row
                0.0 1.0  0.0,  -0.5 0.5  0.0,
               -0.5 0.5  0.0,   0.5 0.5  0.0,
                0.0 1.0  0.0,
            # Fourth row
                0.0 1.0  0.0,  -0.3 0.3 -0.3,
                0.0 0.5 -0.5,   0.3 0.3 -0.3,
                0.0 1.0  0.0,
            # Fifth row
                0.0 1.0  0.0,   0.0 1.0  0.0,
                0.0 1.0  0.0,   0.0 1.0  0.0,
                0.0 1.0  0.0,
            ]
        }
    }
}
```

Figure 19.26   *An elevation grid using a special shading effect.*

Animating Normals

Figure 19.27 extends the square and normals example in Figure 19.21. A **TimeSensor** node is added to act as an animation clock, and a **NormalInterpolator** node is used to interpolate between sets of normal vectors. The output of the **NormalInterpolator** node is routed to the **Normal** node of the square shape. During the animation, the normals on the right side of the face animate from pointing forward along the positive Z axis, to pointing to the right, then back again. The shading of the square varies as the normals vary.

```
#VRML V2.0 utf8
Group {
    children [
    # Animated shape
        Shape {
            appearance Appearance {
                material Material { }
            }
            geometry IndexedFaceSet {
                coord Coordinate {
                    point [
                        -1.0 -1.0  0.0,   1.0 -1.0  0.0,
                         1.0  1.0  0.0,  -1.0  1.0  0.0,
                    ]
                }
                normal DEF AnimNorm Normal {
                    vector [
                        0.0  0.0  1.0,   0.0  0.0  1.0,
                        0.0  0.0  1.0,   0.0  0.0  1.0,
                    ]
                }
                coordIndex  [ 0, 1, 2, 3 ]
                normalIndex [ 0, 1, 2, 3 ]
                normalPerVertex TRUE
            }
        },
    # Animation clock
        DEF Clock TimeSensor {
            cycleInterval 4.0
            loop TRUE
        },
```

Figure 19.27 continues

```
# Animation normals
    DEF NormPath NormalInterpolator {
        key [ 0.0, 0.5, 1.0 ]
        keyValue [
        # time 0.0 normals
            0.0  0.0  1.0,    0.0  0.0  1.0,
            0.0  0.0  1.0,    0.0  0.0  1.0,
        # time 0.5 normals
            0.0  0.0  1.0,    1.0  0.0  0.0,
            1.0  0.0  0.0,    0.0  0.0  1.0,
        # time 1.0 normals
            0.0  0.0  1.0,    0.0  0.0  1.0,
            0.0  0.0  1.0,    0.0  0.0  1.0,
        ]
    }
    ]
}
ROUTE Clock.fraction_changed TO NormPath.set_fraction
ROUTE NormPath.value_changed TO AnimNorm.set_vector
```

Figure 19.27 *A square face and animated normals.*

Summary

A normal indicates the orientation of a face and is used by the VRML browser to determine how brightly to shade a face. Normals can be thought of as arrows pointing outward from the front of a face. The more a normal arrow points at a light, such as the headlight, the brighter the face is shaded. Faces that are oriented directly toward a light have normals that point straight at the light and are shaded the brightest, while faces whose normals point away from a light are shaded darker.

The front of a face is the side where the coordinates of its perimeter appear ordered in a counterclockwise fashion. You can use the right-hand rule to determine which direction a normal will point: Curl the fingers of your right hand in the direction coordinates are ordered around a face's perimeter, then stick your thumb out as if hitchhiking. Your thumb will point in the direction of the face's normal.

The normal for a coordinate or face is computed using three consecutive coordinates: 0, 1, and 2. Compute two vectors, one as the difference between coordinates 1 and 0, and the other as the difference between coordinates 2 and 1. Next, compute the cross product of the two vectors to get a third vector pointing outward from the face. This is the normal for the face at coordinate 1.

To shade a shape using your own normals, specify a list of normals in the **Normal** node. Each field of the **Normal** node includes a list of values. Normals in a list are referred to using normal indices. The first normal in the list has an index of 0, the second an index of 1, and so on.

For elevation grids, when the **normalPerVertex** field value is **FALSE**, one normal from the normal list is used for each grid square. When the **normalPerVertex** field value is **TRUE**, one normal is used for each grid point.

For indexed face sets, you can bind selected normals to selected coordinates by providing a list of normal indexes in the **normalIndex** field of the **IndexedFaceSet** node. When the **normalPerVertex** field value is **FALSE**, one normal index is used for each face in the face set. When the **normalPerVertex** field value is **TRUE**, one normal index is used for each face coordinate.

A shape's normals can be animated by using a **NormalInterpolator** node. The interpolator uses a list of key fractional times in the **key** field and key normal vector sublists in the **keyValue** field. Each key fractional time specifies a time, between 0.0 and 1.0, at which the corresponding key normal vector sublist is to be output from the interpolator node. For input fractional times between key fractional times, the interpolator node interpolates between adjacent, key normal vector sublists in the list and outputs the computed normal vector list.

## CHAPTER 20

Lighting Your Worlds

Lights in a VRML world serve the same purpose as lights in the real world: they brighten a scene and highlight points of interest. Until now you have used only the headlight, a light automatically created by your VRML browser and attached to your current viewpoint. You can also create additional lights and place them anywhere you like within your VRML world.

VRML supports three node types to control lighting: **PointLight, DirectionalLight,** and **SpotLight.** Using these light nodes, you can brighten a dark room corner, highlight a picture on a wall, or add a stage spotlight. Creative lighting can add tremendously to the realism of any world.

Understanding Lighting

Using VRML you can create lights additional to the headlight in your world, placing them at specific locations and aiming them in specific directions. Shape faces are then shaded based on whether they face any of these additional lights, as well as whether they face you and your headlight.

VRML supports three types of lights, each mimicking the attributes of real-world lights: point lights, directional lights, and spotlights.

> **SIDEBAR: THE SHAPE OF LIGHTS** VRML lights have no form or shape. They describe how to light a world, but not what the shape of an actual light is, like a lamp or a sun. Since VRML lights have no shape, you will not be able to see them when they are placed in a world. You see only their lighting effects on the world.

Point Lights

A *point light* is a light located in your world that emanates light in a radial pattern in all directions, as if the light rays were all coming from a single point. In the real world, a lamp with its shade removed acts like a point light.

Figure 20.1 shows the effect of a point light placed in the middle of a world of spheres. The sides of the spheres that face the point light are illuminated, while the sides that face away are not. The arrows in Figure 20.1 show how the light rays of a point light emanate in a radial pattern in all directions from its location.

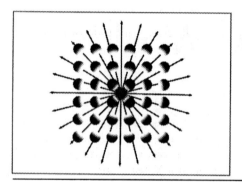

Figure 20.1   *The rays from a point light radiate out from it in all directions.*

In VRML, a point light is created by specifying its 3-D location in your world, its intensity, and its color. Light intensities can be varied from 0.0 (off) to 1.0 (fully on), similar to turning a dimmer knob on a real light.

The color of a light is controlled by an RGB color, just like that used to set a material color. A red light, for instance, gives a red glow to a world. You can similarly use green, blue, or any other color of light for other lighting effects.

Directional Lights

A *directional light* is a light aimed at your world from infinitely far away so that all of its light rays are parallel and point in the same direction. In the real world, the sun is essentially a directional light. It is so far away that by the time the sun's rays reach the Earth, they are nearly parallel.

Figure 20.2 shows a directional light whose parallel light rays shine from left to right on a world of spheres. The sides of the spheres that face the directional light are illuminated, while the sides that face away are not. The arrows in Figure 20.2 show how the light rays of the directional light all project in the same direction.

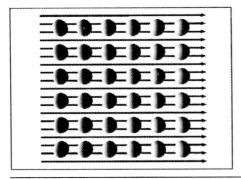

Figure 20.2 *The rays from a directional light all project in the same direction.*

In VRML, a directional light is created by specifying an aim direction for the light. You define an *aim direction* in the same way you define rotation axes: Imagine a line drawn between two points, one always at the origin (0.0, 0.0, 0.0) and the other under your control. As you move the second point around, the line between the origin and your second point changes direction. For instance, if you place your second point at (1.0, 0.0, 0.0), then the line drawn between the origin and your point is a horizontal line pointing to the right. This is an aim direction that aims to the right.

Aim directions can point a directional light in any direction. To point a light straight up the Y axis use an aim direction of (0.0, 1.0, 0.0). To point straight down the negative Z axis, use an aim direction of (0.0, 0.0, -1.0). You can also use diagonal aim directions, for instance, to aim a directional light 45.0 degrees in the positive X, Y, and Z directions at once by using (1.0, 1.0, 1.0).

VRML directional lights also have an intensity and a color, just like point lights.

Spotlights

A *spotlight* is a light placed at a location in your world, aimed in a specific direction, and constrained so that its rays emanate within a light cone. Shapes that fall within that cone of light are illuminated by the spotlight, and others are not.

Figure 20.3 shows the effect of a spotlight placed in the middle of a world of spheres and aimed to the right. The spotlight's cone is tightened to hit only the right spheres and light up their left sides. The remaining spheres are outside the spotlight's cone of light and are shaded dark. The arrows in Figure 20.3 show how the spotlight's cone of light rays emanate from it.

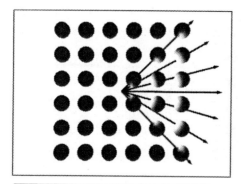

Figure 20.3   *The rays from a spotlight radiate within a strictly defined area.*

In VRML, a spotlight is created by specifying its 3-D location in your world, an aim direction, and two values to control the size and illumination level within an illumination cone: the cutoff angle and the beam width. The *cutoff angle* is the angular spread of the cone of illumination, measured from the central axis of the cone to the outermost edge. A smaller angle makes the cone more narrow, and a larger angle makes the cone wider. The *beam width* is a second spread angle for a smaller cone within the cone of illumination controlled by the cutoff angle. The spotlight's illumination is uniform within the inner cone, and gradually drops off between the inner and outer cones. You can use these two cone angles to control lighting within the spotlight's beam.

VRML spotlights also have an intensity and a color, just like point lights.

Coloring Lights

You may recall from physics classes that white light is made up of all colors of light. When white light shines on a colored surface, some colors of light are absorbed by the surface, while others are reflected. Absorbed light turns into heat, and reflected light bounces off the surface and may, eventually, reach your eye.

The colors of light that are absorbed and reflected by a surface are determined by that surface's color. A blue surface, for instance, reflects blue light and absorbs the rest. So, when a white light shines on a blue surface, the blue components of that white light are reflected, and the remainder is absorbed. What you see when you look at such a surface is the reflected light. White surfaces reflect all colors of light, and black surfaces absorb all colors of light.

In VRML, you set the color of shapes using the **Material, Color,** and texturing nodes. When white light from the headlight shines on those colored shapes, each shape reflects back some of the colors in the light. A blue shape reflects blue light, a red shape reflects red light, and so on. Lighting in VRML, then, works the same way as lighting in the real world.

The headlight is a white light and cannot be colored. Point lights, directional lights, and spotlights that you add to your world may, however, be colored lights.

Unlike white light, colored light contains only a narrow range of light colors. When a colored light shines on a white surface, the only light colors available for reflection are those that are present in the colored light. For instance, a white surface illuminated by a red light will look red since the only reflected light is red light. A white surface lit by a green light will look green, and so on. The color of a shape, then, depends on both its color and the color of light that shines on it.

The situation is trickier when you shine a colored light on a colored surface. A blue surface, for instance, can reflect only blue light. A red light, however, has no blue light in it. So, a blue surface illuminated by a red light appears black since there is no blue light to reflect off of it. Similarly, a blue surface lit by a green light appears black. A blue surface lit by a blue light, however, appears blue.

In VRML, you can set the light color for any point light, directional light, and spotlight. Using colored lights, you can specify creative lighting effects. You can give a room a warm glow by using a yellowish light. You can make a world seem cold and harsh by using a light with a slight blue tinge to it.

Ambient Light

In the real world, surfaces are lit by light sources shining on them directly *and* by light that has bounced off other surfaces. Living room lamps, for instance, may aim straight up at the ceiling, and the light that bounces off the ceiling gives the living room a gentle wash of light.

Direct light is illumination that results from light traveling in a straight, direct, unobstructed line from a light to a shape. The ceiling lit by an upward-pointing living room lamp is being lit by direct light from that lamp.

Ambient light is illumination that results from the scattering and reflection of light as it bounces around a room. The furniture in a room lit by a lamp aimed at the ceiling is being lit by ambient light that originated at that lamp.

In VRML, you can simulate the effects of both direct and ambient light. Parts of shapes that are within a direct line of sight of a **PointLight, DirectionalLight,** or **Spot-Light** node's light are illuminated by direct light. To control ambient light levels in a world, you can provide an *ambient intensity* level for each light. A high value means that the light contributes a great deal to the ambient brightness of a world. A sun, for instance, would have a high ambient intensity. A low ambient-intensity value means that the light doesn't contribute much to the ambient-light level of a world. A flashlight with a tightly focused beam, for instance, would have a low ambient intensity.

When shading a shape, your VRML browser adds together the ambient effects of all nearby lights in your world and uses this intensity to control the ambient-light level for the shape. A low ambient-light level makes the lighting seem stark and gives the scene less contrast, like exploring a dark room by candlelight. A higher ambient-light level softens the room lighting and makes it more natural. A very high ambient-light level washes out a room, reducing the effects of shading and making the room seem more like a cartoon.

Light Attenuation

Light attenuation is a description of how a light's illumination gradually drops off with distance from the light source. Using light attenuation, you can make some lights shine over a large area, while others illuminate only their immediate surroundings.

VRML's **PointLight** and **SpotLight** nodes each provide two light attenuation controls: a set of three attenuation parameters, and a light radius. The *light radius* controls the maximum illumination area of the light. With a small radius, a light only illuminates a small area surrounding the light. With a large radius, the light can illuminate a large part of your world.

The *attenuation parameters* of the **PointLight** and **SpotLight** nodes control how illumination decreases from the center to the edge of the light cone's radius. You can use these parameters to make all points in the illuminated area have the same brightness level, or you can make the illumination level drop off rapidly with distance from the light. This enables you to create a variety of lighting effects.

Since a directional light does not have a location, the **DirectionalLight** node does not have a radius or attenuation parameters. Instead, directional lights are limited to illuminate only those shapes built within the same group, as specified by a parent grouping node such as the **Transform** node. Shapes within the same group as the **DirectionalLight** node are lit by it, while those outside the group are not. This enables you to control the range of a directional light in a manner analogous to the radius of **PointLight** and **SpotLight** nodes.

Multiple Lights

You can use multiple lights in your world. Each one can be of a different type, at a different location, and with a different color. To prevent all of your lights from illuminating all of your shapes, you can use the radius control to restrict point lights and spotlights or **Transform** nodes to restrict directional lights.

TIP 3-D graphics boards usually support only a limited number of simultaneous lights in a world. This limit may be as low as just one, for the headlight, but is typically eight or more. Using more lights in your world than your graphics board can support may cause noticeable slowing or may cause some lights to be skipped when your world is drawn. Check the manuals for your graphics board and your VRML browser to see what light limitations they each have.

The Headlight

The headlight is a white **DirectionalLight** node that is automatically added to your worlds and controlled by the VRML browser. When on, the headlight aims forward and always illuminates anything in front of you.

Most browsers have a feature in one of their menus to turn the headlight on and off. Additionally, VRML's **NavigationInfo** node, discussed in Chapter 26, enables you to turn the headlight on or off for your world. While working with lights, you may want to use these features to turn off the headlight so that you see only the lighting caused by your additional lights and not that caused by the headlight.

Shadows

In the real world, shapes cast shadows when they block light rays. In VRML, however, shapes do not cast shadows. Shadow computation is a complicated and time-consuming operation that cannot easily be performed interactively. Since VRML shapes do not cast shadows, a light can illuminate a shape even if the shape is behind another shape. VRML light travels straight through shapes, unhindered.

Shadows in the real world tell us much about the solidity and positioning of shapes. Without shadows, VRML worlds can look odd and ambiguous. It is sometimes difficult, for instance, to tell whether one shape sits directly on top of another, or whether it is hovering above it. Without a shadow cast by the hovering shape, it is difficult to determine where it actually is.

You can compensate for this lack of shadows in VRML worlds by creating your own fake shadows. For any shape; look at how it would block light and where it should cast a shadow. Then, create a face using, for example, an indexed face set, color it black and semitransparent, and place it where the shadow should be. While not a perfect representation of shadows, the effect is close, easy to do, and can make a huge difference in the realism of your world.

Lighting Flat Shapes

Intuitively, aiming a spotlight at the center of a large cube's face should create a bright spot in the middle of that face. The actual effect, however, may vary with the VRML browser and graphics hardware you are using.

Typical graphics hardware and software computes the effect of lighting only at the coordinates of a shape, such as the corners of a cube's faces. Using those computed, coordinate-lighting values, the hardware or software then shades from one coordinate's value to the next as it shades across the face of the shape. You use a similar shading effect when you assign a different material color to each coordinate of a face and let the VRML browser smoothly vary colors from one to the next across the face.

Now, imagine that you aim a spotlight straight at the center of a square and build the square using typical graphics hardware or software. Each of the four corners of the square is the same distance from the spotlight and has the same computed illumination intensity from the light. Using these four identical values at the four corners of the square, the graphics hardware or software will smoothly vary from one to the next across the face. But since all four coordinate values are identical, no variation occurs and the entire square is drawn at the same brightness. The spotlight's bright spot that should have been drawn at the center of the square is completely missed.

Properly computing the effect of spotlights aimed like the one previously described requires sophisticated graphics hardware that is out of the price range of most individuals. Graphics software can properly compute this type of lighting but at such a cost in drawing time that it is usually impractical for interactive graphics.

As a result, shapes lit by spotlights and point lights in a VRML world will not always show the exact lighting effect you expect from observing the real world.

One way to compensate for these lighting limitations is to create *meshed shapes* that use a kind of mesh, or grid, of coordinates and small faces to create a surface. You can use a mesh even when creating flat shapes.

If you aim a spotlight at the center of a meshed square, lighting is computed at every coordinate in the mesh. Each tiny facet will be shaded independently. Facets near the center of the square mesh and closer to the spotlight are shaded bright. Those farther away at the edges of the square mesh will be shaded dark. This creates a bright spot in the center of the square mesh where the spotlight's light strikes the surface.

Smooth shapes such as cylinders, cones, and spheres are typically already meshed in this way to create their faceted shapes. Boxes, however, are not meshed. You can create your own flat or curved meshed surfaces using **IndexedFaceSet** and **ElevationGrid** nodes.

TIP   While meshing a shape does compensate for lighting problems inherent in typical graphic hardware and software, it also drastically increases the number of coordinates in a shape and the time it takes your computer to draw the shape. Meshing a flat shape should be done only when you must have proper lighting effect on that shape. The rest of your shapes should be left unmeshed in order to achieve maximum drawing performance.

The **PointLight** Node Syntax

The **PointLight** node creates a directional light source whose rays emanate in a radial pattern in all directions.

SYNTAX   **PointLight node**

```
PointLight {
    on                 TRUE          # exposedField  SFBool
    location           0.0 0.0 0.0   # exposedField  SFVec3f
    radius             100.0         # exposedField  SFFloat
    intensity          1.0           # exposedField  SFFloat
    ambientIntensity   0.0           # exposedField  SFFloat
    color              1.0 1.0 1.0   # exposedField  SFColor
    attenuation        1.0 0.0 0.0   # exposedField  SFVec3f
}
```

The **on** exposed field specifies a **TRUE** or **FALSE** value that indicates whether the light is turned on or off. When on, the light's illumination affects the shading of shapes in the world. The default value is **TRUE**, which indicates that the light is turned on.

The value of the **location** exposed field specifies a 3-D coordinate for the location of the light source in the current coordinate system. The default value places the light at the origin.

The value of the **radius** exposed field specifies the radius of a sphere of illumination, centered at the light source location. Shapes within the sphere are illuminated by the light source, while those outside of the sphere are not. The **radius** field value must be greater than or equal to 0.0. The default value creates a sphere of illumination with a radius of 100.0 units.

The light source location and radius are both relative to the current coordinate system, as created by a grouping node like the **Transform** node. Translation, rotation, or scaling of the coordinate system affects both the location and size of the light source's sphere of illumination.

The value of the **intensity** exposed field controls the brightness of the light source. A value of 0.0 turns the light source dark, while 1.0 sets the illumination to full brightness. The default value is 1.0.

The value of the **ambientIntensity** exposed field controls the effect the light source has on the ambient-light level for shapes within the light's sphere of illumination. A value of 0.0 indicates the light source has no effect on the ambient-light level. A value of 1.0 indicates the light affects the ambient-light level a great deal. The default value is 0.0.

The value of the **color** field specifies an RGB color for the light. The color contains three floating-point values, one each for the red, green, and blue components of the color. The default value creates a white light source.

The **intensity** and **color** field values combine to determine the colored-light level for the light source, as follows:

```
lightColor = color x intensity
```

The **intensity** field value acts like a dimmer knob that controls the brightness of the color selected by the **color** field value.

The **intensity, ambientIntensity,** and **color** field values combine to determine the colored, ambient-light level contribution from the light source as follows:

```
lightAmbientColor = color x intensity x ambientIntensity
```

The **intensity** and **ambientIntensity** field values act together like dimmer knobs that control the ambient-light color selected by the **color** field value.

The values of the **attenuation** exposed field specify a set of three control parameters that indicate how the light source's brightness varies from the center of the sphere of illumination outward to the sphere's radius. For a shape coordinate within the sphere of illumination at a distance d from the light's location, the light color brightness at that shape coordinate is determined as follows:

```
attenuatedColor = lightColor / (attenuation[0] + attenuation[1] x d +
attenuation[2] x d²)
```

The first **attenuation** field value **attenuation[0]** controls whether light has a constant brightness within the sphere of illumination. The second value **attenuation[1]** controls how the light brightness drops off with distance from the light. The third value **attenuation[2]** controls how the light brightness drops off with the square of the distance from the light. All three parameters can be used in combination to create various lighting effects. All attenuation values must be greater than or equal to 0.0. The default value for the **attenuation** field creates a light whose illumination is constant within the sphere of illumination.

TIP Some VRML browsers may not support the full range of control offered by the values of the **attenuation** field. These browsers may approximate the actual attenuation.

The point light's attributes can be changed by sending values to the implied **set_on**, **set_location**, **set_radius**, **set_intensity**, **set_ambientIntensity**, **set_color**, and **set_attenuation** eventIns of the exposed fields. When values are received by these inputs, the corresponding field values are changed, and the new values are output using the implied **on_changed**, **location_changed**, **radius_changed**, **intensity_changed**, **ambientIntensity_changed**, **color_changed**, and **attenuation_changed** eventOuts of the exposed fields.

Lighting attributes and how they combine with material attributes are discussed further in Chapter 21.

The **DirectionalLight** Node Syntax

The **DirectionalLight** node creates a directed light source whose rays travel in parallel in a specified direction.

SYNTAX	DirectionalLight node

```
DirectionalLight {
    on                  TRUE            # exposedField  SFBool
    intensity           1.0             # exposedField  SFFloat
    ambientIntensity    0.0             # exposedField  SFFloat
    color               1.0 1.0  1.0    # exposedField  SFColor
    direction           0.0 0.0 -1.0    # exposedField  SFVec3f
}
```

The **on, intensity, ambientIntensity,** and **color** fields are described in the section entitled "The **PointLight** Node Syntax."

The value of the **direction** exposed field specifies a 3-D vector indicating the aim direction for the light source. The aim vector is specified as three floating-point values, one each for the X, Y, and Z components of a 3-D coordinate in the current coordinate system. The light source's light rays travel parallel to an imaginary line drawn between the current coordinate system origin and the 3-D coordinate. The default value of the **direction** field creates a light source aimed forward along the negative Z axis.

The light from a directional light illuminates all shapes built within the current group and its descendants, as built by a parent grouping node for a group containing the **DirectionalLight** node.

The directional light's attributes can be changed by sending values to the implied **set_on, set_direction, set_intensity, set_ambientIntensity,** and **set_color** eventIns of the exposed fields. When values are received by these inputs, the corresponding field values are changed, and the new values are output using the implied **on_ changed, direction_changed, intensity_changed, ambientIntensity_changed,** and **color_changed** eventOuts of the exposed fields.

Lighting attributes and how they combine with material attributes are discussed further in Chapter 21.

TIP Some VRML browsers cannot limit the effects of a directional light to only those shapes built within the same group. For such browsers, directional lights may illuminate all shapes in the world, regardless of the coordinate system in which the **DirectionalLight** node is placed.

The **SpotLight** Node Syntax

The **SpotLight** node creates a light source whose rays emanate in a radial pattern from a location, but only within a cone aimed in a specified direction.

SYNTAX	SpotLight node

```
SpotLight {
        on                  TRUE               # exposedField  SFBool
        location            0.0 0.0  0.0       # exposedField  SFVec3f
        direction           0.0 0.0 -1.0       # exposedField  SFVec3f
        radius              100.0              # exposedField  SFFloat
        intensity           1.0                # exposedField  SFFloat
        ambientIntensity    0.0                # exposedField  SFFloat
        color               1.0 1.0  1.0       # exposedField  SFColor
        attenuation         1.0 0.0  0.0       # exposedField  SFVec3f
        beamWidth           1.570796           # exposedField  SFFloat
        cutOffAngle         0.785398           # exposedField  SFFloat
}
```

The **on, location, radius, intensity, ambientIntensity,** and **color** fields are as described for the **PointLight** node. The **direction** field is described in the section entitled "The **DirectionalLight** Node Syntax."

The value of the **cutOffAngle** exposed field specifies the spread angle of a cone of illumination whose tip is at the spotlight's location and whose cone axis is aligned parallel with the spotlight's aim direction. The cutoff angle specifies an angular spread measured in radians from the cone's axis to the sides of the cone. Shapes within the cone of illumination are lit by the spotlight. Increasing the **cutOffAngle** field value widens the spread of the cone, while decreasing the angle narrows the cone of illumination. The cutoff angle must be between 0.0 and 90.0 degrees (½ radians). The default value is 45.0 degrees (0.785398 radians).

The value of the **beamWidth** exposed field specifies the spread angle of a cone of uniform illumination within the larger cone of illumination controlled by the **cutOffAngle** field value. The tip of the inner cone is at the spotlight's location, and the cone's axis is aligned parallel with the spotlight's aim direction. The beam width specifies an angular spread measured in radians from the cone's axis to the sides of the inner cone. Illumination within the inner cone is a uniform full brightness, as controlled by the **intensity** field value and attenuation. Illumination between the inner and outer cones drops off from full brightness at the inner cone's edge to no brightness at the outer cone's edge. If the **beamWidth** field value is greater than the **cutOffAngle** field value, then illumination within the entire cone of illumination is uniform. The beam-width angle must be between 0.0 and 90.0 degrees (½ radians). The default value for the **beamWidth** field is 90.0 degrees (1.57 radians).

The spotlight's attributes can be changed by sending values to the implied **set_on**, **set_location**, **set_direction**, **set_radius**, **set_intensity**, **set_ambientIntensity**, **set_color**, **set_attenuation**, **set_beamWidth**, and **set_cutOffAngle** eventIns of the exposed fields. When values are received by these inputs, the corresponding field values are changed, and the new values are output using the implied **on_changed**, **location_changed**, **direction_changed**, **radius_changed**, **intensity_changed**, **ambientIntensity_changed**, **color_changed**, **attenuation_changed**, **beamWidth_changed**, and **cutOffAngle_changed** eventOuts of the exposed fields.

Lighting attributes and how they combine with material attributes are further discussed in Chapter 21.

Experimenting with Lighting

The following examples provide a more detailed examination of the ways in which the **PointLight**, **DirectionalLight**, and **SpotLight** nodes can be used to light your world.

Creating a Test World

The **PointLight**, **DirectionalLight**, and **SpotLight** nodes each have several features that can interrelate in complex fashions. It is convenient to begin using these parameters within a simple test world, such as a field of spheres. Several of the following examples use such a sphere world.

Figure 20.4 shows a sphere world containing 36 white spheres arranged in six rows of six. The **Transform** node at the top of the file centers the spheres around the origin. The world in Figure 20.4 is illuminated by the viewer headlight. Later examples that add lights to this sphere world assume it is in a file named "spheres.wrl."

```
#VRML V2.0 utf8
Transform {
    translation -7.5 -7.5 0.0
    children [
        DEF BallRow Group {
            children [
                DEF Ball Shape {
                    appearance Appearance {
                        material Material { }
                    }
                    geometry Sphere { }
                },
                Transform { translation  3.0 0.0 0.0 children USE Ball },
                Transform { translation  6.0 0.0 0.0 children USE Ball },
                Transform { translation  9.0 0.0 0.0 children USE Ball },
                Transform { translation 12.0 0.0 0.0 children USE Ball },
                Transform { translation 15.0 0.0 0.0 children USE Ball }
            ]
        },
        Transform { translation 0.0  3.0 0.0 children USE BallRow },
        Transform { translation 0.0  6.0 0.0 children USE BallRow },
        Transform { translation 0.0  9.0 0.0 children USE BallRow },
        Transform { translation 0.0 12.0 0.0 children USE BallRow },
        Transform { translation 0.0 15.0 0.0 children USE BallRow }
    ]
}
```

Figure 20.4 *A sphere world illuminated by the headlight.*

Creating a Test Mesh

As noted earlier, lighting calculations are typically performed by your VRML browser only for the coordinates of a shape. This can cause some lighting effects, particularly those created by spot and point lights, to be missed by the VRML browser as it shades a shape. One way to avoid this problem is to create a fine mesh of faces instead of using one large face. Such a mesh can be created using an **ElevationGrid** node and a list of 0.0 heights for the grid points. Several of the following examples use such a mesh to illustrate lighting features.

Figure 20.5 shows a square mesh with 144 grid points arranged in 12 rows of 12. The **Transform** node at the top of the file centers the mesh around the origin. The world in Figure 20.5 is illuminated by the viewer headlight. Later examples that use this mesh assume it is in a file named "`mesh.wrl`."

```
#VRML V2.0 utf8
Transform {
    translation -8.25 0.0 -8.25
    children Shape {
        appearance Appearance {
            material Material { }
        }
        geometry ElevationGrid {
            xDimension 12
            zDimension 12
            xSpacing    1.5
            zSpacing    1.5
            solid       FALSE
            height [
                0.0, 0.0, 0.0, 0.0, 0.0, 0.0, 0.0, 0.0, 0.0, 0.0, 0.0, 0.0,
                0.0, 0.0, 0.0, 0.0, 0.0, 0.0, 0.0, 0.0, 0.0, 0.0, 0.0, 0.0,
                0.0, 0.0, 0.0, 0.0, 0.0, 0.0, 0.0, 0.0, 0.0, 0.0, 0.0, 0.0,
                0.0, 0.0, 0.0, 0.0, 0.0, 0.0, 0.0, 0.0, 0.0, 0.0, 0.0, 0.0,
                0.0, 0.0, 0.0, 0.0, 0.0, 0.0, 0.0, 0.0, 0.0, 0.0, 0.0, 0.0,
                0.0, 0.0, 0.0, 0.0, 0.0, 0.0, 0.0, 0.0, 0.0, 0.0, 0.0, 0.0,
                0.0, 0.0, 0.0, 0.0, 0.0, 0.0, 0.0, 0.0, 0.0, 0.0, 0.0, 0.0,
                0.0, 0.0, 0.0, 0.0, 0.0, 0.0, 0.0, 0.0, 0.0, 0.0, 0.0, 0.0,
                0.0, 0.0, 0.0, 0.0, 0.0, 0.0, 0.0, 0.0, 0.0, 0.0, 0.0, 0.0,
                0.0, 0.0, 0.0, 0.0, 0.0, 0.0, 0.0, 0.0, 0.0, 0.0, 0.0, 0.0,
                0.0, 0.0, 0.0, 0.0, 0.0, 0.0, 0.0, 0.0, 0.0, 0.0, 0.0, 0.0,
                0.0, 0.0, 0.0, 0.0, 0.0, 0.0, 0.0, 0.0, 0.0, 0.0, 0.0, 0.0,
            ]
        }
    }
}
```

Figure 20.5   *A flat mesh created using an **ElevationGrid** node.*

Using Point Lights

Figure 20.6*a* inlines the sphere world and adds a point light at the center. The point light's illumination spreads in a radial pattern in all directions, always lighting the sphere sides that face inward toward the middle of the sphere world. Varying the **intensity** field value brightens and darkens the light, and varying the **color** field changes the light source's color. You can also vary the **ambientIntensity** field to brighten the ambient light level in the world. Figure 20.6*b* shows the sphere world and point light with an **ambientIntensity** field value of 0.8. This high ambient intensity reduces the contrast from bright to dark in the world and begins to wash it out.

```
#VRML V2.0 utf8
Group {
    children [
        PointLight {
            location 0.0 0.0 0.0
            radius    12.0
        },
        Inline {
            url "spheres.wrl"
            bboxCenter 0.0 0.0 0.0
            bboxSize   16.0 16.0 1.0
        }
    ]
}
```

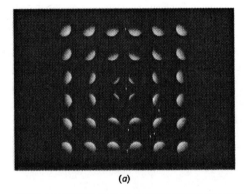
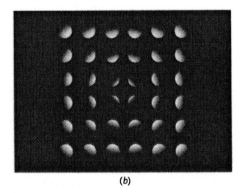

(a)   (b)

Figure 20.6 (a) *A sphere world illuminated by a point light in the center and* (b) *the same sphere world with the point light's ambient intensity set high. (The VRML text in this figure builds the world shown in Figure 20.6a.)*

By varying the **attenuation** field values you can control how illumination varies from the center of the point light's sphere of illumination to its outer edges. The default attenuation values create a constant illumination level within the sphere. The VRML text in Figure 20.7 specifies attenuation values that gradually reduce the illumination level from the center to the edges. This attenuation creates a more realistic lighting.

```
#VRML V2.0 utf8
Group {
    children [
        PointLight {
            location 0.0 0.0 0.0
            radius    12.0
            attenuation 0.0 0.3 0.0
        },
        Inline {
            url "spheres.wrl"
            bboxCenter 0.0 0.0 0.0
            bboxSize   16.0 16.0 1.0
        }
    ]
}
```

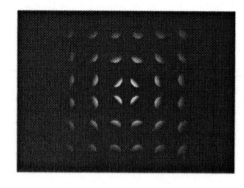

Figure 20.7   *A sphere world illuminated by a point light with attenuation control.*

Varying the point light's **radius** field value increases and decreases the size of the sphere of illumination. Figure 20.8 reduces the radius to half the distance from the center of the sphere world to its edges. Notice that spheres outside the point light's sphere of illumination are unlit by the point light, including the point light's direct and ambient lighting contributions.

```
#VRML V2.0 utf8
Group {
    children [
        PointLight {
            location 0.0 0.0 0.0
            radius    5.0
            ambientIntensity 0.8
        },
        Inline {
            url "spheres.wrl"
            bboxCenter 0.0 0.0 0.0
            bboxSize   16.0 16.0 1.0
        }
    ]
}
```

Figure 20.8   *A sphere world illuminated by a point light with a small radius.*

Building a Glowing Shape Using a Point Light

The radial illumination created using a **PointLight** node is a convenient feature that you can use to make shapes appear to glow. Start by creating a shape, such as a sphere. Give the shape an emissive color or texture so that its brightness is unaffected by lighting. Finally, place the shape in your world and add a point light at the center of the shape. The radial illumination of the point light brightens the sides of things that face your shape, as if that shape is glowing, as shown in Figure 20.9. The ceiling and pillars are from Figure 13.16 and are contained within the file "vaulted.wrl," which inlines "vault.wrl" to build a single piece of the ceiling. The floor is the mesh created in Figure 20.5 and is inlined from the file "mesh.wrl."

```
#VRML V2.0 utf8
Group {
    children [
    # Vaulted ceiling and columns
        Inline {
            url "vaulted.wrl"
            bboxCenter 0.0 1.0 0.0
            bboxSize   6.0 2.0 6.0
        },
    # Floor
        Inline {
            url "mesh.wrl"
            bboxCenter 0.0 0.0 0.0
            bboxSize   15.0 0.0 15.0
        },
    # Glowing sphere
        Transform {
            translation 0.0 1.0 0.0
            children [
                PointLight {
                    location  0.0 0.0 0.0
                    radius    10.0
                    intensity 1.0
                    ambientIntensity 0.2
                    color 0.7 0.5 0.0
                },
                Shape {
                    appearance Appearance {
                        # No material, use emissive texturing
                        texture ImageTexture {
                            url "fire.jpg"
                        }
                    }
                    geometry Sphere { radius 0.2 }
                }
            ]
        },
    # Pedestal pyramid
        Shape {
            appearance DEF White Appearance {
                material Material { }
            }
```

Figure 20.9 continues

```
                    geometry IndexedFaceSet {
                        coord Coordinate {
                            point [
                            # Around the base
                                -0.12 0.03  0.12,    0.12 0.03  0.12,
                                 0.12 0.03 -0.12,   -0.12 0.03 -0.12,
                            # Tip
                                 0.0  0.63  0.0,
                            ]
                        }
                        coordIndex [
                            0, 1, 4, -1,  1, 2, 4, -1,
                            2, 3, 4, -1,  3, 0, 4, -1,
                        ]
                        solid TRUE
                    }
                },
        # Pedestal base
            Transform {
                translation 0.0 0.015 0.0
                children Shape {
                    appearance USE White
                    geometry Box { size 0.4 0.03 0.4 }
                }
            }
        ]
    }
```

Figure 20.9   *A glowing sphere within a gothic building.*

Animating Lights

You can animate any of the fields of a lighting node. For instance, to vary the light's brightness over time, you can use a **TimeSensor** node to clock a **ScalarInterpolator** node that outputs floating-point intensity values routed into the **intensity** exposed field of the light node.

Figure 20.10 creates a blinking lightbulb. To make the lightbulb appear to blink, three circuits are built. The first circuit uses a **TimeSensor** node clock and a **Scalar-Interpolator** node to blink a **PointLight** node's intensity from on to off and back on again during the animation. For realism, when the **PointLight** node is turned off by the animation, the bulb's emissive color should be turned down as well, and the diffuse color turned up. To accomplish this, two additional circuits are wired from the **TimeSensor** node to two **ColorInterpolator** nodes that route to the **diffuseColor** and **emissiveColor** fields of the **Material** node used to color the bulb. Using all three of these circuits, when the animation runs, the light source blinks on and off, and the bulb's shading changes with it. The effect is one of a realistic blinking lightbulb.

```
#VRML V2.0 utf8
Group {
    children [
    # Generic lighting for ambience
        DirectionalLight {
            intensity 0.2
            ambientIntensity 1.0
        },
    # Light bulb
        DEF BulbLight PointLight {
            radius 16.0
            color 1.0 0.0 0.0
        },
    # Light bulb shape
        Shape {
            appearance Appearance {
                material DEF BulbColor Material {
                    emissiveColor 1.0 0.3 0.3
                    diffuseColor  0.0 0.0 0.0
                }
            }
            geometry DEF Bulb Sphere { }
        },
    # Wall
        Transform {
            translation 0.0 0.0 -1.1
            rotation 1.0 0.0 0.0 1.57
            children Inline { url "mesh.wrl" }
        },
    # Animation clock
        DEF Clock TimeSensor {
            cycleInterval 4.0
            loop TRUE
        },
    # Animation brightness and colors
        DEF BulbIntensity ScalarInterpolator {
            key [ 0.0, 0.5, 0.5, 1.0 ]
            keyValue [ 1.0, 1.0, 0.0, 0.0 ]
        },
        DEF BulbDiffuse ColorInterpolator {
            key [ 0.0, 0.5, 0.5, 1.0 ]
            keyValue [
                0.0 0.0 0.0,  0.0 0.0 0.0,
                1.0 0.3 0.3,  1.0 0.3 0.3
            ]
        },
        DEF BulbEmissive ColorInterpolator {
            key [ 0.0, 0.5, 0.5, 1.0 ]
            keyValue [
                1.0 0.3 0.3,  1.0 0.3 0.3,
                0.0 0.0 0.0,  0.0 0.0 0.0,
            ]
        }
    }
    ]
}
```

Figure 20.10 continues

```
ROUTE Clock.fraction_changed       TO BulbIntensity.set_fraction
ROUTE Clock.fraction_changed       TO BulbDiffuse.set_fraction
ROUTE Clock.fraction_changed       TO BulbEmissive.set_fraction
ROUTE BulbIntensity.value_changed  TO BulbLight.set_intensity
ROUTE BulbDiffuse.value_changed    TO BulbColor.set_diffuseColor
ROUTE BulbEmissive.value_changed   TO BulbColor.set_emissiveColor
```

Figure 20.10   *A blinking lightbulb.*

Using Directional Lights

Figure 20.11*a* inlines the sphere world and adds a directional light aiming to the right. The directional light's illumination lights the left sides of spheres in the world. You can aim the directional light in any direction. Figure 20.11*b* uses the same sphere world, but aims the directional light diagonally up and to the right by changing the **direction** field values to 0.5 0.5 0.0.

```
#VRML V2.0 utf8
Group {
    children [
        DirectionalLight {
            direction 1.0 0.0 0.0
        },
        Inline {
            url "spheres.wrl"
            bboxCenter 0.0 0.0 0.0
            bboxSize   16.0 16.0 1.0
        }
    ]
}
```

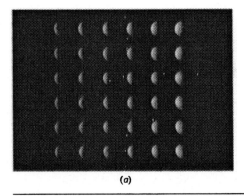 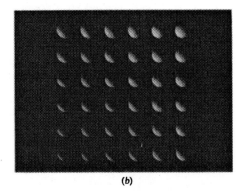

(a)   (b)

Figure 20.11 *(a) A sphere world illuminated by a directional light aiming to the right and (b) aimed up and to the right. (The VRML text in this figure builds the world shown in Figure 20.11a.)*

As with **PointLight** nodes, you can vary the **DirectionalLight** node's **intensity** field value to brighten and darken the light, vary the **color** field value to change the light source's color, and vary the **ambientIntensity** field value to change the ambient light level in the world.

A point light's illumination is limited by attenuation and its radius, a directional light's illumination is limited to those shapes within the light's group. Figure 20.12 uses two **Transform** nodes to create two new groups. The first transform group contains a **DirectionalLight** node aimed to the right and an inline of the sphere world. The second transform group contains a second **DirectionalLight** node aimed to the left and another instance of the sphere world. Since directional lights can only illuminate those shapes built within the same group, the first directional light only illuminates the left sphere world, while the second directional light only illuminates the right sphere world.

```
#VRML V2.0 utf8
Group {
    children [
        Transform {
            translation -9.0 0.0 0.0
            children [
                DirectionalLight {
                    direction 1.0 0.0 0.0
                },
                DEF Spheres Inline {
                    url "spheres.wrl"
                    bboxCenter 0.0 0.0 0.0
                    bboxSize  16.0 16.0 1.0
                },
            ]
        },
        Transform {
            translation 9.0 0.0 0.0
            children [
                DirectionalLight {
                    direction -1.0 0.0 0.0
                },
                USE Spheres
            ]
        }
    ]
}
```

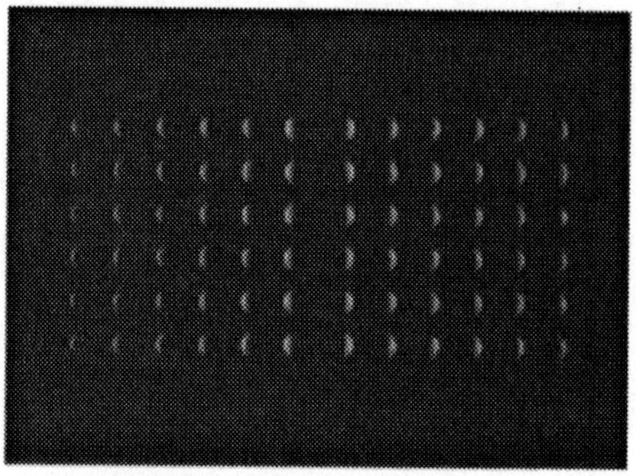

Figure 20.12 *Two sphere worlds illuminated by two directional lights.*

T I P Some VRML browsers cannot limit the illumination effects of directional lights. Using these browsers, both sets of spheres in Figure 20.12 are illuminated by both directional lights.

Simulating Sunlight Using a Directional Light

Technically, the sun is a point light: the sun's rays emanate in all directions in a radial pattern from the sun's location. However, due to the earth's distance from the sun, the tiny spread of the sun's rays that reach the earth are nearly parallel. You can simulate the sun's nearly parallel rays using a **DirectionalLight** node. By varying the aim direction of the light, you can simulate morning, noon, and dusk in a virtual world.

Figure 20.13 builds a world using the gothic ceiling and pillars from Figure 13.16, a flat floor, and a **DirectionalLight** node to simulate the sun. Figure 20.13*a* shows the world with the light's aim direction set to point to the right, and down a little, such as for sunrise. Figure 20.13*b* shows the world with the light's aim direction pointing straight down, such as for noon. Figure 20.13*c* again shows the world, but now with the light's aim direction pointing to the left, and down a little, such as for sunset. To make the lighting more realistic, you can make the light's color more orange during sunrise and sunset and use a higher ambient intensity at noon.

```
#VRML V2.0 utf8
Group {
    children [
        DirectionalLight {
            direction  0.8 -0.2 -0.2
            intensity 1.0
            ambientIntensity 0.3
            color 1.0 0.6 0.0
        },
    # Vaulted ceiling and columns
        Inline {
            url "vaulted.wrl"
            bboxCenter 0.0 1.0 0.0
            bboxSize   6.0 2.0 6.0
        },
    # Floor
        Shape {
            appearance Appearance {
                material Material { }
            }
            geometry Box { size 16.0 0.01 16.0 }
        }
    ]
}
```

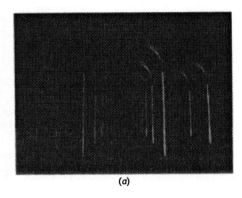

(a)

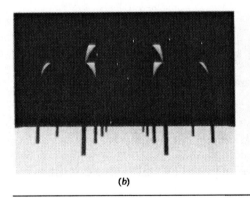

(b)

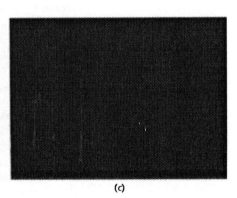

(c)

Figure 20.13 *A directional light used to simulate the sun (a) at sunrise, (b) at noon, and (c) at sunset. (The VRML text in this figure builds the world shown in Figure 20.13a.)*

You can animate the direction of the directional light in the previous example by using a **TimeSensor** node and a **PositionInterpolator** node. The SFVec3f output of the **PositionInterpolator** node can be used to specify a direction instead of a 3-D position. When routed into the **direction** exposed field of a **DirectionalLight** node, the animation causes the lighting direction to change from sunrise to sunset. At the same time, you can vary the light's color and ambient intensity value to create realistic animation. Figure 20.14 uses these animation nodes to cause the sunlight direction to change from sunrise to sunset.

```
#VRML V2.0 utf8
Group {
    children [
    # Animated sunlight
        DEF SunLight DirectionalLight {
            direction  0.8 -0.2 -0.2
            intensity 1.0
            ambientIntensity 0.5
            color 1.0 0.6 0.0
        },
    # Animation clock
        DEF Clock TimeSensor {
            cycleInterval 10.0
            loop TRUE
startTime 1
        },
    # Animation directions
        DEF LightDirection PositionInterpolator {
            key [ 0.0, 0.5, 1.0 ]
            keyValue [ 0.8 -0.2 -0.2, 0.0 -1.0 -0.2, -0.8 -0.2, -0.2 ]
        },
    # Animation colors and ambient intensity
        DEF LightColor ColorInterpolator {
            key [ 0.0, 0.5, 1.0 ]
            keyValue [ 1.0 0.6 0.0, 1.0 0.9 0.7, 1.0 0.3 0.1 ]
        },
        DEF LightAmbient ScalarInterpolator {
            key [ 0.0, 0.5, 1.0 ]
            keyValue [ 0.3, 0.7, 0.2 ]
        },
    # Vaulted ceiling and columns
        Inline {
            url "vaulted.wrl"
            bboxCenter 0.0 1.0 0.0
            bboxSize   6.0 2.0 6.0
        },
    # Floor
        Shape {
            appearance Appearance {
                material Material { }
            }
            geometry Box { size 16.0 0.01 16.0 }
        }
    ]
}
ROUTE Clock.fraction_changed        TO LightDirection.set_fraction
ROUTE Clock.fraction_changed        TO LightColor.set_fraction
ROUTE Clock.fraction_changed        TO LightAmbient.set_fraction
ROUTE LightDirection.value_changed TO SunLight.set_direction
ROUTE LightColor.value_changed      TO SunLight.set_color
ROUTE LightAmbient.value_changed    TO SunLight.set_ambientIntensity
```

Figure 20.14 *The sunlight direction animated using a PositionInterpolator node.*

Using Spotlights

Figure 20.15 inlines the sphere world and adds a spotlight at the center. The spotlight's illumination spreads in a radial pattern within a cone aiming to the right. The sides of spheres that are within the spotlight's cone and are facing the spotlight are illuminated. By varying the **cutOffAngle** field value, you can widen or narrow the spotlight's cone of illumination. Figure 20.15*a* above uses a 22.5-degree cone angle (0.392 radians). Figure 20.15*b* widens this angle to 45.0 degrees (0.785 radians).

```
#VRML V2.0 utf8
Group {
    children [
        SpotLight {
            location  0.0 0.0 0.0
            direction 1.0 0.0 0.0
            radius    12.0
            cutOffAngle 0.393
        },
        Inline {
            url "spheres.wrl"
            bboxCenter 0.0 0.0 0.0
            bboxSize   16.0 16.0 1.0
        }
    ]
}
```

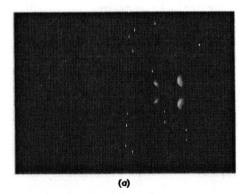
(a)

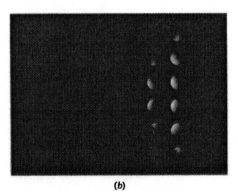
(b)

Figure 20.15   (a) *A sphere world illuminated by a spotlight in the center aiming to the right and (b) by a wide-angle spotlight. (The VRML text in this figure builds the world shown in Figure 20.15a.)*

Within the spotlight's cone of illumination, controlled by the **cutOffAngle** field value, is a second, inner cone whose spread angle is controlled by the **beamWidth** field value. Illumination within the inner cone has a uniform brightness. Illumination between the cones falls off from full brightness at the edge of the inner cone to no brightness at the edge of the outer cone. Shapes outside of the outer cone aren't illuminated at all by the spotlight.

Figure 20.16 shows a spot light aimed at a mesh. Figure 20.16*a* sets inner and outer illumination cones to the same 45.0-degree (0.785-radian) spread angle. This creates uniform lighting within the spotlight. Figure 20.16*b* sets the outer cone to 45.0 degrees and the inner cone to 22.5 degrees (0.392 radians). Illumination within the inner cone is uniform, but drops off between the inner and outer cones. Figure 20.16*c* shows the outer cone set to 45.0 degrees and the inner cone to 0.5 degrees (0.09 radians). With a 0.5 degree spread angle for the inner cone, there is almost no part of the spotlight's beam that has uniform brightness. Illumination falls off from the center of the spotlight to the edges.

```
#VRML V2.0 utf8
Group {
    children [
        SpotLight {
            location  0.0 5.0 0.0
            direction 0.0 -1.0 0.0
            radius    12.0
            intensity 1.0
            cutOffAngle 0.785
            beamWidth   0.785
        },
        Inline {
            url "mesh.wrl"
            bboxCenter 0.0 0.0 0.0
            bboxSize   16.0 1.0 16.0
        }
    ]
}
```

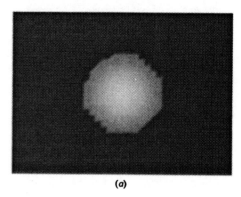

(a)

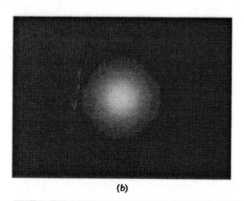

(b)

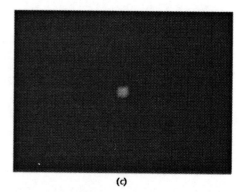

(c)

Figure 20.16 *A mesh illuminated by spotlights with (a) inner and outer cones set to 45.0 degrees, (b) the outer cone set to 45.0 degrees and the inner set to 22.5 degrees, and (c) the outer cone set to 45.0 degrees and the inner set to 0.5 degrees. (The VRML text in this figure builds the world shown in Figure 20.16a.)*

As with **PointLight** nodes, you can vary the **SpotLight** node's **intensity** field value to brighten and darken the light, vary the **color** field value to change the light source's color, and vary the **ambientIntensity** field value to change the ambient-light level in the world. Similar to the **PointLight** node, the **radius** field controls the maximum extent of the spotlight's cone of illumination.

Creating Fake Shadows

As noted earlier, the light from VRML light sources shines straight through shapes and does not create shadows. This can make your worlds look surrealistic. Shapes that are meant to be sitting on top of a surface, like a table or the floor, can appear to be floating, because they cast no shadows onto the surface. To compensate for this lack of shadows, you can create your own fake shadows using dark-colored, semi-transparent geometry placed where the shadows should be.

Figure 20.17 shows a very simple world consisting of three balls floating above a floor and lit from above by a **DirectionalLight**. In Figure 20.17*a* there are no fake shadows. Figure 20.17*b*, however, adds fake circular shadows on the floor, directly beneath the spheres. The addition of these fake shadows makes it much easier to see whether the spheres are floating or not and where they are in relation to each other.

```
#VRML V2.0 utf8
Group {
    children [
    # Lighting
        DirectionalLight {
            direction 0.0 -1.0 0.0
            ambientIntensity 0.5
        },
    # Floor
        Shape {
            appearance Appearance {
                material Material { }
            }
            geometry Box { size 8.0 0.01 8.0 }
        },
    # Spheres and fake shadows
        Transform {
            translation 0.0 4.0 2.0
            children [
                Shape {
                    appearance Appearance {
                        material Material { diffuseColor 1.0 1.0 0.0 }
                    }
                    geometry Sphere { }
                },
            # Shadow
                Transform {
                    translation 0.0 -3.95 0.0
                    children Shape {
                        appearance DEF ShadowAppearance Appearance {
                            material Material {
                                diffuseColor 0.0 0.0 0.0
                                transparency 0.5
                            }
                        }
                    }
```

Figure 20.17 continues

```
                        geometry Cylinder {
                            height 0.0
                            side   FALSE
                            bottom FALSE
                        }
                    }
                }
            ]
        },
        Transform {
            translation 2.0 2.0 -2.0
            children [
                Shape {
                    appearance Appearance {
                        material Material { diffuseColor 0.0 1.0 0.0 }
                    }
                    geometry Sphere { radius 2.0 }
                },
            # Shadow
                Transform {
                    translation 0.0 -1.95 0.0
                    children Shape {
                        appearance USE ShadowAppearance
                        geometry Cylinder {
                            radius 2.0
                            height 0.0
                            side   FALSE
                            bottom FALSE
                        }
                    }
                }
            ]
        },
        Transform {
            translation -2.0 2.5 0.0
            children [
                Shape {
                    appearance Appearance {
                        material Material { diffuseColor 0.0 1.0 1.0 }
                    }
                    geometry Sphere { radius 0.75 }
                },
```

Figure 20.17 continues

```
# Shadow
    Transform {
        translation 0.0 -2.45 0.0
        children Shape {
            appearance USE ShadowAppearance
            geometry Cylinder {
                radius 0.75
                height 0.0
                side    FALSE
                bottom FALSE
            }
        }
    }
   ]
  }
 ]
}
```

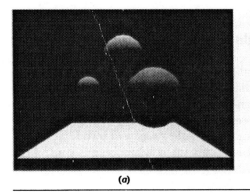 

(a)   (b)

Figure 20.17 *(a) A simple world without fake shadows and (b) with fake shadows. (The VRML text in this figure builds the world shown in Figure 20.17b.)*

The fake shadows created in Figure 20.17b are built using the tops of cylinders, positioned below the spheres. You can also create shadows using other geometric types, typically indexed face sets.

TIP Sometimes it is difficult to figure out exactly what shape a fake shadow should have. This is particularly true when trying to create a fake shadow for a complex shape. One technique for dealing with these situations is to duplicate the original shape, give the duplicate a dark semitransparent color, then squish the shape flat using a **Transform** node and its **scale** field. Place the flattened, dark duplicate beneath the original to create the illusion of a shadow. You can also rotate the duplicate before squishing it in order to create a skewed shadow from a light source that isn't straight up overhead.

Summary

By default, the VRML browser creates only a single light in a world: the headlight. The headlight is a white light attached to your current viewpoint that moves as you move and always points straight ahead into the world.

You can add additional lights to the world with one or more **PointLight, DirectionalLight,** and **SpotLight** nodes. Point lights are lights in the world whose rays emanate in a radial pattern in all directions, like a lamp's lightbulb when the shade is removed. Directional lights are lights that aim in a single direction with all of their light rays parallel, like those of the distant sun. Spotlights are lights that aim in a specific direction from one point in the world and illuminate only those shapes within a cone of light emanating from the spotlight.

All three light nodes have an **on** field for turning the light on and off, an **intensity** field for setting the light's brightness, an **ambientIntensity** field for controlling how the light affects the overall ambient-light level in the world, and a **color** field for setting the light's RGB color.

Point and spot lights are positioned using the **location** field value of the **PointLight** and **SpotLight** nodes. The light location is a 3-D coordinate in the current coordinate system.

Directional lights and spotlights are aimed in a specific direction using the **direction** field value of the **DirectionalLight** and **SpotLight** nodes. The aim direction is a 3-D vector that can be thought of as a 3-D coordinate in the current coordinate system. An imaginary line between the coordinate system origin and this coordinate indicates a direction along which the light's rays will travel.

Point lights have a sphere of illumination whose size is controlled by the **radius** field value of the **PointLight** node. Shapes within the sphere will be illuminated by the light, while those outside the sphere will not.

Spotlights have a cone of illumination whose angular spread is controlled by the **cutOffAngle** field value of the **SpotLight** node. The maximum extent of this cone is controlled by the node's **radius** field. Shapes within the cone will be illuminated by the light, while those outside the cone will not. A second, inner cone, whose angular spread is controlled by the **beamWidth** field value, specifies a cone of uniform illumination. Shapes within the inner cone will be lit by the light's full brightness. Illumination between the inner and outer cones drops off from full brightness at the edge of the inner cone to no brightness at the edge of the outer cone.

Illumination within a point light's sphere, or a spotlight's cone of illumination can drop off, or attenuate, with distance from the light. Attenuation can be controlled using the **attenuation** field values of the **PointLight** and **SpotLight** nodes.

Illumination from a directional light is limited to those shapes built within the same group as the **DirectionalLight** node.

CHAPTER 21

Creating Shiny Shapes Using Materials

Using a **Material** node and its **diffuseColor** field, you control the color used to shade shapes. Whether lit by your headlight or by additional lights, your shapes have so far appeared as if they are made out of a dull, matte material. Using additional fields in the **Material** node, you can direct the VRML browser to build shiny shapes and simulate plastics, metals, and other shiny materials.

The shading of shiny shapes is controlled by **Material** node fields, including the **shininess, specularColor,** and **ambientIntensity** fields. These fields work together with the lighting in your world to control how shiny shapes are drawn.

Understanding How to Create Shiny Shapes

The **Material** node introduced in Chapter 10 has a number of additional fields for creating shiny shapes drawn by the VRML browser. These features are effective when you include one or more point lights, directional lights, or spotlights in your world.

Light Reflection

In the real world when light rays strike a surface, some are absorbed by it, some are reflected off it, and some are transmitted through the surface. For example, a window transmits most light rays and reflects and absorbs the rest. A table, however, transmits no light and reflects or absorbs all of the light that shines on it. In any case, the light that reflects or is transmitted through a surface continues into the world, bouncing from surface to surface to illuminate the scene.

437

The real-world physics of lighting is very complex. The way light reflects off a real-world surface depends on the surface's material, how rough it is, what temperature it is, and what its electrical properties are. All of these surface properties may vary for different colors of light up and down the spectrum. Computer programs written to simulate some or all of these lighting effects can draw astonishingly realistic images of virtual worlds. They also can take hours to draw a single image. To draw virtual worlds quickly, VRML uses a simplified method of simulating real-world lighting.

VRML's simulation of real-world light reflection includes two types of reflection: diffuse reflection and specular reflection. These two reflection types mimic the way light reflects off shapes in the real world. Using them, you can create realistic imagery, often drawn by your VRML browser in less than a second.

Diffuse Reflection

Diffuse reflection bounces light off a surface in random directions, scattering it about. Since each ray striking the surface bounces in a different random direction, the overall effect is one of a gentle, diffuse lighting on a shape. There are no glints, sparkles, or highlights. Instead, a shape drawn based only on diffuse reflection computations will look dull, or matte, as if painted with flat house paint.

Figure 21.1 shows a vase shaded using only diffuse reflection. The **diffuseColor** field of the **Material** node controls the color of the light reflected by diffuse reflection.

Figure 21.1   *A vase shaded using diffuse reflection.*

Specular Reflection

Specular reflection bounces light off a surface in a mathematically predictable way that makes shiny surfaces reflect the world around them. A mirror, for instance, bounces incoming light back out so that you see a perfect reflection of yourself.

Real-world shiny surfaces reflect other shapes in the world, such as a chrome bumper reflecting the sky, ground, and other cars nearby. Such reflections are very time-consuming to compute. VRML simplifies the simulation of real-world lighting by skipping shape reflections and concentrating on light-source reflections. In other words, shiny surfaces in VRML can reflect point-light sources, directional-light sources, and spotlight sources in the world, but not shapes. This is sufficient to create many realistic scenes. In the real world, the reflection of light sources causes glints, sparkles, and highlights on shiny surfaces. By simulating these same light-source reflections, VRML enables you to build shiny surfaces as well as the diffuse, dull surfaces built using only the **diffuseColor** field of a **Material** node.

Figure 21.2 shows a vase shaded using specular reflection. Notice the highlights on the vase. The highlights are reflections of the headlight and of a point-light source above and to the right of the vase.

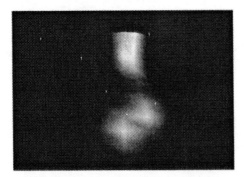

Figure 21.2 *A vase shaded using specular reflection.*

Recall that point lights, directional lights, and spotlights have no actual shape. How, then, are they reflected by a shiny shape in VRML? The highlights on the vase in Figure 21.2 are in a sense, faked. The highlights on this vase are bright spots that reflect distant light sources as if the light sources had tiny dots as their shapes. For point-light sources and spotlight sources, the tiny dot is located at the light source's location. For directional-light sources, the dot is located infinitely far away in the direction from which the light's rays are coming.

Diffuse and Specular Reflections

Real-world surfaces rarely exhibit just diffuse reflection or just specular reflection. Most surfaces exhibit a little of each characteristic. Dull surfaces exhibit diffuse reflection, but only a little specular reflection. Shiny surfaces exhibit some diffuse reflection, and more specular reflection.

Between dull and shiny surfaces, semishiny surfaces exhibit both diffuse and specular reflection. The shininess of a surface is evident by the size of the highlight showing the reflection of a light. A dull surface has a broad highlight, while a shinier surface has a smaller highlight. A very shiny surface has a very small, tightly focused highlight.

Figure 21.3 shows a variety of vases, each lit by the headlight and a point-light source above and to the right of each vase. Figure 21.3*a* shows a dull vase with a broad diffuse highlight. Figure 21.3*b* shows a somewhat shinier surface with a narrower highlight. Figure 21.3*c* shows a shinier surface, and *d* a very shiny surface with a small highlight.

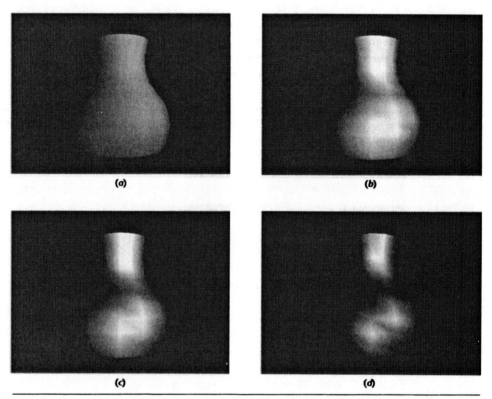

(a)   (b)

(c)   (d)

Figure 21.3   *Vases illustrating a range of shininess levels, including (a) a dull vase, (b) a somewhat shiny vase, (c) a shiny vase, and (d) a very shiny vase.*

The **shininess** field in the **Material** node provides you control over the amount of diffuse and specular reflection exhibited by any shape. Using this field, you can control the size of the specular reflection highlight to simulate shiny or dull shapes.

Specular Colors

The color of a real-world, specular-reflection highlight on a real-world shiny surface depends partly on the surface material and partly on the color of the light being reflected. Some surfaces, like shiny plastics, reflect white lights as white highlights. Other surfaces, such as metals, reflect white lights as gold-, silver-, or copper-colored highlights.

Computation of real-world, colored-highlight effects takes too long to compute for interactive graphics applications, such as VRML browsers. Instead, VRML enables you to set the color of a specular reflection highlight yourself by using the **specularColor** field of the **Material** node. By choosing the color of the highlight, you can simulate plastics and metals.

Ambient Light

Ambient light is light that has bounced from surface to surface many times and provides a general, overall illumination for a room. A living room lamp aimed at the ceiling, for instance, bounces light off the ceiling to create a gentle wash of ambient light for the room.

The **ambientIntensity** field of **PointLight**, **SpotLight**, and **DirectionalLight** nodes provides the principal control of the ambient-light level in a world. You can also control how a shape responds to ambient light by using the **ambientIntensity** field of the shape's **Material** node. Using a high ambient intensity for a shape makes it subject to lighting by the world's ambient-light level, which is determined by the light sources in use. A low ambient intensity for a shape makes it less subject to ambient lighting. Shiny shapes, for instance, are typically not illuminated by ambient lighting, while dull shapes are.

The **Material** Node Syntax

The **Material** node specifies material attributes and may be used as the value for the material field of an **Appearance** node.

SYNTAX	**Material node**

```
Material {
    diffuseColor       0.8 0.8 0.8    # exposedField  SFColor
    emissiveColor      0.0 0.0 0.0    # exposedField  SFColor
    transparency       0.0            # exposedField  SFFloat
    ambientIntensity   0.2            # exposedField  SFFloat
    specularColor      0.0 0.0 0.0    # exposedField  SFColor
    shininess          0.2            # exposedField  SFFloat
}
```

The **diffuseColor, emissiveColor,** and **transparency** fields are as described in Chapter 10.

The value of the **ambientIntensity** exposed field controls how the material is affected by the ambient-light level of the world. A high value makes the material highly affected by the ambient-light level, while a low value reduces the ambient lighting effect on the material. Values must be between 0.0 and 1.0. The default value for this field creates a low ambient effect for the material.

The value of the **specularColor** exposed field specifies the RGB specular color of light reflected off a shape by specular reflections. This controls the color of the highlight on shiny shapes. For many real-world materials, the specular color is the same as that of the light sources shining on the shape (typically white). For metals, however, the specular color tends more toward the color of the material, as specified by the **diffuseColor** field value. The default value for the **specularColor** field is black, which disables specular reflections for the shape.

The value of the **shininess** exposed field controls the shininess of the material. A value of 0.0 makes shapes dull and matte. Higher values make shapes appear more shiny. The visual effect is a reduction in the size of the specular reflection highlight. Typical values are between 0.0 and 0.5. The default value for the field creates a moderately shiny material when a specular color is specified.

The ambient intensity, specular color, and shininess of a material can be changed by sending values to the implied **set_ambientIntensity**, **set_specularColor**, and **set_shininess** eventIns of the **ambientIntensity**, **specularColor**, and **shininess** exposed fields. When values are received by these inputs, the corresponding field values are changed, and the new values are output using the implied **ambientIntensity_changed**, **specularColor_changed**, and **shininess_changed** eventOuts of the exposed fields.

SIDEBAR: MATERIAL FEATURE SUPPORT Some VRML browsers may not support the full range of features specified by the **Material** node. Table 21.1 shows how VRML browsers may handle unsupported **Material** node features. For more information about how browsers may handle other unsupported features, see Table 10.4

Table 21.1 How VRML Browsers May Handle Unsupported Material Node Features

Unsupported Feature	*Action*
Ambient intensity	When a VRML browser cannot support ambient intensities, the **ambientIntensity** field value may be ignored. Browsers that do not support a different ambient intensity setting for each shape in the world, may average the ambient intensities of all shapes in the world and use that single ambient intensity to control the overall ambient-light level in the world.
Specular color and shininess	When a VRML browser cannot support specular reflection, the **specularColor** and **shininess** fields are ignored. For browsers that only support a specular intensity, the browser converts the color specified in the **specularColor** field to a brightness level by multiplying the red value by 0.32, the green value by 0.57, and the blue value by 0.11.

Experimenting with Advanced Materials

The following examples provide a more detailed examination of the ways in which the **Material** node can be used and how it interacts with nodes and fields discussed in previous chapters.

Making Shapes Shiny

Figure 21.4 shows a variety of vases, each built by an **Extrusion** node and lit by the headlight and a point-light source above and to the right of the vase. Figure 21.4*a* shows a dull vase with a broad diffuse highlight. Figure 21.4*b* shows a somewhat shinier surface with a narrower highlight. Figure 21.4*c* shows a shinier surface, and Figure 21.4*d* shows a very shiny surface with a small highlight. Table 21.2 provides the **Material** node values used for each of the four vases.

```
#VRML V2.0 utf8
Group {
    children [
        PointLight {
            location 3.0 3.0 3.0
            ambientIntensity 0.2
        },
        Shape {
            appearance Appearance {
                material Material {
                    ambientIntensity 0.2
                    diffuseColor 0.10 0.10 0.10
                    specularColor 0.80 0.80 0.80
                    shininess 0.16
                }
            }
            geometry Extrusion {
                creaseAngle 1.57
                endCap FALSE
                solid  FALSE
                crossSection [
                # Circle
                    1.00  0.00,    0.92 -0.38,
                    0.71 -0.71,    0.38 -0.92,
                    0.00 -1.00,   -0.38 -0.92,
                   -0.71 -0.71,   -0.92 -0.38,
                   -1.00 -0.00,   -0.92  0.38,
                   -0.71  0.71,   -0.38  0.92,
                    0.00  1.00,    0.38  0.92,
                    0.71  0.71,    0.92  0.38,
                    1.00  0.00
                ]
```

Figure 21.4 continues

```
spine [
# Straight-line
    0.0 0.0 0.0,   0.0 0.4 0.0,
    0.0 0.8 0.0,   0.0 1.2 0.0,
    0.01 1.6 0.0,  0.02 2.0 0.0,
    0.02 2.4 0.0,  0.02 2.8 0.0,
    0.03 3.2 0.0,  0.03 3.6 0.0,
    0.0 4.0 0.0
]
scale [
    1.8  1.8,  1.95  1.95,
    2.0  2.0,  1.95  1.95
    1.8  1.8,  1.5   1.5
    1.2  1.2,  1.05  1.05,
    1.0  1.0,  1.05  1.05,
    1.15 1.15,
]
        }
     }
  ]
}
```

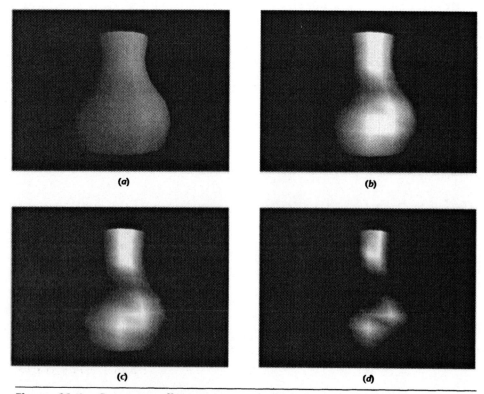

(a)   (b)

(c)   (d)

Figure 21.4 *Gray vases illustrating a range of shininess levels, including (a) a dull vase, (b) a somewhat shiny vase, (c) a shiny vase, and (d) a very shiny vase. (The VRML text in this figure builds the world shown in Figure 21.4d.)*

Table 21.2 **Material** Node Values for the Vases Shown in Figure 21.4

Figure	ambientIntensity	diffuseColor	specularColor	shininess
21.4a	0.2	0.4 0.4 0.4	0.0 0.0 0.0	0.2
21.4b	0.4	0.15 0.15 0.15	0.7 0.7 0.7	0.05
21.4c	0.4	0.15 0.15 0.15	0.7 0.7 0.7	0.08
21.4d	0.2	0.10 0.10 0.10	0.8 0.8 0.8	0.16

Making Shiny Metallic and Plastic Shapes

In the real world, metal shapes reflect different colors of light differently. This has the effect of coloring the highlight on shiny metal shapes. Copper, for instance, has a slightly orange highlight, while gold has a somewhat yellow one. Aluminum's highlight is slightly blue.

The specular highlight of a shiny plastic is always the same color as the light source illuminating the shape, regardless of the color of plastic. If the light source is white, then the specular highlight is white, even when the plastic is red or blue.

Figure 21.5 shows a vase like those in Figure 21.4. The vase's **Material** node uses field values to make the vase look like shiny gold. By using alternate field values for the vase's **Material** node, you can create aluminum, copper, and other metallic and plastic materials. Table 21.3 provides some sample values to try.

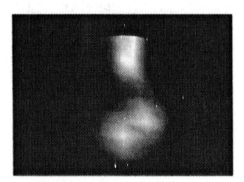

Figure 21.5 *A shiny gold vase.*

Table 21.3 **Material** Node Values Used to Create Metallic and Plastic Material Effects

Effect	ambientIntensity	diffuseColor	specularColor	shininess
Aluminum	0.3	0.30 0.30 0.50	0.70 0.70 0.80	0.10
Copper	0.26	0.30 0.11 0.00	0.75 0.33 0.00	0.08
Gold	0.4	0.22 0.15 0.0	0.71 0.70 0.56	0.16
Metallic purple	0.17	0.10 0.03 0.22	0.64 0.00 0.98	0.20
Metallic red	0.15	0.27 0.00 0.00	0.61 0.13 0.18	0.20
Plastic blue	0.1	0.20 0.20 0.71	0.83 0.83 0.83	0.12

Summary

Real-world light reflection is simulated in VRML using two types of reflection: diffuse reflection and specular reflection. Diffuse reflection scatters light randomly as it reflects off a shape. Specular reflection bounces light in a regular, predictable way, like a mirror. The highlight on a shiny shape is a specular reflection of a light source.

The **diffuseColor** field of a **Material** node controls the color of reflected light from diffuse reflection.

The **specularColor** field controls the color of reflected light from specular reflection. For plastics, this is the same color as the light in the scene (usually white). For metals, this is the metal's color, such as a bright yellow for gold or a bright orange for copper.

The **shininess** field controls how shiny a shape is by varying the size of the highlight on a shape. A **shininess** field value of 0.0 creates dull, matte shapes, while higher values create shinier shapes with smaller highlights.

The **ambientIntensity** field controls the effect the ambient light level has on the material. Low values make the material relatively unaffected by the ambient light level, while higher values do the opposite.

CHAPTER 22

Adding a Background

When building a virtual world, the nodes discussed in prior chapters are typically used to create the immediate surroundings of the viewer, including floors, ceilings, walls, furniture, and so forth. By using clever world design, you can limit the viewer's view of the world by building walls and zig-zag hallways in the way. These limiting tricks enable you to reduce the number of shapes your browser must draw each time the viewer moves. This reduces drawing time and increases the responsiveness of your browser while viewing your world.

View-limiting tricks can get oppressive. There are times when letting the viewer out of the enclosed, limited world is desirable and necessary. At such times the viewer gains an unobstructed view of your world's sky or distant horizon. You can use 3-D shapes to build a sky or to place buildings or mountains at the horizon. However, if the viewer is never intended to fly up to look at the sky closely or walk all the way to the horizon, using shapes to build these 3-D world features is a waste of the browser's drawing time.

To create efficient world backgrounds, VRML provides the **Background** node. Using this node you can control the sky and ground colors and set up a panorama of background images to create distant mountain ranges or cityscapes. This enables you to provide an outer environment for your world without having to create 3-D shapes for sky and horizon features.

Understanding Backgrounds

VRML's background features provide you control over your world's sky and ground colors and enable you to specify a set of panorama images to be placed around, above, and below your world.

Sky Colors

Conceptually, VRML's sky is an infinitely large sphere placed around the world. All of the worlds built in prior chapters have used a default black color for the sky sphere. Using the **Background** node you can specify other colors for the sky sphere.

For a simple sky, you can color the entire sky sphere a single color, such as sky blue. To create more realistic, horizon-coloring effects, you can color the sky sphere with a gradient of colors, ranging from blue directly above, down to lighter or darker colors at the horizon.

When creating a sky-color gradient, each of your gradient colors is listed within the skyColor field of the **Background** node, starting with a color for the sky sphere's upper pole directly overhead, proceeding down the sky sphere toward the lower pole directly below. For each sky color except the first, you also provide an angle in the skyAngle field. Each sky angle measures an angle down from the upper pole at which a sky color should be applied on the sky sphere. Colors between sky angles are smoothly graded to create a sky-color gradient. Using sky angles you can precisely specify how color should change from directly above to the horizon and below.

For example, you can create a sky-color gradient using the colors and sky angles in Table 22.1.

Table 22.1 Sky Angles and Colors Used to Create a Sky-Color Gradient

Sky Angle (radians)	Sky Color (RGB)
upper pole	0.0 0.2 0.7
0.785	0.0 0.5 1.0
1.571	1.0 1.0 1.0

The first sky color is always used for the upper pole of the sky sphere. The second sky color is placed at the angular location specified by the first sky angle. The sky sphere region between the upper pole and the first sky angle is filled with a smooth gradient from the first to the second sky color. Similarly, the third sky color is placed at the angular location specified by the second sky angle, and so on. If you provide *n* sky colors, you need only provide *n*–1 sky angles.

Table 22.1 specifies a sky blue color for the upper pole of the sky sphere. A gradient to a brighter blue is created down to the 75.0-degree (1.309-radian) angle on the sphere. From there, a color gradient to white is created down to the horizon at the 90.0-degree (1.571-radian) angle.

You can specify sky colors all the way down to the lower pole of the sky sphere at the 180.0-degree (3.142-radian) angle. If you stop short of 180.0 degrees, as in Table 22.1, the last color is used to color the rest of the sky sphere down to the lower pole.

Ground Colors

Like the sky, VRML's ground is an infinitely large sphere placed around the world. Using features similar to those for the sky sphere, you can specify color gradients for the ground sphere. To enable you to use the sky and ground spheres together, the ground sphere is slightly inside the sky sphere. Uncolored portions of the ground sphere let the sky sphere show through.

Using the **Background** node, you can provide a list of ground gradient colors within the **groundColor** field and a list of angles in the **groundAngle** field. The first ground color specifies the color of the ground sphere at the lower pole directly below. The second ground color is placed at the angular location specified by the first ground angle, and so on up the ground sphere. If you provide *n* ground colors, you need only provide *n*–1 ground angles.

You can specify ground colors all the way up to the upper pole of the ground sphere at the 180.0-degree (3.142-radians) angle. Typically, however, the ground colors are only provided up to a horizon at around 90.0 degrees (1.571 radians). When you stop short of 180.0 degrees, the remaining, upper portion of the ground sphere is made invisible so that the sky sphere can be seen outside the ground sphere. By combining ground and sky sphere coloring you can create ground color gradients for the lower portion of your world- and sky-color gradients for the upper portion.

For example, you can create a ground shading effect using the colors and ground angles in Table 22.2.

Table 22.2   Ground Angles and Colors Used to Create Ground Shading

Ground Angle (radians)	Ground Color (RGB)
lower pole	0.1 0.10 0.0
1.309	0.4 0.25 0.2
1.571	0.6 0.60 0.6

Table 22.2 specifies a brown color for the lower pole of the ground sphere. A gradient to a grayer brown is created up to the 75.0-degree (1.309-radian) angle on the sphere. From there, a color gradient to a brownish gray is created to the horizon at the 90.0-degree (1.571-radian) angle.

Panorama Images

Sky and ground spheres provide basic background colors for your world. To this background you can add a panorama of images to create mountains or a cityscape on the horizon. Conceptually, this panorama is built using an infinitely large box placed just inside the sky and ground spheres. On each side of this panorama box, you can place images of mountains, cities, or whatever.

Panorama images on the panorama box cover the ground and sky spheres outside of the box. To allow those spheres to show through, you can use panorama images with pixel transparency values. This creates holes in the panorama image, exactly like the holes created by texture images used in Chapter 17. Through the panorama-image holes, the outer ground and sky spheres are visible.

You can provide a different image for each of the six sides of the panorama box by using the **frontUrl, backUrl, leftUrl, rightUrl, topUrl,** and **bottomUrl** fields of the **Background** node. The outer ground and sky spheres show through any side for which you do not provide an image. Panorama images are typically not provided for the top and bottom sides of the panorama box. This lets the sky and ground show through above and below.

Understanding Background Binding

There can be only one background for your world. Nevertheless, there are times when you need to change the background from, say, a bright noon sky to an orange sunset sky. To accomplish this effect, you can create multiple **Background** nodes in your world and use background binding to switch between the **Background** nodes so that at any given time only one of them is in use.

The Background Stack

Your VRML browser maintains a *stack* of available background nodes, ordered like a stack of playing cards. The stack of background nodes has a bottom and a top. You can place any **Background** node on top of the stack. You can also take any **Background** node off the stack, and put it aside. The **Background** node on top of the stack is the one your VRML browser uses to color the background of your world.

Background Binding

Background binding is the process of placing a **Background** node on top of the background stack. When a **Background** node is *bound*, it is put on top of the stack. When a **Background** node is *unbound*, it is taken off the stack. You can bind a **Background** node by sending TRUE to the node's **set_bind** eventIn, and you can unbind it by sending FALSE to the **set_bind** eventIn.

When a **Background** node is bound and placed on top of the stack, it sends TRUE using its **isBound** eventOut. When a **Background** node is on top of the stack, the new **Background** node overrides it, and the old **Background** node sends FALSE using its **isBound** eventOut. Using these outputs of the **Background** node, you can create a circuit that keeps track of which **Background** node is on top of the stack.

Using binding, you can place many **Background** nodes on the stack. If you unbind the top **Background** node, then the next **Background** node in the stack becomes the current **Background** node, and it controls the background coloring of your world. If you unbind all the nodes on the stack, leaving an empty background stack, then your VRML browser colors the background of your world using the default values of a **Background** node. These default values create a black background, like the background of the examples in the previous chapters.

When your world is read by your browser, the first **Background** node your VRML browser finds is automatically bound to the top of the background stack.

The **Background** Node Syntax

The **Background** node creates a background for the world using a textured panorama box, a ground sphere outside that box, and a sky sphere outside the ground sphere. The box and both spheres are conceptually infinitely large and surround the virtual world. The viewer can turn to look at different portions of the box and spheres, but can never approach them.

SYNTAX | **Background node**

```
Background {
    skyColor        [ 0.0 0.0 0.0 ]    # exposedField  MFColor
    skyAngle        [ ]                # exposedField  MFFloat
    groundColor     [ ]                # exposedField  MFColor
    groundAngle     [ ]                # exposedField  MFFloat
    backUrl         [ ]                # exposedField  MFString
    bottomUrl       [ ]                # exposedField  MFString
    frontUrl        [ ]                # exposedField  MFString
    leftUrl         [ ]                # exposedField  MFString
    rightUrl        [ ]                # exposedField  MFString
    topUrl          [ ]                # exposedField  MFString
    set_bind                           # eventIn       SFBool
    bind_changed                       # eventOut      SFBool
}
```

The values of the **skyColor** exposed field specify a list of RGB colors used to color the sky sphere. The default value for the **SkyColor** exposed field is a single, black color.

The values of the **skyAngle** exposed field indicate sphere angles at which the sky colors are used. Sky angles are measured from 0.0 degrees (0.0 radians) at the upper pole of the sphere to 90.0 degrees (1.571 radians) at the sphere's equator and 180.0 degrees (3.141 radians) at the lower pole of the sphere. Sky angles must be listed in increasing order. If the last sky angle is less than 180.0 degrees, then the last sky color is used to fill the rest of the sky sphere down to the lower pole. The default value for the **skyAngle** exposed field is an empty list of angles.

The first sky color is placed at the upper pole of the sky sphere. The second sky color is placed at the first sky angle, the third color at the second angle, and so on. For points between any two sky angles, a color gradient is created that smoothly varies from the sky color associated with the first sky angle to that for the second. If there are *n* sky colors, there must be *n*–1 sky angles. The default values for the **skyColor** and **skyAngle** fields create a black sky sphere.

The values of the **groundColor** exposed field specify a list of RGB colors used to color the ground sphere. The default value is an empty list of colors.

The values of the **groundAngle** exposed field indicate sphere angles at which the ground colors are used. Ground angles are measured from 0.0 degrees (0.0 radians) at the lower pole of the sphere to 90.0 degrees (1.571 radians) at the sphere's equator and 180.0 degrees (3.141 radians) at the upper pole of the sphere. Ground angles must be listed in increasing order. If the last ground angle is less than 180.0 degrees, the rest of the ground sphere is left transparent. This enables the sky sphere outside the ground sphere to show through. The default value of the **groundAngle** exposed field is an empty list of angles.

The **groundColor** and **groundAngle** exposed fields act in an analogous manner to the **skyColor** and **skyAngle** fields. If there are *n* ground colors, then there must be *n*–1 ground angles. The default values for the **groundColor** and **groundAngle** fields create a transparent ground sphere.

The values of the **frontUrl**, **backUrl**, **leftUrl**, **rightUrl**, **topUrl**, and **bottomUrl** exposed fields each specify an image to be applied to the corresponding side of a panorama box built in the current coordinate system and surrounding the viewer. The front of the box is forward along the negative Z axis, and the back of the box is backward along the positive Z axis. Similarly, the left and right sides of the box are left along the negative X axis and right along the positive X axis, respectively. The top of the box is up along the positive Y axis, and the bottom of the box is down along the negative Y axis.

Each **url** field value specifies a prioritized list of URLs, ordered from highest priority to lowest. The VRML browser tries to open the file specified by the first URL in the list. If the file cannot be found, the browser tries the second URL in the list, and so on. When a URL is found that can be opened, the image in the file is read and used to texture a side of the panorama box. If none of the URLs can be opened, then no texturing takes place. The default value for each of these fields is an empty list of URLs.

Panorama image files must be in the JPEG, GIF, or PNG image-file formats. Images in these formats provide color or grayscale values for each pixel and can include a pixel transparency value for each pixel (depending on the abilities of the file format—see chapter 17 for discussions about image-file formats).

When a panorama image includes pixel transparency values, transparent portions of the panorama image let the outer sky and ground spheres show through. If no panorama image is provided for one or more sides of the panorama box, the outer sky and ground spheres are visible through that side of the box. Typically, the top and bottom sides of the box are left without images, and the images on the front, back, left, and right sides of the box use pixel transparency values to let the sky show through behind mountains or city skylines.

The sky sphere, ground sphere, and panorama box are not affected by lighting in the world. All three are shaded as if using an emissive material.

The **Background** node may be the child of any grouping node, and it builds the background within the current coordinate system. However, the background is affected only by rotation of the current coordinate system and not by translation or scaling. This ensures that a viewer can turn to look at different portions of the spheres and panorama box but cannot move closer to them.

The VRML browser maintains a background stack containing **Background** nodes. The top node on the stack is the bound **Background** node and is used by the VRML browser to control the world's background coloring. A **Background** node can be placed on top of the stack or removed from the stack by sending **TRUE** or **FALSE** values to the node's **set_bind** eventIn. When a **Background** node's **set_bind** eventIn receives a value, the resulting actions depend on the value received and the position of the specified **Background** node in the stack.

When **TRUE** is sent to a specified **Background** node's **set_bind** eventIn, and the new **Background** node is on top of the stack, nothing happens. Otherwise, the following actions take place:

- The **Background** node currently on top of the stack sends **FALSE** using its **isBound** eventOut.
- The new **Background** node is moved to the top of the background stack and becomes the current background.
- The new current **Background** node sends **TRUE** using its **isBound** eventOut.

When **FALSE** is sent to a specified **Background** node's **set_bind** eventIn, and the specified **Background** node is not in the background stack, nothing happens. If the specified **Background** node is in the stack, but is not on top of the stack, it is removed from the stack, and nothing else happens. If the specified **Background** node is on top of the stack, the following actions take place:

- The specified **Background** node sends **FALSE** using its **isBound** eventOut.
- The specified **Background** node is removed from the background stack.
- The next node on the stack becomes the new current background.
- The new current **Background** node sends **TRUE** using its **isBound** eventOut.

In the preceding cases, when the **Background** nodes on top of the stack and previously on top of the stack both send values using their **isBound** eventOuts, those values are sent simultaneously.

If the background stack is emptied by removing all **Background** nodes from the stack, no **Background** node is currently bound. In this case, the VRML browser uses default **Background** node values to control the world's background coloring.

When a VRML world is read by the browser, the first **Background** node encountered in the top-level file (not within any inlined files) is automatically moved to the top of the background stack, and bound. If there are no **Background** nodes in the top-level file, the background stack remains empty until a **Background** node is bound through the actions of a circuit.

The colors and panorama images of a background can be changed by sending values to the implied **set_groundAngle**, **set_groundColor**, **set_skyAngle**, **set_skyColor**, **set_backUrl**, **set_bottomUrl**, **set_frontUrl**, **set_leftUrl**, **set_rightUrl**, and **set_topUrl** eventIns of the exposed fields. When values are received on these inputs, the corresponding field values are changed, and the new values are output using the implied **groundAngle_changed**, **groundColor_changed**, **skyAngle_changed**, **skyColor_changed**, **backUrl_changed**, **bottomUrl_changed**, **frontUrl_changed**, **leftUrl_changed**, **rightUrl_changed**, and **topUrl_changed** eventOuts of the exposed fields.

Experimenting with Backgrounds

The following examples provide a more detailed examination of the ways in which the **Background** node can be used and how it interacts with nodes discussed in previous chapters.

Coloring the Sky

The VRML text in Figure 22.1 uses a **Background** node to create a color gradient across the sky sphere using a list of sky colors and a list of angles at which each color should appear on the sky sphere. The node specifies a dark blue for the upper pole of the sky sphere, a gray-blue at the 75.0-degree (1.309-radian) point, and white for the horizon. The last sky color is automatically used by the VRML browser to fill in the lower portion of the sky sphere. The ground sphere and panorama box are left at their default values, which make both invisible so that the sky sphere shows through. Since Figure 22.1 has only a single **Background** node, that node is automatically bound as the world's background.

```
#VRML V2.0 utf8
Background {
    skyColor [
        0.0 0.2 0.7,
        0.0 0.5 1.0,
        1.0 1.0 1.0
    ]
    skyAngle [ 1.309, 1.571 ]
}
```

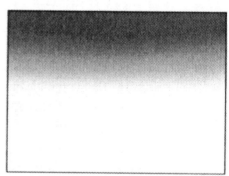

Figure 22.1   *A sky sphere with multiple colors.*

Coloring the Ground

Figure 22.2 uses a **Background** node to color the lower half of the ground sphere. Colors vary from dark brown at the lower pole of the ground sphere to gray-brown at 75.0 degrees (1.309 radians) and gray at the horizon. Since the last angle is less than 180.0 degrees, the upper portion of the ground sphere is left transparent so that the sky sphere (using the colors shown in Figure 22.1) can show through.

```
#VRML V2.0 utf8
Background {
    skyColor [
        0.0 0.2 0.7,
        0.0 0.5 1.0,
        1.0 1.0 1.0
    ]
    skyAngle [ 1.309, 1.571 ]
    groundColor [
        0.1 0.10 0.0,
        0.4 0.25 0.2,
        0.6 0.60 0.6,
    ]
    groundAngle [ 1.309, 1.571 ]
}
```

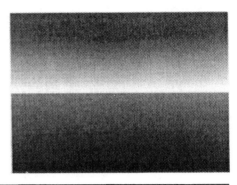

Figure 22.2 *A background with multiple ground and sky colors.*

Adding a Panorama

You can use the **Background** node's panorama box to add images of distant mountains and cities to the horizon of your world. Figure 22.3*a* shows an image of several mountains, and *b* shows the pixel transparency image of the mountains. Notice that the sky and the lower part of the image are transparent. Figure 22.3*c* uses this image for the front, back, left, and right sides of the panorama box. To avoid a visible seam at the corners of the box, the mountain image is designed to match side to side. Sky and ground colors are also provided so that transparent parts of the mountain image reveal the sky and ground.

The mountain panorama in Figure 22.3*c* does not use images for the top and bottom of the panorama box. This enables the sky and ground colors to show through. You can provide images for these box sides as well. An image of clouds, for instance, is appropriate for a top panorama image. The pixel transparency values for cloud pixels should be opaque, while those for sky pixels should be transparent. This creates holes in the sky panorama image wherever there aren't clouds. Through the holes, the background sky sphere's colors are visible.

```
#VRML V2.0 utf8
Background {
    skyColor [
        0.0 0.2 0.7,
        0.0 0.5 1.0,
        1.0 1.0 1.0
    ]
```

Figure 22.3 continues

```
skyAngle [ 1.309, 1.571 ]
groundColor [
    0.1 0.10 0.0,
    0.4 0.25 0.2,
    0.6 0.60 0.6,
]
groundAngle [ 1.309, 1.571 ]
frontUrl  "mountns.png"
backUrl   "mountns.png"
leftUrl   "mountns.png"
rightUrl  "mountns.png"
}
```

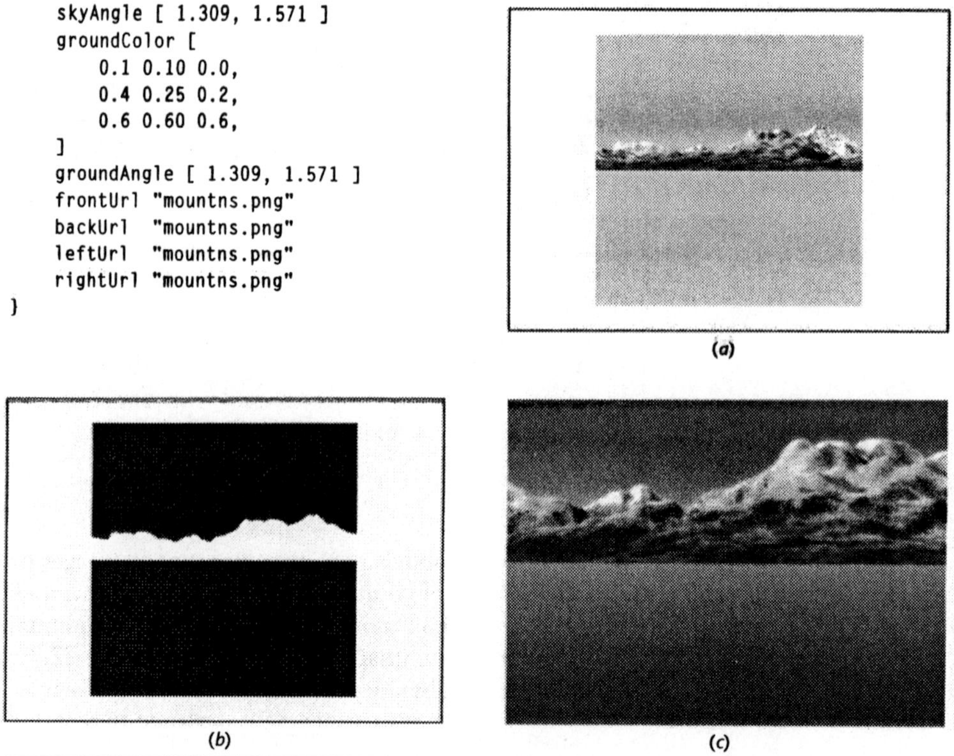

(a)

(b)

(c)

Figure 22.3 *A mountain image showing the (a) color and (b) pixel transparency parts of the image. (c) A background with a mountain panorama image all around. (The VRML text in this figure builds the world shown in Figure 22.3c.)*

Binding and Unbinding Backgrounds

Recall that you can use a **TouchSensor** node to turn a shape into a button. When the pointing device button is pressed while over a sensed shape, the **TouchSensor** node outputs **TRUE** using its **isActive** eventOut. When the button is released, the sensor outputs **FALSE** using its **isActive** eventOut. You can route these values to the **set_bind** eventIn of a **Background** node to bind and unbind when you press and release the pointing-device button on a shape.

Figure 22.4 creates a world with three **Background** nodes and two shapes: a red cube and a blue sphere. The first **Background** node is automatically bound when the world is read. That node creates the sky- and ground-color background used in previous examples. The second and third **Background** nodes create a fire red sky and a dark blue sky. A **TouchSensor** node sensing the red cube is routed to the red sky background's **set_bind** eventIn, and a **TouchSensor** node sensing the blue sphere is routed to the blue background's **set_bind** eventIn.

```
#VRML V2.0 utf8
Group {
    children [
    # Initial background
        Background {
            skyColor [ 0.0 0.2 0.7,  0.0 0.5 1.0,  1.0 1.0 1.0 ]
            skyAngle [ 1.309, 1.571 ]
            groundColor [ 0.1 0.1 0.0,  0.4 0.25 0.2,  0.6 0.6 0.6 ]
            groundAngle [ 1.309, 1.571 ]
        },
    # Alternate backgrounds
        DEF AltBack1 Background {
            skyColor [ 1.0 0.0 0.0,  1.0 0.4 0.0,  1.0 1.0 0.0 ]
            skyAngle [ 1.309, 1.571 ]
            groundColor [ 0.1 0.1 0.0,  0.5 0.25 0.2,  0.6 0.6 0.2 ]
            groundAngle [ 1.309, 1.571 ]
        },
        DEF AltBack2 Background {
            skyColor [ 1.0 0.0 0.8,  0.5 0.0 0.8,  0.0 0.0 0.8 ]
            skyAngle [ 1.309, 1.571 ]
            groundColor [ 0.0 0.0 0.1,  0.0 0.1 0.3,  0.3 0.3 0.6 ]
            groundAngle [ 1.309, 1.571 ]
        },
    # Shapes to act as buttons
        Transform {
            translation -2.0 0.0 0.0
            children [
                Shape {
                    appearance Appearance {
                        material Material {
                            diffuseColor 1.0 0.0 0.0
                        }
                    }
                    geometry Box { }
                },
                DEF TouchBox TouchSensor { }
            ]
        },
        Transform {
            translation 2.0 0.0 0.0
            children [
                Shape {
                    appearance Appearance {
                        material Material {
                            diffuseColor 0.0 0.0 0.8
                        }
                    }
                    geometry Sphere { }
                },
```

Figure 22.4 continues

```
                 DEF TouchSphere TouchSensor { }
          ]
       }
    ]
}
ROUTE TouchBox.isActive    TO AltBack1.set_bind
ROUTE TouchSphere.isActive TO AltBack2.set_bind
```

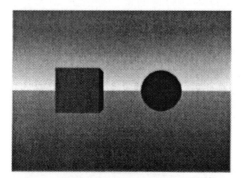

Figure 22.4 *Backgrounds bound and unbound by touching a red cube or a blue sphere.*

When you press the pointing-device button on the cube, the red sky background is moved to the top of the background stack and bound, making the sky turn red. When you release the pointing-device button, the red sky background is removed from the top of the stack, and the initial background returns. Similarly, when you press the pointing-device button on the blue sphere, the blue sky background is bound, and when you release the pointing-device button, the blue sky is unbound, and the initial background returns.

Summary

The **Background** node controls the creation of a background for your world. That background consists of a sky sphere, a ground sphere just inside the sky sphere, and a panorama box just inside the ground sphere. Both spheres and the panorama box are conceptually infinitely far away and enclose the entire world. The viewer can turn to look at the sky and panorama from different angles but can never get closer to them.

The **skyColor** field provides a list of colors for controlling a color gradient from the upper pole of the sky sphere to the lower pole. Colors are placed on the sphere at angles specified in the **skyAngle** field.

The **groundColor** field provides a list of colors for controlling a color gradient from the lower pole of the ground sphere to the upper pole. Colors are placed on the ground sphere at angles specified in the **groundAngle** field. The portion of the ground sphere past the last ground angle is transparent, thereby providing a view of the sky sphere outside the ground sphere.

The **frontUrl, backUrl, leftUrl, rightUrl, topUrl,** and **bottomUrl** fields each use a URL for a texture image to be applied to the corresponding side of the panorama box. If you don't provide an image for a box side, then that side is transparent and reveals the ground and sky spheres behind it. Images with pixel transparency values can be used to create holes in the panorama, revealing the ground and sky spheres.

The VRML browser maintains a background stack of **Background** nodes. The top node on the stack is bound and used to specify the appearance of the world's background. Sending **TRUE** to a **Background** node's **set_bind** eventIn moves the node to the top of the stack and binds it. Sending **FALSE** to a **Background** node's **set_bind** eventIn removes the node from the stack, unbinding it (if it was on top of the stack).

The first **Background** node found when reading in your world is automatically moved to the top of the background stack and bound. If there are no **Background** nodes in your world, or the stack becomes empty, then the default values of a **Background** node are used to specify the world's background.

CHAPTER 23

Adding Fog

After building the shapes for your world, you can add the effect of a virtual atmosphere by using the **Fog** node. You can use the **Fog** node to create a light haze or a thick, pea-soup fog, and you can vary the fog color.

Understanding Fog

VRML's fog features provide you control over your world's atmosphere. Like real-world fog, VRML's virtual fog has two attributes: the fog's color and the fog's thickness.

Fog color is controlled by specifying a color for the fog. By default the fog color is white, but you can create fog of any color. One common technique is to use a black fog color. This darkens distant parts of the world and is often used to create a moody feel in environments like dungeons.

Fog thickness is controlled by specifying a visibility range for the fog. The visibility range specifies the distance from the viewer to the point where the fog completely obscures shapes in your world. Shapes near the viewer are seen more clearly through the fog, but distant shapes near the visibility range are almost entirely obscured by the fog. If you use a large distance for the visibility range, you create a light haze in your world. If you shorten the distance for the visibility range, you thicken the fog and reduce the visibility in your world.

You can also control fog thickness by specifying a fog type. A *linear* fog type increases fog thickness linearly as the distance from the viewer increases. An *exponential fog* type increases fog thickness exponentially with distance and creates more realistic and thicker-seeming fog.

Shape and Fog Colors

In the real world, fog obscures our view of the edges and colors of shapes because small water droplets suspended in the atmosphere get in the way. In a perfect simulation of real-world fog, a computer would compute the effect of each and every water droplet suspended in a virtual world's atmosphere. Unfortunately, the computational effort this requires is well beyond our current computational abilities.

Rather than compute the exact effect of each virtual water droplet in a virtual atmosphere, VRML uses a considerably simpler method of simulating fog. VRML fog changes the apparent color of shapes. Shapes that are far away and deep in the virtual fog are washed out and take on the color of the fog. Shapes that are nearby retain most of their shape color and are only washed out a little bit by the fog.

Imagine, for instance, that your world has a red cube in it and that you've added a **Fog** node with a white fog color. When you are near the red cube, the cube appears red, as it should. As you move away from the cube, the fog begins to get in the way, and the cube color is gradually changed to match the fog color. When you reach the visibility range for your fog, the red cube is completely obscured by the fog and turns white, the color of the fog.

Fog and Backgrounds

The background specified by a **Background** node is independent of any fog effects that you apply to the shapes in your world. For instance, a distant mountain range painted on the background's panorama box is not washed out by fog, like shapes are.

To use backgrounds and fog most effectively, you should design both at the same time. For example, if you're using a light hazy-gray fog, then you should consider adding a bit of painted-on gray fog to the images you use for the background panorama. If you don't, the background may appear too crisp and perfect to match the effect the fog has on the shapes in your world. If you are using a very thick, brown fog, then you should consider skipping the background panorama altogether and just color the background sphere the same color as your fog. By coordinating the background and fog settings, you can create very realistic environments.

Understanding Fog Binding

Like the backgrounds discussed in Chapter 22, you can specify fog only once for your world. Nevertheless, there are times when you need more than one fog selection, such as for different amounts of fog at different times of day. To accomplish this, you can create multiple **Fog** nodes in your world, and use fog binding to switch between the **Fog** nodes so that at any given time, only one of them is in use.

The Fog Stack

Your VRML browser maintains a stack of available fog nodes, exactly like the background stack used for **Background** nodes. You can place any **Fog** node on top of the stack or remove any **Fog** node from the stack and put it aside. The **Fog** node on top of the stack is the one your VRML browser uses to control the fog color and thickness in your world.

Fog Binding

Fog binding is the process of placing a **Fog** node on top of the fog stack. When a **Fog** node is *bound*, it is put on top of the stack. When a **Fog** node is *unbound*, it is taken off the stack. You can bind a **Fog** node by sending **TRUE** to the node's **set_bind** eventIn, and you can unbind it by sending **FALSE** to the set_bind eventIn.

When a **Fog** node is bound and placed on the top of the stack, it sends **TRUE** using its **isBound** eventOut. If there was a **Fog** node already on the top of the stack, the new **Fog** node overrides it, and the old **Fog** node sends **FALSE** using its **isBound** eventOut. Using these outputs of the **Fog** node, you can create a circuit that keeps track of which **Fog** node is on top of the stack.

Using binding, you can place many **Fog** nodes on the stack. If you unbind the top **Fog** node, then the next **Fog** node in the stack becomes the current **Fog** node, and it controls the fog in your world. If you unbind all the nodes on the stack, leaving an empty fog stack, then your VRML browser controls the fog in your world using the default values of the **Fog** node. These default values turn off fog.

When your world is first read by your browser, the first **Fog** node your VRML browser finds is automatically bound to the top of the fog stack.

The **Fog** Node Syntax

The **Fog** node creates a foglike atmospheric effect in your worlds.

| SYNTAX | **Fog** node |

```
Fog {
    color              1.0 1.0 1.0    # exposedField  SFColor
    visibilityRange    0.0            # exposedField  SFFloat
    fogType            "LINEAR"       # exposedField  SFString
    set_bind                          # eventIn       SFBool
    bind_changed                      # eventOut      SFBool
}
```

The value of the **color** exposed field specifies the RGB color of the fog. An RGB color is specified as three floating-point values between 0.0 and 1.0 that specify the amount of red (R), green (G), and blue (B) light to be mixed together to form the fog color. The default value for the field is white.

The value of the **visibilityRange** exposed field specifies the distance from the viewer, measured in the current coordinate system, at which shapes in the world become completely obscured by the fog. A large visibility range creates a fog that thickens gradually over a large distance, creating the visual effect of a light haze. A small visibility range creates a fog that thickens quickly in a short distance, like a thick fog. A visibility range of 0.0 or less disables the **Fog** node. The default value for the field is 0.0 units.

The value of the **fogType** exposed field specifies the fog type. When the fog type is "LINEAR", fog thickness increases linearly with distance from the viewer. When the fog type is "EXPONENTIAL", fog thickness increases exponentially with distance from the viewer. The default value for the field is "LINEAR".

Fog affects the color of shapes built in the world. Shapes that are more distant than the visibility range are drawn without shading, using only the fog color. Shapes that are closer retain some shading, and some of their original color is mixed with the fog color. Shapes that are very close to the viewer retain all of their shape color and shading, and are unaffected by the fog color.

The VRML browser maintains a fog stack containing **Fog** nodes. The top node on the stack is the bound **Fog** node and is used by the VRML browser to control the amount of fog in the world. A **Fog** node can be placed on top of the stack or removed from the stack by sending **TRUE** or **FALSE** values to the node's **set_bind** eventIn. When a **Fog** node's **set_bind** eventIn receives a value, the resulting actions depend on the value received and the position of the specified **Fog** node in the stack.

When **TRUE** is sent to a specified **Fog** node's **set_bind** eventIn, and the new **Fog** node is on top of the stack, nothing happens. Otherwise, the following actions take place:

- The **Fog** node currently on top of the stack sends **FALSE** using its **isBound** eventOut.
- The new **Fog** node is moved to the top of the fog stack and becomes the current description of the world's fog.
- The new current **Fog** node sends **TRUE** using its **isBound** eventOut.

When **FALSE** is sent to a specified **Fog** node's **set_bind** eventIn, and the specified **Fog** node is not in the fog stack, nothing happens. If the specified **Fog** node is in the stack, but is not on top of the stack, it is removed from the stack, and nothing else happens. If the specified **Fog** node is on top of the stack, the following actions take place:

- The specified **Fog** node sends **FALSE** using its **isBound** eventOut.
- The specified **Fog** node is removed from the fog stack.
- The next node on the stack becomes the new current description of the world's fog.
- The new current **Fog** node sends **TRUE** using its **isBound** eventOut.

In the preceding cases, when the **Fog** nodes on top of the stack and previously on top of the stack both send values using their **isBound** eventOuts, those values are sent simultaneously.

If the fog stack is emptied by removing all **Fog** nodes from the stack, no **Fog** node is currently bound. In this case, the VRML browser uses default **Fog** node values to control the world's fog effects.

When a VRML world is read by the browser, the first **Fog** node encountered in the top-level file (not within any inlined files) is automatically moved to the top of the fog stack and bound. If there are no **Fog** nodes in the top-level file, the fog stack remains empty until a **Fog** node is bound through the actions of a circuit.

The color and thickness of fog can be changed by sending values to the implied **set_color, set_visibilityRange,** and **set_fogType** eventIns of the exposed fields. When values are received using these inputs, the corresponding field values are changed, and the new values output using the implied **color_changed, visibilityRange_ changed,** and **fogType_changed** eventOuts of the exposed fields.

Experimenting with Fog

The following examples provide a more detailed examination of the ways in which the **Fog** node can be used and how it interacts with nodes discussed in previous chapters.

Creating a Test World

The VRML text in Figure 23.1 builds a simple test world used for each of the following examples. The test world contains an ambient directional light, a green floor, and two rows of beige cylinders receding into the distance. If you type in this example, place it in a file named `"fogworld.wrl."` Each of the examples following this one inline this file and add **Fog** and **Background** nodes.

```
#VRML V2.0 utf8
Group {
    children [
    # Ambient lighting
        DirectionalLight {
            direction 0.0 -1.0 -1.0
            intensity 0.2
            ambientIntensity 1.0
        },
    # Floor
        Shape {
            appearance Appearance {
                material Material {
                    ambientIntensity 0.5
                    diffuseColor 0.2 0.8 0.2
                }
            }
            geometry Box { size 50.0 0.01 50.0 }
        },
```

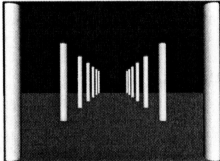

Figure 23.1 continues

```
# Pair of columns
    DEF ColumnPair Group {
        children [
            Transform {
                translation -4.0 3.0 0.0
                children DEF Column Shape {
                    appearance Appearance {
                        material Material {
                            diffuseColor 1.0 0.8 0.5
                        }
                    }
                    geometry Cylinder {
                        radius 0.3
                        height 6.0
                    }
                }
            },
            Transform {
                translation 4.0 3.0 0.0
                children USE Column
            }
        ]
    },
# Several more pairs of columns
    Transform { translation 0.0 0.0  -8.0  children USE ColumnPair },
    Transform { translation 0.0 0.0   8.0  children USE ColumnPair },
    Transform { translation 0.0 0.0 -16.0  children USE ColumnPair },
    Transform { translation 0.0 0.0  16.0  children USE ColumnPair },
    Transform { translation 0.0 0.0 -24.0  children USE ColumnPair },
    Transform { translation 0.0 0.0  24.0  children USE ColumnPair },
    ]
}
```

Figure 23.1 *A test world for experimenting with fog.*

Using Linear Fog

The VRML text in Figure 23.2 inlines the test world, adds a **Background** node with a white sky color, and adds a **Fog** node. The fog color is white, and the type is "LINEAR". The visibility range in Figure 23.2*a* is 0.0; which turns off the fog and creates a clear atmosphere in the world. The visibility range in Figure 23.2*b* is 40.0 to create a light haze in the world. Try walking down the line of columns and notice how the column colors gradually change as you approach them. Distant columns take on the white color of the fog, while closer columns retain their beige shape color. Using the same world, try decreasing the visibility range to 30.0 and then to 20.0. Notice how the fog thickness increases as you reduce the visibility range. Figure 23.2*c* shows the effect when the visibility range is 30.0, and *d* shows the effect when the visibility range is 20.0.

```
#VRML V2.0 utf8
Group {
    children [
        Fog {
            color 1.0 1.0 1.0
            fogType "LINEAR"
            visibilityRange 40.0
        },
        Background { skyColor 1.0 1.0 1.0 },
        Inline { url "fogworld.wrl" }
    ]
}
```

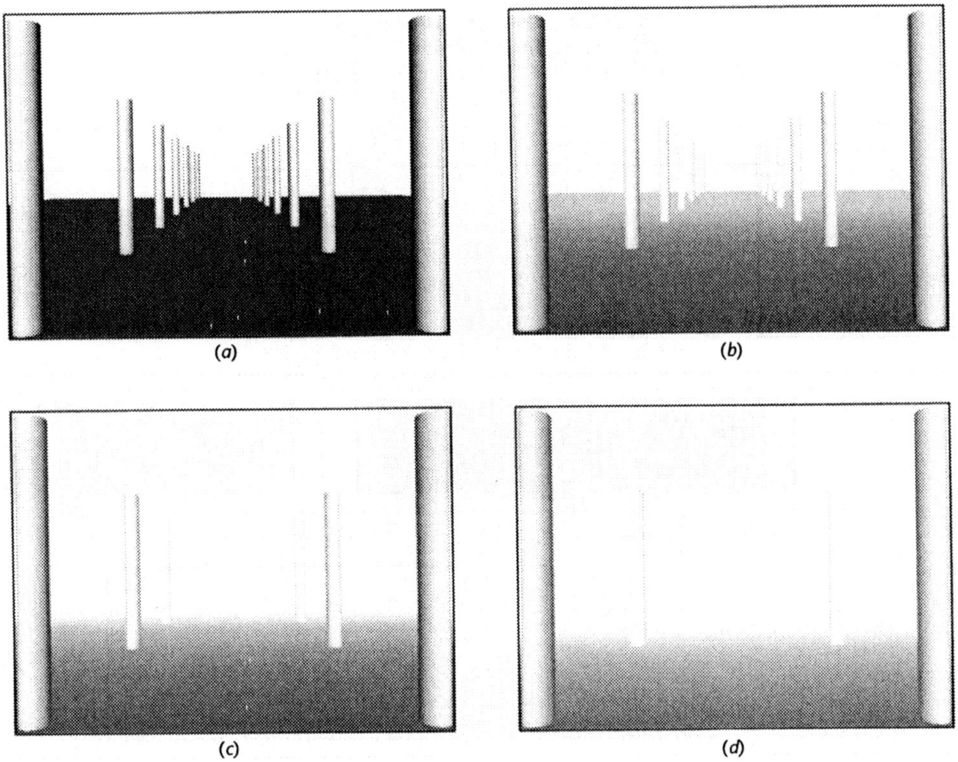

Figure 23.2 *A linear, foggy world with a visibility range of (a) 0.0, (b) 40.0, (c) 30.0 and (d) 20.0. (The VRML text in this figure builds the world shown in Figure 23.2b.)*

Using Exponential Fog

When the fog type is "LINEAR", the fog thickness varies linearly with the distance to a shape. This works well for creating haze effects, but it isn't realistic when you use thicker fog. For more realistic fog, the "EXPONENTIAL" fog type works better.

Figure 23.3 shows the foggy test world with the fog type changed to "EXPONENTIAL". Figure 23.3*a* uses a visibility range of 100.0, *b* shows a visibility range of 40.0, and *c* a visibility range of 20.0. Notice that changing the fog type to "EXPONENTIAL" creates a thicker fog effect.

```
#VRML V2.0 utf8
Group {
    children [
        Fog {
            color 1.0 1.0 1.0
            fogType "EXPONENTIAL"
            visibilityRange 40.0
        },
        Background { skyColor 1.0 1.0 1.0 },
        Inline { url "fogworld.wrl" }
    ]
}
```

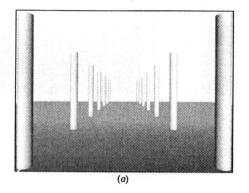

(a)

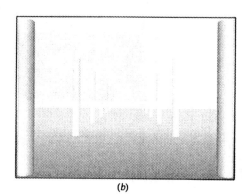

(b)

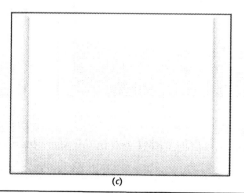

(c)

Figure 23.3   *An exponential foggy world with a visibility range of (a) 100.0, (b) 40.0, and (c) 20.0. (The VRML text in this figure builds the world shown in Figure 23.3b.)*

Using Colored Fog

Using the test world, the VRML text in Figure 23.4 specifies black fog instead of white fog. The **Background** node is also removed, letting the background default to a black sky color. Notice how the use of black fog creates a moody atmosphere.

```
#VRML V2.0 utf8
Group {
    children [
        Fog {
            color 0.0 0.0 0.0
            fogType "EXPONENTIAL"
            visibilityRange 40.0
        },
        Inline { url "fogworld.wrl" }
    ]
}
```

Figure 23.4 *A foggy world using black fog.*

Binding and Unbinding Fog

The VRML text in Figure 23.5 adds two **Fog** and **Background** nodes to the test world again. The first **Fog** node and the first **Background** node are each automatically bound when the world is read in. These nodes create a light white fog and a white background. The second **Fog** and **Background** nodes create a red fog and background.

A **TouchSensor** node sensing the columns and ground of the test world is routed into the **set_bind** eventIn of the red **Fog** and **Background** nodes. When you press the pointing-device button on any part of the world, the red fog and background are each bound. When you release the button, both nodes are unbound, and the original white fog and background are restored.

```
#VRML V2.0 utf8
Group {
    children [
    # Initial fog and background
        Fog {
            color 1.0 1.0 1.0
            fogType "LINEAR"
            visibilityRange 40.0
        },
        Background { skyColor 1.0 1.0 1.0 },
    # Alternate fog background
        DEF AltFog Fog {
            color 1.0 0.0 0.0
            fogType "LINEAR"
            visibilityRange 30.0
        },
        DEF AltBack Background { skyColor 1.0 0.0 0.0 },
```

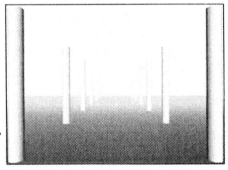

Figure 23.5 continues

```
# Test world
    Transform {
        children [
            Inline { url "fogworld.wrl" },
            DEF TouchWorld TouchSensor { }
        ]
    }
]
}
ROUTE TouchWorld.isActive TO AltFog.set_bind
ROUTE TouchWorld.isActive TO AltBack.set_bind
```

Figure 23.5   *Fog and backgrounds bound and unbound by clicking within the world.*

Summary

The **Fog** node controls the creation of fog in your world. The fog **color** field specifies the color of the fog. The **visibilityRange** field controls the fog thickness by setting a limit beyond which shapes are obscured by the fog. The **fogType** field specifies a value of "LINEAR" or "EXPONENTIAL" to indicate whether fog should increase linearly or exponentially with distance.

Fog affects the color of shapes drawn in the world. Distant shapes are washed out with the fog color, while shapes nearby are largely unaffected by the fog. Backgrounds specified by the **Background** node are not affected by fog. For the most realistic effect, the background color should be set to the fog color.

The VRML browser maintains a fog stack of **Fog** nodes. The top node on the stack is bound and used to specify the appearance of the world's fog. Sending **TRUE** to a **Fog** node's **set_bind** eventIn moves the node to the top of the stack and binds it. Sending **FALSE** to a **Fog** node's **set_bind** eventIn removes the node from the stack and unbinds it if it was the top of the stack.

The first **Fog** node found when reading a world is automatically moved to the top of the fog stack and bound. If there are no **Fog** nodes in the world, or the stack becomes empty, then the default values of a **Fog** node are used to specify the world's fog.

## CHAPTER 24

Adding Sound

You can increase the realism of your virtual worlds by adding sounds using the **AudioClip, MovieTexture,** and **Sound** nodes. You can create ambient sound, such as background music in a virtual mall or spooky screams in a dungeon. You can also add sounds that are triggered by circuits, such as a door slam when an animated door closes. You can even position sounds in your world so that when a door to the viewer's left slams shut, the door slam sound comes from the left when heard over the viewer's speakers or headphones.

Understanding Sound

Adding sound to your world involves two components: the sound source and the sound emitter. The source and emitter act like components in a home audio system. The *sound source* provides a sound signal, like a CD player or VCR, and the *sound emitter* turns the source's signal into sound you can hear, like speakers in an audio system.

Sound Sources

In VRML, a sound source is typically described by the **AudioClip** node. The **AudioClip** node provides a **url** field whose value specifies one of two types of sound files to play as the sound source:

- A digital sound file, which stores digitally recorded sounds, such as music and sound effects. VRML supports one of the most common methods for storing digital sound: the WAV file format. (See the sidebar entitled "The WAV File Format.")
- A General MIDI type 1 file, which stores instructions for performing a piece of music. These instructions are understood by the sound

synthesizer hardware found on most sound cards. General MIDI is a special variant of MIDI used for general music performances played on PCs and Macintoshes. (See the sidebar entitled "The MIDI File Format.")

SIDEBAR: THE WAV FILE FORMAT WAV is short for "waveform." Microsoft's WAV file format stores low-, medium-, or high-quality digital-sound, waveform information. WAV files are the standard sound file format for Microsoft Windows and can be created using a variety of tools on PC, Macintosh, and UNIX systems. See Appendix B for references to further information on the WAV file format.

On PC and UNIX systems, WAV files are typically named with a ".wav" file name extension. On a Macintosh, the WAV format has no standard file type, but is nevertheless widely supported by Macintosh sound applications.

A sound source also can be described by the **MovieTexture** node, which you can use to specify a movie to play as a sound source. By using the same **MovieTexture** node for both a texture and a sound source, you can create a synchronized multimedia presentation within your world. For instance, you can create a virtual television that plays an MPEG video clip on the television screen while playing the associated sound through the television's virtual speakers.

SIDEBAR: THE MIDI FILE FORMAT MIDI stands for "Musical Instrument Digital Interface." MIDI is an international standard developed to enable communications between sound synthesizers used during a musical performance. MIDI instructions indicate performance information, such as when to start playing a note, when to stop, and how loud to play. These instructions indicate *when* to play a sound, but not *what* sound to play. For instance, the same MIDI note instruction can be used to play a kick drum sound, a cymbal crash, a piano note, or a trombone glissando. The choice of sounds to play is largely up to the sound synthesizer being used and how it is set up.

Without knowing how a sound synthesizer has been set up, the composer of a MIDI performance can only hope that when the MIDI file plays a note intended for a piano sound, the user actually has a piano sound programmed into the sound synthesizer instead of, for example, a bagpipe sound. To provide more regularity to this situation, the *General MIDI* standard specifies a set of common sounds all synthesizers should support, including pianos, strings, horns, kick drums, and so forth. By composing for the General MIDI sounds, a composer can be assured that the piano sonata will be performed using a synthesized piano sound and not a bagpipe. VRML supports General MIDI for all MIDI files used as sound sources. See Appendix B for references to further information on MIDI and General MIDI.

On PC systems, MIDI files are typically named with a ".mid" file name extension. On UNIX systems, MIDI files usually have a ".midi" file name extension. On a Macintosh, MIDI files have a "Midi" file type.

WAV files, General MIDI files, and MPEG files provide a rich set of possible sound sources for your world. You can even use all three within the same world. Typically,

WAV files are used for playing short sound effects or bits of speech. General MIDI files are used to play background music, and MPEG files are used to describe short movie clips to play as synchronized textures and sounds. (See the sidebar entitled "Comparing File Sizes.")

TIP A sound editing application is an essential tool for creating and manipulating digital sound files. Similarly, a MIDI music composition and playback application is an essential tool for creating and manipulating MIDI files. Many excellent tools are available as shareware on the Internet. If you don't have the tools or the time to create your own sounds or MIDI files, you can purchase libraries of sounds on CD-ROM or browse the Internet for sounds and MIDI files created by sound designers and composers.

SIDEBAR: COMPARING FILE SIZES To create an accurate representation of a sound, digital sound files may use as many as 44,100 two-byte numbers for each second of sound (double that for stereo sound). A single minute of digital sound may require as much as 10 megabytes of disk space.

MIDI files store sound performance instructions instead of a digital representation of a sound. A one-minute MIDI file performance of a moderately complex piece of piano music may require only a few kilobytes of disk space.

The small size of MIDI files makes them particularly appropriate for describing background music in your world. Digital sound files are typically used only for short sound effects.

Sound Source Control

The **AudioClip** and **MovieTexture** nodes both provide fields that enable you to control how and when a sound source plays. For both nodes, the **startTime** and **stopTime** fields specify the absolute times at which a sound starts and stops playing. Both nodes also provide a **loop** field with which you can indicate whether a sound should be played just once or played repeatedly in a loop.

You can control the speed with which a sound source is played by using the **pitch** field of the **AudioClip** node or the **speed** field of a **MovieTexture** node. Both fields specify a speed increase or decrease factor. A speed or pitch value of 0.5, for instance, plays the sound source at half speed, while a value of 2.0 plays the source at double speed. To play a sound or movie at normal speed, you specify a value of 1.0.

Sound Emitters

The **Sound** node describes a sound emitter in your world, similar to a speaker hooked to a home audio system. The node's **source** field value specifies an **AudioClip** or **MovieTexture** node that provides a source of sound. The **location** and **direction** fields of the **Sound** node enable you to position the sound emitter and aim it in a specified direction. The **Sound** node's **intensity** field gives you a master volume control for the sound.

In the real world, sound diminishes in volume as you move farther away from a sound emitter. You can mimic this real-world effect in your virtual worlds by using **Sound** node fields to specify the size of two invisible, sound-range *ellipsoids*, or oblong spheres.

An inner *minimum-range ellipsoid* and an outer *maximum-range ellipsoid* both define 3-D regions of your world surrounding the **Sound** node's location. As a viewer moves within these regions, the volume of the emitted sound changes as follows:

- If the viewer is inside the minimum-range ellipsoid, the viewer is close to the sound emitter, and the sound is heard at full volume.

- If the viewer is between the minimum- and maximum-range ellipsoids, the viewer is farther away from the sound. The emitted sound is heard at a diminished volume that decreases from full volume at the edge of the minimum-range ellipsoid to zero volume at the edge of the maximum-range ellipsoid.

- If the viewer is outside the maximum-range ellipsoid, the viewer is too far away to hear the emitted sound at all, and the volume is zero.

The size of the minimum-range ellipsoid is controlled by the values of the **minFront** and **minBack** fields of the **Sound** node. The **minFront** field value specifies a distance from the sound emitter to the front edge of the ellipsoid, and the **minBack** field value specifies a distance to the back edge of the ellipsoid. The size of the maximum-range ellipsoid is similarly controlled by the values of the **maxFront** and **maxBack** fields of the **Sound** node. For both ellipsoids, the front and back distances are measured along an imaginary line aimed in the direction the sound emitter is facing.

Using these two range ellipsoids, you can achieve very precise control over the area in your world within which a viewer can hear an emitted sound. For instance, you can use a **Sound** node to play background music in one room in a virtual building and simultaneously use a second **Sound** node to play cheering crowd noises in another room. Using range ellipsoids for both **Sound** nodes, you can limit both sounds so that the viewer hears only the music when they are in the first room and only the crowd noises when they are in the second room.

Sound-Emitter Priorities

You can have any number of **Sound** nodes in your world. Typically, some **Sound** nodes are used to play background music and noises, while other **Sound** nodes are triggered by circuits to cause sound effects to play. Using the range ellipsoids, you can limit the effect of each **Sound** node so that they aren't all heard at once.

There are times when multiple **Sound** nodes are playing and the viewer is within range of all of them. In such cases, it may not be possible to play all of the sounds simultaneously. Most sound hardware, for instance, can only play between four and eight simultaneous sounds. In these cases, your VRML browser must decide which sounds to play, and which not to play. You can help your browser by prioritizing sounds using the **priority** field of the **Sound** node. Sounds with higher priorities are played in preference to those with lower priorities. For instance, it is typical to chose higher priorities for sound effects such as laser blasts or warning messages and to choose lower priorities for background sounds and music. Using priorities, you can ensure that important sounds are always heard.

Sound Spatialization

Sound spatialization is a digital signal processing technique that makes a digital sound appear to emit from a specific point in 3-D space. The panning controls on a home audio system are a limited form of spatialization. You can use panning to slide a sound left and right. Using spatialization, however, you can slide a sound up and down, forward and back, and even spin it around your head. (See the sidebar entitled "Sound Spatialization.")

You can enable the use of sound spatialization for a sound emitter by setting the value of the **spatialize** field to **TRUE** in a **Sound** node. Thereafter, any sound emitted by the node is processed digitally to make it sound like it is being played at the emitter's 3-D location. This can be very effective when used with sound effects. For instance, a door slamming to the left of the viewer emits a sound to the left of the viewer.

When the **spatialize** field value is **FALSE,** the sound emitted by a **Sound** node is not spatialized. Nonspatialized sounds are useful for sounds that are intended to sound as if they are coming from all around the viewer. Wind noises, earthquake rumbles, and rain are sounds typically not spatialized.

SIDEBAR: SOUND SPATIALIZATION   When you hear a sound in the real world, each of your ears receives a slightly different version of the sound, depending upon the sound's location. Your brain automatically detects the left- and right-ear sound differences and from them it determines the location of the real-world sound. These sound differences result from an arrival time difference and a frequency-content difference caused by the way sound travels in the real world.

Imagine, for instance, that a friend standing to your right snaps his or her fingers. The sound waves caused by the finger snap travel outward from the fingers and arrive at your right ear, and a split second later they arrive at your left ear. This slight, split-second, *arrival-time difference* is detected by your auditory system and interpreted as meaning that the finger snap occurred to your right.

For high-frequency sounds, your ear has a hard time detecting arrival-time differences. In this case, it must rely instead on *frequency-content differences* in the sounds that arrive at your left and right ear. For instance, when the finger-snap sound waves pass your head to reach your left ear, your head muffles the sound slightly, causing the sound's frequency content to be different when it gets to your left ear. Your brain detects the frequency-content difference between the sound heard at your left and right ears and, again, interprets that to mean that the finger snap occurred to your right.

Sound spatialization recreates these arrival time and frequency content differences. If you listen to just the left or just the right output of your sound card, you won't hear these slight changes being made to the sound. But when you put on a pair of headphones and listen to the left and right outputs simultaneously, you'll hear realistic 3-D sound.

The **AudioClip** Node Syntax

The AudioClip node describes a sound source and can be specified as the value of the **source** field in a **Sound** node.

| SYNTAX | **AudioClip node** |

```
AudioClip {
    url                    [ ]      # exposedField  MFString
    duration               ""       # exposedField  SFString
    startTime              0.0      # exposedField  SFTime
    stopTime               0.0      # exposedField  SFTime
    pitch                  1.0      # exposedField  SFFloat
    loop                   FALSE    # exposedField  SFBool
    isActive                        # eventOut      SFBool
    duration_changed                # eventOut      SFFloat
}
```

The value of the **url** field specifies a prioritized list of URLs ordered from highest priority to lowest. The VRML browser typically tries to open the file specified by the first URL in the list. If the file cannot be found, the browser tries the second URL in the list, and so on. When a URL is found that can be opened, the sound in the file is read and used as a sound source. If none of the URLs can be opened, then no sound is played. The default value for the **url** field is an empty list of URLs.

Sound source files must be General MIDI type 1 files or digital sound files in the WAV file format. General MIDI type 1 files store instructions for performing a piece of music on a sound card's sound synthesizer. WAV files store digital recordings of sound that can be played back using a sound card's waveform playback features.

General MIDI and WAV files both include within them an indication of the duration of the sound they describe. As soon as either sound file type is read by the VRML browser, the sound's duration (measured in seconds) is determined and output on the **duration_changed** eventOut. The output duration is independent of the playback speed selected by the **pitch** field. If there is a problem with the sound file, or the duration cannot be determined for some reason, a -1 is output on the **duration_changed** eventOut instead of the sound's duration.

The value of the **description** exposed field specifies a text string describing the sound. VRML browsers that cannot play sounds may display the description text instead.

The value of the **startTime** exposed field specifies the time at which the sound starts playing. The **startTime** field value is an absolute time measured in seconds since 12:00 midnight, GMT, January 1, 1970. The default value is 0.0 seconds.

The value of the **stopTime** exposed field specifies the time at which the sound stops playing. The **stopTime** field value is an absolute time and has a default value of 0.0 seconds.

The value of the **pitch** exposed field specifies a multiplication factor for speeding up or slowing down playback of the sound. A value of 1.0 plays the sound at its normal speed. A value between 0.0 and 1.0 slows the sound playback speed, decreasing its pitch. A value greater than 1.0 increases the sound playback speed, increasing its pitch. The **pitch** field value must be greater than 0.0. The default value of 1.0 plays the sound at normal speed.

The value of the **loop** exposed field specifies whether the sound playback loops. If the field value is **TRUE**, the sound plays repeatedly. If the loop field value is **FALSE**, the sound plays once before stopping. The default value for the **loop** field is **FALSE**.

The **startTime, stopTime, speed,** and **loop** field values work together to control the **AudioClip** node's playback. An **AudioClip** node remains dormant until the start time is reached. At the start time the **AudioClip** node becomes active, outputs TRUE using the **isActive** eventOut and begins playing through the sound. If the loop field value is FALSE, the **AudioClip** node generates sound until either the stop time is reached or one cycle through the sound has been completed at (**startTime** + duration/**pitch**), whichever comes first. If the **loop** field value is TRUE, the **AudioClip** node generates sound continually, through a potentially infinite number of playback cycles, until the stop time is reached. In the special case where the stop time is earlier than the start time, the stop time is ignored. This can be used to create sounds that loop forever. When the sound stops playing, FALSE is output using the **isActive** eventOut.

The **startTime, stopTime, pitch,** and **loop** field values can be used together to create several standard effects listed in Table 24.1.

Table 24.1   Standard Effects Based on startTime, stopTime, pitch, and loop Field Values

loop field value	*startTime, stopTime, and pitch field value relationships*	*Effect*
TRUE	stopTime £ startTime	Run forever.
TRUE	startTime < stopTime	Run until **stopTime**.
FALSE	stopTime £ startTime	Run for one cycle, then stop at (**startTime** + duration/**pitch**).
FALSE	startTime < (startTime + duration/pitch) £ stopTime	Run for one cycle, then stop at (**startTime** + duration/**pitch**).
FALSE	startTime < stopTime < (startTime + duration/pitch)	Run for less than one cycle, then stop at **stopTime**.

The value of the **pitch** exposed field can be changed by routing an event to the exposed field's implied **set_pitch** eventIn. If the node is active when the new value is received, the new value is ignored. Otherwise, the new pitch value sets the exposed field and is output using the exposed field's implied **pitch_changed** eventOut.

The value of the **url** and **description** exposed fields can be changed by routing an event to the exposed field's implied **set_url** and **set_description** eventIns, respectively. The new value changes the field value and is output using the exposed field's implied **url_changed** and **description_changed** eventOuts, respectively.

The value of the **loop** exposed field can be changed by routing a **TRUE** or **FALSE** event to the exposed field's implied **set_loop** eventIn. If the **loop** field value is changed from **TRUE** to **FALSE**, and the **AudioClip** node is currently active and playing a sound during a cycle, then the playback continues until the end of the cycle, or until the stop time, before stopping. If the **loop** field value is changed from **FALSE** to **TRUE**, and the node is currently active, then the playback loop continues until the stop time. In any case, the **loop** field value is changed, and the new value is output the exposed field's implied **loop_changed** eventOut.

The value of the **startTime** exposed field can be changed by routing an event to the exposed field's implied **set_startTime** eventIn. If the node is active when a new value is received, the new value is ignored. Otherwise, the new value sets the exposed field and is output using the exposed field's implied **startTime_changed** eventOuts.

If the **AudioClip** node is not active when a new start time is received, the node's start time is changed. This may cause the node to become active if the new start time is the current time or is recent enough that the current time is less than (startTime + duration/pitch).

The value of the **stopTime** exposed field can be changed by routing an event to the exposed field's implied **set_stopTime** eventIn. If a new stop time is earlier than the start time, the new stop-time value is ignored. Otherwise, the new stop time changes the **stopTime** field value and is output using the exposed field's implied **stopTime_changed** eventOut. The new stop time is also used to reevaluate whether it is time to stop the sound playback based on the current time, the duration, the pitch, and the new stop time.

The **MovieTexture** Node Syntax

The MovieTexture node specifies texture mapping attributes and may be used as the value for the **texture** field of an **Appearance** node. When a movie file containing audio is used, the MovieTexture node specifies sound that can be played back when the node is used as the value of the **source** field of the **Sound** node.

| SYNTAX | MovieTexture node |

```
MovieTexture {
    url                 [ ]        # exposedField  MFString
    startTime           0.0        # exposedField  SFTime
    stopTime            0.0        # exposedField  SFTime
    speed               1.0        # exposedField  SFFloat
    loop                FALSE      # exposedField  SFBool
    repeatS             TRUE       # field         SFBool
    repeatT             TRUE       # field         SFBool
    isActive                       # eventOut      SFBool
    duration_changed               # eventOut      SFFloat
}
```

The fields of the **MovieTexture** node are discussed in Chapters 17 and 18.

A **MovieTexture** node may be used as a sound source only if the movie file referenced by the **url** field is in the MPEG-1 Systems (audio and video) format. Audio-only MPEG files are not supported.

To synchronize audio and video playback, the same **MovieTexture** node may be used both as a source for a texture and a source for a sound. The **MovieTexture** node should be given a defined name using **DEF**, and then simultaneously used as the value of the **texture** field in an **Appearance** node and for the value of the **source** field in a **Sound** node.

The **Sound** Node Syntax

The **Sound** node creates a sound emitter whose sound can be heard within an ellipsoidal region.

SYNTAX | **Sound node**

```
Sound {
    source        NULL            # exposedField  SFNode
    intensity     1.0             # exposedField  SFFloat
    location      0.0 0.0 0.0     # exposedField  SFVec3f
    direction     0.0 0.0 1.0     # exposedField  SFVec3f
    minFront      1.0             # exposedField  SFFloat
    minBack       1.0             # exposedField  SFFloat
    maxFront      10.0            # exposedField  SFFloat
    maxBack       10.0            # exposedField  SFFloat
    priority      0.0             # exposedField  SFFloat
    spatialize    TRUE            # field         SFBool
}
```

The value of the **source** exposed field provides a node that specifies a sound source for the emitted sound. Typical **source** field values include the **AudioClip** and **Movie-Texture** nodes. The default **NULL** value for this field indicates that no sound source is used and no sound is emitted.

The value of the **intensity** exposed field acts as a master volume control for the sound emitter. Field values must be between 0.0 and 1.0. A value of 1.0 sets the emitter to full volume. Values between 0.0 and 1.0 reduce the emitter volume, reducing the volume range of the sound source. A value of 0.0 reduces the volume to zero, turning off the sound emitter. The default value is 1.0.

The value of the **location** exposed field specifies a 3-D coordinate for the location of the sound emitter in the current coordinate system. The default value places the sound emitter at the origin.

The value of the **direction** exposed field specifies a 3-D vector indicating the aim direction for the sound emitter. The aim vector is specified as three floating-point values, one each for the X, Y, and Z components of a 3-D vector. The default value of the **direction** field creates a sound emitter aimed forward along the positive Z axis.

The values of the **minFront** and **minBack** exposed fields specify the size of a minimum-range ellipsoid surrounding the sound emitter. The **minFront** and **min-Back** field values specify distances to the front and back ends of the ellipsoid, measured in the current coordinate system forward and backward from the emitter location and along an imaginary line parallel to the emitter direction. If the **minFront** and **minBack** field values are equal, the region is a sphere centered on the emitter location. The **minFront** and **minBack** field values both must be greater than or equal to 0.0. The default values for the **minFront** and **minBack** fields specify a spherical region with a radius of 1.0 unit.

The values of the **maxFront** and **maxBack** exposed fields specify the size of a maximum-range ellipsoid in a manner identical to that for the minimum-range ellipsoid. The **maxFront** and **maxBack** field values both must be greater than or equal to 0.0. The default values of the **maxFront** and **maxBack** fields specify a spherical region with a radius of 10.0 units.

The minimum- and maximum-range ellipsoids work together to specify how the sound emitted by a **Sound** node varies in volume as a viewer moves away from the emitter's location.

Between the minimum- and maximum-range ellipsoids, sound volume decreases with the square of the distance between the viewer and the nearest edge of the minimum-range ellipsoid. This matches the way sound volume diminishes in the real world. Within the minimum-range ellipsoid, the sound is heard at full and constant volume. Outside the maximum-range ellipsoid, the sound's volume is zero, and the sound is not heard.

Typically, the minimum-range ellipsoid is fully contained within the maximum-range ellipsoid. However, if the **maxFront** or **maxBack** field values are either one less than the corresponding **minFront** and **minBack** field values, then the maximum-range ellipsoid may be partially or fully contained within the minimum-range ellipsoid. In this case, the minimum-range ellipsoid takes precedence, and sound volume drops to zero immediately outside of the minimum-range ellipsoid.

The value of the **priority** field specifies a prioritization hint to the VRML browser for use when there are more sounds to be played than the sound generation hardware can support. Sound priority values range between 0.0 and 1.0, where 1.0 is the highest priority. Typically, low-priority values are used for background music and sounds, while high-priority values are used for special sound cues, such as sound effects. The default sound priority is 0.0.

If the VRML browser has more sounds to play than the hardware can support, it sorts the sounds to produce a list ordered from highest to lowest priority, as follows:

- Sounds are sorted from highest to lowest by **priority** field values.
- Among sounds with the same priority, where the priority is greater than 0.5, sounds are sorted in increasing order based on the length of time the sound has been playing (the current time minus the sound source's **startTime** field value).
- Among sounds with the same priority and playing time, sounds are sorted in decreasing order based on the volume of the sound at the viewer's location.

Once sorted, the sounds at the top of the list are played in preference to those farther down in the list. This sorting approach ensures that high-priority sounds take precedence over lower-priority sounds. The approach also ensures that among sounds with the same priority, those that have started recently or that are nearby take precedence.

SIDEBAR: MIDI VERSUS DIGITAL SOUND PRECEDENCE On most systems, the number of digital sound sources that can be played is independent of the number of MIDI sound sources that can be played. On these systems, the VRML browser may maintain two sorted sound lists, one for digital sound sources and one for MIDI sound sources.

The value of the **spatialize** field specifies a **TRUE** or **FALSE** value that indicates whether the sound is processed to provide a 3-D sound localization effect. When the field value is **TRUE,** the sound source is converted to a monaural signal, spatially processed, and played over the sound hardware's left and right outputs. Sound processing typically creates a 3-D localization effect that makes a sound appear to come from a 3-D location in space. When the **spatialize** field value is **FALSE,** the sound source is played over the sound hardware's left and right outputs without monaural conversion or spatialization processing. Whether the field is TRUE or FALSE, the emitted sound's volume is controlled by the minimum- and maximum-range ellipsoids. The default value for the **spatialize** field is **TRUE.**

TIP Some VRML browsers or sound cards do not support the digital signal processing necessary to spatialize a sound. On such systems, setting the **spatialize** field value to **TRUE** converts the sound to monaural and pans it appropriately left and right without additional signal delay and frequency-content processing.

The sound emitter's attributes can be changed by sending values to the implied **set_source, set_intensity, set_location, set_direction, set_minFront, set_minBack, set_maxFront, set_maxBack,** and **set_priority** eventIns of the exposed fields. When values are received by these inputs, the corresponding field values are changed, and the new values are output using the implied **source_changed, intensity_changed, location_changed, direction_changed, minFront_changed, minBack_changed, max-Front_changed, maxBack_changed,** and **priority_changed** eventOuts of the exposed fields.

The sound emitted by a **Sound** node can be heard only if the **Sound** node is encountered by the VRML browser as it draws the world. For instance, if a **Sound** node is the child of a **Switch** node, but the **Switch** node's **whichChoice** field value specifies a different child, the **Sound** node is not encountered by the VRML browser during drawing and no sound is emitted from the node.

Experimenting with Sound

The following examples provide a more detailed examination of the ways in which the **AudioClip, MovieTexture,** and **Sound** nodes can be used.

The following examples all use digital sound files, MIDI files, and MPEG files available on the book's CD-ROM, including the files listed in Table 24.2.

Table 24.2   Digital Sound Files, MIDI Files, and MPEG Files Available on the Book's CD-ROM

Sound File	Type	Length	Description
bachfuge.mid	MIDI	4 minutes, 54 seconds	Bach fugue, played on guitar
drone1.wav	WAV	18.41 seconds	Ominous low drone
ghostly1.wav	WAV	28.07 seconds	Ghostly drone
tone1.wav	WAV	1.59 seconds	Simple tone
tv.mpg	MPEG	14.06 seconds	Television animation
willow1.wav	WAV	28.77 seconds	Wispy New Age drone

Creating Emitter Markers

The **Sound** node creates no shapes to mark its location or the extent of its minimum- and maximum-range ellipsoids. When experimenting with sound, it is often convenient to create a set of temporary shapes to mark the emitter's location and range. This can help make it clear where a sound emitter is and over what range it can be heard.

Many of the following examples use a set of generic emitter marker shapes created and stored in "sndmark.wrl." The VRML text in Figure 24.1 shows this marker file and consists of:

- An emissive white sphere to mark an emitter's location.
- A pink circle to mark the extent of an emitter's minimum-range ellipsoid.
- A purple circle to mark the extent of an emitter's maximum-range ellipsoid.

All of the emitter-marker shapes are centered at the origin. The minimum-range ellipsoid marker has a radius of 5.0 units, and the maximum-range ellipsoid has a radius of 10.0 units.

```
#VRML V2.0 utf8
Group {
    children [
```

Figure 24.1 continues

```
# Emitter marker
    Shape {
        appearance Appearance {
            material Material {
                diffuseColor  0.0 0.0 0.0
                emissiveColor 1.0 1.0 1.0
            }
        }
        geometry Sphere { radius 0.25 }
    },
# Minimum range ellipsoid (circle) marker
    DEF MinMarker Shape {
        appearance Appearance {
            material Material {
                diffuseColor  0.0 0.0 0.0
                emissiveColor 1.0 0.0 0.5
            }
        }
        geometry Cylinder {
            radius 5.0
            height 0.01
            side   FALSE
            bottom FALSE
        }
    },
# Maximum range ellipsoid (circle) marker
    DEF MaxMarker Shape {
        appearance Appearance {
            material Material {
                diffuseColor  0.0 0.0 0.0
                emissiveColor 0.5 0.0 1.0
            }
        }
        geometry Cylinder {
            radius 10.0
            height 0.001
            side   FALSE
            bottom FALSE
        }
    },
    ]
}
```

Figure 24.1 *A set of emitter markers indicating the emitter's location, minimum-range ellipsoid, and maximum-range ellipsoid.*

Creating an Ambient Sound

An *ambient sound* is one that plays continually. Ambient sounds are typically used to play background music or to play sounds that set a mood for the virtual environment.

To make a sound play continually, you can set the **loop** field value to **TRUE** in an **AudioClip** node. When the world is read by the browser the sound begins playing immediately and repeats forever.

The VRML text in Figure 24.2 builds a world with an ambient sound emitter at the origin. The sound is emitted by a **Sound** node that uses an **AudioClip** node as the sound source. The **AudioClip** node plays a repeating digital sound from the file "willow1.wav." The **Sound** node's minimum-range ellipsoid is configured with front and back values of 5.0 units. The maximum-range ellipsoid is configured with front and back values of 10.0 units. To make it easier to understand the location of the emitter and the extent of its range ellipsoids, the generic emitter marker shapes built in Figure 24.2 are inlined from the file "sndmark.wrl."

```
#VRML V2.0 utf8
Group {
    children [
    # Sound emitter
        Sound {
            source AudioClip {
                url "willow1.wav"
                loop TRUE
            }
            minFront 5.0
            minBack  5.0
            maxFront 10.0
            maxBack  10.0
        },
    # Sound emitter markers
        Inline { url "sndmark.wrl" }
    ]
}
```

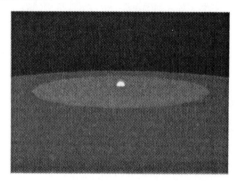

Figure 24.2 *A world with ambient sound and a set of emitter markers.*

With this ambient sound world read by the browser, try walking toward and away from the sound emitter marked by the glowing white sphere in the middle of the world. When you are outside the outer-marker circle (purple), the sound's volume is zero. When you enter the region between the outer- and inner-marker circles (between pink and purple), the sound's volume rises. Finally, when you enter the inner-marker circle (pink), the sound reaches full volume and stays at that level as you move within the inner-marker circle.

As you move through this world, try wearing a pair of headphones. Your VRML browser automatically spatializes the sound so that it changes as you move in the space. For instance, if you enter the inner-marker circle then turn so that the sound emitter is on your left, the sound you hear pans to the left. If your VRML browser supports full spatialization processing, the sound is processed to create a 3-D effect.

The example in Figure 24.2 uses a digital sound file as the sound source. You can also use a MIDI file as the sound source selected by an **AudioClip** node. In the above example, try replacing the **AudioClip** node's **url** field value with the file "bachfuge.mid" to select a Bach fugue as the sound to play in the world.

You can include multiple **Sound** nodes within the same world. As viewers move through the world, they hear the emitted sound from all nearby **Sound** nodes.

Triggering a Sound

You can use a circuit to trigger a sound to begin. For instance, to trigger a sound when a shape is touched, use a **TouchSensor** node and route its **touchTime** eventOut to the implied **set_startTime** eventIn of an **AudioClip** node.

The VRML text in Figure 24.3 builds a world with a triggered sound at the origin. A **Sound** node creates a sound emitter that uses an **AudioClip** node as the sound source. The **AudioClip** node plays a digital sound from the file "tone1.wav." The **loop** field value is set to **FALSE** so that the sound plays from beginning to end and stops without looping. The generic emitter-marker shapes are inlined from "sndmark.wrl" and sensed by a **TouchSensor** node. The **TouchSensor** node's **touchTime** eventOut is routed to the **AudioClip** node's implied **set_startTime** eventIn to trigger the sound whenever any of the marker shapes are touched.

```
#VRML V2.0 utf8
Group {
    children [
    # Sound emitter
        Sound {
            source DEF Source AudioClip {
                url "tone1.wav"
                loop FALSE
            }
            minFront 5.0
            minBack  5.0
            maxFront 10.0
            maxBack  10.0
        },
    # Sound emitter markers
        Inline { url "sndmark.wrl" },
    # Sensor
        DEF Touch TouchSensor { }
    ]
}
ROUTE Touch.touchTime TO Source.set_startTime
```

Figure 24.3 *A world with a sound triggered by touching a set of emitter markers.*

Changing the Pitch of a Sound

The **pitch** field of the **AudioClip** node controls the speed at which a sound is played. As the speed increases, the pitch increases as well. You can use this effect to create a virtual musical instrument in your world.

Figure 24.4 builds four keys of a virtual keyboard. Each key has a shape (a **Box** node), a **TouchSensor** node, an **AudioClip** node specifying an audio source, and a **Sound** node to emit a sound when the key shape is touched. Each key's **AudioClip** node uses a different **pitch** field value to set the pitch of the sound played for the key.

```
#VRML V2.0 utf8
Group {
    children [
    # Middle C (C4)
        Transform {
            children [
                DEF WhiteKey Shape {
                    appearance Appearance {
                        material Material { }
                    }
                    geometry Box { size 0.23 0.1 1.5 }
                },
                DEF C4 TouchSensor { },
                Sound {
                    source DEF PitchC4 AudioClip {
                        url "tone1.wav"
                        pitch 1.0
                    }
                }
            ]
        },
    # C# above middle C (Cs4)
        Transform { translation 0.125 0.1 -0.375
            children [
                DEF BlackKey Shape {
                    appearance Appearance {
                        material Material {
                            diffuseColor 0.4 0.4 0.4
                        }
                    }
                    geometry Box { size 0.2 0.1 0.75 }
                },
                DEF Cs4 TouchSensor { }
                Sound {
                    source DEF PitchCs4 AudioClip {
                        url "tone1.wav"
                        pitch 1.059
                    }
                }
            ]
        },
    # D above middle C (D4)
        Transform { translation 0.25 0.0 0.0
            children [
                USE WhiteKey,
                DEF D4 TouchSensor { }
                Sound {
                    source DEF PitchD4 AudioClip {
                        url "tone1.wav"
                        pitch 1.122
                    }
                }
            ]
        },
```

Figure 24.4 continues

```
# D# above middle C (Ds4)
    Transform { translation 0.375 0.1 -0.375
        children [
            USE BlackKey,
            DEF Ds4 TouchSensor { }
            Sound {
                source DEF PitchDs4 AudioClip {
                    url "tone1.wav"
                    pitch 1.189
                }
            }
        ]
    }
  ]
}
ROUTE C4.touchTime   TO PitchC4.set_startTime
ROUTE Cs4.touchTime  TO PitchCs4.set_startTime
ROUTE D4.touchTime   TO PitchD4.set_startTime
ROUTE Ds4.touchTime  TO PitchDs4.set_startTime
```

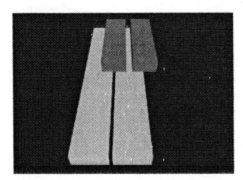

Figure 24.4   *Four keys on a virtual keyboard.*

You can extend this virtual keyboard to complete an octave by adding more keys using the **pitch** values shown in Table 24.3 for the keyboard's white and black keys.

Table 24.2   Pitch Values for Building a Virtual Keyboard

Keyboard Key	Key Type	Pitch	Keyboard Key	Key Type	PitchF
C-1	white	0.031	F#2	black	0.354
C#-1	black	0.033	G2	white	0.375
D-1	white	0.035	G#2	black	0.397
D#-1	black	0.037	A3	white	0.420
E-1	white	0.039	A#3	black	0.445
F-1	white	0.042	B3	white	0.472
F#-1	black	0.044	C3	white	0.500
G-1	white	0.047	C#3	black	0.530
G#-1	black	0.050	D3	white	0.561
A0	white	0.053	D#3	black	0.595
A#0	black	0.056	E3	white	0.630
B0	white	0.059	F3	white	0.667
C0	white	0.062	F#3	black	0.707
C#0	black	0.066	G3	white	0.749
D0	white	0.070	G#3	black	0.794
D#0	black	0.074	A4	white	0.841
E0	white	0.079	A#4	black	0.891
F0	white	0.083	B4	white	0.944
F#0	black	0.088	C4 (middle-C)	white	1.000
G0	white	0.094	C#4	black	1.059
G#0	black	0.099	D4	white	1.122
A1	white	0.105	D#4	black	1.189
A#1	black	0.111	E4	white	1.260
B1	white	0.118	F4	white	1.335
C1	white	0.125	F#4	black	1.414
C#1	black	0.132	G4	white	1.498
D1	white	0.140	G#4	black	1.587
D#1	black	0.149	A5	white	1.682
E1	white	0.157	A#5	black	1.782
F1	white	0.167	B5	white	1.888
F#1	black	0.177	C5	white	2.000
G1	white	0.187	C#5	black	2.119
G#1	black	0.198	D5	white	2.245
A2	white	0.210	D#5	black	2.378
A#2	black	0.223	E5	white	2.520
B2	white	0.236	F5	white	2.670
C2	white	0.250	F#5	black	2.828
C#2	black	0.265	G5	white	2.997
D2	white	0.281	G#5	black	3.175
D#2	black	0.297	A6	white	3.364
E2	white	0.315	A#6	black	3.564
F2	white	0.334	B6	white	3.775

Table 24.2 continues

Table 24.2   Pitch Values for Building a Virtual Keyboard

Keyboard Key	Key Type	Pitch	Keyboard Key	Key Type	Pitch
C6	white	4.000	F#7	black	11.314
C#6	black	4.238	G7	white	11.986
D6	white	4.490	G#7	black	12.699
D#6	black	4.757	A8	white	13.454
E6	white	5.040	A#8	black	14.254
F6	white	5.339	B8	white	15.102
F#6	black	5.657	C8	white	16.000
G6	white	5.993	C#8	black	16.951
G#6	black	6.350	D8	white	17.959
A7	white	6.727	D#8	black	19.027
A#7	black	7.127	E8	white	20.159
B7	white	7.551	F8	white	21.357
C7	white	8.000	F#8	black	22.627
C#7	black	8.476	G8	white	23.973
D7	white	8.980	G#8	black	25.398
D#7	black	9.514	A9	white	26.909
E7	white	10.079	A#9	black	28.509
F7	white	10.679	B9	white	30.204

Animating Sound Location

You can use the **location** field of a **Sound** node to specify the emitter location within the current coordinate system. You can also use a **Transform** node to translate, rotate, and scale the coordinate system in which a sound emitter is placed. Using a circuit, you can move sounds around in a world.

Figure 24.5 extends the ambient sound example found in Figure 24.2 by doubling the ambient sound and adding nodes to animate the coordinate system enclosing each sound emitter. Two **TimeSensor** nodes clock the animation, while two **OrientationInterpolator** nodes specify coordinate system rotations for the two sound emitters. The first emitter's clock and path takes it in a slow, counterclockwise circle around the origin, while the second emitter's clock and path take it in a faster clockwise circle around the origin. A glowing cyan sphere is placed at the origin to mark the center of the world. The movement of the two sounds is most pronounced if you walk to the cyan sphere and remain stationary as the sounds move around you.

```
#VRML V2.0 utf8
Group {
    children [
    # Origin marker
        Shape {
            appearance Appearance {
                material Material {
                    diffuseColor 0.0 0.0 0.0
                    emissiveColor 0.0 1.0 1.0
                }
            }
            geometry Sphere { radius 0.5 }
        },
    # Sound emitter 1
        DEF Emitter1 Transform {
            translation 5.0 0.0 0.0
            center -5.0 0.0 0.0
            children [
                Sound {
                    source AudioClip {
                        url "willow1.wav"
                        loop TRUE
                    }
                    intensity 0.5
                    minFront 5.0
                    minBack  5.0
                    maxFront 10.0
                    maxBack  10.0
                },
                DEF SoundMarker Inline { url "sndmark.wrl" }
            ]
        },
        DEF Emitter1Clock TimeSensor {
            cycleInterval 15.0
            loop TRUE
        },
        DEF Emitter1Path OrientationInterpolator {
            key [ 0.0, 0.5, 1.0 ]
            keyValue [ 0.0 1.0 0.0 0.0, 0.0 1.0 0.0 3.14, 0.0 1.0 0.0 6.28 ]
        },
    # Sound emitter 2
        DEF Emitter2 Transform {
            translation -5.0 0.0 0.0
            center 5.0 0.0 0.0
```

Figure 24.5 continues

```
            children [
                Sound {
                    source AudioClip {
                        url "drone1.wav"
                        loop TRUE
                    }
                    intensity 0.5
                    minFront 5.0
                    minBack  5.0
                    maxFront 10.0
                    maxBack  10.0
                },
                USE SoundMarker
            ]
        },
        DEF Emitter2Clock TimeSensor {
            cycleInterval 7.0
            loop TRUE
        },
        DEF Emitter2Path OrientationInterpolator {
            key [ 0.0, 0.5, 1.0 ]
            keyValue [ 0.0 1.0 0.0 0.0, 0.0 1.0 0.0 3.14, 0.0 1.0 0.0 6.28 ]
        },
    ]
}
ROUTE Emitter1Clock.fraction_changed TO Emitter1Path.set_fraction
ROUTE Emitter2Clock.fraction_changed TO Emitter2Path.set_fraction
ROUTE Emitter1Path.value_changed     TO Emitter1.set_rotation
ROUTE Emitter2Path.value_changed     TO Emitter2.set_rotation
```

Figure 24.5 *Two ambient sounds circling the origin.*

Controlling Sound Direction

Most real-world sound emitters do not emit sound uniformly in all directions. Instead, they emit sound primarily in one direction. A speaker on a home audio system, for instance, strongly emits sound in the speaker's forward direction.

You can use the **Sound** node's direction and range ellipsoid values to cause a sound emitter to emit primarily in one direction. For example, the VRML text in Figure 24.6 builds a world with a single sound emitter. The emitter is aimed to the right, along the positive X axis, by setting its direction field value to 1.0 0.0 0.0. The emitter's minimum-range ellipsoid is stretched to the right, along the emitter direction, by setting the **minFront** field value to 5.0 units and the **minBack** field value to 1.0 unit. Similarly, the emitter's maximum-range ellipsoid is stretched to the right by setting the **maxFront** field value to 10.0 units and the **maxBack** field value to 2.0 units.

To mark the size and location of the emitter and the range ellipsoids, marker shapes are added to the world. The generic marker shapes used in previous examples assume the range ellipsoids are spheres centered on the emitter. In this example, however, the range ellipsoids are both oblong spheres stretched to the right and positioned off-center from the emitter's location. To mark these ellipsoids, Figure 24.6 shows a custom-built set of marker shapes created by translating and scaling marker spheres like those in the generic marker shape built in Figure 24.1.

```
#VRML V2.0 utf8
Group {
    children [
    # Directed sound emitter
        Sound {
            source AudioClip {
                url "willow1.wav"
                loop TRUE
            }
            direction 1.0 0.0 0.0
            minFront 5.0
            minBack  1.0
            maxFront 10.0
            maxBack  2.0
        },
    # Emitter marker
        Shape {
            appearance Appearance {
                material Material {
                    diffuseColor  0.0 0.0 0.0
                    emissiveColor 1.0 1.0 1.0
                }
            }
            geometry Sphere { radius 0.25 }
        },
    # Minimum range ellipsoid marker
        Transform {
            translation 2.0 0.0 0.0
            scale 3.0 2.0 2.0
            children DEF MinMarker Shape {
                appearance Appearance {
                    material Material {
                        diffuseColor  0.0 0.0 0.0
                        emissiveColor 1.0 0.0 0.5
                    }
                }
                geometry Cylinder {
                    radius 1.0
                    height 0.01
                    side   FALSE
                    bottom FALSE
                }
            }
        },
    # Maximum range ellipsoid marker
        Transform {
            translation 4.0 0.0 0.0
            scale 6.0 4.0 4.0
```

Figure 24.6 continues

```
children DEF MaxMarker Shape {
    appearance Appearance {
        material Material {
            diffuseColor  0.0 0.0 0.0
            emissiveColor 0.5 0.0 1.0
        }
    }
    geometry Cylinder {
        radius 1.0
        height 0.001
        side   FALSE
        bottom FALSE
    }
}
        ]
    }
}
```

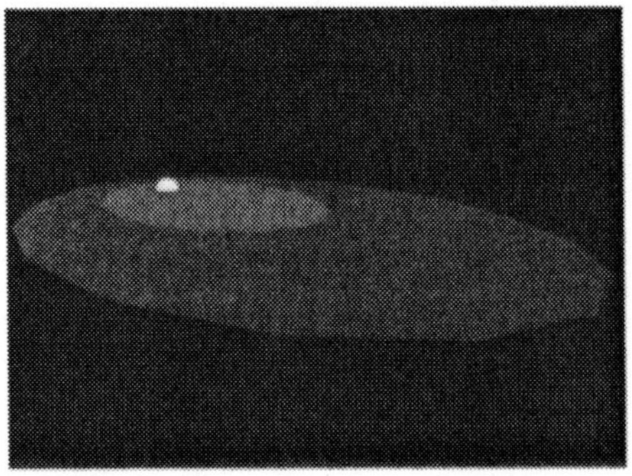

Figure 24.6 *An ambient sound aimed to the right.*

Using MPEG Sound Sources

You can use a **MovieTexture** node to specify a sound source for a **Sound** node, while simultaneously using the same node as a texture source for texture mapping a shape. These features of VRML enable you to create virtual televisions and movie screens that show animated imagery while playing synchronized sound.

Figure 24.7 builds a virtual television using a **Box** node to build the chassis, two **IndexedFaceSet** nodes to build the television screen and control panel, a **MovieTexture** node to play images on the television screen, and a **Sound** node to emit the television audio. A **TouchSensor** node sensing the television triggers the playback of the movie images and sound.

```
#VRML V2.0 utf8
Group {
    children [
    # Chassis
        Shape {
            appearance Appearance {
                material Material { diffuseColor 0.3 0.3 0.3 }
            }
            geometry Box { size 5.0 3.5 2.0 }
        },
```

Figure 24.7 continues

```
# Controls
    Shape {
        appearance Appearance {
            material Material { }
            texture ImageTexture {
                url "tvcntrl.jpg"
                repeatS FALSE
                repeatT FALSE
            }
        }
        geometry IndexedFaceSet {
            coord Coordinate {
                point [
                    1.75 -1.5 1.01,   2.40 -1.5 1.01,
                    2.40  1.5 1.01,   1.75  1.5 1.01,
                ]
            }
            coordIndex [ 0, 1, 2, 3 ]
            texCoord TextureCoordinate {
                point [
                    0.0 0.0,   1.0 0.0,
                    1.0 1.0,   0.0 1.0
                ]
            }
        }
    },
# Screen
    Shape {
        appearance Appearance {
            material Material {
                diffuseColor 0.0 0.0 0.0
                emissiveColor 1.0 1.0 1.0
            }
            texture DEF TV MovieTexture {
                url "tv.mpg"
                loop FALSE
                repeatS FALSE
                repeatT FALSE
            }
        }
        geometry IndexedFaceSet {
            coord Coordinate {
                point [
                    -2.35 -1.5 1.01,
                     1.65 -1.5 1.01,
                     1.65  1.5 1.01,
                    -2.35  1.5 1.01
                ]
            }
            coordIndex [ 0, 1, 2, 3 ]
        }
    },
```

Figure 24.7 continues

```
# Sound
    Sound {
        # Use MovieTexture as sound source
        source USE TV
        minFront 30.0
        minBack  30.0
        maxFront 100.0
        maxBack  100.0
    },
# Trigger on touch
    DEF Touch TouchSensor { }
  ]
}
ROUTE Touch.touchTime TO TV.set_startTime
```

Figure 24.7 *A virtual TV.*

Summary

The **Sound** node specifies a sound emitter in the environment. The **source** field of the **Sound** node selects a sound source, described by either an **AudioClip** node or a **MovieTexture** node. The **intensity** field of the **Sound** node acts as a master volume control for the sound source. The **location** and **direction** fields of the **Sound** node specify the location of the sound emitter and the direction in which it faces.

The **minFront** and **minBack** fields of the **Sound** node specify the size of a minimum-range ellipsoid for the emitter, while the **maxFront** and **maxBack** fields specify the size of a maximum-range ellipsoid. When the viewer is inside the minimum-range ellipsoid, the emitted sound is heard at full volume. When the viewer is outside the maximum-range ellipsoid, the sound is too far away to be heard and has zero volume. When the viewer is between the minimum- and maximum-range ellipsoids, the emitted sound is heard at a volume that diminishes with the square of the distance from the emitter.

The **priority** field of the **Sound** node specifies a priority for the sound. Priorities are used by the VRML browser to specify which of multiple, simultaneous sounds should be played when the sound hardware cannot play them all at once.

The **spatialize** field of the **Sound** node enables or disables the use of digital signal processing that creates a 3-D effect to position emitted sounds around the head of the listener.

The **url** field of the **AudioClip** node selects a WAV digital sound file or a MIDI file for playback as a sound source. The **description** field specifies an optional message that a VRML browser may display instead of playing the sound if the computer does not support sound playback. The **startTime** and **stopTime** fields specify when the sound is played, and the **loop** field indicates whether the sound is played repeatedly.

The **pitch** field of the **AudioClip** node specifies a speed multiplier for sound playback. Values greater than 1.0 increase the pitch of the sound, while values between 0.0 and 1.0 reduce the sound's pitch.

## CHAPTER 25

Controlling Detail

As you add more detail to your worlds, your VRML browser takes longer to build them, and they seem less interactive. You are forced to strike a balance between lots of detail for maximum realism and quick drawing for maximum interactivity.

One technique that can help you control world detail is to take advantage of the fact that shapes farther away from you in the world need not be drawn with as much detail as those close to you. Shapes very distant need not be drawn at all since you can hardly see them anyway. By reducing the detail of distant shapes, you give your VRML browser less to draw, and thus increase interactivity. You can control these different levels of detail using the VRML **LOD** (level of detail) node.

Understanding Detail Control

The level-of-detail technique comes from computer graphics flight simulators used to train aircraft pilots. In such a simulator, the pilot flies a simulated plane over a simulated landscape, practicing takeoff, landing, and other flight maneuvers. Realism is important, but so is interactivity.

To make a flight simulator feel realistic, the terrain needs lots of detail, including shapes for buildings, streets, cars, trees, and so on. Since the aircraft can fly anywhere over a large terrain, that same detail is needed throughout. With trees, buildings, and so on, in close proximity and far away, the realism of the simulator is great, but the interactivity is poor. Drawing all the detail slows down the system.

To increase the speed of the system, flight simulator designers noted that less detail is needed for distant terrain, than for that directly below the aircraft. Drawing each individual tree for a distant forest is a waste of time since the aircraft pilot can't see that far away anyway. By replacing distant trees with simpler shapes, such as a single green face for the entire forest, the flight simulator can draw the world more quickly and increase interactivity. Only when the aircraft flies close to the forest does the simulator replace the green face with individual tree shapes.

This same technique can be used for buildings, cars, streets, and so on. Each shape is created in multiple versions, typically with high, medium, and low detail. The high-detail version is used only when the aircraft is in close proximity. The medium-detail version is used when the aircraft is farther away, and the low-detail version is used when the aircraft is far away. For greater control, there can be more detail levels, though typically two or three is enough.

You can use this same detail-control technique when designing your own VRML worlds. For complex shapes, create two or three versions. The high-detail version has all the detail needed for realism, but it is used only when the viewer is close to the shape. The medium-detail version has only the essential components of the shape and is used when the viewer is farther away. The low-detail version has very few components, providing only the basic parts necessary when the shape is seen from far away.

Understanding Level-of-Detail Groups

After creating several different versions of a shape in varying levels of detail, you can enclose them within a level-of-detail group built by an **LOD** node. The different detail versions are included in the group by listing them in the **level** field of the node. The highest detail version is listed first, then the second highest, and so forth.

Within the node, you also provide your browser with information to help it automatically switch between the different versions based on how far away the viewer is from them. This distance between the viewer and a shape is called the *range*. If you have *three* different detail versions of a shape, then you need to specify *two* different range values in the **range** field of the **LOD** node. The first range value specifies the distance at which to switch from the first to the second version of the shape. The second range value specifies the distance at which to switch from the second version to the third.

The range is a measure of the distance between the viewer and the center of your shape in the **LOD** node. By default, the center of the shape is at the coordinate system's origin. If you've designed your shape to be centered somewhere other than the origin, you can specify the actual center of your shape by using the **center** field in the **LOD** node.

Range values are used by your VRML browser as hints about when to switch between versions. Your browser may follow your directions exactly, or it may choose to switch versions based on performance considerations. For instance, if your browser is trying to keep movement in your world as interactive as possible, it may choose to use a lower detail version of shapes while the viewer is moving, then switch to a higher detail version when the viewer stops moving.

You can pass detail-switching control entirely over to your VRML browser by providing no range values yourself. In this case, the **range** field of the node is left empty.

The **LOD** Node Syntax

VRML nodes describing different detail levels of a shape can be grouped together using the **LOD** node.

SYNTAX	LOD node

```
LOD {
    center   0.0 0.0 0.0   # field         SFVec3f
    level    [ ]           # exposedField  MFNode
    range    [ ]           # field         MFFloat
}
```

The value of the **level** exposed field specifies a list of child nodes to be included in the group. Typical **level** field values include **Shape** nodes and other grouping nodes. The group as a whole is presumed to describe a single shape, with each child in the **level** field value list describing a different version of that shape. The first child provides the highest-detail version of the shape, and subsequent children provide lower-detail versions. Based on the distance from the viewer to the center of the **LOD** group node, measured in the current coordinate system, a single child from the **level** field value list is selected and drawn. As the viewer moves closer and farther away from the group, different children are selected. The default value for this field is an empty list of children.

The value of the **center** field specifies the 3-D coordinate in the current coordinate system for the center of the shape built within the **LOD** node. The distance between the viewer and the center coordinate is used to select between the versions of the shape provided in the **level** field value list. The default value for the **center** field is the origin.

The value of the **range** field specifies a list of viewer-to-shape distances at which the browser should switch from one level of detail to another. If there are n different detail versions of a shape in the **level** field value list, then there should be $n - 1$ ranges listed in the **range** field. Alternatively, if the **range** field value is an empty list, then the VRML browser uses its own algorithm for selecting between versions of the shape. The default value for the **range** field is an empty list.

Range values in the **range** field must be positive and must be listed in increasing order. When the viewer is closer than the first range, the first child in the **level** field list is drawn. When the viewer is between the first and second ranges, the second child in the **level** field list is drawn, and so on. If there are fewer children in the **level** field value list than there are ranges, then the last child in the list is used for the extra ranges. If there are more children in the **level** field value list than there are ranges, then the extra children are ignored.

Range values should be chosen so that a switch from one detail version to the next is barely noticeable. When specified, range values are always treated as hints to the VRML browser. The browser is free to ignore range values and use its own algorithm for selecting between detail versions. For best results, specify range values only when necessary. The rest of the time, use an empty range list for the **range** field in order to give the browser the greatest freedom in controlling detail selection to optimize drawing speed.

The group's children can be changed by sending values to the implied **set_level** eventIn of the **level** exposed field. When a value is received on this input, the field value is changed, and the new value is output using the implied **level_changed** eventOut.

The shape built within the **LOD** node is built within the current coordinate system. The translation, rotation, and scaling features of a **Transform** node affect the shape, as well as the **center** and **range** field values.

Nodes within any of an **LOD** node's children continue to receive and send events, even when they are not specified to be drawn.

Experimenting with Level of Detail

The following examples provide a more detailed examination of the ways in which the **LOD** node can be used and how it interacts with nodes discussed in previous chapters.

Creating Multiple Detail Versions of a Shape

An **LOD** node is, conceptually, a description of a single shape. Each child in the **LOD** node is a different version of that same shape. These different versions may be constructed the same, or differently. For example, a high-detail version of a shape may use several **IndexedFaceSet** nodes, but lower-detail versions may use primitive shapes like **Sphere** and **Box** nodes.

The detail versions of a shape are typically highly related. The highest-detail version may include textures and small features only visible when the viewer is close by. A mid-detail version of the shape may drop the small features but keep the larger features and textures. Finally, a low-detail version of the shape may drop the textures and all but the most basic visual features of the shape.

The following examples build three different versions of a torch to be placed on the wall of a dungeon. Each version of the torch has a handle, a fire pot, and one or more flames in the fire pot. The way these parts of the torch are built varies from the high- to the low-detail version of the torch.

Figure 25.1 creates the high-detail version of the torch. The torch handle is built using a **Cone** node. The fire pot is built using two **Cylinder** nodes and several faces in an **IndexedFaceSet** node. The flames in the fire pot are built using several faces in an **IndexedFaceSet** node. Finally, a mounting bracket for the torch is created using several **Box** nodes.

```
#VRML V2.0 utf8
Transform {
    translation 0.0 0.0 0.2
    scale 0.5 0.5 0.5
    children [
    # Torch handle
        Transform {
            translation 0.0 -0.75 0.0
            rotation 1.0 0.0 0.0 3.14
            children Shape {
                appearance DEF Gray Appearance {
                    material Material {
                        diffuseColor  0.4 0.4 0.4
                        specularColor 0.7 0.7 0.7
                    }
                }
                geometry Cone {
                    height 1.5
                    bottomRadius 0.15
                }
            }
        },
    # Fire pot
        DEF Ring Shape {
            appearance USE Gray
            geometry Cylinder {
                height 0.1
                radius 0.4
                top    FALSE
                bottom FALSE
            }
        },
        Transform { translation 0.0 0.2 0.0 children USE Ring },
    # Fire pot detail
        DEF Bar Shape {
            appearance USE Gray
            geometry IndexedFaceSet {
                coord Coordinate {
                    point [
                        0.04 0.00 0.38,  0.04 0.35 0.38,
                       -0.04 0.35 0.38, -0.04 0.00 0.38,
                    ]
                }
                coordIndex [ 0, 1, 2, 3 ]
            }
        },
        Transform { rotation 0.0 1.0 0.0 -1.571 children USE Bar },
        Transform { rotation 0.0 1.0 0.0 -0.785 children USE Bar },
        Transform { rotation 0.0 1.0 0.0  0.785 children USE Bar },
        Transform { rotation 0.0 1.0 0.0  1.571 children USE Bar },
```

Figure 25.1 continues

```
# Mounting bracket
    Transform {
        translation 0.0 -0.35 0.0
        children [
            Shape {
                appearance USE Gray
                geometry Cylinder {
                    height 0.15
                    radius 0.20
                }
            },
            Transform {
                translation 0.0 0.0 -0.2
                children Shape {
                    appearance USE Gray
                    geometry Box { size 0.45 0.25 0.39 }
                }
            }
        ]
    },
# Flames
    DEF Flames Shape {
        # No appearance, use emissive shading
        geometry IndexedFaceSet {
            coord Coordinate {
                point [
                     0.25 0.0 0.00,  0.15 1.0 0.10,
                     0.05 0.0 0.15,  0.18 0.0 0.05,
                     0.00 1.2 0.05, -0.10 0.0 0.05,
                    -0.00 0.0 0.15, -0.13 0.8 0.10,
                    -0.25 0.0 0.00,
                ]
            }
            color Color {
                color [
                    1.0 0.0 0.0,  0.9 0.5 0.0,
                    1.0 0.0 0.0,  0.9 0.3 0.0,
                    1.0 1.0 0.0,  0.9 0.3 0.0,
                    0.7 0.1 0.2,  0.9 0.8 0.0,
                    1.0 0.0 0.0,
                ]
            }
            coordIndex [
                0, 1, 2, -1,  3, 4, 5, -1,  6, 7, 8, -1,
            ]
        }
    },
# Additional Flames
    Transform {
        rotation 0.0 1.0 0.0 1.57
        scale    0.9 0.9 1.0
        children USE Flames
    },
```

Figure 25.1 continues

```
Transform {
    rotation 0.0 1.0 0.0 -1.57
    scale    0.9 0.9 1.0
    children USE Flames
    }
  ]
}
```

Figure 25.1 *A high-detail torch.*

You can get a rough idea of the complexity of the high-detail torch by counting the number of coordinates used by all of its shapes. Though the number of coordinates used by a primitive shape, such as a **Cone** node, varies from browser to browser and with distance. Table 25.1 provides representative numbers.

Table 25.1   Approximate Number of Coordinates in the High-Detail Torch

Torch Part	VRML Shapes	Approximate Number of Coordinates
Handle	Cone	17
Fire pot	Two cylinders	$2 \times 32 = 64$
Fire pot detail	Five faces	$5 \times 4 = 20$
Mounting bracket	Box and cylinder	$8 + 32 = 40$
Flames	Faces	9
Additional flames	Two flames	$2 \times 9 = 18$
TOTAL		168

The total complexity of the high-detail torch is approximately 168 coordinates. While this is by no means a perfect measure of how hard this shape is for the VRML browser to draw, it is at least a partial measure and something you can look at when trying to reduce the shape's detail to create medium- and low-detail versions.

When the torch is some distance from the viewer, some of the detail can be dropped without the viewer noticing. In particular, the fire pot can be built more simply by eliminating the vertical faces. The wall-mounting bracket can be skipped, and the two additional sets of flames can be eliminated. These simplifications reduce the shape's coordinate count by 78 coordinates—approximately a 46 percent reduction from the original shape. Figure 25.2 shows the medium-detail version of the torch.

```
#VRML V2.0 utf8
Transform {
    translation 0.0 0.0 0.2
    scale 0.5 0.5 0.5
    children [
    # Torch handle
        Transform {
            translation 0.0 -0.75 0.0
            rotation 1.0 0.0 0.0 3.14
            children Shape {
                appearance DEF Gray Appearance {
                    material Material {
                        diffuseColor  0.4 0.4 0.4
                        specularColor 0.7 0.7 0.7
                    }
                }
                geometry Cone {
                    height 1.5
                    bottomRadius 0.15
                }
            }
        },
    # Fire pot
        DEF Ring Shape {
            appearance USE Gray
            geometry Cylinder {
                height 0.1
                radius 0.4
                top    FALSE
                bottom FALSE
            }
        },
        Transform { translation 0.0 0.2 0.0 children USE Ring },
    # Fire pot detail (eliminated)
    # Mounting bracket (eliminated)
    # Flames
        DEF Flames Shape {
            # No appearance, use emissive shading
            geometry IndexedFaceSet {
                coord Coordinate {
                    point [
                         0.25 0.0 0.00,  0.15 1.0 0.10,
                         0.05 0.0 0.15,  0.18 0.0 0.05,
                         0.00 1.2 0.05, -0.10 0.0 0.05,
                        -0.00 0.0 0.15, -0.13 0.8 0.10,
                        -0.25 0.0 0.00,
                    ]
                }
        }
```

Figure 25.2 continues

```
            color Color {
                color [
                        1.0 0.0 0.0,   0.9 0.5 0.0,
                        1.0 0.0 0.0,   0.9 0.3 0.0,
                        1.0 1.0 0.0,   0.9 0.3 0.0,
                        0.7 0.1 0.2,   0.9 0.8 0.0,
                        1.0 0.0 0.0,
                ]
            }
            coordIndex [
                0, 1, 2, -1,  3, 4, 5, -1,  6, 7, 8, -1,
            ]
        }
    }
    # Additional Flames (eliminated)
    ]
}
```

Figure 25.2 *A medium-detail torch.*

Finally, when the torch is quite distant, the shape can be simplified considerably. The cylinders for the fire pot can be drawn as simple 2-D faces. Similarly, the torch handle can be changed to a downward-pointing, 2-D triangular face. The flames can be reduced to a single orange triangle. The resulting shape uses only 14 coordinates—approximately a 92 percent reduction from the original shape. Figure 25.3 builds the low-detail version of the torch.

```
#VRML V2.0 utf8
Transform {
    translation 0.0 0.0 0.2
    scale 0.5 0.5 0.5
    children [
    # Torch handle (simplified)
        Shape {
            appearance DEF Gray Appearance {
                material Material { diffuseColor 0.4 0.4 0.4 }
            }
            geometry IndexedFaceSet {
                coord Coordinate {
                    point [
                        -0.15 0.0 0.0,   0.0 -1.5 0.0,
                        0.15 0.0 0.0,
                    ]
                }
                coordIndex [ 0, 1, 2 ]
            }
        },
```

Figure 25.3 continues

```
# Fire pot (simplified)
    DEF Ring Shape {
        appearance USE Gray
        geometry IndexedFaceSet {
            coord Coordinate {
                point [
                # First ring
                    -0.40 -0.05 0.1,  0.40 -0.05 0.1,
                     0.40  0.05 0.1, -0.40  0.05 0.1,
                # Second ring
                    -0.40  0.15 0.1,  0.40  0.15 0.1,
                     0.40  0.25 0.1, -0.40  0.25 0.1,
                ]
            }
            coordIndex [ 0, 1, 2, 3, -1,  4, 5, 6, 7, -1 ]
        }
    },
# Fire pot detail (eliminated)
# Mounting bracket (eliminated)
# Flames (simplified)
    DEF Flames Shape {
        # No appearance, use emissive shading
        geometry IndexedFaceSet {
            coord Coordinate {
                point [
                    0.18 0.0 0.05,  0.00 1.2 0.05,
                    -0.18 0.0 0.05,
                ]
            }
            color Color {
                color [
                    1.0 0.0 0.0,  0.9 0.5 0.0,
                    1.0 0.0 0.0,
                ]
            }
            coordIndex [ 0, 1, 2 ]
        }
    }
# Additional Flames (eliminated)
]
}
```

Figure 25.3 *A low-detail torch.*

Switching Among Shapes

Figure 25.4 builds all three torch versions created in the previous examples. The torches are inlined from the files "torch1.wrl" (high-detail), "torch2.wrl" (medium detail), and "torch3.wrl" (low detail).

```
#VRML V2.0 utf8
Group {
    children [
    # High-detail
        Transform {
            translation -0.5 0.0 0.0
            children Inline { url "torch1.wrl" }
        },
    # Medium-detail
        Inline { url "torch2.wrl" },
    # Low-detail
        Transform {
            translation 0.5 0.0 0.0
            children Inline { url "torch3.wrl" }
        }
    ]
}
```

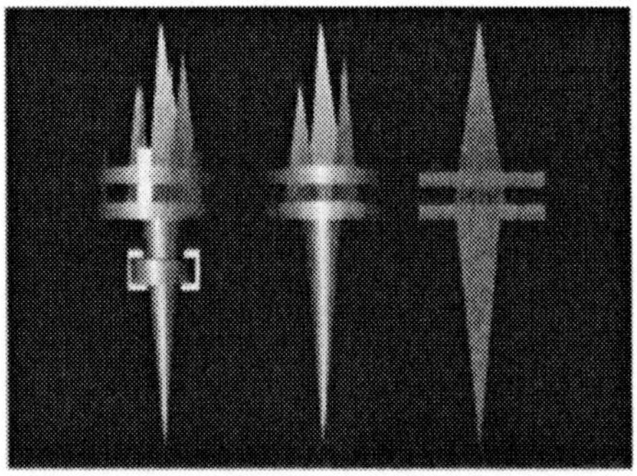

Figure 25.4 *The three torches side by side.*

T I P You can use the preceding three-torch file to help you decide what range to specify for each torch version. Using your browser, start with all three torches close up, then gradually move back in the world. Stop moving when the high- and medium-detail torches appear approximately the same. Since you can no longer see the added detail of the high-detail torch, this distance is a good point to switch from the high- to medium-detail torch. Many VRML browsers have a menu item to show you the current viewpoint position. Jot down this position. Now move farther away from the torches until the medium- and low-detail versions of the torches look approximately the same. Jot down this viewpoint position.

Ranges of 7.5 and 12.0 units work well for switching among the three torch versions. Using these ranges, you can place all three torches within an **LOD** node to direct your VRML browser to switch among them automatically. Figure 25.5 groups together the three versions of the torch—listed within the group from high detail to low detail—within an **LOD** node. The **range** field is set to two range switch points: 7.5 units and 12.0 units. Because the torch is built centered at the origin, the **LOD** node's **center** field is set to 0.0 0.0 0.0.

```
#VRML V2.0 utf8
LOD {
    center 0.0 0.0 0.0
    range [ 7.5, 12.0 ]
    level [
    # High-detail
        Inline { url "torch1.wrl" },
    # Medium-detail
        Inline { url "torch2.wrl" },
    # Low-detail
        Inline { url "torch3.wrl" }
    ]
}
```

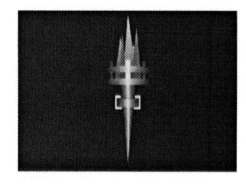

Figure 25.5   *Three torches within an LOD node.*

The **LOD** node groups together the three versions of the torch, listed from high detail to low detail within the group. The range field is set to two range switch points: 15.0 units and 25.0 units. Since the torch was built centered at the origin, the center field of the LOD node is set to 0.0 0.0 0.0.

Using your VRML browser, you can experiment to confirm that the range values are right and adjust them if they are not. Start close to the torch. The high-detail torch version is drawn, since the distance between you and the torch is less than the first range value. Slowly move back away from the torch. At 15.0 units away, the torch is switched from the high-detail version to the medium-detail version. At 25.0 units away the torch is switched again, this time from the medium-detail version to the low-detail version. As you move still farther away, the low-detail version will dwindle in size but will not change again. The low-detail version remains in use for any distances beyond 25.0 units.

Turning Shapes On and Off Automatically

When building a virtual world, you typically start with the individual shapes, like the torches in the previous examples, and place them in a larger context, such as a dungeon room. The room is then combined with other rooms to create the dungeon level of a castle, and the dungeon level is combined with others to create the entire castle, and so on. A single dungeon room, with torches, a treasure chest, assorted wizard's paraphernalia, and so on, can be quite complex. As you add more and more rooms, such as those necessary for an entire dungeon level, the number of shapes to draw increases, and the VRML browser can slow noticeably when trying to draw all of them.

Notice, however, that while inside one room, all further rooms need not be drawn since they are on the other side of opaque walls. The VRML browser can't automatically skip drawing unseen rooms since it can't easily figure out which rooms are needed. You could, for instance, have a semitransparent window or an open doorway that reveals a distant room. An automatic algorithm to remove unseen rooms would need to take these into account. It is typically not possible, however, to determine these things automatically within the VRML browser.

You can help the browser by using an **LOD** node around individual rooms. Consider, for example, that each dungeon room can have two detail versions. The high-detail version contains a full description of the room and is used only when the room is visible to the viewer, such as when the viewer is in it. The low-detail version of a room contains nothing: no walls, floor, ceiling, torches, or anything. It is a completely empty shape and is used only when the room is not visible to the viewer, such as when the viewer and room are on opposite sides of an opaque wall.

Using these two versions of a room, you can switch between them using an **LOD** node. Set the node's **range** field value to draw the full room when the room gets within sight of the viewer and to build the empty shape when the viewer can't see the room. This technique enables you to turn the room on and off as needed. By turning off all rooms that are out of sight of the viewer, you can dramatically reduce the amount of work your VRML browser does to draw your world.

The following examples build a portion of a dungeon to illustrate the use of **LOD** nodes to turn rooms on and off and to illustrate a few design principles to follow when creating worlds that use this feature. To start, build a simple room in the dungeon. The room contains a floor, a ceiling, left and right walls, and places a torch at the center of each wall. Figure 25.6 shows the floor, contained in the file "dfloor.wrl." The floor is later used to create the ceiling as well by instancing the floor and placing it at ceiling level. Notice the use of an **ElevationGrid** node to build the floor. This creates a mesh of faces like the meshes used in Chapter 20 to enhance lighting effects. The mesh floor used in Figure 25.6 enhances lighting effects introduced in Figure 25.8 when point lights are added for each torch in the dungeon.

```
#VRML V2.0 utf8
Transform {
    translation -5.0 0.0 -2.5
    children Shape {
        appearance Appearance {
            material Material { diffuseColor 1.0 1.0 1.0 }
            texture ImageTexture { url "stone2.jpg" }
            textureTransform TextureTransform {
                scale 16.0 8.0
            }
        }
    }
```

Figure 25.6 continues

```
        geometry ElevationGrid {
            xDimension 8
            zDimension 8
            xSpacing    1.4285714
            zSpacing    0.7142857
            solid       FALSE
            height [
                0.0, 0.0, 0.0, 0.0, 0.0, 0.0, 0.0, 0.0,
                0.0, 0.0, 0.0, 0.0, 0.0, 0.0, 0.0, 0.0,
                0.0, 0.0, 0.0, 0.0, 0.0, 0.0, 0.0, 0.0,
                0.0, 0.0, 0.0, 0.0, 0.0, 0.0, 0.0, 0.0,
                0.0, 0.0, 0.0, 0.0, 0.0, 0.0, 0.0, 0.0,
                0.0, 0.0, 0.0, 0.0, 0.0, 0.0, 0.0, 0.0,
                0.0, 0.0, 0.0, 0.0, 0.0, 0.0, 0.0, 0.0,
                0.0, 0.0, 0.0, 0.0, 0.0, 0.0, 0.0, 0.0,
            ]
        }
    }
  }
}
```

Figure 25.6 *A dungeon-room floor.*

Figure 25.7 shows the wall for the room, contained in the file "dwall.wrl." The wall is later used to create the left and right walls of a room. Notice the use of an **ElevationGrid** node to create mesh walls.

```
#VRML V2.0 utf8
Transform {
    translation 0.0 3.5 -2.5
    rotation 0.0 0.0 1.0 -1.57
    children Shape {
        appearance Appearance {
            material Material { diffuseColor 1.0 1.0 1.0 }
            texture ImageTexture { url "stonewal.jpg" }
        }
```

Figure 25.7 continues

```
    geometry ElevationGrid {
        xDimension 8
        zDimension 8
        xSpacing   0.5
        zSpacing   0.7142857
        solid      FALSE
        height [
            0.0, 0.0, 0.0, 0.0, 0.0, 0.0, 0.0, 0.0,
            0.0, 0.0, 0.0, 0.0, 0.0, 0.0, 0.0, 0.0,
            0.0, 0.0, 0.0, 0.0, 0.0, 0.0, 0.0, 0.0,
            0.0, 0.0, 0.0, 0.0, 0.0, 0.0, 0.0, 0.0,
            0.0, 0.0, 0.0, 0.0, 0.0, 0.0, 0.0, 0.0,
            0.0, 0.0, 0.0, 0.0, 0.0, 0.0, 0.0, 0.0,
            0.0, 0.0, 0.0, 0.0, 0.0, 0.0, 0.0, 0.0,
            0.0, 0.0, 0.0, 0.0, 0.0, 0.0, 0.0, 0.0,
        ]
    }
  }
}
```

Figure 25.7 *A dungeon-room wall.*

Figure 25.8 combines the floor, wall, and torches to create a simple dungeon room with a floor, ceiling, left and right walls, and a torch in the middle of each wall. The torches are built by inlining the file "torches.wrl," which contains the **LOD** node and torch inlines discussed with the torches in Figure 25.5. A point light is added at each torch to make the room glow as if it is lit by the torches. (For the best effect, turn off your browser's headlight.)

```
#VRML V2.0 utf8
Group {
    children [
    # Floor (two strips)
        Transform {
            translation 0.0 0.0 2.5
            children DEF Floor Inline { url "dfloor.wrl" }
        },
        Transform { translation 0.0 0.0 -2.5 children USE Floor },
    # Ceiling (reuse the floor)
        Transform { translation 0.0 3.5  2.5 children USE Floor },
        Transform { translation 0.0 3.5 -2.5 children USE Floor },
```

Figure 25.8 continues

```
# Left wall with torch
    Transform {
        translation -5.0 0.0 0.0
        children [
            Transform {
                translation 0.0 0.0 2.5
                children DEF Wall Inline { url "dwall.wrl" }
            },
            Transform { translation 0.0 0.0 -2.5 children USE Wall },
            Transform {
                translation 0.0 2.25 0.0
                rotation 0.0 1.0 0.0 1.57
                children [
                    PointLight {
                        location 0.0 0.25 0.2
                        color 1.0 0.4 0.2
                        intensity 0.8
                        attenuation 0.0 0.6 0.0
                        radius 10.0
                    },
                    DEF Torch Inline { url "torches.wrl" }
                ]
            }
        ]
    },
# Right wall with torch
    Transform {
        translation 5.0 0.0 0.0
        children [
            Transform { translation 0.0 0.0  2.5 children USE Wall },
            Transform { translation 0.0 0.0 -2.5 children USE Wall },
            Transform {
                translation 0.0 2.25 0.0
                rotation 0.0 1.0 0.0 -1.57
                children [
                    PointLight {
                        location 0.0 0.25 0.2
                        color 1.0 0.4 0.2
                        intensity 0.8
                        attenuation 0.0 0.6 0.0
                        radius 10.0
                    },
                    USE Torch
                ]
            }
        ]
    }
]
}
```

Figure 25.8 *A dungeon room.*

Before continuing to build a piece of a dungeon, try walking about within the dungeon room created in Figure 25.8. Notice that the two torches each change from low-, to medium-, to high-detail versions as you move closer. Also notice that the two torches change independently. So, if the viewer is close to one torch and far from the other, the nearer torch is shown in high-detail, while the more distant torch is shown in low-detail.

Using the dungeon built room in Figure 25.8, you can build two adjacent rooms. While in the first room, the second room should not be drawn, and while in the second room, the first room should not be drawn. To accomplish this, each room is controlled by an **LOD** node. To make this effect easier to see no wall is placed between the rooms in Figure 25.9 which shows the two rooms placed one after the other.

```
#VRML V2.0 utf8
Group {
     children [
     # First room
        LOD {
             range [ 20.0 ]
             level [
                 Inline { url "droom.wrl" }
                 Group { }
             ]
        },
     # Second room
        Transform {
             translation 0.0 0.0 -10.0
             children LOD {
                 range [ 20.0 ]
                 level [
                     Inline { url "droom.wrl" },
                     Group { }
                 ]
             }
        }
     ]
}
```

Figure 25.9   *Two dungeon rooms controlled by* **LOD** *nodes.*

Notice that as you walk forward into the first room, the second room appears. If you walk into the second room, and turn around and look back, the first room has disappeared. If you walk back toward the first room, it reappears. The **LOD** nodes surrounding each room automatically turn the rooms on and off as you approach them.

The sudden appearance and disappearance of entire rooms is disconcerting. If you place a wall and doorway between the two rooms, you can reduce this effect. If viewers can see through the doorway into the next room, however, they still see the room appear as they approach and disappear as they walk away. You can avoid this problem by adding a door to the doorway. Only when the door is opened should the second room appear.

Figure 25.10 shows a wall with a doorway in a file called "dwall2.wrl." Figure 25.11 shows a door (contained in a file called "ddoor.wrl") to be placed in the wall's doorway.

```
#VRML V2.0 utf8
Shape {
    appearance Appearance {
        material Material { diffuseColor 1.0 1.0 1.0 }
        texture ImageTexture { url "stonewal.jpg" }
    }
    geometry IndexedFaceSet {
        coord Coordinate {
            point [
                -5.0 0.0 0.0, -1.5 0.0 0.0,
                -1.5 2.5 0.0,  1.5 2.5 0.0,
                 1.5 0.0 0.0,  5.0 0.0 0.0,
                 5.0 3.5 0.0, -5.0 3.5 0.0,
            ]
        }
        texCoord TextureCoordinate {
            point [
                0.0 0.0,  0.7 0.0,  0.7 0.7,  1.3 0.7,
                1.3 0.0,  2.0 0.0,  2.0 1.0,  0.0 1.0
            ]
        }
        coordIndex [ 0, 1, 2, 3, 4, 5, 6, 7 ]
        convex FALSE
        solid FALSE
    }
}
```

Figure 25.10   *A dungeon wall with a doorway.*

```
#VRML V2.0 utf8
Shape {
    appearance Appearance {
        material Material { diffuseColor 1.0 1.0 1.0 }
        texture ImageTexture { url "panel.jpg" }
    }
```

Figure 25.11 continues

```
geometry IndexedFaceSet {
    coord Coordinate {
        point [
            -0.75 0.0 0.0,  0.75 0.0 0.0,
            0.75 2.5 0.0, -0.75 2.5 0.0,
        ]
    }
    texCoord TextureCoordinate {
        point [
            0.0 0.0,  1.0 0.0, 1.0 2.0,  0.0 2.0,
        ]
    }
    coordIndex [ 0, 1, 2, 3 ]
    solid FALSE
  }
}
```

Figure 25.11   *A dungeon door.*

Figure 25.12 adds to the world in Figure 25.9 a wall and pair of sliding doors between the two rooms. To cause the doors to slide open at a touch, Figure 25.12 uses a **TouchSensor** node sensing the doors, and a circuit that slides the doors open, pauses, then slides them closed again after five seconds.

The addition of the wall and doors in Figure 25.12 helps to ensure that the viewer can't see into the second room until the **LOD** node for that room turns it on. It is possible, however, for a viewer to touch and open the doors while standing far enough away that the second room's **LOD** node has not yet turned on that room. To fix this problem, you can use one of several types of proximity sensors to enable the doors to be opened only when the viewer is close to them. This prevents the doors from opening until the viewer is close enough to trigger the **LOD** node to turn on the second room. Proximity sensors are discussed in Chapter 27.

```
#VRML V2.0 utf8
Group {
    children [
    # First room
        LOD {
            range [ 20.0 ]
            level [
                Inline { url "droom.wrl" },
                Group { }
            ]
        },
```

Figure 25.12 continues

```
# Second room
    Transform {
        translation 0.0 0.0 -10.0
        children LOD {
            range [ 20.0 ]
            level [
                Inline { url "droom.wrl" },
                Group { }
            ]
        }
    },
# Wall between first and second rooms
    Transform {
        translation 0.0 0.0 -5.0
        children Inline { url "dwall2.wrl" }
    },
# Left and right door panels
    Transform {
        translation 0.0 0.0 -4.95
        children [
            DEF LeftDoor Transform {
                children Transform {
                    translation -0.75 0.0 0.0
                    children DEF Door Inline { url "ddoor.wrl" }
                }
            },
            DEF RightDoor Transform {
                children Transform {
                    translation 0.75 0.0 0.0
                    children USE Door
                }
            },
            DEF TouchDoor TouchSensor { }
        ]
    },
# Animation clock
    DEF Clock TimeSensor {
        cycleInterval 5.0
    },
# Animation paths for the left and right doors
    DEF LeftOpen PositionInterpolator {
        key [ 0.0, 0.1, 0.9, 1.0 ]
        keyValue [
            0.0 0.0 0.0, -1.3 0.0 0.0,
            -1.3 0.0 0.0,  0.0 0.0 0.0
        ]
    },
```

Figure 25.12 continues

```
    DEF RightOpen PositionInterpolator {
        key [ 0.0, 0.1, 0.9, 1.0 ]
        keyValue [
            0.0 0.0 0.0,   1.3 0.0 0.0,
            1.3 0.0 0.0,   0.0 0.0 0.0
        ]
    }
]
}
ROUTE TouchDoor.touchTime        TO Clock.set_startTime
ROUTE Clock.fraction_changed     TO LeftOpen.set_fraction
ROUTE Clock.fraction_changed     TO RightOpen.set_fraction
ROUTE LeftOpen.value_changed     TO LeftDoor.set_translation
ROUTE RightOpen.value_changed    TO RightDoor.set_translation
```

Figure 25.12 *Two dungeon rooms controlled by* **LOD** *nodes and separated by a wall and a pair of sliding doors.*

TIP Another way of obscuring the appearance and disappearance of the room controlled by the **LOD** node is to limit the viewer's ability to see very far. Instead of placing a simple wall between the rooms, create a zigzag hallway between the rooms. The hallway blocks the viewer's direct view of the next room, enabling an **LOD** node to turn the next room on and off without being obvious about it.

The room-and-hallway technique is used throughout dungeon-based, 3-D games. The game player's view of the world is always cleverly restricted so that the appearance and disappearance of rooms is hidden. If you could watch the game player move through the game from a bird's-eye view, you'd see a circle of turned-on rooms around the game player. As the player moves about in the game, the nearby rooms are always turned on just as they are needed, while the rest of the game world is turned off. You can use this same technique to help optimize your VRML worlds.

Summary

The more detail you add to a world, the longer it takes the VRML browser to draw it. To maintain both high realism and high interactivity, you can control the detail level at which the VRML browser draws shapes by using **LOD** nodes.

For key shapes in your world, create multiple versions, typically high-, medium-, and low-detail versions. For the high-detail version, include all the detail needed to make the shape look realistic when you're near it. For the medium-detail version, delete some of the extra detail to simplify the shape for viewing from medium distances. For the low-detail version, reduce the shape to the bare essentials needed to make the shape look right from far away.

Collect together each of the detail versions of a shape and place them within a level-of-detail group managed by an **LOD** node. The **center** field of the **LOD** node indicates the center of the shape. The **LOD** node's range field provides a list of viewer-to-shape-center distances at which a switch from a higher- to a lower-detail version is made. When the viewer is closer than the first range value, the first detail version in the group is drawn. When the viewer is farther away than the first range value, but closer than the second, the second detail version in the group is drawn, and so on. For $n - 1$ different versions of a shape, there should be $n - 1$ range values indicating where to switch from one to the next.

Using **LOD** nodes, you can switch between different detail versions of the same shape or turn entire groups of shapes on and off based upon the viewer's proximity.

CHAPTER 26

Controlling the Viewpoint

In previous chapters, you used your VRML browser to move around within a world and view it from different positions and orientations. At each new viewing position, the browser snaps a picture, as if using a virtual camera, and displays the picture on your screen. Your movements in the world continually position and orient that camera.

It is often convenient to set up a predefined camera viewpoint in a world. Each time that world's VRML file is loaded, the browser automatically positions the viewer at that predefined viewpoint position. From there, the viewer can move around in the world and view the world from additional positions and orientations. VRML provides two node types for setting up predefined viewpoints and specifying how the viewer can move about in the world: **Viewpoint** and **NavigationInfo**.

Understanding Viewpoints

A *viewpoint* is a predefined viewing position and orientation in your world, like a recommended photograph location at a tourist attraction. You can specify the location and viewing direction for the viewpoint. When the **Viewpoint** node is a child of a **Transform** node, the viewpoint's location and orientation are in that **Transform** node's coordinate system. If the coordinate system moves, so does the viewpoint.

Using a circuit or features of the VRML browser's user interface, you can cause the viewer's position and orientation to jump to those in a **Viewpoint** node. For instance, you can provide multiple viewpoints in your world, and use a circuit that makes the viewer's camera jump from viewpoint to viewpoint and give a guided tour of the area.

Understanding the Viewpoint Field of View

A viewpoint acts like a camera through which a viewer can see your world. In the real world, you can use different camera lenses to control how much of the world in front of you can be seen through the camera. A wide-angle lens, for instance, enables you to see a broad expanse of the world, while a telephoto lens focuses instead on a small part of the world.

One type of real-world lens is called "wide-angle" because it enables the viewer to see a wide area of the world, measured as an angle (called a *field-of-view angle*) from the left edge to the right edge of what the camera sees. In VRML, you can control this angle. A large angle widens the viewpoint to see a broad expanse of your world, like a real-world wide-angle lens. A small angle narrows the view to a smaller portion of your world, like a real-world telephoto lens.

The range of the world that is visible to a VRML viewpoint can be illustrated by a tapered box with the narrow end at the viewpoint and the wide end at the horizon (called a *frustrum* by mathematicians). Any shape that falls within the box is visible, while those outside the box are beyond the viewer's peripheral vision or behind the viewer's back. As you decrease the field-of-view angle, you taper the box, making it more narrow and decreasing the range of the world that is visible. If you widen the field-of-view angle, you widen the box and increase the range of the world that is visible.

A frustrum that describes the range of the world visible from a viewpoint is called a *viewing-volume frustrum*. A **Viewpoint** node specifies a viewing-volume frustrum such as this to indicate to the browser the amount of your world that should be visible from the viewpoint's position and orientation. The VRML browser draws only those shapes that fall within this viewing-volume frustrum.

Figure 26.1 shows two viewing-volume frustrums: (*a*) one with a narrow 30.0-degree field of view and (*b*) the other with a normal 45.0-degree field of view. You can use field of view angles as large as 180.0 degrees. However, angles larger than about 60.0 degrees begin to create an unnatural distortion.

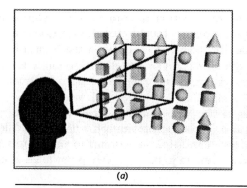 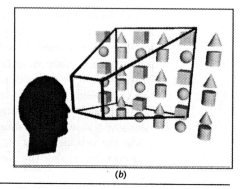

(a)   (b)

Figure 26.1 *Two viewing-volume frustrums: (a) one with a narrow field of view and (b) one with a normal field of view.*

When your browser is drawing into a square window on your screen, the viewpoint's field-of-view angle specifies the left-to-right and top-to-bottom spread of the viewing-volume frustrum. However, when your browser is drawing into a rectangular window, the field-of-view angles for left-to-right and top-to-bottom must be different or the image appears warped. To compensate, when the window is wider than it is tall, the field-of-view angle you specify is used by your browser for the left-to-right angle, and the top-to-bottom angle is automatically computed to be somewhat smaller. Similarly, when the window is taller than it is wide, your field-of-view angle is used for the top-to-bottom angle, and the left-to-right angle is automatically computed to be somewhat smaller.

SIDEBAR: HEAD-MOUNTED DISPLAYS Some VRML browsers support *head-mounted displays*, or *HMDs*. HMDs place small screens near your eyes, one for each eye. Lenses in front of your eyes widen the screen images to give you peripheral vision. A sensor on the HMD is used by your VRML browser to determine the location of your head and the direction you are looking. This information is used to change your viewing position and orientation so that you can look about in your virtual world without using a mouse or keyboard. Due to the lens optics used for HMDs, the field of view must be carefully computed by your browser, so when using HMDs or any other form of virtual reality viewing equipment, your browser may use its own field-of-view angle and ignore your value in the **fieldOfView** field.

Understanding Viewpoint Binding

You can have any number of viewpoints in your world. Each one defines a new recommended viewing position, orientation, and field of view for a viewer of your world. However, only one of these viewpoints can be in use at a time. *Viewpoint binding* enables you to control which viewpoint is in use and to switch from viewpoint to viewpoint.

The Viewpoint Stack

Your VRML browser maintains a *stack* of available viewpoint nodes, exactly the same as the background and fog stacks used for **Background** and **Fog** nodes discussed in Chapters 22 and 23, respectively. You can place any **Viewpoint** node on top of the stack or remove any **Viewpoint** node from the stack and put it aside. The **Viewpoint** node on top of the stack is the *current viewpoint* and the one your VRML browser uses to control the viewer's position and orientation in your world.

As viewers move about, their position and orientation changes relative to the current viewpoint and the coordinate system in which the current viewpoint is positioned. If the coordinate system of the current viewpoint translates or rotates, then the viewers are translated or rotated as well. You can use this effect to move viewers about—as if, for example, they are moving upward with a rising elevator—or to fly them about as if they are in an airplane.

You can use a circuit to move **Viewpoint** nodes on and off the viewpoint stack. Most VRML browsers also provide a menu of available viewpoints in your world. The viewer can select between these viewpoints, which places a new **Viewpoint** node on top of the viewpoint stack and makes it the current viewpoint. You can specify a meaningful name for your viewpoint (in a browser menu) by setting the value of the **description** field in the **Viewpoint** node. If you omit a description, the viewpoint is not placed in the browser's menu.

Viewpoint Binding

Viewpoint binding is the process of making a **Viewpoint** node the current viewpoint by placing it on top of the viewpoint stack. When a **Viewpoint** node is *bound*, it is put on top of the stack. When a **Viewpoint** node is *unbound*, it is taken off the stack. You can bind a **Viewpoint** node by sending **TRUE** to the node's **set_bind** eventIn, and you can unbind it by sending **FALSE** to the **set_bind** eventIn.

When a **Viewpoint** node is bound and placed on top of the stack, it sends **TRUE** using its **isBound** eventOut. If there was a **Viewpoint** node already on the top of the stack, the new **Viewpoint** node overrides it, and the old **Viewpoint** node sends **FALSE** using its **isBound** eventOut. Using these outputs of the **Viewpoint** node, you can create a circuit that keeps track of which **Viewpoint** node is on top of the stack.

Using binding, you can place many **Viewpoint** nodes on the stack. If you unbind the top **Viewpoint** node, then the next **Viewpoint** node in the stack becomes the current **Viewpoint** node. If you unbind all the nodes on the stack, leaving an empty viewpoint stack, then your VRML browser uses the default values of a **Viewpoint** node. These default values create a viewpoint 10.0 units from the origin along the positive Z axis, looking down the negative Z axis. All the examples in the previous chapters use this default viewpoint.

When your world is read by the browser, the first **Viewpoint** node your VRML browser finds is automatically bound to the top of the viewpoint stack and used as the initial viewing position and orientation for your world. For instance, if you want a new viewer to arrive at the doorstep of a castle door when your world is read, you can set the first **Viewpoint** node to be at that doorstep.

Each time a new **Viewpoint** node is placed on top of the stack, the **Viewpoint** node that was previously on top saves the viewer's current position and orientation. This saved information is used when switching between viewpoints.

Switching between Viewpoints

VRML's **Viewpoint** node can create two subtly different styles of viewpoint: jump and no-jump. The jump viewpoint style is specified when the node's **jump** field value is **TRUE**. When this field value is **FALSE,** the no-jump viewpoint style is specified.

Jump Viewpoints

When a *jump* viewpoint is placed on top of the viewpoint stack, by selecting it from a browser menu for example, the viewer automatically jumps to that **Viewpoint** node's position, orientation, and field of view (some browsers quickly fly the viewer to the new position and orientation). Once viewers are located at the new viewpoint, they are free to move about in the world or select another predefined viewpoint and jump to that location.

Each time viewers jump to a new jump viewpoint, the new viewpoint becomes their current **Viewpoint** node. Their subsequent movements are relative to the viewpoint and the coordinate system in which the viewpoint is built.

Each time a **Viewpoint** node is placed on top of the stack, the previous top viewpoint saves the viewer's current position and orientation. When a **Viewpoint** node is removed from the top of the viewpoint stack, the VRML browser automatically looks at the next **Viewpoint** node on the stack and makes it the current viewpoint. If that **Viewpoint** node is a jump viewpoint, then the viewer is jumped to that viewpoint's saved position and orientation.

Jump viewpoints are typically used to specify important and interesting places to view in your world. They provide a shortcut mechanism so that a viewer can quickly get to those views without walking to each of them.

The viewpoint stack is particularly effective when used with jump viewpoints. In a typical scenario, the viewer selects a viewpoint from a browser menu and jumps to a point of interest. The viewer moves about a bit, then selects another viewpoint from the browser menu and jumps again. Each time the viewer jumps, the current position and orientation are saved away on the stack. Later, the viewer can retrace previous steps by removing the top viewpoint from the stack, one by one. Each time the top viewpoint is removed, the viewer jumps back to the saved position and orientation of the next viewpoint on the stack. This feature of VRML enables a viewer to quickly detour to a point of interest, and then jump back to a prior location and continue from there.

No-jump Viewpoints

When a *no-jump* viewpoint is placed on top of the viewpoint stack, by selecting it from a browser menu for example, the viewpoint becomes the current viewpoint, but the viewer's position, orientation, and field of view are *not* changed. Instead, the viewer remains stationary. The viewer's movements, however, are now relative to the new current **Viewpoint** node and to the coordinate system in which that viewpoint is built.

The need for no-jump viewpoints is subtle and useful when using a circuit to make a world interactive. To illustrate, first imagine a world containing a room and an elevator. The room is built inside a room coordinate system created by a room **Transform** node. Similarly, the elevator is built in an elevator coordinate system created by an elevator **Transform** node. Each coordinate system also contains a **Viewpoint** node. The VRML text that follows shows a rough outline of this world:

```
Group {
    children [
    # Room
        Transform {
            children [
                Viewpoint { . . . },
                . . .
            ]
        },
    # Elevator
        Transform {
            children [
                Viewpoint { . . . },
                . . .
            ]
        }
    ]
}
```

Using sensor and interpolator nodes, the elevator is set up so that pushing a button does two things:

- The viewer's current viewpoint is switched from the room **Viewpoint** node to the elevator **Viewpoint** node.

- The **translation** field of the elevator's **Transform** node is animated so that the elevator rises. Since the viewer is now using the elevator's **Viewpoint** node, the viewer rises along with the elevator.

Using this imaginary world, consider this scenario: a viewer enters the world using the room **Viewpoint** node, walks to the elevator, enters, stands to the left, and pushes an elevator button. What happens next depends on whether the elevator **Viewpoint** node style is jump or no-jump

If the elevator **Viewpoint** node is a jump viewpoint, when the viewer pushes the elevator button, the viewer's current viewpoint is changed to the elevator's **Viewpoint** node. Since the elevator viewpoint is a jump viewpoint, the viewer's position and orientation instantly jump to that of the elevator viewpoint. Imagine that the elevator viewpoint is positioned in the center of the elevator. Prior to pushing the elevator button, the viewer is standing to the left. Jumping the viewer's viewpoint instantly moves the viewer from standing to the left to standing in the center of the elevator. This jump jars the viewer visually.

If the elevator **Viewpoint** node is a no-jump viewpoint when the viewer pushes the elevator button, the viewer's current viewpoint is changed to the elevator's **Viewpoint** node. This time, though, since the elevator viewpoint is a no-jump viewpoint, the viewer's position is *not* changed. The viewer is allowed to stand still or move about within the elevator. They are *not* rudely pushed into the middle of the elevator just because they pushed an elevator button.

For both viewpoint styles, the viewer's current **Viewpoint** node is changed to the one in the elevator. When the elevator starts to rise, the viewer rises with it. The difference in the two viewpoint styles is whether the viewer is pushed to the center of the elevator when the viewpoint is changed.

Jump and no-jump viewpoints both have their uses. As noted earlier, jump viewpoints are typically used to set up predefined viewing positions for attractions in your world. Selecting a jump viewpoint jumps the viewer to a predefined position so that the viewer can see what you want to be seen. In contrast, no-jump viewpoints are typically used to set up smooth transitions from one coordinate system to another. In the example above, the no-jump viewpoint in the elevator is used to transition the viewer from the stationary coordinate system of the room to the rising coordinate system in the elevator.

As noted earlier, when the top **Viewpoint** node on the viewpoint stack is removed, the VRML browser automatically makes the next **Viewpoint** node on the stack the current viewpoint. If that new current viewpoint is a no-jump viewpoint, the viewer's position and orientation are *not* changed. Further movements by the viewer are relative to the new current viewpoint and the coordinate system in which it is built.

The no-jump removal of viewpoints from the top of the stack is analogous to the no-jump placement of viewpoints on top of the stack. This ensures that when the viewer leaves the elevator, for example, the viewer isn't rudely pushed to a new position.

Understanding Navigation Information

In virtual reality, an *avatar* is a symbolic-virtual-world representation of a real-world person. Using an avatar, the real-world person moves through the virtual world, seeing what the avatar sees, and interacting by telling the avatar what to do.

In a multi-user virtual reality environment, each user in the environment chooses a 3-D shape as a representative in that environment. If you were in such an environment, you'd see these avatar shapes move and turn as the real-world person controlling them walks about in the virtual world. Depending on the features of the environment, you might be able to walk your avatar up to other people's avatars and chat with them.

The features of an avatar can be divided into two groups:

- Those that describe what an avatar looks like
- Those that describe how an avatar can move

Many VRML browsers provide menus to specify the appearance of your avatar. The movement features of the avatar, however, are primarily controlled by the **NavigationInfo** node.

The **NavigationInfo** node works in concert with the current **Viewpoint** node; the **Viewpoint** node describes how to view a world, and the **NavigationInfo** node describes how to move about in that world.

Avatar Navigation Types

Navigation is the process of moving about and getting where you want to be, whether in the real world or within a virtual world. Two common ways of moving in the real world are by walking and by flying. Both of these *navigation types* enable you to move forward, turn about, and navigate to where you want to be. When walking, you follow the terrain; flying enables you to rise above the terrain, unconstrained by the bumpiness of it. VRML provides analogs of these navigation types.

Different navigation types are appropriate for different situations. If your virtual world is a dungeon, then the walking navigation type is probably most appropriate. However, if your world is intended for use in a flight simulator, then flying is probably a better navigation type to use.

Using the **NavigationInfo** node, you can specify which navigation type you expect the viewer's avatar to use when moving through your world. The navigation type is specified using the **type** field, which can have one of the four standard values shown in Table 26.1.

Table 26.1   The Four VRML Navigation Types and Valid Values of the type Field

type Field Value	Description
"WALK"	Enables the viewer's avatar to explore your virtual world as if it were walking. The viewer always has a sense of up and down, both of which are aligned with the current **Viewpoint** node's coordinate system Y axis. The avatar is typically constrained to follow the terrain and pulled downward along the Y axis by gravity.
"FLY"	Enables the viewer's avatar to fly around your world. Provides the viewer with a sense of up and down that is aligned with the current **Viewpoint** node's Y axis. The avatar is not constrained to follow the terrain, and typically there are no effects of gravity.
"EXAMINE"	Enables the viewer to treat the world like an object held out in front of them. The viewer can turn the object about and zoom in to look at it more closely. This type does not impose a sense of up and down on the viewer. The viewer's avatar is not constrained to follow terrain and is not affected by gravity.
"NONE"	Provides the viewer with no way to navigate through the world; navigation is disabled. The viewer can only move about using animation features authored by the world's creator.

The navigation type you specify in the **type** field of the **NavigationInfo** node is a hint to the VRML browser and the viewer. Most VRML browsers provide a menu to select between these navigation types. Using this menu, a viewer of your world can override your navigation type hint. This enables a viewer to walk, fly, and examine portions of your world as necessary.

Avatar Navigation Speed

The rate at which a viewer's avatar moves through your world should be appropriate for the kind of world you've created. For instance, if your world is a virtual anthill, then movement within the anthill should probably be a few centimeters per second. However, if your VRML file describes a quadrant of a galaxy, then a speed of a few light years per second might be more appropriate.

You can specify the preferred avatar motion speed in your world by using the **speed** field of a **NavigationInfo** node. The value in this field specifies the number of units per second at which an avatar should move. When walking or flying, this controls the avatar's forward and side-to-side motion speed. When using the examine navigation type, the navigation speed controls how quickly the viewer can slide the shape side-to-side or zoom in to it.

The navigation speed you select in the **speed** field is a hint to the VRML browser and the viewer. This speed provides an initial speed for avatar movement. Most VRML browsers provide menu items to speed up or slow down the avatar's movement, overriding your speed hint. This enables a viewer's avatar to move quickly or slowly depending on what it is trying to do.

Avatar Size

Though an avatar's shape is typically specified using VRML browser menus, the avatar's overall size is specified using the **NavigationInfo** node's **avatarSize** field. That size includes the three parameters shown in Table 26.2 and illustrated in Figure 26.2.

Table 26.2 The avatarSize Field's Three Parameters

Size Parameter	Description
width (parameter #1 in Figure 26.2)	Specifies how close an avatar can get to a shape before the avatar collides with it; expressed as a radius and roughly equivalent to the shoulder-to-shoulder width–back-to-stomach depth of the avatar. (Collision detection is discussed in Chapter 27.)
height (parameter #2 in Figure 26.2)	Specifies how far above the ground the current viewpoint should be kept when following a terrain using the walk navigation type. Roughly equivalent to the distance from the avatar's eyes to its toes.
step height (parameter #3 in Figure 26.2)	Specifies how high an obstacle the avatar can step on or over while using the walk navigation type. Obstacles taller than this are too big for the avatar to pass without walking around them. Roughly equivalent to the maximum height an avatar can raise its leg.

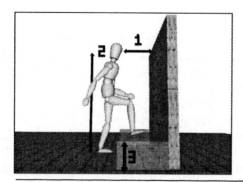

Figure 26.2 *An avatar with width, height, and step height indicated.*

The Avatar Headlight

Recall that the VRML browser provides you a default headlight to illuminate the virtual world when there are no other lights in the world. This headlight is attached to the head of the viewer's avatar. As the avatar moves, so does the headlight.

Using the **NavigationInfo** node and its **headlight** field, you can turn the avatar's headlight on and off. The headlight choice you specify in the **headlight** field is a hint to the VRML browser and the viewer. Most VRML browsers provide a menu item to turn the headlight on and off, overriding your hint. This enables the viewer to add or remove the extra illumination provided by the headlight.

Avatar Visibility Limits

The viewing-volume frustrum controlled by the **Viewpoint** node specifies the breadth of the world that is visible from the current viewpoint. Using the **NavigationInfo** node, you can also control the depth of the world that is visible. To do this, the **NavigationInfo** node's **visibilityLimit** field controls the distance from the viewpoint to the farthest end of the viewing-volume frustrum. In a sense, the visibility limit specifies the avatar's seeing ability. Shapes farther away than the avatar's visibility limit are outside of the viewing-volume frustrum, are not drawn, and are out of the viewer's sight.

The distance to the near end of the viewing-volume frustrum can also be controlled. Most VRML browsers use the avatar's width (from the **avatarSize** field divided by 2.0) as the distance to the near limit of the viewing-volume frustrum. Shapes closer than this near limit are not drawn.

Figure 26.3a shows a viewing-volume frustrum with the near limit very close and the visibility limit far away. Figure 26.3b shows the near limit moved further away (by changing the avatar size), and the far limit moved closer (by changing the visibility limit). This change constricts the viewing-volume frustrum so that the browser only draws a narrow slice of the world.

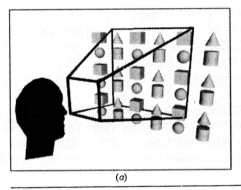 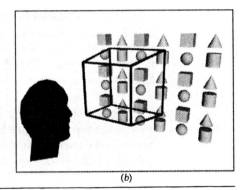

(a) (b)

Figure 26.3 *Two viewing-volume frustrums (a) one with normal near- and far-visibility limits and (b) one with the near limit moved farther away and the far limit moved closer.*

You can use the visibility limits to reduce the amount of your world that is visible, giving your browser less to build and enabling it to build your world more quickly. You can disable the use of a far visibility limit by setting the **visibilityLimit** field to 0.0. Using this value, the visibility limit is infinite and all shapes in your world are drawn, regardless of their distance from the viewer.

Understanding Navigation Binding

Like backgrounds, fog, and viewpoints, there can be only one current **NavigationInfo** node at a time for your world. Nevertheless, there are times when you need more than one **NavigationInfo** node. To handle multiple avatar characteristics, you can create multiple **NavigationInfo** nodes in your world and use navigation binding to switch between the **NavigationInfo** nodes so that only one of them is in use at a time.

The Navigation Stack

Your VRML browser maintains a *stack* of available **NavigationInfo** nodes, exactly like the background, fog, and viewpoint stacks. You can place any **NavigationInfo** node on top of the stack or remove a **NavigationInfo** node from the stack and put it aside. The **NavigationInfo** node on top of the stack is the current **NavigationInfo** node and the one your VRML browser uses to control the viewer's avatar characteristics.

Navigation Binding

Navigation binding is the process of placing a **NavigationInfo** node on top of the navigation stack. When a **NavigationInfo** node is *bound*, it is put on top of the stack. When a **NavigationInfo** node is *unbound*, it is taken off the stack. You can bind a **NavigationInfo** node by sending **TRUE** to the node's **set_bind** eventIn, and you can unbind it by sending **FALSE** to the **set_bind** eventIn.

When a **NavigationInfo** node is bound and placed on top of the stack, it sends **TRUE** using its **isBound** eventOut. If there was a **NavigationInfo** node already on the top of the stack, the new **NavigationInfo** node overrides it, and the old **NavigationInfo** node sends **FALSE** using its **isBound** eventOut. Using these outputs of the **NavigationInfo** node, you can create a circuit that tracks which **NavigationInfo** node is on top of the stack.

Using binding, you can place many **NavigationInfo** nodes on the stack. If you unbind the top **NavigationInfo** node, then the next **NavigationInfo** node in the stack becomes the current **NavigationInfo** node, and it controls the viewer's avatar. If you unbind all the nodes on the stack, leaving an empty navigation stack, then your VRML browser controls the avatar using default **NavigationInfo** node values.

When your world is read by your browser, the first **NavigationInfo** node your VRML browser finds is automatically bound to the top of the navigation stack.

Using Viewpoint and Navigation Information Together

The current **NavigationInfo** node always describes how an avatar can move and see through the viewpoint described by the current **Viewpoint** node. Recall that a viewpoint is specified in the coordinate system that contains the **Viewpoint** node. If that coordinate system translates, rotates, or scales, the viewpoint is affected as well. Since a **NavigationInfo** node describes the avatar viewer at a viewpoint, changing the viewpoint's coordinate system also affects avatar navigation information. The coordinate system in which the **NavigationInfo** node is created is ignored. Only the current viewpoint's coordinate system matters.

When the current viewpoint's coordinate system is scaled up or down, the avatar size, speed, and visibility limit are affected as well. This ensures that the avatar's size and movement always match the viewpoint's environment. If that environment is scaled, the avatar is scaled as well.

The **Viewpoint** Node Syntax

The **Viewpoint** node specifies a viewing location within a coordinate system.

SYNTAX	Viewpoint node

```
Viewpoint {
    position      0.0 0.0 1.0          # exposedField   SFVec3f
    orientation   0.0 0.0 1.0    0.0   # exposedField   SFRotation
    fieldOfView   0.785398            # exposedField   SFFloat
    description   ""                   # field          SFString
    jump          TRUE                 # exposedField   SFBool
    set_bind                           # eventIn        SFBool
    isBound                            # eventOut       SFBool
    bindTime                           # eventOut       SFTime
}
```

The value of the **position** exposed field specifies a 3-D coordinate for the location of the viewpoint in the current coordinate system. The default value places the viewpoint 10.0 units along the positive Z axis from the coordinate system's origin.

The initial viewpoint is aimed down the negative Z axis, with the positive X axis pointing to the right, and the positive Y axis pointing straight up. The **orientation** exposed field values provide a rotation axis about which to rotate the viewpoint and a rotation angle specifying the amount by which to rotate around that axis. The first three values in the field specify the X, Y, and Z components of a 3-D direction vector. The fourth value in the **orientation** field specifies the positive or negative rotation angle, measured in radians. The default values for the **orientation** field indicate that no rotation is to occur.

The value of the **fieldOfView** exposed field specifies an angle, in radians, indicating the spread angle of the viewpoint's viewing-volume frustrum. A large angle creates a wide-angle camera-lens effect, while a small angle creates a telephoto camera-lens effect. Angles must be between 0.0 and 180.0 degrees (0.0 and 3.142 radians). The default value for the **fieldOfView** exposed field is 45.0 degrees (0.785398 radians), which creates a normal field of view. Field-of-view angles beyond 60.0 degrees create noticeable distortion.

When building into a square screen window, the field-of-view angle controls the vertical and horizontal spread of the viewing-volume frustrum. To avoid image warping when drawing into a wide rectangular window, the field-of-view angle controls the horizontal spread of the viewing frustrum, while a somewhat smaller angle is used for the vertical spread. Similarly, when building into a tall rectangular window, the field-of-view angle controls the vertical spread of the frustrum, while a somewhat smaller angle is used for the horizontal spread.

The field-of-view angle is a hint to the VRML browser. The browser may ignore the field-of-view angle, particularly when using *head-mounted displays* (HMDs) or similar virtual reality display equipment. In these cases, the lens optics of the display dictate the use of specific field-of-view angles, overriding any specified in the **fieldOfView** field of **Viewpoint** nodes.

The **description** field value specifies a text string used to describe the viewpoint. Viewpoint descriptions should be short and are typically used as menu items in a viewpoint menu provided by most VRML browsers. If the viewpoint description is the empty string, the viewpoint is not listed in the browser's viewpoints menu. The default value for the **description** field is an empty string.

The VRML browser maintains a viewpoint stack containing **Viewpoint** nodes. The top node on the stack is said to be the bound viewpoint node and is used by the VRML browser to control the viewer's position, orientation, and field of view. A **Viewpoint** node can be placed on top of the stack or removed from the stack by sending **TRUE** or **FALSE** values to the node's **set_bind** eventIn. A VRML browser also may provide user-interface features that automatically send **TRUE** or **FALSE** values to the node's **set_bind** eventIn to change a viewpoint. Whether sent by way of a circuit or a user-interface control, when a **Viewpoint** node's **set_bind** eventIn receives a value, the resulting actions depend on the value received and the position of the specified **ViewPoint** node in the stack.

When **TRUE** is sent to a specified **Viewpoint** node's **set_bind** eventIn and the new Viewpoint node is on top of the stack, nothing happens. Otherwise, the following actions take place:

- The viewer's current position and orientation are saved within the **Viewpoint** node currently on top of the stack.
- The **Viewpoint** node currently on top of the stack sends **FALSE** using its **isBound** eventOut and sends the current absolute time using its **bindTime** eventOut.
- The new **Viewpoint** node is moved to the top of the viewpoint stack and becomes the current viewpoint.
- The new current **Viewpoint** node sends **TRUE** using its **isBound** eventOut and sends the current absolute time using its **bindTime** eventOut.
- If the new current **Viewpoint** node's **jump** field value is **TRUE**, the viewer's position and orientation are set to the position and orientation in the **Viewpoint** node, causing the viewer to jump to the new current viewpoint. If the **jump** field value is **FALSE**, the viewer's position and orientation are left unchanged.

When **FALSE** is sent to a specified **Viewpoint** node's **set_bind** eventIn, and the specified **Viewpoint** node is not in the viewpoint stack, nothing happens. If the specified **Viewpoint** node is in the viewpoint stack but not on top of the stack, it is removed from the stack, and nothing else happens. If the specified **Viewpoint** node is on top of the stack, the following actions take place:

- The specified **Viewpoint** node sends **FALSE** using its **isBound** eventOut and sends the current absolute time using its **bindTime** eventOut.
- The specified **Viewpoint** node is removed from the viewpoint stack.
- The next node on the stack becomes the new current viewpoint.
- The new current **Viewpoint** node sends **TRUE** using its **isBound** eventOut and sends the current absolute time using its **bindTime** eventOut.
- If the new current **Viewpoint** node's **jump** field value is **TRUE**, the viewer's position and orientation are set to the position and orientation saved earlier, causing the viewer to jump to the saved viewpoint. If the **jump** field value is **FALSE,** the viewer's position and orientation are left unchanged.

In the above cases, when the **Viewpoint** nodes on top of the stack and previously on top of the stack both send values using their **isBound** eventOuts, those values are sent simultaneously.

If the viewpoint stack is emptied by removing all **Viewpoint** nodes from the stack, no **Viewpoint** node is currently bound. In this case, the VRML browser uses default **Viewpoint** node values to control the viewer's viewpoint.

When a VRML world is read by the browser, the first **Viewpoint** node encountered in the top-level file (not within any inlined files) is automatically moved to the top of the viewpoint stack and bound. If there are no **Viewpoint** nodes in the top-level file, the viewpoint stack remains empty until a **Viewpoint** node is bound through the actions of a circuit.

If a **Viewpoint** node is a child of an **LOD** or **Switch** node, and it is bound but is not the currently selected child, the results are undefined. **LOD** nodes are discussed in Chapter 25 and **Switch** nodes in Chapter 11.

If binding a **Viewpoint** node results in collision with a shape, then the VRML browser may adjust the viewer position to step back from the collision. Collision detection is discussed in Chapter 27.

Viewpoint attributes can be changed by sending values to the implied **set_position**, **set_orientation**, **set_fieldOfView**, and **set_jump** eventIns of the exposed fields. When values are received by these inputs, the corresponding field values are changed, and the new values are output using the implied **position_changed**, **orientation_changed**, **fieldOfView_changed**, and **jump_changed** eventOuts of the exposed fields.

The viewpoint's position and orientation are specified relative to the viewpoint's coordinate system. Translating, rotating, or scaling that coordinate system changes the viewpoint as well.

The **NavigationInfo** Node Syntax

The **NavigationInfo** node provides information about the viewer's avatar and how it navigates using the current viewpoint.

SYNTAX	NavigationInfo node

```
NavigationInfo {
    type             "WALK"                # exposedField   MFString
    speed            1.0                    # exposedField   SFFloat
    avatarSize       [ 0.25, 1.6, 0.75 ]   # exposedField   MFFloat
    headlight        TRUE                   # exposedField   SFBool
    visibilityLimit  0.0                    # exposedField   SFFloat
    set_bind                                # eventIn        SFBool
    isBound                                 # eventOut       SFBool
}
```

The value of the **type** exposed field specifies the style of motion the viewer's avatar uses. Four standard navigation types—"**WALK**", "**FLY**", "**EXAMINE**", and "**NONE**"—are available, as shown in Table 26.1.

TIP Some VRML browsers support additional navigation types. These browser-specific types should be used with care, since they may not be available to viewers that use different browsers to view your world.

The value of the **type** exposed field provides a prioritized list of preferred navigation types, ordered from most preferred to least. If the first type listed in the field is recognized by the browser, it is used and the remainder of the **type** field values are ignored. If the first type is not recognized, the second value in the field is checked and used, if recognized, and so on. If none of the types are recognized, the browser uses the "WALK" navigation type. The default value of the **type** field is "WALK".

The navigation type specified by a **NavigationInfo** node is a *hint* to the VRML browser and viewer. Most browsers provide a menu that enables the viewer to select a different navigation type, overriding that specified by the **NavigationInfo** node's **type** field value.

The value of the **speed** exposed field specifies the recommended avatar motion speed, measured in units per second. Larger values increase the avatar's speed, while lower values slow down the avatar. The default value is 1.0 unit per second.

Avatar speed typically controls only the forward, back, and side-to-side motion of the avatar. Turning rates are not affected by the avatar speed.

The avatar speed specified by a **NavigationInfo** node is a hint to the VRML browser and viewer. Most browsers provide menu items that enable the viewer to increase or decrease the movement speed, overriding that specified by the **NavigationInfo** node's **speed** field value.

The values of the **avatarSize** exposed field describe the size characteristics of the viewer's avatar. The field contains a variable-length list of values. The meanings of the first three values in this list are shown in Table 26.3.

Table 26.3   Avatar Size Indexes, Default Values, and Their Meanings

Avatar Size Index	Default Value	Meaning
0	0.25	Avatar's width, expressed as a radius
1	1.60	Avatar's viewing height
2	0.75	Avatar's maximum step size

TIP Some VRML browsers support additional avatar size controls. These browser-specific controls should be used with care, since they may not be available to viewers that use different browsers to view your world.

Some VRML browsers may not support the specification of avatar sizes. For these browsers, the **avatarSize** field values are ignored and overridden by the browser's information.

The **headlight** exposed field specifies a **TRUE** or **FALSE** value that turns the avatar's headlight on or off. The headlight is a **DirectionalLight** node with an intensity of 1.0, an ambient intensity of 0.0, a color of 1.0 1.0 1.0, and a direction of 0.0 0.0 -1.0. The default value of the **headlight** field is **TRUE**.

The headlight status specified by a **NavigationInfo** node is a hint to the VRML browser and viewer. Most browsers provide a menu that enables the viewer to turn the headlight on and off, overriding that specified by the **NavigationInfo** node's **headlight** field value.

The value of the **visibilityLimit** exposed field specifies the distance to the far end of the viewing-volume frustrum and establishes the farthest distance the viewer can see. Shapes built more distant than this limit may not be drawn by the browser. Alternately, the browser can fade distant shapes to the background color or ignore the limit altogether. A visibility limit of 0.0 specifies an infinitely distant limit. The default limit is 0.0.

Some VRML browsers may use the avatar width divided by 2.0 to set the distance to the near end of the viewing-volume frustrum. Shapes closer than this near limit are not drawn.

The VRML browser maintains a navigation stack containing **NavigationInfo** nodes. The top node on the stack is said to be the bound **NavigationInfo** node and is used by the VRML browser to control the viewer's avatar. A **NavigationInfo** node can be placed on top of the stack or removed from the stack, by sending **TRUE** or **FALSE** values to the node's **set_bind** eventIn. When this occurs, the resulting actions depend on the value received and the position of the specified **NavigationInfo** node in the stack.

When **TRUE** is sent to a specified **NavigationInfo** node's **set_bind** eventIn, and the new **NavigationInfo** node is already the top node in the stack, nothing happens. Otherwise, the following actions take place:

- The **NavigationInfo** node currently on top of the stack sends **FALSE** using its **isBound** eventOut.
- The specified **NavigationInfo** node is moved to the top of the navigation stack and becomes the new current **NavigationInfo** node.
- The new current **NavigationInfo** node sends a **TRUE** value using its **isBound** eventOut.

When **FALSE** is sent to a specified **NavigationInfo** node's **set_bind** eventIn, and the specified **NavigationInfo** node is not in the navigation stack, nothing happens. If the specified **NavigationInfo** node is on the stack but is not on top of the stack, it is removed from the stack, and nothing else happens. If the specified **NavigationInfo** node is on top of the stack, the following actions take place:

- The specified **NavigationInfo** node sends **FALSE** using its **isBound** eventOut.
- The specified **NavigationInfo** node is removed from the navigation stack.
- The next node down on the stack becomes the new current **NavigationInfo** node.
- The new current **NavigationInfo** node sends **TRUE** using its **isBound** eventOut.

In the above cases, when the **NavigationInfo** nodes on top of the stack and previously on top of the stack both send values using their **isBound** eventOuts, those values are sent simultaneously.

If the navigation stack is emptied by removing all **NavigationInfo** nodes from the stack, there is no currently bound **NavigationInfo** node. In this case, the VRML browser uses default **NavigationInfo** node values to control the viewer's avatar.

When a VRML world is read by the browser, the first **NavigationInfo** node encountered in the top-level file (not within any inlined files) is automatically moved to the top of the navigation stack and bound. If there are no **NavigationInfo** nodes in the top-level file, the navigation stack remains empty until a **Navigation-Info** node is bound through actions of a circuit.

The avatar attributes can be changed by sending values to the implied **set_type, set_speed, set_avatarSize, set_headlight,** and **set_visibilityLimit** eventIns of the exposed fields. When values are received by these inputs, the corresponding field values are changed, and the new values are output using the implied **type_changed, speed_changed, avatarSize_changed, headlight_changed,** and **visibilityLimit_ changed** eventOuts of the exposed fields.

Navigation information applies to the current **Viewpoint** node. The avatar size, speed, and visibility limit are measured relative to the coordinate system of the viewpoint, not relative to that of the **NavigationInfo** node. Scaling the coordinate system containing the viewpoint changes the size, speed, and visibility limit of the avatar.

Experimenting with Viewpoints and Navigation Information

The following examples provide a more detailed examination of the ways in which the **Viewpoint** and **NavigationInfo** nodes can be used and how they interact with nodes discussed in previous chapters.

Building a Test Environment

To provide an environment in which to experiment with viewpoints and navigation information, all of the following examples use the dungeon rooms with sliding doors created in Chapter 25. If you typed the dungeon example, save it in "dungeon.wrl"; it is inlined in each of the following examples

Positioning the Viewpoint

The VRML text in Figure 26.4 builds a world by inlining the dungeon from "dungeon.wrl." To this world is added a **Viewpoint** node to position the viewer at the room's entrance. A **NavigationInfo** node is used to set the viewer's avatar size (width, height, step size) and speed. The navigation type is set to "WALK" so that the viewer can walk about the dungeon. Since the inlined dungeon has its own light sources, the headlight is unneeded and is turned off by the **NavigationInfo** node.

```
#VRML V2.0 utf8
Group {
    children [
        Viewpoint {
            description "Forward view"
            position 0.0 1.6 5.0
        },
        NavigationInfo {
            type "WALK"
            speed 1.0
            headlight FALSE
            avatarSize [ 0.5, 1.6, 0.5 ]
        },
        Inline { url "dungeon.wrl" }
    ]
}
```

Figure 26.4 *A viewpoint positioned at the entrance to the dungeon.*

Orienting the Viewpoint

The VRML text in Figure 26.5 moves the viewpoint in Figure 26.4 to the right wall and orients it to face the doorway. To orient the viewpoint, the **orientation** field value specifies a vertical rotation axis and a rotation angle of 35.0 degrees (0.611 radians).

```
#VRML V2.0 utf8
Group {
    children [
        Viewpoint {
            description "Corner view"
            position 3.0 1.6 3.0
            orientation 0.0 1.0 0.0 0.611
        },
        NavigationInfo {
            type "WALK"
            speed 1.0
            headlight FALSE
            avatarSize [ 0.5, 1.6, 0.5 ]
        },
        Inline { url "dungeon.wrl" }
    ]
}
```

Figure 26.5 *A viewpoint positioned at the right wall and turned to look toward the doorway.*

Controlling the Field of View of the Viewpoint

Using the **fieldOfView** field of the **Viewpoint** node, you can widen or narrow the viewing-volume frustrum and create wide-angle or telephoto lens effects. The default field of view is 45.0 degrees, which creates a normal viewing frustrum. Figure 26.6a uses a wider, 60.0-degree (1.047-radian) field of view. Figure 26.6b shows the field of view widened even further to 90.0 degrees (1.57 radians). Notice that with wider fields of view, the image becomes distorted. Typically, field-of-view angles are between 45.0 degrees and 60.0 degrees.

```
#VRML V2.0 utf8
Group {
    children [
        Viewpoint {
            description "60.0 FOV degree corner view"
            position 3.0 1.6 3.0
            orientation 0.0 1.0 0.0 0.611
            fieldOfView 1.047
        },
        NavigationInfo {
            type "WALK"
            speed 1.0
            headlight FALSE
            avatarSize [ 0.5, 1.6, 0.5 ]
        },
        Inline { url "dungeon.wrl" }
    ]
}
```

(a)	(b)

Figure 26.6 (a) A viewpoint with a 60.0-degree field of view and (b) with a 90.0-degree field of view. (The VRML text in this figure builds the world shown in Figure 26.6a.)

Using Multiple Viewpoints

You can have any number of **Viewpoint** nodes in the same world. The first **Viewpoint** node found is used by your VRML browser as the initial viewpoint when a viewer first enters the world. Later, using menu options provided by the browser, the viewer can switch between the initial viewpoint and the remaining viewpoints in your world. Using the **description** field of each **Viewpoint** node, you can provide meaningful menu names for the viewpoints.

Figure 26.7 combines all of the viewpoints used in the previous examples, placing them all in the same world. This example places all the **Viewpoint** nodes at the top of the file. You can also include **Viewpoint** nodes elsewhere in your file.

```
#VRML V2.0 utf8
Group {
    children [
    # Viewpoints
        Viewpoint {
            description "Forward view"
            position 0.0 1.6 5.0
        },
        Viewpoint {
            description "Corner view"
            position 3.0 1.6 3.0
            orientation 0.0 1.0 0.0 0.611
        },
        Viewpoint {
            description "60.0 FOV degree corner view"
            position 3.0 1.6 3.0
            orientation 0.0 1.0 0.0 0.611
            fieldOfView 1.047
        },
        Viewpoint {
            description "90.0 FOV degree corner view"
            position 3.0 1.6 3.0
            orientation 0.0 1.0 0.0 0.611
            fieldOfView 1.57
        },
    # Navigation
        NavigationInfo {
            type "WALK"
            speed 1.0
            headlight FALSE
            avatarSize [ 0.5, 1.6, 0.5 ]
        },
    # World
        Inline { url "dungeon.wrl" }
    ]
}
```

Figure 26.7 *The dungeon with multiple viewpoints available.*

Summary

The **Viewpoint** node specifies a predefined viewing location for viewing your world. The **position** field value specifies the viewpoint's location. The **orientation** field value rotates the viewpoint to look in a desired direction.

The **fieldOfView** field value of a **Viewpoint** node specifies the angular spread of the viewpoint's viewing-volume frustrum. A large angle spreads the frustrum out, creating a wide-angle lens effect. A small angle narrows the frustrum, creating a telephoto lens effect. A 45.0 degree angle is typical, and angles above about 60.0 degrees create noticeable distortion.

The **description** field value of a **Viewpoint** node provides a short description of the viewpoint. The browser uses these viewpoint descriptions to create a viewpoint menu. The viewer can select viewpoints from the menu to move from one viewpoint to the next.

The VRML browser maintains a viewpoint stack of **Viewpoint** nodes. The top node on the stack is bound and used to control the viewer's position and orientation. Selecting a viewpoint from a browser menu or sending **TRUE** to a **Viewpoint** node's **set_bind** eventIn moves the node to the top of the stack and binds it. Sending **FALSE** to a **Viewpoint** node's **set_bind** eventIn removes the node from the stack, unbinding it if it was on top of the stack.

The first **Viewpoint** node found when reading your world is automatically moved to the top of the viewpoint stack and bound. If there are no **Viewpoint** nodes in your world, or the stack is emptied, the default values of a Viewpoint node are used to control the viewer's position and orientation.

Viewer motion is relative to the current viewpoint and the coordinate system in which that viewpoint is built.

A jump viewpoint is one for which the jump field has a TRUE value. When a jump viewpoint is selected, such as from a menu, the viewer's position, orientation, and field of view jumps to those specified by the **Viewpoint** node. Jump viewpoints are useful for specifying important vantage points in your world.

A no-jump viewpoint is one for which the **jump** field has a **FALSE** value. When a no-jump viewpoint is selected, the viewer's position, orientation, and field of view are left unchanged. No-jump viewpoints are useful for handling smooth transitions from one coordinate system to another.

A NavigationInfo node describes characteristics of an avatar: a virtual-world incarnation of the viewer. The **type** field specifies how the viewer can move in the world: "WALK", "FLY", "EXAMINE", or "NONE". Walking follows the terrain and is subject to gravity. Flying doesn't follow the terrain and ignores gravity. The examine type treats the world similar to an object that can be turned about as if held in a viewer's hands. When the **type** field value is "NONE", the viewer cannot move at all and must rely on viewer controls provided by animation circuits in the world itself.

The NavigationInfo node's **avatarSize** field value specifies the width, height, and maximum step height of the viewer's avatar. The **speed** field specifies how quickly the avatar can move, measured in units per second.

The **headlight** field of the **NavigationInfo** node turns the avatar's headlight on or off.

The **visibilityLimit** field controls the maximum distance the avatar can see. Shapes beyond this maximum distance are not drawn.

The VRML browser maintains a navigation stack of **NavigationInfo** nodes. The top node on the stack is bound and used to control the viewer's avatar. Sending **TRUE** to a **NavigationInfo** node's **set_bind** eventIn moves the node to the top of the stack and binds it. Sending **FALSE** to a **NavigationInfo** node's **set_bind** eventIn removes the node from the stack, unbinding it if it was on top of the stack.

The first **NavigationInfo** node found when reading your world is automatically moved to the top of the navigation stack and bound. If there are no **NavigationInfo** nodes in your world or the stack is emptied, the default values of a **NavigationInfo** node are used to control the viewer's avatar.

The avatar size, speed, and visibility limits for a **NavigationInfo** node are all relative to the coordinate system of the current **Viewpoint** node. Scaling that coordinate system up or down affects the avatar size, speed, and visibility limits.

CHAPTER 27

Sensing Viewer Proximity

You can use **TouchSensor** nodes to detect when a viewer touches a shape with the pointing device, and you can use **PlaneSensor, SphereSensor,** and **Cylinder-Sensor** nodes to detect when a viewer drags the pointing device over a shape. VRML provides three additional nodes you can use to sense the viewer: the **VisibilitySensor, ProximitySensor,** and **Collision** nodes.

The **VisibilitySensor** node senses when the viewer is within sight of a region in your world. The **ProximitySensor** node senses when the viewer has moved into a region in your world. The **Collision** node detects when a viewer has collided with a shape in your world. You can use the outputs of all three of these sensors to start and stop animations and trigger sounds based on viewer proximity.

Understanding How Viewer Proximity Is Sensed

Viewer proximity is sensed using three methods: sensing a viewer's visibility, sensing a viewer's proximity, and via collision detection.

Visibility Sensors

Visibility sensors sense whether a box-shaped region in your world is visible from the viewer's position and orientation. You can use these sensors to start and stop animation or to control other actions that are only necessary when a sensed region of your world is visible.

You specify the region of your world sensed by a **VisibilitySensor** node by indicating its center and size. Each time any part of the region enters the viewing-volume frustrum, the sensor outputs the current, absolute time using its **enterTime** eventOut. Similarly, each time the region exits the viewing-volume frustrum, the sensor outputs the time using the **exitTime** eventOut. Using these two eventOuts, you can wire circuits to start activities when a region becomes visible and to stop them when a region is no longer visible.

Proximity Sensors

Proximity sensors sense when a viewer enters and moves about within a box-shaped region in your world. You can use these sensors to start an animation when the viewer approaches and to stop it when the viewer leaves. For instance, you can wire a **ProximitySensor** node to an animated sliding door so that when the viewer approaches the door, the door automatically slides open. When the viewer leaves the door area, the door automatically slides closed again.

You specify the region of your world sensed by a **ProximitySensor** node by indicating its center and size. Each time the viewer enters the region, the sensor outputs the current, absolute time using its **enterTime** eventOut. Similarly, each time the viewer leaves the region, the sensor outputs the time using the **exitTime** eventOut. Each time the viewer changes position or orientation while within the sensed region, the **ProximitySensor** node outputs that position and orientation using its **position_changed** and **orientation_changed** eventOuts, respectively. You can use these outputs to track the viewer's movements within a region of interest.

Collision Detection

Collision detection detects when the viewer comes close to and collides with shapes in your world. This occurs when the viewer runs into shapes, similar to running into a wall.

The **Collision** node is a grouping node similar to the **Group** node introduced in Chapter 11. Like the **Group** node, the **Collision** node has a list of children in its **children** field, and a bounding box center and size for those children.

The **Collision** node does two things when it detects a viewer collision:

- It outputs the current absolute time using its **collideTime** eventOut.
- It alerts the browser.

You can use the **collideTime** eventOut to trigger animation or sound. For example, you can route the **collideTime** eventOut to the **startTime** field of an **AudioClip** node to play an "Ow!" sound whenever the viewer runs into a wall.

When the **Collision** node alerts the browser that a collision has occurred, the browser checks the current navigation type, specified by the **NavigationInfo** node. If the current navigation type is "EXAMINE" or "NONE", then the browser typically does nothing when a viewer collides with a shape. If the current navigation type is "WALK" or "FLY", the browser typically stops the viewer's motion, as if they have run into a solid wall. This prevents a viewer from walking or flying through solid shapes in your world and dramatically increases realism.

By default, your entire world is contained within a **Collision** node group automatically built for you by the browser. You can add additional **Collision** nodes so that you can sense when the viewer runs into particular shapes, like walls. You can also use the node's **collide** field to turn collision detection off entirely for all shapes within the group. This doesn't change the way the child shapes look, but the viewer is free to walk straight through them. This enables you to create shapes that you want the viewer to be able to walk through, such as the semitransparent surface of a lake or a secret-passage doorway in a dungeon.

Detecting whether a viewer has or has not collided with a shape can be very time-consuming for your VRML browser. A good way to help speed your browser's collision detection is to provide a proxy shape in the **Collision** node's **proxy** field. The *proxy shape* should be a simpler, alternate representation of the complex shape built by the **Collision** node's children. For instance, if the group's children describe a detailed piano and its 88 keys, then a reasonable proxy shape might be a simple box the approximate size and shape of the piano. When your VRML browser checks for viewer collision with the piano, it can save a tremendous amount of time by only checking for collision with a simple, box proxy shape instead of checking for collision with every single feature of the detailed piano shape.

The **VisibilitySensor** Node Syntax

The **VisibilitySensor** node may be the child of any group, and it senses when a box-shaped region in the current coordinate system is visible from the current viewer position and orientation.

| SYNTAX | Syntax: VisibilitySensor node |

```
VisibilitySensor {
    enabled      TRUE              # exposedField  SFBool
    center       0.0 0.0 0.0       # exposedField  SFVec3f
    size         0.0 0.0 0.0       # exposedField  SFVec3f
    isActive                       # eventOut      SFBool
    enterTime                      # eventOut      SFTime
    exitTime                       # eventOut      SFTime
}
```

The value of the **enabled** exposed field specifies whether the sensor is turned on or off. If the field value is **TRUE,** the sensor is on and can generate outputs. If the field is **FALSE,** the sensor is off and no outputs are generated, except those generated in response to a change in an exposed field (for example, **enabled_changed**). The default value for the field is **TRUE.**

The value of the **center** exposed field specifies the 3-D coordinate at the center of a sensed region in the current coordinate system. The default region center is the origin.

The value of the **size** exposed field specifies the dimensions of a sensor's box-shaped region with a width, a height, and a depth measured along the X, Y, and Z axes of the current coordinate system. The default region size is a point at the origin.

When any part of the sensed region is contained within the viewing-volume frustrum, the sensor node outputs **TRUE** using the **isActive** eventOut and outputs the current absolute time using the **enterTime** eventOut. When all parts of the sensed region are outside the viewing-volume frustrum, **FALSE** is output using the **isActive** eventOut, and the current absolute time is output using the **exitTime** eventOut.

The sensor attributes can be changed by sending values to the implied **set_ enabled, set_center,** and **set_size** eventIns of the exposed fields. When values are received by these inputs, the corresponding field values are changed, and the new values are output using the implied **enabled_changed, center_changed,** and **size_ changed** eventOuts of the exposed fields.

If a sensor is instanced using **DEF** and **USE,** the visibility region is sensed within each instance of the sensor.

The **ProximitySensor** Node Syntax

The **ProximitySensor** node may be the child of any group, and it senses when the viewer enters, exits, and moves about within a box-shaped region in the current coordinate system.

| SYNTAX | **ProximitySensor node** |

```
ProximitySensor {
    enabled              TRUE           # exposedField   SFBool
    center               0.0 0.0 0.0    # exposedField   SFVec3f
    size                 0.0 0.0 0.0    # exposedField   SFVec3f
    isActive                            # eventOut       SFBool
    enterTime                           # eventOut       SFTime
    exitTime                            # eventOut       SFTime
    position_changed                    # eventOut       SFVec3f
    orientation_changed                 # eventOut       SFRotation
}
```

The values of the **enabled, center,** and **size** exposed fields are discussed in the section entitled "The **VisibilitySensor** Node Syntax." A proximity sensor with a **size** field of 0.0 0.0 0.0 turns off the sensor.

When the viewer enters the sensed region, the sensor node outputs **TRUE** using the **isActive** eventOut and outputs the current absolute time using the **enterTime** eventOut. When the viewer exits the sensed region, **FALSE** is output using the **isActive** eventOut, and the current absolute time is output using the **exitTime** eventOut.

Each time the viewer's position or orientation changes within the sensed region, the viewer's new position and orientation are output using the **position_changed** and **orientation_changed** eventOuts, respectively. Both values are measured in the coordinate system of the **ProximitySensor** node. The viewer's changed position and orientation may be the result of any of several actions, including movement by the viewer using the browser's user interface, movement of the coordinate system containing the current **Viewpoint** node, binding of a new current **Viewpoint** node, movement of the sensed region while the viewer remains stationary, and so on.

The sensor attributes can be changed by sending values to the implied **set_enabled, set_center,** and **set_size** eventIns of the exposed fields. When values are received by these inputs, the corresponding field values are changed, and the new values are output using the implied **enabled_changed, center_changed,** and **size_changed** eventOuts of the exposed fields.

If a sensor is named using **DEF** and instanced using **USE,** the sensor senses the proximity region within each instance of the sensor.

The **Collision** Node Syntax

The **Collision** group node senses when the viewer collides with any shape within the group.

SYNTAX | **Collision node**

```
Group {
    children           [ ]                # exposedField  MFNode
    bboxCenter         0.0  0.0  0.0      # field         SFVec3f
    bboxSize           -1.0 -1.0 -1.0     # field         SFVec3f
    collide            TRUE               # exposedField  SFBool
    proxy              NULL               # field         SFNode
    collideTime                           # eventOut      SFTime
    addChildren                           # eventIn       MFNode
    removeChildren                        # eventOut      MFNode
}
```

The value of the **children** exposed field specifies a list of children nodes to be included in the group. Typical **children** field values include **Shape** nodes and other grouping nodes. The VRML browser builds the group by building each of the shapes and groups contained within the group. The default value for this field is an empty list of children.

The value of the **bboxSize** field specifies the size of a bounding box large enough to contain all of the shapes within the group. The first value gives the width of the box in the X direction, the second value the height of the box in the Y direction, and the third the depth of the box in the Z direction. The default for this field is a bounding box with a -1.0-unit width, height, and depth, which indicates that the VRML browser automatically computes the bounding box.

The value of **bboxCenter** field specifies the center of the bounding box. The field value is a 3-D coordinate within the group's coordinate system. The default value is the origin. If the VRML browser automatically computes the bounding-box size, it automatically computes the bounding-box center, as well.

The **collide** exposed field specifies a **TRUE** or **FALSE** value that enables or disables collision detection for the children in the group. When the field value is **TRUE,** the group's shapes are subject to collision detection each time the viewer moves while using the "WALK" or "FLY" navigation types specified by the **NavigationInfo** node. When the viewer collides with a shape in the group, the browser is notified, and the viewer's motion is typically stopped. When the **collide** field value is **FALSE**, collision detection is disabled for the group, and the viewer can walk through the group's shapes. The default value for the **collide** field is **TRUE**.

The children of a **Collision** node may include **Collision** nodes. This creates a family tree of collision control. During collision detection, the VRML browser examines the collision family tree, starts with the top-most parent, and checks each child one at a time. If a **Collision** node parent enables collision detection for its children, then the VRML browser checks for collision with each child of that parent, and their children, and so on down the tree.

While examining the collision family tree, if the VRML browser encounters a **Collision** node parent that disables collision detection for its children, then the VRML browser skips any further collision checking for those children and their descendants. Any **Collision** node that sets its **collide** field value to **FALSE** overrides any descendant **Collision** nodes further down in the tree.

The VRML browser always creates a hidden **Collision** node that surrounds the entire world and has a **collide** field value of **TRUE**. This ensures that collision detection is on by default for the entire world while "WALK" or "FLY" navigation types are in use.

Collision between the viewer and a shape occurs when the distance from the viewer to the shape is less than or equal to the avatar's width as specified by the **avatarSize** field of the **NavigationInfo** node. When a collision occurs with a shape, each **Collision** node containing the shape outputs the current, absolute time using its **collideTime** eventOut.

A single shape may be the descendant of multiple **Collision** nodes, such as when a **Collision** node contains a **Collision** node as a child, which in turn contains another **Collision** node, and so on down to the shape. If all of the **Collision** nodes leading down to a shape enable collision detection on their children, and the viewer runs into that shape, then all of the **Collision** nodes down to the shape register the collision and output the time on their **collideTime** eventOuts.

The value of the **proxy** field specifies an optional shape used as an alternate and simpler representation of the child shapes. During collision detection, the proxy shape is used instead of the child shapes. The children shapes are actually built, and the proxy shape is ignored. The default value for the **proxy** field is the **NULL** shape.

If a **Collision** node has no children but does have a proxy shape, then the proxy shape specifies the size and shape of an invisible shape in the world. This can be used to create transparent shapes, such as windows.

All geometry nodes, except the **PointSet** and **Indexed LineSet** nodes, create collidable shapes.

The value of the **collide** field can be changed by routing an event to the implied **set_collide** eventIn of the exposed field. When a value is received, the field value is changed, and the new value is output using the implied **collide_changed** eventOut of the exposed field.

You can set, add to, or remove values from the list of children in the group using the implied **set_children** eventIn of the **children** exposed field and the **addChildren** and **removeChildren** eventIns. When a list of node values is sent to the implied **set_children** eventIn, the children list value of the **children** field is replaced with the incoming node list. When a list of node values is sent to the **addChildren** eventIn, each node in the incoming list is added to the list of nodes in the **children** field (if the node isn't already in that child list). Finally, when a list of node values is set to the **removeChildren** eventIn, each node is removed from the child list (if the node is in that child list). In all three cases, if the child list is changed, the new list of children is sent using the implied **children_changed** eventOut of the **children** exposed field.

Experimenting with Proximity Sensing

The following examples provide a more detailed examination of the ways in which the **VisibilitySensor, ProximitySensor,** and **Collision** nodes can be used.

Triggering Animation by Sensing Visibility and Proximity

Figure 27.1 illustrates the use of a **VisibilitySensor** node to trigger animation that opens and closes a sliding door in a dungeon. Added to the dungeon built in Chapter 25 are two **Sound** nodes and their **AudioClip** nodes to play sounds when the door slides open or closed. Two **TimeSensor** nodes act as clocks for opening and closing the doors, and four **PositionInterpolator** nodes specify a translation path to slide the left and right doors when opened and closed.

The **VisibilitySensor** node's enter time triggers the playback of a door-opening sound and starts the door-opening **TimeSensor** node. That node routes to two **PositionInterpolator** nodes to slide the doors apart. Similarly, the **VisibilitySensor** node's exit time triggers playback of a door closing sound and starts the door-closing **TimeSensor** node. That node routes to two **PositionInterpolator** nodes to slide the doors closed.

If the viewer turns to face the doors and then quickly turns away, the **VisibilitySensor** node's enter time and exit time are very close together. In this situation, the doors may still be opening when the exit time triggers their closing animation. To avoid having two animations attempt to change the position of the doors at the same time in opposite directions, the **VisibilitySensor** node's outputs are also used to stop animations. In particular, while the **VisibilitySensor** node's enter time starts an opening animation, it also stops a closing animation by routing the enter time to the **stopTime** field of the door closing **TimeSensor** node and the closing **AudioClip** sound. Similarly, the **VisibilitySensor** node's exit time starts a door-closing animation and stops a door-opening animation.

After displaying the world shown in Figure 27.1 with your browser, try turning to face the doors, and then move away again. Each time you see the doors, they slide open with a clunk. Each time you turn away from the doors, they slide shut with a clunk.

```
#VRML V2.0 utf8
Group {
    children [
        NavigationInfo { headlight FALSE },
    # Room
        Inline { url "droom.wrl" },
    # Wall
        Transform {
            translation 0.0 0.0 -5.0
            children Inline { url "dwall2.wrl" }
        },
    # Left and right door panels
        Transform {
            translation 0.0 0.0 -4.95
            children [
                DEF LeftDoor Transform {
                    children Transform {
                        translation -0.75 0.0 0.0
                        children DEF Door Inline { url "ddoor.wrl" }
                    }
                },
                DEF RightDoor Transform {
                    children Transform {
                        translation 0.75 0.0 0.0
                        children USE Door
                    }
                },
            # Visibility Sensor
                DEF DoorSense VisibilitySensor {
                    center 0.0 1.75 0.0
                    size 3.0 2.5 1.0
                }
            ]
        },
    # Sounds
        Sound {
            source DEF OpenSound AudioClip { url "clunk1.wav" }
            minFront 20.0 minBack 20.0
            maxFront 60.0 maxBack 60.0
        },
        Sound {
            source DEF CloseSound AudioClip { url "clunk1.wav" }
            minFront 20.0 minBack 20.0
            maxFront 60.0 maxBack 60.0
        },
    # Animation clocks
        DEF OpenClock TimeSensor {
            cycleInterval 0.5
        },
        DEF CloseClock TimeSensor {
            cycleInterval 0.5
        },
```

Figure 27.1 continues

```
# Animation paths for the left and right doors
    DEF LeftOpen PositionInterpolator {
        key [ 0.0, 1.0 ]
        keyValue [ 0.0 0.0 0.0, -1.3 0.0 0.0 ]
    },
    DEF LeftClose PositionInterpolator {
        key [ 0.0, 1.0 ]
        keyValue [ -1.3 0.0 0.0, 0.0 0.0 0.0 ]
    },
    DEF RightOpen PositionInterpolator {
        key [ 0.0, 1.0 ]
        keyValue [ 0.0 0.0 0.0, 1.3 0.0 0.0 ]
    },
    DEF RightClose PositionInterpolator {
        key [ 0.0, 1.0 ]
        keyValue [ 1.3 0.0 0.0, 0.0 0.0 0.0 ]
    }
  ]
}
ROUTE DoorSense.enterTime          TO OpenSound.set_startTime
ROUTE DoorSense.exitTime           TO OpenSound.set_stopTime
ROUTE DoorSense.enterTime          TO OpenClock.set_startTime
ROUTE DoorSense.exitTime           TO OpenClock.set_stopTime

ROUTE DoorSense.exitTime           TO CloseSound.set_startTime
ROUTE DoorSense.enterTime          TO CloseSound.set_stopTime
ROUTE DoorSense.exitTime           TO CloseClock.set_startTime
ROUTE DoorSense.enterTime          TO CloseClock.set_stopTime

ROUTE OpenClock.fraction_changed   TO LeftOpen.set_fraction
ROUTE OpenClock.fraction_changed   TO RightOpen.set_fraction
ROUTE CloseClock.fraction_changed  TO LeftClose.set_fraction
ROUTE CloseClock.fraction_changed  TO RightClose.set_fraction

ROUTE LeftOpen.value_changed       TO LeftDoor.set_translation
ROUTE LeftClose.value_changed      TO LeftDoor.set_translation
ROUTE RightOpen.value_changed      TO RightDoor.set_translation
ROUTE RightClose.value_changed     TO RightDoor.set_translation
```

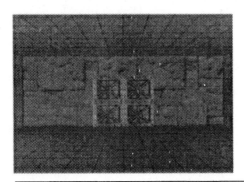

Figure 27.1 *A dungeon door that slides open and closed based on visibility.*

In a manner analogous to the **VisibilitySensor** node, you can route the outputs of the **ProximitySensor** node into **TimeSensor** and **AudioClip** nodes to cause animation and sound to start when the viewer moves into a region. You can modify Figure 27.1 by replacing the **VisibilitySensor** node with the following **ProximitySensor** node:

```
# Proximity sensor
    DEF DoorSense ProximitySensor {
        center 0.0 1.75 4.0
        size 16.0 3.5 8.0
    }
```

Using the **ProximitySensor** node, the door slides open when the viewer moves into the region immediately in front of the door, and it slides closed when the viewer moves out of the region.

Triggering Animation by Sensing Collision

You can use a **Collision** group node to sense when the viewer collides with any shape in a group. By routing the **collideTime** eventOut of the **Collision** node to a **TimeSensor** or **AudioClip** node, you can start animation and sound when the viewer runs into something.

The VRML text in Figure 27.2 modifies the sliding door example from Figure 27.1 to build the door shapes within a **Collision** group node. The group's **collideTime** eventOut triggers a clunk sound and an animation to open the door.

Unlike the **VisibilitySensor** and **ProximitySensor** nodes, the **Collision** node has no second output to use to close the doors behind the viewer. This example uses a **ProximitySensor** node's **exitTime** eventOut to close the doors when the viewer walks away.

```
#VRML V2.0 utf8
Group {
    children [
        NavigationInfo {
            headlight FALSE
            avatarSize [ 1.0, 1.6, 0.75 ]
        },
    # Room
        Inline { url "droom.wrl" },
    # Wall
        Transform {
            translation 0.0 0.0 -5.0
            children Inline { url "dwall2.wrl" }
        },
    # Left and right door panels in a collision group
        DEF DoorCollide Collision {
            children Transform {
                translation 0.0 0.0 -4.95
```

Figure 27.2 continues

```
            children [
                DEF LeftDoor Transform {
                    children Transform {
                        translation -0.75 0.0 0.0
                        children DEF Door Inline { url "ddoor.wrl" }
                    }
                },
                DEF RightDoor Transform {
                    children Transform {
                        translation 0.75 0.0 0.0
                        children USE Door
                    }
                },
                DEF DoorSense ProximitySensor {
                    center 0.0 1.75 0.0
                    size 6.0 3.5 8.0
                }
            ]
        }
    },
# Sounds
    Sound {
        source DEF OpenSound AudioClip { url "clunk1.wav" }
        minFront 20.0 minBack 20.0
        maxFront 60.0 maxBack 60.0
    },
    Sound {
        source DEF CloseSound AudioClip { url "clunk1.wav" }
        minFront 20.0 minBack 20.0
        maxFront 60.0 maxBack 60.0
    },
# Animation clocks
    DEF OpenClock TimeSensor {
        cycleInterval 0.5
    },
    DEF CloseClock TimeSensor {
        cycleInterval 0.5
    },
# Animation paths for the left and right doors
    DEF LeftOpen PositionInterpolator {
        key [ 0.0, 1.0 ]
        keyValue [ 0.0 0.0 0.0, -1.3 0.0 0.0 ]
    },
    DEF LeftClose PositionInterpolator {
        key [ 0.0, 1.0 ]
        keyValue [ -1.3 0.0 0.0, 0.0 0.0 0.0 ]
    },
    DEF RightOpen PositionInterpolator {
        key [ 0.0, 1.0 ]
        keyValue [ 0.0 0.0 0.0, 1.3 0.0 0.0 ]
    },
```

Figure 27.2 continues

```
            DEF RightClose PositionInterpolator {
                key [ 0.0, 1.0 ]
                keyValue [ 1.3 0.0 0.0, 0.0 0.0 0.0 ]
            }
        ]
    }
    ROUTE DoorCollide.collideTime      TO OpenSound.set_startTime
    ROUTE DoorSense.exitTime           TO OpenSound.set_stopTime
    ROUTE DoorCollide.collideTime      TO OpenClock.set_startTime
    ROUTE DoorSense.exitTime           TO OpenClock.set_stopTime

    ROUTE DoorSense.exitTime           TO CloseSound.set_startTime
    ROUTE DoorCollide.collideTime      TO CloseSound.set_stopTime
    ROUTE DoorSense.exitTime           TO CloseClock.set_startTime
    ROUTE DoorCollide.collideTime      TO CloseClock.set_stopTime

    ROUTE OpenClock.fraction_changed   TO LeftOpen.set_fraction
    ROUTE OpenClock.fraction_changed   TO RightOpen.set_fraction
    ROUTE CloseClock.fraction_changed  TO LeftClose.set_fraction
    ROUTE CloseClock.fraction_changed  TO RightClose.set_fraction

    ROUTE LeftOpen.value_changed       TO LeftDoor.set_translation
    ROUTE LeftClose.value_changed      TO LeftDoor.set_translation
    ROUTE RightOpen.value_changed      TO RightDoor.set_translation
    ROUTE RightClose.value_changed     TO RightDoor.set_translation
```

Figure 27.2 *A dungeon door that slides open when the viewer collides with it and closes when the viewer walks away.*

Using Proxy Shapes for Collision Detection

Sensing collision with a complex shape can be time-consuming. Typically, it is sufficient to detect if the viewer has collided with a simple proxy shape, such as a box, that surrounds the complex shape. Using a simple proxy shape reduces the computation required to check for collision and speeds the VRML browser.

Figure 27.3 shows a pedestal and sphere enclosed within a **Collision** node group. Collision with the pedestal or sphere triggers the animation and sound effects. To reduce the computation required to check for collision, the **Collision** node uses a **Box** node as a proxy shape, positioned and sized to surround the sphere and pedestal. Notice that the **Shape** node used for the **Box** node doesn't include an **Appearance** node. Since the **Box** node is only used for collision detection and is never drawn, there is no need to include appearance information in the proxy shape. Similarly, there is no need to include sounds, lights, or other information unless it pertains to the size and position of the proxy shape.

```
#VRML V2.0 utf8
Group {
    children [
        NavigationInfo {
            headlight FALSE
            avatarSize [ 1.0, 1.0, 0.75 ]
        },
    # Floor (two strips)
        Transform {
            translation 0.0 0.0 2.5
            children DEF Floor Inline { url "dfloor.wrl" }
        },
        Transform { translation 0.0 0.0 -2.5 children USE Floor },
    # Collision group
        DEF OrbCollide Collision {
            proxy Transform {
                translation 0.0 0.6 0.0
                children Shape {
                    geometry Box { size 0.4 1.2 0.4 }
                }
            }
            children [
            # Glowing orb with sound effects
                DEF OrbSpin Transform {
                    translation 0.0 1.0 0.0
                    children [
                    # Orb light
                        PointLight {
                            location 0.3 0.0 0.0
                            radius 10.0
                            ambientIntensity 0.2
                            color 0.7 0.5 0.0
                        },
                    # Orb itself
                        Shape {
                            appearance Appearance {
                                # No material, use emissive texturing
                                texture ImageTexture { url "fire.jpg" }
                            }
                            geometry Sphere { radius 0.2 }
                        },
                    # Orb sounds
                        Sound {
                            source AudioClip {
                                url "drone1.wav"
                                loop TRUE
                            }
                            intensity 0.5
                        },
```

Figure 27.3 continues

```
                                DEF WispyAmp Sound {
                                    source DEF Wispy AudioClip {
                                        url "willow1.wav"
                                        stopTime 1.0
                                    }
                                    intensity 0.0
                                }
                            ]
                        },
                # Pedestal pyramid
                    Shape {
                        appearance DEF PedestalColor Appearance {
                            material Material { }
                        }
                        geometry IndexedFaceSet {
                            coord Coordinate {
                                point [
                                # Around the base
                                    -0.12 0.03  0.12,    0.12 0.03  0.12,
                                     0.12 0.03 -0.12,   -0.12 0.03 -0.12,
                                # Tip
                                     0.0  0.63  0.0,
                                ]
                            }
                            coordIndex [
                                0, 1, 4, -1,  1, 2, 4, -1,
                                2, 3, 4, -1,  3, 0, 4, -1,
                            ]
                            solid TRUE
                        }
                    },
                # Pedestal base
                    Transform {
                        translation 0.0 0.015 0.0
                        children Shape {
                            appearance USE PedestalColor
                            geometry Box { size 0.4 0.03 0.4 }
                        }
                    },
                ]
            }
        # Animation clock
            DEF Clock TimeSensor {
                cycleInterval 28.0
            },
        # Orb animation and volume control
            DEF OrbSpinner OrientationInterpolator {
                key [ 0.0, 0.5, 1.0 ]
                keyValue [
                    0.0 1.0 0.0 0.0,
                    0.0 1.0 0.0 3.14,
                    0.0 1.0 0.0 6.28
                ]
            },
```

Figure 27.3 continues

```
         DEF WispyVolume ScalarInterpolator {
             key      [ 0.0, 0.1, 0.9, 1.0 ]
             keyValue [ 0.0, 0.6, 0.6, 0.0 ]
         }
     ]
}
ROUTE OrbCollide.collideTime    TO Clock.set_startTime
ROUTE OrbCollide.collideTime    TO Wispy.set_startTime
ROUTE Clock.fraction_changed    TO OrbSpinner.set_fraction
ROUTE Clock.fraction_changed    TO WispyVolume.set_fraction
ROUTE OrbSpinner.value_changed  TO OrbSpin.set_rotation
ROUTE WispyVolume.value_changed TO WispyAmp.set_intensity
```

Figure 27.3   *An orb that animates when the viewer collides with its box proxy shape.*

Summary

A **VisibilitySensor** node senses when a box-shaped region in the world is visible from the viewer's position and orientation. The region's location and size are specified by the **center** and **size** fields of the node. When any part of the region enters the viewing-volume frustrum, the sensor outputs **TRUE** using its **isActive** eventOut and the current absolute time using its **enterTime** eventOut. When the entire sensed region exits the viewing-volume frustrum, the sensor outputs **FALSE** using its **isActive** eventOut and the current absolute time using its **exitTime** eventOut.

A **ProximitySensor** node senses when the viewer enters, exits, or moves within a box-shaped region in the world. The region's location and size are specified by the **center** and **size** fields of the node. When the viewer enters the region, the sensor outputs **TRUE** using its **isActive** eventOut and the current, absolute time using its **enterTime** eventOut. When the viewer exits the region, the sensor outputs **FALSE** using its **isActive** eventOut and the current, absolute time using its **exitTime** eventOut. Each time the viewer moves within the region, the viewer's position and orientation are output using the **position_changed** and **orientation_changed** eventOuts.

A **Collision** node manages a group of children listed in its **children** field. If the **collide** field value is **TRUE,** collision detection is enabled for the group, and the viewer is prevented from walking or flying through the group's shapes. If the **collide** field value is **FALSE**, collision detection is disabled for the group, and the viewer can walk or fly through them unhindered. To speed up collision detection, an optional proxy shape can be specified in the node's **proxy** field. The proxy shape is used for collision detection calculations instead of checking the more complex child shapes of the group. In any case, when a collision occurs, the current, absolute time is output using the node's **collideTime** eventOut.

## CHAPTER 28

Adding Anchors

As a Web technology, VRML provides you with the ability to link VRML worlds together. Using links, you can connect a door in your world to a destination VRML world described elsewhere on the Web. One of the doors in *that* world can link back to your world or to yet another destination world. Linking puts the entire Web at your fingertips, enabling you to explore the Web as if wandering through a vast building, stepping through door after door between virtual worlds.

VRML world links are bound, or *anchored*, to specific shapes in your world. When a viewer clicks on an anchor shape, the VRML browser follows the link, fetches the destination world from the Web, and displays it for the viewer. You can use any shape as an anchor shape, including doors in a room, books in a library, a painting on a room wall, and so on. Any shape you can build using a series of VRML nodes can be an anchor leading to another world.

VRML anchors are specified using the **Anchor** node and a URL indicating the Web address of a destination VRML world on the Web. The file specified in the URL is the world to which the viewer travels with a click on the anchor shape.

Understanding Anchors

Anchors are built using the **Anchor** grouping node. Contained within the node's **children** field are the nodes making up an anchor shape. The node's **url** field value specifies the URL of a destination Web page to which the viewer travels when the viewer clicks on the anchor shape.

The **parameter** field value specifies parameters that are interpreted by your Web browser when the destination Web page is retrieved from the Web. Using anchor parameters, you can access the full set of features available in your Web browser, including features like HTML frames.

When the viewer moves the cursor over an anchor shape, many VRML browsers highlight the shape or display a description of the link, provided by you in the Anchor node's **description** field. The description enables the viewer to see where an anchor door leads before clicking on it.

The **Anchor** Node Syntax

The **Anchor** grouping node encloses a group of shapes. When the viewer clicks on these shapes, the browser reads a new world.

SYNTAX	Anchor node			
Anchor {				
children	[ ]	# exposedField	MFNode
bboxCenter	0.0 0.0 0.0	# field	SFVec3f
bboxSize	-1.0 -1.0 -1.0	# field	SFVec3f
url	[ ]	# exposedField	MFString
parameter	[ ]	# exposedField	MFString
description	""	# exposedField	SFString
addChildren		# eventIn	MFNode
removeChildren		# eventOut	MFNode
}				

The value of the **children** exposed field specifies a list of children nodes to be included in the anchor group and that, collectively, describe an anchor shape. Typical **children** field values include **Shape** nodes and other grouping nodes. The default value for this field is an empty list of children.

The value of the **bboxSize** field specifies the size of a bounding box large enough to contain all of the shapes within the group. The first value gives the width of the box in the X direction, the second value the height of the box in the Y direction, and the third the depth of the box in the Z direction. The default for this field is a bounding box with a -1.0-unit width, height, and depth, which indicates that the VRML browser automatically computes the bounding box.

The value of **bboxCenter** field specifies the center of the bounding box. The field value is a 3-D coordinate within the group's coordinate system. The default value is the origin. If the VRML browser automatically computes the bounding-box size, it automatically computes the bounding-box center, as well.

The shapes within the **children** field specify an anchor shape. When the viewer clicks on the anchor shape using a pointing device, such as a mouse, the VRML browser loads a destination Web page specified by the URLs in the node's **url** field. The destination Web page can be a VRML world or any other page type supported by the Web browser.

The value of the **url** exposed field specifies a prioritized list of URLs for a destination Web page, ordered from highest priority to lowest. When the viewer clicks on the anchor shape, the VRML browser tries to open the Web page specified by the first URL in the list. If the Web page cannot be found, the browser tries the second URL in the list, and so on. When a URL is found that indicates a destination Web page that can be opened, the destination Web page is loaded into the browser. If the destination Web page is a VRML world, the current VRML world is put aside, and the groups and shapes within the destination world are read and displayed. If none of the URLs can be opened, then nothing happens when the viewer clicks on the anchor shape. The default value for the **url** field is an empty list of URLs.

The value of the **description** exposed field is a short text string that describes the destination Web page. Most VRML browsers display the description text when the viewer moves the cursor over the anchor shape without clicking on it. If no description text is provided, most VRML browsers display the destination-Web-page URL. Some browsers provide menu options to select a user preference to display the description, the URL, both, or neither as the viewer moves the cursor over an anchor shape. The default value of the **description** field is an empty string.

The values of the **parameter** exposed field specify additional information optionally used by the Web browser when a destination Web page is read in. Each string value in the parameter field's value list consists of a keyword, an equal sign (=), and a value. The keywords and their possible values, depend on the features of your Web browser. Some browsers, for instance, support the `target` keyword to select a frame in the current Web page into which the destination Web page is read. In this case, the value for the `target` keyword is the name of the frame to receive the destination Web page (e.g., `target=myframe`). See the manual for your Web browser for a list of keywords and values that it supports. The default value for the **parameter** field is an empty list of parameters.

Any URL in the **url** field may include an optional viewpoint selection by ending the URL with a pound sign (#) followed by the name of a **Viewpoint** node in the destination world (e.g., `http://www.somewhere.org/myworld.wrl#CoolView`). **Viewpoint** node names are created using the **DEF** syntax (for example, **DEF CoolView Viewpoint** { . . . }). When the destination world is read by the VRML browser, the viewer is initially positioned at the selected **Viewpoint** node. If the **Viewpoint** node name is not found in the destination world, or no viewpoint selection is added to the end of the URL, then the viewer is initially positioned at the default starting viewpoint of the destination world (see Chapter 26 on **Viewpoint** nodes).

A URL in the **url** field may include a viewpoint selection but contain an empty Web page address (for example, `#CoolView`). An empty address specifies the current world as the destination world. When the viewer clicks on the anchor shape, the viewer's position and orientation are switched to the specified **Viewpoint** node in the current world. You can use this effect to simulate the viewpoints menu found on most VRML browsers.

An **Anchor** node may be the child of another **Anchor** node, which may be the child of another **Anchor** node, creating a family tree of anchor shapes. An anchor shape built by a child **Anchor** node is simultaneously part of an anchor shape built by its parent **Anchor** node, and so on up the family tree. When the viewer clicks on an anchor shape that is the descendant of multiple **Anchor** nodes in the family tree, the **Anchor** node lowest in the tree takes precedence. The browser reads the destination Web page of the **Anchor** node taking precedence and ignores any ancestor **Anchor** nodes further up in the tree.

You can set, add to, or remove from the list of children in the group using the implied **set_children** eventIn of the **children** exposed field and the **addChildren** and **removeChildren** eventIns. When a list of node values is sent to the implied **set_children** eventIn, the children list value of the **children** field is replaced with the incoming node list. When a list of node values is sent to the **addChildren** eventIn, each node in the incoming list is added to the list of nodes in the **children** field (if the node isn't already in that list of children). Finally, when a list of node values is sent to the **removeChildren** eventIn, each node in the incoming list is looked up in the children list, and if found, the node is removed from the child list. In all three cases, if the child list is changed, the new list of children is sent the implied **children_changed** eventOut of the **children** exposed field.

Anchor attributes can be changed by sending a value to the implied **set_url**, **set_parameter**, and **set_description** eventIns of the exposed fields. When a value is received by this input, the corresponding field value is changed, and the new value is output using implied **url_changed**, **parameter_changed**, and **description_changed** eventOuts of the exposed fields.

Experimenting with Anchors

The following examples provide a more detailed examination of the ways in which the **Anchor** node can be used and how it interacts with nodes discussed in previous chapters.

Building an Anchor Shape

To set up an anchor example, you need two worlds: the departure world and the destination world. For the destination world, the following examples use the dungeon built in Chapter 25. For the departure world, the following examples use a partial room and door using some of the same components used to build the dungeon.

Figure 28.1 shows the destination world file, named `"dngnwrld.wrl."` Viewpoint nodes in the world describe available viewing positions within a dungeon. The **Inline** node inlines the dungeon description from `"dungeon.wrl."`

```
#VRML V2.0 utf8
Group {
    children [
    # Viewpoints
        DEF Forward Viewpoint {
            description "Forward view"
            position 0.0 1.6 5.0
        },
        DEF Corner Viewpoint {
            description "Corner view"
            position 3.0 1.6 3.0
            orientation 0.0 1.0 0.0 0.611
        },
    # Navigation
        NavigationInfo { headlight FALSE },
    # World
        Inline { url "dungeon.wrl" }
    ]
}
```

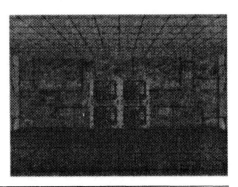

Figure 28.1   *A dungeon destination world.*

Figure 28.2*a* builds a departure world. Using components from the dungeon, the room is inlined from the file "droom.wrl," the back wall from "dwall2.wrl," and the door from "ddoor.wrl." An **Anchor** node contains the door, turning the door into an anchor shape.

The **Anchor** node's destination URL is the destination world built in Figure 28.1 and named "dngnwrld.wrl." When the viewer clicks on the door in the partial room, the dungeon destination world is read by the VRML browser, and the viewer is positioned at the first **Viewpoint** node in the dungeon.

```
#VRML V2.0 utf8
Group {
    children [
        NavigationInfo { headlight FALSE },
    # Room
        Inline { url "droom.wrl" },
    # Dungeon wall
        Transform {
            translation 0.0 0.0 -5.0
            children DEF Wall Inline { url "dwall2.wrl" },
        },
    # Anchor doors
        Anchor {
            url "dngnwrld.wrl"
            description "The Dungeon"
            children [
            # Left door panel
                Transform {
                    translation -0.75 0.0 -4.95
                    children DEF LeftDoor Transform {
                        children DEF Door Inline { url "ddoor.wrl" }
                    }
                },
```

Figure 28.2 continues

```
# Right door panel
    Transform {
        translation 0.75 0.0 -4.95
        children DEF RightDoor Transform {
            children USE Door
        }
    }
]
}
]
}
```

Figure 28.2 *A world with a door anchor shape that, when clicked on, jumps to the dungeon destination world shown in Figure 28.1.*

Using Viewpoint Anchors

You can add a pound sign (#) and the name of a **Viewpoint** node to the end of a destination URL. When the viewer clicks on the anchor shape, the destination Web page is read, and the viewer is positioned at the named **Viewpoint** node in the destination world.

For example, you can modify the **url** field value of the departure world's **Anchor** node. The new **url** field value, which follows, adds "#Corner" to specify the destination world's "Corner" **Viewpoint** node as the starting viewing position when the viewer clicks on the anchor door in the departure world.

```
Anchor {
    url "dngnwrld.wrl#Corner"
    description "The Dungeon"
    children [ ... ]
}
```

Summary

The **Anchor** grouping node describes an anchor in your world that links your world to another on the Web. The shapes within the node's **children** field build an anchor shape. The **url** field value specifies the URL of a destination world. When the viewer clicks on the anchor shape, the destination world is retrieved from the Web and read by the VRML browser.

The **parameter** field value specifies optional browser parameters to control the way in which a destination world is read by the browser.

The **description** field value provides a short description of the destination world. The destination description is typically displayed by the browser when the viewer moves the cursor over an anchor shape.

## CHAPTER 29

Providing Information About Your Worlds

After completing a world, you can title it and sign it. You should include this information as comments in any VRML file you write. You can also include this information within a **WorldInfo** node. Unlike comments, the information you place in a **WorldInfo** node can be easily extracted by your VRML browser and displayed to a viewer of your world. This enables you to title and sign your work and lets others see your title and signature when they view your work.

Understanding World Information

The **WorldInfo** node enables you to declare the title of your world and any additional commentary you'd like to provide. That commentary often includes a copyright notice, your name, the date you finished the world, a revision history of the world, and perhaps some comments about what the world is for and what is interesting within it.

The **WorldInfo** node does not create shapes in your world. Instead, this information is typically made available by your VRML browser through a special menu item. When the user selects this menu item, a window is displayed showing your world title and commentary. Some browsers also place the world's title on the browser window's title bar.

You can have any number of **WorldInfo** nodes in your world, but only the first one encountered is displayed by your browser.

The **WorldInfo** Node Syntax

The **WorldInfo** node provides information about your world.

SYNTAX   WorldInfo node

```
WorldInfo {
    title    ""     # field  SFString
    info     [ ]    # field  MFString
}
```

The value of the **title** field is a text string that specifies the title for your world. Titles should be short so that they can be placed on the title bar of the browser's window. The default title is the empty string.

The value of the **info** field is a list of text strings that provide commentary about your world. The default value is an empty list.

A world may contain multiple **WorldInfo** nodes, but a VRML browser will only use the first one it encounters.

Experimenting with World Information

The following example provides a more detailed examination of the ways in which the **WorldInfo** node can be used.

Providing a Title and Commentary About Your World

The VRML text Figure 29.1 inlines a dungeon world and specifies a title and commentary for it using a **WorldInfo** node. The dungeon is contained in the file "dungeon.wrl" and is composed of the room, door, and torches built in Chapter 27.

```
#VRML V2.0 utf8
Group {
    children [
        WorldInfo {
            title "The Dungeon"
            info [
                "(c) Copyright 1997, Ames, Nadeau, and Moreland",
                "Created for The VRML 2.0 Sourcebook",
                "Published by John Wiley & Sons."
            ]
        },
```

Figure 29.1 continues

```
NavigationInfo { headlight FALSE },
Inline { url "dungeon.wrl" }
    ]
}
```

Figure 29.1 *A title and commentary for the dungeon.*

Summary

The **WorldInfo** node provides information about your world to the VRML browser and the viewer. The **title** field value specifies the title of the world, and the **info** field values provide additional commentary about the world.

## CHAPTER 30

Creating Program Scripts

The past chapters have discussed a wide variety of animation nodes, including the **TimeSensor** node, the various interpolator nodes, nodes that sense the viewer's touch or drag operations, and nodes that sense the viewer's proximity and collision with a shape in your world. Using routes, you can wire these sensors and interpolators to portions of your world to animate shapes.

The animation abilities provided by VRML's sensors and interpolators are intended for relatively straightforward animation. For complex animation, VRML's interpolators and sensors are sometimes too limiting. In these situations, you can use one or more of VRML's general-purpose **Script** nodes.

A **Script** node is a shell of a node: It has fields, eventIns, and eventOuts, but it has no actions of its own. Instead, you can provide your own **Script** node actions by providing a program script. *Program scripts* are miniature applications typically written in the Java or JavaScript programming languages.

Using a program script and a **Script** node, you can create nodes to perform complex actions. Typical program script actions include the output of computed animation paths, like the path of an object falling and bouncing due to gravity. Other typical program script actions include handling the artificial intelligence of a monster in a dungeon game or tracking a game player's health and inventory. You can use program scripts to communicate with remote computers over the Internet and track the activities of players in multiplayer environments.

The **Script** node, together with program scripts written in the Java and JavaScript languages, provide a powerful extension to VRML with which you can program your own sensors and interpolators.

Understanding **Script** Nodes

The **Script** node can describe a custom-made sensor or interpolator. Like any sensor or interpolator, the node requires a list of fields, eventIns, and eventOuts.

The custom-made sensor or interpolator also requires a description of what the node does with those fields, eventIns, and eventOuts.

The fields, eventIns, and eventOuts of the custom-made sensor or interpolator describe the *interface* to the node's actions. For instance, a **Script** node that computes the path of a falling shape, might have fields whose values specify the gravity strength, the initial height of the shape, the initial forward velocity, and so forth. The same gravity **Script** node may include a fractional time eventIn, such as from a **Time-Sensor** node, and a 3-D position eventOut that can be routed to a falling shape's **Transform** node. All of these fields, eventIns, and eventOuts define the gravity **Script** node's interface.

In addition to the interface, the custom-made sensor or interpolator also needs a description of what to do. This description is a program script that is typically written in Java or JavaScript. For instance, the program script for a gravity **Script** node does the actual computations needed to generate a falling-shape path for an animation.

Defining an Interface

When you build a custom sensor or interpolator, the fields, eventIns, and eventOuts of the node's interface are named and defined by you.

The **Script** node provides special syntax for defining the interface to a custom sensor or interpolator. That syntax has three forms, one each for defining a field, an eventIn, and an eventOut.

Defining an Interface Field

Each interface field in your custom sensor or interpolator must have a field data type, a name, and an initial value. All three of these are listed within a **Script** node.

```
Script {
    ...
    field fieldType fieldName initialValue
    ...
}
```

A line in a **Script** node that starts with the word field begins the definition of an interface field for your custom sensor or interpolator. Following the word field is the name of a field data type (fieldType), like those listed in Table 2.1. After the field data type, you specify the name for your interface field (fieldName), such as gravity or velocity. Finally, at the end of the field definition, you provide an initial value (initialValue) for the field, such as -9.8 or 1.0 0.0 0.0

The following are all examples of possible field interface definitions within a **Script** node:

```
field SFBool     enabled          TRUE
field SFColor    diffuseColor     0.8 0.8 0.8
field MFColor    spacecraftColor  [ 1.0 0.0 0.0, 0.0 0.0 1.0 ]
field SFFloat    intensity        1.0
field MFFloat    attenuation      [ 1.0, 0.0, 0.0 ]
field SFImage    textureImage     0 0 0
```

```
field SFInt32        phoneNumber         5551234
field MFInt32        indicatorChoice     [ 42, 531, 5 ]
field SFNode         texture             NULL
field MFNode         children            [ ]
field SFRotation     orbitAngle          0.0 0.0 1.0 0.0
field MFRotation     orientation         [ 0.0 0.0 1.0 0.0 ]
field SFString       robotName           "Marvin"
field MFString       dwarves             [ "Sneezy", "Sleepy", "um..." ]
field SFTime         startTime           0.0
field SFVec2f        texTranslation      0.0 0.0
field MFVec2f        plotterPoint        [ 0.0 0.0 ]
field SFVec3f        galacticCoordinate  0.0 0.0 0.0
field MFVec3f        vector              [ ]
```

You can name your interface fields anything you like, following the naming restrictions imposed for names defined using **DEF** (see Chapter 2 for **DEF** naming rules). By VRML convention, names start with a lowercase character, and each subsequent word in the name is capitalized. You can also use underbars and numbers in interface field names.

You can have any number of interface field definitions within the same **Script** node. For instance, a node designed to track the characteristics of a dungeon explorer might have fields for the explorer's strength, intelligence, wisdom, dexterity, charisma, and so forth.

Defining an Interface EventIn

Like interface fields, each interface eventIn for your custom sensor or interpolator must have a data type and a name. Both of these are specified within a **Script** node.

```
Script {
    ...
    eventIn eventInType eventInName
    ...
}
```

A line in a **Script** node that starts with the word eventIn begins the definition of an interface eventIn for your custom sensor or interpolator. Following the word eventIn is the name of a data type (*eventInType*), such as those listed in Table 2.1. After the data type, you specify the name for your interface eventIn (*eventInName*), such as set_startTime or addChildren. The following are all examples of possible eventIn interface definitions within a **Script** node:

```
eventIn SFBool       set_enabled
eventIn MFColor      set_skyColor
eventIn SFFloat      set_height
eventIn SFImage      set_texture
eventIn SFInt32      set_population
eventIn MFNode       addChildren
eventIn SFRotation   set_orbitAngle
eventIn SFString     set_candyFlavor
eventIn SFTime       set_stopTime
eventIn MFVec2f      set_point
eventIn MFVec3f      set_position
```

Similar to interface fields, you can name your interface eventIns anything you like, following the **DEF** naming restrictions. By VRML convention, eventIn names always start with set_ unless they deal with adding or removing children from a group. By following this convention, you create custom sensors and interpolators that fit well into the rest of the language.

Interface eventIn names typically start with a lowercase character, and each subsequent word in the name is capitalized. You can also use underbars and numbers in interface eventIn names.

You can have any number of interface eventIn definitions for the same custom sensor or interpolator defined by a **Script** node. For instance, a node designed to track the activities of a monster in a dungeon game might have interface eventIns to set its position, orientation, intelligence, weaponry, anger level, and so on.

Defining an Interface EventOut

You can define interface eventOuts for your custom sensor or interpolator similar to the way you define interface eventIns. Each interface eventOut definition must have a data type and a name, both of which are specified within a **Script** node.

```
Script {
    ...
    eventOut eventOutType eventOutName
    ...
}
```

A line in a **Script** node that starts with the word eventOut begins the definition of an interface eventOut for your custom sensor or interpolator. Following the word eventOut is the name of a data type (eventOutType), such as those listed in Table 2.1, and the name for your interface eventOut (eventOutName), such as fraction_changed or isBound. The following are all examples of possible eventOut interface definitions within a **Script** node:

```
eventOut SFBool        isActive
eventOut SFColor       eyeColor_changed
eventOut MFFloat       stockIndexes_changed
eventOut SFImage       panorama_changed
eventOut SFInt32       age_changed
eventOut SFNode        shape_changed
eventOut SFRotation    orientation_changed
eventOut SFString      fontFamily_changed
eventOut SFTime        creationTime
eventOut SFVec2f       point_changed
eventOut MFVec3f       coordinate_changed
```

You can name interface eventOuts anything you like, following the **DEF** naming restrictions. By VRML convention, eventOut names always end in _changed unless they are a Boolean value or a time value. Boolean eventOut names always start with is, and time eventOut names usually have the word Time at the end.

Like interface field and eventIn names, interface eventOut names typically start with a lowercase character, and each subsequent word in the name is capitalized. You can also use underbars and numbers in interface eventIn names.

You can have any number of interface eventOut definitions within the same **Script** node. For instance, a node designed to track the orbits of the planets in our solar system might have one eventOut for each planet, including `mercury_changed`, `venus_changed`, `earth_changed`, and so on.

Using Fields, EventIns, and EventOuts in an Interface Definition

Using the above syntax features of the **Script** node, you can specify the interface fields, eventIns, and eventOuts for your custom sensor or interpolator. For example, the following VRML text shows the interface definition for a **Script** node that computes the path for a falling shape:

```
Script {
    field    SFFloat gravity  -9.8
    field    SFVec3f velocity 1.0 0.0 0.0
    field    SFVec3f position 0.0 0.0 0.0
    eventIn  SFVec3f set_position
    eventOut SFVec3f position_changed
    eventIn  SFFloat set_fraction
}
```

You cannot create exposed fields in your interface definitions. However, you can create the equivalent of an exposed field by providing interface field, eventIn, and eventOut definitions that work together. For instance, the preceding example includes a **position** interface field, an associated **set_position** interface eventIn, and an associated **position_changed** interface eventOut.

Defining a Program Script

Once an interface is defined for your custom sensor or interpolator, you need to provide a program script that performs the sensor or interpolator actions. Program scripts may be in any programming language supported by your VRML browser. Typically, program scripts are written in Java or JavaScript.

A program script is associated with a **Script** node by placing the script in a file and providing the URL to that file as the value of the **Script** node's url field. For example, the following VRML text uses the JavaScript program script in "myscript.js" to define the actions of a custom sensor or interpolator:

```
Script {
    url "myscript.js"
    field ...
    eventIn ...
    eventOut ...
}
```

When using JavaScript, you can also include the program script within the **url** field, instead of referring to a program script file on the Web. To include the script directly, use a URL that starts with the word "javascript:" and follow it with the program script. For instance, the following VRML text includes a JavaScript program script within a **Script** node's **url** field:

```
Script {
    url "javascript:
        function set_position( pos, time ) {
            position - pos;
        }
    "
    field ...
    eventIn ...
    eventOut ...
}
```

Including a JavaScript program script directly in the **Script** node's **url** field can be very handy. Typically, VRML worlds that use **Script** nodes tend to include a lot of them. If each program script you create has to go in a separate file, referenced by a separate **Script** node, you can easily end up with dozens of small, program-script files everywhere. It is much more convenient to include the program script directly within the **Script** node inside the appropriate part of your world.

Whether included directly in the **Script** node or stored in a separate file, the program script for the **Script** node defines the actions of that node. Those actions can include responding to inputs received by interface eventIns, computing new values, storing those values in the node's interface fields, sending new values using the node's interface eventOuts, and more. The way in which these actions are accomplished depends on the features of the programming language being used.

TIP   VRML 2.0 does not require that a browser support any specific programming language for program scripts. The VRML 2.0 specification does, however, provide language documentation for those browsers that chose to provide support for either Java or JavaScript. Most browsers will support one or both of these languages for program scripts. Check your browser manual for information on its scripting-language support.

Controlling Program-Script Behavior

The **Script** node provides two additional fields that control how a program script behaves: the **mustEvaluate** and **directOutput** fields.

Evaluation Control

Conceptually, a **Script** node executes, or *evaluates*, the program script every time a value is received by an interface eventIn. The program script typically computes something, then sends one or more values using its interface eventOuts.

If you have a large number of **Script** nodes, sensors, and interpolators, your VRML browser can get quite busy constantly evaluating all these nodes each time something changes. To avoid slowing the drawing of the world, your VRML browser may postpone evaluating a **Script** node's program script until a more convenient time. In this case, two or more values may arrive at the node's interface eventIns before the VRML browser evaluates the program script.

When the VRML browser evaluates a **Script** node's program script, the program script should receive all pending interface eventIns, perform its computation, and generate its outputs. Once complete, the VRML browser may not get back to the **Script** node for quite awhile, depending on how busy it is with other activities, such as drawing your world.

In most cases, postponing evaluation is not a problem. In fact, all of VRML's standard sensors and interpolators have postponed evaluation. There are cases, however, when a **Script** node's program script must be evaluated immediately every time a new value is received by an interface eventIn. You can alert the VRML browser to this situation by setting the value of the **Script** node's **mustEvaluate** field to TRUE.

The **mustEvaluate** field value is typically set to TRUE for program scripts that communicate over the Internet to remote multi-user environment servers, such as those used for games. In this kind of situation, every viewer action must be immediately communicated to the game server so that the server can register whether the viewer has fallen into a fiery pit, run into a monster, fired a weapon, or fallen prey to an evil beast. Postponed evaluation delays this information and can cause inaccuracies in the game server's management of the situation.

Typically, the **mustEvaluate** field value is left at the default **FALSE** value and evaluation is postponed by the VRML browser when it needs to. Setting this field value to **TRUE** should be done sparingly. Program-script evaluation takes time, and if the browser is forced to spend its time evaluating lots of program scripts every time an interface eventIn receives a value, then the browser has less time to spend drawing the world or performing other animation actions.

Output Control

A program script can react to new values received by its interface eventIns and compute new values to send using its interface eventOuts. A program script can also get the values in its interface fields and save values back to those interface fields. For most program scripts, this is the only interaction the program script needs with the rest of the VRML world.

There are times when it is necessary for a program script to gain more control over the VRML world to change the values of fields of other nodes in the world. For instance, you might write a program script that automatically creates circuits by building routes between relevant nodes in your world. Building routes is a global action that affects your VRML world in general and requires more power than typical program scripts have.

You can set the **directOutput** field value of a **Script** node to TRUE to indicate that the node's program script should have the power to manipulate the VRML world directly. Typically this field's value is **FALSE**, and program scripts do not have direct access to the VRML world.

When the **directOutput** field value is **FALSE**, a program script can access a limited range of world features, including its own interface eventIns, eventOuts, and fields, as well as the exposed fields of any node value provided to the program script. A program script with the **directOutput** field value set to **FALSE** cannot access anything else in the VRML world. Such a program script is relatively isolated from the world. This isolation enables the VRML browser to optimize animation and shapes in the world, resulting in increased drawing speed and interactivity.

When the **directOutput** field value is **TRUE**, a program script has additional abilities at its disposal. Such a program script can send values to the eventIns of any node value, access the value last sent using any eventOut of any node value, and build its own routes between nodes. This kind of program script can cause a great number of changes in the VRML world and is no longer as isolated as one with a **FALSE** value for the **directOutput** field. This means that the VRML browser is less free to optimize and can result in poorer browser performance.

Typically, most program scripts in a world use a **directOutput** field value of **FALSE**. Only special program scripts involved in making sweeping changes to a world use a **TRUE** value for a **Script** node's **directOutput** field and pay the associated performance penalty in the browser.

Writing Java and JavaScript Program Scripts

Java is a full-featured programming language developed by Sun Microsystems. *JavaScript* is a simpler language developed by Netscape Communications. Both languages enable you to add animation to Web pages or control activities within a VRML world. Despite the similarity in their names, the languages are considerably different. JavaScript is easier to learn, while Java provides extensive features needed for larger programming projects. Either language can be used to write program scripts for a **Script** node.

The Java and JavaScript languages are documented in numerous books. An explanation of their language features is beyond the scope of this book. Appendix B lists references to materials on Java and JavaScript. The following sections assume you have some knowledge of Java and/or JavaScript and focus on the features a VRML browser provides to Java or JavaScript program scripts so that they can access and change the VRML world.

The features the VRML browser must provide to a Java or JavaScript program script are generically classified as part of the language's *API*, which stands for *Application Programming Interface*. The program script API includes features in the following categories:

- Access to the interface fields and eventOuts of the program script's **Script** node

- Conversion between VRML's data types and those of the programming language

- The ability to initialize and shutdown a program script and to respond to incoming events

- Access to the browser to change world content or load a new world

Accessing Interface Fields and EventOuts

A program script must be able to read the values in its interface fields, write new values back to those fields, and send values using its interface eventOuts.

- In Java, the API provides a suite of classes and methods that a program script can call to access interface fields and eventOuts. The **getField** method, for instance, gets a handle to an interface field. Using the value returned by the **getField** method, the Java program script can read and write interface fields. Similarly, the **getEventOut** method gets a handle to an interface eventOut. Using the eventOut handle, the Java program script can send events using the eventOut.

- In JavaScript, the API automatically creates an interface variable for each interface field or eventOut. Using an interface variable, the JavaScript program script can read or write interface fields. Similarly, the JavaScript program script can write to an eventOut's interface variable to send events using the eventOut.

Each event written to an eventOut and received by an eventIn has two components: an event value and an event time stamp.

- An *event value* is a value, such as a 3-D position, generated by a node and sent using an eventOut.

- An *event time stamp* is a value that contains the absolute time at which an event is created and sent using a route. Event time stamps are automatically created by the browser each time an event value is sent.

Events that arrive at a node's eventIn are always sorted so that those that were sent first, arrive first.

Converting between Data Types

Java and JavaScript each provide their own data types for managing numeric data, string data, and other data types.

- In Java, the API provides an extensive set of classes for each of the VRML data types. Methods in those classes provide data-type conversion between VRML and Java data types.

- In JavaScript, the API automatically converts VRML data types into JavaScript data types without the need for any function calls. Complex VRML data types, such as those with multiple components (like an RGB color) or multiple values (such as a list of coordinates), are automatically converted to JavaScript single- and multi-dimensional arrays.

The Java and JavaScript APIs both provide a special data type designed to hold a node value. Using API features, the program script can read and write the exposed fields, eventIns, and eventOuts of any node to which it has access. One common way of gaining access to a node is to pass that node to the program script as a value in an interface field or eventIn.

Access to a node value gives a program script the opportunity to change that node without using a route wired to its exposed fields or eventIns. This kind of direct access, however, is strictly controlled by the **directOutput** field value of the program script's **Script** node. If the **directOutput** field value is **FALSE**, the program script can read from, but not write to, another node's exposed fields, eventIns, and eventOuts. If the **directOutput** field value is **TRUE**, the program script can write, as well as read.

Delivering Events

A program script can respond to three types of activities:

- Initialization
- Shutdown
- Event receipt

Initialization occurs when the program script is first read and before any events have been sent to it. This is a program script's opportunity to set up initial values and prepare for the receipt of future events.

- In Java, the API enables the program-script author to create an **initialize** method that is called when the program script is initialized.
- In JavaScript, the API enables the program-script author to create an **initialize** function that is called when the program script is initialized.

Shutdown occurs when the program script is discarded, perhaps as the result of quitting the browser or reading a new world. Shutdown is the time for a program script to clean up anything it has left to do.

- In Java, the API enables the program-script author to create a **shutdown** method that is called when the program script is discarded.
- In JavaScript, the API enables the program-script author to create a **shutdown** function that is called when the program script is discarded.

For both Java and JavaScript, the initialization and shutdown method or function is passed with no arguments.

Event receipt occurs when a new input event is received by a program script's eventIn. At this time, the program script should receive the new event value, compute something with it, and generate one or more events using its interface eventOuts.

- In Java, the API enables the program-script author to create one method for each interface eventIn; the method is named the same as the interface eventIn.
- In JavaScript, the API enables the program-script author to create one function for each interface eventIn; the function is named the same as the interface eventIn.

For both Java and JavaScript, the eventIn method or function is passed two arguments: the new event value and the new event time stamp. The method may compute a result using the new event and output events to the program script's interface eventOuts.

Responding to Multiple Events

Recall that the VRML browser can postpone program-script evaluation if the **Script** node's **mustEvaluate** field is **FALSE** (the typical case). In such situations, a program script may collect a backlog of pending events, all waiting to be delivered to the program script the next time the browser evaluates it.

When a program script is evaluated and there is a backlog of pending events, each appropriate eventIn function is called for each pending event. If the program script performs a lengthy computation for each new event, then processing the backlog may take a while. This lengthy processing can slow the browser and reduce the interactivity experienced by the viewer.

Typically, a program script computes a new output event each time it receives an input event. In this case, processing a backlog of pending events can generate a flurry of output events that pile up at other nodes waiting for evaluation. In many cases, however, only the latest event received at a node is of interest. Any intermediate events piled up in the backlog can be safely ignored.

For instance, when an event is received on a **Transform** node's **set_translation** eventIn, the coordinate system is instantly translated by the new translation value. If a flurry of ten events are received by the **Transform** node, then the coordinate system is instantly translated ten times in a row. When finished with the flurry of events, the coordinate system is left translated based on the last event the node received, exactly as if that had been the only event it received. In this case, the first nine of the ten events waste time when only the last event received is necessary.

The Java and JavaScript APIs both enable the program-script author to create an **eventsProcessed** method or function to resolve this problem. The **eventsProcessed** function is called without parameters by the VRML browser after some or all of the pending events in a backlog have been processed by calling the appropriate eventIn functions. Because the **eventsProcessed** function is called after a flurry of events have been processed, the **eventsProcessed** function provides a more efficient location for doing lengthy computations. Any events generated by the function have as their time stamp the time stamp of the last event processed.

For example, imagine a circuit containing a **TouchSensor** node sensing a button shape, a **Script** node with a JavaScript program script, and a room filled with 1,000 bouncing Ping-Pong balls. Each time the viewer clicks on the button, an event is sent to the program script to compute a new position for each of the 1,000 Ping-Pong balls. If the viewer clicks on the button shape quickly, several times in a row, a backlog of pending events waiting for the program script to finish computing Ping-Pong-ball positions is generated after the first click. If the viewer gets impatient at seeing nothing happening on the screen and clicks a dozen more times, the backlog of pending events can get large, and it may take a while for the browser to catch up.

In this kind of situation, time can be saved by computing Ping-Pong-ball locations only after emptying the backlog of pending events. The program script relegates its lengthy Ping-Pong-ball computations to the **eventsProcessed** function and uses short, quick eventIn functions only to count the incoming events instead of computing Ping-Pong-ball positions for each one.

Accessing the Browser

In addition to accessing parts of the VRML world, a program script can also access features of the browser itself.

- In Java, the API provides the **getBrowser** method of the **Script** class. The returned object is an instance of the **Browser** class, which provides methods for querying the browser, changing world content, and reading a new world.

- In JavaScript, the API provides an automatically created **browser** object. The object provides methods for querying the browser, changing world content, and reading a new world.

Java and JavaScript program scripts can access the browser to query the URL of the current world, get the viewer's movement speed, and ask for the current frame rate. Program scripts can also create new nodes or groups of nodes, add routes, delete routes, and instruct the browser to read new worlds.

The **Script** Node Syntax

The **Script** group node defines the fields, eventIns, and eventOuts of a node containing a program script.

SYNTAX	Script node

```
Script {
    url               [ ]      # exposedField  MFString
    mustEvaluate      FALSE    # field         SFBool
    directOutput      FALSE    # field         SFBool
# Any number of
    field      fieldType      fieldName      initialValue
    eventIn    eventInType    eventInName
    eventOut   eventOutType   eventOutName
}
```

The value of the **url** exposed field specifies a prioritized list of URLs, ordered from highest priority to lowest. The VRML browser typically tries to open the file specified by the first URL in the list. If the file cannot be found, the browser tries the second URL in the list, and so on. When a URL is found that can be opened, the program script within the file is read and used to define the actions of the **Script** node. If none of the URLs can be opened, then no program script is read, and the **Script** node performs no actions. The default value for the **url** field is an empty list of URLs.

The program script referenced by a URL value in the **url** field may be in any language supported by the VRML browser. Typical supported languages are Java and JavaScript.

JavaScript functions and statements may be included directly within the **url** field value itself, instead of in a separate file, by beginning the URL value with `"javascript:"`. The remainder of the URL value, through the closing double quotation mark, is treated as JavaScript text and interpreted by the browser's JavaScript interpreter. JavaScript that contains string literal text should use single quotation marks rather than double quotation marks to avoid confusion with the double quotation mark that ends the URL value.

The **mustEvaluate** field specifies a TRUE or FALSE value that specifies how the program script is evaluated. When the field value is TRUE, the program script is evaluated by the browser each time a new value is received by an eventIn for the node. When the field value is FALSE, program script evaluation may be postponed by the browser until a more convenient time. This may cause a delay between the delivery of an event to the node and evaluation of the node's actions to handle the event. If multiple events are delivered to the node while evaluation is postponed, a backlog of pending events may develop. Typical program scripts use a FALSE value for the **mustEvaluate** field. The default value is FALSE.

TIP For maximum performance, a **FALSE** value for the **mustEvaluate** field should be used. Browser performance depends, in part, on the number of program scripts it must evaluate each time an event is sent. Using a **TRUE** value for the **mustEvaluate** field increases the browser's workload and may cause a reduction in drawing frequency and interactivity.

The **directOutput** field specifies a TRUE or FALSE value indicating how the program script's outputs are limited. When the field value is FALSE, the program script may read the value of any exposed field and eventOut for any node value to which it has access (such as one passed to the **Script** node as the value of a field or eventIn). When the **directOutput** field value is TRUE, the program script may also write the value of any exposed field, and send a value to any eventIn of any node value to which it has access. Additionally, when the **directOutput** field value is TRUE, the program script may add and delete routes from the world. Typical program scripts use a FALSE value for the **directOutput** field. The default value is FALSE.

TIP For maximum performance, a **FALSE** value for the **directOutput** field should be used. Browser performance depends, in part, on its ability to optimize the internal structure of the shapes in the world. Using a **TRUE** value for the **directOutput** field reduces the range of optimizations available to the browser, increases the browser's workload, and may cause a reduction in drawing frequency and interactivity.

The URL list can be changed by sending a value to the implied **set_url** eventIn of the **url** exposed field. When a value is received on this input, the corresponding field value is changed, and the new value is output by the implied **url_changed** eventOut of the exposed field. When the URL list of the **Script** node is changed, the prior program script, if any, is shut down. The new program script is read and initialized.

The **field, eventIn,** and **eventOut** syntax of the **Script** node each define an interface between the **Script** node and the program script indicated by the **url** field value. The **field** syntax defines an interface field with a data type, an interface field name, and an initial value. Valid data types are listed in Table 2.1. Interface field names can be any sequence of letters, numbers, and underbars, but cannot start with a number. Some program script languages impose further limitations on interface field names based on the naming conventions of the language and the list of the language's reserved keywords.

The **eventIn** syntax of the **Script** node defines an interface eventIn with a data type and an interface eventIn name. Valid data types are listed in Table 2.1. Interface eventIn names have the same limitations as those for interface field names.

The **eventOut** syntax of the **Script** node defines an interface eventOut with a data type and an interface eventOut name. Valid data types are listed in Table 2.1. Interface eventOut names have the same limitations as those for interface field and eventIn names.

A **Script** node may have any number of interface field, eventIn, and eventOut definitions. Interface field, eventIn, and eventOut names must be unique for the node.

The program script associated with a **Script** node is evaluated in three standard situations:

- Initialization
- Shutdown
- Event receipt

Initialization occurs when the program script is first read. The mechanism and syntax for initializing the program script depends on the programming language used.

Shutdown occurs when the program script is removed from the browser. This occurs when the current world is replaced with a new world. Shutdown also occurs when a portion of the world containing the program script's **Script** node is removed or when the **url** field of the **Script** node is changed. The mechanism and syntax for shutting down a program script depends on the programming language used.

Event receipt occurs when a value is received by the **Script** node using an interface eventIn. This may occur when a value follows a route connected to the interface eventIn or when another program script with direct output access assigns a value to the interface eventIn. The mechanism and syntax for performing a program script action in response to receipt of the event value depends on the programming language used.

Some programming languages may provide additional standard situations in which the program script is evaluated.

Each programming language supplies its own API (Application Programming Interface) that provides the program script access to features of the VRML browser and the execution environment.

While no specific programming language is required of all VRML browsers (at the time this was written), it is expected that most will support either Java or JavaScript.

The **Script** node creates no shapes and has no visible effect on a world. A **Script** node may be included as the child of any grouping node, but is independent of the coordinate system in use, and is not affected by child choice changes, such as those made within **Switch** and **LOD** nodes. Typically, **Script** nodes are placed at the end of the outermost group of a VRML file.

The Java and JavaScript APIs

Documenting the Java and JavaScript APIs is beyond the scope of this book; however, two documents on the CD-ROM provide a short description of the APIs.

Experimenting with Scripts

The following examples provide a more detailed examination of the ways in which the **Script** node can be used.

All of the following examples create program scripts in the JavaScript programming languages. The VRML APIs for Java and JavaScript provide equivalent functionality, so any of the example program scripts can be translated into Java.

Creating an Interpolator

An interpolator takes an incoming fractional time value, such as values output by a **TimeSensor** node, and generates a position, rotation, or other value. You can create your own interpolators by using a **Script** node and a program script.

To build an interpolator, the VRML text in Figure 30.1 creates a **Script** node defining an interface with one eventIn and one eventOut:

```
DEF Mover Script {
    url "move1.js"
    eventIn SFFloat set_fraction
    eventOut SFVec3f value_changed
}
```

The **set_fraction** interface eventIn is intended to receive a floating-point fractional time from a **TimeSensor** node.

The **value_changed** interface eventOut is used to output a new 3-D position suitable for routing to the **set_translation** eventIn of a **Transform** node.

The **url** field specifies a JavaScript program script (`"move1.js"`) to perform the interpolator's actions.

```
// Move a shape in a straight path
function set_fraction( fraction, eventTime ) {
    value_changed[0] - fraction; // X component
    value_changed[1] - 0.0;      // Y component
    value_changed[2] - 0.0;      // Z component
}
```

Recall that the program script is evaluated in three situations: initialization, shutdown, and upon event receipt. The preceding interpolator program script needs neither initialization nor shutdown, so functions for these actions are omitted. Event delivery on the node's **set_fraction** interface eventIn is handled by the program script's **set_fraction** eventIn function.

When a new fraction value is received by the **set_fraction** interface eventIn, the eventIn function is called with two arguments: the fraction value and the time stamp. The time stamp is unused by this interpolator, but the fraction value is used to set the X component of a 3-D coordinate sent by the program script using the **value_changed** interface eventOut. The Y and Z components of the 3-D coordinate are both set to zero.

Each time a fractional value is received by the program script, a new 3-D coordinate is output that uses the fractional value as the X component. When routed to a **Transform** node's **set_translation** eventIn, the new interpolator's output slides a shape to the right along the X axis, starting at the origin when the fraction is 0.0 and ending at (1.0, 0.0, 0.0) when the fraction is 1.0.

The VRML text in Figure 30.1 builds a world with a white floor and a red sphere. A **TimeSensor** node provides a clock with its **fraction_changed** eventOut routed to the **Script** node. The **Script** node acts as an interpolator and routes its **value_changed** interface eventOut to a **Transform** node surrounding the red sphere. As the clock ticks, the **Script** node generates new translation values and the red sphere moves to the right. At the end of a clock cycle, the fraction output by the **TimeSensor** node returns to 0.0, the **Script** node generates a 3-D coordinate for the origin, and the red sphere jumps back to the origin and starts sliding to the right again.

```
#VRML V2.0 utf8
Group {
    children [
        Background {
            skyColor    [ 1.0 0.0 0.8,  0.5 0.0 0.8,  0.0 0.0 0.8 ]
            skyAngle    [ 1.309, 1.571 ]
            groundColor [ 0.0 0.0 0.1,  0.0 0.1 0.3,  0.3 0.3 0.6 ]
            groundAngle [ 1.309, 1.571 ]
        },
    # Floor
        Shape {
            appearance Appearance {
                material Material { }
            }
            geometry Box { size 2.0 0.01 0.5 }
        },
    # Animating red ball
```

Figure 30.1 continues

```
      Transform {
          translation 0.0 1.1 0.0
          children DEF BallTransform Transform {
              children Shape {
                  appearance Appearance {
                      material Material {
                          diffuseColor 1.0 0.3 0.3
                      }
                  }
                  geometry Sphere { radius 0.1 }
              }
          }
      },
  # Animation clock
      DEF Clock TimeSensor {
          cycleInterval 4.0
          loop TRUE
      },
  # Script
      DEF Mover Script {
          url "move1.js"
          eventIn  SFFloat set_fraction
          eventOut SFVec3f value_changed
      }
  ]
}
ROUTE Clock.fraction_changed TO Mover.set_fraction
ROUTE Mover.value_changed    TO BallTransform.set_translation
```

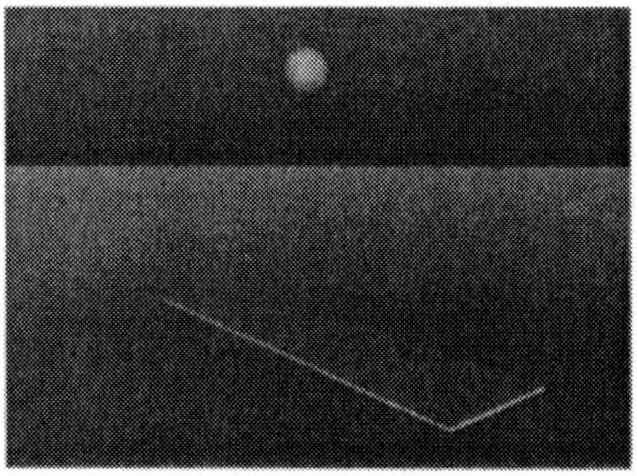

Figure 30.1 *A moving red sphere and a custom interpolator.*

Creating a Sine-Wave Interpolator

The interpolator built in Figure 30.1 generates a simple, straight-line animation path. You can modify the interpolator to generate a more complicated path by changing the program script. For instance, you can generate an animation path in the shape of a sine wave by using the JavaScript **Math.sin** function.

```
// Move a shape in a sine wave path
function set_fraction( fraction, eventTime ) {
   value_changed[0] - fraction;
   value_changed[1] - Math.sin( fraction * 6.28 );
   value_changed[2] - 0.0;
}
```

The new program script ("move2.js") is identical to that in the previous example, except that it uses the **Math.sin** function to compute a sine-wave path for the Y component of the output 3-D coordinate. The **fraction** event value is multiplied by 6.28 (2π) to produce an angle (in radians) that varies from 0.0 to 6.28 radians. The **Math.sin** function returns a value that varies from -1.0 to 1.0. The resulting 3-D coordinates from the interpolator slide a shape from left to right, while moving it up and down in a sine-wave path.

To use the new interpolator program script with the world built in Figure 30.1, change the **url** field value of the **Script** node to load the new JavaScript file: "move2.js."

Creating a Helical Interpolator

You can extend the interpolator script to generate a helical path by also setting the Z component of each 3-D coordinate output by the interpolator.

```
// Move a shape in a helical path
function set_fraction( fraction, eventTime ) {
    value_changed[0] - fraction;
    value_changed[1] - Math.sin( fraction * 6.28 );
    value_changed[2] - Math.cos( fraction * 6.28 );
}
```

The new program script ("move3.js") uses the **Math.cos** function to compute a Z component for each 3-D coordinate. The Y and Z components of the coordinate now trace out a circle, while the X component follows a straight-line path. Together, the coordinates describe a helical path.

To use the new interpolator program script with the world built in Figure 30.1, change the **url** field value of the **Script** node built in Figure 30.1 to load the new JavaScript file: "move3.js".

To give you more control over the helical interpolator's path, you can add interface fields to the **Script** node that provide motion parameters, such as the radius of the helix and the number of 360.0-degree turns the helix goes through as the fraction value varies from 0.0 to 1.0.

```
DEF Mover Script {
    url "javascript:
        // Move a shape in a helical path
        function set_fraction( fraction, eventTime ) {
            value_changed[0] - fraction;
            value_changed[1] - radius * Math.sin( turns * fraction * 6.28 );
            value_changed[2] - radius * Math.cos( turns * fraction * 6.28 );
        }"
    field    SFFloat radius 1.0
    field    SFFloat turns 1.0
    eventIn  SFFloat set_fraction
    eventOut SFVec3f value_changed
}
```

Replace the **Script** node in Figure 30.1 with the preceding **Script** node, and try different values for the **radius** and **turns** fields.

Using program scripts like these, you can create interpolators that generate arbitrarily complex paths. Try experimenting with other math functions to generate the X, Y, and Z components of a motion path.

Building a Boolean Event Filter

The events output by the standard VRML sensors and interpolators satisfy most animation needs. There are times, however, when it is convenient to filter a node's event outputs, processing them to match your own needs.

You can build an event filter using a **Script** node and program script. The filter receives an event of interest using an interface eventIn and sends out new events using one or more interface eventOuts. The new events are typically closely based on the received event.

For example, the following **Script** node filters an **SFBool** event received by its **set_boolean** interface eventIn. If the Boolean value is TRUE, TRUE is output using its **true_changed** interface eventOut. If the Boolean value is FALSE, TRUE is output using its **false_changed** interface eventOut.

```
DEF Filter Script {
    url "javascript:
        function set_boolean( bool, eventTime ) {
            if ( bool == true ) { true_changed  = true; }
            else                 { false_changed = true; }
        }"
    eventIn  SFBool set_boolean
    eventOut SFBool true_changed
    eventOut SFBool false_changed
}
```

You can use this Boolean event filter to construct a group of *radio buttons*, standard user-interface elements that present a list of choices, one of which may be selected at a time. For instance, you might use a group of radio buttons to select between sky backgrounds in your world, each one built using the **Background** node.

A first attempt at constructing radio buttons to select among backgrounds could use several **TouchSensor** nodes, each sensing a different button shape in your world. Each **TouchSensor** node's **isActive** eventOut is routed to the **set_bind** eventIn of a **Background** node. When the viewer presses the mouse button on the sensed shape, the **TouchSensor** node outputs a TRUE value, which binds the selected **Background** node and changes the background color of the world. Unfortunately, when the viewer releases the mouse button, the **TouchSensor** node's **isActive** eventOut sends a FALSE value, which unbinds the selected **Background** node, returning it to the prior background. Instead, the mouse-button release should do nothing, leaving the newly selected **Background** node as the currently bound background.

To accomplish this, you can use the Boolean event filter wired to the circuit between the **TouchSensor** node's **isActive** eventOut and the **Background** node's **set_bind** eventIn. When the viewer touches the sensed shape, the TRUE value output from the **isActive** eventOut travels to the filter, which generates a TRUE value using its **true_changed** interface eventOut, and that travels to the **Background** node's **set_bind** eventIn to cause the background to be bound. When the viewer releases the mouse button, the FALSE generated by the **TouchSensor** node's **isActive** eventOut travels into the event filter, which is not output to its **true_changed** interface eventOut. The FALSE value is filtered out by the Boolean filter, and a TRUE value is sent to the unused **false_changed** interface eventOut. Since no **FALSE** value is passed to the **Background** node's **set_bind** eventIn, the node is not unbound and is left as the current background.

If you use multiple **TouchSensor** nodes, multiple sensed shapes, multiple **Background** nodes, and multiple Boolean filters, you can create a group of radio buttons that each select a different background. Pressing the mouse button on a sensed shape selects the background. Releasing the mouse button does nothing. The VRML text in Figure 30.2 shows the construction of such a world with three **Background** nodes and three touchable shapes.

```
#VRML V2.0 utf8
Group {
    children [
    # Bindable Backgrounds (cyan, red, blue)
        DEF Back1 Background {
            skyColor    [ 0.0 0.2 0.7,  0.0 0.5 1.0,  1.0 1.0 1.0 ]
            skyAngle    [ 1.309, 1.571 ]
            groundColor [ 0.1 0.1 0.0,  0.4 0.25 0.2,  0.6 0.6 0.6 ]
            groundAngle [ 1.309, 1.571 ]
        },
        DEF Back2 Background {
            skyColor    [ 1.0 0.0 0.0,  1.0 0.4 0.0,  1.0 1.0 0.0 ]
            skyAngle    [ 1.309, 1.571 ]
            groundColor [ 0.1 0.1 0.0,  0.5 0.25 0.2,  0.6 0.6 0.2 ]
            groundAngle [ 1.309, 1.571 ]
        },
        DEF Back3 Background {
            skyColor    [ 1.0 0.0 0.8,  0.5 0.0 0.8,  0.0 0.0 0.8 ]
            skyAngle    [ 1.309, 1.571 ]
            groundColor [ 0.0 0.0 0.1,  0.0 0.1 0.3,  0.3 0.3 0.6 ]
            groundAngle [ 1.309, 1.571 ]
        },
    # Shapes to act as buttons (cyan, red, blue)
        Transform { translation -3.0 0.0 0.0
            children [
                Shape {
                    appearance Appearance {
                        material Material {
                            diffuseColor 0.0 0.5 0.8
                        }
                    }
                    geometry Box { }
                },
                DEF BackButton1 TouchSensor { }
            ]
        },
```

Figure 30.2 continues

```
Group {
    children [
        Shape {
            appearance Appearance {
                material Material {
                    diffuseColor 1.0 0.3 0.3
                }
            }
            geometry Sphere { }
        },
        DEF BackButton2 TouchSensor { }
    ]
},
Transform { translation 3.0 0.0 0.0
    children [
        Shape {
            appearance Appearance {
                material Material {
                    diffuseColor 0.2 0.2 0.8
                }
            }
            geometry Cone { }
        },
        DEF BackButton3 TouchSensor { }
    ]
},
# Scripts
DEF Filter1 Script {
    url "javascript:
        function set_boolean( bool, eventTime ) {
            if ( bool -- true ) { true_changed  - true; }
            else                 { false_changed - true; }
        }"
    eventIn  SFBool set_boolean
    eventOut SFBool true_changed
    eventOut SFBool false_changed
},
DEF Filter2 Script {
    url "javascript:
        function set_boolean( bool, eventTime ) {
            if ( bool -- true ) { true_changed  - true; }
            else                 { false_changed - true; }
        }"
    eventIn  SFBool set_boolean
    eventOut SFBool true_changed
    eventOut SFBool false_changed
},
DEF Filter3 Script {
    url "javascript:
        function set_boolean( bool, eventTime ) {
            if ( bool -- true ) { true_changed  - true; }
            else                 { false_changed - true; }
        }"
```

Figure 30.2 continues

```
             eventIn  SFBool set_boolean
             eventOut SFBool true_changed
             eventOut SFBool false_changed
         },
     ]
}
ROUTE BackButton1.isActive TO Filter1.set_boolean
ROUTE BackButton2.isActive TO Filter2.set_boolean
ROUTE BackButton3.isActive TO Filter3.set_boolean
ROUTE Filter1.true_changed TO Back1.set_bind
ROUTE Filter2.true_changed TO Back2.set_bind
ROUTE Filter3.true_changed TO Back3.set_bind
```

Figure 30.2 *A filter used to make a group of radio buttons that select among backgrounds.*

The Boolean-filter script enabled the creation of a group of 3-D radio buttons in your world. You can use similar techniques to create a variety of 3-D, user-interface controls. For instance, you can create an on-off toggle-button script that sends **TRUE** on a first click, **FALSE** on the next, then **TRUE** on the third, and so on:

```
DEF OnOffToggle Script {
    url "javascript:
        function set_boolean( bool, eventTime ) {
            if ( bool -- false ) { return; }
            if ( value -- true ) { value - false; }
            else                 { value - true; }
            value_changed - value;
        }"
    field    SFBool value FALSE
    eventIn  SFBool set_boolean
    eventOut SFBool value_changed
}
```

You can use this script to create an on-off toggle button by routing a **TouchSensor** node's **isActive** eventOut to the **Script** node's **set_boolean** eventIn. Route the **Script** node's **value_changed** eventOut to anything you'd like to turn on and off, such as the **isBind** eventIn of a **Background**, **Fog**, or **Viewpoint** node, the **on** eventIn of any lighting node, or the **enabled** eventIn of any sensor node, such as a **TimeSensor** node. Each time the viewer clicks on the shape sensed by a **Touch-**

Sensor node, the on-off toggle script switches from **TRUE**, to **FALSE**, to **TRUE** again, and so on.

Using a similar technique, you can create a script that cycles between a list of choices, stepping to the next choice each time the viewer clicks on a shape sensed by a **TouchSensor** node:

```
DEF CycleSelector Script {
    url "javascript:
        function set_boolean( bool, eventTime ) {
            if ( bool -- false ) { return; }
            whichChoice - whichChoice + 1;
            if ( whichChoice > 2 )  { whichChoice - 0; }
            if ( whichChoice -- 0 ) { choice0_changed - true; }
            if ( whichChoice -- 1 ) { choice1_changed - true; }
            if ( whichChoice -- 2 ) { choice2_changed - true; }
        }"
    field    SFInt32 whichChoice 0
    eventIn  SFBool  set_boolean
    eventOut SFBool  choice0_changed
    eventOut SFBool  choice1_changed
    eventOut SFBool  choice2_changed
}
```

You can use this script to cycle between turning on one of three items. For instance, you can use this script to select among the three **Background** nodes shown in Figure 30.2.

Scripts like the Boolean filter, the toggle script, and the choice-selector script form the basis of many of the user interface controls used in today's 2-D user interfaces. You can use these scripts, and their variations, to build 3-D user interfaces in your world. For instance, you can add light switches to your lamps, buttons to doors to make them open and close, control panels to elevators to select among floors, buttons to select among channels on a virtual television playing back movie textures, and so on.

Building a Time-Stamp Filter

A time-stamp filter outputs only the time stamp of an incoming event. The event value itself is ignored.

```
DEF Filter Script {
    url "javascript:
        function set_boolean( bool, timeStamp ) {
            eventTime - timeStamp;
        }"
    eventIn  SFBool set_boolean
    eventOut SFTime eventTime
}
```

You can use this kind of filter to detect when an event value occurs, ignoring the value itself. For instance, the **TouchSensor** node's **touchTime** eventOut sends the current absolute time when the viewer releases the mouse button while on the shape. However, the node does not provide an eventOut for sending the absolute time when the viewer first presses the mouse button on the shape. The sensor provides an **isActive** eventOut that sends **TRUE** when the viewer presses the mouse button. Since every event has a time stamp, you can use a time-stamp filter to take an incoming Boolean event from a **TouchSensor** node's **isActive** eventOut and send out the event's time stamp.

Figure 30.3 uses a **TouchSensor** node, a time-stamp filter, a **Sound** node, and an **AudioClip** node within a world with a single touchable sphere. Pressing the mouse button on the sphere starts the sound, and releasing the mouse button stops it. This is accomplished by routing the **isActive** eventOut of the **TouchSensor** node to the Boolean filter, and then routing the **true_changed** interface eventOut of the Boolean filter to the time-stamp filter. The time-stamp filter's event time is then routed to the **set_startTime** eventIn of the **AudioClip** node to start the sound when the sensed shape is touched. To stop the sound, the **TimeSensor** node's **touchTime** eventOut is routed directly to the **set_stopTime** eventIn of the **AudioClip** node.

The effect of all this filtering is to turn the sphere in Figure 30.3 into a momentary on-off switch. Pressing the switch starts the sound, and releasing the switch stops it. You could use this to turn lights on and off, start and stop animation, and so on.

```
#VRML V2.0 utf8
Group {
    children [
    # Background
        Background {
            skyColor    [ 1.0 0.0 0.0,  1.0 0.4 0.0,  1.0 1.0 0.0 ]
            skyAngle    [ 1.309, 1.571 ]
            groundColor [ 0.1 0.1 0.0,  0.5 0.25 0.2,  0.6 0.6 0.2 ]
            groundAngle [ 1.309, 1.571 ]
        },
    # On-off switch
        Shape {
            appearance Appearance {
                material Material {
                    diffuseColor 1.0 0.3 0.3
                }
            }
            geometry Sphere { }
        },
        DEF Touch TouchSensor { },
    # Sound
        Sound {
            source DEF Audio AudioClip {
                url "willow1.wav"
                loop TRUE
                stopTime 1.0
            }
        },
    # Filters
        DEF Filter Script {
            url "javascript:
```

Figure 30.3 continues

```
                    function set_boolean( bool, eventTime ) {
                        if ( bool -- true ) { true_changed  - true; }
                        else                 { false_changed - true; }
                    }"
                eventIn  SFBool set_boolean
                eventOut SFBool true_changed
                eventOut SFBool false_changed
            },
            DEF TimeFilter Script {
                url "javascript:
                    function set_boolean( bool, timeStamp ) {
                        eventTime - timeStamp;
                    }"
                eventIn  SFBool set_boolean
                eventOut SFTime eventTime
            }
        ]
    }
}
ROUTE Touch.isActive        TO Filter.set_boolean
ROUTE Filter.true_changed   TO TimeFilter.set_boolean
ROUTE TimeFilter.eventTime  TO Audio.set_startTime
ROUTE Touch.touchTime       TO Audio.set_stopTime
```

Figure 30.3   *A pair of filters used to create a momentary on-off switch.*

Building a Route Debugger

As you may have discovered, complicated animation circuits sometimes can be confusing and hard to debug. One trick is to create a debug filter that converts an incoming event value to a text string that you can route to the **string** field of a **Text** node. You can wire this filter to a node's eventOut and see the values being sent using that eventOut.

```
DEF Debug Script {
    url "javascript:
        function initialize( ) {
            string_changed[0] - label + ':';
        }
        function set_float( f, ts ) {
            string_changed[0] - label + ': (' + ts + ') ' + f;
        }"
    field    SFString label "fraction"
    eventIn  SFFloat  set_float
    eventOut MFString string_changed
}
```

The preceding program script responds to floating-point values sent to its **set_float** interface eventIn. For each new value, the program script creates a text string and outputs it using its **string_changed** interface eventOut. Each text string contains two values: a message label and the floating-point event value. When routed to a **Text** node's **set_string** eventIn, the text string provides a handy debugging message that enables you to monitor any floating-point eventOut.

The **label** interface field of the **Script** node provides a message label that is placed in front of the output text string. If you use multiple debug filters to monitor multiple eventOuts, you can use the message label to identify each debug message.

The program script uses an **initialize** function to generate an initial text string that contains only the label. This ensures that any **Text** node to which the debug filter is routed starts off immediately with a properly labeled, though empty, debug message.

Figure 30.4 uses the debug filter in conjunction with a general-purpose, helical-path world. The **fraction_changed** eventOut of the world's **TimeSensor** node is routed to the debug filter, and the debug message it generates is routed to the **set_string** eventIn of a **Text** node. Thereafter, as the animation progresses, the **Time-Sensor** node's fractional time is constantly displayed in the world.

You can extend this debug filter by adding inputs for other types of data. For instance, you could add an interface eventIn for **SFVec3f** data, and then use the filter to display the output of the general-purpose, helical interpolator.

```
#VRML V2.0 utf8
Group {
    children [
        Background {
            skyColor    [ 1.0 0.0 0.8,  0.5 0.0 0.8,  0.0 0.0 0.8 ]
            skyAngle    [ 1.309, 1.571 ]
            groundColor [ 0.0 0.0 0.1,  0.0 0.1 0.3,  0.3 0.3 0.6 ]
            groundAngle [ 1.309, 1.571 ]
        },
    # Floor
        Shape {
            appearance Appearance {
                material Material { }
            }
            geometry Box { size 2.0 0.01 0.5 }
        },
    # Animating red ball
        Transform {
            translation 0.0 1.1 0.0
            children DEF BallTransform Transform {
                children Shape {
                    appearance Appearance {
                        material Material {
                            diffuseColor 1.0 0.0 0.0
                        }
                    }
                    geometry Sphere { radius 0.1 }
                }
            }
        },
```

Figure 30.4 continues

```
# Animation clock
    DEF Clock TimeSensor {
        cycleInterval 4.0
        loop TRUE
    },
# Script
    DEF Mover Script {
        url "javascript:
            function set_fraction( fraction, eventTime ) {
                value_changed[0] - fraction;
                value_changed[1] - radius * Math.sin( turns * fraction * 6.28 );
                value_changed[2] - radius * Math.cos( turns * fraction * 6.28 );
            }"
        field    SFFloat radius 1.0
        field    SFFloat turns  1.0
        eventIn  SFFloat set_fraction
        eventOut SFVec3f value_changed
    }
# Debugger
    DEF Debug Script {
        url "javascript:
            function initalize( ) {
                string_changed[0] - label + ':';
            }
            function set_float( f, ts ) {
                string_changed[0] - label + ': ' + f;
            }"
        field    SFString label "fraction"
        eventIn  SFFloat  set_float
        eventOut MFString string_changed
    },
    Transform {
        translation 0.0 0.01 -0.15
        children Shape {
            appearance Appearance {
                material Material {
                    diffuseColor  0.0 0.0 0.0
                    emissiveColor 1.0 1.0 1.0
                }
            }
            geometry DEF Message Text {
                fontStyle FontStyle {
                    size 0.35
                    justify "MIDDLE"
                }
            }
        }
    }
    ]
}
```

Figure 30.4 continues

```
ROUTE Clock.fraction_changed  TO Mover.set_fraction
ROUTE Mover.value_changed     TO BallTransform.set_translation
ROUTE Clock.fraction_changed  TO Debug.set_float
ROUTE Debug.string_changed    TO Message.set_string
```

Figure 30.4   *A debug filter used to monitor the output of a **TimeSensor** node.*

Controlling a Shape with a Program Script

The debug filter built in the previous example modifies the geometry of a text shape by repeatedly changing the shape's text string. You can use this same approach to build program scripts that modify other geometry types.

The **Extrusion** node can be used to create a huge variety of shapes. However, the fields of the node are so general-purpose that it can be difficult to create relatively straightforward extruded shapes, such as donuts. A donut shape is, perhaps, best described by two radii: the radius of the circular donut cross section and the radius of the circular spine through which that cross section is swept. These radii can be used to automatically generate the cross section and spine in an **Extrusion** node.

You can build a donut-maker program script that automatically generates cross-section and spine values for routing to an **Extrusion** node. The **Script** node in Figure 30.5 defines the interface for such a program script. The interface includes fields to specify the radii of the cross section and spine and to specify the number of points (the *resolution*) used in the circular paths for the cross section and spine. Interface eventIns enable you to change the cross-section and spine radii with a circuit. Finally, interface eventOuts are defined for sending computed cross-section and spine values.

The following program script (donutmkr.js) handles the work of building cross-section and spine coordinate lists. The **generateCrossSection** and **generateSpine** functions each compute circular paths for the cross section and spine, respectively. Both functions use the appropriate resolution to decide how many coordinates to generate and use the appropriate radius to decide how large to make the circular paths. The generated cross section and spine are each output using the interface eventOuts.

The program script's **initialize** function calls **generateCrossSection** and **generate-Spine** to build the initial cross section and spine. Later, each of the eventIn functions respond by regenerating the cross section or spine using the latest radius values.

```
function initialize( ) {
    generateCrossSection( );
    generateSpine( );
}
function set_crossSectionRadius( csr, ts ) {
    crossSectionRadius = csr;
    generateCrossSection( );
}
function set_spineRadius( sr, ts ) {
    spineRadius = sr;
    generateSpine( );
}
function generateCrossSection( ) {
    angle = 0.0;
    delta = 6.28 / crossSectionResolution;
    for ( i = 0; i < crossSectionResolution; i++ ) {
        crossSection_changed[i][0] = crossSectionRadius * Math.cos( angle);
        crossSection_changed[i][1] = -crossSectionRadius * Math.sin( angle);
        angle += delta;
    }
}
function generateSpine( ) {
    angle = 0.0;
    delta = 6.28 / spineResolution;
    for ( i = 0; i < spineResolution; i++ ) {
        spine_changed[i][0] = spineRadius * Math.cos( angle );
        spine_changed[i][1] = 0.0;
        spine_changed[i][2] = -spineRadius * Math.sin( angle );
        angle += delta;
    }
}
```

The VRML text in Figure 30.5 uses the donut-maker program script to automatically generate an extrusion donut shape.

```
#VRML V2.0 utf8
Group {
    children [
    # Donut, initially empty
        Shape {
            appearance Appearance {
                material Material { }
            }
            geometry DEF Donut Extrusion {
                crossSection [ ]
                spine [ ]
                creaseAngle 1.57
                beginCap FALSE
                endCap   FALSE
            }
        },
```

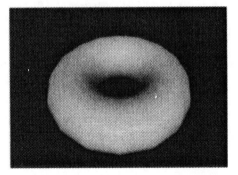

Figure 30.5 continues

```
# Donut maker
   DEF DonutMaker Script {
      url "donutmkr.js"
      field    SFFloat crossSectionRadius    1.0
      field    SFFloat spineRadius           2.0
      field    SFInt32 crossSectionResolution 16
      field    SFInt32 spineResolution        16
      eventIn  SFFloat set_crossSectionRadius
      eventIn  SFFloat set_spineRadius
      eventOut MFVec2f crossSection_changed
      eventOut MFVec3f spine_changed
   }
  ]
}
ROUTE DonutMaker.crossSection_changed TO Donut.set_crossSection
ROUTE DonutMaker.spine_changed        TO Donut.set_spine
```

Figure 30.5 *A donut shape built with a donut-maker program script.*

The previous donut-maker example illustrates the use of program scripts to do more than act as custom sensors, interpolators, or filters. Using shape-building program scripts, you can automatically generate elevation grids using fractal-mountain techniques, build groups of shapes to construct fractal trees, and provide interfaces to existing geometry nodes to enable easy generation of walls, doors, stairways, and other useful shapes. You can also use program scripts to automatically compute texture coordinates, shape normals, and colors. By setting the **directOutput** field value to **TRUE** in a **Script** node, you can create program scripts that generate routes or make sweeping changes to world content, such as globally changing colors, lighting, or shape sizes. Program scripting is the back door into the VRML browser, and scripting enables you to extend VRML to support additional custom sensors, interpolators, appearances, geometry, and more.

Summary

The **Script** node provides a mechanism for creating custom sensors and interpolators. The node uses an interface definition to define the fields, eventIns, and eventOuts of a custom node. The actions of the node are defined by a program script written in any language the browser supports but are typically written in Java or JavaScript.

The **url** field of the **Script** node specifies the program script. The special `"javascript:"` syntax for a URL indicates that the JavaScript program-script text is included as the value of the **url** field instead of within a file named by the URL.

The **mustEvaluate** field indicates whether the program script must be evaluated immediately each time an event is delivered to one of its eventIns. When the field value is **TRUE**, the program script is evaluated on each new event. When the field value is **FALSE**, the program script's evaluation may be postponed until the browser has time to evaluate it.

The **directOutput** field indicates whether the program script has direct access to nodes in the world. When the field value is **TRUE,** the program script can read any exposed field or eventOut and write to any exposed field or eventIn of any node to which it has access. When the field value is **FALSE,** the program script can only read the exposed fields and eventOuts of nodes to which it has access.

The **field, eventIn,** and **eventOut** syntax of the **Script** node define the interface between the **Script** node and the program script. The **field** syntax defines the data type, name, and initial value of an interface field. The **eventIn** and **eventOut** syntax define the data type and name of an interface eventIn or eventOut.

The program script associated with a **Script** node is evaluated in three main situations:

- Initialization
- Shutdown
- Upon receipt of an event

At initialization, a program script can set up its initial state. At shutdown, a program script can finalize its actions before the program script is discarded.

A program script may respond to the receipt of a new event by one of its interface eventIns by accessing the new value, converting it to an appropriate data type for the programming language in use, computing something based on the new value, and then outputting a new event using one of its eventOuts. The program script can also access features of the browser directly to change world content or to load a new world.

The mechanism by which a program script handles initialization, shutdown, event delivery, data-type conversion, and browser access is defined in the programming language's API (Application Programming Interface). The Java and JavaScript APIs both provide features with which a program script can perform these actions.

CHAPTER 31

Creating New Node Types

VRML provides over 50 different node types for creating shapes, selecting colors, specifying animation, and more. To this set of standard node types, you can add your own node types.

Each new node type you create has a node-type name, a list of fields, eventIns, and eventOuts; and a node body. The *node-type name* is any name you like for your new node type. For instance, if your new node type creates a fractal mountain, then you might use **FractalMountain** as the node-type name.

Called the *node interface*, the new node type's fields, exposed fields, eventIns, and eventOuts describe the interface to your node type, similar to the program script interface declared in a **Script** node. A **FractalMountain** node, for instance, may have fields whose values indicate the desired height of the mountain, its width and depth, its color, and the amount of detail to build into the mountain shape.

The *node body* of a new node type describes what the node does and how it does it. A node body is defined using any combination of any of VRML's nodes. For instance, a **FractalMountain** node's body can use an **ElevationGrid** node to describe the geometry for the mountain, plus a **Script** node and program script to compute the elevations used in the **ElevationGrid** node.

New node types are created using a **PROTO** definition (**PROTO** is short for *prototype*). Features of the **PROTO** definition enable you to define the new node type's name, fields, exposed fields, eventIns, eventOuts, and the node body.

You can place **PROTO** definitions in separate VRML files and build up a library of your own new node types. To use one of your new node types in a world, you can reference the node definition by using an EXTERNPROTO declaration (**EXTERNPROTO** is short for *external prototype*).

603

Understanding Prototypes

A **PROTO** definition describes a new node type. Like any node type, the new node type requires a node name; a list of fields, exposed fields, eventIns, and eventOuts; and a description of what the node does.

```
PROTO nodeTypeName [ nodeInterface ] { nodeBody }
```

A **PROTO** definition starts with the word **PROTO** followed by the new node type's name. Following the name is a list of fields, exposed fields, eventIns, and eventOuts making up the node's interface. The node interface is defined within square brackets. Following the interface is the node body, defined within curly braces.

Defining a Node-Type Name

The *node-type name* can be any word that starts with a letter, and it can include letters, numbers, and punctuation with the same limitations as **DEF** names (see Chapter 2). New node-type names must be different from any of the existing VRML node-type names and from any other new node types you define in the same VRML file.

VRML's convention is to capitalize the first letter of each word in a node-type name, including the first word in the name. This is why all VRML node-type names start with an uppercase character. You are encouraged to follow this same node-type naming convention, but you don't have to.

Defining a Node Interface

The fields, exposed fields, eventIns, and eventOuts, of the new node type describe the interface to the node's actions. For instance, a new node type that builds a grandfather clock might have fields whose values specify the clock's wood texture and the tone of its chimes, while eventIns and eventOuts for the clock set the clock and output the time at regular intervals.

Defining an interface for a new node type uses definitions that are nearly identical to that used to define program-script interfaces in the **Script** node. The interface definition syntax has four forms, one each for defining a field, exposed field, eventIn, and eventOut. All of the interface definitions are enclosed within square brackets following the node-type name in a **PROTO** definition.

Defining an Interface Field

You can define an interface field for your new node type by specifying a data type for the field, a name for the field, and a default value. All of these are specified within a **PROTO** interface definition line that starts with the word field followed by the data-type name, your chosen name for the field, and the default value.

```
PROTO MyNode [
    ...
    field fieldType fieldName defaultValue
    ...
] { ... }
```

A *data-type name* (`fieldType`) indicates the type of information the new node's field stores. The data types available in VRML are listed in Table 2.1.

Interface field names (`fieldName`) can be anything you like, following the same limitations used for **DEF** names. By VRML convention, interface names start with a lowercase character, and capitalize each additional word in the name. You can also use underbars and numbers in interface field names.

Defining an Interface Exposed Field

You can define interface exposed fields for your new node type using the same approach used for defining interface fields. For each interface exposed field, you provide an interface definition line that starts with the word `exposedField`, followed by a data-type name (`fieldType`), a name for the exposed field (`fieldName`), and a default value (`defaultValue`).

```
PROTO MyNode [
    ...
    exposedField fieldType fieldName defaultValue
    ...
] { ... }
```

Defining an Interface EventIn

Like interface fields and exposed fields, each interface eventIn for your new node must have a data type and a name. No default value is needed for interface eventIns. The data type and name are specified within a **PROTO** definition by using an interface definition line starting with `eventIn` followed by a data-type name (`eventInType`), and a name (`eventInName`) for the eventIn.

```
PROTO MyNode [
    ...
    eventIn eventInType eventInName
    ...
] { ... }
```

Similar to interface fields and exposed fields, you can name your interface eventIns anything you like, per **DEF** name limitations. By VRML convention, eventIn names always start with `set_` unless they deal with adding or removing children from a group. By following this convention, you create new node types that fit well into the rest of the language.

Defining an Interface EventOut

Interface eventOuts are defined in a manner analogous to that for interface eventIns. Each interface eventOut is specified in a **PROTO** definition using an interface definition line that starts with eventOut and is followed by a data-type name (*eventOut-Type*), and a name for the eventOut (*eventOutName*).

```
PROTO MyNode [
    ...
    eventOut eventOutType eventOutName
    ...
] { ... }
```

You can name interface eventOuts anything you like, per the **DEF** name limitations. By VRML convention, eventOut names always end in changed, unless they are a Boolean value or a time value. Boolean eventOut names always start with is, and time eventOut names usually have the word Time at the end.

Defining Multiple Interface Fields, Exposed Fields, EventIns, and EventOuts

Using **PROTO** interface definitions, you can specify all the interface fields, exposed fields, eventIns, and eventOuts for your new node type. For example, the following VRML text shows the interface definition of a **PROTO** definition for a grandfather clock shape node.

```
PROTO GrandfatherClock [
    eventIn SFTime set_time
    field MFNode chimeSources [ ]
    field SFNode woodTexture NULL
    eventOut SFTime chimeTime
] { ... }
```

The **GrandfatherClock** node defined by the **PROTO** definition has an eventIn for setting the clock time and an eventOut that sends the current, absolute time at the start of each chime on each quarter hour. The **chimeSources** interface field is intended to contain a list of four **AudioClip** nodes used to play the clock's quarter-hour chimes. The **woodTexture** interface field is intended to contain a texture node to specify the wood grain texture for the clock's cabinet.

Once a new node type has been defined you can use the node later in your world, exactly as if it were a standard VRML node. For instance, you can use a **Grandfa-therClock** node in this way:

```
GrandfatherClock {
    chimeSources [
        AudioClip { url "chhour.wav" },
        AudioClip { url "ch15min.wav" },
        AudioClip { url "ch30min.wav" },
        AudioClip { url "ch45min.wav" }
    ]
    woodTexture ImageTexture { url "oak.jpg" }
}
```

Similar to any other node, you can route events to the **GrandfatherClock** node's eventIns and from its eventOuts.

Defining a Node Body

Once an interface is defined for your new node type, you need to provide a node body that describes what your new node type does and how it does it. A *node body* is a list of any VRML nodes, including grouping nodes, shape nodes, appearance nodes, sensors, interpolators, **Script** nodes, and other node types you previously defined using a **PROTO** definition. A node body can also contain routes to wire these nodes together into a circuit.

For example, the **GrandfatherClock** node's body may include several **Indexed-FaceSet** nodes to build the clock's shape, a pair of **TimeSensor** and **OrientationInterpolator** nodes to turn the hands on the clock face, another **TimeSensor** node and **OrientationInterpolator** node to swing the clock's pendulum, and four **Sound** nodes to play the clock's chimes. The **GrandfatherClock** node's body also may include a **Script** node that monitors the current time and sends an event to each chime **AudioClip** node when its time to ring a clock chime.

The ability to include any list of nodes and routes within the body of a new node type is one of the most powerful features of VRML. Using this feature, you can take any shape you can build and turn it into a new node type just by dropping the shape's nodes into a node body, defining an interface, and adding a name. For instance, if you've created standard wall, floor, and door shapes that you use frequently when building rooms, you can create **Wall, Floor,** and **Door** node types that include, as their node bodies, the appropriate nodes to create a wall, floor, or door.

Node Use

The standard VRML node types each have rules about where they can be used. A **Material** node, for instance, can be used as the value of a **material** field in an **Appearance** node, but it can't be used to describe geometry in the **geometry** field of a **Shape** node. Similarly, an **AudioClip** node can describe a sound source for a **Sound** node, but it can't describe a font style in a **Text** node.

Just like standard VRML node types, your new node type has rules about where it can be used. These rules are determined automatically based upon the type of node that appears first in the node body. For example, if the first node in the body is a **Shape** node, then your new node type can be used anywhere a **Shape** node can be used. If the first node in the body is a **Material** node, then your new node type can be used anywhere a **Material** node can be used.

Abiding by these rules you can create a new node type that acts similar to any other node in VRML. You can create new geometry nodes, new shape nodes, new grouping nodes, new material and texture nodes, new sound nodes, and so on. In every case, the use rules for the first node in the node body determine the use rules for the new node type.

Accessing the Interface from the Node Body

The node body can make an automatic connection between any interface item and any appropriate field, exposed field, eventIn, or eventOut in the node body. Each connection is specified using the **IS** syntax following a field, exposed field, eventIn, or eventOut name within any node in the node body.

```
AnyNode {
    anyField IS anyInterfaceItem
}
```

For example, the following **PROTO** definition creates a **Cube** node type that builds a white cube shape using a **Shape** node and a **Box** node. The node interface defines a **cubeSize** field that the node body connects to the **Box** node's **size** field by using `size IS cubeSize`.

```
PROTO Cube [
    field SFVec3f cubeSize 0.0 0.0 0.0
] {
    Shape {
        appearance Appearance {
            material Material { }
        }
        geometry Box {
            size IS cubeSize
        }
    }
}
```

The new **Cube** node type can be used to build parts of your world. Each time you use the node, the value in the **cubeSize** field is automatically used as the value of the **size** field for the **Box** node contained within the **Cube** node.

You can connect the same interface item to multiple body nodes. For example, you can create a **DoubleCube** node type that creates two shapes using **Box** nodes and connect a single **cubeSize** interface field to the **size** field of both **Box** nodes.

You can also use the **IS** syntax to connect interface eventIns and eventOuts to eventIns and eventOuts of nodes in the node body. For example, the following **PROTO** definition connects a **set_position** interface eventIn to the implied **set_translation** eventIn of a **Transform** node's **translation** field, and connects an interface **position_changed** eventOut to the **Transform** node's implied **translation_changed** eventOut.

```
PROTO Positioner [
    eventIn SFVec3f set_position
    eventOut SFVec3f position_changed
] {
    Transform {
        set_translation IS set_position
        translation_changed IS position_changed
        children [ ... ]
    }
}
```

The data type for the interface item and the item in the node body must be the same when the **IS** connection is used. For instance, you can connect an **SFVec3f** interface field to any body field, exposed field, eventIn, or eventOut that is an **SFVec3f**, but you can't connect it to a body field that is an **MFColor** or **SFBool**.

Interface eventIns can only connect to the eventIns or implied eventIns of exposed fields in the node body. Similarly, interface eventOuts can only connect to the eventOuts or implied eventOuts of exposed fields. Interface fields can only connect to fields or exposed fields in the node body, and interface exposed fields can only connect to exposed fields in the node body. Table 31.1 summarizes these connection rules.

Table 31.1   Rules Governing Connections between Interface eventIns and eventOuts and the eventIns and eventOuts in the Node Body

Node Body Item	Node Interface Item			
	field	*exposed field*	*eventIn*	*eventOut*
field	allowed	not allowed	not allowed	not allowed
exposed field	allowed	allowed	allowed	allowed
eventIn	not allowed	not allowed	allowed	not allowed
eventOut	not allowed	not allowed	not allowed	allowed

Using **DEF** and **USE** within a Node Body

You can use **DEF** and **USE** to name and use nodes within a node body. You can also use **DEF** to name nodes used in **ROUTE** statements inside the node body. The names you give to nodes in a node body are not recognized outside that node body, and the names you give to nodes outside of a node body are not recognized within a node body.

Creating Multiple New Node Types

You can create as many new node types as you like by including multiple **PROTO** definitions within a world. Any node type defined by a **PROTO** definition can be used anywhere later in the same file. Typically, **PROTO** definitions are placed at the top of VRML files.

You can even create a **PROTO** definition nested inside the node body of a larger **PROTO** definition. The node type created by a nested **PROTO** definition contained within a larger **PROTO** definition is only available within the node body of the larger **PROTO** definition.

For example, the following VRML text declares an **Inside** node type using a **PROTO** definition nested within an **Outside PROTO** definition's node body. The **Inside** node type can be used inside the **Outside** node type's node body but not outside that node body.

```
PROTO Outside [ ... ] {
    PROTO Inside [ ... ] { ... }
    Inside { ... }
}
```

Understanding External Prototypes

A **PROTO** definition creates a new node type that you can use anywhere in the rest of the same world file. There are times, however, when it is more convenient to put **PROTO** definitions in external files, such as when maintaining a library of your own new node types. In these cases, you can access those **PROTO** definitions by using an **EXTERNPROTO** declaration in a world file.

An **EXTERNPROTO** declaration is a reduced version of a **PROTO** definition: it specifies a node type name and an interface declaration, but does not specify the default values for interface fields and exposed fields. Instead of a node body, the **EXTERNPROTO** declaration specifies a URL that points to the external file containing the **PROTO** definition. The default field values and the node body are both satisfied by the referenced **PROTO** definition. The interface declarations specified in the **EXTERNPROTO** declaration must match or be a subset of those in the **PROTO** definition.

```
EXTERNPROTO nodeTypeName [ nodeInterface ] [ urls ]
```

An **EXTERNPROTO** declaration starts with the word EXTERNPROTO followed by the new node type's name and a list of fields, exposed fields, eventIns, and eventOuts making up the node's interface. Following the interface is a URL or list of URLs (in square brackets) that reference an external file containing the corresponding **PROTO** definition.

When the VRML browser encounters the **EXTERNPROTO** declaration, it finds the new node-type definition in the file specified by the URL. That new node type is then available for use anywhere in the rest of the world file.

Typically, the node-type name you provide in an **EXTERNPROTO** declaration is the same as the node-type name for the associated **PROTO** definition in the file specified by the URL. However, you can use a different name if you like. For example, if a **PROTO** definition creates a new node type named "Torus," you can use an **EXTERNPROTO** declaration to establish an alternate name, such as "Donut."

Creating Multiple New Node Types in the Same File

You can create libraries of new node types by including multiple **PROTO** definitions in the same external file. By default, an **EXTERNPROTO** declaration uses only the first **PROTO** definition found in the file specified by the URL. You can direct that a specific **PROTO** definition be used from a file containing multiple **PROTO** definitions by adding a pound sign (#) and node-type name to the end of the URL used in an **EXTERNPROTO** declaration. For instance, the following two **EXTERNPROTO** declarations reference **PROTO** definitions contained in the same external file "mylib.wrl." Both declarations add a node-type-name specification to the URL:

```
EXTERNPROTO MyNewNode1 [ ... ] "mylib.wrl#MyNewNode1"
EXTERNPROTO MyNewNode2 [ ... ] "mylib.wrl#MyNewNode2"
```

The **PROTO** Definition Syntax

The **PROTO** definition syntax creates a new node type specifying a node interface and node body.

SYNTAX **PROTO**

```
PROTO nodeTypeName [
# Any number of:
    field          fieldType        fieldName        defaultValue
    exposedField   fieldType        fieldName        defaultValue
    eventIn        eventInType      eventInName
    eventOut       eventOutType     eventOutName
] {
    nodeBody
}
```

The *nodeTypeName* in the **PROTO** definition specifies the name for the new node type. Node-type names can be any sequence of letters and numbers conforming to the rules used for **DEF** names.

The **field, exposedField, eventIn,** and **eventOut** syntax of the **PROTO** definition each declare an interface for the new node type.

The **field** syntax defines an interface field with a data type, an interface field name, and a default value. Valid data types are listed in Table 2.1. Interface field names may be any sequence of letters and numbers conforming to the rules used for **DEF** names.

The **exposedField** syntax defines an interface exposed field with a data type, an interface exposed-field name, and a default value. Valid data types are listed in Table 2.1. Interface exposed-field names have the same limitations as those for interface field names.

The **eventIn** syntax defines an interface eventIn with a data type and an interface eventIn name. Valid data types are listed in Table 2.1. Interface eventIn names have the same limitations as those for interface field names.

The **eventOut** syntax defines an interface eventOut with a data type and an interface eventOut name. Valid data types are listed in Table 2.1. Interface eventOut names have the same limitations as those for interface field names.

The *nodeBody* in the **PROTO** definition defines the content and actions of the new node type. The node body may contain any number of nodes, and those nodes can be of any type. The first node in the body determines the use rules that apply to the new node type: Anywhere the first node can be used, the new node type can be used.

DEF names defined outside the node body are not recognized within the node body. **DEF** names defined inside the node body are not recognized outside the node body.

The new node type defined by a **PROTO** definition can be used anywhere in the remainder of the file, including the **PROTO** definition, and in any file that references the definition using an **EXTERNPROTO** declaration.

PROTO definitions included inside the node body are not recognized outside the node body.

The **IS** syntax may be used to connect interface fields, exposed fields, eventIns, and eventOuts to fields, exposed fields, eventIns, and eventOuts within the node body.

The **EXTERNPROTO** Declaration Syntax

The **EXTERNPROTO** declaration syntax creates a new node type specifying a **PROTO** definition contained within another file.

SYNTAX   **EXTERNPROTO**

```
EXTERNPROTO nodeTypeName [
# Any number of:
    field         fieldType        fieldName
    exposedField  fieldType        fieldName
    eventIn       eventInType      eventInName
    eventOut      eventOutType     eventOutName
] url or [ urlList ]
```

The `nodeTypeName` in the **EXTERNPROTO** declaration specifies the name for the new node type. Node-type names can be any sequence of letters and numbers conforming to the rules used for **DEF** names.

The **field, exposedField, eventIn,** and **eventOut** syntax of the **EXTERNPROTO** declaration each declare an interface for the new node type.

The **field** syntax declares an interface field with a data type and an interface field name. Valid data types are listed in Table 2.1. Interface field names may be any sequence of letters and numbers conforming to the rules used for **DEF** names.

The **exposedField** syntax declares an interface exposed field with a data type and an interface exposed-field name. Valid data types are listed in Table 2.1. Interface exposed field names have the same limitations as those for interface field names.

The **eventIn** syntax declares an interface eventIn with a data type and an interface eventIn name. Valid data types are listed in Table 2.1. Interface eventIn names have the same limitations as those for interface field names.

The **eventOut** syntax declares an interface eventOut with a data type and an interface eventOut name. Valid data types are listed in Table 2.1. Interface eventOut names have the same limitations as those for interface field names.

The **EXTERNPROTO** declaration creates a complete node-type definition by retrieving a **PROTO** definition found in an external file. The `url` following the closing square bracket of the interface declarations provides a URL for the external file.

Optionally, a list of URLs may be provided within square brackets and prioritized from highest priority to lowest priority. The VRML browser tries to open the file specified by the first URL in the list. If the file cannot be found, the browser tries the second URL in the list, and so on. When a URL is found that can be opened, the first **PROTO** definition found in the file is associated with the **EXTERNPROTO** declaration. If none of the URLs can be opened, the node-type declaration is incomplete. If the browser encounters any node of this type, the node is ignored.

If the same external file contains multiple **PROTO** definitions, the **EXTERN-PROTO** declaration may specify a node type by adding a pound sign (#) and node-type name to the end of the **EXTERNPROTO** declaration's URL. The **PROTO** definition with the specified node-type name is retrieved and associated with the **EXTERNPROTO** declaration.

The node-type name used in the **EXTERNPROTO** declaration need not match that used in the associated **PROTO** definition. When node-type names differ, the new node type created by the **EXTERNPROTO** declaration uses the **EXTERN-PROTO** declaration's node-type name.

The **EXTERNPROTO** declaration may specify some or all of the interface fields, exposed fields, eventIns, and eventOuts found in the associated **PROTO** definition. The **EXTERNPROTO** declaration cannot include interface items not found in the **PROTO** definition. The data types specified in **EXTERNPROTO** declarations must match those found in the associated **PROTO** definition.

The **IS** Connection Syntax

The **IS** syntax creates a connection between an interface field, exposed field, eventIn, or eventOut in a **PROTO** definition and a field, exposed field, eventIn, or eventOut in the definition's node body.

SYNTAX	IS

   fieldName IS interfaceItem

The *fieldName* is any field, exposed field, eventIn, or eventOut for any node or **Script**-node interface within a **PROTO** definition's node body.

The *interfaceItem* is any interface field, exposed field, eventIn, or eventOut within a **PROTO** definition's interface.

The **IS** syntax establishes a connection from the interface item to the node-body item. Once connected, the interface field or exposed-field value is automatically used as the value of the corresponding body-node field or exposed field. Similarly, interface and exposed-field implied eventIns automatically route events to body-node or implied eventIns, and body-node and exposed field implied eventOuts automatically route events using interface and implied eventOuts.

The data type of the interface item and the item in the node body must be the same.

Interface eventIns can only connect to eventIns or implied eventIns of exposed fields in the node body. Similarly, interface eventOuts can only connect to eventOuts or implied eventOuts of exposed fields. Interface fields can only connect to fields or exposed fields in the node body, and interface exposed fields can only connect to node-body exposed fields.

The **IS** syntax can be used to connect the same interface field, exposed field, eventIn, or eventOut to multiple node-body fields, exposed fields, eventIns, and eventOuts.

Experimenting with New Node Types

The following examples provide a more detailed examination of the ways in which **PROTO** and **EXTERNPROTO** declarations can be used and how they interact with nodes discussed in previous chapters.

Creating a New Material Node Type

Typically, worlds are carefully designed so that the same colors and textures are used throughout for consistency. In this regard, designing a world involves many of the same skills used by an interior designer to create an attractive, real-world, building interior.

You can build a library of colors used within a world by creating a new node type for each color. You can, for instance, create a new node type named **WallColor** whose node body contains a **Material** node with an RGB value specified for the **diffuseColor** field. Every time you need to build a shape colored with your standard wall color, you can use your **WallColor** node instead of a **Material** node. If at some later time you need to change the RGB color for the **WallColor** node, you can make the change once—in the **PROTO** definition—the rest of the world's shapes are automatically updated the next time you display the world.

Figure 31.1 uses a **PROTO** definition to create a new **WallColor** node type based on a **Material** node. Since the wall color is intended to be unchanging, the new **Wall-Color** node has no fields, exposed fields, eventIns, or eventOuts.

```
#VRML V2.0 utf8
PROTO WallColor [ ] {
    Material {
        diffuseColor 0.0 0.6 1.0
    }
}

Shape {
    appearance Appearance {
        material WallColor { }
    }
    geometry Box { size 10.0 2.0 0.1 }
}
```

Figure 31.1 *Definition and use of a* **WallColor** *node type.*

Once the **WallColor** node type has been defined, you can use the new **WallColor** node anywhere in the rest of the file. Since the first node in the **WallColor** node's body is a **Material** node, the use rules for **Material** nodes apply to the new **WallColor** node: The new node can be used anywhere a **Material** node can be used, such as for the value of the **material** field in an **Appearance** node. The world in Figure 31.1 uses the **WallColor** node to set the color of a flattened box that can be used as a room wall.

Often it is more convenient to place commonly used node-type definitions in external files, and then use an **EXTERNPROTO** declaration to pull in those definitions when you need them in a world. This enables you to maintain a library of standard new node types that you can use over and over again as you build different shapes and worlds.

Figure 31.2 rearranges the VRML text from Figure 31.1, placing it in two separate files. Figure 31.2 shows the file "matlib.wrl," which contains the **PROTO** definition for the **WallColor** node. This file also contains additional node-type definitions for other standard materials in a library of materials.

```
#VRML V2.0 utf8
PROTO WallColor [ ] {
    Material {
        diffuseColor 0.0 0.6 1.0
    }
}
PROTO Gold [ ] {
    Material {
        ambientIntensity 0.4
        diffuseColor 0.22 0.15 0.0
        specularColor 0.71 0.70 0.56
        shininess 0.16
    }
}
```

Figure 31.2 continues

```
PROTO Aluminum [ ] {
    Material {
        ambientIntensity 0.3
        diffuseColor 0.30 0.30 0.50
        specularColor 0.70 0.70 0.80
        shininess 0.10
    }
}
PROTO Copper [ ] {
    Material {
        ambientIntensity 0.26
        diffuseColor 0.30 0.11 0.00
        specularColor 0.75 0.33 0.00
        shininess 0.08
    }
}
```

Figure 31.2 *An external file containing a material library with the* **WallColor** *node type definition.*

Figure 31.3 shows a world containing the box shape from Figure 31.1. The world uses the **WallColor** node after referencing it with an **EXTERNPROTO** declaration specifying the URL for the "matlib.wrl" material library created in Figure 31.2. Notice that a #WallColor is added at the end of the URL. This ensures that the material library's "WallColor" **PROTO** definition is associated with the **EXTERN-PROTO** declaration.

```
#VRML V2.0 utf8
EXTERNPROTO WallColor [ ] "matlib.wrl#WallColor"

Shape {
    appearance Appearance {
        material WallColor { }
    }
    geometry Box { size 10.0 2.0 0.1 }
}
```

Figure 31.3 *A world that uses an externally declared node type.*

Creating a New Appearance Node Type

In the same way that a set of new material node types can be used to standardize colors in your world, a set of new appearance node types can be used to standardize appearances that include colors and textures. For instance, in a dungeon world you may need standard appearances for stone walls, tiled floors, wood doors, and so on.

For each standard appearance, you can create a new appearance node type that has within its node body an **Appearance** node along with its **Material** and texture nodes. Figure 31.4 creates a pair of wood-grain appearances. Each appearance uses a grayscale wood texture ("wood_g.jpg") and a **Material** node with a **diffuseColor** field value to color the grayscale texture.

```
#VRML V2.0 utf8
PROTO DarkOak [
    exposedField SFNode textureTransform NULL
] {
    Appearance {
        material Material { diffuseColor 1.0 0.45 0.23 }
        texture ImageTexture { url "wood_g.jpg" }
        textureTransform IS textureTransform
    }
}
PROTO LightOak [
    exposedField SFNode textureTransform NULL
] {
    Appearance {
        material Material { diffuseColor 1.0 0.65 0.53 }
        texture ImageTexture { url "wood_g.jpg" }
        textureTransform IS textureTransform
    }
}
```

Figure 31.4 *An external file containing an appearance library with wood appearances.*

When a wood-grain appearance is used, it may be necessary to include an appropriate **TextureTransform** node to translate, rotate, and scale the wood texture. Since you cannot determine these transform needs ahead of time and embed them within the new node's body, you need an interface exposed field. Each of the new appearance node types in Figure 31.4 include a **textureTransform** interface exposed field that expects an **SFNode** value for a **TextureTransform** node. Within the new node's body, the **IS** syntax is used to connect the interface exposed field to the **textureTransform** exposed field of the embedded **Appearance** node.

The appearances created in Figure 31.4 can be used to build shapes in your world using **EXTERNPROTO** declarations. Figure 31.5 builds a world with two side-by-side boxes that use the two wood-grain appearances from the external file "applib.wrl" shown in Figure 31.4. Since the first node in the body of each new node type is an **Appearance** node, the new wood appearance nodes can be used anywhere an **Appearance** node can be used, such as for the value of the **appearance** field in the **Shape** nodes that build the two boxes.

```
#VRML V2.0 utf8
EXTERNPROTO DarkOak [
    exposedField SFNode textureTransform
] "applib.wrl#DarkOak"

EXTERNPROTO LightOak [
    exposedField SFNode textureTransform
] "applib.wrl#LightOak"

Group {
    children [
        Transform { translation -1.5 0.0 0.0
            children Shape {
```

Figure 31.5 continues

```
                    appearance DarkOak { }
                    geometry Box { }
                }
            },
            Transform { translation 1.5 0.0 0.0
                children Shape {
                    appearance LightOak {
                        textureTransform TextureTransform {
                            translation 0.5 0.0
                            scale 2.0 1.0
                        }
                    }
                    geometry Box { }
                }
            }
        ]
    }
```

Figure 31.5 *Two spheres using appearance-node types from an external appearance library file.*

Creating a New Geometry Node Type

Recall from Chapter 30 the program script created to automatically generate donut geometry within an **Extrusion** node. Figure 31.6 encapsulates this **Extrusion** node and the associated donut-maker **Script** node within a **PROTO** definition to create a new **Donut** node type. Each of the fields, eventIns, and eventOuts of the donut-maker **Script** node are connected to corresponding interface fields, eventIns, and eventOuts.

```
#VRML V2.0 utf8
PROTO Donut [
    field    SFFloat crossSectionRadius     1.0
    field    SFFloat spineRadius            2.0
    field    SFInt32 crossSectionResolution 16
    field    SFInt32 spineResolution        16
    eventIn  SFFloat set_crossSectionRadius
    eventIn  SFFloat set_spineRadius
    eventOut MFVec2f crossSection_changed
    eventOut MFVec3f spine_changed
] {
    DEF Ext Extrusion {
        spine         [ ]
        crossSection  [ ]
        creaseAngle   1.57
        beginCap      FALSE
        endCap        FALSE
    }
    DEF DonutMaker Script {
```

Figure 31.6 continues

```
            url "donutmkr.js"
            field    SFFloat crossSectionRadius    IS crossSectionRadius
            field    SFFloat spineRadius           IS spineRadius
            field    SFInt32 crossSectionResolution IS crossSectionResolution
            field    SFInt32 spineResolution       IS spineResolution
            eventIn  SFFloat set_crossSectionRadius IS set_crossSectionRadius
            eventIn  SFFloat set_spineRadius       IS set_spineRadius
            eventOut MFVec2f crossSection_changed  IS crossSection_changed
            eventOut MFVec3f spine_changed         IS spine_changed
        }
        ROUTE DonutMaker.crossSection_changed TO Ext.set_crossSection
        ROUTE DonutMaker.spine_changed        TO Ext.set_spine
}
```

Figure 31.6 *A donut node type.*

Figure 31.7 uses the new **Donut** node by providing an **EXTERNPROTO** declaration that references the **Donut** node **PROTO** definition from within the file "donutpro.wrl" shown in Figure 31.6. The donut shape is shaded using the **LightOak** appearance node created earlier. Notice that since the first node in the **Donut** node's body is a geometry node (the **Extrusion** node), the new **Donut** node type can be used anywhere a geometry node can be used, such as for the value of the **geometry** field in a **Shape** node.

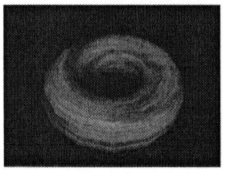

```
#VRML V2.0 utf8
EXTERNPROTO Donut [
    field    SFFloat crossSectionRadius
    field    SFFloat spineRadius
    field    SFInt32 crossSectionResolution
    field    SFInt32 spineResolution
    eventIn  SFFloat set_crossSectionRadius
    eventIn  SFFloat set_spineRadius
    eventOut MFVec2f crossSection_changed
    eventOut MFVec3f spine_changed
] "donutpro.wrl#Donut"

EXTERNPROTO LightOak [
    exposedField SFNode textureTransform
] "applib.wrl#LightOak"

Shape {
    appearance LightOak {
        textureTransform TextureTransform {
            translation 0.5 0.0
        }
    }
    geometry Donut {
        crossSectionRadius 1.0
        spineRadius        2.0
    }
}
```

Figure 31.7 *A donut shape built using the **Donut** geometry node and the **LightOak** appearance node.*

The **Donut** node's **EXTERNPROTO** declaration used in Figure 31.7 is lengthy because of the number of features in the **Donut** node type. However, the actual use of the **Donut** node later in the file doesn't use most of the node's features. In this situation, you can drop the declaration for those interface items you don't use in the file.

Creating a New Filter Node Type

In Chapter 30 you built several types of event filters, including the Boolean event filter that converts an input Boolean event into two output Boolean events. Figure 31.8 encapsulates the Boolean filter's **Script** node within a **PROTO** definition to create a **BooleanFilter** node. Since the first node in the filter's node body is a **Script** node, the new **BooleanFilter** node can be used anywhere a **Script** node can be used. You can use this same approach to encapsulate any **Script** node and create new sensors and interpolators.

```
#VRML V2.0 utf8
PROTO BooleanFilter [
    eventIn  SFBool set_boolean
    eventOut SFBool true_changed
    eventOut SFBool false_changed
] {
    Script {
        eventIn  SFBool set_boolean    IS set_boolean
        eventOut SFBool true_changed   IS true_changed
        eventOut SFBool false_changed  IS false_changed
        url "javascript:
            function set_boolean( bool, eventTime ) {
                if ( bool == true ) { true_changed  = true; }
                else                 { false_changed = true; }
            }"
    }
}
```

Figure 31.8   *A Boolean-filter node type.*

Creating a Spin-Group Node Type

In addition to materials, geometry, and scripts, you can also include sensors, interpolators, and other VRML animation features within a new node type. For example, Figure 31.9 uses a **PROTO** definition to create a **SpinGroup** grouping node that automatically spins around the Y axis the shapes contained within the group.

To create the **SpinGroup** node, the **PROTO** definition starts with an interface definition that includes exposed fields for the group node's list of children and for parameters to control the cycle interval, looping type, start time, and stop time for the group's automatic spinning. Within the **PROTO** definition's body, the new node-type is created using a **Transform** node that is automatically animated using **TimeSensor** and **OrientationInterpolator** nodes. The interface's exposed fields are connected to exposed fields within the body using the **IS** syntax. Once defined, Figure 31.9 uses the **SpinGroup** node to automatically spin a group of three green boxes.

```
#VRML V2.0 utf8
PROTO SpinGroup [
    exposedField MFNode    children        [ ]
    exposedField SFTime    cycleInterval  1.0
    exposedField SFBool    loop           FALSE
    exposedField SFTime    startTime       0.0
    exposedField SFTime    stopTime        0.0
] {
    DEF SpinMe Transform {
        children      IS children
    },
    DEF Clock TimeSensor {
        cycleInterval IS cycleInterval
        loop          IS loop
        startTime     IS startTime
        stopTime      IS stopTime
    },
    DEF Spinner OrientationInterpolator {
        key [ 0.0, 0.5, 1.0 ]
        keyValue [
            0.0 1.0 0.0 0.0,
            0.0 1.0 0.0 3.14,
            0.0 1.0 0.0 6.28
        ]
    },
    ROUTE Clock.fraction_changed TO Spinner.set_fraction
    ROUTE Spinner.value_changed  TO SpinMe.set_rotation
}

SpinGroup {
    cycleInterval 4.0
    loop TRUE
    children [
        Shape {
            appearance DEF Green Appearance {
                material Material { diffuseColor 0.0 1.0 0.3 }
            }
            geometry Box { size 25.0 2.0 2.0 }
        },
        Shape {
            appearance USE Green
            geometry Box { size 2.0 25.0 2.0 }
        },
        Shape {
            appearance USE Green
            geometry Box { size 2.0 2.0 25.0 }
        }
    ]
}
```

Figure 31.9 *A SpinGroup node type used to automatically spin a group of three boxes.*

Using a **PROTO** definition, you can create arbitrarily complicated new node types. Your new node types can select colors, apply textures, build shapes, animate those shapes, and use **Script** nodes to do computations. The **PROTO** definition ability in VRML enables you to arbitrarily extend VRML to meet your own needs.

Summary

A **PROTO** definition creates a new node type with a specified name, interface, and body. Once defined, the new node type can be used throughout the rest of the VRML file.

The **field, exposedField, eventIn,** and **eventOut** definitions of the **PROTO** declaration specify the interface for the new node type. The **field** syntax declares the data type, name, and default value of an interface field. The **exposedField** syntax defines the data type, name, and default value of an interface exposed field. The **eventIn** and **eventOut** syntax defines the data type and name of an interface eventIn or eventOut.

The node body for a **PROTO** definition contains one or more nodes that create shapes or perform actions for the new node type. The VRML use rules for the first node in the node body determine the use rules for the new node type.

The **IS** syntax creates a connection between an interface field, exposed field, eventIn, or eventOut and a field, exposed field, eventIn, or eventOut within the node body.

The **EXTERNPROTO** declaration creates a new node type with a specified name and interface defined by a **PROTO** definition contained within an external file referenced by a URL or list of URLs. An optional pound sign (#) and node-type name may be appended to a URL to specify a particular **PROTO** definition from within a file containing multiple definitions.

APPENDIX A

Radians and Degrees

Several of VRML's nodes have fields whose values include an angle measured in *radians*.

Most people find it easier to measure angles using *degrees* rather than radians. This means you'll probably be converting a lot from degrees to radians, and back again, as you create your VRML worlds.

In degrees, an angle measures the size of an arc from 0.0 *degrees* to 360.0 degrees, counterclockwise around a full circle. Halfway around the circle is 180.0 degrees, and a quarter of the way is 90.0 degrees. On a clock face, for instance, if 0.0 degrees is at 12 o'clock, then 9 o'clock is 90.0 degrees counterclockwise around the clock face. 6 o'clock is 180.0 degrees around, and 3 o'clock is 270.0 degrees around.

In radians, an angle measures the same arc but instead varies from 0.0 radians to $2\pi = 6.283$ radians full circle. Halfway around the circle is $\pi = 3.142$ radians, and a quarter of the way is $0.5\pi = 1.571$ radians. Figure A.1 shows the correspondence between degrees and radians as they measure out points around a circle.

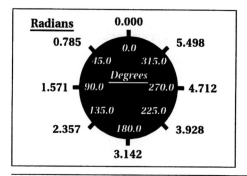

Figure A.1   *Degrees and radians and their correspondence to each other and a clock face.*

Radians are convenient for computer computations, while degrees are more convenient for people. To convert from an angle in degrees to one in radians, use this simple formula:

```
rad - deg ÷ 180.0 x 3.142
```

For instance, 30.0 degrees is 0.524 radians:

```
0.524 - 30.0 ÷ 180 x 3.142
```

To convert from radians back to degrees, use the reverse formula:

```
deg - rad ÷ 3.142 x 180.0
```

For instance, 0.785 radians is 45.0 degrees:

```
45.0 - 0.785 ÷ 3.142 x 180.0
```

Table A.1 provides the degree and radian values for several common angles.

Table A.1   Common Angles in Degrees Converted to Radian Values

Degrees	Radians
0.0	0.000
1.0	0.017
2.0	0.035
5.0	0.087
10.0	0.175
20.0	0.349
30.0	0.524
45.0	0.785
90.0	1.571
180.0	3.142
270.0	4.712
360.0	6.283

Recommended Resources

This appendix lists resources we recommend for VRML authors, including Web sites and traditional, printed resources.

Recommended Web Sites

Using your Web browser, you can access a phenomenal amount of information on the Web. Educational, commercial, and personal Web sites provide free software, product information, tips on product use, price comparisons, technical specifications, news, rumors, answers to frequently asked questions, and examples on using VRML, HTML, and other computing technologies.

Web Starting Points

The Web is changing so quickly that we do not recommend the purchase of any so-called *Web yellow pages* books. Such books provide a snapshot of the Web that, because of publishing production schedules, are always at least three months out of date. Instead, we recommend that you become familiar with a few major Web starting points. Any good starting point provides a searchable index of a portion of the Web's content. Some starting points also provide additional services to help you quickly find the information you need. We recommend the following major Web-search starting points:

- Yahoo!
  `http://www.yahoo.com`
- Alta Vista
  `http://altavista.digital.com`
- Netscape Communications
  `http://home.netscape.com/home/internet-search.html`

The VRML Repository

The VRML Repository is the principal Web site for information about VRML and related technologies. If you're looking for information on VRML, the VRML Repository is always the best place to start.

```
http://www.sdsc.edu/vrml
```

The VRML Repository is hosted by the San Diego Supercomputer Center (SDSC) and maintained by the authors of this book. The repository includes a tremendous amount of information about available VRML browsers, VRML authoring tools, graphics display hardware, and input hardware. The repository provides links to the official VRML specification, tutorials on VRML, documents that answer frequently asked questions, and links to other important specifications. The repository also provides information on VRML object libraries, texture libraries, and sound libraries, as well as links to VRML worlds available all over the Web. The repository's content is updated daily to track the rapid evolution of VRML. We recommend the VRML Repository as the starting point for any VRML-related Web search.

The Wiley Web Site

This book's CD-ROM includes all of the examples, texture images, sounds, and scripts discussed in the book. This information is also available on the Web at the John Wiley & Sons Web site. Also included at the Wiley Web site is an errata document, as well as notes on additions and changes made to the VRML specification since this book was printed.

```
http://www.wiley.com/compbooks/
```

Specification Documents

VRML 2.0 integrates a number of key technologies to enable you to create compelling multimedia environments. The official, detailed specifications for VRML and related technologies are available on the Web, maintained by several standards organizations including:

- International Standards Organization (ISO)
- Internet Engineering Task Force (IETF)
- VRML Consortium
- World Wide Web Consortium (W3C)

VRML Specification

The VRML 2.0 specification provides the official definition of the features of VRML 2.0. The language specification is maintained by the VRML Consortium and is available at the following addresses:

```
http://vag.vrml.org
http://vrml.sgi.com/moving-worlds/spec
```

Java and JavaScript Specifications

The Java and JavaScript language specifications are available at the following addresses:

- Java Language Specification
  `http://www.javasoft.com/doc/language_specification/j.title.doc.html`
- Java Application Programming Interface (API) Specification
  `http://java.sun.com/doc/language.html`
- JavaScript Language Specification
  `http://home.netscape.com/eng/mozilla/3.0/handbook/javascript`

Image-File Format Specifications

The GIF, JPEG, MPEG, and PNG specifications are defined by ISO and W3C documents available at the following addresses:

- GIF 1987 Specification
  `http://www.w3.org/pub/WWW/Graphics/GIF/spec-gif87.txt`
- GIF 1989 Revised Specification
  `http://www.w3.org/pub/WWW/Graphics/GIF/spec-gif89.txt`
- JPEG Specification (ISO 10918)
  `http://www.iso.ch/isob/switch-engine-cate.pl?KEYWORDS=10918&searchtype=refnumber`
- JPEG Frequently Asked Questions
  `http://www.cis.ohio-state.edu/hypertext/faq/usenet/jpeg-faq/top.html`
- MPEG Specification (ISO 11172)
  `http://www.iso.ch/isob/switch-engine-cate.pl?KEYWORDS=11172&searchtype=refnumber`
- MPEG Frequently Asked Questions
  `http://www.crs4.it/HTML/LUIGI/MPEG/mpegfaq.html`
- PNG Specification
  `http://www.w3.org/pub/WWW/TR/WD-png`

Sound-File Format Specifications

The MIDI synthesizer-performance-file format specification is available from the International MIDI Association at the following address:

`http://home.earthlink.net/~mma/specinfo.htm`

The WAV digital-sound-file format is also known as the RIFF or WAV RIFF format. The WAV specification is available in Microsoft technical documentation, and is briefly described at the following address:

`ftp://ftp.cwi.nl/pub/audio/RIFF-format`

Language Specifications

Language tags are used in the **FontStyle** node to specify variations in font use particular to a selected language. Language tags themselves are the subject of the IETF RFC 1766 specification available at the following address:

```
http://ds.internic.net/rfc/rfc1766.txt
```

Each language tag contains a *language code* and a *territory* (country) *code*. Language and territory codes are the subject of the ISO 639 and ISO 3166 standards, respectively. Both standards are available for purchase at ISO's site. The essential lists of standard language and territory codes, however, are freely available on the Web.

- Language Code Specification (ISO 639)—sales information
  ```
  http://www.iso.ch/cate/d4766.html
  ```
- Territory Code Specification (ISO 3166)—sales information
  ```
  http://www.iso.ch/cate/d22748.html
  ```
- Language codes
  ```
  http://sizif.mf.uni-lj.si/linux/cee/std/ISO_639.html
  ```
- Territory codes
  ```
  http://sizif.mf.uni-lj.si/linux/cee/std/ISO_3166.html
  ```

Internet Specifications

MIME types, used to identify broad categories of Web information, are the subject of the IETF RFC 1521 and 1522 standards available at the following address:

```
http://ds.internic.net/rfc/rfc1521.txt
http://ds.internic.net/rfc/rfc1522.txt
```

The structure of URLs and relative URLs is the subject of the IETF RFC 1738 and RFC 1808 standards available at the following address:

- URL Specification (IETF RFC 1738)
  ```
  http://ds.internic.net/rfc/rfc1738.txt
  http://www.w3.org/pub/WWW/Addressing/rfc1738.txt
  ```
- Relative URL Specification (IETF RFC 1808)
  ```
  http://ds.internic.net/rfc/rfc1808.txt
  http://www.w3.org/pub/WWW/Addressing/rfc1808.txt
  ```

UTF-8, or *UCS (Universal Character Set) Transformation Format 8*, is a computer encoding scheme (transformation format) for storing characters from a very large international character set that includes English characters, as well as those for Russian, Japanese, Chinese, Korean, and many other languages. The eight in the UTF-8 name indicates that the basic unit of encoding is an 8-bit byte.

The UCS is defined by the ISO 10646-1:1993 standard and the pDAM 1-5 extension. The UCS specification is available for sale only. ISO sales information is available at the following address:

http://www.iso.ch/cate/d18741.html

The UTF-8 character encoding scheme specification is available at the following address:

http://www.dkuug.dk/JTC1/SC2/WG2/docs/n1335

Recommended Reading

As the popularity of computer graphics, virtual reality, and the Web has grown, hundreds of books have become available. In this section we list some of our favorite texts on these subjects. They are available in most technical and university bookstores.

Java and JavaScript Programming

There are over a hundred books on Java available. For a light introduction to Java, we recommend:

van Hoff, Arthur, Sami Shaio, and Orca Starbuck, *Hooked on Java*, Reading, MA: Addison-Wesley, 1996.

For detailed, authoritative Java programming information, we recommend the following books, written by the inventors of Java at Sun Microsystems:

Arnold, Ken, and James Gosling, *The Java Programming Language*, Reading, MA: Addison-Wesley, 1996.

Gosling, James, Frank Yellin, and The Java Team, *The Java Application Programming Interface, Volume 1, Core Packages*, Reading, MA: Addison-Wesley, 1996.

Gosling, James, Frank Yellin, and The Java Team, *The Java Application Programming Interface, Volume 2, Window Toolkit and Applets*, Reading, MA: Addison-Wesley, 1996.

While there are several JavaScript programming books available, we recommend that you use the JavaScript documentation and tutorials available at Netscape Communications' Web site.

Introduction to Computer Graphics

Readers interested in learning more about the field of computer graphics are encouraged to read any of several introductory texts:

Angel, Edward, *Computer Graphics*, Reading, MA: Addison-Wesley, 1990.

Foley, James D., Andries van Dam, Stephen K. Feiner, John F. Hughes, and Richard L. Phillips, *Introduction to Computer Graphics*, Reading, MA: Addison-Wesley, 1994.

Glassner, Andrew S., *3D Computer Graphics: A User's Guide for Artists and Designers*, Design Press, 1989.

Pokarny, Cornel K., and Curtis F. Gerald, *Computer Graphics: The Principles Behind the Art and Science*, Franklin, Beedle & Associates, 1989.

Watt, Alan, *3D Computer Graphics*, Reading, MA: Addison-Wesley, 1993.

Of these texts, *3D Computer Graphics: A User's Guide for Artists and Designers* is a particularly easy-to-read and informative introductory book designed specifically for readers without mathematics and computer programming backgrounds. The remaining books in the list are written for the computer programmer and are frequently used as textbooks for university courses on computer graphics.

Advanced Computer Graphics

The following books provide more advanced information on computer graphics:

Arvo, James, ed. *Graphics Gems II*, Boston, MA: Academic Press, 1991.

Foley, James D., Andries van Dam, Stephen K. Feiner, John F. Hughes, and Richard L. Phillips, *Computer Graphics: Principles and Practice*, Reading, MA: Addison-Wesley, 1995.

Glassner, Andrew S., ed. *Graphics Gems*, Boston, MA: Academic Press, 1990.

Glassner, Andrew S., *Principles of Digital Image Synthesis, Volume 1 and 2*, San Mateo, CA: Morgan Kaufmann, 1995.

Heckbert, Paul S., ed. *Graphics Gems IV*, Boston, MA: Academic Press, 1994.

Kirk, David, ed. *Graphics Gems III*, Boston, MA: Academic Press, 1992.

Paeth, Alan W., ed. *Graphics Gems V*, Boston, MA: Academic Press, 1995.

Watt, Alan, and Mark Watt, *Advanced Animation and Rendering Techniques, Theory and Practice*, Reading, MA: Addison-Wesley, 1992.

Advanced Animation and Rendering Techniques, Theory and Practice and *Computer Graphics: Principles and Practice* cover computer graphics topics in depth. The latter text is generally considered the principle technical reference used by computer graphics professionals.

Principles of Digital Image Synthesis is a two-volume set that covers the underlying physics and mathematics behind computer graphics and requires a good foundation in mathematics and physics.

The *Graphics Gems* series of books provide dozens of algorithmic shortcuts, tricks, and techniques for computer graphics programmers.

Geometric Modeling

VRML's **IndexedFaceSet** node provides a flexible way to define complex, faceted shapes. However, it is often more intuitive to work with mathematically defined surfaces, such as those created by splines. Most geometric modeling done in the computer graphics industry is based on splines or similar mathematical surfaces. The following texts cover geometric modeling techniques. All include a fair amount of mathematics and are written for the computer programmer.

Bartels, Richard H., John C. Beatty, and Brian A. Barsky, *An Introduction to Splines for Use in Computer Graphics & Geometric Modeling*, San Mateo, CA: Morgan Kaufmann, 1987.

Farin, Gerald, *Curves and Surfaces for Computer Aided Geometric Design, second edition*, Boston, MA: Academic Press, 1990.

Mortenson, Michael E., *Geometric Modeling, second edition*, New York, NY: John Wiley & Sons, 1996.

Image Manipulation

Texture images can be based on real-world photographs, image-application artwork, or texture-generation algorithms. The following text provides a technical discussion of the mathematics and algorithms involved in texture generation.

Ebert, David S., F. Kenton Musgrave, Darwyn Peachey, Ken Perlin, and Steven Worley, eds., *Texturing and Modeling, A Procedural Approach*, Boston, MA: Academic Press, 1994.

VRML supports the JPEG, PNG, GIF, and MPEG image and movie formats. There are, however, hundreds of other widely used image file formats. We recommend the following technical text on image file formats.

Murray, James D., and William vanRyper, *Encyclopedia of Graphics File Formats* Sebastopol, CA: O'Reilly & Associates, Inc., 1994.

Virtual Reality

The following texts each discuss techniques for developing and using virtual reality hardware and software.

Burdea, Grigore, and Philippe Coiffet, *Virtual Reality Technology*, New York, NY: John Wiley & Sons, 1994.

Gradecki, Joe, *The Virtual Reality Construction Kit*, New York, NY: John Wiley & Sons, 1994.

Gradecki, Joe, *The Virtual Reality Programmer's Kit*, New York, NY: John Wiley & Sons, 1994.

Watkins, Christopher, and Stephen R. Marenka, *Virtual Reality ExCursions with Programs in C*, Boston, MA: Academic Press, 1994.

Sound spatialization techniques for virtual reality are discussed in depth in the following text.

Begault, Durand R., *3-D Sound for Virtual Reality and Multimedia*, Boston, MA: Academic Press, 1994.

Game Programming

VRML's features were specifically designed to facilitate virtual reality games. Programming games in VRML involve many of the same design and algorithm concerns required for games programmed using other computer graphics technologies. The following texts all provide technical discussions of game development.

Anderson, Greg, Peter Freese, Brenda Garno, Eagle Jones, Tab Julius, Steve Larsen, Andrew Lehrfeld, Erik Lorenzen, Tim Melton, Michael J. Norton, Bob Pendleton, Wayne Russell, Mark Seminatore, Lee Taylor, Keith Weiner, and Brad Whitlock, *More Tricks of the Game-Programming Gurus*, Indianapolis, IN: Sams Publishing, 1995.

LaMothe, André, *Black Art of 3D Game Programming*, Corte Madera, CA: Waite Group Press, 1995.

LaMothe, André, John Ratcliff, Mark Seminatore, and Denise Tyler, *Tricks of the Game Programming Gurus*, Indianapolis, IN: Sams Publishing, 1994.

Sawyer, Ben, *The Ultimate Game Developer's Sourcebook*, Coriolis Group Books, 1996.

Index

Page references in italic type indicate definitions. Page references in bold type indicate syntax discussions. Page references followed by lowercase roman t indicate material in tables. Terms beginning with 2-D and 3-D are located as if spelled out as "two-D" and "three-D" respectively.

Unusual terms

. designations [edu, gov, com, org], 7
.wrl extension, 11

A

Absolute time, *110–111*
addChildren field:
    Anchor node, 562
    Billboard node, 192
    Collision node, 548–549
    Group node, 30, 189–190
    Transform node, 191
Adjustable desk lamp, 88–90, 155–158
Advanced shape geometries, *17–18*
Aim direction, directional lights, *409*
Airplane, scaling, 94–95
Alta Vista, 625
ambientIntensity field:
    DirectionalLight node, 416, 427, 441
    Material node, 441
    PointLight node, 415, 420, 441
    SpotLight node, 417, 432, 441
Ambient light, *411*, 441
Ambient sound, *483*–485
Anchor node, 559–560
    summarized, 564–565
    syntax, **560–562**
Anchors, 2, *559–560*
    summarized, 560–565
    viewpoint anchors, 564
Anchor shapes, 562–564
Angles, 623–624
Animation, *109–110*, 121–122. *See also* Program scripts
    colors, 166–167, 175–176
    coordinates, 222, 236–238
    keyframe, *112–113*
    linear interpolation, 113–115
    multiple interpolators, 128–131
    multiple shapes, one interpolator, 127–128
    multiple time sensors, 131–133
    normals, 390, 403–404
    rotation, 114, 115, 124–125

scaling, 115, 125–129
sound location, 489–491
spines, 270–273
summarized, 133
texture transforms, 370–371
time and, 109–112
translation, 114, 115, 122–123
transparency, 182–183
triggering:
    with cursor proximity sensing, 148–149
    with touch, 149–150
    with viewer proximity sensing, 549–554
APIs, *580*, 582
Appearance, 17, 161–162. *See also* ColorInterpolator node; ScalarInterpolator node
    blinking effects, *see* Blinking effects
    colors, *see* Coloring
    glowing effects, *see* Glowing effects
    multiple shapes, 174
    shading, *see* Shading
    summarized, 184–185
    transparency, 165, 180–181
    animation, 182–183
appearance field, Shape node, 161, 168
Appearance node, 25, 161–162
    for coloring, 275, 277
    summarized, 184
    syntax, **27**, **168**, **307**, **352**
    texture nodes as input, 303
    using with Material node, 173–184
Application Programming Interfaces (APIs), *578*, 582
Archway, 73–75, 87–88, 103–105
    using inlining, 205–207
Ascii character set, 13
Asterisk, 85–87
attenuation field:
    PointLight node, 412, 415–416, 417
    SpotLight node, 412, 418
Attributes, of shapes, 17
Audio, *see* Sound
AudioClip node, 471–472, 473, 484
    summarized, 495
    syntax, **476–478**
    using in time-stamp filter, 594